# History of Multicultural Education, Volume VI

## Volume VI

Teachers and Teacher Education

# History of Multicultural Education
*Edited by Carl A. Grant and Thandeka K. Chapman*

# History of Multicultural Education, Volume VI

## Teachers and Teacher Education

Edited by

### Carl A. Grant
*University of Wisconsin, Madison*

### Thandeka K. Chapman
*University of Wisconsin, Milwaukee*

Routledge
Taylor & Francis Group

NEW YORK AND LONDON

First published 2008
by Routledge
270 Madison Ave, New York, NY 10016

Simultaneously published in the UK
by Routledge
2 Park Square, Milton Park, Abingdon, Oxon OX14 4RN

*Routledge is an imprint of the Taylor & Francis Group, an informa business*

© 2008 Taylor & Francis

Typeset in Sabon by
RefineCatch Limited, Bungay, Suffolk

*Library of Congress Cataloging in Publication Data*
History of multicultural education / edited by Carl A. Grant and Thandeka K. Chapman.
  p.cm.
Includes bibliographical references and index.

ISBN 978-0-8058-5439-8 (hardback, volume i : alk. paper) – ISBN 978-0-8058-5441-1 (hardback, volume ii : alk. paper) – ISBN 978-0-8058-5443-5 (hardback, volume iii : alk. paper) – ISBN 978-0-8058-5445-9 (hardback, volume iv : alk. paper) – ISBN 978-0-8058-5447-3 (hardback, volume v : alk. paper) – ISBN 978-0-8058-5449-7 (hardback, volume vi : alk. paper)

1. Multicultural education–United States.  I. Grant, Carl A.  II. Chapman, Thandeka K.
LC1099.3.H57 2008
370.1170973–dc22                                                                2008016735

ISBN10: 0-8058-5449-5 (hbk)
ISBN10: 0-415-98889-6 (set)

ISBN13: 978-0-8058-5449-7 (hbk)
ISBN13: 978-0-415-98889-6 (set)

# CONTENTS

# PREFACE TO THE SIX-VOLUME SET

## How we came to this work

We were invited by a large publishing house to create a multi-volume set on what we are calling the history of multicultural education. A change within the organizational structure of the publishing house resulted in the discontinuation of the initial project. However, over the course of the last seven years, the project was embraced by a second publishing house that later merged with our first publishing home. Our 360 degree turn has been both a professional challenge and an amazing opportunity. The project has grown and expanded with these changes, and given us the opportunity to work with many different people in the publishing industry.

We relate this series of events for multiple reasons. First we want to encourage new scholars to maintain their course of publication, even when manuscripts are not accepted on the first or second attempt to publish. Second, we would like to publicly thank Naomi Silverman and Lawrence Erlbaum Associates for throwing us a necessary lifeline for the project and for their vision concerning this project. Lastly, we would also like to thank Routledge Press for warmly welcoming us back to their publishing house and providing ample resources to support the publication of the six-volume set.

## What we got out of it and what we saw

Over the course of six years, we have worked to complete these volumes. These volumes, separately or as a set, were marketed for libraries and resources rooms that maintain historical collections. For Thandeka it was an opportunity to explore the field of multicultural education in deep and multifaceted ways. For Carl, it was a bittersweet exploration of things past and an opportunity to reflect on and re-conceptualize those events and movements that have shaped multicultural education. Collectively, the time we spent viewing the articles, conceptualizing the volumes, and writing the introductions was also a meaningful chance to discuss, critique, lament, and celebrate the work of past and present scholars who have devoted time to building and expanding the literature on equity and social justice in schools.

Looking across journals and articles we noticed patterns of school reform that are related to political and social ideas that constantly influence and are influenced by the public's perceptions of the state of education and by professionals working in the field of education. We would also like to recognize authors who have made consistent contributions in journals to multicultural education. These authors have cultivated lines of inquiry concerning multicultural education with regard to teachers, students, parents, and classroom events for decades. Although we would like to list these scholars, the fear of missing even one significant name keeps us from making this list.

Moreover, we recognize that a good deal of the significant work in the field was not published in journal articles or that articles were greatly altered (titles, tone, examples, word choice) to suit the editors and perceived constituents of the journal. There are many stories that are told between the lines of these articles that may go unnoticed by readers who are less familiar with the field, such as the difficulty authors had with finding publication outlets, and questions and criticism from colleagues about conducting research and scholarship in the areas of multi-cultural education. Although these pressures cannot be compared across groups, scholars of color, white scholars, men and women all felt marginalized because they chose to plant their careers in the rich but treacherous soil of multicultural education.

Just as we can see career patterns, we also saw patterns of journals that were willing to publish articles that focused on multicultural education. While many journals have created an *occasional* special issue around topics of equity, social justice, and students of color, there are journals that have consistently provided outlets for the work of multicultural scholars over the past three decades.

## Our hopes for the use of the volumes

We began this project with the desire to preserve and recount the work conducted in multicultural education over the past three decades. As scholars rely more heavily on electronic resources, and funding for ERIC and other national data-bases is decreased, we are concerned that older articles (articles from the late 60s thru the early 80s) that may never be placed in this medium would eventually be lost. The volume set is one attempt to provide students, teacher educators, and researchers with a historical memory of debates, conceptualizations, and pro-gram accounts that formed and expanded the knowledge-base of multicultural education.

# GENERAL INTRODUCTION TO
# THE VOLUMES

Multicultural education's rich and contested history is more than thirty years old; and is presently having an impact on the field of education, in particular, and society in general. It is time to provide a record of its history in order that the multiple accounts and interpretations which have contributed to the knowledge base, are maintained and documented. Whereas this account is not comprehensive, it nevertheless serves as a historically contextualized view of the development of the field and the people who have contributed to the field of multicultural education.

The paradigm of multicultural education as social reconstruction asserts the need to reform the institutional structures and schooling practices that maintain the societal status quo. These reforms are fashioned by socially reconstructing the ways that educators and politicians approach issues of equity and equality in our public schools. Multicultural education has become the umbrella under which various theoretical frameworks, pedagogical approaches, and policy applications are created, shared, critiqued, and implemented through on-going struggles for social justice in education. These campaigns for educational reform influence and benefit all citizens in the United States.

As a movement, multicultural education has brought forth an awareness of and sensitivity to cultural differences and similarities that continues to permeate the highest institutional infrastructures of our nation. Although the movement is rooted in struggles for racial equality, multicultural education readily includes physical disabilities, sexual orientation, issues of class and power, and other forms of bias affecting students' opportunities for academic and social success. The inclusion of other forms of difference beyond skin color is one way that multicultural education acknowledges diversity in a myriad of forms and dismantles the assumptions of homogeneity within racial groups.

The purpose of this set of volumes on the history of multicultural education is to locate, document, and give voice to the body of research and scholarship in the field. Through published articles spanning the past thirty years, this set of books provides readers with a means for knowing, understanding, and envisioning the ways in which multicultural education has developed; been implemented and resisted; and been interpreted in educational settings. By no means consistent in definition, purpose, or philosophy, multicultural education has influenced policy, pedagogy, and content in schools around the United States and the world. In addition, it has stimulated rigorous debates around the nature and purpose of schooling and how students and teachers should be educated to satisfy those purposes.

This set of volumes draws attention to how scholars, administrators, teachers, students, and parents have interpreted and reacted to various political and social events that have informed school policy and practices. Each volume in the set documents and tells a story of educators' attempts to explicate and advocate for the social and academic needs of heterogeneous and homogeneous communities. Through their struggles to achieve access and equity for all children, different scholars have conceptualized the goals, roles, and participants of multicultural education in numerous ways. Through the academic arena of scholarly publications, and using diverse voices from the past thirty years, the *History of Multicultural Education* acknowledges the challenges and successes distinguished through struggles for equity in education.

## Methods for collecting articles and composing the volumes

It is because of the multifaceted nature of multicultural education that we have taken multiple steps in researching and collecting articles for this volume set. Keeping in mind the many ways in which this set of volumes will enrich the study and teaching of education, we have approached the task of creating the texts using various methods. These methods reflect the spirit of inclusion intrinsic to scholarship in multicultural education and respect for diversity in the academic communities that promote and critique multicultural education. This was a multiple step process that included the following stages of data collection.

In the Spring of 2000, we began collecting articles using an electronic data bank called the *Web of Science*. This program allows the Editors to discover the number of times articles have been referenced in a significant number of refereed journals. We submitted proper names, article titles, and subject headings to create lists of articles that have been cited numerous times. The number of citations gave us an initial idea of how frequently the article had been cited in refereed journals. Using the *Web of Science* we established a list of articles, which because of their extensive referencing, have become seminal and historical works in the field of multicultural education. The authors cited in these pieces generated the names of over forty scholars who are both highly recognized or not immediately recognized for their scholarship in the area of multicultural education.

To extend the breadth and depth of these volumes, we returned to the *Web of Science* and used various subject headings to uncover other articles. The articles found in our second round of searching were also highly referenced by various scholars. The two searches were then cross-referenced for articles and authors. Through this process we attempted to reveal as many significant articles that dealt with multicultural education as possible. Some articles are foundational pieces of literature that have been copiously cited since their publication, while other articles represent a specific area of scholarship that has received less attention. For example, articles specific to early childhood and middle school education were not as easily identified as conceptual pieces that articulated various aspects of multicultural education.

The *Web of Science* program has some limitations. Articles that were published in less mainstream or more radical journals may not appear. The creation of a list of articles based solely on this program begs the questions of "What knowledge is of most worth?" and "How do we validate and acknowledge those significant contributions that have been marginalized in educational discourses?"

As multicultural educators, we were cautious not to re-instantiate those very discourses and practices that marginalize academic conversations. Therefore we used other educational and social science databases and traditional library-stack searches to present a more comprehensive set of texts that represent the field of multicultural education. For example, the reference sections in the first two searches were cross-referenced for articles that may not have appeared on-line. These articles were manually located, assessed, and used for their reference pages as well.

The main program limitation that haunted us was the lack of articles from the late 1960s and early 1970s that appeared in the electronic searches. We realized that educational research is lacking a comprehensive knowledge of its history because many scholars only cite articles written in the last ten to fifteen years when reporting their findings in academic journals. The lack of citations from the early years of multicultural education scholarship forced us to take a third approach to researching articles.

Using the ERIC files from 1966–1981 and manually sifting through bounded journals from the 1960s and 1970s, we were able to uncover other significant articles to include in the volumes. The decision to include or exclude certain articles rested primarily on the editors and other scholars who reviewed earlier drafts of the introductions to each volume and the references cited for that volume. We used the feedback from these scholars to complete our search for articles.

The volumes are a reflection of the field of research in multicultural education as well as a reflection of the community of scholars who contribute to the discourse(s) concerning issues of equity and equality in public schools. Our concern with shouldering such an awesome responsibility and our desire to include the voices from the many communities of multicultural education scholarship lead us to the final approach to finding quality articles. We solicited the opinions of over twenty multiculturalists. We asked them to choose the articles they believed belong in the volumes and suggest articles or areas that were not represented. Several scholars such as Sonia Nieto, Carlos Ovando, and Christine Sleeter answered our request and provided us with valuable feedback.

Polling various academic communities made the project a more inclusive effort, but also served as a tool to communicate the work of multicultural scholars. We appreciated the opportunity to engage with other scholars during the creation of these volumes. The multi-step research methodology for this project strengthens and enhances the finished product, making the volumes a valuable contribution to the field of education. This set of volumes, because it represents the voices of many scholars, is a spirited set of articles that reflects the tenets of multicultural education, its history, its present, its ideas for the future, and the people who believe in equity and social justice for all citizenry.

## Features of the volumes

Each volume in the set includes a diverse group of authors that have written in the field of multicultural education. The array of work is based on the article's contribution to educational scholarship; they represent well-known and lesser-known points of view and areas of scholarship. The volumes do not promote one scholar's vision of multicultural education, but include conflicting ideals that inform multiple interpretations of the field.

Many of the articles from the early 1970s and 1980s are difficult for students to obtain because technology limits the number of years that volumes can be accessed through web databases. Volumes in the set provide students with access to the foundational articles that remain solely in print. Students and veteran scholars doing historical research may be especially interested in the volumes because of the rich primary sources.

The volumes are delineated by six subject groupings: *Conceptual Frameworks and Curricular Content, Foundations and Stratifications, Instruction and Assessment, Policy and Governance, Students and Student Learning*, and *Teachers and Teacher Education*. These six, broadly defined areas reflect the diversity of scholarship dealing with issues of equity and social justice in schooling. The articles illustrate the progression of research and theory and provide a means for readers to reflect upon the changes in language and thought processes concerning educational scholarship. Readers also will see how language, pedagogical issues, policy reforms, and a variety of proposed solutions for equity attainment have been constructed, assimilated, and mutated over the thirty year time period.

## Volume I: Conceptual Frameworks and Curricular Issues

The articles in this volume illustrate the initial and continued debates over the concepts, definitions, meanings, and practices that constitute multicultural education. The authors articulate how best to represent the history and citizens of the United States, what types of content should be covered in public schools, and the types of learning environments that best serve the needs of all students. For example, this volume shows how multicultural education challenged the representations of people of color that are presented or ignored in textbooks. Conversely, articles that challenge conceptions of multicultural education are also included. Content wars over the infusion of authors of color, the inclusion of multiple historical perspectives, and an appreciation for various scientific and social contributions from people of color that reflect challenges to Eurocentric knowledge and perspectives are presented in this volume.

## Volume II: Foundations and Stratifications

This volume presents theoretical and empirical articles that discuss the institutional factors that influence schooling. Issues such as the historical configurations of schools, ideologies of reproduction and resistance, and administrative structures that often maintain imbalances of power and equity in schools are discussed. In addition, articles explicating the various ways that students and educational opportunities are racially and socio-economically stratified are present in this volume.

## Volume III: Instruction and Assessment

The articles in this volume elucidate general pedagogical approaches and specific instructional approaches with consideration given to content areas and grade level. Diverse instructional practices and the relationships between students and their teachers are discussed. Although content and pedagogy are difficult to separate, the work in this volume addresses the dispositions of the teacher and his/her awareness of learning styles, and his/her ability to incorporate aspects of students' culture and community affiliations into pedagogy. Also included in this volume are theories and models of multicultural assessment tools that reflect the needs of diverse learning communities.

## Volume IV: Policy and Policy Initiatives

This volume on policy and governance explores the effects of federal and state mandates on school reforms dealing with equity in education. The articles in this volume show how educational organizations and associations have attempted to influence and guide school policy, instructional practices, and teacher-education programs. In addition, the volume presents articles that discuss how interest groups (e.g., parents and concerned teachers) influence enactments of education policy in schools.

## Volume V: Students and Student Learning

This volume on "Students and Student Learning" focuses on students as individuals, scholars, and members of various social and cultural groups. The articles highlight different aspects of students' lives and how they influence their academic behaviors and includes students' affective responses to their schooling and their beliefs about the value of education. The articles also address how schools socially construct student learning through the lenses of race, class, and gender. In addition, the articles show how students act as political agents to structure, direct, and often derail their academic progress. Arguing that multicultural education is necessary for everyone, the articles highlight specific racial and cultural groups as well as offer generalizations about the academic needs of all students.

## Volume VI: Teachers and Teacher Education

The teacher education volume addresses issues of multicultural education for preservice and experienced teachers. The articles cover the racial and social demographics of the past and current teaching force in the United States and the impact of these demographics on the structure of multicultural teacher education programs. Several articles speak to the role(s) of the university concerning multicultural preservice and in-service education classes, field placements, and institutional support for veteran teachers. These articles explore the nature of teaching for social justice in higher education, the desire to attract teachers of color, and the juncture between theory and practice for newly licensed teachers.

# ACKNOWLEDGEMENTS

There are many who deserve a public thank you for their support of and participation in this project. We would like to thank the many colleagues and graduate students who offered constructive criticism, suggested articles, read drafts of the introductions, and helped to conceptualize the placement of articles in the different volumes. These people include: Barbara Bales, Anthony Brown, Keffrelyn Brown, Nikola Hobbel, Etta Hollins, Gloria Ladson-Billings, Sonia Nieto, Carlos Ovando, Christine Sleeter, and Michael Zambon.

We would like to offer a special thank you to the journals that, because of the nature of the project, reduced or forgave their fees for re-printing.

Thanks to Director JoAnn Carr and the staff in the Center for Instructional Materials and Computing (CIMC) for putting up with our large piles of bound and unbound journals that we pulled from the shelves and made unavailable for others for days at a time. Thank you for re-shelving all the publications (sometimes over and over again) and never reprimanding us for the amount of work we created.

A super big thank you to Jennifer Austin for compiling, organizing, and maintaining our files of publishers' permission requests. Jennifer also contacted and reasonably harassed folks for us until they gave her the answers we needed. Brava!

Thank you to our families for their support and only occasionally asking "Aren't you finished yet?"

# STATEMENT CONCERNING ARTICLE AVAILABILITY AND THE CONFLICT WITH REPRINT COST

During this insightful, extensive process, the goal was to share re-printings of all the articles with our readers. However, as we moved to the end of our journey, we discovered that it was financially unfeasible to secure permissions from the publishers of all the articles. We found most publishers more than willing to either donate articles or grant us significant breaks on their re-printing prices. Other publishers were more intractable with their fees. Even if the budget allowed for the purchasing of the 200-plus articles, the price of the books would have become prohibitive for most readers. Therefore, the printed articles found in the volumes do not represent all the articles that met the criteria outlined in the Preface and are discussed in each of the volumes' introductions.

At first we decided not to summarize these articles and use them solely as support for the rest of the volume(s). As we refined our introductions and re-read (and read again) the articles, we could not discount how these pieces continued to provide significant knowledge and historical reflections of the field that are unique and timely. Therefore, if the volumes are to represent the most often referenced examples and keenly situated representations of multicultural education and paint a historically conceptualized picture of the field, we had no choice but to include the works of these scholars in our introductions. Unfortunately, for the reasons explained here, some of these articles are not included in these volumes. In Appendix 2, we have provided a list of all the publishers and publishing houses so that individuals and organizations may access these articles from their local or university libraries or web services free of charge.

# LIST OF JOURNALS REPRESENTED IN THE SIX-VOLUME SET

*Action in Teacher Education*
*American Association of Colleges for Teacher Education*
*American Educational Research Association*
*American Journal of Education*
*American Sociological Association*
*Anthropology and Education*
*Association for Supervision and Curriculum Development*
*Comparative Education Review*
*Curriculum and Teaching*
*Education*
*Education and Urban Society*
*Educational Horizons*
*Educational Leadership*
*Educational Research Quarterly*
*Educators for Urban Minorities*
*English Journal*
*Exceptional Children*
*FOCUS*
*Harvard Educational Review*
*Interchange*
*Journal of Curriculum Studies*
*Journal of Curriculum and Supervision*
*Journal of Teacher Education*
*Journal of Research and Development in Education*
*Journal of Negro Education*
*Journal of Literacy Research* (formerly *Journal of Reading Behavior*)
*Journal of Educational Thought*
*Journal of Teacher Education*
*Language Arts*
*Momentum*
*Multicultural Education*
*National Catholic Educational Association*
*National Council for the Social Studies*
*National Educational Service*
*Negro Educational Review*
*Peabody Journal of Education*

# INTRODUCTION TO VOLUME VI

More so than any other volume, we experienced great difficulty when paring down the articles to present in this book. The field of multicultural teacher education and research on teachers' dispositions is expansive. Since the early 1970s, scholars have been advocating for teacher education programs to better reflect the changing demographics of American schools. As mentioned in the other volumes, the idea that multicultural education is for teaching students of color or students unlike the teacher, and not white students, is deeply imbedded in the ideology of multicultural education programs. The consistent decrease in students of color from the limited pool of applicants in teacher education has left multicultural teacher educators to rigorously focus on ways to change pre-service white teachers' dispositions in diverse classrooms. Thus it becomes the job of multicultural teacher education to re-program teachers' attitudes through course work and field experiences that provide a wider lens for them to view culture beyond their perceived naïve backgrounds and limited interactions with people of color. The desire to mold teachers' perceptions of difference in order to better serve students is part of the binary created in the multicultural literature between white teachers and students of color. That being said, multicultural teacher education seeks to produce teachers that can relate to student populations unlike the teacher's own friends and family in ways that are empowering for the student, regardless of the teacher's racial and cultural backgrounds. The goal to reshape teachers' attitudes about diversity, the focus on students of color as the beneficiaries of multicultural education, and the view of multicultural teacher education as a site of social reform are themes throughout this teacher education volume.

In part, this ideology stems from the historical past of schools and the purpose of schooling. Public schools were indeed created to assimilate the masses of ethnic immigrants moving into the country. Teachers were responsible for creating democratic citizens who were prepared to contribute to their new country. While scholars have always questioned the merits of the "melting pot" school model, the notion of assimilation did not become largely contested until the late 1960s and early 1970s when students of color were bused to all white schools and teachers of color were forced out of classrooms to privilege white teachers. It is this juncture of history, when dropout rates for students of color soared and achievement severely declined, that multicultural teacher education made its debut.

The conceptions of multicultural teacher education rest upon the reality of an unchanging population of teachers who are predominantly white middle-class women. The politics of race, class, and gender in public schools is bound to the demographics of students and teachers in public schools. The enrollment in pre-K-12 classrooms reflects the changing racial, ethnic, socioeconomic, and sexual orientation demographics of the United States.

Although the nature of multicultural education promotes reform for all student populations, teacher education programs implementing multicultural education have done little to structure white teacher candidates' teacher preparation to teach multicultural education to homogenous white populations. The conversations over programming, teachers' dispositions, and teacher educator initiatives primarily center around the ability to transform white teachers with limited understandings of culture and diversity into thoughtful, critical agents of change in classrooms with students who do not reflect their racial, ethnic, and socioeconomic class background.

In the thirty years of multicultural teacher education, the field has come to some consensus. These areas of consensus are prevalent in policy and classroom practices in higher education, secondary education, and elementary education. Who multicultural teachers should be and how they should act extends to an almost precise theory, but quite imprecise assessment of practice. In short, multicultural education scholars know the dispositions and ideology that embody a multicultural teacher, but have not perfected ways to sustain these behaviors and ideals in teachers as they teach.

In this volume, the articles have been separated into four categories that reflect the cultivation of ideal multicultural education teachers: dispositions of teachers, teacher education programs, the model teacher, and reflections of praxis. These four areas cover research reports from the field and theories concerning the social, emotional, and sometimes academic needs of teachers.

## Teacher Dispositions

Teacher educators lament the fact that the current population of white female preservice teachers will not be changing in the near future. Although programs have been established to recruit and support teachers of color, those scholars in multicultural teacher education must work with their somewhat immobile population. In order to better understand what was occurring in classrooms, teacher disposition research became quite popular in the 1970s and 1980s. The analyzed data from these surveys of preservice and veteran teachers confirmed that white teachers held deficit views of their students of color and their poor students.

Gollub and Sloan (1978) reviewed the literature on teacher dispositions and found that teachers seemed to base their subjective predictions regarding student's future academic success on their perceptions of race and class. They established that teachers did not like to have their perceptions of students disrupted by alternative examples of progress or behavior. The authors recognized that their work did not prove a connection between academic achievement and teacher beliefs, however they advocated for more research to be conducted in this area of study. They called for future research on the relationship between disposition and student success.

In response to multicultural mandates, scholars began testing students and evaluating programs to gage the possibilities of multicultural teacher education reform. Psychological and sociological studies of teachers' perceptions of students in the 1970s and early 1980s demonstrated the ideological depth and affirmation of the deficit model in teacher practices. In the mid- to late 80s, these surveys of teacher attitudes were used to assess how well teacher education programs responded to NCATE mandates to provide "evidence of planning for multicultural education in its teacher education curricula including both the general and professional studies components" (1977, p. 4). At the preservice level, surveys were used to predict teachers' capabilities for teaching diverse students or to measure preservice teachers' development after undergoing some form of multicultural education training. Giles and Sherman (1982) piloted a Multicultural Attitude Questionnaire to characterize preservice teachers' attitudes towards diverse populations of students. While they successfully quantified aspects of preservice teachers, they were unable to make connections between these attributes and successful teacher practices.

Other surveys sought to measure how seasoned teachers were implementing multicultural education. Washington's survey (1982) showed that most elementary school teachers believed multicultural education was important, but few practiced it. The teachers' limited understandings of the field, lack of professional development, and the scarcity of materials were the main reasons teachers gave for not implementing multicultural education. Similarly, Rueda, Rodriguez, and Prieto (1981) conducted a needs assessment survey of teachers in bilingual/multicultural exceptional classrooms to gain insight into the ways in which instruction was being taught for this population of students. These scholars also found a significant gap between teacher knowledge and practice and advocated for more in-services that connected the university to schools through on-going professional development opportunities.

As the field evolved, scholars became more critical of academic institutions and structures. Gomez's (1993) review of the research on prospective teachers' beliefs yields a number of implications for teacher education. Gomez pointed out that the lack of cohesion between and among schools, colleges of education, and universities prevents the institutionalization of multicultural teacher education. She stated that without a commitment to and an understanding of the promotion of equity and equality from all parties involved in the education and indoctrination of teachers, multicultural education programs will continue to fall short of their goal for addressing institutional and structural inequalities.

Almost ten years later, McAllister and Irvine (2002) reviewed the research concerning pre-service and in-service teachers' dispositions on multicultural education. This thorough overview of articles, books, unpublished presentations, and research documents serves as a resource for scholars who wish to continue this vein of research. McAllister and Irvine make a solid argument for the benefits of attitudinal research; however, much like the body of the research itself, they do not look closely at the issues of power and privilege between students and professors that are bound in the data collection process. Although they highlight the disconnect between teachers' beliefs and practices, they do not provide rationales for this occurrence. The missing explanation for this discrepancy begs the question of what measures must be provided in order for a teacher to reform her practice and become a change agent.

## Teacher Preparation

The academic needs of teachers have not been a primary focus for multicultural teacher education. While grade level and subject area programs struggle to balance the number of courses students need in their content area versus the number of courses students need in instructional methods, multicultural teacher education has not focused on this issue. Perhaps it is because the field assumes subject competency and chooses to focus on pedagogy and reflection, or because when teacher education as a field evolved there was already a heavy emphasis on knowledge in the content areas. Briefly, Competency Based Teacher Education (CBTE) in the 1970s and the National Commission on Teaching and America's Future (*What matters most: Teaching for America's future*, 1996) in the 1990s connected multicultural education to content specificity at all levels of public schools. And while some scholars made connections between the two movements, it seems that CBTE and multicultural education ran parallel, with a few scholarly intersections (Hunter, 1974). Regardless of the reasons for this slight to content knowledge, the literature shows that the connection between a teacher's content competency and their ability to relate that knowledge to all children was lacking in the field. Few scholars continue to push the often lost connection between quality instruction and multicultural education.

One focus in multicultural teacher education has been the need for ample and diverse field placements. In the literature, scholars agree that students must have opportunities to interact with communities and students as soon as possible. While all the articles speak to this issue, Baker (1977), Grant and Koskela (1986) and Mahan (1982) provided concrete examples of teacher education programs that have specific field experiences tied to African American, Native American and Latino communities. These programs try to place students in racially and culturally diverse settings both in and out of the classroom. The assumption is that preservice teachers should become acclimated to contexts different from their own experiences in order to learn the value of these settings.

Baker, Grant and Koskela, and Mehan addressed the struggle to provide students with diverse field experiences in university settings that lack heterogeneous communities. They also observe that the mere fact that a placement has a diverse student or teaching population does not mean that the work being done is multicultural. Moreover, they recognized that the placement may be working through a deficit model that contrasts with the teacher's university instruction. This mis-match between the university and the field site calls for a better relationship with existing teachers and a cultivation of talent that has pedagogically invested in multicultural education.

Other articles in this section explore the gamut of practices and program designs that facilitate multicultural teacher education. Cochran-Smith's (1995) and Sleeter's (2001) reviews of research in multicultural teacher education provided comprehensive overviews of the field and recommendations for improving programs. These recommendations keep in mind the demographics of preservice teachers and their dispositions towards teaching and learning. In addition, both authors stressed the need for programs that maintain a focus on diversity that is not limited to a few instructors or classes in the institution.

Hollins (1995) also called for restructuring that touches all aspects of the teacher education program. Using the theory of culturally mediated instruction, Hollins suggested that preservice teachers receive support during their field experiences at the university as well as their induction period into the profession. This next step to supporting teachers in the field has become a crucial element to the retention of new teachers and the eventual practice of multicultural education.

Oakes (1996) heeded the call for multicultural teacher education and created Center X. She articulated her vision for the center and shared the processes that shaped the planning and opening of the professional education programs. Oakes discussed the various ways the center is tracking their students and their experiences in the program as well as in the profession. Her work is one of a handful of articles in the field of education that catalogues the planning and development of a multicultural teacher education program with a focus on issues of social justice.

Other scholars have sought to combine multicultural education with bilingual and special teacher education (Carriker & Berdine, 1979). Rueda and Prieto (1979) and Amos and Landers (1984) examine the confluence between multicultural education and exceptional education for teacher education programs. These authors articulated the differences in exceptional education and regular education and how they are intertwined with regard to the needs of students of color who are exceptional.

From the onset of these programs, scholars believed that teachers were agents of change. Whereas they have been historically used to reinforce the status quo and reinscribe notions of white superiority, multicultural teacher education sought to use teachers to challenge the unchallenged. Although it was not until the 1980s that the word "critical" and "social justice" were frequently used to describe programmatic goals, there has been an emphasis on creating teachers that will shape a critical democracy by asking students to interrogate the ways they understand their communities and society. Articles by Shor (1986) and Giroux and McLaren (1986), represent the shift in the 1980s towards "emancipatory pedagogy" (Gordon, 1986). The authors explored the meaning of democratic citizenship and the teacher's role in promoting this concept. In addition, Shor and Giroux and McLaren place teachers at the crux of reform and school change. They asserted that teachers must be seen as competent pedagogues who have the power to mold students' perceptions of the world.

## The Model Teacher

In the literature there exist multiple portraits of the model multicultural teacher. Scholars point out that being a multicultural educator can lead to isolation from other teachers and administrators who do not share the same vision of schools or children. Who is the ideal teacher? Reading across the literature, a multicultural teacher is:

- someone who knows the difference between fair and equal,
- holds a wealth of knowledge about the subject,
- connects to students homes and communities on personal and academic levels,
- makes learning meaningful and contextual,
- models a critique of society and knowledge,
- provides multiple opportunities for students to learn,
- understands culture and its impact on children,
- regards pupils in high esteem.

In addition, this ideal multicultural teacher has reflected upon experiences and biases that benefit or hamper the ability to teach in multicultural ways. Interestingly enough, the literature shows that conversations about what multicultural teachers should know and be able to do have changed very little in the last forty years.

As early as 1963 (Rousseve, 1963), teacher educators were concerned with how teachers were communicating culture and acceptance to students of color. Even in Rousseve's deficit portrait of African American students, he recognized that the model teacher must understand the institutional barriers, the presence of racism and classism, and the cultural divide that teachers must overcome to teach "disadvantaged youth."

Grant's (1977) article demonstrates how the teachers' roles in the classroom are constantly shifting with the times. Just as social constructions of culture, race, and class are transformed, so are the expectations of teachers. Grant advocated for an expanded conceptualization of the role "mediator of culture" that incorporates acceptance and affirmation of students' backgrounds.

In the mid-1970s, the National Council for the Accreditation of Teacher Education (NCATE) provided an extensive rationale and model for teacher education programs to embrace in order to produce multicultural teachers. This rationale provided both a definition of multicultural education and a series of competencies teachers must learn in order to produce a multicultural citizen. James (1978) responded to the definition of the model teacher, and recognized that multicultural education is an on-going process that moves beyond higher education.

Gay (1978) used the term "respect" to convey how teachers should feel about their students and their racial and cultural backgrounds. She provided a model of the multicultural teacher that includes provisions for students' home languages to be spoken in the classroom and for cross-cultural engagement to naturally occur. Gay's work is significant because she included both black and white teachers in her argument for multicultural education, whereas the majority of the research focuses on the white teacher's need to understand and connect with their racialized and socialized identities. Her recommendations for reforming teacher preparation speak to preservice teachers from middle-class backgrounds. She acknowledged that both white and black teachers support and dismiss students because of their race and socioeconomic status. In keeping with scholarship that details the roles of the multicultural teacher, Gay asserted that teachers should examine their own personal identities and how their backgrounds impact their beliefs and expectations for students.

Twenty years later Haberman and Post's (1998) list of twelve attributes that teachers need to become multicultural echoes the statements of Gay (1978). This progression is important because it demonstrates the length of time and the unfailing appeal by multicultural educators to find ways to cultivate specific dispositions in teachers. Ironically, it also demonstrates how little the field has been able to move past these areas because they are so difficult to accomplish.

## Professional Development

This volume attempts to illustrate the trends and themes that have shaped multicultural teacher education. An assessment of the field is incomplete without the mention of in-service programs and research in the field. Although many of the articles in this volume give some attention to in-service programs, there has not been substantial documentation in this area. That is not to say that work has not been done (Howe & Pang, 2000; Leistyna, 2001; White, 1981; Yao, 1983). The success of these programs rested on cohort support, common concerns of the participating teachers, and well-conceived curriculum plans. Beyond these studies, much of the work in professional development has been conducted in specific subject matter areas. The documentation of successful professional programs that address the total reformation of school programs is a significant void in the body of multicultural scholarship. There are several potential reasons for the cavity: one-time in-services, non-tenure related work, lack of general regard by the field, and difficult roles of the researcher as facilitator and evaluator. However, as more educators utilize action research paradigms, perhaps these projects will begin to accumulate and yield rich fruit.

## Reflections of Praxis

The desire to shape the minds of tomorrow's citizens and impact the world through multicultural education also is present in the section on reflections of praxis. No one knows how difficult the list of attributes is to achieve better than those who have changed their teacher education practices to move theory into practice. In the field of teacher education, there is a substantial amount of self-study and reflection that demonstrates the trials and tribulations of invoking multicultural education. These anecdotes and case studies recognize the difficulties of changing all levels of education. The case studies represent teacher educators' attempts at "praxis," or the blending together of theory and practice. When conducting praxis, multicultural teacher educators find themselves caught between their strong beliefs and how to best represent them in their classrooms. As with these pieces, scholars find that changing a person's system of beliefs is extremely difficult, if not impossible. Yet, because the field of research and practice deems it highly important for teachers to hold a particular ideology towards children in order to become multicultural teachers, multicultural educators design comprehensive programs and use their individual courses to whittle away at pre-service teachers' narrow understandings of the world and supplant their beliefs with a critical social justice focus.

As early as 1981 Mahan and Boyle (1981) found that teacher educators had difficulty agreeing upon the integral features needed for multicultural teacher education programs. Thus, many teacher educators use their own classrooms to expose their preservice students to multicultural issues. Using her work with preservice teachers, Ahlquist (1991) explicated the tensions that arise between preservice students and teacher educators when instructors try to interrupt students' deeply imbedded notions of students of color and the role(s) of the teacher. Her work is a frank look at the difficulties multicultural teacher educators face when they push students' to reflect on their own racism and limited understandings of the world.

King defines preservice students' limited understandings of race and racism as "dysconscious racism" (King, 1991). In this seminal piece, King presented her approach to praxis as a model for other teacher educators. This small study of her practice explored how preservice teachers' beliefs changed during the course of a foundation class.

In contrast, Kumashiro's (2000) piece highlighted his reflections on the process of praxis and his desire to create critical dissonance among both high school and preservice students. As an instructor, Kumashiro realized that he was imposing a specific ideology upon the students much like the traditional ideology they were constantly exposed to throughout their education. Kumashiro's open critique of his practice humanizes the process of praxis and impresses upon the reader the ongoing evolution of a multicultural educator's pedagogy.

The acknowledgement of preservice teacher resistance poses an ethical dilemma for teacher educators. These authors represent the few studies that question the ramifications of requiring students to reconstruct their thinking and behaviors. Students in multicultural teacher education programs often are asked to move away from their former comfort levels that may or may not be shrouded by a lack of knowledge about racism, and embrace a critical consciousness.

## Conclusion

As issues of accountability become more complex and teacher education programs are forced to prove their worth in the current political contexts, the need for more longitudinal data on students from multicultural teacher education programs becomes paramount. The authors represented in these texts, and many more who are not included, have a forty-year-old vision of the ideal teacher that they believe produces academically successful and emotionally balanced citizens. Yet where is the proof?

## References

Ahlquist, R. (1991). Position and imposition: Power relations in a multicultural foundations class. *Journal of Negro Education, 60*(2), 158–169.

Amos, O. E., & Landers, M. F. (1984). Special education and multicultural education: A compatible marriage. *Theory Into Practice, 23*(2), 144–150.

Baker, G. (1977). Multicultural imperatives for curriculum development in teacher education. *Journal of Research and Development in Education, 11*(1), 70–83.

Carriker, W. R., & Berdine, W. H. (1979). Multiculture and special education teacher education accreditation. *TEASE, 2*(4), 65–68.

Cochran-Smith, M. (1995). Color blindness and basket making are not the answer: Confronting the dilemmas of race, culture, and language diversity in teacher education. *American Educational Research Journal, 32*(3), 493–522.

Gay, G. (1978). Multicultural preparation and teacher effectiveness in desegregated schools. *Theory Into Practice, 17*(2), 149–156.

Giles, M. B., & Sherman, T. M. (1982). Measurement of multicultural attitudes of teacher trainees. *Journal of Educational Research, 75*(4), 204–209.

Giroux, H., & McLaren, P. (1986). Teacher education and the politics of engagement: The case for democratic schooling. *Harvard Educational Review, 56*(3), 213–238.

Gollub, W. L., & Sloan, E. (1978). Teacher expectations and race and socioeconomic status. *Urban Education, 13*(1), 95–106.

Gomez, M. L. (1993). Prospective teachers' perspectives on teaching diverse children: A review with implications for teacher education and practice. *Journal of Negro Education, 62*(4), 459–474.

Gordon, B. (1986). The use of emancipatory pedagogy in teacher education. *The Journal of Educational Thought, 20*(2), 59–66.

Grant, C. (1978). Education that is multicultural—Isn't that what we mean? *Journal of Teacher Education, 29*(5), 45–48.

Grant, C. A. (1977). The mediator of culture: A teacher role revisited. *Journal of Research and Development in Education, 11*(1), 102–117.

Grant, C. A., & Koskela, R. A. (1986). Education that is multicultural and the relationship between preservice campus learning and field experiences. *Journal of Educational Research, 79*(4), 197–204.

Haberman, M., & Post, L. (1998). Teachers for multicultural schools: The power of selection. *Theory Into Practice, 37*(2), 96–104.

Hollins, E. (1995). Revealing the deep meaning of culture in school learning: Framing a new paradigm for teacher preparation. *Action in Teacher Research, 17*(1), 70–79.

Howe, W. A., & Pang, V. O. (2000). Overcoming resistance to multicultural discourse through the use of classroom simulations. *MultiCultural Review, 9*(3), 32.

Hunter, W. A. (Ed.) (1974). *Multicultural education through competency based teacher education.* Washington D.C.: AACTE.

James, R. (1978). Multicultural education: NCATE standard rationale. *Journal of Teacher Education, 29*(1), 13–20.

King, J. (1991). Dysconscious racism: Ideology, identity, and the miseducation of teachers. *Journal of Negro Education, 60*(2), 133–146.

Kumashiro, K. (2000). Teaching and learning through desire, crisis, and difference: Perverted reflections on anti-oppressive education. *Radical Teacher, 58*(Fall), 6–11.

Ladson-Billings, G. (1995). "But that's just good teaching": The case for culturally relevant pedagogy. *Theory Into Practice, 34*(3), 159–165.

Leistyna, P. (2001). Extending the possibilities of multicultural professional development in public schools. *Journal of Curriculum and Supervision, 16*(4), 282–304.

Mahan, J. (1982). Community involvement components in culturally-oriented teacher preparation. *Education, 103*(2), 163–172.

Mahan, J., & Boyle, V. (1981). Multicultural teacher preparation: An attitudinal survey. *Educational Research Quarterly, 6*(3), 97–103.

McAllister, G., & Irvine, J. J. (2002). The role of empathy in teaching culturally diverse students: A qualitative study of teachers' beliefs. *Journal of Teacher Education, 53*(5), 433–443.

National Council for Accreditation of Teacher Education (NCATE) (1977). *Standards for the Accreditation of Teacher Education.* Washington D.C.

Oakes, J. (1996). Making the rhetoric real: UCLAs struggle for teacher education that is multicultural and social reconstructionist. *Multicultural Education, 4*(2), 4–10.

Rousseve, R. (1963). Teachers of culturally disadvantaged American youth. *Journal of Negro Education, 33*(2), 114–121.

Rueda, R., & Prieto, A. G. (1979). Cultural pluralism: Implications for teacher education. *TEASE, 2*(4), 4–10.

Rueda, R., Rodriguez, R., & Prieto, A. G. (1981). Teachers' perceptions of competencies for instructing bilingual/multicultural exceptional children. *Exceptional Children, 48*(3), 268–270.

Shor, I. (1986). Equality is excellence: Transforming teacher education and the learning process. *Harvard Educational Review, 56*(4), 406–426.

Sleeter, C. (2001). Preparing teachers for culturally diverse schools: Research and the overwhelming presence of whiteness. *Journal of Teacher Education, 52*(2), 94–106.

Washington, V. (1982). Implementing multicultural education: Elementary teachers' attitudes and professional practices. *Peabody Journal of Education, 59*(3), 190–200.

*What matters most: Teaching for America's future* (1996). New York: National Commissions on Teaching and America's Future.

White, J. G. (1981). Improving multicultural teacher in-service: A CIPP planning model. *The High School Journal, 64*(5), 217–221.

Yao, E. L. (1983). A training program in Asian-American culture for elementary school teachers. *Contemporary Education, 54*(2), 86–92.

# PART 1

**■■■**

# TEACHER DISPOSITIONS

# CHAPTER 1

# TEACHER EXPECTATIONS AND RACE AND SOCIOECONOMIC STATUS (1978)

*Wendy Leebov Gollub and Earline Sloan*

Given the present social structure in the United States and the vested interest of the upper and middle classes in maintaining this structure (Stein, 1971), certain inequalities of opportunity exist among classes and races of people. According to American rhetoric, public school education offers equal opportunity to all and should, therefore, be a significant factor in equalizing the inequalities among members of social groups. Obviously, public education is not living up to the rhetoric that supports it. As the Coleman Report so bluntly states:

> One implication stands out above all: That schools bring little influence to bear on a child's achievement that is independent of his background and general social context; and that this very lack of independent effect means that the inequalities imposed on children by their home, neighborhood, and peer environment are carried along to become the inequalities with which they confront adult life at the end of school. For equality of educational opportunity through the schools must imply a strong effect of schools that is independent of the child's immediate social environment, and that strong independent effect is not present in American Schools [Coleman et al., 1966: 325].

In the late 1960s Rist (1970) conducted a three year study in which he concluded that one very important reason that a student's academic achievement is so closely tied to his/her social background is that a teacher's expectations regarding the academic potential of a child in his/her first year of schooling, frequently kindergarten, are based almost totally on racial and socioeconomic facts about the child. A large body of research concurs in the Rist findings. Differential treatment from the teacher based on these expectations then contributes to the realization of the expectations. Thereafter, the initial achievement level of the child in his/her first year of schooling is reinforced by each subsequent teacher. The cycle goes on.

It is the purpose of this article to synthesize the bulk of research that establishes the relationship between the teacher expectancy effect and the social evils of poverty and prejudice and thereby offer some insight into the operation of this pernicious phenomenon.

## Teacher expectations and student socioeconomic status

Miller and associates (1969) asked teachers to predict the future academic success of four fictional first-grade students based on case history reports. The students were matched for I.Q., school grades, and history of behavior problems. However, teachers were led to believe that two of the students came from middle class homes and two from lower class homes. Teachers rated the middle class students higher on ten of twelve scales even though students were matched on the seemingly more relevant variables.

Similarly, Goodwin and Sanders (1969) asked teachers to rank the importance of seven variables as predictors of future success for first- and sixth-grade students. Socioeconomic status was ranked number one for the first-grade pupils followed by I.Q., standardized test scores, age, sex, anecdotal notes, and, finally, grade-point average. For the sixth graders, standardized test scores were first followed by grade-point average. Socioeconomic status still ranked above I.Q., age, and anecdotal notes.

Friedman and Friedman (1973) studied twenty-four fifth- and sixth-grade classrooms to ascertain the relationship between teacher reinforcing behavior and student social class. They found that significantly more total reinforcements, and especially nonverbal reinforcements, were given to middle class children than to lower class children. In 1940 Davis and Dollard found similar results.

Leacock (1969) compared second- and fifth-grade classrooms in four New York City schools matched or contrasted according to certain socioeconomic and racial criteria. Included in the study were one lower-income Black school, one lower-income white school, one middle-income Black school, and one middle-income white school. Classroom observation as well as teacher and student interview data were analyzed in detail according to the following categories:

1    the nature and clarity of the teacher's teaching concept, particularly with regard to the integration and development of curriculum content;
2    the depth, richness, and variety of the curriculum content;
3    the style of learning and thought being encouraged in the classroom;
4    the value content of classroom materials; and
5    the relation of curriculum content to the children's experiences (Leacock, 1969: 23).

Leacock points to the feedback pattern of the second-grade teacher in the lower-income Black school as illustrative of the failure syndrome created in such schools. "The teacher in the low-income all-Negro school both reflects and creates the expectation of defeat for the children in her class. She is the teacher whose response to the children's work was negative twice as often as it was positive" (Leacock, 1969: 139).

Leacock reports further:

The teachers of the fifth and second grades in the lower-income Negro school, at first impression did not seem unsupportive of the children. . . . Both, however, shared a derogatory attitude toward the children and their potentialities as groups. The second-grade teacher denied much of what the children offered from their own experience. . . . The fifth-grade teacher . . . continually derogated and undermined the children's academic contributions. In both classrooms, the children were constantly receiving the message, "You are not going to do very much." The researchers were struck by the fact that standards in the low-income Negro classrooms were low for both achievement and behavior. They had assumed that the middle-income schools would stress achievement and that the lower-income schools would emphasize behavior.

Yet it was in the middle-income schools, both Negro and white, that the strictest demands were made (1969: 155).

Leacock's findings emphasize in particular the differences in teachers' goal-setting statements for the different socioeconomic status students.

> What we observed in the classroom was not the attempt to "impose middle-class goals" on the children, but rather a tacit assumption that these goals were not open to at least the vast majority of them. The "middle-class values" being imposed on the low-income Negro children defined them as inadequate and their proper role as one of deference. Despite the fact that some teachers in the low-income schools stated they felt a responsibility to set "middle-class standards" for the children, their lowered expectations were expressed by a low emphasis on goal-setting statements altogether. In a three-hour period, clear-cut overt goal-setting statements numbered 12 and 13 for the low-income Negro school, 15 and 18 for the low-income white school and 43 and 46 for the middle-income white school (Leacock, 1969: 205).

Rist, in his provocative study (1970), identified the role that cultural expectations play in the formation of low teacher expectations and the resulting effect on student achievement. The teachers he observed were all Black teachers dealing with Black students.

The study began at the kindergarten level. Each kindergarten teacher in the study had several sources of information available to him/her before the students ever came to school, although not a single source was related directly to the *academic* potential of the incoming kindergarten child. "Rather, they concerned various types of social information revealing such facts as the financial status of certain families, medical care of the child, presence or absence of a telephone in the home, as well as the structure of the family in which the child lived, i.e., number of siblings, whether the child lived with both, one or neither of his natural parents" (Rist, 1970: 418).

Within eight days of starting school, the students had been placed in "ability" reading groups which were shown to remain basically the same in composition until at least the end of the Rist study three years later.

As Rist observed students in the reading groups, he discovered that the students at tables 1, 2, and 3 became increasingly dissimilar according to a number of criteria. First of all, students' physical appearances were noticeably different. Students with darkest skin, shabbiest clothes, and worst body odor were all at table 3. Second, students at table 1 seemed most at ease in their interactions with one another and the teacher, especially when initiating contacts with the teacher. The use of language within the classroom appeared to be the third major differentiation among the children. While students at the first table were most verbal and used more standard English, students at the third table were least verbal and used more dialect. The final criterion by which the children at the first table were quite noticeably different from those at the other tables consisted of a series of social factors which were known to the teacher prior to her seating the children.

Rist hypothesized that the above criteria became for teachers indicative of expected success and others become indicative of expected failure. Those children who closely fit the teachers' "ideal type" of the successful child were chosen for seats at table 1. Rist further speculated that the criteria upon which the teachers

*Table 1.1* Distribution of socioeconomic status factors by seating arrangement at the three tables in the kindergarten classroom

| | Seating arrangement* | | |
|---|---|---|---|
| Factors | Table 1 | Table 2 | Table 3 |
| Income | | | |
| 1) Families on welfare | 0 | 2 | 4 |
| 2) Families with father employed | 6 | 3 | 2 |
| 3) Families with mother employed | 5 | 5 | 5 |
| 4) Families with both parents employed | 5 | 3 | 2 |
| 5) Total family income below $3,000. /yr** | 0 | 4 | 7 |
| 6) Total family income above $12,000. /yr** | 4 | 0 | 0 |
| Education | | | |
| 1) Father ever grade school | 6 | 3 | 2 |
| 2) Father ever high school | 5 | 2 | 1 |
| 3) Father ever college | 1 | 0 | 0 |
| 4) Mother ever grade school | 9 | 10 | 8 |
| 5) Mother ever high school | 7 | 6 | 5 |
| 6) Mother ever college | 4 | 0 | 0 |
| 7) Children with pre-school experience | 1 | 1 | 0 |
| Family Size | | | |
| 1) Families with one child | 3 | 1 | 0 |
| 2) Families with six or more children | 2 | 6 | 7 |
| 3) Average number of siblings in family | 3–4 | 5–6 | 6–7 |
| 4) Families with both parents present | 6 | 3 | 2 |

*Source:* Rist, 1970: 421.

\* There are nine children at table 1, eleven at table 2, and ten children at table 3.
\*\* Estimated from stated occupation.

constructed this ideal version of the successful student rested in their perception of certain attributes in the child that they believed constituted success in the larger society. One particular teacher's normative reference group, for example, was a mixed Black-White, well-educated middle class. Those attributes most desired by educated members of the middle class became the basis for her evaluation of the children. "The organization of the kindergarten classroom according to the expectation of success or failure after the eighth day of school became the basis for the differential treatment of the children for the remainder of the school year. . . . The fundamental division of the class into those expected to learn and those expected not to permeated the teacher's orientation to the class" (Rist, 1970: 423).

By the time the children reached the second grade, their grouping assignments appeared to be based not on the teacher's expectations of how the child might perform, but rather on the basis of past performance of the child. Still there was no mobility between groups.

When Mackler (1969) studied the effects of tracking systems in Harlem, he reported findings similar to Rist's. Kindergarten teachers grouped children according to such valued traits as politeness, passivity, and listening to and following directions. Eventually it was the kindergarten teachers' evaluation of students along these dimensions that determined the "track" the students were placed in early in the first grade. Students who had not attended kindergarten were automatically placed in the lower tracks. Once placed, students in subsequent years rarely changed from their original first-grade placement.

Three of the largest studies analyzing the effects of ability grouping (Douglas, 1964; Goldberg et al., 1966; Husen and Svensson, 1960) support the above findings. Children of higher socioeconomic status tend to be placed in higher tracks than their measured ability would predict. Furthermore, once placed in a given track, students tend to stay there. Less than 5% move, and that movement is most often downward.

Tuckman and Bierman (1971) experimented with reassigning students in a tracking system. Four hundred twenty-one Black junior high and senior high students were randomly and unobtrusively assigned to the next higher ability group in a suburban city school system. Three hundred eighty-four comparable students were retained as controls. At the end of the year teachers recommended that 54% of those moved up be retained in the higher tracks. Only 1% of the controls were recommended for a higher placement. Experimental students in the higher tracks scored as well on achievement tests, received comparable grades, and attended school as regularly as other highs. They did significantly better in every way than the controls who remained in their original placements. Lows who had been reassigned to a middle track did not do as well as controls according to report card grades. However, they did do significantly better than controls according to test scores and their attendance and school-satisfaction ratings were similar.

The tracking system unquestionably affects the attitudes and expectations of students, teachers, and parents and contributes to the continued failure of many students. On the other hand, parents and teachers in attempting to change this system could find themselves in a double bind. Wasserman (1974) claims that the absence of tracking in low socioeconomic schools, particularly Black schools, is equivalent to thrusting the entire student body in the "low group." A tracking system gives a small portion of students labeled "fast" a semblance of a chance because colleges and potential employers might consider them exceptions.

## Teacher expectations and race

The degree to which race is a determiner of teacher expectations is greatly confounded by an overlapping of race with socioeconomic status. In our society, controlling for socio-economic status too frequently has the effect of controlling for race as well. Despite the fact that Leacock (1969) found it difficult to locate middle class Black schools for her study, she was able to conclude that socioeconomic status was more relevant a variable than race. However, she did uncover a disturbing race-related finding.

> In the middle-income white school, the children toward whom the teacher felt most positive had an average I.Q. score some eleven points higher than those toward whom she felt negative. Those toward whom she felt neutral fell in between, although closer to the high than the low scorers. This was not the case in the low-income Negro school. Here the children about whom the teacher felt positive or neutral had an average I.Q. score *almost ten points lower* than those about whom she felt negative. As to "ability" and achievement, the average reading-achievement scores in the middle-income classroom

followed the I.Q. scores, while they did not in the low-income Negro school. In the latter, average reading achievement was the same for the different I.Q. groups. Although far from being completely culture-free, I.Q. tests are at least more so than reading-achievement tests, and they indicate the untapped abilities of those more creative hence often more problematical children who are rebelling against the constrictions of school and society. That they often express the frustration felt by the group as a whole is suggested by a further finding. In the middle-income school the popularity of the better readers and unpopularity of the poorer readers was clear. In the low-income school, however, it was the slightly better readers with the average I.Q. who were, as a group, more unpopular than the poorer readers with the higher I.Q. [Leacock, 1969: 136–137].

In a study using white and black students with the same white teachers, Rubovits and Maehr (1973) found that the "gifted Black" students were the least liked, most ignored, and most criticized students even in comparison to their "non-gifted" Black counterparts. Attitudes and behaviors on the part of teachers could not be accounted for by student behavior because the students in this study had been randomly labeled as gifted or nongifted.

The teachers in the Rubovits and Maehr study were relatively inexperienced in dealing with Black students and probably did not expect to find gifted Blacks. If so, Rubovits and Maehr's findings are not surprising. There is much evidence to show that teachers are not happy with students who violate their expectations even when these "violations" are in a positive rather than negative direction (Rosenthal, 1973; Brophy and Good, 1974; Jeter and Davis, 1973; Shore, 1969).

Coates (1972) conducted an experimental study similar to Rubovits and Maehr's. In this study adult men and women taught learning problems to one of four nine-year-old boys (two Black, two White) who were following the directions of the experimenters. While each adult worked with a child, he or she could see the child, but not his responses. The adults received feedback suggesting that the child was slowly and gradually learning the problem. After each response from the child, the adult received information about the correctness of that response. The experimenter gave the same feedback to all adult participants about each of the four children. The adult then had to select a feedback statement for the child from a list of five that represented a scale from criticism to praise. When the session with one child was completed, the adult filled out an adjective-description rating of that child. Data analysis of the feedback statements the adults made to children during the teaching time revealed that the women treated the Black and White children similarly, while the men showed greater negativity toward the Black children. However, on sixteen of the nineteen trait-rating scales, the child's race proved to be a significant factor for both men and women. They rated the Black boys more negatively (e.g., as dull, unfriendly, and passive) than they rated the white boys.

In Yee's (1968) study of teacher and student attitudes, student race and ethnicity as well as student socioeconomic status were shown to influence teacher attitudes. Middle class White students were viewed most favorably by teachers, followed by lower class White students, lower class Mexican-American students, and finally lower class Black students. This held true despite the fact that most teachers of the Black students were Black.

While the influence of race on the formation of teacher expectations has probably not as yet been adequately researched, evidence to date does suggest that being Black or a member of any minority for that matter (Kleinfeld, 1972; Yee, 1968) can negatively affect teachers' expectations. Certainly being both Black and poor at this time in history is an ill-fated combination that is likely to breed teacher behaviors that impede student success in school.

## Summary

Much of the most powerful and striking literature on teacher expectations establishes teacher expectations as a social, as well as an educational, problem. Research has demonstrated a high correlation between low teacher expectations and certain socioeconomic and racial characteristics of students.

Teachers' subjective predictions regarding students' future academic success (particularly when these students are still in the lower grades), seem to be based on characteristics associated with the race of the student and the income-level of the students' families. Research also shows that teachers tend to treat minority students and students from low-income families less appropriately than they treat students from middle-income families. Based on his observations, Rist hypothesized that a teacher's normative reference group (usually the educated middle class), becomes the basis for the teacher's evaluation of a student's potential; and on this basis, children are sorted into those expected to learn and those not expected to learn. This division is accomplished through ability grouping within a classroom and institutionalized through the tracking systems in the schools.

The racial and socioeconomic bases for teacher expectations is one important reason schools in America are not making an impact on students independent of their background and general social context.

## References

Brophy, J. and T. Good (1974) Teacher-Student Relationships. New York: Holt, Rinehart & Winston.

Coates, B. (1972) "White adult behavior toward Black and White children." Child Development 43: 143–154.

Coleman, J. S. et al. (1966) Equality of Educational Opportunity. Washington, DC: Government Printing Office.

Davis, O. and J. Dollard (1940) Children of Bondage. Washington, DC: American Council on Education.

Douglas, J. (1964) The Home and the School. London: MacGibbon & Kee.

Friedman, H. and P. Friedman (1973) "Frequency and types of teacher reinforcement given to lower- and middle-class students." Presented at the annual meeting of the American Educational Research Association.

Goldberg, M., A. Passow, and J. Justman (1966) The Effects of Ability Grouping. New York: Teachers College Press.

Goodwin, W. and J. Sanders (1969) "An exploratory study of the effect of selected variables upon teacher expectation of pupil success." Presented at the annual meeting of the American Educational Research Association.

Husen, T. and N. Svennson (1960) "Pedagogic milieu and development of intellectual skills. School Rev. 68: 36–51.

Jeter, U. and O. Davis (1973) "Elementary school teachers' differential classroom interaction with children as a function of differential expectations of pupil achievements." Presented at the annual meeting of the American Educational Research Association.

Kleinfeld, J. (1972) "Instructional style and the intellectual performance of Indian and Eskimo students." Final Report, Project No. 1-J-027, Office of Education, U.S. Department of Health, Education, and Welfare.

Leacock, E. (1969) Teaching and Learning in City Schools. New York: Basic Books.

Mackler, B. (1969) "Grouping in the ghetto." Education and Urban Society 2: 80–96.

Miller, C., J. McLaughlin, J. Haddon, and N. Chansky (1969) "Socio-economic class and teacher bias." Psych. Reports 23: 806.

Rist, R. C. (1970) "Student social class and teacher expectations: the self-fulfilling prophecy in ghetto education." Harvard Educational Rev. 40, 3 (August): 411–450.

Rosenthal, R. (1973) "The pygmalion effect lives." Psychology Today (September): 56–63.

—— and L. Jacobson (1968) Pygmalion in the Classroom. New York: Holt, Rinehart & Winston.

Rubovits, P. D. and M. L. Maehr (1973) "The effect of the labels 'gifted' and 'non-gifted' on teachers' interaction with Black and White students." (unpublished)

Shore, A. (1969) "Confirmation of expectancy and changes in teachers evaluations of student behaviors." Dissertation Abstracts 30: 1878–1879.

Stein, A. (1971) "Strategies for failure." Harvard Educational Rev. 41, 2 (May).

Tuckman, B. and M. Bierman (1971) "Beyond pygmalion: galatea in the schools." Presented at the annual meeting of the American Educational Research Association.

Wasserman, M. (1974) Demystifying School. New York: Praeger.

Yee, A. "Interpersonal attitudes of teachers and advantaged and disadvantaged pupils." J. of Human Resources 3: 327–332.

# CHAPTER 2

# MEASUREMENT OF MULTICULTURAL ATTITUDES OF TEACHER TRAINEES (1982)

*Mary B. Giles and Thomas M. Sherman*

The National Council for Accreditation of Teacher Education (NCATE) has mandated that each teacher training program shall provide "evidence of planning for multicultural education in its teacher education curricula including both the general and professional studies components" (NCATE, 1977, p. 4). This standard has created the necessity not only of training teachers in multicultural education but also of assessing the development of multicultural attitudes among teacher trainees. For assessment to be possible, however, the dimension or dimensions that constitute multicultural attitudes must be clearly defined. NCATE indicated that "multicultural education is viewed as an intervention and an on-going assessment process to help institutions and individuals become more responsive to the human condition, individual cultural integrity, and cultural pluralism in our society" (p. 4). The implication seems to be that multicultural education will result in increased knowledge as well as changes in attitudes about teaching in multicultural settings.

Nevertheless, an explicit delineation of what constitutes cultural differences and what is an appropriate attitude toward differences is not easily determined. There are many points of view on what should be the outcomes of multicultural education. There appears, however, to be relatively broad agreement that the concept of culture is pervasive rather than confined to a single issue such as racial classification or economic status. In essence, the issue appears to be one regarding the acceptability of socially, economically, culturally, and racially based differences.

NCATE presented a minimum of four purposes for multicultural education:

1  the promotion of analytical and evaluative abilities to confront issues such as participatory democracy, racism and sexism, and the parity of power
2  the development of skills for values clarification including the study of the manifest and latent transmission of values
3  the examination of the dynamics of diverse cultures and the implications for developing teaching strategies
4  the examination of linguistic variations and diverse learning.

Although the NCATE emphasis is on the acquisition of information and skills, the basis for examination of an attitude rather than a body of knowledge lies in the assumption that receptivity to multicultural education would be preceded or accompanied by an attitude of openness to new ideas and an acceptance of the legitimacy of different points of view within the social system. Though an accepting attitude does not encompass all facets of multicultural education, the difficulty in identifying the content of the knowledge to be transmitted as well as the belief that changes in information are likely to be accompanied by changes in attitude, led to the decision to attempt to define and measure a positive multicultural attitude. This investigation was predicated on the hypothesis that the acceptance of cultural diversity within society was grounded in a generalized acceptance of other people, an openness to new ideas, acceptance of self, and, to some degree, an exposure to culturally different groups.

## Method

The data were collected from 381 undergraduate teacher trainees in a large, Southern, land-grant university as part of an on-going assessment of the teacher training program. The student population is largely white and middle class. Students from all class levels were represented and all students were required to complete this and several other instruments at the same time.

Several constructs that appeared related to multicultural attitudes were assembled into a Multicultural Attitude Questionnaire (MAQ) with six sections.

### *Variety in family and friends*

Variety in an individual's circle of friends in college was assessed by a Diversity Among Friends scale. Students who indicated that they had no close friends on the college campus did not complete this section. The remaining students were asked to jot down the names of four people with whom they spent the most time. They were then directed to answer six questions, derived from the sociogram construct, about these four friends. The questions were:

1   How many of these four friends come from the same home town as you?
2   How many come from the same state as you?
3   How many share your religious background?
4   How many of them are of the same ethnic and racial background as you?
5   How many of them grew up in family situations more like than different from yours?
6   How many of them are generally in the same income range as you and your family?

The response options were:

0—if the question applies to one friend.
1—if the question applies to two friends.
2—if the question applies to three friends.
3—if the question applies to all four friends.
4—if you don't know.

The responses were summed to provide a total score on the scale with a low score indicating high diversity.

The lack of a "none" option was an unfortunate omission in response options and created some problems for responding accurately to these items. As a result, more cases were eliminated from this section because of incomplete responses than from any other.

## Social distance

Part II of the MAQ provided a list of nine activities and asked students to respond on a 5-point (0 to 4) Likert-type scale as to the degree of interest or disinterest they had in engaging in the activities with students from racial or ethnic backgrounds different from theirs. The lower scores indicated a greater degree of interest. The midpoint of the scale (2) was considered a neutral point. The nine activities fell into a clear two-factor structure and were divided into two scales as follows:

Casual Activities Scale

1   eating in a public place or the dining hall
2   eating privately in your apartment or a friend's apartment
3   participating in a sports event
4   going to a movie, concert, or sports event

Personal Activities Scale

1   going dancing
2   dating
3   taking home to spend weekend with you and your parents
4   marrying
5   living with

These scales were based on the concept of social distance (Bogardus, 1958).

## Acceptance of others

Part III of the MAQ was composed of items from the Acceptance of Others Scale and the Perceived Acceptance by Others Scale, devised by Fey (1955). Both scales are answered on a 5-point (0 to 4) Likert-type scale ranging from "almost always" to "very rarely." Some of the items are reverse-scored and were coded so that a low score indicates lower acceptance.

## Opinions on specific groups

Parts IV and V of the MAQ were used only during the first administration of the instrument. These were the only sections in which opinions about specific racial/ethnic groups were solicited by name. In Part IV six groups (White Americans, Black Americans, Asian Americans, Spanish Americans, American Indians, and the foreign-born) were presented with four semantic differential scales (good-bad; foolish-smart; clean-dirty; harmful-helpful). In Part V comparisons between families with different racial/ethnic backgrounds were given with a 5-point Likert-type scale ranging from extremely similar to extremely dissimilar.

When confronted with these items, some students became openly hostile during the testing session and others complained subsequently to their faculty advisors about the nature of these items. Analysis of the data showed that almost all of the students had chosen either the positive end of the scale or the neutral point for all items; thus, the data were essentially useless. While information of this type seems to be at the heart of the multicultural attitude question, it was obvious that it could not be gained from these groups of students by such a direct approach, and subsequent groups of students were told to skip these two sections. No analyses of these data are included in this report.

## Ethnic composition

The final section of the MAQ asked students to identify the primary racial/ethnic composition of their high school and neighborhood. The overwhelming majority (over 90%) of the students in the group were from white high schools and from white neighborhoods and, thus, there was little variance in their responses. This section is not included in the analyses that follow, although it will be kept in the questionnaire because it seems to be potentially useful with more diverse groups of students.

## Results

Descriptive statistics for the scales within the MAQ are shown in Table 2.1. All scales, with the exception of the Acceptance by Others Scale, showed satisfactory internal consistency reliability coefficients, particularly in light of the shortness of some of the scales. A principal components factor analysis with varimax rotation of the five items on the Acceptance by Others Scale revealed two clear factors: the first, with two items, explaining 45% of the variance; and the second, with three items, explaining an additional 30% of the variance. However, given the inherent instability of extremely short scales of only two and three items, it was decided not to divide the scale on the basis of the factor analysis.

There was considerable overlap among the scales, suggesting that they may measure dimensions of the same construct. The maximum variance in one scale explained by another was approximately 61% for the Diversity Among Friends and the Personal Activities Scale. This particular relationship suggests that those students who report having more friends from different racial/ethnic backgrounds are also more interested in closer contact with different students. The differences in the correlations between Casual and Personal Activities and the two Acceptance Scales suggest that different mechanisms may operate in the Casual and Personal Activities scores, even though the correlation between the two scales was relatively high (.69).

To examine the hypothesized link between the scales of the MAQ and a generalized acceptance of self, the scales from the Adjective Check List (Gough and Heilbrun, 1965), the Rokeach Dogmatism Scale (Rokeach, 1960), and the Rotter Internal-External Locus of Control Scale (Rotter, 1966) were regressed on the MAQ scales. In addition, because multicultural attitudes, as defined here, should be independent of intellectual ability, scores from the *Missouri College English Test* (Callis & Johnson, 1964) were included as an indicator of verbal skills. A preliminary examination of the *Missouri College English Test* scores showed small or negligible correlations between these scores and the scales of the Adjective Check List and the MAQ scales.

Because of numerous high intercorrelations among the scales of the Adjective Check List, and the problem of multicollinearity in the regression analysis, a principal components factor analysis with varimax rotation was performed on the 24 Adjective Check List scales. A five-factor solution was obtained. The factor loadings from this solution are presented in Table 2.2.

Table 2.1 Descriptive statistics for MAQ scales

| Scale name | Alpha reliability | Score range | No of students | X̄ Scale score | SD | Intercorrelations | | | |
| --- | --- | --- | --- | --- | --- | --- | --- | --- | --- |
| | | | | | | CA | PA | AO | AB |
| Diversity Among Friends (DF) (Low score = high diversity) | .87 | 0–24 | 225 | 7.49 | 5.89 | .52 | .78 | .41 | .76 |
| Casual Activities (CA) (Low score = higher interest) | .92 | 0–16 | 371 | 3.77 | 3.70 | – | .69 | .05 | .21 |
| Personal Activities (PA) (Low score = high interest) | .92 | 0–20 | 349 | 10.83 | 6.67 | | – | .21 | .45 |
| Acceptance of Others (AO) (Low score = low acceptance) | .84 | 0–80 | 377 | 41.23 | 10.95 | | | – | .47 |
| Acceptance by Others (AB) (Low score = low acceptance) | .39 | 0–20 | 369 | 14.17 | 2.74 | | | | – |

To facilitate further discussion of the factors, a subjective interpretation of the patterns of the largest loading variables was made and the factors were named. The scales loading most heavily on Factor 1 reflected a positive attitude toward life, an effort to do well and to achieve objectives, and to attempt to understand one's own behavior and that of others. This factor was named Well-Adjusted. Factor 2 appeared to describe a more forceful, dominant, confident individual who is determined to do well and sure of his ability. Factor 2 was named Decisive. Factor 3 suggested an individual who likes change, is perceptive and alert, and welcomes challenge. The Lability scale, which loaded highly on this factor, is one of the more unstable scales of the Adjective Check List, and most of the interpretive emphasis was placed on the Need for Change scale and the positive aspects of the Lability scale. Factor 3 was named Flexible. Factor 5 appeared to describe an uncomplicated, outgoing, pleasure-seeking outlook, and

*Table 2.2* Factor loadings on rotated 5-factor solution for 24 scales from the Adjective Check List

| Scale | Factor 1[a] | Factor 2[b] | Factor 3[c] | Factor 4[d] | Factor 5[e] |
|---|---|---|---|---|---|
| No. Adjectives Checked | .05 | .00 | .09 | −.09 | .87 |
| No. Favorable Adjectives | .83 | .22 | .10 | .24 | .21 |
| No. Unfavorable Adjectives | −.57 | .07 | −.22 | −.03 | .27 |
| Defensiveness | .82 | .18 | −.16 | .27 | .07 |
| Self-Confidence | .16 | .84 | .11 | .13 | .03 |
| Self-Control | .81 | −.24 | −.28 | −.03 | −.10 |
| Lability | .08 | .17 | .74 | .04 | −.05 |
| Personal Adjustment | .85 | .03 | −.02 | .20 | −.02 |
| Need for Achievement | .57 | .69 | −.12 | −.06 | .12 |
| Need for Dominance | .30 | .90 | −.03 | .09 | .05 |
| Need for Endurance | .72 | .35 | −.46 | −.03 | −.06 |
| Need for Order | .69 | .21 | −.53 | −.18 | .08 |
| Need for Intraception | .83 | −.06 | .06 | −.04 | .06 |
| Need for Nurturance | .76 | −.17 | .05 | .47 | −.05 |
| Need for Affiliation | .65 | .14 | .17 | .53 | .09 |
| Need for Heterosexuality | .15 | .22 | .13 | .73 | .20 |
| Need for Exhibition | −.35 | .67 | .14 | .46 | .09 |
| Need for Autonomy | −.46 | .69 | .31 | −.13 | .10 |
| Need for Aggression | −.73 | .52 | .03 | −.11 | .07 |
| Need for Change | −.06 | .26 | .75 | .09 | .19 |
| Need for Succorance | −.48 | −.59 | −.20 | .02 | .29 |
| Need for Abasement | .13 | −.86 | −.09 | −.09 | .09 |
| Need for Deference | .48 | −.73 | −.30 | .10 | −.09 |
| Counseling Readiness | −.19 | .05 | .02 | −.72 | .28 |
| Variance explained by rotated factor | 7.66 | 5.29 | 2.10 | 2.05 | 1.24 |

[a] Well-adjusted factor
[b] Decisive factor
[c] Flexible factor
[d] Sociable factor
[e] Enthusiastic factor

was named Sociable. The single scale loading unambiguously on Factor 5 reflects surgency, drive, and a relative absence of repressive tendencies and may indicate an exuberance that is essentially shallow. This factor was summarized as Enthusiastic.

When factor scores from these five Adjective Check List factors, the Rokeach Dogmatism Scale, the Rotter Locus of Control Scale, and the *Missouri College English Test* were regressed on the five MAQ scales, significant total regressions were obtained for all MAQ scales except the Casual Activity Scale. A summary of these regression results is given in Table 2.3.

In general, the regression analysis followed expectation. More flexible and better-adjusted individuals showed greater diversity of backgrounds among their close friends. These individuals also showed greater interest in the personal contact with students of other racial/ethnic groups. It was somewhat surprising, however, to find that individuals scoring toward the external end of the locus of control continuum, i.e., those who tended to believe that the control of reinforcement lay outside themselves, reported greater diversity among their friends.

High acceptance of others was associated with high scores on the Sociable and Enthusiastic scales and with more internal scores on the locus of control scale. High dogmatism scores, i.e., and tendency towards a closed belief system, were associated with low acceptance of others as were high scores on the Flexible factor. This result for the Flexible factor seems somewhat contradictory to the relationship between Flexibility and the Diversity Among Friends scale. It is not clear what this may imply. Scores on the *Missouri College English Test* showed a significant beta-weight in this regression only. On the Acceptance by Others scale, higher scores on the Well-Adjusted, the Decisive, the Sociable, and the Enthusiastic factors were associated with a perception of greater acceptance by others. Individuals with a more internal locus of control also felt that people were more accepting of them.

To determine whether differences between groups could be detected using the MAQ scale scores, a series of *t* tests was performed on the various scales using demographic data. One limitation to this analysis was the very low proportion of racial/ethnic groups other than white in the group of teacher trainees. Only 16 of the students indicated nonwhite racial identification and, thus, an examination of the effects of race could not be made.

The variables examined for all scales were sex, religious affiliation, type of community in which the majority of precollege years were spent, father's education, mother's education, family income level, the importance of college to parents, and area of educational interest. Students whose mothers did not go to college and who were interested in secondary education as well as males and Protestants exhibited significantly less diversity in selecting friends than did elementary education students, students whose mothers attended college, and females and non-Protestants. Students who grew up in metropolitan areas and elementary education students were more interested in both casual and personal relationships with students from other racial/ethnic groups. Females were more amenable to casual activities than males, and students with religious affiliations other than Protestant were more accepting of personal activities with students of other racial/ethnic groups. Protestants were also significantly less accepting of others than students indicating other religious preferences. These results are summarized in Table 2.4.

*Table 2.3* Summary of multiple linear regressions of personality factor scores, attitude and ability measures on MAQ Scales

| Scale | Multiple r | r² | F | df | F-test for beta-weights Variable | F |
|---|---|---|---|---|---|---|
| Diversity Among Friends | .49 | .24 | 4.35* | 8,112 | Well-Adjusted (−) | 14.81* |
| | | | | | Decisive (+) | 0.67 |
| | | | | | Flexible (−) | 10.62* |
| | | | | | Sociable (+) | 0.49 |
| | | | | | Enthusiastic (+) | 2.21 |
| | | | | | Dogmatic (−) | 0.76 |
| | | | | | I-E (−) | 7.24* |
| | | | | | Test (+) | 0.59 |
| Casual Activities | .19 | .04 | 1.53 | 8,313 | Well-Adjusted (−) | 2.72 |
| | | | | | Decisive (+) | 0.03 |
| | | | | | Flexible (−) | 2.80 |
| | | | | | Sociable (−) | 1.34 |
| | | | | | Enthusiastic (−) | 0.14 |
| | | | | | Dogmatic (+) | 0.32 |
| | | | | | I-E (+) | 0.87* |
| | | | | | Test (−) | 3.53 |
| Personal Activities | .29 | .09 | 3.43* | 8,294 | Well-Adjusted (−) | 4.28* |
| | | | | | Decisive (+) | 0.11 |
| | | | | | Flexible (−) | 20.08* |
| | | | | | Sociable (+) | 0.42 |
| | | | | | Enthusiastic (+) | 0.52 |
| | | | | | Dogmatic (+) | 0.17 |
| | | | | | I-E (−) | 0.05 |
| | | | | | Test (+) | 2.49 |
| Acceptance of Others | .46 | .22 | 10.99* | 8,320 | Well-Adjusted (−) | 0.02 |
| | | | | | Decisive (+) | 0.34 |
| | | | | | Flexible (−) | 7.39* |
| | | | | | Sociable (+) | 3.84* |
| | | | | | Enthusiastic (+) | 10.00* |
| | | | | | Dogmatic (−) | 21.65* |
| | | | | | I-E (−) | 32.43* |
| | | | | | Test (+) | 4.64* |
| Acceptance by Others | .45 | .20 | 9.76* | 8,311 | Well-Adjusted (+) | 7.65* |
| | | | | | Decisive (+) | 6.63* |
| | | | | | Spontaneous (+) | 0.00 |
| | | | | | Sociable (+) | 18.02* |
| | | | | | Enthusiastic (+) | 10.40* |
| | | | | | Dogmatic (+) | 0.02 |
| | | | | | I-E (−) | 22.58* |
| | | | | | Test (+) | 3.77 |

* $p \leq .05$

Table 2.4  *t* tests for scales and descriptive variables showing significantly different means[a]

| Scale | Variable | Categories | N | X̄ | SD | t | df |
|---|---|---|---|---|---|---|---|
| Diversity Among Friends | Sex | Male | 37 | 10.46 | 4.92 | 3.64 | 154 |
| | | Female | 119 | 6.57 | 5.88 | | |
| | Religious preference | Protestant | 105 | 8.70 | 5.65 | 3.81 | 154 |
| | | Non-Protestant | 51 | 5.02 | 5.67 | | |
| | Mother's education | No college | 55 | 9.35 | 5.72 | 2.97 | 154 |
| | | Some college | 101 | 6.49 | 5.77 | | |
| | Area of educational interest | Elementary | 80 | 5.60 | 6.01 | −4.52 | 150 |
| | | Secondary | 72 | 9.67 | 4.96 | | |
| Casual Activities | Sex | Male | 108 | 4.67 | 3.69 | 3.02 | 369 |
| | | Female | 263 | 3.40 | 3.65 | | |
| | Community type | Metropolitan | 189 | 3.33 | 3.64 | −2.36 | 369 |
| | | Other | | | | | |
| | Area of educational interest | Elementary | 155 | 2.94 | 3.54 | −4.06 | 361 |
| | | Secondary | 208 | 4.50 | 3.68 | | |
| Personal Activities | Religious preference | Protestant | 223 | 11.77 | 6.39 | 3.53 | 347 |
| | | Non-Protestant | 126 | 9.18 | 6.85 | | |
| | Community type | Metropolitan | 173 | 9.83 | 6.73 | −2.81 | 347 |
| | | Other | 176 | 11.82 | 6.48 | | |
| | Area of educational interest | Elementary | 152 | 9.22 | 7.37 | −4.06 | 281[b] |
| | | Secondary | 188 | 12.18 | 5.73 | | |
| Acceptance of Others | Religious preference | Protestant | 240 | 42.31 | 10.26 | 2.45 | 375 |
| | | Non-Protestant | 137 | 39.35 | 11.87 | | |
| Acceptance by Others | No significantly different means | | | | | | |

[a] *p* ≤ .05 for two-tail test.
[b] Approximate *t* with adjusted degrees of freedom because of significant difference in variances.

## Discussion

Overall, the MAQ appears to be a promising instrument from which a more stable and clearly defined questionnaire may be developed. It shows acceptable reliability, and many relationships between the MAQ and other instruments fell within expected limits suggesting that the MAQ possesses a considerable degree of construct validity, as the construct was defined in this study. Obviously, observations of behavior are needed to establish the relationship of the self-reported attitudes and behaviors on the MAQ to performance in situations in which diverse cultural/racial backgrounds are found.

In its present stage, however, the MAQ can detect differences between groups of students and, to the extent that the dimensions it measures are facets of attitudes toward multicultural differences, the MAQ offers a place to begin in assessing developmental shifts in multicultural attitudes as students progress through a teacher education program. This sensitivity to differences makes possible program specific evaluation and research on those program components that have been designed to achieve the aims of the NCATE multicultural standard.

## References

Bogardus, E. S. Racial distance changes in the United States during the past thirty years. *Sociology and Social Research*, 1958, *43*, 127–134.

Callis, R., & Johnson, W. *Missouri college English test.* New York: Harcourt, Brace & World, Inc., 1965.

Fey, W. F. Acceptance by others and its relation to acceptance of self and others: A revaluation. *Journal of Abnormal and Social Psychology*, 1955, *50*, 274–276.

Gough, H. G., & Heilbrun, A. B., Jr. *The adjective check list.* Palo Alto, California: Consulting Psychologists Press, 1965.

NCATE, *Standards for the Accreditation of Teacher Education.* Washington, D.C.: National Council for Accreditation of Teacher Education, May, 1977.

Rokeach, M. *The open and closed mind.* New York: Basic Books, 1960.

Rotter, J. B. Generalized expectancies for internal versus external control of reinforcement. *Psychological Monographs*, 1966, *80* (Whole No. 609).

# CHAPTER 3

# IMPLEMENTING MULTICULTURAL EDUCATION (1982)

## Elementary teachers' attitudes and professional practices

*Valora Washington*

Surprisingly little research investigates teachers' roles in desegregated education. Because it focuses on student outcomes, school desegregation research has failed largely to delineate factors interacting with those outcomes. While our education literature clearly suggests that teachers hold different attitudes toward and expectations about advantaged, disadvantaged white and nonwhite pupils, salient behaviors and attitudes are not identified specifically in ways which facilitate change (Washington, 1980). A critical issue is the relationship between attitudes and behavior and the assumption that multicultural teacher training can mediate the interaction between those two variables.

Indeed, calls for multicultural teacher training imply that teacher racism and/or ignorance stunts minority children's learning potential. Though based on legitimate concerns and needs for minority education, advocates for teacher change often present models of what should be without adequate information about what is. This procedure often results in implementation strategies lacking a specific focus (other than goodwill); these implementors (e.g., colleges of education) can only assume the quality or quantity of incongruence between models of multicultural education and local educational practice.

In their review of the literature, Washington and Woolever (1979) found no surveys of teacher attitudes and practices regarding multicultural education which we could compare to theoretical constructs or employ as a basis for implementing multicultural teacher training. This lack of information underlines the need to survey teachers about multicultural education practice. Such information is vital to the provision of effective and efficient educational leadership. According to Washington and Woolever (1979) colleges of education, now required by certification agencies to devise multicultural education programs may utilize such information as a data base underlying educational change. In this way, services to preservice and inservice teachers can be guided by educational reality rather than be tailored to general, and often vague, models of multicultural education. Given this problem and this goal, the primary objectives of the research reported here involved surveying teachers to determine (a) their attitudes toward multiethnic or integrated schooling, (b) their access to multicultural materials and methods, and (c) their degree of utilization of multicultural materials and methods.

## Subjects

All school systems in North Carolina with at least 20% minority enrollment, according to 1978–79 statistics, were invited to participate in this research. From this population, 69 school systems, over 47% of the state/local education units, chose to participate. Within each school system, teachers of first, third, and fifth grade students (Note 1) were asked to complete the survey.

The North Carolina Multicultural Education Survey sampled the attitudes and behaviors of 3,017 elementary school teachers. These teachers represent the three grade levels selected. Thirty-two percent taught first grade; 31%, third grade; 24%, fifty grade; and 13% taught more than one of those three grades. Of the respondents, 95% were female; only 5% male.

## Procedure

### Implementation strategy

Most cooperating school systems selected a liaison (usually an elementary school supervisor or assistant superintendent) to assist in distributing and collecting surveys. Therefore, we mailed surveys to the central administrative office, liaisons distributed them to teachers, and central office personnel returned them to us. In a few instances, however, school systems provided mailing lists of eligible teachers. Also, several small school systems enlisted the support of the elementary school principal(s) in distributing and collecting the surveys.

On the basis of both theoretical and intuitive guidelines, survey construction began July 1, 1979. In conjunction with a teacher training effort, we field-tested the instrument during August 1979 (Note 2), and made revisions continually through December 1979 based on the pretest data and collaboration with survey research specialists, teacher educators, elementary school teachers, and public school administrators. We administered the survey in January and February 1980.

### Instrumentation

The survey instrument included the following information and scales (Note 3):

1  *General information:* Provided data about the school system population and the respondents' place of education, gender, race, North Carolina region, years of teaching experience, subject area specialty, the highest academic degree, percentage of "special" (handicapped, poor, and ethnic minority) children taught, and the quality of his/her professional life (e.g., job satisfaction, attitudes toward the profession).
2  *Scale 1: Desegregation attitudes* (sum Items 20–25). Indicated attitudes toward desegregation and its effects on the educational system or on pupils. 6 to 30 points possible.
3  *Scale 2: Multicultural education attitudes* (sum Items 26–31). Indicated attitudes toward multicultural education and its effects on the quality of schooling. 6 to 30 points possible.
4  *Scale 3: Availability of multicultural materials or methods* (sum Items 32–37). Indicated whether respondents believe that they have access to a variety of instructional methods and materials which facilitate multicultural education. 6 to 30 points possible.

5   *Scale 4: Classroom behavior* (sum Items 38–44). Indicated the frequency with which the respondents actually utilized or implemented teaching activities which reflect multicultural education concerns or techniques. 7 to 35 points possible.

## Analysis

We computed a separate score for each scale in the survey. To evaluate teacher responses within scales, each level of response was assigned to numerical rating of 1 to 5. High scores (5) indicate the most positive responses; i.e., high scores suggest more active and fulfilling professional lives, are disposed favorably toward desegregated and multicultural schooling or believe its effects beneficial, believe they enjoy access to a wider variety of multicultural materials and methods, and tend to utilize these materials and methods as integral parts of instruction. The results include general descriptions of teacher multicultural attitudes and behavior; determinations of statistical variance between groups of respondents (by race, sex, grade level, etc.); and discussion of the congruence between multicultural education theory and practice, with concern for professional development.

## General results

Generally, teachers' desegregation attitudes were relatively neutral or slightly positive, $\bar{x} = 18$. For example, 49% of respondents agreed and 24% disagreed that the United States government has a moral obligation to desegregate schools. Similarly, 49% of the teachers disagreed and 24% agreed that school desegregation has caused more harm than good. Only 40% clearly disagreed that democracy is threatened by forced busing, while 31% agreed with that statement. About half (46%) disagreed that public school desegregation has lowered the quality of education; over one-third of the teachers (36%) agreed with that statement. Almost equal proportions of teachers agreed (38%) and disagreed (34%) that children's moral and social education has been enhanced by attendance at desegregated schools. Yet, a small minority (22%) agreed and a majority (55%) disagreed that everyone has benefited from school desegregation.

Compared to their attitudes toward school desegretation, teachers' feelings toward multicultural schooling were more positive, $\bar{x} = 21$. A clear majority (71%) agreed and only a fraction (17%) disagreed that children should know the contributions of minorities in every subject they study. A majority (65%) also indicated that attention to multicultural education will (not) distract young children from learning basic skills; however, 16% believed there would be a distraction. Similarly 61% disagreed and 18% agreed that multicultural education leads to lower academic standards. Rather, a majority (62%) believed and 15% disagreed that multicultural education helps minority and white children. Nonetheless, only 44% disagreed and 9% agreed that emphasis on cultural pluralism and bilingualism in education destroys social cohesion. Almost equal proportions agreed (37%) and disagreed (30%) that the state department of education should require local school districts to have multicultural curricula. The survey also assessed teacher opinions regarding the availability of multicultural materials and methods. Teachers indicated repeatedly that multicultural curricula methods and materials were inaccessible to them, $\bar{x} = 16$.

A variety of instruments and techniques for testing and counseling ethnic groups were not usually available to 60% of the respondents; 2% had such instruments. Similarly, 55% reported that their curriculum did not include information written by or about ethnic groups for teaching content skills such as math and reading. Forty-nine percent did not have and 29% had access to a handbook of ideas, approaches, materials, or activities supporting multicultural activities. Also, 49% did not report inservice training or assistance which included multicultural or bilingual education concerns; 23% did report multicultural training. About one-third reported yes (34%) and one-third indicated no (31%) when asked: Do your school assemblies, decorations, speakers, holidays, and heroes reflect ethnic differences? Nonetheless, most teachers (52%) reported that their school library or resource center included a wide variety of material on the histories, experiences, and cultures of many ethnic groups; only 18% did not include these materials.

Given teacher inassessibility, it is not surprising that teachers report that they did not utilize multicultural materials and methods, $\bar{x} = 11$. Eighty-four percent within the past school year had never taken any field trips which were related to cross-cultural experiences. Results show 71% had never utilized parent or community resources to support multicultural education in the curricula; 64% had never planned activities whereby students could try out cross-cultural experiences and reflect upon them. Fifty percent had never put up bulletin boards or other displays related to different groups, or had multiracial and multiethnic bulletin boards; 37% used multicultural bulletin boards once or twice. Within the past month, 47% had one or two subject content lessons which had included information about the contributions of minorities; 38% had not had such lessons. Within the past month, 42% of the teachers had one or two occasions in which they read to students, or required students to read books which had ethnic minorities in the primary roles; 37% did not offer multicultural readings.

In assessing the primary reason for difficulty in implementing multicultural education concepts, most teachers (61%) indicated that appropriate materials were unavailable; 18% cited that reasons for difficulty would be the teacher's lack of time on the project. Some of the teachers (17%) reported the primary cause of difficulty as disinterested children. Only 4% suggested that the school administration or parents would discourage them.

To further profile North Carolina teachers and their classrooms, respondents were asked to indicate the extent to which pupils segregated themselves by race, sex, and social class. One-fourth of the teachers (26%) indicated that students never segregate themselves along racial lines. Similarly, one-third of the respondents (33%) believe that students rarely group racially. Few teachers (12%) believe students grouped themselves by race often or most of the time. More than race or social class segregation, teachers inclined to indicate that students segregate themselves by gender. Thirty-two percent of the teachers responded that students never or rarely segregate themselves by gender. On the other hand, 27% of the respondents indicate that students do separate themselves by sex often and most of the time.

## Variance between teacher groups

Analysis of variance procedures were utilized to determine whether significant differences were present between identified teacher groups. The dependent variables included desegregation attitudes, multicultural methods and materials, classroom behavior, perceptions of student segregation, and reasons for difficulty in establishing multicultural education (see Table 3.1).

*Table 3.1* Checklist of significant differences between teacher groups on the North Carolina Multicultural Education Survey

| Teacher groups ↓ / Measures → | Access to desegregation attitudes | Education attitudes | Materials and methods | Reasons for classroom utilization | Student segregation | Multicultural failure |
|---|---|---|---|---|---|---|
| Large vs. Small Towns | | | X | | | X |
| Educated In vs. Out of N.C. | X | | | | | |
| Different Grade Levels | | X | X | X | X | |
| Gender Differences | | | | | X | |
| Racial Differences | X | X | X | X | X | X |
| Within-State Regional Differences | X | X | | X | X | X |
| Differences in Proportions of Poor Children Taught | X | X | | X | X | X |
| Differences in Proportions of Minority Children Taught | X | X | | X | X | X |
| Subject Specialty | | | X | X | X | |
| Degree of Professional Experience | X | | X | X | | X |
| Bachelor's vs. Graduate Degrees | X | X | X | X | | |

## Population

Analyses were made of two levels of responses (residents of towns under or over 10,000 people). Teachers serving larger school systems indicated greater access to multicultural materials and methods, $F(1, 2663) = 8.92, p < .003$. Also, differences occurred in the reasons given for the difficulties in establishing a multicultural learning environment, $F(1, 2489) = 6.60, p < .01$.

## Place of education

Although 90% of the teachers were educated in North Carolina, a large number (291) were not. Teachers educated outside the state held more favorable desegregation attitudes, $F(1, 2846) = 4.24, p < .04$.

## Grade

Four grade levels were delineated: first, third, fifth, and combination (more than one grade level). Combination classroom teachers were most favorable in their attitudes toward multicultural education, $F(3, 2814) = 5.48, p < .001$, and in the perceptions of the availability of multicultural materials and methods, $F(3, 2820) = 2.55, p < .05$. Nonetheless, the actual integration of multicultural education ranked greatest among third and fifth grade teachers, $F(3, 2803) = 3.39, p < .02$. According to teachers, pupils increasingly segregated themselves by race, sex, or social class from first to fifth grades, $F(3, 2814) = 94.94, p < .0001$. Figure 3.1 illustrates mean scores by grade levels instructed by the respondents.

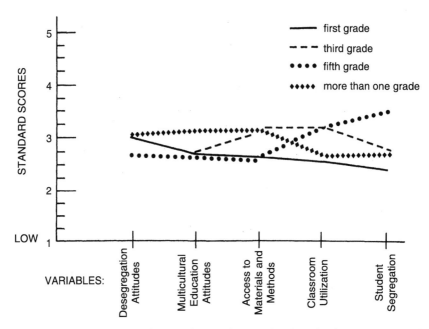

*Figure 3.1* Mean scores on the North Carolina Multicultural Education Survey by grade levels instructed by the respondents

## Gender

Of the respondents, 95% were females; 133 indicated that they were males. Recognizing this limitation, gender differences were indicated in teacher perceptions of student segregation. Males indicated more segregation by gender, race, or social class than females did, $F(1, 2843) = 19.25, p < .0001$. Figure 3.2 illustrates mean scores on the survey scales by gender.

## Race

Of the respondents, 3% were American Indians, 32% were Afro-Americans, and 64% were whites. Compared to white teachers, minority teachers (Indian and black) had more favorable attitudes toward school desegregation, $F(1, 2839) = -332.93, p < .0001$. Minority teachers also held more favorable attitudes toward multicultural education, $F(1, 2826) = 301.77, p < .0001$. White teachers, however, indicated that multicultural materials and methods were more available to them than minorities indicated, $F(1, 2832) = 30.76, p < .0001$. Nonetheless, blacks and Indians actually utilized multicultural methods and materials more than white teachers did, $F(1, 2815) = 57.30, p < .0001$. Similarly, racial groups expressed different reasons for the difficulties in implementing multicultural education in the classroom, $F(1, 2638) = 80.37, p < .0001$. Figure 3.3 illustrates mean scores on the survey scales by race. Also, whites indicated more student segregation, $F(1, 2826) = 44.65\ p < .0001$.

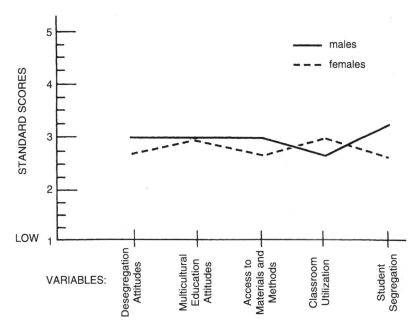

*Figure 3.2* Mean scores on the North Carolina Multicultural Education Survey by gender of the respondents

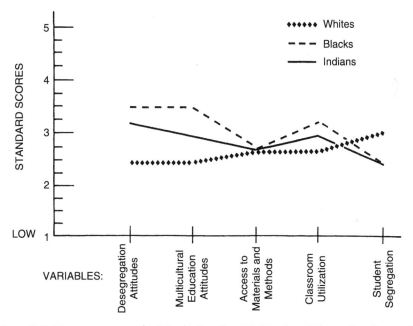

*Figure 3.3* Mean scores on the North Carolina Multicultural Education Survey by race of the respondents

## Region

North Carolina can distinguish three geographical areas: the Piedmont, Coastal Plains, and Mountains. Although we exerted efforts to include all three regions in this survey, we note that, given the criteria of 20% minority enrollment in the participating school systems, many Mountain schools were excluded; most black and Indian North Carolineans reside in the Piedmont or Coastal Plains. Therefore, in descending order, mean desegregation attitude scores varied from the Piedmont, to the Coastal Plains to the Mountains, $F (2, 2766) = 8.01, p < .0003$. Multicultural education attitudes showed a similar pattern of variability, $F(2, 2754) = 10.02, p < .0001$. Although the regions did not vary in indications of multicultural education materials availability, differences did appear in the extent to which teacher behavior reflected multicultural practice, $F (2, 2746) = 4.22, p < .01$. The regions also varied in perceptions of student segregation, $F (2, 2755) = 3.66, p < .03$, and in reasons for difficulty in establishing a multicultural curricula, $F (2, 2574) = 13.18, p < .0001$.

## Proportions of poor children instructed

More than half of the teachers (52%) taught fewer than 50% poor children, and 49% of the teachers taught more than 50% poor children. Both desegregation and multicultural education attitudes were most favorable among teachers of more poor children, $F (1, 2823) = 36.10, p < .0001$, and $F (1, 2810) = 56.57, p < .0001$ respectively. Although no significant differences appear in teachers' access to multicultural materials and methods, teachers of more poor children actually utilized multicultural concepts to a greater extent, $F (1, 2802) = 8.04, p < .005$. Yet, teachers of fewer poor children indicated more segregation among students, $F (1, 2811) = 9.86, p < .001$. These two groups of teachers also held varying opinions on reasons for multicultural education failure $F (1, 2630) = 7.80, p < .005$.

## Proportion of minority children instructed

Equal proportions (50%) of teachers taught less and more than 50% minority children. Teachers of more minority children held the most favorable attitudes toward school desegregation, $F (1, 2813) = 47.47, p < .0001$, and teachers of more minorities inclined most favorably toward multicultural education concepts, $F (1, 2801) = 72.88, p .0001$. Also, teachers of more minority children tended to utilize multicultural materials and methods more often, $F (1, 2793) = 16.06, p < .0001$. Yet, teachers of fewer minority children indicated that children segregate themselves along gender, race, or social class lines more often, $F (1, 2801) = 28.09, p < .0001$. These two teacher groups also varied in their reasons for multicultural education failure, $F (1, 2621) = 33.31, p < .0001$.

## Subject specialty

Subjects were grouped also according to teaching specialty. Of the teachers, 33% were language arts specialists, 46% had more than one teaching specialty, 11% had a "nonlanguage arts" specialty, and 10% had no specialty. Nonspecialists had the lowest mean scores (15.6) and language arts specialists scored highest ($\bar{x} = 16.6$) in indications of the availability of multicultural materials and methods, $F$

$(3, 2787) = 3.72$, $p < .01$. Similarly, nonlanguage arts specialists and nonspecialists actually utilized multicultural methods and materials to a lesser extent than language arts specialists and those teachers with more than one specialty, $F$ $(3, 2771) = 6.66$, $p < .0002$. These teacher groups also varied in perceptions of student segregation, $F$ $(3, 2781) = 13.03$, $p < .0001$.

## Teaching experience

Two levels of teaching experience were compared: fewer than 10 years (47% of respondents) and 10 years or more (53% of respondents). Teachers having more experience had more positive attitudes toward school desegregation, $F$ $(1, 2883) = 13.14$, $p < .0003$. More experienced teachers also indicated greater access to multicultural materials and methods, $F$ $(1, 2876) = 23.31$, $p < .0001$. More experienced teachers also utilized multicultural materials and methods to a greater extent, $F$ $(1, 2859) = 44.87$, $p < .0001$. The two teacher groups also varied in the reason expressed for difficulties in implementing multicultural education, $F$ $(1, 2680) = 4.70$, $p < .03$.

## Degree

Most teachers (79%) held a bachelor's degree only, but 21% of the teachers held graduate degrees. Teachers holding graduate degrees had more favorable attitudes toward both school desegregation, $F$ $(1, 2873) = 6.58$, $p < .01$, and towards multicultural education, $F$ $(1, 2860) = 11.85$, $p < .0006$. Also, teachers holding graduate degrees indicated that they enjoyed greater access to multicultural materials and methods, $F$ $(1, 2866) = 7.30$, $p < .007$; these teachers also utilized these materials more than did teachers holding bachelor's degrees only, $F$ $(1, 2849) = 11.08$, $p < .0009$.

## Discussion

Generally, teachers are divided evenly in opinion and commitment to the concept of school desegregation and its impact. Nonetheless, within the integrated classrooms, most teachers apparently hold attitudes indicating a commitment to educational practice denoting equal treatment and equal opportunity for development of each individual to the fullest of his or her potential.

Teachers, however, generally indicated a lack of access to materials to enhance implementation of multicultural education theory in classrooms. Consequently, while the attitude measures indicate teacher receptivity to multicultural education, teachers do not have access to materials to enable them to act in accordance with their favorable predispositions.

Access to materials is important since actual instructional practice is essential to multicultural education. Favourable attitudes are necessary for multicultural education but are not sufficient without their behavioral correlates. Yet, this survey found that most teachers do not employ multicultural materials and methods at all, or that their use of these techniques remains negligible. For example, despite federal and state emphasis on parent involvement with schools, during 1979–80 most teachers stated that they had never utilized parent or community resources to support multicultural education in the curricula. Also, since bulletin boards are often central features of primary classrooms, it is noteworthy that half of the teachers had never, during 1979–80, created any bulletin boards or other displays related to different groups or had multiracial and multiethnic bulletin boards. Multicultural materials and methods were seriously lacking in educational practice.

Given the teachers' relatively favorable attitudes toward theoretical concepts of multicultural education, a training focus on consciousness raising would not be warranted. Rather, teachers may benefit most from training which includes provision of materials and model strategies for selecting and using these materials. Although teachers did indicate access to a number of school library resources, it is feasible that, given the absence of multicultural inservice training, teachers remain unaware of creative use of these materials, or ways they can integrate these materials into existing curricula.

The importance of providing materials to teachers, and of providing training as to their varied usages, is underlined by the fact that almost two-thirds (61%) of the teachers responded that multicultural failure probably would result because appropriate materials were not available. Yet, teacher training including model uses of multicultural materials may be required to alter perceptions that pluralistic instruction mandates much teacher time and requires "something extra." Training would need to focus on multicultural education as an integral part of existing curricula, as part of typical lesson plans.

Given the emphasis on materials, training would be most effective given hands-on experiences, rather than lecture-discussion workshops for pre- or in-service teachers. An administrative resource person in each school/school system could support and encourage using multicultural materials and methods. Workshops demonstrating model teaching and learning strategies or providing teachers with opportunities for sharing experiences may generate interest and increase implementation. An extended training program should include opportunities for discussion and for peer-learning among teachers of similar content-areas of grade levels.

A critical feature of training would be opportunities for work within the classroom setting, including the provision of multicultural materials, examples of model or alternative instructional methodology, and assistance in observing, identifying, and capitalizing upon the unique strenghs of individual learners. According to Washington (in press), training which has involved lectures and discussion, though enjoyed by teachers, has not proved effective in altering classroom practice.

Training involving peer learning is indicated further since data analysis demonstrates relatively successful multicultural practice among some teacher groups. Notably, more successful examples of multicultural classroom behavior were found among third- and fifth-grade teachers, blacks/Indians, residents of the North Carolina Piedmont, teachers with larger proportions of poor or minority children, more experienced teachers, and those holding degrees.

The North Carolina Multicultural Education Survey has identified and validated needs of local educators in responding to the challenge presented by multicultural education requirements. Specifically, teachers need materials as well as innovative and creative training in utilizing these materials. Since the teachers themselves appear to exhibit favorable attitudes toward and interest in multicultural instruction, it may be important to alert local and state education administrators of the gaps in theory and practice. Perhaps, these administrators may require consciousness-raising and assistance in realizing and allocating necessary resources required for implementation.

Our study is an important assessment tool. The identification of what *is* occurring in integrated, multicultural classrooms provides a data base for both research and programs which hope to mediate what *is* with what *should be* or what *is required*. In this way, the current study is an innovative step toward understanding the outcomes of desegregated schooling in terms of their causation. Competency and achievement tests continue to alert educators that the educational gap between blacks and whites is not narrowing, despite over a decade of school desegregation. It is, indeed, timely to move beyond legal requirements of integrated schooling to facilitating teaching-learning processes which will fulfill the promise of the *Brown* decisions.

## Notes

1   Research indicates that primary school children are most susceptible to teacher behavior and attitudes (see Washington, 1976, 1979a, 1979b). Also, we reasoned that, if multicultural education is being implemented at all, it would most likely occur at the elementary school level.
2   Field testing of the instrument became part of an investigation entitled, "The Impact of Anti-Racism/Multicultural Education Training on Elementary Teachers' Attitudes and Behavior" by Valora Washington. A report of this investigation will appear in a forthcoming issue of *The Elementary School Journal*.
3   Protocols of scale 4 were administered in the fall of 1976 to preservice teachers at Indiana University. Protocols of scales 2 and 4 were administered to teachers of the Indianapolis Public School System in the fall of 1977. Protocols of scales, 3, 4, 5, 6, and 7 were administered in a North Carolina School System during August 1979 (see note 2).

## References

Washington, V. Impact of antiracism/multicultural education training on elementary teachers attitudes and classroom behavior. *The Elementary School Journal*, 1981, n.p.
Washington, V. Learning racial identity. In R.C. Granger and J.C. Young (Eds.), *Demythologizing the inner city child*. Washington, DC: National Association for the Education of Young Children, 1976, pp. 85–98.
Washington, V. Noncognitive effects of instruction: A look at teacher behavior and effectiveness. *Educational Horizons*, Spring 1979b, 57, n.p.
Washington, V. The role of teacher behavior in school desegregation. *Educational Horizons*, Spring 1979a, 57, 145–51.
Washington, V. Teachers in integrated classrooms: Profiles of attitudes, perceptions and behavior. *Elementary School Journal*, 1980, 80, 193–201.
Washington, V., & Woolever, R. Preparing teachers for diversity: An urban necessity. In W.J. Wicker (Ed.), *Perspectives on urban affairs in North Carolina*. Chapel Hill, NC: Urban Studies Council/University of North Carolina Press, 1979, pp. 57–66.

# CHAPTER 4

# CULTURAL PLURALISM (1979)
## Implications for teacher education
*Robert Rueda and Alfonso G. Prieto*

Describing the impact of cultural pluralism on teacher training is an interesting yet elusive task, given the present state of the art. To address this issue systematically, it is imperative that we attempt to establish some common definitions for some of the terminology. The first term that needs defining is *culture*. Granted, there are many definitions of *culture*; however, Aragon's (1973) definition appears to be extremely useful for our purposes. He contends that the concept of a culture involves five criteria:

1  A common language or pattern of communication which is unique to that group;
2  A common basic diet and method of food preparation;
3  Similarities in dress or costuming;
4  Predictable interpersonal, interfamilial interactions, or common socialization patterns;
5  A common set of values, beliefs, and ethics.

*Cultural pluralism* can be defined as the degree of cultural differences which are fostered and encouraged by the society. De Sola Pool (1972) points out that there are three dimensions which allow us to determine the level of cultural pluralism within a given culture: "(1) the number of different cultures within it, or (2) the degree of difference between them, or (3) the strength of the people's identification with the ethnic subcultures" (pp. 321–322). In examining each of these dimensions, it is evident that cultural pluralism exists, at least to some degree, in the United States.

Using de Sola Pool's first criterion, we may be able to identify a variety of groups within the United States that would meet Aragon's definition of a culture. The second criterion is the degree to which the cultures differ. Unfortunately, there is no viable way to assess the specific degree of difference between cultures adequately. In a gross sense, however, it is possible to distinguish between cultures that are significantly discrepant. The third and probably the most important criterion identified by de Sola Pool is the strength of cultural identification. To many of us, two groups may appear to share many similarities, when in reality the members of the groups themselves are primarily concerned with their differences. This dimension may well be the most significant in terms of both service delivery to children and teacher training. Again it is difficult to establish the degree of identification, since it tends to be a very individualized and personal phenomenon.

It is at the level of identification, however, that our educational institutions find themselves in conflict with the populations they purport to serve. The fact that we meet these three criteria in the United States reaffirms the idea that the "melting pot" concept is a figment of a naive and immature socialization mentality.

Since we can argue that the United States is a culturally pluralistic society, we can begin to examine that concept within the structure of education. The American Association of Colleges for Teacher Education in 1973 adopted a "No One Model American" policy, which pointed out the need to recognize cultural and linguistic differences among our population. From the perspective of that policy statement, cultural pluralism, as applied to the institution of education, would discount the assimilation concept of the melting pot as well as the separate but equal position. The policy enjoins us to truly celebrate the differences and the unique contribution that various divergent groups bring to this society. Furthermore, it suggests that our educational institutions should incorporate this philosophy into their on-going daily operations. It is further suggested that this may be accomplished by developing and using multicultural education programs.

One of the major objectives of cultural pluralism is the understanding and appreciation of multiculturalism and multilingualism. In its broadest sense, *multicultural education* may be viewed as an educational process which in some way is concerned with all the different cultural groups represented in a given society (Banks, 1977). Although it is important for us to maintain that philosophical position, the reality of the present state of affairs requires us to attempt to address the issue more specifically.

If we are to be successful in providing appropriate and relevant educational experiences using a multicultural model, it is necessary that we initially limit the focus of our effort. This position is based on our current level of empirical evidence and knowledge in the area, and the practical restrictions we face in program implementation and curriculum development. Banks (1977) has suggested that we restrict the parameters of multicultural education so that we specifically focus on those populations which have suffered discrimination because of their unique cultural characteristics.

One of the major focuses of multicultural education should be to understand, as well as compare and examine, the major issues of discrimination, prejudice, and alienation which have affected these groups. One method of achieving that goal in the past has been to establish ethnic studies programs. While those programs may be considered to be a small component of multicultural education, their focus and boundaries are much too limited to achieve the goals of multicultural education. In the past, those programs have dealt with affective and sensitizing experiences and only superficially addressed the serious issues of multicultural education.

Another more comprehensive and functional approach is multiethnic education, which is a major component of multicultural education. The major goal of *multiethnic education* is to modify the educational milieu in such a way that it becomes more representative and incorporates the ethnic differences seen in our society (Banks, 1977). The changes should be designed so that the value of cultural diversity is emphasized within the institution. If that goal is to be accomplished, educational institutions must engage in a process of self-evaluation designed to determine the extent to which they are monoethnic, and then develop strategies for change (Banks, 1977).

In its truest sense, multicultural education must permeate the entire educational environment. Its goals and objectives must be included in all areas of the curriculum rather than be attached as an appendage to an existing monoethnic curriculum. One avenue by which that objective can be reached is through multi-ethnic education programs. Furthermore, teacher-training institutions must incorporate into their multiethnic training programs certain content that is unique to the target populations that will be receiving the services of their graduates. This content must reflect not only the superficial aspects of the culture, but a variety of culturally related differences which may be associated with educational achievement.

## Culturally associated variables related to education

The "melting pot" view of American social structure led to attempts to consolidate all subcultures into a new and superior culture. Formal educational institutions, namely American public schools, have played a major role in this process (Katz, 1975). However, it has become increasingly apparent that this approach has led to unfavorable outcomes for certain cultural/linguistic groups. It is being increasingly recognized among educators that the cultural/linguistic characteristics of certain groups have often been used to deny them equal educational opportunity (Hunter, 1974; Mercer, 1973; U.S. Commission on Civil Rights, 1974).

The negative outcomes of a monocultural educational approach have been opposed on philosophical, legal, and humanistic grounds (Klassen & Golnick, 1977). Yet if meaningful and lasting changes are to be made in educational practice, the arguments must be based on more than philosophy and humaneness. Specifically, we must establish an empirical basis to support, maintain, and perhaps modify a pluralistic approach to education in the United States. Empirical evidence to support a pluralistic approach to education has begun to accumulate from several diverse areas. Systematic investigation of educationally related variables associated with cultural/linguistic difference is relatively recent. However, a growing body of related empirical knowledge demands further consideration of cultural/linguistic factors in educational practice.

There are several correlates of cultural/linguistic background which may directly influence successful outcomes in school. Although it is premature to specify causal relationships between cultural/linguistic background and these correlated variables, we can say that a relationship does exist. These variables include but are not limited to cognitive, perceptual, personality, and learning characteristics. A brief review of representative research in the areas of personality/social development and cognitive style will illustrate the nature of the observed differences in these dimensions.

### Personality/social development

A number of investigations comparing Anglo-American and Mexican-American children have demonstrated that Anglo-American children are more competitive and less cooperative than Mexican-American children (Avellar & Kagan, 1976; Kagan & Madsen, 1971; Madsen & Shapira, 1970). Typically these studies have employed experimental games which allow a measurement of prosocial or competitive behavior, either in dyadic or group interaction situations (McClintock, 1974) or in peer-absent situations (Kagan, Zahn, & Gealy, 1977).

Although some studies have methodological flaws, e.g., confounding culture and socioeconomic status (SES) (McClintock, 1974), a recent study by Knight and Kagan (1977) controlled SES, urbanization level, and even school attended.

A four-alternative choice experimental game was employed to measure the frequency of two prosocial and two competitive alternatives in 197 subjects of various SES and ethnic background combinations. The researchers found that developmental differences between ethnic groups existed, consistent with earlier research.

It has been proposed that differences in social motivation may account for lower achievement in school (McClintock, 1974). In a test of this hypothesis, Kagan et al. (1977) found that only in kindergarten and second grade was competitiveness significantly related to school achievement. However, it appears that the Mexican-American sample in the study was relatively acculturated. This interpretation is supported by the fact that the differences in competitiveness and prosocial behavior between the two ethnic groups were smaller than observed in previous studies. In spite of this one study, ethnic differences have reliably and consistently been reported in this area, and further studies are needed to document the role of this difference on school achievement.

## Cognitive styles

It has become increasingly apparent that there are meaningful and stable differences in ways in which individuals select and organize input from their environment. These individual differences have come to be known as *cognitive style*. In a review by Keogh (1973), it was concluded that there is general agreement that "the term 'cognitive style' refers to individual consistencies in information seeking and information processing across a variety of problem-solving situations."

One aspect of cognitive style which has received considerable attention is Witkin's field dependence-independence construct (Witkin, Lewis, Hertzman, Machover, Meissner, & Wapner, 1954). Those who are able to overcome the influence of a surrounding perceptual field by differentiating or distinguishing parts from the whole are described as *field independent*; those more influenced by context or background are called *field dependent* (Witkin, Dyk, Faterson, Goodenough, & Karp, 1962).

Several studies have examined cultural background as a correlate of cognitive style. For example, Anglo-American children have consistently been found to be more field independent than Mexican-American children (Buriel, 1975; Kagan & Zahn, 1975; Ramirez & Price-Williams, 1974; Sanders, Scholz, & Kagan, 1976). Most recently, however, a methodological controversy has arisen in regard to the instruments used to measure this construct. When more than one method was used to measure field dependence-independence in a sample of 40 Mexican-American and Anglo-American children, Buriel (1978) found cultural differences on only one of the three measures used and found, in general, low correlations between the three measures for the Mexican-American but not the Anglo-American children.

The interest in cultural differences in cognitive styles on the part of researchers is understandable in the context of educational implications. One major impetus to crosscultural research in cognitive styles is the assumed relationship between preferred cognitive style and school achievement. For example, Kagan and Zahn (1975) found a correlation between field dependence and lowered reading and math achievement test scores. These results are not unequivocal, however. Buriel (1978) found no significant main effects of culture or field dependence in comparing the relationship of three separate field dependence measures to reading and math achievement scores. It appears that further work is needed on the relation of cognitive style and academic achievement for Mexican-American children. Nevertheless, there appears to be some evidence to support the favored position of field independence and educational achievement for exceptional and nonexceptional populations. In a comprehensive review of research with both normal and exceptional populations, Keogh (1973) concluded that, "It seems reasonable that some educational environments are especially facilitating for children with particular modes of perceptual organization, whereas other environments might be debilitating to children with these styles."

In addition to the relationship between cognitive style and school achievement, there is at least one other reason why differences in cognitive style might be important. This reason deals with value orientation. It has been unambiguously proposed that field dependence and field independence do not differ in value or worth (Witkin, et al., 1962). Yet descriptors of field dependence tend to be less positive than those used to describe field independence. For example, field dependence has been associated with a more conciliatory and accommodating interpersonal style (Oltman, Goodenough, Witkin, Freedman, & Friedman, 1975). In addition, some investigators have described field independence with more positive words than field dependence (Rubel & Nakamura, 1972). This implicit value orientation associated with cognitive style difference led Keogh (1973) to conclude that "overall there is a kind of unstated opinion favoring the field independent strategy." It is appropriate but speculative at this point to hypothesize that this attitude may be reflected in the design of formal educational programs.

Although reliable differences have been documented in the area of cognitive styles, nevertheless there are unresolved problems. For example, although we can find reliable differences in the measurement of different cognitive styles, there are problems with the interpretation of these differences. Specifically, while the concept is primarily measured in terms of perceptions, the differences are interpreted in terms of cognitive functioning and even personality and social characteristics. In addition, the complex relationship among the variables of culture, cognitive style, and school achievement remains to be definitively resolved. This relationship becomes even more complex when the variable of exceptional/nonexceptional is added. In spite of these difficulties, it appears that these issues can no longer be ignored in the design of educational programs.

This review of selected investigations provides a brief but documented view of some crosscultural differences, specifically in personality/social development and cognitive style. Yet there are several points that need to be clarified to put this empirical knowledge into proper perspective. First, this brief review was not meant to provide a comprehensive overview of research in these areas. Rather, it only demonstrates representative crosscultural work with possible implications for exceptional children. Second, there are several other culturally related domains which could have been included, such as crosscultural differences in maternal teaching strategies (Feshbach, 1973; Laosa, 1978; Steward & Steward, 1973). A third point which is often overlooked is that there may be as much intracultural variation on a given domain as there is crosscultural variation (Laosa, 1978). A fourth point which is clearly evident is that, at this point, many of the implications of crosscultural differences for exceptional populations must be extrapolated from research employing nonexceptional populations. There is currently a significant lack of research on crosscultural differences with exceptional children.

A final point deserves mention with respect to cultural/linguistic differences on various dimensions. It is entirely conceivable to review research related to differences in these areas and to conclude that cultural/linguistic differences are automatically deficits or negative characteristics. For example, we have already discussed the possible consequences of a field dependent orientation or a lack of competitive behavior in relation to school achievement. We firmly maintain that cultural/linguistic differences are in fact differences and *not deficits*. That is, differences in educational outcomes may reflect the characteristics of schools as much as they reflect child-related characteristics. In any case, certain characteristics of cultural/linguistic minorities may in fact be advantageous. Recent studies relating bilingualism to linguistic development suggest that childhood bilingualism, for example, can promote an awareness of linguistic operations, a more analytic orientation to linguistic input, greater sensitivity to linguistic feedback cues, and ability to analyze ambiguities in sentence structure (Ben-Zeev, 1977a; Cummins, 1978; Cummins & Mulcahy, 1978; Feldman & Shen, 1971; Ianco-Worrall, 1972). These findings are suggestive but remain to be duplicated with exceptional populations. In addition, recent work suggests that the context in which a skill or characteristic is exhibited may be as salient a factor as the strength of that skill or characteristic in terms of its expression (Cole et al., 1971; La Belle, 1976). But in spite of the difficulties, it is possible at this point to consider some implications of the emerging specialization of bilingual/multicultural special education.

## Implications for teacher education

Up to this point we have been focusing on the concept of culture and how different culturally related variables may influence school achievement. We used this approach to indicate the growing empirical base upon which we can base multicultural special education. This approach has rather direct implications for that aspect of multicultural education associated with teacher training.

Multicultural education has been approached in a variety of ways. Traditionally, educational institutions have addressed the issues of cultural awareness and acceptance by introducing specific activities into the established monocultural curriculum. These activities have included special lessons or readings on the contributions of certain minority ethnic groups, courses on pluralism and ethnic studies, music, art, story telling, crafts, observance of special ethnic holidays and celebrations, as well as other areas and activities (Rivlin, 1977). The goals of these activities reflect concern with issues such as increased ethnic pride and crosscultural understanding.

It is not our intention at this point to disparage either the goals or activities of these multicultural programs. Rather, we suggest that a narrow focus on the overt aspects of culture may not be sufficient to meet the educational needs of children of diverse cultural and linguistic backgrounds. Teachers will need to be trained not only in the overt aspects of cultural/linguistic differences, but will need to become familiar with culturally associated characteristics that may be directly related to educational attainment. As discussed earlier, these variables might include perceptual, cognitive, social, and learning differences. As the brief review of literature demonstrated, a growing body of empirical knowledge is developing. For multicultural education to survive as a part of the educational structure, both overt and covert aspects of cultural/linguistic differences will need to be incorporated in the preparation of teachers of bilingual/multicultural exceptional children. Teacher-training institutions are the logical beginning point for this activity. Therefore, the content of teacher-training programs needs to be broadened to reflect our developing empirical knowledge of cultural/linguistic differences.

A related implication concerns the activities of teacher trainers themselves. The brief review of studies in this article suggests that although some empirical research is available to teacher trainers, problems do exist. For example, the available empirical studies are sometimes inconsistent and contradictory, probably as a function of the newness of the field of study. In addition, in many cases the exact relation between culturally associated factors (the covert or "deeper" aspects of culture) and school achievement is unclear. Therefore, often results of the studies are only suggestive for practice. Finally, much of this research has been done with nonexceptional populations. Therefore, the results must be extrapolated to exceptional populations until such time as findings can be validated with exceptional students. At any rate, it is evident that teacher trainers must become familiar with empirical research in the areas under discussion. Furthermore, teacher trainers need to become aware of the limitations of this knowledge base before attempting to translate the research into practice.

These implications for teacher-training programs in the area of multicultural special education focus primarily on content issues. A related, but by no means less important, consideration concerns process. More specifically, we need to direct our attention toward the manner in which teachers are trained. At present many multicultural teacher-training programs are separate entities in the institutions in which they are located. An example of this would be a Master's degree program offering a specialization in multicultural education.

An alternative approach would consist of infusing the content of multicultural education into entire training programs. We suggest that the multicultural content perhaps should not be separated and labeled as a distinct entity to be dealt with in a few courses. A much more thorough approach would appear to be to incorporate this content in all aspects and phases of teacher-training programs. Multicultural content cuts across various specific study areas such as evaluation, methods of instruction, and other traditional teacher-training curricular areas. Separating multicultural education as a distinct entity within an institution often allows the concept, philosophy, and activities of multicultural education to be ignored or bypassed in the mainstream teacher-training program.

Although these ideas pose a possible alternative to the present structure of teacher-training programs, there are certain practical problems. For example, multicultural special education is a relatively new direction in special education. It is probable that this move in a new direction will be challenged either by some professionals in the field or by others controlling educational economic resources. Therefore, because of political and/or funding reasons, it may be advantageous to maintain multicultural special education as a separate entity until it is securely established. But the ultimate goal of teacher-training programs should be to incorporate a multicultural orientation in all phases of their activities. The pluralistic composition of the U.S. population is a definite indicator of the direction that needs to be followed.

We need to stress a final consideration clearly at this point. A major thrust of this article has been to advocate a broader, empirically based approach to teacher-training in the area of multicultural special education. We have suggested several possibilities based on this approach. However, any new directions in teacher-training programs and in the development of multicultural education should be based on empirical data to the maximum extent possible. Constant formative evaluation such as that advocated by Laosa (1974) is needed to empirically determine the ultimate value of any one approach as opposed to alternative approaches. The development of programs to prepare personnel to meet the educational needs of multicultural exceptional children clearly presents a challenge to special education—a challenge that can only be met by careful attention to empirical knowledge and modification of programs based on solid empirical data.

## References

American Association of Colleges for Teacher Education, Commission on Multicultural Education. No one model American. *Journal of Teacher Education*, 1973, *24*, 264–265.
Aragon, J. Cultural conflict and cultural diversity in education. In L. Bransford, L. Baca, & K. Lane (Eds.), *Cultural diversity and the exceptional child*. Reston, Va.: The Council for Exceptional Children, 1973.
Avellar, J., & Kagan, S. Development of competitive behaviors in Anglo-American and Mexican-American children. *Psychological Reports*, 1976, *39*, 191–198.
Banks, J. The implications of multicultural education for teacher education. In F. Klassen & D. Gollnick (Eds.), *Pluralism and the American teacher: Issues and case studies*. Washington, D.C.: American Association of Colleges for Teacher Education, 1977.
Ben-Zeev, S. The influence of bilingualism on cognitive development and cognitive strategy. *Child Development*, 1977, *48*, 1009–1018. (a)
Ben-Zeev, S. The effect of bilingualism in children from Spanish-English low economic neighborhoods on cognitive development and cognitive strategy. *Working Papers in Bilingualism*, 1977 (No. 14), 83–122. (b)
Buriel, R. Cognitive styles among three generations of Mexican-American children. *Journal of Cross-Cultural Psychology*, 1975, *6*, 417–429.
Buriel, R. Relationship of three field-dependence measures to the reading and math achievement of Anglo American and Mexican American children. *Journal of Educational Psychology*, 1978, *70*, 167–174.
Cole, M., et al. *The cultural context of learning and thinking*. New York: Basic Books, 1971.
Cummins, J. Bilingualism and the development of metalinguistic awareness. *Journal of Cross-Cultural Psychology*, 1978, *9*, 131–149.
Cummins, J., & Mulcahy, R. Orientation to language in Ukranian-English bilingual children. *Child Development*, 1978, *49*, 1239–1242.
de Sola Pool, I. Plural society in the southwest: A comparative perspective. In E. Spicer & R. Thompson (Eds.), *Plural society in the Southwest*. Albuquerque: University of New Mexico Press, 1972.
Feldman, C., & Shen, M. Some language-related cognitive advantages of bilingual five-year olds. *Journal of Genetic Psychology*, 1971, *118*, 235–244.
Feshbach, N. D. Cross-cultural studies of teaching styles in four-year-olds and their mothers. In A. E. Pick (Ed.), *Minnesota symposia on child psychology*. Vol. 7. Minneapolis: University of Minnesota Press, 1973.
Hunter, W. A. *Multicultural education through competency-based teacher education*. Washington, D.C.: American Association of Colleges for Teacher Education, 1974.
Ianco-Worrall, A. Bilingualism and cognitive development. *Child Development*, 1972, *43*, 1390–1400.
Kagan, S., & Madsen, M. C. Cooperation and competition of Mexican, Mexican-American, and Anglo-American children of two ages under four instructional sets. *Developmental Psychology*, 1971, *5*, 32–39.
Kagan, S., & Zahn, G. L. Field dependence and the school achievement gap between Anglo-American and Mexican-American children. *Journal of Educational Psychology*, 1975, *67*, 643–650.
Kagan, S., Zahn, G. L., & Gealy, J. Competition and school achievement among Anglo-American and Mexican-American children. *Journal of Educational Psychology*, 1977, *69*, 432–441.
Katz, M. B. *Class, bureaucracy, and schools: The illusion of educational change in America*. New York: Praeger, 1975.
Keogh, B. Perceptual and cognitives styles: Implications for special education. In L. Mann

& D. Sabatino (Eds.), *The first review of special education*. Philadelphia: Journal of Special Education Press, 1973.

Klassen, F. H., & Gollnick, D. M. *Pluralism and the American teacher: Issues and case studies*. American Association of Colleges for Teacher Education, 1977.

Knight, G. P., & Kagan, S. Development of prosocial and competitive behaviors in Anglo-American and Mexican-American children. *Child Development*, 1977, *48*, 1385–1394.

La Belle, T. Deficit, difference, and contextual explanations for the school achievement of students from minority ethnic backgrounds. *UCLA Educator*, 1976, *19*(1), 25–29.

Laosa, L. Maternal teaching strategies in Chicano families of varied educational and socio-economic levels. *Child Development*, 1978, *49*, 1129–1135.

Laosa, L. Toward a research model of multicultural competency-based teacher education. In W. A. Hunter (Ed.), *Multicultural education through competency-based teacher education*. Washington, D.C.: American Association of Colleges for Teacher Education, 1974.

Madsen, M. C., & Shapira, A. Cooperative and competitive behavior of urban Afro-American, Anglo-American, Mexican-American, and Mexican village children. *Developmental Psychology*, 1970, *3*, 16–20.

McClintock, C. G. Development of social motives in Anglo-American and Mexican-American children. *Journal of Personality and Social Psychology*, 1974, *29*, 348–354.

Mercer, J. *Labeling the mentally retarded*. Berkeley: University of California Press, 1973.

Oltman, P. K., Goodenough, D. R., Witkin, H. A., Freedman, N., & Friedman, F. Psychological differentiation as a factor in conflict resolution. *Journal of Personality and Social Psychology*, 1975, *32*, 730–736.

Ramirez, M., III, & Price-Williams, D. R. Cognitive styles of children of three ethnic groups in the United States. *Journal of Cross-Cultural Psychology*, 1974, *5*, 212–219.

Rivlin, H. N. Research and development in multicultural education. In F. H. Klassen & D. M. Gollnick (Eds.), *Pluralism and the American Teacher: Issues and case studies*. American Association of Colleges for Teacher Education, 1977.

Rubel, D. N., & Nakamura, C. Y. Task versus social orientation in young children and their attention to relevant social cues. *Child Development*, 1972.

Sanders, M., Scholz, J. P., & Kagan, S. Three social motives and field independence-dependence in Anglo-American and Mexican-American children. *Journal of Cross-Cultural Psychology*, 1976, *7*, 451–462.

Steward, M. S., & Steward, D. S. The observation of Anglo-, Mexican-, and Chinese-American mothers teaching their young sons. *Child Development*, 1973, *44*, 329–337.

U.S. Commission on Civil Rights. *Toward quality education for Mexican Americans. Report VI: Mexican-American education study*. Washington, D.C.: February 1974.

Witkin, H. A., Dyk, R. B., Faterson, H. F., Goodenough, D. R., & Karp, S. A. *Psychological differentiation*. New York: Wiley, 1962.

Witkin, H. A., Lewis, H. B., Hertzman, M., Machover, K., Meissner, P., & Wapner, S. *Personality through perception*. New York: Harper, 1954.

# CHAPTER 5

# PROSPECTIVE TEACHERS' PERSPECTIVES ON TEACHING DIVERSE CHILDREN (1993)

## A review with implications for teacher education and practice

*Mary Louise Gomez*

I am a teacher educator who aims to prepare prospective teachers to work effect-ively with all children regardless of their life experiences, language backgrounds, skin colors, or family socioeconomic status. In my work, I have observed that prospective teachers often turn to experiences from their own pasts for clues on how to interpret and respond to the contemporary behaviors of the children whom they teach. My White, middle-class, English-speaking university students often believe that their particular personal experiences from their own suburban mid-western childhoods are directly transferrable to the situations they encounter in teaching children unlike themselves living in another time and place. Reliance on these experiences frequently leads to prospective teachers' failure to support or to increase the learning and achievement of the increasingly heterogeneous student population with which they work.

As I pondered the dilemmas of new teachers at my university and the chal-lenges that they pose for me as a teacher educator, I sought information regarding the perspectives of other new teachers about the children whom they will teach. I searched for the responses of other teacher educators who had also taken these perspectives into account in their programs of teacher preparation.[1] The follow-ing questions guided my investigations: Who are prospective teachers in the United States and what are their perspectives on the diverse children they teach? How have other teacher educators developed campus and classroom experiences for prospective teachers so that they can best meet diverse learners' needs?[2] This article presents my synthesis of the answers to these questions and offers implications for programs of teacher preparation.

## A portrait of the prospective teacher population

Who will be the teachers of the future and whom will they teach? There is pres-ently an undisputed mismatch in the race, social-class, and language backgrounds of teachers and students in the United States. In 1990, when the kindergarten through grade 12 school population of the nation was 40% children of color, nearly 90% of teachers were White (National Center for Education Statistics [NCES], 1992). According to Hodgkinson (1991) and others, the race of those teaching and those taught will continue to differ in the future as numbers of school-age children of color increase and numbers of teachers of color decrease in the United States. Social-class differences between students and their teachers are also increasing. In 1989, for example, 15% of White children, 44% of African American children, and 36% of Latino children lived in poverty; these numbers continue to rise (Children's Defense Fund, 1991). Nearly half of all children living in poverty in the United States live in central cities (Children's Defense Fund, 1991). In contrast, most U.S. teachers come from lower-middle-class and middle-class homes and were raised in rural and suburban areas of the nation (Zimpher, 1989). There are also increasing gaps in language background between U.S. teachers and students. There were two million limited-English-proficient students enrolled in grades K–12 in the U.S. in 1990; this marks a 36% increase from 1986 (Olsen, 1991). However, most of the nation's teachers continue to be monolingual in English (Zimpher, 1989).

The data presented above show only that teachers and many of their pupils differ from one another in the United States. At first glance, it may not appear to be a problem that representatives of one group—White, middle-class, English-speaking people, most of whom are females—teach most of the children in the United States. However, when we add to these data findings from several large-scale studies commissioned by the American Association of Colleges for Teacher Education (AACTE) (e.g., Zimpher, 1989; and AACTE, 1990), the Metropolitan Life Insurance Company (Louis Harris & Associates, 1991), and the federally funded National Center for Research on Teacher Education (NCRTE) (Paine, 1989), and a smaller study conducted by Sears (1992), we develop a sharper picture of the nation's prospective teachers. From this picture, we can begin to understand how the race, social-class, sexual orientations, and language backgrounds of prospective teachers affect their attitudes toward Others—persons different from themselves—and their willingness to live near and be a part of communities of Others, to teach Others, and to expect that Others can learn.

The 1990 AACTE study examined questionnaire responses from 472 prospective teachers (60% White, 40% persons of color) enrolled in the third or fourth year of elementary, secondary, and early childhood teacher preparation programs located in 42 AACTE-member institutions. Nearly all of the Whites surveyed grew up in White neighborhoods, attended institutions of higher education also mostly populated by Whites, and reported spending most to all of their time at school with other Whites. Their counterparts who were Black, Latino, and Asian were more likely to live near, go to school with, and spend time with other people of color—especially those who were members of their racial or ethnic group. English was the native language of nearly all of the Whites and Blacks, 50% of the Latinos, and 40% of the Asians surveyed. A majority of the prospective teachers surveyed travelled 100 miles or less from their homes to attend college.

Despite the limitations of their home and school experiences with persons unlike themselves, nearly 100% of Blacks, Latinos, and Asians and over 80% of Whites surveyed felt prepared to work with persons from a different cultural background than their own. However, when asked if they preferred a "majority" (predominantly White setting) as opposed to a "minority" or predominantly non-White setting in which to teach, 80% of Whites, Blacks, and Latinos, and 60% of Asians indicated a preference for a "majority" setting for a teaching assignment.

Zimpher (1989) reports results of an earlier AACTE-sponsored three-phase longitudinal study of teacher education known as RATE (Research About Teacher Education) for which 2,700 prospective elementary and secondary teachers enrolled in 90 institutions preparing teachers were surveyed. From this study, Zimpher developed a portrait of a typical teacher candidate: she is White; from a suburban or rural hometown; monolingual in English; and selected her college for its proximity to home, its affordability and its accessibility. She has travelled little beyond her college's 100-mile or less radius from her home and prefers to teach in a community similar to the one in which she grew up. She hopes to teach middle-income, average (not handicapped or gifted) children in traditional classroom settings.

The Metropolitan Life Insurance Company study surveyed 1,007 teachers who completed their first year of teaching in the United States in 1991. This sample was drawn from elementary, middle school, and secondary public school teachers who graduated from AACTE-member teaching colleges in 1990 and taught for the first time in a public school that year. Eighty percent were female and over 90% were White. In their initial year of teaching, nearly all of the novices had children of color in their classrooms. Nearly three-quarters of the group taught some children who lived in poverty. Responses from these novice teachers indicate that early in their careers, many teachers locate children's problems of learning and achievement not as outcomes of teachers' beliefs about and behaviors toward children in school, but as consequences of children's outside-of-school lives beyond the purview of teachers, schools, and schooling. Over 80% of those sampled strongly agreed with the statement, "I can really make a difference in the lives of my students" before they began teaching. Twenty-five percent fewer strongly agreed with this statement after they had taught for one year. Half of those sampled strongly agreed with the statement that "Many children come to school with so many problems that it's very difficult for them to be good students" before they began to teach; 20% more strongly agreed with this statement after one year of teaching.

Findings from Goodlad's (1990) study of teacher education in the United States corroborate those from the Metropolitan Life study regarding new teachers' willingness to relinquish responsibility for some children's learning and achievement. Goodlad found that many teachers "were less than convinced that all students can learn. They voiced the view that they should be kind and considerate to all, but they accepted as fact the theory that some simply can't learn" (p. 264).

Paine's (1989) analyses of data from another large-scale study of teachers portray an equally dispiriting picture of prospective teachers' beliefs about diverse child populations. Paine drew on baseline data collected in the NCRTE's study of teacher education. Paine analyzed and categorized the orientations toward diversity of 233 teachers at the beginning of their teacher education programs at five preservice sites (Dartmouth College, Illinois State University, Michigan State University, Norfolk State University, and the University of Florida). This sample of prospective teachers included 174 elementary education majors and 59 English and mathematics majors who intended to teach in secondary schools. All respondents completed the surveys, and a 62-person subset of teacher candidates was interviewed about their orientations toward teaching diverse students. Paine found that these prospective teachers identified family background, motivation, student attitudes, and ability as differences that are important for teachers to consider. For the most part, the subjects were oriented toward individual differences, (e.g., people are different in size, age, skin color, etc.) rather than categorical differences (e.g., individuals are categorized by common characteristics such as race, class, or gender groups). While they voiced concerns about equity and justice, these student teachers were uncertain about how to operationalize their concerns in the classroom. Many saw diversity as a problem for schools and teachers. As Paine notes, they generally brought to their teaching "approaches to diversity that have the potential for reproducing inequality and reflect larger social and historical dilemmas" (p. 20).

Sears' (1992) findings concerning the attitudes and feelings of prospective teachers toward gays, lesbians, and bisexuals echo those of Paine concerning their perspectives toward persons differing from themselves in race, socioeconomic status, and language background. Although the 258 prospective teachers that Sears surveyed and interviewed (in South Carolina) expressed supportive feelings toward all students, Sears contends that their "countervailing expressions of high levels of personal prejudice, ignorance, and fear" (p. 29) about gay, lesbian, and bisexual students make it likely that they will reproduce rather than reform the generally narrow-minded and oppressive treatment of homosexuals in the U.S.

Summaries and critiques of extant research on teacher education for diversity (Grant & Secada, 1990; Zeichner, 1992) also indicate that the perspectives of many U.S. teachers can be barriers to the effective instruction of substantial numbers of students. For example, in their summary of research concerning demographic diversity and teacher education, Grant and Secada point out that young, White, female, suburbanite, novice teachers are often assigned to classrooms and schools where their more-experienced colleagues do not wish to teach. These are often classrooms populated with children of color and students labelled as low-skilled. As the AACTE and Metropolitan Life surveys indicate, these are also not the children that novices hoped to teach. Nor are they, as Grant and Secada further point out, the children that these novice teachers were prepared to teach by their academic programs.

## Challenging prospective teachers' perspectives about others

In his review of the literature concerning what "teachers need to be like, to know, and to be able to do, to successfully teach ethnic and language minority students," Zeichner (1992) contends that little has changed since 1969 in terms of the population of teachers recruited into teacher education or in the ways in which these teaching recruits are educated once they are enrolled in programs of preparation. Zeichner uses Smith's 1969 report of the task force report of the National Institute for Advanced Study in Teaching Disadvantaged Youth, as a kind of "watershed" for his critique of teacher education. In this document, Smith decries the race, class, and gender biases that permeated processes of teacher selection as well as programs of preparation for teachers in that era, and warns that their continuation would reap a bleak harvest for U.S. school children's learning and achievement. Nearly two decades after the release of Smith's report, a number of other calls for the reform of teacher education and teaching have been issued. For the most part, these reports (AACTE, 1986, 1991; Carnegie Forum on Education and the Economy, 1986; Goodlad, 1990; Holmes Group, 1986, 1990, 1991) locate issues of race, class, gender, and poverty at the margins of their concerns for teacher education. Regardless of the attention to teaching for diversity received in these reports, some researchers and teacher educators have heeded calls to reappraise who we prepare for teaching and how we do so (Ahlquist, 1991; Cooper, Beare & Thorman, 1990; Gomez & Tabachnick, 1991, 1992; Kleinfeld, 1992; Ladson-Billings, 1991; Larke, 1990; Larke, Wiseman, & Bradley, 1990; Murrell, 1992; Noordhoff & Kleinfeld, 1990, 1991). They have studied prospective teachers' perspectives on persons unlike themselves and have attempted to modify courses, field experiences, and entire programs of teacher preparation to interrupt, challenge, and change the ways teachers think about themselves and Others.

In all of the studies of prospective teachers discussed in this section, the researchers looked closely at the views of preservice teachers enrolled in an entire program of teacher education or in a single course or field experience in which the researchers were also faculty or staff members. The studies were conducted, in part, to better understand the impact of the course, field experience, or programs on their participants and to provide data that would assist program faculty in modifying these to better meet their goals for teacher preparation.

## Programs of teacher education focusing on diversity

Noordhoff and Kleinfeld (1990, 1991) and Gomez and Tabachnick (1991, 1992) studied the perspectives on teaching diverse students held by preservice teachers enrolled in two different programs of teacher preparation. Each pair of researchers studied the changing perspectives and practices of prospective teachers working across a set of coordinated courses, field experiences, and seminars in a program of teacher education designed for teaching particular populations of learners.

Noordhoff and Kleinfeld, co-directors of the "Teachers for Alaska" program at the University of Alaska, studied post-baccalaureate non-education majors preparing to teach native Alaskan (Eskimo, Indian, and Aleut) peoples in rural secondary schools. In addition to more traditional experiences of teacher preparation such as on-campus course work, students in the program are also expected to spend time living and practice teaching in communities of native peoples. The prospective teachers use a three-phase set of classroom and community experiences—"an analyzed apprenticeship"—as well as narratives or cases about teaching in rural Alaska as tools for reflection on what good teaching means in this setting. Noordhoff and Kleinfeld (1990) present the case readings and the field experiences as posing "problems of design" for teaching with the intent that their students will explore "ways of transforming present situations into preferred situations" (p. 167). Their analyses of the changes in the perspectives and practices of the first two cohorts of teachers enrolled in this program reveal that, at its close, teachers "began to take more account of a primary facet of the teaching context—their students—in preparing and implementing lessons" (p. 181). As these researchers conclude, their students initiate shifts in perspective over the year from "seeing instruction as a certain task under their control to viewing teaching as a more uncertain and problematic act that is dependent on contextual factors" (p. 181).

Gomez and Tabachnick also use narratives as a means of preparing elementary teachers in the "Teaching for Diversity" program that they co-direct at the University of Wisconsin-Madison. Students in this program are asked to uncover and challenge their perspectives about educating diverse populations of learners by telling one another stories about their teaching. These stories are then questioned and critiqued by their peers and teacher educators. Students enrolled in the three semesters of professional course work, field experiences, and seminars comprising the program conduct all field experiences in one of two sets of elementary schools with highly diverse student bodies. Each school enrolls approximately 50% students of color, who like their White peers, are from varied language, cultural, and socioeconomic status backgrounds. Like Noordhoff and Kleinfeld, Gomez and Tabachnick report that changing teachers' perspectives on diverse Others is a long and labor-intensive process, even in programs expressly designed with a coordinated set of experiences to challenge and enhance prospective teachers' notions about teaching those unlike themselves. Only after two or more semesters of carefully coordinated course work, practica, and seminars did the prospective teachers in their study demonstrate any substantial reconsideration of the ideas about diverse learners they held when they entered the program.

## Courses focusing on diversity issues

Given the concerns of teacher educators who are attempting to effect change in preservice teachers' perspectives about Others through a coordinated effort over multiple semesters, it is not surprising that others challenging and studying the perspectives of students enrolled in one or two facets of a teacher education program have raised analogous questions about their efforts. For example, Ahlquist (1991), Ladson-Billings (1991), and Beyer (1991), have attempted to challenge and change the perspectives about Others of students enrolled in their teacher education courses. They report limited success in their efforts, noting that students often bring to their courses images of the accomplishments, needs, and goals of Others that are grounded in ignorance, fear, and/or indifference.

Ahlquist attempted to confront and interrupt the pejorative beliefs about Others held by 30 prospective secondary teachers (27 of whom were White women) in her "Multicultural Foundations of Education" course at San Jose State University. Her purpose was to teach her students "to challenge the status quo in the hopes that they, as the teachers of the future, will choose to take a stand in the interests of social justice" (p. 158). She reports that although her students expressed curiosity about multicultural education at the beginning of the course, they also contended that sexism and racism no longer existed and that Ahlquist was "utopian and idealistic for advocating cultural diversity" (p. 160). Reflecting on her experiences in teaching this course, Ahlquist asserts that she may have misunderstood and underestimated the complex dynamics of power and the resistance to diversity and change in her classroom. She also concedes that she may have expected too many changes in students' thinking in too brief a period of time, and writes: "Now I realize that deep understanding of an issue grows out of reflective examination of one's own experience, and true consciousness often comes very slowly" (p. 167).

Ladson-Billings's goals for her undergraduate "Introduction to Teaching in a Multicultural Society" course at Santa Clara University were similar to Ahlquist's. Through readings, the viewing of films, class discussion, and a 10-hour field experience in a human service agency (including drop-in shelters, soup kitchens, and child care centers for low-income people), this class was designed to help preservice elementary student teachers develop a "critical consciousness" toward societal inequities and injustices. Students were guided to "examine critically the ways that culture mediates our ways of knowing the world, the ways that schools structure inequality, and the ways in which they, as prospective teachers, could make a commitment to social justice and social change" (p. 4). While many of those enrolled in the course demonstrated new and different understandings of racism and the causes of poverty (as shown in their journals and in class discussions), Ladson-Billings reports no significant differences in the subsequent attitudes and beliefs of preservice elementary teachers who took her course and those who did not.

Beyer's analyses of how a course he teaches at Knox College affects preservice teachers may provide clues about why Ladson-Billings failed to realize substantive changes in preservice teachers' beliefs about Others. Beyer questions whether teacher educators spend too much time in what he calls "crucial and essential" theoretical analysis and too little time nurturing "the affective, existential quality of moral engagement and commitment" (p. 127). Therefore, he includes in his course on "School and Society" a 25-hour community service component. Students may fulfill this requirement by working in either a human service agency or an individual home. In his assessment of how this course differently affected three preservice teachers, Beyer writes that "an important dimension of this difference involves the previous commitments and consciousness of political, economic, and social issues that students bring with them" (p. 127). Accordingly, students' perspectives on diversity, their existing moral and political commitments, and prior personal experiences play pivotal roles both in how they understand their community service and the different meanings they derive from it. For example, for some of the teacher candidates in Beyer's study, their first awareness of social and economic injustice in U.S. society came about while engaging in the required community service work. Only then did these students begin to question how and why Others end up on public assistance or in poverty rather than in the work force. On the other hand, some students come to teacher education fully cognizant about how prejudice against Others creates and sustains poverty in the U.S. Through community service, Beyer notes, these prospective teachers become more articulate about how and why Others face such dilemmas and renew their sense of personal commitment to social and political change.

## Field experiences focusing on diversity issues

Other teacher educators have developed field experience components of programs designed to challenge the perspectives of their students regarding people unlike themselves (Cooper, Beare, & Thorman, 1990; Larke, 1990; Larke, Wiseman, & Bradley, 1990; Mahan, 1982a, 1982b; Murrell, 1992). While their efforts differ on a number of dimensions, they demonstrate the scope of activity surrounding field experiences as sites for challenging and changing prospective teachers' perspectives.

One type of effort is described by Murrell of Alverno College, who arranges field placements for White, middle-class female teacher candidates in inner-city schools in Milwaukee, where the college's teacher education program is located. In these settings, the prospective teachers are often in the minority in terms of social class and race. Murrell studied the beliefs about good teaching evidenced by 15 White female prospective teachers enrolled in the seminar that accompanied their 25-hour field placement experience, noting that, "Pre-service teachers' perceptions of what it means to be a teacher are profoundly shaped by their early field experiences as interpreted through their past experiences as students in public schools" (p. 16). He further reports that prospective teachers' accommodation of their beliefs to those of their teaching colleagues and to the school culture at-large worked against the maintenance of a program-advocated critical stance toward teaching diverse children in an urban setting. Murrell's study supports earlier work conducted by Zeichner and Tabachnick (1985), who conclude that novice teachers take from their teacher education programs those ideals most like their own entering beliefs or sharpen their own perspectives via their contrast with those of the program.

While Murrell's location in Milwaukee facilitates the placement of teacher candidates in ethnically, economically, and racially diverse schools, other teacher educators have sought out-of-area placements to provide experiences with diverse learners for their teacher candidates. For example, Cooper, Beare, and Thorman report that, since 1985, selected prospective teachers enrolled at Moorehead State University in Minnesota have conducted their student teaching in a south Texas community with a prevailing Latino culture. The purpose of this option to the university's traditional student teaching experiences is to "redirect teaching practice from the vantage point of a different cultural setting" (p. 2). Once in Texas, student teachers participate in weekly seminars and keep journals of their experiences and observations. Following their return to Minnesota, the researchers compared the responses of 18 of the student teachers in one Texas cohort with those of 85 student teacher-peers (who did their student teaching in Minnesota) via the Self-Assessment in Multicultural Education Instrument (SAME), a Likert-scale instrument. Although no data on the two groups of teachers' classroom practices was reported, results from the SAME survey indicate encouraging differences in the Texas-placed student teachers' attitudes toward the role that race and culture play in classroom interactions and students' learning and achievement. A critical component of the power of this field experience to change teacher candidates' perspectives toward Others may have been the immersion of the student teachers in a culture in which they became the Other.

Mahan reports similar shifts in teachers' perspectives in a program he has directed for two decades at Indiana University. In this program, selected prospective teachers leave their White, midwestern campus to student teach in one of three sites with populations of people unlike themselves. These student teachers can work with Navajo and Hopi Indians living on reservations, Latinos living in towns on the border of Arizona and Mexico and in the Rio Grande Valley of Texas, or low-income Black children living in inner-city Indianapolis. Prior to leaving for 16 to 17 weeks of student teaching, they must take a course focusing on the target cultural group. In addition to traditional expectations for student teaching, all participants must fulfill additional hours of community involvement and service. Mahan (1982a) reports that "structured, semester-long field experiences in cultural communities produce a significant positive response from preservice teachers" (p. 171).

Larke and her colleagues at Texas A & M University have experimented with a different kind of field experience called the Minority Mentorship Project. This experience is added to more traditional program requirements of practica and student teaching. Through it, preservice teachers in the elementary education program are paired with a Black or Latino school-aged youngster for a minimum five-semester period in which they are encouraged to befriend and mentor the child and attend a one-credit seminar to share and evaluate their experiences. Pre- and post-test measures obtained via survey of the prospective teachers' attitudes toward persons of color and low-income persons suggest that frequent contact with a culturally different child over a number of months, coupled with opportunities to think and talk about the experience, can influence positively the attitudes of White, middle-class prospective teachers toward Others.

As outcomes of the field experience programs reviewed in the present study, changes in teachers' perspectives toward Others appear affected by a variety of factors. These include the diversity of the student population taught, the school and community contexts in which the experiences took place, the ongoing support for challenging and changing teacher candidates' perspectives during the field experience, and the degree of dissonance experienced by teachers when they themselves are the Others. The latter factor has been found to be among the most promising practices for challenging and changing preservice teachers' perspectives, especially when combined with seminars or other ongoing conversations guiding students' self-inquiry and reflection about teaching and working with persons different from themselves.

## Implications for reforming teacher education

Perhaps the most remarkable finding gleaned from the studies of teacher education courses, field experiences, and programs discussed in this article is the amount of agreement found among the teacher educator-authors that their work just begins the critical self-inquiry demanded if prospective teachers are to successfully educate diverse learners. Perhaps their uniformity of response would not be so striking if all of the prospective teachers had, in a sense, unknowingly enrolled in components of programs designed to challenge and change their perspectives, as we are led to believe those taught by Ahlquist, Beyer, Ladson-Billings, or Murrell had done. Nonetheless, Noordhoff and Kleinfeld and Gomez and Tabachnick—who educate students competing for limited numbers of places in programs specifically designed for such purposes—also indicate that their students often only develop the requisite understandings for successfully teaching diverse students one-half or two-thirds of the way through their programs, when little time is left to practice implementing these new understandings.

Why are the perspectives of prospective teachers so difficult to alter, and what implications does the length of time it takes to alter these have for reforms of teacher education? Haberman (1991a, 1991b) targets the early stages of the recruitment and selection processes as the critical points for reform if we are to achieve different outcomes for teacher education—different commitments, knowledge, and skills in teachers as well as different results for diverse children, their greater learning, and achievement. Haberman makes two important arguments. First, he (1991a) contends that attempting to educate prospective teachers who are young people still engaged in the struggle to develop their own identities lies at the heart of the problem. He dismisses the cohort of young, White, female prospective teachers in the United States as too immature and inexperienced to educate youths facing poverty, racism, and other serious challenges of our world, and argues for the recruitment into teaching of older persons with diverse work and other life experiences as one means of responding to diverse students' unmet classroom needs. Second, he (1991b) argues that research on values formation suggests that a single course or field experience in a teacher education program only rarely if ever has the power to interrupt or change values formed over a lifetime. In particular, Haberman maintains that isolated reforms of teacher education programs on campuses and in communities where the majority culture supports prospective teachers' maintenance of distorted images of Others are subsequently misguided and doomed to failure. Popkewitz (1991) draws conclusions similar to those of Haberman regarding the outcomes of such isolated efforts, but he frames the problems differently. Rather than ask how teacher educators can alter the selection processes or schooling for individual teacher candidates, Popkewitz asks teacher educators to examine how we have come to regard society's grave economic and social problems as being within the scope and responsibility of resolution by individuals. Further, he asks how we have come to regard school children as the locus of reform and salvation for our nation's woes. Popkewitz questions both the resolution of problems of equity and justice by individual teachers working within institutions structured for purposes other than social and economic justice, and the notion that it is through children that striking societal changes might be effected.

I heed the words of both scholars in forming the discussion that follows. As a teacher educator engaged in challenging and attempting to change the perspectives toward Others of young, White, monolingual-in-English, heterosexual females from suburbia, I am keenly aware of the difficulties and ironies of the tasks I and my colleagues have set for ourselves. I recognize that it is unlikely that a few semesters in a teacher education program can turn racists or homophobes into teachers who carefully and joyfully educate the children of Others. I also appreciate the inherent contradictions of participating in an endeavor that focuses its efforts on individual females as change agents in schools where this work contravenes the institution's tacit and explicit purposes, and in a society that devalues the labor of women (who now and will continue to be the majority of U.S. teachers), particularly when that labor is related to caring for and working with children. Nonetheless, I remain convinced that despite its tensions, the effort to provide a safe, nurturing, and encouraging environment for everyone's children for the 13,000 hours they will spend in school is a worthy one.

Four factors assure me that as teacher educators we will, for some time in the future, continue to educate prospective teachers resembling those in our current cohort to teach increasingly diverse populations of children. These factors are: (1) the predictions of demographers regarding the characteristics of and numbers of different incoming student populations (see Hodgkinson, 1985, 1991, for discussion of contemporary population trends); (2) the increased pressure from groups within and outside of education for "professionalizing" teaching (e.g., the National Board of Professional Teaching Standards; various state department mandates for selection, credentialing, and licensure) that often result in rejecting or sifting out people unlike those already credentialed; (3) the continuing availability of higher status, higher paying positions in professions outside of teaching for people of color; and (4) the pervasive racism, sexism, and homophobia marking life in the United States that prevents the encouragement and induction of diverse people into teaching.

Given these caveats, I return to the problem at hand: What fruitful options appear likely to challenge and change the perspectives of prospective U.S. teachers, and concomitantly, their classroom practices with and for Other people's children? As Haberman suggests, the recruitment and selection processes for teaching require re-examination and action. While it appears unlikely that large numbers of diverse persons will enter teaching in the near future, we can, as teacher educators, more carefully select from our existing pool of applicants people with a variety of work and life experiences demonstrating their existing commitments to social and economic justice and equity for Others. Through interviewing and documenting teacher candidates' prior experiences and giving greater weight in the selection process to factors such as these, we may be able to abbreviate the time required to challenge and alter prospective teachers' perspectives about Others, and in so doing, allocate more time in teacher education courses and field experiences to crafting excellent, just, and equitable practices of teaching.

Beyond recruitment and selection, questions of teacher education reform lead us to consider what we do and where and when we do it in all facets of a teacher's education. While none of the studies reviewed herein speak directly to the liberal arts preparation of future teachers, that portion of a teacher's education certainly requires scrutiny if we are to challenge and change candidates' perspectives toward Others. The portrait of our collective history (and of those who shaped and wrote it) presented in the liberal arts can serve either to reinforce or disrupt the stereotypes and confusion that most prospective teachers bring regarding the contributions of diverse people. Therefore, increased dialogue and collaboration with our colleagues in the arts and sciences is necessary regarding the nature of the courses in which we enroll prospective teachers.

Further, the length, character, and quality of field experiences we require must be examined. As the encouraging work of Larke and her colleagues, Cooper and his colleagues, Mahan, and others show, positive personal relationships and investments in Others' lives and futures can occur when prospective teachers are carefully placed and carefully supervised in field experiences in which they have the opportunity to interact over time and across occasions with people different from themselves. The need for both careful placement and careful supervision is highlighted by Beyer and Ladson-Billings when they discuss the effects of community action components in their courses. Clear to both is the tendency for the greatest benefits of these experiences to accrue to those students who come to teacher education predisposed to the reflection-in-action and reflection-on-action required by their courses.

Finally, Murrell's research concerning how mainstream prospective teachers learn to teach in schools with large numbers of diverse children adds a heretofore missing dimension to this discussion. Murrell found that preservice teachers' perspectives of Others as deficient—perspectives that they brought to their practicum and its accompanying seminar—were often reinforced by their cooperating teachers, other teachers, and staff. As a teacher educator who was also a person of color, he was often a lone, dissonant voice challenging these perspectives. Murrell's work points out the futility of university- and college-based teacher educators' working alone to alter teacher candidates' perspectives on Others. He further stresses the importance of developing concerted, coherent programs in which prospective teachers' perspectives are challenged in the classroom as well as on the campus.

## Conclusion

What principles might we derive from the work of the teacher educators described here? First, the problems that we face in educating all of our children cannot be resolved when we act alone. The reform of teacher education for diversity must take place in partnership with multiple communities within colleges and universities and with our colleagues in public schools, as well as with the various communities from which the children in our schools come. Second, no single activity—whether it be reading case studies; conducting community service; living with, tutoring, or practice teaching with people unlike oneself; telling stories of one's teaching; reading about and listening to Others' stories; participating in seminars accompanying practica or student teaching; or being an Other oneself— is adequate preparation for teaching diverse populations of children. Third, no isolated component, no single course or lone field experience of teacher education, can provide adequate reform. Fourth, no program of teacher education acting apart from its constituent partners in the college or university and the public schools can adequately prepare teachers for classrooms with diverse populations of children. Finally, no individual teacher can, working without partners inside and outside of schools, effect the changes our institutions and our society require. To date, no reform report on teacher education nor any single teacher education program has adequately addressed the complexity and the urgency of the challenges that lay before us in educating all of our children.

## Notes

1   As Tabachnick, Zeichner, Densmore, and Hudak (1983) point out, the notion of perspective has its theoretical roots in the work of Mead (1938) and his concept of the "act." Contemporary uses of the term "perspective" to discuss teachers' beliefs about their work and the classroom actions that give meaning to these date back to Becker, Geer, Hughes, and Strauss's (1961) study of medical students' socialization. This latter study defines "perspectives" as "a coordinated set of ideas or actions a person uses in dealing with some problematic situation; a person's ordinary way of thinking about and acting in such a situation" (p. 34).
2   In this article, I use the terms "diverse learners" and "Others" (upper-cased) throughout to encompass the various groups of people who are often disenfranchised by schools and schooling (e.g., persons of color; persons from low-income families; those with limited proficiency in English; those who are gay, lesbian, or bisexual). Grumet (1988) uses the phrase "Other people's children" to awaken a sense of obligation to teach all children—those of people unlike as well as like oneself—responsibly and well. Delpit (1988) uses the same phrase to challenge teachers to acknowledge how their participation in the "culture of power" constrains their understanding and teaching of diverse children.

## References

Ahlquist, R. (1991). Position and imposition: Power relations in a multicultural foundations class. *Journal of Negro Education, 60*(2), 158–169.
American Association of Colleges for Teacher Education (AACTE). (1986). *A call for change in teacher education.* Washington, DC: AACTE.
American Association of Colleges for Teacher Education. (1990). *AACTE/Metropolitan Life survey of teacher education students.* Washington, DC: AACTE.
American Association of Colleges for Teacher Education. (1991). *What college and university leaders can do to help change teacher education.* Washington, DC: AACTE.
Becker, H., Geer, B., Hughes, E., & Strauss, A. (1961). *Boys in white.* Chicago: The University of Chicago Press.
Beyer, L. E. (1991). Teacher education, reflective inquiry, and moral action. In B. R. Tabachnick & K. M. Zeichner (Eds.), *Inquiry-oriented practices in teacher education* (pp. 113–129). New York: Falmer Press.
Carnegie Forum on Education and the Economy. (1986). *A nation prepared: Teachers for the 21st century.* New York: Carnegie Corporation.
Children's Defense Fund. (1991). *The state of America's children: 1991.* Washington, DC: Children's Defense Fund.
Cooper, A., Beare, P., & Thorman, J. (1990). Preparing teachers for diversity: A comparison of student teaching experiences in Minnesota and South Texas. *Action in Teacher Education, 12*(3), 1–4.
Delpit, L. D. (1988). The silenced dialogue: Power and pedagogy in educating other people's children. *Harvard Educational Review, 58*(3), 280–289.
Gomez, M. L., & Tabachnick, B. R. (1991, April). *"We are the answer": Preparing pre-service teachers to teach diverse learners.* Paper presented at the annual meeting of the American Educational Research Association, Chicago, IL.
Gomez, M. L., & Tabachnick, B. R. (1992). Telling teaching stories. *Teaching Education, 4*(2), 129–138.
Goodlad, J. (1990). *Teachers for our nation's schools.* San Francisco: Jossey-Bass.
Grant, C. A., & Secada, W. G. (1990). Preparing teachers for diversity. In W. R. Houston (Ed.), *Handbook of research on teacher education* (pp. 403–422). New York: Macmillan.
Grumet, M. R. (1988). *Bitter milk: Women and teaching.* Amherst, MA: University of Massachusetts Press.
Haberman, M. (1991a). The rationale for training adults as teachers. In C. E. Sleeter (Ed.), *Empowerment through multicultural education* (pp. 275–286). Albany, NY: State University of New York Press.
Haberman, M. (1991b). Can cultural awareness be taught in teacher education programs? *Teaching Education, 4*(1), 25–32.

Hodgkinson, H. L. (1985). *All one system: Demographics of education—Kindergarten through graduate school.* Washington, DC: Institute for Educational Leadership.

Hodgkinson, H. L. (1991, April 10). Remarks made during the AACTE/ERIC Clearinghouse on Teacher Education video teleconference, "Who's Missing from the Classroom? The Need for Minority Teachers," Washington, DC.

The Holmes Group. (1986). *Tomorrow's teachers.* East Lansing, MI: The Holmes Group.

The Holmes Group. (1990). *Tomorrow's schools: Principles for the design of professional development schools.* East Lansing, MI: The Holmes Group.

The Holmes Group. (1991). *Toward a community of learning: The preparation and continuing education of teachers.* East Lansing: The Holmes Group.

Kleinfeld, J. (1992). Learning to think like a teacher: The study of cases. In J. Shulman (Ed.), *Case methods in teacher education* (pp. 33–49). New York: Teacher's College Press.

Ladson-Billings, G. (1991, April). *When difference means disaster: Reflections on a teacher education strategy for countering student resistance to diversity.* A paper presented at the annual meeting of the American Educational Research Association, Chicago, IL.

Larke, P. J. (1990). Cultural diversity awareness inventory: Assessing the sensitivity of preservice teachers. *Action in Teacher Education, 12*(3), 23–30.

Larke, P. J. Wiseman, D., & Bradley, C. (1990). The minority mentorship project: Changing attitudes of preservice teachers for diverse classrooms. *Action in Teacher Education, 12*(3), 5–12.

Louis Harris & Associates, Inc. (1991). *The Metropolitan Life survey of the American teacher, 1991. The first year: New teachers' expectations and ideals.* New York: Metropolitan Life Insurance Company.

Mahan, J. (1982a). Community involvement components in culturally oriented teacher preparation. *Education, 103*(2), 163–172.

Mahan, J. (1982b). Native Americans as teacher trainers: Anatomy and outcomes of a cultural immersion project. *Journal of Educational Equity and Leadership, 2*(2), 100–110.

Mead, G. H. (1938). *The philosophy of the act.* Chicago: The University of Chicago Press.

Murrell, P., Jr. (1992, April). *Deconstructing informal knowledge of exemplary teaching in diverse urban communities: Apprenticing preservice teachers as case study researchers in cultural sites.* Paper presented at the annual meeting of the American Educational Research Association, San Francisco.

National Center for Education Statistics. (1992). *American education at a glance.* Washington, D. C.: Office of Education Research and Improvement.

Noordhoff, K., & Kleinfeld, J. (1990). Shaping the rhetoric of reflection for multicultural settings. In R. T. Clift, W. R. Houston, & M. C. Pugach (Eds.), *Encouraging reflective practice in education* (pp. 163–185). New York: Teacher's College Press.

Noordhoff, K., & Kleinfeld, J. (1991, April). *Preparing teachers for multicultural classrooms: A case study in rural Alaska.* A paper presented at the annual meeting of the American Educational Research Association, Chicago, IL.

Olsen, R. (1991). Results of a K–12 and adult ESL enrollment survey—1991. *TESOL Matters, 1*(5), 4.

Paine, L. (1989). *Orientation towards diversity: What do prospective teachers bring?* (Research Report 89–9). East Lansing, MI: National Center for Research on Teacher Education.

Popkewitz, T. S. (1991). *A political sociology of educational reform.* New York: Teacher's College Press.

Sears, J. (1992). Educators, homosexuality, and homosexual students: Are personal feelings related to professional beliefs? In K. M. Harbeck (Ed.), *Coming out of the closet: Gay and lesbian students, teachers, and curricula* (pp. 29–79). New York: The Haworth Press.

Smith, B. O. (1969). *Teachers for the real world.* Washington, DC: AACTE.

Tabachnick, B. R., Zeichner, K. M., Densmore, K., & Hudak, G. (1983, April). *The development of teacher perspectives.* Paper presented at the annual meeting of the American Educational Research Association, Montreal, Canada.

62    *Mary Louise Gomez*

Zeichner, K. M. (1992). *Educating teachers for cultural diversity*. East Lansing, MI: National Center for Research on Teacher Education.
Zeichner, K. M., & Tabachnick, B. R. (1985). The development of teacher perspectives: Social strategies and institutional control in the socialization of beginning teachers. *Journal of Education for Teaching, 11*(1), 1–25.
Zimpher, N. (1989). The RATE Project: A profile of teacher education students. *Journal of Teacher Education, 40*(6), 27–30.

CHAPTER 6

# CROSS CULTURAL COMPETENCY AND MULTICULTURAL TEACHER EDUCATION (2000)

*Gretchen McAllister and Jacqueline Jordan Irvine*

Teachers in multicultural classrooms face increasing challenges in providing an appropriate classroom environment and high standards of instruction that foster the academic achievement of all students, particularly students of color from low socioeconomic backgrounds. Inconsistent findings in the research have hindered the field of teacher education from developing effective strategies that produce desired changes in teachers' beliefs, attitudes, and behaviors that result in school success for culturally diverse students.

In order for teachers to be effective with diverse students, it is crucial that they first recognize and understand their own worldviews; only then will they be able to understand the worldviews of their students (M. J. Bennett, 1993). Researchers assert that in order for teachers to interact effectively with their students they must confront their own racism and biases (Banks, 1994; Gillette & Boyle-Baise, 1995; Nieto & Rolon, 1995), learn about their students' cultures, and perceive the world through diverse cultural lenses (Banks, 1994; Gillette & Boyle-Baise, 1995; Nieto & Rolon, 1995; Sleeter, 1992; Villegas, 1991).

Although these principles are frequently espoused in teacher education, there is scant research about the process by which teachers develop a cross-cultural competence that enables them effectively to teach diverse students in their classrooms. A person who is considered cross-culturally competent is one "who has achieved an advanced level in the process of becoming intercultural and whose cognitive, affective, and behavioral characteristics are not limited but are open to growth beyond the psychological parameters of only one culture. . . . The intercultural person possesses an intellectual and emotional commitment to the fundamental unity of all humans and, at the same time, accepts and appreciates the differences that lie between people of different cultures" (Gudykunst & Kim, 1984, p. 230). Christine Bennett (1995) adds to this definition a commitment to combating racism and "all forms of prejudice and discrimination, through the development of appropriate understanding, attitudes, and social action skills" (p. 263).

Existing teacher training and professional development models do not adequately develop the type of cross-cultural competence defined by Gudykunst and Kim (1984), Bennett (1995), and others and deemed essential for teachers of diverse students (Cochran-Smith, 1995; Little, 1993; Lawrence & Tatum, 1996).

One conceptual framework that has not been thoroughly examined in multicultural teacher education research is process-oriented models. Some of these models have been used in the fields of counseling and intercultural relations to describe the cognitive, behavioral, and affective changes related to how adults develop cross-cultural competence. The authors recommend the infusion of these models into teacher education to assist teachers in becoming more effective with their diverse learners.

## Purpose

The purpose of this review is to examine process-oriented models that appear to be applicable to the development of teachers who work in multicultural school settings. Specifically, this review will address the following two questions:

(a)  What research supports process-oriented models used to structure cross-cultural learning?
(b)  How do these models contribute to our understanding of multicultural professional development for teachers?

This paper consists of three sections: the first provides a rationale for using process-oriented models to understand the development of cross-cultural competence; the second section presents and compares the models and critiques the research that has used the models; the third presents implications for the models' use in multicultural professional development.

## Process frameworks

In this review three different models of cross-cultural development will be explored. They include Helms's Racial Identity Theory, Banks's Typology of Ethnicity, and Milton Bennett's Developmental Model of Intercultural Sensitivity. These models emerge from different disciplines and are based on different premises, but all three describe a process (often broken down into stages or strata) that can be used to increase understanding of how people change their behavior and attitudes about themselves and others as cultural beings.

Although non-process models, such as those developed by Hoopes (1979) and Gudykunst and Hammer (1983) have been found to be useful, they do not provide the advantages of process models. Process-oriented models, which describe how people grow in terms of their cultural identities or worldviews, can assist educators in three areas: understanding teachers' behaviors (including resistance), sequencing course content, and creating conducive learning environments.

First, process-oriented models help situate teachers' behaviors, attitudes, as well as their interactions with students of color. Carter and Goodwin (1994), in their literature review of racial identity theory in education, point out that the "racial identity levels of educators themselves influence how they perceive and interact with children of color" (p. 307). Moreover, teachers' racial identities and worldviews influence their behaviors, attitudes, and cognitive frames (Bennett, 1986), which in turn shape teachers' responses to and participation in professional development programs for multicultural education.

Teachers enrolled in multicultural courses are often resistant and appear disinterested in learning. Teacher educators often characterize this resistance by asserting that "they are not ready" (Zeichner, 1994), that "they just don't get it," or that teachers simply are willing "to stay dumb" (Martin, 1995). Others contend that teachers are racist and unwilling to change their attitudes. Process-oriented models offer a framework for understanding resistance as well as providing appropriate support for effective interventions.

A second advantage of process models is their structure for designing and sequencing effective course and program interventions. Researchers of multicultural education have noticed that most teachers, teacher educators, and cross-cultural consultants do not connect topics and course purposes to an overall theory or some pre-defined structure (Grant & Secada, 1990; York, 1994). Courses are often arranged in a topical or chronological order that may not support cross-cultural development. For example, a course curriculum or inservice workshop may present a difficult topic such as "White privilege" too early in the course, before teachers have gained the ability to recognize their own or others' cultural views, norms, values, and biases. The structuring of topics and learning experiences along a process framework fosters environmental congruence (Helms, 1990) between students' levels of understanding and the course content and pedagogy. Some believe that such congruence can foster the development of cross-cultural beliefs, attitudes, and behaviors (M. J. Bennett, 1993; Helms, 1990; Widick, Knefelkamp, & Parker, 1975).

The third advantage of process models is that they provide instructional and pedagogical strategies to create conducive learning environments for students. In his stage-based model of moral development, Kohlberg (1984) suggests various techniques that provide students with opportunities to gain an understanding of other perspectives, a critical component of cross-cultural learning. In the case of multicultural teacher professional development, teachers are provided opportunities to experience diversity, either indirectly, through readings, simulations, watching videos, or directly, by interacting with people from other cultures. Other learning strategies include reflection (Banks, 1994; Cadray, 1995), role playing (Helms, 1990; Taylor, 1994), participation in consciousness-raising groups that promote self-awareness and self-assessment (Greeley, Garcia, Kessler, & Gilchrest, 1992), and community inquiry into questions concerning race, class, and culture (Cochran-Smith & Lytle, 1995). Some researchers and educators nurture cross-cultural growth by creating a balance between experiential learning and reflection (Taylor, 1994), and between support and challenge (J. Bennett, 1993; Carney & Kahn, 1984; Widick et al., 1975), and by making sure that adequate time is given for the learning experience (Taylor, 1994).

Process models have their critics. These models have been accused of lacking empirical evidence, oversimplifying complex problems (Jones, 1990), generalizing across race and gender, and diminishing personal agency (Meyers et al., 1991). For example, some researchers (Jones, 1990; Loevinger, 1976; Phinney, 1990; Prosser, 1978; Taylor, 1994) state that cross-cultural learning and identity development are complex processes that involve many factors such as age, gender, ethnicity, race, social-class, and sexual orientation. They claim that some models simplify the concept of identity by focusing on a single factor such as race.

Process-oriented models have been criticized for their generalization to other groups. One classic example is Gilligan's (1982) criticism of Kohlberg's work (1984) on moral development. Questions have also been raised regarding the broad application of ethnic identity and cultural awareness models to both majority and minority populations (Helms, 1990). Another area of contention regarding these models concerns the lack of personal agency. Meyers et al. (1991) contend that process models ignore an individual's ability to control his or her responses to the environment.

This review argues that, despite these limitations, process models should not be dismissed summarily and should be reviewed for their applicability and utility in teacher education research and practice in the area of cultural diversity.

## Three process models of ethnic and racial identity

Three process models, Helms's (1984, 1990) Racial Identity Development, Banks's (1984) Typology of Ethnicity, and M. J. Bennett's (1993) Developmental Model of Intercultural Sensitivity, were selected to inform the studies included in this review. Each research study reviewed in this paper employed one of the three models, used adults as study participants, and addressed the need to develop some area of cross-cultural competency.

### Helms's racial identity model

Predominant in the counseling field, racial identity development models focus on how people develop racial and ethnic identity. More recently, racial identity theory has been suggested as a tool for examining the development of racial identity and for facilitating meaningful interactions and instruction in classrooms (Carter & Goodwin, 1994; Tatum, 1992). Specifically, racial identity refers to a "sense of group or collective identity based on one's perception that he or she shares a common racial heritage with a particular racial group" (Helms, 1990, p. 3). Racial identity models address the psychological implications of racial group membership, "that is, belief systems that evolve in reaction to perceived differential racial-group membership" (p. 4).

Several process models have been developed for specific racial groups, such as White (Helms, 1984), Black, (Cross, 1978; Helms, 1984), and Asian (Sue, 1981), while others include several races in one multiracial model (Atkinson, Morten, & Sue, 1983). In each of these racial identity development models the authors contend that an individual moves from a "racially defined identity to a more healthy, self-defined racial transcendence" (Helms, 1990, p. 17).

It must be noted that racial identity models grew out of Black racial identity models that emerged in the 1970s in response to the Civil Rights Movement (Helms, 1990). William Cross's (1978) model, which consists of four stages (*pre-encounter, encounter, immersion/emersion, internalization*), was one of the predominant Black racial identity development models that appeared during this era. Because most of the research regarding issues of cross-cultural learning has focused on white preservice teachers (Dilworth, 1998), there is insufficient research employing Cross's black identity model that examines the development of cross-cultural competence.

Until recently, most of the discussions regarding Whites and racism have focused on identifying types of racism, such as institutional, personal, and cultural (Jones, 1990) or models of White defensiveness. In the 1980s, researchers (Hardiman, 1982; Helms, 1984) recognized that an understanding of White identity development might provide more insight into White racism. These models describe how White people shift from one set of understandings of racism to another. In their models, White people progress in a linear fashion toward increasing recognition of a White racial consciousness and an increasing personal responsibility for racism. Hardiman (1982) and Helms (1994) have both published in this area. However, because Helms's model has received more empirical verification it will be used as an example of White racial identity development.

Helms's model of White racial identity development consists of two sections with three stages each. The first section consists of the stages that describe the process of abandoning racism (*contact, disintegration*, and *reintegration*), while the second section describes the development of a positive White identity (*pseudo-independence, immersion/emersion,* and *autonomy*). People enter the first stage, *contact,* when they first encounter or meet a Black person. White people at this stage have not had a lot of information about or interaction with Black people and do not recognize any real differences between a Black or White cultural experience. The duration of this stage depends upon White people's previous experiences with and knowledge of Black people.

As Whites interact with more Blacks and learn about Black culture, they enter the next stage, *disintegration,* which is characterized by anxiety as Whites begin consciously to realize their ethnicity and its associated privilege. At this point they experience cognitive dissonance between the beliefs, values, and behaviors learned early in their lives and the information and contradictory experiences they presently encounter. White people often experience guilt and fear at this point. Such feelings may prompt them to move into the next stage, *reintegration,* in which these emotions are transformed into anger toward Black people and a feeling of their own racial superiority. This guilt, anger, and fear precipitate a retreat into White culture. It usually takes some jarring experience or situation to shift an individual from this racist phase.

In the next stage, *pseudo-independence,* White people begin to redefine their racial identity in more positive ways. Helms (1990) states that in this stage White people attempt to understand the Black culture and interact more with Blacks, but often within a White cultural framework. At this point White people have not been able to step outside their own cultural frame of reference. In the next stage, *immersion/emersion,* White people seek correct information regarding their participation in a racist society and shift their focus from paternalism to helping other Whites change. The last stage, *autonomy,* constitutes an ongoing process in which people internalize a positive racial identity and engage people from other cultures. Able to identify oppressive structures, they can now work toward eliminating them.

## Research studies on Helms's racial identity model

A total of seven studies that employed racial identity development models from the fields of counseling, education, and psychology were examined. Four studies were found that used quantitative measures to examine different aspects of racial identity development and its relationship to multicultural competencies. The predominant instrument used in these four quantitative studies was the White Racial Identity Attitude Scale designed by Helms and Carter (1990). This inventory, a self-report, Likert instrument consisting of 50 attitudinal statements, measures White participants' attitudes in relation to the five stages on the White Racial Identity Scale. A similar instrument exists to measure the racial identity attitudes of African Americans, the Black Racial Identity Attitude Scale (BRIAS).

Brown, Parham, and Yonker (1996) employed the White Racial Identity Scale to measure change in the White racial identity of thirty-five white graduate students who participated in a sixteen-week multicultural course. Eighty per cent of the participants had previous multicultural training and most of them had had experiences with people from at least two different racial backgrounds, though the nature of these experiences is not defined. The authors designed the course based on three areas—acquisition of self knowledge, cultural knowledge, and cross-cultural skills—and they used a variety of teaching methods such as lectures, talks by guest speakers, and simulations. Results indicated that at the end of the course women endorsed more items than men did in the pseudo-independence stage on the White Racial Identity Scale, and men endorsed more items than women did in the autonomy stage. The authors drew a causal relationship between the course and those changes found in the group.

Neville, Heppner, Louie, and Thompson (1996) also examined the change in White racial identity as well as the multicultural self-efficacy of thirty-eight graduate counseling students who were enrolled in the same course, multicultural psychology, in three different universities. Though this particular sample was racially mixed (twenty-nine Whites, four Blacks, two Asians, one Latino, one Native American, and one "other"), only the results of the White students were reported because the sample for the students of color was too small to yield any significant results. The influence of the race of the instructors for the course—two were African American and one was White American—was not discussed. The course, fifteen weeks in length with three, one-hour classes per week, involved a variety of techniques to help raise students' awareness regarding their racial and ethnic backgrounds and the socio-cultural realities of minorities in the United States.

Neville et al. (1996) administered a pre- and post-course White Racial Attitude Scale and the Multicultural Awareness Knowledge and Skills Survey (MAKSS). The latter survey measured the effects of instructional methods on students' cross-cultural awareness. Correlating the findings on MAKSS with student attitudes on the WRIAS, the authors found that White students in the higher stages, pseudo-independence and autonomy, reflected a stronger endorsement of multicultural therapy competencies, as measured by MAKSS. The authors drew a causal relationship between the course and increased racial identity attitudes in the upper stages. A one year follow-up survey, with a sixty-six percent return rate, revealed that students sustained changes over time.

Whereas the two previous studies took place in classroom settings, Taylor's (1994) study provided an opportunity to measure, using the WRIAS and other instruments, the effect of a diversity course in a natural setting. Two trainers, a White female and a Native American female, were invited by three non-profit organizations to deliver on-site diversity awareness training. Taylor was interested in the relationship between knowledge of diversity, moral development, and racial identity development. In addition, she wanted to examine the influence of varying training schedules on the moral and identity development of the participants and on their acquisition of knowledge. Cognitive and racial identity development and the use of intentionally structured groups guided the course. Unlike the other researchers, Taylor modified her intervention according to her findings on the pre-test of racial identity (WRIAS) and an instrument to assess moral development. Due to the small number of people of color, she did not analyze the Black participants' responses to the BRIAS. Though her overall results show no strong significance for any of her questions, she did find a positive correlation between moral development and the autonomy stages on the Racial Identity Development scale. These findings suggest that there may be a correlation between individuals' attitudes toward their own racial groups and their attitudes toward other groups as well as a relationship between such attitudes and complex moral issues such as social justice, equality, and racism. Taylor also noticed that the participants from one of the training sites manifested more resistance to training than participants from the other sites, which may be attributed to lack of readiness to accept the diversity training.

Unlike the other three studies, that conducted by Ottavi, Pope-Davis, and Dings (1994) employed the WRIAS and other instruments to measure the correlation between four different competencies—skills, relationship, awareness, and knowledge—and the stages on the White Racial Identity Scale, rather than the effects of an intervention. Ottavi et al. measured the racial identity attitudes of 128 White graduate counseling students using WRIAS, and their self-reported multicultural competencies using Multicultural Counseling Instrument (MCI). Using multiple regression they found that the WRIAS explained the incremental variance in the MCI subscales. In other words, there seemed to be a relationship among the higher stages of racial identity and self-reported multicultural competency.

These studies revealed that higher stages of racial identity attitudes were associated with increasing multicultural competencies (Ottavi et al., 1994; Neville et al., 1996; Taylor, 1994). Several of the researchers believed that the higher stages of racial identity models reflected certain cross-cultural capacities, such as an increased ability to accept racial difference, to appreciate the influence of racial attitudes on people of color, and to exhibit less racist behavior (Brown et al., 1996; Helms, 1990; Neville et al., 1996). Neville et al. revealed that participants at the lower three stages were not as affected by training. The other studies do not include a discussion of the experiences of those people at the lower stages, perhaps because there were not many people at the lower levels, or if entrance into the course was voluntary, perhaps only those at the higher levels were willing to join the course.

Three of the seven studies used qualitative research methods such as interviews and observations (Lawrence & Tatum, 1996, 1997; Sleeter, 1992) to examine Helm's model. In their first study, Lawrence and Tatum (1996) examined 26 White classroom teachers engaged in a 45-hour anti-racist professional development program based on Racial Identity Development theory. In a second study (Lawrence & Tatum, 1997), the authors examined 84 White classroom teachers involved in the same program at a different time of the year. In both of the studies these teachers participated in the course with teachers and administrators from different ethnicities. The course involved a variety of teaching methods including lecture, discussion, and video.

Lawrence and Tatum (1996, 1997) found in their two studies that teachers changed their thinking, attitudes, and behavior regarding race. In the 1997 study forty-eight percent of the eighty-four teachers exhibited some form of anti-racist behavior in their professional lives. These behaviors included interrupting racist practices in their schools and other aspects of their professional life, integrating the topic of racism into the curriculum and classroom discourse, increasing interactions with parents and students of color, and raising expectations of students in their classrooms. In the 1996 study Lawrence and Tatum reported that teachers changed in their racial identity development, especially in regard to their commitment to anti-racist actions. Using teachers' self-report data, the authors identified changes from Helms's pseudo-independence to immersion/emersion stages.

Contrary to Lawrence and Tatum, Sleeter (1992) did not find many systematic changes in teachers' practices and thinking, even though the teachers themselves reported changes. Sleeter used participant observations and interviews to study thirty-two classroom teachers enrolled in a multicultural professional development program. The teachers participated in a weekly awareness building inservice program for two years. Data collection consisted of approximately three to five interviews and observations per year. Observations by Sleeter and her research associates revealed that after the professional development program, teachers enhanced what they had already been doing. The greatest change, even for teachers involved with the program for two years, was increased attention to Black students (not described thoroughly in her study) and increased use of cooperative learning activities. Though Sleeter does not report changes on the racial identity development scale or use it systematically to analyze change, she does employ anecdotes that allude to the changes she observed.

All seven studies provided insights as well as raised questions regarding the use of racial identity models to examine changes in teachers' beliefs, attitudes, and behaviors. Six of the seven studies reported positive results from an intervention, as well as a positive correlation between multicultural competencies and higher stages on the White Racial Identity Development model. The studies provided information on both an aggregate and individual level. Researchers who used the WRIAS reported aggregate scores reflecting the overall change of the group. Although aggregate scores can help to discriminate the nature of racial identity models (Helms, 1990; Thompson, 1994), they may also distort findings. For example, if a few individuals change dramatically while the rest of the participants remained the same or changed little the aggregate score on the White Racial Identity Attitude Scale would reveal significant group changes. Not knowing who changed and how much they changed does not help researchers and teacher educators to understand the complex picture of cross-cultural development. The qualitative studies, which also have their methodological weaknesses, did provide richer and deeper insights into how teachers changed individually in terms of reported behavior, attitudes, and knowledge (Lawrence & Tatum, 1996, 1997). But the studies lack a description of the *process* of that change. In addition, researchers do not inform the readers about how they employed the White Racial Identity Developmental Model as an analytical framework.

Four of the seven studies focused only on White participants (Brown et al., 1996; Lawrence & Tatum, 1996, 1997; Ottavi et al., 1994). The other three studies with racially mixed samples were unable to report the results from the Black Racial Identity Attitude Scale because of small numbers of Black participants (Helms, 1990). The focus on White participants also may have stemmed from researchers' concern with White counselors' (Ponterotto, 1988) and White teachers' (Lawrence & Tatum, 1996, 1997) abilities to work effectively with diverse populations. Perhaps there is a common belief that people from marginalized groups may already be bicultural and hence have the necessary skills to interact effectively with people from diverse backgrounds. However, some researchers have questioned assumptions about the biculturality of marginalized groups. M. J. Bennett (1993), for instance, argues that marginalized people "may understand and even respect differences with which they are familiar, but they may be unable to recognize or use this sensitivity as part of a generalized skill in adapting to cultural differences" (p. 56). This might be the case with an African American teacher who speaks Spanish and feels a cultural connection with her Hispanic students but is insensitive to her Vietnamese students.

In four of the studies, researchers measured participants as they applied their newly acquired knowledge to their work settings (Lawrence & Tatum, 1996, 1997; Sleeter, 1992; Taylor, 1994). According to adult learning theory (Oja, 1980), learners' levels of interest and application will be enhanced when learning is immediately applied and contextualized in naturalistic work settings. Adopting the insight of adult learning theory—that learners' levels of interest and application will be enhanced when learning is immediately applied and contextualized in naturalistic work settings—four of the studies measured participants as they applied their newly acquired knowledge in work settings. Only Taylor's research (1994) discusses the influence of the work environment on the participants' response to the diversity workshop. She notes that immediate application may be impeded by other contextual factors such as changes in leadership.

Sleeter (1992) and Lawrence and Tatum (1996) write that observation is key to measuring change. Although researchers found changes on the White Racial Identity Scale as well as a correlation between certain variables and White Racial Identity Development, none of these researchers actually observed changes in people or people at different stages. Many researchers (Brown et al., 1996; Helms, 1990; Neville et al., 1996; Ottavi et al., 1994; Sabnani, Ponterotto, & Borodovsky, 1991) believe that changes in attitude will affect behavior, Sleeter's (1992) study shows otherwise. Although teachers in her study reported changes in their practice and thinking, these changes were not reflected in the teachers' classroom practices. This suggests that in studies using self-report instruments or interviews, participants may overrate their multicultural competencies or misrepresent their attitudes.

The timing of the administration of the instrument may also have influenced findings. Most researchers administered the White Racial Identity Attitude Scale at the end of the intervention (e.g., Brown et al., 1996; Ottavi et al., 1994). Only Neville et al. (1996) re-administered the survey a year later, finding that participants in their study remained on the same level as when they were measured at the end of the intervention. None of the other studies examined any possible Hawthorne effects. If cross-cultural learning is considered continuous, then it would not be unusual to find these effects (M. J. Bennett, 1993; Helms, 1990; Oja, 1990).

The various types of interventions measured may have also biased the findings, hence raising methodological questions. Only two researchers designed interventions that were based on process frameworks, such as racial identity development (Lawrence & Tatum, 1996, 1997) or moral and racial identity development (Taylor, 1994). Caution should be taken when comparing studies with different interventions. There may be a relationship between the type of intervention and the changes in participants' attitudes, behaviors, and knowledge. Interventions that were constructed based on a process-oriented model, such as racial identity development (Lawrence & Tatum, 1996, 1997) may produce greater changes in participants than interventions that took a more eclectic approach (e.g., Sleeter, 1992).

Despite the complexity and the many limitations of measuring changes in racial identity development, the studies revealed that the White Racial Identity Attitude Scale may help teacher educators in designing and assessing courses and programs in multicultural teacher education.

## Banks's Typology of Ethnic Identity

Most of the racial identity models originated in the field of psychology and deal specifically with ego development in ethnic identity rather that "acquisition of ethnic identity" as reflected in the work of James Banks (Tomlinson, 1995). Though similar to racial identity models, Banks's (1994) Typology of Ethnic Identity is distinctive in its inclusion of multiple ethnicities and its focus in education. Banks's typology is not race specific and can be used with individuals of any ethnic or racial group. Banks has further distinguished his model by aligning his work with schools and curriculum in multicultural education.

Banks's model involves six stages: *ethnic psychological captivity, ethnic encapsulation, ethnic identity clarification, bi-ethnicity, multi-ethnicity and reflective nationalism,* and *globalism and global competency* (Banks, 1994). These stages exist as points along a dynamic and multidimensional typology or "ideal-type construct" (p. 223). He states that each stage is a "gradual and developmental process. . . . The stages should not be viewed as strictly sequential and linear. I am hypothesizing that some individuals may never experience a particular stage" (p. 227). He further states that every ethnic group is highly diverse and dynamic and that each person within a single ethnic group may not begin at the same stage in the culture learning process—persons from marginalized ethnic groups will have identity development journeys different from those characteristic of members of the dominant culture. But Banks does hypothesize that "once an individual experiences a particular stage, he or she is likely to experience the stages above it sequentially and developmentally" (p. 227).

Stage one, *ethnic psychological captivity,* demonstrates the socio-historical nature of Banks's model. Members of the dominant culture will most likely not experience this stage as strongly as some marginalized groups, if at all. During the stage of *ethnic psychological captivity,* people internalize negative racial and ethnic stereotypes and beliefs. The greater the stigmatization, the more people internalize the oppression.

Continuing with Bank's positional framework, in stage two, *ethnic encapsulation,* the dominant culture internalizes the myth about the inferiority of other groups, while marginalized groups become insular either out of fear or strong ethnic identity. The stronger the experiences in stage one, the higher the level of ethnocentrism in the second stage. Gradually, people begin to resolve the conflict around their ethnic identity, which leads them into the next stage.

In stage three, *ethnic identity clarification,* all ethnic groups begin to see both positive and negative aspects of their own groups. Racial identity development in one's own group is not based on hatred or fear of other groups. An important aspect of this stage revolves around self-acceptance. Banks (1994) states that:

> Self-acceptance is a prerequisite to accepting and responding positively to other people. Individuals are more likely to gain self acceptance when they have experienced positive contact with other groups as well as achieved some measure of economic and psychological security (p. 225).

In stage four, *bi-ethnicity,* individuals have the skills and the desire to function in two cultures. They learn how to do this in different ways depending on their social location in society. In order to gain economic mobility, some groups, such as African Americans and Latinos, must learn to function in the dominant culture as well as in their own. Certain groups living in homogeneous environments may not achieve this stage quickly; it seems that arrival at this stage would necessitate certain experiences, such as contact with other groups.

Stage five, *multi-ethnicity and reflective nationalism,* includes individuals who have developed a cross-cultural competency that enables them to move beyond the obvious aspects of a culture, such as the holidays and food, in order to understand and appreciate the values, symbols, and institutions of other cultures. People at this point along the continuum should be able to switch comfortably between cultures and become responsible, reflective, and active citizens.

The sixth and final stage, *globalism and global competency,* is an extension of the fifth in that people learn increasingly how to balance their three identities: ethnic, national, and global. Throughout this stage people learn when to use which identity and in which context (Banks, 1994).

## Research studies using Banks's typology

Three studies employing Banks's typology (Cox, 1982; Martin & Atwater, 1992; Smith, 1983) used teachers and one included administrators (Smith, 1983) as their participants. Unlike studies using Helms's racial identity theory, these studies included results from participants of different races (Cox, 1982; Martin & Atwater, 1992), ages (Cox, 1982; Martin & Atwater, 1992; Smith, 1983), genders (Cox, 1982; Martin & Atwater, 1992; Smith, 1983), and teaching experiences (Martin & Atwater, 1992; Smith, 1983).

All three studies employed the Teacher Survey Instrument developed by Ford (1979, cited in Smith, p. 128) to measure stage placement and change on Banks's Typology of Ethnicity. The five-point Likert scale instrument consists of 42 items that match each stage in the typology. Both Cox (1983) and Martin and Atwater (1992) measured the construct validity of the Teacher Survey Instrument prior to using it. Smith (1983) failed to do this and presented this omission as one of his study's limitations.

Cox (1983) sent demographic surveys and the Teacher-Student Interaction Instrument (TSI) to a racially diverse sample of 350 classroom teachers in order to determine their placement on Banks's typology of ethnicity. She found that her participants were distributed along Banks's typology with the majority predominately focused in the bi-ethnicity stage (sixty-three percent), as well as stage five. Having measured the correlation between stages and demographic factors, she concludes that certain demographic factors seemed to be correlated with people's placement at various stages on Banks's typology. For example, among her participants, women, people of color, individuals with multicultural experiences, and younger respondents tended to place in higher stages.

Smith (1983) focused his dissertation more closely on the relationship between teachers' self-reported preparedness in multicultural education and their stages on Banks's typology. He measured the stages using the TSI and used the Multicultural Learning Opportunity Inventory (MLO) to measure respondents' experiences. The three-part survey consisted of statements designed to assess formal and informal daily experiences with diversity. Smith used a third instrument Multicultural Preparedness Inventory to generate self-assessed levels of preparedness in multicultural education. The surveys were mailed to 315 certificated elementary school personnel from a suburban district in the Pacific North-west. Most of the sample were experienced teachers, White, female, and in their thirties. Out of nine hypotheses, only five of Smith's produced positive, though weak, correlations. The two that addressed ethnic awareness (Banks's stages) included a positive but weak relationship between preparedness and ethnic awareness and a positive relationship between informal learning opportunities and ethnic awareness. Beyond stating the correlations, Smith did not provide a more detailed description of the relationship between the stages and the variables of preparedness and informal learning opportunities.

Martin and Atwater's (1992) study measured the effects of a multicultural math and science summer program on the development of ethnic identity. Two-thirds of the sixty-six teachers and administrators who participated were female and African American; one half were middle and high school teachers. Martin and Atwater's research was part of a larger study that included pre-service students as well. The participants in the study attended a twelve-day Science and Math summer workshop for three hours per day; of the twelve days, five were devoted to diversity issues. The effect of the workshop in creating "multicultural science teachers" was measured by changes on Banks's Typology of Ethnic Identity. The authors defined a multicultural science teacher as one who placed at Stage 4 or higher on Banks's typology. Martin and Atwater (1992) found fifty-seven percent of the teachers had ethnic identity levels in stage four or higher, and they found no significant differences between gender, years of teaching experience, grade levels, and content specialty.

The attempts by the authors of all three studies to determine if the stages on Banks's typology were associated with other variables resulted in contradictory findings. Cox (1983) found that gender and experience were salient variables, while Martin and Atwater (1992) did not. Cox (1983) and Smith (1983) found contradictory results regarding the role of multicultural experience and level of ethnic identity. A lack of common definitions may have created the contradictory evidence. For example, Cox and Smith defined multicultural experience differently. Cox added on several questions to the TSI and Smith used an established instrument, the MLO, to measure multicultural experiences. This lack of a common definition of multiculturalism creates difficulty in comparing studies. In addition, studies published in previous decades may not provide appropriate comparisons to current research.

Some results may have been influenced by biased samples. For example, teachers in the Martin and Atwater study (1992) may have been enrolled in the summer course because of their interest and commitment to multicultural education. Her results should be interpreted differently from Cox's research that used a random sample of 350 teachers.

The weakest aspect of all three studies is their inadequate methodology and cursory or inadequate data reporting. The Cox (1983) study is representative of these weaknesses. Cox neither included a full discussion of her methodology nor a complete presentation of the statistics. The associations between variables provide interesting information regarding the multicultural learning process, but no causal relationship nor direction of influence was discussed. Insufficient research analysis may also explain why some of these studies were not published in refereed journals.

Overall, the studies revealed that people were at different levels of ethnic awareness and identity development, as shown by the varying placements on Banks's Typology of Ethnicity (Banks, 1994), and that placement at the higher stages is generally associated with multicultural competencies (Smith, 1983) and greater interest in multicultural courses (Martin & Atwater, 1992). The methodological issues, however, caution against drawing firm conclusions.

## Bennett's Developmental Model of Intercultural Sensitivity

Milton J. Bennett's (1993) model, Developmental Model of Intercultural Sensitivity (DMIS), suggests a significant departure from those of Helms and Banks. However, the DMIS describes similar changes in a person's behavior, cognition, and affect and deals with the learner's subjective experience in understanding how different cultures "create and maintain world views" (Bennett, 1986, p. 25). Difference is the organizing key to Bennett's model, in that each stage represents a new way of experiencing cultural difference. The model has two aspects; the first part of the continuum has three stages of decreasing levels of ethnocentrism (*denial, defense,* and *minimization*) and the second has three stages of increasing ethnorelativism (*acceptance, adaptation, integration*).

The first stage of the model, *denial,* represents the lack of knowledge of difference. People assume that their world views are the only world views and behave accordingly. In the second stage, *defense*, they realize differences exist but, in an ethnocentric fashion, they strive to preserve their own cultural views. People may do this in one of three ways: (a) they may put down or denigrate another culture; (b) they may uplift their own as superior; or (c) if living in a community outside their own, they may uplift that particular community as superior. Bennett noted that elevating another's community as superior is often misinterpreted as cultural sensitivity, but the uplifting of the other culture in this case is done in an egotistical fashion by "presenting one's self as more culturally sensitive" (Bennett, 1986, p. 187). The third stage of the ethnocentric half of the continuum, *minimization*, represents those people who claim they are "color blind." People at this level minimize the differences and continue to interact within their own cultural paradigms, living under the assumption that their behaviors and perceptions are shared by others. No awareness of their own cultures has occurred yet.

Movement to stage four, *acceptance*, represents a critical change from ethnocentrism to the first stage of ethnorelativism. At this stage people recognize that others have different values and world views, and people begin to accept and respect different behaviors and communication styles. "Characteristic of this shift is the subjective reconstrual of difference as a 'thing' to difference as a 'process' " (Bennett, 1986, p. 185). People move away from a reactive mode of always seeing the "other," to one of interaction, where the individual and the other become a "we-creating reality."

Stage five, *adaptation*, reflects the behavioral changes in individuals when they are more able to act in an ethnorelative fashion. Bennett (1986) views this stage as a crucial point. People are finally able to (a) change their processing of reality; (b) modify their behaviors so that they are more appropriate; and (c) be able to think and/or to act from another cultural perspective, or as Bennett puts it, to exhibit empathy (Bennett, 1986).

In the sixth and final stage, *integration*, people are not merely sensitive to other cultures, but rather they are in the process of becoming a part of and apart from a given cultural context (Adler, 1977, p. 26). This stage has two subphases: one, *contextual evaluation* in which people can evaluate a phenomenon from another perspective or within the cultural context; and, two, *constructive marginality*, in which people see outside of themselves continuously and stand outside of all cultural frameworks.

## Studies on Bennett's model

Two studies were found that employed the Developmental Model of Intercultural Sensitivity. An education dissertation by Watanabe (1992) used the model to assess students' stage developments, and the other, a master's thesis in the field of intercultural communication (Turner, 1990), employed the model to assess the placement of expatriates on the DMIS and the relationship between this placement and their coping skills.

Watanabe's (1992) dissertation examined the effect of a peer multicultural workshop intervention in a residence hall. He used a semi-structured interview to assess the stage placement of four students and found that after the intervention the students progressed further on the various stages of the DMIS. Unfortunately, this author provided no information about how the stages and terms were operationalized. His work provided little information about the methodology, the use of the DMIS, interview structure, or results. However, his is one of the few studies that created a developmentally based intervention.

Turner's (1990) research centered on the stage placements of fifteen American expatriates who had been living and working in Kuwait for over two years. Most of her participants had been in the country for at least six years. Turner (1990) provided a detailed methodology in her work. She coded each part of the interviews and determined the stages of the participants. In addition, she also developed a structured interview to assess each participants' level on the Developmental Model of Intercultural Sensitivity in four areas: interactions with cultural others, cross-cultural communications skills, stress management, and satisfaction with being immersed in a different culture. Participants' stages were determined by the largest percentage of responses in a stage.

Turner's (1990) use of the interview method reflected the dynamic nature and "messiness" of participants' thoughts. None of the participants' responses fell neatly into one stage, but rather their responses were spread across two or three stages (Bennett, 1993; Turner, 1990).

Although all of the expatriates had lived in Kuwait for two years or more, only three were categorized as ethnorelative on the Developmental Model of Intercultural Sensitivity. Turner also found that some expatriates at ethnocentric stages were satisfied with their experience and had adjusted to Kuwaiti culture. These results raised questions regarding the relationship between intercultural effectiveness and intercultural sensitivity. Despite these findings, Turner concluded that in order for people to achieve greater levels of cross-cultural interaction and for them to interact in different contexts more ethnorelative levels of intercultural sensitivity would be needed.

In sum, Watanabe's use of the Developmental Model of Intercultural Sensitivity does not provide much information regarding its viability as a research tool or a structure for designing interventions. Turner's study provides a stronger methodology that could be further refined and validated for use by other researchers. The DMIS has been used in training (Paige, 1993), and found to be helpful identifying and assessing people at different stages of development. However, more rigorously designed research is needed to determine its effectiveness as a tool for teacher educators and researchers.

The three models (Cross and Helms's Racial Identity Development, Banks's Typology of Ethnicity, and Bennett's Developmental Model of Intercultural Sensitivity) share certain similarities. Despite the fact that the models emanate from different disciplines, they share several characteristics, such as their structure and assumptions. The structures of the models are similar in that they are all process-oriented cognitive models in which individuals move through a set of stages or statuses (e.g. Helms, 1994). The stages progress from little differentiation or conception of complexity to higher levels of abstraction and differentiation (Mezirow, 1978). According to the models, people move from a self-centered state to identification with society and eventually to the larger global community, improving their ability to place their identities or those of others within an increasingly larger perspective. As people mature or move through the models they become increasingly "inclusive, discriminating and more integrative of experience" (Mezirow, 1978, p. 106) until they approach a common telos or ultimate end. The final stage of each model contain capacities desired for teaching in a culturally diverse classroom, such as perspective-taking and reflection skills. These later stages are considered desirable because, ostensibly, teachers have gained skills and understanding that facilitate the achievement of their culturally diverse students.

The difference in the models center on how they are have been used in training, either in anti-racism or cultural-difference training. Racial identity development models have been used by researchers and teacher educators to encourage anti-racist thinking and behavior (Carter & Goodwin, 1994; Lawrence & Tatum, 1996), and encourage teachers to examine the institutional, individual, and cultural racism that exists in schools and society (Kailin, 1994; Lawrence & Tatum, 1996; Sleeter, 1992). Educators adhering to this approach believe that societal structures as well as racist attitudes and behaviors support the academic failure of poor urban children (Sleeter, 1992; Villegas, 1991).

The second approach focuses on the cultural differences between the school and children's cultures (Banks, 1995; Villegas, 1991). While cultural difference theory shifts the responsibility for children's academic success to schools and teachers, this approach encourages teachers to learn continuously about their children's cultures, as well as adapt their classrooms, pedagogy, and personal behaviors and thinking to meet the needs of the children and their cultures (Villegas, 1991). The Developmental Model of Intercultural Sensitivity supports the desired goals of this approach because of its focus on cultural differences and increased understanding of cultural nuances. It also provides a useful framework for understanding teachers' cross-cultural growth.

## Summary and implications

Having presented and reviewed three process-oriented models that appear to be applicable to the development of teachers who work in multicultural school settings, do we conclude that these models contribute to our understanding of multicultural professional development for teachers?

The first conclusion from this review is that process models of cross-cultural competence do provide some conceptual insight into how teachers can be more effective with their culturally diverse students. The models reviewed support Grant and Secada's (1990) call to better understand how teacher cognition and beliefs develop. As Grant and Secada stated: "If we could map how teachers move from the former to the latter, we might be able to plan teacher education programs to help teachers develop these skills" (p. 419). Pajares (1992) argues that the study of teachers' beliefs is critical in understanding teachers' behaviors and that inquiry into this area has powerful implications for teacher efficacy and student achievement.

Although the quantity and quality of extant research studies are limited, the studies' findings do have relevance for teacher education. It can be assumed that teachers, like the participants in the reviewed studies, are at different levels of multicultural awareness (Cox, 1982; Helms, 1990; Martin & Atwater, 1992; Turner, 1990) and that higher levels are positively associated with multicultural competency (Neville et al., 1994; Ottavi et al., 1996), non-racist behavior (Lawrence & Tatum, 1996, 1997), and knowledge about other cultures and races (Lawrence & Tatum, 1996; Taylor, 1994). This review concluded that levels of racial identity or cross-cultural awareness vary (Cox, 1982; Ottavi et al., 1994; Smith, 1983; Turner, 1990), and that teachers do not start with the same type of cross-cultural understanding. Process models can help to identity and differentiate racial attitudes (Cross, 1978; Helms, 1990; Sabnani et al., 1991), understandings of cultural difference (Bennett, 1993), and acceptance and understanding of one's own ethnicity and others (Banks, 1994). These findings have implications for assessing readiness to learn, designing effective learning opportunities, and providing appropriate support and challenge for teachers.

First, concerning learner readiness, the research suggests that individuals in the ethnocentric stage of any of the models will be more hesitant, more vulnerable, and less open (Taylor, 1994). Those in the higher ethnorelative stages will be more interested in learning about other cultures and more willing to take risks (M. J. Bennett, 1993; Meijer, 1993). Teacher educators' knowledge of the general level of readiness of their pre- and in-service teachers in multicultural professional development courses can facilitate the development of appropriate course and field work. As diagnostic tools, the models inform teacher educators of possible stages and readiness levels of their students (J. Bennett, 1993). If teacher educators are aware of their students' readiness then they can make appropriate decisions about how to instruct them in the area of diversity.

Second, the structure of the intervention can provide support and challenge when designed in ways that reflect the process and not just the content of cross-cultural learning (J. Bennett, 1993). Sequencing topics in a process framework provides more support for the learner and fosters greater development (e.g., Lawrence & Tatum, 1996). For example, self-awareness regarding one's culture has been identified as a key prerequisite and a first step for learners in multi-cultural programs (Brown et al., 1996; Sabnani et al., 1991; York, 1994). When participants explore their own culture in the early stages of an intervention they are more likely to move toward a multicultural frame of reference. Banks (1994) and others suggest that individuals do not become sensitive and open to different ethnic groups until and unless they develop a positive sense of self, including an awareness and acceptance of their own ethnic group.

Third, there are implications for both support and challenge for teacher educa-tion students. Personal reflections on the self and discussions on issues of racism can be difficult for pre- and in-service teachers as well as teacher educators (Martin, 1995; Paige, 1993). There is a need to encourage risk-taking to foster cross-cultural growth (Taylor, 1994), but too much risk discourages learners from engaging in the process and encourages resistance (J. Bennett, 1993; Helms, 1990). Some of these risks include: (a) a sense of fear emanating from reflections on cultures which people do not have a lot of experience with (Paige, 1993), (b) feelings of guilt and confusion from discussing highly personalized behaviors and being involved in affective learning (Paige, 1993), and (c) a sense of frustration and excitement as people uncover new ways of understanding the world and the nature of life (Brislin, 1981; Paige, 1993). The intentional use of groups has been one source of support as well as challenge for learners and provide opportunities for learners to interact with people of diverse backgrounds, experiences, and beliefs (Brown et al., 1996; Helms, 1990; Ottavi et al., 1994; Neville et al., 1996; Sleeter, 1992). Group support, however, must be well designed and as authentic as possible. Merely plunging teachers into a new setting with little support or at the inappropriate time according to their developmental level may increase stereotyping and produce negative feeling on the part of the learner (M. J. Bennett, 1993).

## Recommendations

This review and its implications provide insights for teacher educators working with pre-service and in-service teachers. They include: (a) constructing multi-cultural courses using process models to decrease resistance and increase support for the learner; (b) using support groups to provide opportunities for reflection, support, and challenge; (c) providing opportunities for students to interact with individuals from other ethnic backgrounds in authentic cultural settings;

(d) examining the level of awareness of the teacher education faculty or in-service staff to signal possible conflicts of learning goals and purposes between students and their teachers; (e) providing on-going professional development to increase the knowledge and skills of the faculty; and (e) using adult and student developmental theory in conjunction with cross-cultural and racial identity models to enhance the cross-cultural learning process (Parham, 1989; Watanabe, 1992).

More research must be conducted regarding these models' effectiveness in teacher education, particularly well-designed observational studies in naturalistic classroom settings. Measuring change, especially cross-cultural change, is a complex and difficult process. As researchers gain more understanding regarding the challenging environment in which teachers work, they must expand their methods and ways of thinking regarding the measurement of cross-cultural change.

In order to apply the stage-based models, practitioners must have more information regarding their effectiveness in producing change in attitudes, behaviors, and belief. Teachers must also believe that theories and research apply to their particular situations and contexts. Therefore, development needs to be viewed in its full complexity. Teachers' personalities and school contexts must be examined for their possible influences on the growth process. The relationship among attitude, behavior, and beliefs needs closer attention: Do people develop these various capacities simultaneously? Does context influence the independent growth of these different capacities? The structure of the interventions, such as their content and pedagogy, must be more closely examined. Hopefully, future research areas will assist teacher educators, teachers, and researchers in enhancing cross-cultural knowledge, skills, and attitudes that reverse the cycle of school failure for far too many culturally diverse students.

# References

Atkinson, D., Morten, G., & Sue, D. (1983). *Counseling American minorities: A cross-cultural perspective*. Dubuque, IA: William C. Brown.
Banks, J. (1994). *Multiethnic education: Theory and practice*. Needham Heights, MA: Allyn and Bacon.
Bennett, C. (1995). Preparing teachers for cultural diversity and national standards of academic excellence. *Journal of Teacher Education, 46*, 259–266.
Bennett, J. (1993). Cultural marginality: Identity issues in training. In M. Paige (Ed.), *Cross-cultural orientation* (pp. 109–136). Lanham, MD: University Press of America.
Bennett, M. J. (1986). A developmental approach to training for intercultural sensitivity. *International Journal of Intercultural Relations, 10*, 179–195.
Bennett, M. J. (1993). Towards ethnorelativism: A developmental model of intercultural sensitivity. In M. Paige (Ed.), *Education for the intercultural experience* (pp. 21–72). Yarmouth, ME: Intercultural Press.
Brislin, R. (1981). *Cross-cultural encounters*. Elmsford, NY: Pergamon.
Brown, S. P., Parham, T. A., & Yonker, R. A. (1996). Influence of a cross-cultural training course on racial identity attitudes of White women and men: Preliminary perspectives. *Journal of Counseling & Development, 74*, 510–516.
Cadray, J. P. (1995). Enhancing multiculturalism in a teacher preparation program: A reflective analysis of a practitioner's intervention. *Dissertation Abstracts International, 57*(8). (University Microfilms No. 9701563).
Carney, C. G., & Kahn, K. B. (1984). Building competencies for effective cross-cultural counseling. *The Counseling Psychologist, 12*, 111–119.
Carter, R. T., & Goodwin, A. L. (1994). Racial identity and education. In L. Darling-Hammond (Ed.), *Review of Research in Education, Vol. 20* (pp. 291–336). Washington, DC: AERA.
Cochran-Smith, M. (1995, November). *Knowledge, skills, and experiences for teaching*

*culturally diverse learners: A perspective for practicing teachers.* Paper presented at the Invitational conference on Defining the Knowledge Base for Urban Teacher Education, Emory University, Atlanta, GA.

Cochran-Smith, M., & Lytle, S. L. (1995). *Inside/outside: Teacher research and knowledge.* New York: Teachers College.

Cox, B. B. (1982). *A research study focusing on Banks's Stages of Ethnicity Typology as related to elementary teachers multicultural experiences.* Unpublished doctoral dissertation, University of Houston, Houston, Texas.

Cross Jr., W. E. (1978). The Thomas and Cross models of psychological nigrescence: A review. *Journal of Black Psychology 5*, 13–31.

Dilworth, M. E. (1998). Old messages with new meanings. In M. E. Dilworth (Ed.), *Being responsive to cultural differences: How teachers learn* (pp. 197–202). Washington, DC: AACTE.

Gillette, M., & Boyle-Baise, M. (1995, April). *Multicultural education at the graduate level: Assisting teachers in developing multicultural perspectives.* Paper presented at the annual meeting of the American Education Research Association, San Francisco, CA.

Gilligan, C. (1982). *In a different voice: Psychology theory and women's development.* Cambridge, MA: Harvard University.

Grant, C., & Secada, W. G. (1990). Preparing teachers for diversity. In W. R. Houston (Ed.), *Handbook of research on teacher education* (pp. 403–422). New York: Macmillan.

Gudykunst, W. B., & Hammer, M. R. (1983). Basic training design: Approaches to intercultural training. In D. Landis & R. Brislin (Eds.), *Handbook for intercultural training: Vol. 1. Issues in design and theory* (pp. 118–154). New York: Pergamon.

Gudykunst, W. B., & Kim, Y. Y. (1984). *Communicating with strangers: An approach to intercultural communication.* Reading, MA: Addison-Wesley.

Guskey, T. R. (1986). Staff development and the process of teacher change. *Educational Researcher, 15*, 5–12.

Hardiman, R. (1982). White identity development: A process oriented model for describing the racial consciousness of White Americans. *Dissertation Abstracts International, 43*, 104A.

Helms, J. E. (1984). Toward a theoretical explanation of the effects of race on counseling: A Black and White model. *Counseling Psychologist, 12*, 153–165.

Helms, J. E. (Ed.). (1990). *Black and White racial identity: Theory, research, and practice.* New York: Greenwood.

Helms, J. E. (1994). The conceptualization of racial identity and other "racial" constructs. In E. Trickett, R. Watts, & D. Birman (Eds.), *Human diversity: Perspectives on people in context* (pp. 285–311). San Francisco: Jossey-Bass.

Helms, J. E., & Carter, R. T. (1990). Development of the White Racial Identity Inventory. In J. E. Helms (Ed.), *Black and White racial identity: Theory, research, and practice* (pp. 67–80). New York: Greenwood.

Hoopes, D. S. (1979). Intercultural communication concepts and the psychology of intercultural experience. In M. A. Pusch (Ed.), *Multicultural education: A cross-cultural training approach* (pp. 9–38). Yarmouth: Intercultural Press.

Jones, W. T. (1990). Perspectives on ethnicity. In L. Moore (Ed.), *Evolving theoretical perspectives on students* (pp. 59–72). San Francisco: Jossey-Bass.

Kailin, J. (1994). Anti-racist staff development for teachers: Considerations of race, class, and gender. *Teaching and Teacher Education, 10*(2), 169–184.

Kohlberg, L. (1984). *The psychology of moral development. The nature and validity of moral stages.* San Francisco: Harper & Row.

Lawrence, S. M., & Tatum, B. D. (1996, February). *Teachers in transition: The impact of anti-racist professional development on classroom practice.* Paper presented at the Teachers College Cross-cultural Roundtable on Psychology and Education.

Lawrence, S. M., & Tatum, B. D. (1997). White educators as allies: Moving from awareness to action. In M. Fine, L. Weiss, L. Powell, and M. Wong (Eds.), *Off White: Critical perspectives on race* (pp. 332–342). New York: Routledge.

Little, J. W. (1993). Teachers' professional development in a climate of educational reform. *Educational Evaluation and Policy Analysis, 15*, 129–151.

Loevinger, J. (1976). *Ego development: Conceptions and theories.* San Francisco: Jossey-Bass.

Martin, H. J., & Atwater, M. M. (1992). *The stages of ethnicity of preservice teachers and in-service personnel involved in multicultural education experiences.* (ERIC Document Reproduction Services No. ED 397 203).

Martin, R. (Ed.). (1995). *Practicing what we preach: Confronting diversity in teacher education.* Albany, NY: State University of New York.

Meyers, L. J., Speight, S. L., Highlen, P. S., Chickaco, I. C., Reynolds, A. L., Adams, E. M., & Hanley, C. P. (1991). Identity development and world view: Toward an optimal conceptualization. *Journal of Counseling & Development, 70,* 54–63.

Mezirow, J. (1978). Perspective transformation. *Adult Education, 28,* 100–110.

Neville, H. A., Heppner, J. J., Louie, C. E., & Thompson, C. I. (1996). The impact of multicultural training on White racial identity attitudes and therapy competencies. *Professional Psychology: Research & Practice, 27,* 83–89.

Nieto, S., & Rolon, C. (1995, November). *The preparation and professional development of teachers: A perspective from two Latinas.* Paper presented at the invitational conference on Defining the Knowledge Base for Urban Teacher Education, Emory University, Atlanta, GA.

Oja, S. N. (1980). Adult development is implicit in staff development. *The Journal of Staff Development, 1,* 7–55.

Oja, S. N. (1980). *Developmental theories and the professional development of teachers.* (ERIC Document Reproduction Service No. ED 248 227).

Ottavi, T. M., Pope-Davis, D. B., & Dings, J. G. (1994). Relationship between white racial identity attitudes and self-reported multicultural counseling competencies. *Journal of Counseling Psychology, 41,* 149–154.

Paige, M. (1993). On the nature of intercultural experiences and intercultural education. In M. Paige (Ed.), *Cross-cultural orientation* (pp. 1–21). Lanham, MD: University Press of America.

Pajares, F. (1992). Teachers' beliefs and educational research: Cleaning up a messy construct. *Review of Educational Research, 62,* 307–332.

Parham, T. A. (1989). Cycles of psychological nigrescence. *The Counseling Psychologist, 17*(2), 187–226.

Phinney, J. S. (1990). Ethnic identity in adolescents and adults: Review of research. *Psychological Bulletin, 108,* 499–514.

Ponterotto, J. G. (1988). Racial consciousness development among White counselor trainees: A stage model. *Journal of Multicultural Counseling and Development, 16,* 146–156.

Prosser, M. H. (1978). *The cultural dialogue: An introduction to intercultural communication.* Boston: Houghton Mifflin.

Sabnani, H. B., Ponterotto, J. G., & Borodovsky, L. G. (1991). White racial identity development and cross-cultural counselor training: A stage model. *The Counseling Psychologist, 19,* 76–102.

Sleeter, C. E. (1992). *Keepers of the American dream: A study of staff development and multicultural education.* Washington, DC: The Falmer Press.

Smith, A. J. (1983). *The relationship of teachers preparedness in multicultural education to levels of ethnic awareness and multicultural exposure among elementary school certificated personnel.* Unpublished doctoral dissertation, University of Washington, Pullman, Washington.

Sue, D. W. (1981). *Counseling the culturally different.* Canada: John, Wiley and Sons.

Taylor, T. Y. (1994). *A study of the effectiveness of a cognitive-developmental program to promote cross-cultural sensitivity among employees.* Unpublished doctoral dissertation, North Carolina State University, Asheville, NC.

Thompson, C. E. (1994). Helm's White Racial Identity Theory: Another look. *Counseling Psychologist, 22,* 645–649.

Tomlinson, L. M. (1995). *The effects of instructional interaction guided by a typology of Ethnic Identity Development: Phase One, reading research report no. 44.* (ERIC Document Reproduction Service No. ED 390 029).

Turner, D. (1990). *Assessing intercultural sensitivity of American expatriates in Kuwait.* Unpublished masters thesis, Portland State University, Portland, OR.

Villegas, A. M. (1991). Culturally responsive pedagogy for the 1990s and beyond. *Trends and Issues Paper No. 6.* Washington, DC: ERIC Clearinghouse on Teacher Education.

Watanabe, G. C. (1992). *A comprehensive developmentally-based undergraduate diversity education model at Washington State University.* Unpublished doctoral dissertation, Washington State University.

Widick, C., Knefelkamp, L., & Parker, C. A. (1975). The counselor as a developmental instructor. *Counselor Education and Supervision, 14,* 286–296.

York, D. E. (1994). *Cross-cultural training programs.* Westport, CN: Bergin & Garvey.

Zeichner, K. M. (1994). Teacher socialization for cultural diversity. In J. Sikula, T. Buttery, & E. Guyton (Eds.), *Handbook of research on teacher education* (329–348). New York: Macmillan.

# PART 2

# TEACHER PREPARATION

■

# CHAPTER 7

# MULTICULTURAL TEACHER PREPARATION (1981)
## An attitudinal survey
*James Mahan and Virginia Boyle*

Educating teachers to be sensitive and responsive to the multicultural needs of students should be a priority of teacher educators throughout this nation. Several conditions including the mobility of the population, the increase in immigration, the implementation of open attendance laws, and the expansion of school bussing are changing communities so that they are becoming more culturally diverse. This diversity tends to reflect, in many instances, the make-up of the general population. As a result, neighborhoods may quickly change from whatever constituency they currently have to one that is different ethnically and culturally. The influx of Vietnamese, Haitians, Cubans, and Iranians is one example of this kind of change. Teachers who have previously been successful teaching in communities that are undergoing change are discovering that what had worked for them in the past no longer works. As a result, new methods are needed.

## Background

These changes pose a serious dilemma for teacher educators. Many questions are being raised about the effectiveness of teacher education programs in terms of the preparation of teachers to cope with the multicultural conditions which exist in our society. The following questions are representative of these concerns:

In a nation of increasing cultural diversity, are teacher attitudes, knowledge, and skills meeting the needs of students from differing cultural and ethnic backgrounds? And, are teacher education institutions preparing teachers to sufficiently meet the needs of culturally diverse students?

Data resulting from a survey of teacher educators throughout the country serve to strengthen this article's assumptions that multicultural teacher preparation is a necessity—a necessity which should be provided in depth through comprehensive programs. In its "standards" paper (1977), the National Council for Accreditation of Teacher Education stated emphatically that provision should be made for instruction in multicultural education in teacher education programs and that multicultural education should receive attention in courses, seminars, directed readings, laboratory and clinical experiences, practicum, and other types of field experiences.

The American Association for Colleges of Teacher Education surveyed 786 institutions in late 1977 concerning the status of multicultural teacher education

(Gollnick, 1978). Responses were received from 387 teacher education institutions. Some provision for multicultural and/or bilingual education was reported by 78.8% of the responding institutions (Gollnick, p. 132). The information presented in the AACTE Survey states responses but did not attempt to assess qualitatively any multicultural teacher preparation education at any of the responding institutions. The data are enlightening, but, more information is needed about the implementation and effects of multicultural teacher education.

## Multicultural teacher education survey

In order to determine how teacher educators assess the status of multicultural teacher education at universities and colleges, a survey was designed and administered during the 1978 and 1979 National Conference of the Association of Teacher Educators. Sixty-six directors of student teaching and/or field experiences responded anonymously to this survey. The respondents, who represented 25 different states, were all school of education educators.

The midwest, eastern and southwest states were best represented. The Pacific Northwest, deep south (except Florida), and the northern plains states (Dakotas, Montana) were under-represented. Respondents described their positions held as characterized by such activities as counseling with student teachers, determining the academic eligibility of prospective student teachers, placing student teachers at field sites, selecting supervising teachers, providing university supervision for student teachers, evaluating student teacher performance, preparing and placing early experience students. The 66 respondents stated they: 1) were knowledgeable about the teacher preparation courses and experiences completed by their own student teachers; 2) were also acquainted with the classrooms in which their student teachers taught; 3) understood the nature of the student bodies of the cooperating public schools; and, 4) reorganized the challenges faced daily by student and classroom teachers.

In addition to the descriptive data, the survey consisted of 12 questions. Many of these questions designed for the survey called for attitudinal responses of feelings or opinions. Some questions did call for factual information.

## Survey findings

The first item asked respondents to identify the degree to which they felt preservice teachers had access to multicultural teacher preparation. Response choices ranged along a Likert type scale from 1 to 6, with 1 representing "No institutions provide it" and 6 representing "All institutions provide it." The mean score of 2.49 was low and the standard deviation of .88 was small, indicating that responding educators appear to believe that multicultural education is not experienced by students in many schools of education.

The second survey item was as follows: "On the national scene, do you feel that multicultural teacher education is a) losing momentum; b) holding its own; c) gaining momentum?" Approximately one-third of the respondents revealed a belief that multicultural teacher preparation is expanding and improving. The remaining two-thirds saw no gains in momentum.

Using the same type of response choice as with the first item, the third survey question tapped respondent feelings about extent of preparation of preservice teachers at respondent institutions. Response choice 1 was equivalent to, "No preservice teachers receive it," and 6 was equivalent to, "All preservice teachers receive it." Results showed a mean of 2.81 and a standard deviation of 1.38.

The teacher educator respondents gave this item a somewhat higher mean than Item #1, and the standard deviation indicates more heterogenous responses. However, a 2.81 mean obviously indicates that the respondents were not much more willing to circle optimum numbers in regard to their own local program than they were in the case of programs elsewhere in the nation.

The survey also asked respondents to estimate at their own institutions the percentage of preservice teachers who sincerely desired multicultural preparation experience. The data reveal that 65% of the respondents felt that only 0% to 40% of the preservice teachers on their campuses desired such experience (see Table 7.1).

On the other hand, 83% of the respondents said that every preservice teacher should be required to experience multicultural teacher preparation. Additionally, 62% stated that public school employers preferred to employ beginning teachers who had well-documented multicultural teacher preparation experiences and that public school employers would view such preparation as a very positive asset: 23% felt that employers were neutral about such preparation and 6% indicated that they believed employers would view such preparation as a liability.

The survey also sought reaction to the quantity and quality of multicultural experiences. For example, Item #7 was as follows:

> Many multicultural teacher preparation programs are composed of both campus academic courses and field-based experiences. In your opinion, what part of a total multicultural program should be *field based* in multicultural school and/or community?

All respondents were in favor of some multicultural experiences in an appropriate field setting. Suggested percentages ranged from 5% to 100%, with 40% and 50% being the bimodal responses. The preference trend here is toward more field-based experience than is likely to be required on most campuses today (see Table 7.2).

The next survey item had to do with the percentage of student teaching experience that should occur in a multicultural school or community. An analysis of findings revealed that more of the responding teacher educators were willing to make multicultural experiences a greater portion of the student teaching assignment than were willing to make them a greater portion of the total teacher preparation sequence. Responses ranged from 0 to 100% with a majority of respondents indicating that half or more of all student teaching should be

*Table 7.1* Respondent estimation of percentage of preservice teachers desiring multicultural preparation experiences

| % desiring | # of respondents | % of respondents |
| --- | --- | --- |
| 2–20 | 28 | 42% |
| 21–40 | 15 | 23% |
| 41–60 | 12 | 18% |
| 61–80 | 8 | 12% |
| 81–100 | 3 | 5% |

*Table 7.2* Respondent opinion about extent of field-based experience in a multicultural setting

| % of field based experience | # of respondents | % of respondents |
| --- | --- | --- |
| 0–20 | 8 | 12% |
| 21–40 | 20 | 30% |
| 41–60 | 28 | 43% |
| 61–80 | 8 | 12% |
| 81–100 | 2 | 3% |

performed in a multicultural setting. Specifically, these educators marked the response choices as follows: 11% said 0–20% of the student teaching should occur in a multicultural school or community; 11% said 21–40% of experience should occur there; 36% said 41–60% of the experiences should occur in the stated setting: and, 20% indicated 61–80% of the experience should occur in a multicultural school or community.

Thirty-nine educators noted they were familiar with the structure and objectives of a multicultural teacher preparation program for preservice teachers presently in use in another college or university. Those who were aware of other multicultural programs were asked to evaluate the effectiveness of these programs with respect to the extent to which respondents felt these programs were being implemented.

Nearly 50% felt that institutions may have ineffectively implemented multicultual programs. Only 10 respondents out of 39 were familiar with institutions where a multicultural program appeared to be a functioning reality. Multicultural endeavors are frequently among these "purported" rather than "existing" programs.

Again using a Likert type scale (1 through 6) with 1 representing "Limited and Superficial" and 6 representing "Comprehensive and Intense," respondents were asked to rate how comprehensive and intense was the average multicultural teacher preparation program in the nation today. The mean response was 2.32, (standard deviation = .99) indicates the current programs are neither comprehensive nor intense, thus identifying an area that teacher educators need to examine and closely review.

The final survey item was as follows: "Think about the last ten student teachers and/or first-year teachers you have taught, supervised, known or observed. How many of the ten had all multicultural preparation you feel that they would need to teach today in the following types of schools?" School descriptions were: "Inner city school (in one of largest 10 cities); Low income, white rural school; Upper middle class suburban school; Migrant/agricultural school; Whatever school the teacher acquaintance was in."

Respondents definitely perceived more preservice and beginning teachers as being prepared to serve in upper middle class schools than in any other type. They only perceived 3.9 out of 10 teachers in the above category as being fully prepared to teach in the school which they were actually working or desired to work. Very few (1.6) beginning teachers were perceived as being prepared for schools serving inner city or migrant youth. The data also suggest that since 7.5 beginning teachers were considered fully prepared for suburbia, and only 3.9 were considered prepared for the positions they were in. Many obviously did *not* obtain suburban jobs and contracted to teach in schools for which they were not perceived as being properly prepared.

## Conclusion

This survey was an attempt to determine attitudes about multicultural teacher preparation as viewed by teacher educators. Results show that most of the respondents are supportive of multicultural teacher preparation, are aware of the various related issues and knowledgeable about current programs. However, responses appear to raise issues around the commitment and implementation of the aspects of multicultural teacher education.

In the areas of access and growth, survey respondents indicated that accessibility to multicultural teacher education is limited but growing, that preservice teachers should have multicultural education in some part of their program and that employers would view this type of preparation as valuable. Respondents noted that 40% to 50% of a multicultural teacher education program should be field based and that 50% of the student teaching experience should be in a multicultural setting. Only 10 respondents could identify programs that were effectively operationalized. Respondents felt that only four out of 10 teachers were prepared to teach in the school in which they were currently working or in the school in which they desired to work. An important survey finding is that only 1.6 teachers are prepared to teach inner city youth or migrant youth.

Teacher education in the eighties will face many critical issues. One of these is the preparation of teachers in the knowledge and techniques of multicultural education. Future teachers must be prepared to educate a highly mobile, multiethnic student population. This issue affects society at its core—the ability of people to relate to one another and the ability of the individual to participate effectively in an educational system. Teacher education, on a large scale, must devote some time to the analysis of this issue. Input should be sought from several sources including the broad base of the society. Logical, practical solutions should be sought. From there, perhaps programs can be designed to develop teachers who are capable of coping with their classes and of assisting students to function in the multicultural society in which we live.

By no means is it suggested that teacher education alone is the answer to the concern that is pervasive in our society. It will take the cooperation of other institutions and the community to attempt to resolve the issue of multicultural education.

## References

Gollnick, D.M. (Ed.) *Multicultural education in teacher education: The state of the scene.* Accreditation Standards for Multicultural Teacher Education Project, American Association of Colleges for Teacher Education, One Dupont Circle, Washington, D.C., 1978.

National Council for Accreditation of Teacher Education (NCATE). *Standards for the accreditation of teacher education.* Washington, D.C.: National Council for Accreditation of Teacher Education, May 1977.

# CHAPTER 8

# EDUCATION THAT IS MULTICULTURAL AND THE RELATIONSHIP BETWEEN PRESERVICE CAMPUS LEARNING AND FIELD EXPERIENCES (1986)

*Carl A. Grant and Ruth A. Koskela*

Two areas of preservice teacher education in need of research attention are multicultural education and the relationship between campus learning and the field experience. Many educators have called for teacher educators to make their programs multicultural (Baker, 1973, 1977; Deslone, 1973; Gezi, 1981; Grant, 1975, 1983; Klassen & Gollnick, 1977; Rivlin, 1977). However, this call for the most part goes unanswered even as schools receive more and more diverse students to educate (see, for example, "The New Ellis Island," 1983) and student teachers reportedly are not being prepared to teach them (Mahon & Boyle, 1981). Dawson (1981) accurately and succinctly captures the disposition of teacher educators concerning multicultural education: "Educational leaders appear to agree that multicultural education should be a part of teacher training programs and public school curricula, but the interest has yet to become reality" (p.5). In explaining why multicultural education has not become a reality, she points out that teacher educators at historically black institutions of higher education believe that their commitment to minorities is sufficient evidence of their involvement in multicultural education. Teacher educators at traditionally white colleges and universities in monocultural and monosocial geographical regions believe that, since their institutions and communities have only a few minorities, they have no obligation to commit time and resources to multicultural education. This attitude, as she correctly and appropriately describes, is "erroneous and typifies the *exemption syndrome*" (p. 5, italics added).

A second area of concern is the use preservice students make during the field experience of what they have learned in their campus coursework. Educators are seeking to understand how the classroom environment affects the students' university training (Copeland, 1979), how laboratory skill learning (microteaching) affects classroom performance (Copeland & Doyle, 1973), how the ecology and context of the classroom affect the student teacher's use of learned skills (Corcoran, 1982; Doyle & Ponder, 1975), whether what is learned in methods courses has a long-term effect on the beliefs and teaching practices of preservice students (Hodges, 1982), how dissonance can be reconciled between preservice preparation and teaching practice (McCaleb, 1979), and to what extent preservice students implement multicultural concepts in these field experiences (Grant, 1981). This research suggests that what is learned at the university is often not used in the field experience; teacher educators are attempting to understand what factors facilitate use of campus learning and what hinder it. For example, Copeland (1979) argues that "student teachers' ability to use many skills they learn during their university training depends not only on the quality of the initial training they receive, but on the environment in which they must practice those skills, their student teaching classroom" (p. 194). Hodges (1982) sought to discover if what is learned in (reading) methods courses has a long-term effect on the beliefs and teaching practices of preservice students. She concluded, "that preservice teachers . . . often act in ways that are dissonant with views they espoused immediately after taking a reading course and in some cases, they even change their views toward reading instruction" (p. 29). Grant (1981) found that during the field experience, students' attention to multicultural concepts learned at the university greatly depended upon the attention given to these concepts by their cooperating teachers or university supervisors. He also found that implementation of multicultural concepts and skills learned at the university was not given serious attention during the field experience.

The purpose of this study is to develop an understanding of the implementation of multiculturalism in a teacher education program and the relationship between campus learning and the field experience. Five questions gave direction to the study: (a) To what extent were undergraduate students in a teacher preparation program receiving additional information on education that is multicultural (EMC: For a discussion of the differernce between EMC and multicultural education, see Grant, 1977, pp. 65–66. Briefly, *multicultural education* suggests a specialty or focus on one part of education, as opposed to the more comprehensive and integrative sense of *education that is multicultural*) after receiving baseline knowledge about the concept in an introductory course? (b) What was the nature and quality of the multicultural information received? (c) What was the nature and quality of EMC the students saw in the school? (d) To what extent did students attempt to use the concepts of EMC during their student teaching experience or in assignments in their university courses? (e) To what extent did students feel comfortable discussing problems and issues related to EMC in university classes and during their field experiences?

This study replicates a previous study by one of the authors (Grant, 1981). The first study followed a sample of students through their preservice program. These students had received baseline instruction in EMC in their introductory course. The study sought to examine, by interviewing the students each semester, what additional information they were receiving on EMC and how they were using this information in their student teaching. The study here has the same purpose but adds interviews with university instructors regarding what they taught about EMC and observations of a sub-sample during student teaching to find out exactly what they actually did with the information.

# Method

Subjects of this study were 23 white students (20 women and 3 men) in an elementary teacher education program at a large midwestern university. The students were followed through their elementary preservice program, which includes a four-semester sequence of professional courses. Students enter the program as second-semester sophomores or first-semester juniors. The first semester in the sequence includes Introduction to Elementary Education. The second semester includes Reading and Language Arts methods courses, with a practicum that requires students to be in an elementary school for three half-days per week for eight weeks. The third semester includes methods courses in mathematics, social studies, and science, with a practicum in the same areas, also for three half-days per week for eight weeks. The fourth semester involves 15 weeks of student or intern teaching. Along with student teaching and the other practica, students participate in a seminar designed to tie the theory and practice of teaching together and to encourage student teachers to reflect upon what they are doing and why they are doing it. Besides the methods courses, students are required to take a course in mainstreaming for teachers and a minimum of seven semester credits in foundations courses consisting of developmental and learning psychology and educational policy.

Sample students' field placements for their first practicum (reading and language arts) were mostly in predominantly white, upper middle or middle-class schools with small minority populations. Only eight of these placements were in the metropolitan school district. Twenty of the placements for the second practicum (science, social studies, and math) were in the metropolitan school district. Most of the schools were white middle class, but 17 had some students of color attending.

Nineteen of the 23 students did their student teaching in the metropolitan school district. Of these 19 students, only 5 taught in schools where there was little or no racial diversity, and 9 taught in schools in upper middle-class areas. The remaining four students taught in predominantly white, middle-class schools outside the metropolitan area.

The sample received instruction on EMC in Introduction to Elementary Education, where they participated in experiences and activities that gave them an awareness and understanding of EMC. For example, they participated in discussions about societal attitudes toward race, sex, class, and handicap and how these are reinforced or ameliorated by the school. These discussions included analyses of instructional materials for race, sex, social class, and handicap bias. The students heard lectures and participated in discussions on various aspects of education that were presented from a multicultural perspective, such as governance and law. Discussions of law and education included issues in school desegregation litigation as well as the constitutional rights of students in schools. The students did assignments and class reports related to the lecture topics that required them to use what they had learned.

Based on their final essay examination and their written assignments, it was determined that the students had an awareness and fairly good understanding of EMC and were able to integrate many EMC concepts into their assignments. For example, in the final examination students pointed out the importance of including multicultural concepts when teaching the basic skills, how the hidden curriculum serves to condition how one group of people thinks about another, and how math anxiety impacts upon female career opportunities. Even if the subjects received no further instruction from a multicultural perspective, they had demonstrated enough understanding of how to integrate EMC into their subsequent university coursework and classroom teaching that one would expect them to do so. Also, it could be reasoned that they could recognize instruction in EMC in their subsequent coursework.

The students were interviewed by experienced interviewers at the end of their second and third semesters and at the end of their student teaching semester. Each interview lasted approximately 40 to 50 minutes. The interviews were taped and then transcribed for analysis. Students were encouraged to bring class notebooks to the interview in order to help their recall of information. Eleven students were observed during their student teaching semester. Eight were observed three times and the others, two times; all 11 were seen at least once during lead teaching weeks. To validate the students' responses, the interviewers also spoke with 17 of the university staff responsible for teaching the methods courses and practicum seminars and supervising the students during their field experience.

The instrument for this study was an interview inventory of 15 questions. The questions were designed to answer the five questions directing the study. The questions explored instruction students received about providing an education that is multicultural, university assignments or projects students did that were related to EMC, the amount of EMC they saw in the school, their use of EMC concepts in the classroom, such as in classroom planning and teaching strategies, and their comfort level while using EMC. The same questions were asked in each of the three interviews, and probing questions were asked for clarification and illumination of responses. During the student teaching semester, the questions focused on the extent to which the student attempted to affirm EMC in his or her classroom.

## Results

The results of this study are presented as follows: (a) What the student teachers were taught, (b) what they saw in the field, and (c) what they did. Only 19 students were interviewed for the second interview. Data were examined and crosschecked by the researchers in order to minimize their individual biases.

## *What the student teachers were taught*

### *Additional instruction*

When asked in the first interview whether they had received additional instruction in EMC since their introductory course, 18 of the 23 students reported that they had received some, mainly in the areas of bias in textbooks and reading dialects and mostly in language arts and reading methods courses. Five of the 18 students made special mention of the mainstreaming class as a place where they received EMC information.

In the second interview, all 19 students reported receiving additional instruction in EMC, mainly in the social studies methods course. Students, for example, made a field trip to a Native American reservation and discussed differences in family structure, African culture, and global education. They also examined instructional materials for race and sex bias. In both the first and second interviews, several students mentioned that the university instructors seem to stress their own EMC special topics (e.g., bias in textbooks) and after these topics were discussed, they rarely returned to EMC. Also, they said that the information they received was more about individual differences among children than about race, sex, and class differences and inequalities that are promoted because of these latter differences.

Ten of the 12 university staff members who worked with the students during this time reported discussing EMC concepts with the students. For example, the staff reported discussing deprivation models as an explanation for low achievement, the use of oral communication in different societies, the melting pot theory, and reading readiness in terms of sex and culture differences.

In the third interview—after student teaching—none of the 23 students reported receiving instruction in EMC. However, four of the five university staff members who supervised students during student teaching reported giving the students information they said was on EMC but which was mostly about individual learning differences in children rather than differences related to race, class, gender, or handicap.

## Classroom planning
When the students were asked during the first interview if anyone (e.g., professors, supervisors, cooperating teachers) had helped them learn how to incorporate EMC into classroom planning, only seven replied affirmatively. During the second interview, five of the 19 replied affirmatively. The major help the students reported receiving was how to make their instructional materials nonbiased. During the third interview, none of the students reported being helped to incorporate EMC into their classroom planning and activities on an ongoing basis, either while working as a student teacher or during their two weeks of lead teaching. The reasons students gave for not incorporating EMC were that they "didn't have help," and "it was a sink or swim situation," and they "did not have time." Eight of the university staff reported helping the students in this area, and nine reported not giving the students help. For example, of the eight giving help, four reported helping the students broaden their conceptual view of concepts they were teaching. One said he helped a student on an inquiry lesson. Another said she introduced students to various ethnic group literature.

## Hidden curriculum
During the first and second interview sessions, 13 students reported both receiving additional information about the hidden curriculum and examining its operation in the classroom. However, several of these students pointed out that it was just mentioned, not "really discussed," and often the examples used to explain its meaning were unclear. During the third interview, 16 students said they both received more information on the hidden curriculum and examined the classroom to see how it was operating. The information students reported receiving was very often related to sexism, teachers' nonverbal behavior, and teacher-pupil rapport. During their classroom teaching, students were most concerned about examining the messages they were sending pupils. Fifteen university staff members reported that they discussed the hidden curriculum in their classes, which included the topics identified by the students as well as other topics, for example, authority in the classroom.

## Teaching strategies
In responding to the question "Did anyone discuss adapting different teaching strategies to various learning styles?" all of the students reported "yes" during each of the three interviews. These discussions took place with university staff members and classroom teachers and included when to use the language experience and basal reading approaches and how to individualize teaching to meet the needs of the students. Only one of the university staff said that the point was not emphasized in his or her teaching. Several students also said their cooperating teachers gave them assistance in this area.

## School-community relations
During their first interview, 21 students responded "yes" to the question "Was there any discussion about the teacher's role in school-community relations?" Sixteen students during the second interview and 17 during the third interview also said "yes." These discussions took place equally at both the school and the

university. At the university, the importance of home-school relations was stressed, and reasons for problems associated with home-school relationships were discussed. In the school, cooperating teachers often had the practicum students participate in parent-teacher conferences. Sixteen university staff members reported discussing school-community relations with their students.

## What the student teachers saw in the field

### Classroom environment
During the first interview, when the students were asked if they had seen any classroom environment that reflected EMC during their practicum visits, only two responded positively. Five of the students voiced concern about the absence of EMC concepts in the school environment, especially in the classrooms that included students of color and working-class students.

During the second interview, 6 of the 19 students reported that classroom environments reflected some aspect of EMC, mainly a bulletin board or poster on Native Americans. During the third interview, 9 of the 23 students reported seeing classroom environments that reflected some aspect of EMC. Once again, this was mainly a bulletin board or poster of a special day, for example, Martin Luther King's Birthday or a poster of a Native American. When the students were asked if during their student teaching they had tried to make the classroom environment show their own affirmation of EMC, only one student responded positively; she had used a bulletin board. Eleven of the university staff reported that the classroom environments they saw did not reflect EMC.

### Contributions of people from various groups
Students were asked if they heard any mention of contributions women, handicapped people, and people of color in the classes they had observed. Seven students during the first interview, 11 during the second, and 17 during the third responded affirmatively to the question. Most often these contributions related to race and were mentioned during Black History Week or a Hispanic celebration. Reports from university staff corroborated what students said. Six of the university staff members who regularly visited the schools reported hearing discussions of contributions, mostly related to an ethnic holiday; six staff members said they did not hear such discussions.

## What the student teachers did

### Assignments or projects
When asked during the first interview if they had any assignments or projects during the semester that included EMC, 11 of the 23 students said "yes." Most indicated that this involved examining curriculum materials for racial and sex bias. During the second interview, 16 of the 19 students said they did an assignment that included EMC; these were mostly papers or units for social studies methods. Eight of these students said they also tried to include multicultural concepts that grew out of their methods courses in their practicum work; however, they reported accomplishing very little. During the third interview, none of the students reported doing an assignment or a project related to EMC for any university class or the seminar they were taking. Eight of the 17 university staff members reported that

their students included EMC in an assignment or project. These were the classes reported by the students where the EMC work had taken place.

## Bias in curriculum materials
In response to the question, "Did you examine any curriculum materials that you used in your class or the school for bias?" 17 students responded "yes" during the first interview, 19 during the second, and 19 during the third. This examination covered a variety of textbooks, for example, social studies, reading, and math. Only three of the university staff members said that they had not provided instruction on examining curriculum material for bias as part of their course content.

## Comfort level
When asked, "How comfortable did you feel raising questions about multicultural issues in your university classes, and in your student teaching classroom?" 11 of the students during the first interview said they felt comfortable at both places, 5 said they were uncomfortable at the school, and 6 said they were uncomfortable at the university. During the second interview, only two felt uncomfortable at the school and one at the university. By the time of the third interview all the students reported feeling comfortable discussing EMC issues at both places. The main reason students said they felt uncomfortable in the school was that the majority of the students and staff were white and they didn't have enough information about EMC. Not having enough information and concern about what peers would think was the major reason for not discussing EMC on campus. Eleven of the university staff members believed that the students felt comfortable discussing EMC at both places.

## Affirming EMC
When asked, "During your student teaching, did you do anything to affirm or implement EMC in your classroom?" seven students responded in the affirmative. However, they did not report attempts to make their teaching multicultural; for example, three presented a unit on Mexico, one discussed sex roles in society, two had a unit on differences in family structures, one put up a bulletin board for International Day at her school, and one of the students who did the Mexico unit also took her students on a blind walk. When the students were asked "why not?" many said there was "no reason" why they didn't; others said they were "too busy." Additionally, the students who had reported examining the classroom for the hidden curriculum and their textbooks for bias (see above) did not see these activities as affirming EMC in their classrooms. Only three of the university staff reported that they saw any students implementing EMC in the school.

## Observations
Observations of the subsample (11 students) during the student-teaching semester confirm the data from the interviews. Student teachers attempted and accomplished very little EMC. Most of the observed lessons followed the textbook, and these lessons did not include EMC, nor did the student teachers integrate EMC into their teaching of the lesson. There were opportunities to readily include EMC, but they were not pursued. For example, one opportunity concerned stereotypic information in a social studies text about Native Americans, and another concerned a Hispanic week celebration program. These opportunities were forfeited.

The student teachers did, however, demonstrate a concern about the children's self-esteem by way of making certain they knew and understood their assignments—what they were supposed to do and how they were supposed to do it. They also paid attention to the children's learning rates and skill needs. In summarizing what was observed, student teachers were mainly concerned with the mechanics of the lesson, especially discipline. EMC was not an important aspect.

## Discussion

The results from the study show that the students were receiving additional instruction in EMC after receiving baseline knowledge in the introductory course. However, many of the students saw this information as not comprehensive, mainly stressing a particular interest of the instructor. One student referred to it as the instructor's "bandwagon." If one looks at the nature of the EMC information students received during the second, third, and fourth semesters of the sequence, one is struck by its fragmented and piecemeal quality and its emphasis on individual differences. One can discuss differences among people without referring to how race, gender, and class impact on them. For example, one can alert students to interests of individual children or to the fact that some are visual learners while others are auditory learners. Whereas this is important, it is not the same as sensitizing students to children's cultural backgrounds or to the impact of discrimination or how useful students see school.

When instruction went beyond individual differences, it focused mainly on race and gender, although class (poor kids) did receive some attention. Most commonly, students received isolated segments addressing bias in textbooks, student learning styles, and the hidden curriculum. Many students believed that the activity of analyzing curriculum materials for race and sex bias was done too often and that this assignment did not really add to their repertoire of knowledge after they did it one or two times. The students seemed to feel positive regarding the information they received about adapting different teaching strategies to learning styles. Individualizing instruction was presented in a diverse manner and did not seem repetitious. Most of the university staff members explained how to diversify the subject matter to meet children's varying learning rates and styles. More positive responses were collected from this question than any of the other questions asked of the students.

Many of the students seemed very interested in the hidden curriculum because they saw it as directly related to their work. Several noted that this concept had made them more aware of their facial expression in the classroom and sex stereotypes in teacher-student interaction. It should be noted however, that the students did not discuss the hidden curriculum very broadly. For example, they did not mention analyzing the authority structure in the classroom, what their teaching procedures and curriculum were teaching about what counts as learning and as knowledge, or what the time schedule was teaching students about institutional life (see, for example, Giroux & Penna, 1979; Swartz & Bourdieu, 1977).

The report that students received very little or no information on EMC during the time of their student teaching could suggest that the university supervisors, cooperating teachers, and students saw dealing with the more "practical" aspects of teaching as more important than EMC during this time. Quite likely the student teachers, in spite of the information on EMC they were taught, retained a traditional view of what teaching and classroom learning entail. Their first concern was likely to learn to reproduce teaching and management practices they observed other teachers, including their cooperating teacher, performing. With this view in mind, they probably saw EMC as something that could be added on after they had learned to reproduce traditional teaching behaviors, rather than as something that would give direction to teaching and classroom learning. Also, since student teaching and the seminar were the only two formal university experiences most students had for the semester, the opportunities to receive EMC information were greatly reduced.

Why did the students see so very little EMC in the schools throughout the school year? One thesis is that the "return" to basics has caused teachers to spend more time stressing the three R's. Another thesis is that there has not been a strong, sincere commitment from those in authority. The school community is predominantly white middle class, and Dawson's "exemption syndrome" seemed to be in operation. We don't believe that there is a conspiracy to exclude EMC in the school, but a lethargic feeling of what Kirp (1979) refers to as "doing good by doing little." In other words, if ethnic celebrations take place regularly and there is no blatant overt discrimination in schools related to race, class, and gender, those in charge may see little need to promote EMC actively.

Many of the students included EMC in their university assignments, and some tried to include EMC in their practicum work that grew out of their methods courses. It should be noted that, especially during the first interview, this consisted mainly of examining curriculum materials for race and sex bias. Why did only seven students report doing something with EMC while student teaching? There are several possible explanations. First, Grant (1981) suggests that students pay attention to EMC mainly when the university instructors and cooperating teachers pay attention to it. Yee (1969) made a similar observation when he noted that cooperating teachers seem to influence the teaching behavior of student teachers. McCaleb (1979) has argued that the attitudes developed in the security of the university environment appear to need reinforcement when confronted with dissonance in student teaching. Thus, since the student teachers did not have active role models for implementing EMC, their actions in this area were passive. We believe students need instructors and teachers to show them how to implement EMC concepts into the daily curriculum and a field placement that supports and encourages their efforts. Although Becker and Ade (1982) did not discover a strong relationship between the modeling of good practice and the student teachers' final performance, we would argue that deliberate active modeling as opposed to passive, occasional modeling is necessary and would probably provide a more positive result. Another explanation could be, as Iannaconne (1963) observed, that student teachers in their transition from the campus to the classroom are not adventuresome, they want to apply what works and gets the students through the lesson. Since they had not had very much experience implementing EMC they did not want to take the chance. Success for student teachers, according to Iannaccone, "is achieved by the setting of low levels of expectations and by classroom management" (p. 78). Another explanation could be that the students' white, middle-class backgrounds (their biographies) have a greater impact upon their behavior (especially when they see their cooperating teachers and supervisors doing very little) than the training they learned at the university. Lortie's (1975) thesis regarding the importance of biography over formal training would give support to this argument. Also, Peters (1977) reminds us, "The effect of training programs on the practice of teachers in classroom is negatively compared with the influence of models in their past with whom they identify and of demands springing from their own personalities" (p. 162).

Still another explanation could be the ecology of the classroom (Copeland, 1979; Doyle & Ponder, 1975). For example, Doyle and Ponder suggest that environmental conditions in the classroom affect what can fit in: "Recommended teaching patterns legitimized by external criteria ... may not have ecological validity in the classroom. That is, such patterns of behavior may conflict with the ecological demands of operating a classroom group" (p. 187). For example, a student teacher teaching in a rural area that is predominantly (or all) white in ideology, practices, and population would have a difficult time "fitting" EMC into the classroom. We would argue that a combination of these explanations could be why EMC was attempted by only a few students. It must be clearly recognized that, while we applaud the attempts of these few students, they had only begun to teach multiculturally. In order for EMC to be comprehensively implemented in the schools, it would have to be integrated into every fiber of one's teaching. It seems that the preservice program the students experienced was far short of preparing them to do this.

By the third interview, most of the students reported that they felt comfortable raising questions about EMC. However, most of the students did not teach EMC concepts during their student teaching. An obvious observation is that they had very little reason to feel uncomfortable about EMC, especially since most were not teaching the concepts, and those who were did so only occasionally. In other words, these responses seem to be based more upon speculation of actions than on past performance.

## Comparison of studies

How did the results of this study compare with the previous study (Grant, 1981)? For the most part the results were very similar, with a few exceptions. Students in both studies received EMC information. Although the nature of the information was very similar, students in the second study reported receiving a little more variety. The quality of the information, although improved in the second study, still seemed mostly to relate to awareness and understanding of EMC concepts, and very little attention was given to application and integration of the concept into the classroom curriculum. Thus, the small increase in both variety and quality of information received in the second study did not have any real additional increase in EMC implementation in the school. Also, both studies point out that analyzing textbooks for sex and race bias is often the heart of the EMC work in many courses.

Both studies found an absence of EMC in the classroom environment, although students in the previous study reported seeing more attention paid to EMC in the classroom. In both studies, students reported feeling comfortable for the most part working with EMC. However, most of the student teachers in both studies did not attempt to integrate EMC into their curriculum. The reasons for not doing so were the same: "not enough time," "predominantly white classroom," and "no reason."

## Conclusion

The EMC concepts that were learned on the campus were not readily integrated into the school curriculum by the students. This observation supports the concern of teacher educators (see Turney, 1982) that the practicum curriculum be studied and that teacher preparation institutions develop their curriculum with well-planned field experiences that relate to the objectives and ideas of their program.

More explicitly, this study recommends that research on teacher socialization also needs to consider the ideology of the curriculum and those in charge in relationship to the socialization process.

Students seem to include EMC mostly when it is promoted by someone in charge. Those aspects of EMC that are more frequently integrated into the curriculum relate to individualizing for skill-related needs of children rather than for issues of race, class, and gender. Attention to race, class, and gender within the total teacher training program needs to be addressed.

In order to help students to transfer campus learning to their classroom teaching, not only must they be given information, they must be shown how to put that information into practice in the daily curriculum. Joyce and Weil (1972) have argued the importance of deliberate modeling or demonstration followed by guided practice to stimulate learning. Student teachers need to see teachers modeling EMC. Students also need a comprehensive integrated multicultural preparation program. Baker (1977) and Grant (1981) have argued that sporadic, isolated, and narrow-focus training in EMC does not prepare students to implement the concepts in their classroom teaching.

Additionally, this study suggests that there needs to be greater communication between the campus and the classroom related to the integration of EMC concepts into the curriculum. Finally, this study suggests a need to understand why EMC is given more attention—although minimal—on the campus than in the school, when the campus classrooms in preservice education are practically all white, mostly female, and mostly middle-class, and the school classrooms have some children of color, working-class students, and a fairly equal distribution of both boys and girls.

## References

Baker, G. (1973). Multicultural training for student teachers. *Journal of Teacher Education* (Winter), 307.

Baker, G. (1977). Two preservice training approaches. *Journal of Teacher Education, 28,* 31–33.

Becker, R., & Ade, W. E. (1982). Relationship of field placement characteristics and students' potential field performance abilities to clinical experience performance rating. *Journal of Teacher Education, 33,* 24–30.

Copeland, W. (1979). Student teachers and cooperating teacher: An ecological relationship. *Theory into Practice, 18,* 194–199.

Copeland, W., & Doyle, W. (1973). Laboratory skill training and student teacher classroom performance. *Journal of Experimental Education, 42,* 16–21.

Corcoran, E. (1982). Classroom contexts as settings for learning to teach: A new direction for research in teacher education. *Action in Teacher Education, 6,* 52–55.

Dawson, M. (1981, February). A matter of linkage: Multicultural education and educational equity. In M. E. Dawson et al. (Eds.), *Educational equity.* (pp. 1–14). Washington, DC: ERIC Clearinghouse on Teacher Education.

Deslone, J. (1973). *Multicultural in-service training: A collaboration of higher education, country schools and local school districts.* (Title IV contract number OEG 9–72–0133) San Francisco: HEW Regional Office.

Doyle, W., & Ponder, G. (1975). Classroom ecology: Some concerns about a neglected dimension of research on teaching. *Contemporary Education, 46,* 183–188.

Gezi, K. (1981). Effective evaluation in bilingual education. *Educational Research Quarterly, 6,* 104–112.

Giroux, H., & Penna, A. (1979). Social education in the classroom: The dynamics of the hidden curriculum. *Theory and Research in Social Education, 7*(1), 21–42.

Grant, C. (1975). Exploring the contours of multi-cultural education. In C. A. Grant (Ed.),

*Sifting and winnowing: An exploration of the relationship between multi-cultural education and CBTE*. Madison, WI: Teacher Corps Associates.

Grant, C. (1978). Education that is multicultural, isn't that what we mean? *Journal of Teacher Education, 29*, 45–48.

Grant, C. (1981). Education that is multicultural and teacher preparation: An examination from the perspectives of preservice students. *Journal of Educational Research, 75*, 95–101.

Grant, C. (1983). Multicultural teacher education—renewing the discussion: A response to Martin Haberman. *Journal of Teacher Education, 34*, 29–32.

Hodges, C. (1982). Implementing methods: If you can't blame the cooperating teacher who can you blame? *Journal of Teacher Education, 33*, 25–29.

Iannaconne, L. (1963). Student teaching: A transitional stage in the making of a teacher. *Theory into Practice, 2*, 73–80.

Joyce, B., & Weil, M. (1972). *Models of teaching*. Englewood Cliffs, NJ: Prentice Hall.

Kirp, D. (1979). *Doing good by doing little*. Berkeley: University of California Press.

Klassen, F., & Gollnick, D. (1977). *Pluralism and the American teacher: Issues and case studies*. Washington, DC: American Association of Colleges for Teacher Education.

Lortie, D. (1975). *Schoolteacher*. Chicago: University of Chicago Press.

McCaleb, J. (1979). On reconciling dissonance between preparation and practice. *Journal of Teacher Education, 30*, 50–53.

Mahon, J., & Boyle, V. (1981). Multicultural teacher preparation: An attitudinal survey. *Educational Research Quarterly. 6*, 97–103.

The New Ellis Island. (1983, June 13). *Time*, 18–25.

Peters, R. (1977). *Education and the education of teachers*. London: Routledge & Kegan Paul.

Rivlin, H. (1977). Research and development in multicultural education. In F. H. Klassen & D. M. Gollnick (Eds.), *Pluralism and the American teacher*. Washington, DC: American Association of Colleges for Teacher Education (pp. 81–115).

Swartz, D., & Bourdieu, P. (1977). The cultural transmission of social inequality. *Harvard Educational Review, 47*(4), 545–555.

Turney, C. (1982). *The practicum in teacher education*. Sydney, Australia: Sydney University Press.

Yee, A. (1969). Do cooperating teachers influence the attitudes of student teachers? *Journal of Educational Psychology, 60*, 327–332.

# CHAPTER 9

# COLOR BLINDNESS AND BASKET MAKING ARE NOT THE ANSWERS (1995)

Confronting the dilemmas of race, culture, and language diversity in teacher education

*Marilyn Cochran-Smith*

Although the present American educational system is dysfunctional for disproportionately large numbers of children who are not part of the racial and language mainstream,[1] there are no universal strategies for teaching about cultural diversity or for teaching children who are culturally and linguistically different from one another, from their teachers, or from the "majority" students for whom instructional materials and school expectations are tailored and whose best interests are served by continuation of the current situation. Indeed, it has been pointed out that it is contradictory to the concept of cultural diversity itself to expect that educational experts can enumerate specific practices that teachers should learn and then apply across schools and communities with different histories and different needs.[2] But it is also not advisable for teachers or children to mistake color blindness for educational equity or to learn "the characteristics" of people of various races and cultures. These practices decontextualize teaching and learning[3] and often result in either bolstering the very stereotypes they are intended to dispel or alienating parents and others who regard them as racist activities in and of themselves.[4]

To alter a system that is deeply dysfunctional, the system needs teachers who regard teaching as a political activity and embrace social change as part of the job[5]—teachers who enter the profession not expecting to carry on business as usual but prepared to join other educators and parents in major reforms. In this article, I argue that teacher educators cannot carry on business as usual either. The ways we have traditionally initiated students into the discourses and practices of teaching—especially through widespread versions of "the lesson plan" based on linear analysis of objectives and methods for teaching and management—are not likely to result in an activist's stance on teaching nor meet the needs of an increasingly diverse population of schoolchildren. I argue, then, that what we need in teacher education is not better generic strategies for "teaching multicultural education" or "teaching for diversity" nor more lessons about basket making and other customs in non-Anglo cultures.[6] Instead, I propose that what we need are generative ways for prospective teachers, experienced teachers, and teacher educators alike to work together in communities of learners—to explore and reconsider their own assumptions, understand the values and practices of families and cultures that are different from their own, and construct pedagogy that takes these into account in locally appropriate and culturally sensitive ways.

In the first section of this article, I contrast the images of teaching and learning that underlie a lesson plan-centered approach to learning to teach with those that underlie an inquiry-centered approach. Next I draw on the teacher research projects of student teachers working in urban schools to demonstrate how inquiry creates opportunities for prospective teachers to develop the perspectives on teaching, learning, and schooling that are central to an activist's stance. I conclude with a call for teacher educators' and student teachers' increased involvement in communities that foster intellectually vital and socially significant inquiries into the dilemmas of race, culture, and language diversity in teaching and learning to teach.

## Learning the discourse of teaching: Contrasting approaches

A nearly universal tradition in preservice education is to introduce student teachers to teaching by having them write and carry out "the lesson plan." Most models of lesson planning have a series of steps: explicitly stating objectives and goals, choosing appropriate learning activities, organizing and sequencing those activities, and specifying evaluation procedures.[7] A growing body of research on teacher planning and teacher thinking suggests that experienced teachers do not proceed in a linear fashion when planning for teaching. Instead, they plan in ways that are significantly more recursive and cyclical, more learner-centered, and structured around larger chunks of content and time than those of the single lesson. In fact, although experienced teachers use a wide range of planning strategies over the course of a school year, *lesson* planning appears to play a modest or even insignificant role. Nevertheless, the lesson endures as the major unit for planning and improving teaching in preservice education, and lesson plans endure as the single form of planning taught explicitly in programs across the country.[8] Hence, they continue to represent what is arguably the most visible way teacher education institutions initiate student teachers into the discourses and practices of teaching.[9]

Although it is troubling to consider the mismatch between the lesson plan assignments that dominate preservice teacher education, on the one hand, and experienced teachers' actual ways of preparing for and thinking about teaching, on the other, it is even more troubling to expose the images of teaching that lesson plans perpetuate. Taken as artifacts of the cultures of teaching and teacher education, typical lesson plan assignments imply that both planning for teaching and teaching itself are linear activities that proceed from a preplanned opening move to a known and predetermined endpoint. They suggest that knowledge, curriculum, and instruction are static and unchanging, transmitted through a one-way conduit from teacher to students, rather than socially constructed through the transactions of teachers, children, and texts. This perspective assumes that we can accurately predict how children make sense of ideas, texts, and information and that all children understand and connect these to their own prior knowledge and experience in the same ways. Most importantly, writing and conducting lessons of the sort described here endorse and perpetuate the primacy of mastery, scripture, and method.

Implicit in the lesson plan and other similar assignments is the notion that uniform mastery of bits of information and knowledge is the goal of every lesson. In elementary school teaching, both the bits to be mastered and the sequence of steps for getting there are spelled out in detail in the teachers' manuals that increasingly accompany textbooks in every curricular area from spelling and language to math, health, and science. The tyranny of the teacher's manual is most apparent, however, in basal reading programs, which provide carefully scripted plans for every single lesson and which are pervasive throughout elementary teaching, accounting for some 90% of reading instruction nationwide and the lion's share of total instructional time at the elementary level.[10] Basal scripts not only tell the teacher exactly when and what to say but also control the children's part in the script by stipulating precisely which responses are to be elicited and accepted. Notwithstanding occasional directives to the teacher to "accept any reasonable answer," it is clear that both teacher and children are expected to honor the authority of scripture and stick to the script, which leaves little room for improvisation, originality of perspective, or diversity. The skills and information to be mastered in each lesson are pre-established and static, and the parts of each actor, including a starring role for the teacher and bit parts for the students, are clearly enumerated. Variations in the cultural and linguistic resources that children bring to school with them, in the verbal and nonverbal interaction patterns to which they are accustomed, and in the kinds of knowledge and prior experiences they may have had are not figured in. In the end, then, because both the content and the sequence of events are established at the outset of a lesson plan and, more often than not, provided for in prepackaged materials, the major task for the prospective teacher is not to learn how to understand the diversity of ways children construct meanings—or what Dewey called the "mind to mind" relationship of teacher to child.[11] Rather, the major task is to develop a repertoire of methods for getting through lessons with a reasonable amount of decorum—methods for establishing order, keeping children on the task at hand, pacing questions and activities, occupying those who finish more quickly than others, and maintaining control.

The image of teaching underlying an inquiry- or teacher-research-centered[12] approach to teaching directly challenges the primacy of mastery, scripture, and method. When teacher research plays a central role in teacher education,[13] student teachers are invited to treat their classrooms and schools as research sites embedded in the contexts of culture and community, to understand their work by raising questions and collecting data, and to discover meanings in the variations in children's behaviors and interpretations of classroom events and interactions. Teacher research is based on the notion that teachers and children together construct knowledge and curriculum through their ongoing classroom interactions by drawing on and mingling their varied language and cultural resources and experiences. Teacher research is not intended as a strategy to help student teachers implement or translate theory into plans for practice. Rather, it is intended to help student teachers uncover and develop "theories of practice" or "theories in practice"—that is, neither theories divorced from practice nor practice unaware of its own underlying theories.[14] Implicit in teacher research is the image of teachers (as one group) among those who construct knowledge about teaching, learning, and schooling and who regard knowledge from the academy as potential frameworks for thinking about and altering practice rather than as scripture for reproducing practice and, hence, ultimately reproducing the inequities embedded in schooling.

## Constructing and confronting the dilemmas

There are five perspectives on race, culture, and language diversity that I think are essential to preparing teachers who see themselves as both educators and activists, who work with others to do what I have called "teach against the grain"[15] of the institutions of schooling that are dysfunctional and inequitable for large numbers of minority students, and who know how to learn to meet the needs of students within particular local contexts. When they are initiated into teaching through systematic and self-critical inquiry, student teachers have opportunities to develop these perspectives: (1) *reconsidering personal knowledge and experience*, (2) *locating teaching within the culture of the school and the community*, (3) *analyzing children's learning opportunities*, (4) *understanding children's understanding*, and (5) *constructing reconstructionist pedagogy*. In the pages that follow, I analyze these perspectives and show a way that they may be developed through various teacher inquiry projects during the preservice period.[16]

## *Reconsidering personal knowledge and experience*

In order to learn to teach in a society that is increasingly culturally and linguistically diverse, prospective teachers, as well as experienced teachers and teacher educators, need opportunities to examine much of what is usually unexamined in the tightly braided relationships of language, culture, and power in schools and schooling.[17] This kind of examination inevitably begins with our own histories as human beings and as educators; our own experiences as members of particular races, classes, and genders; and as children, parents, and teachers in the world. It also includes a close look at the tacit assumptions we make about the motivations and behaviors of other children, other parents, and other teachers and about the pedagogies we deem most appropriate for learners who are like us or not like us. In Project START, student teachers are invited to examine these assumptions by drawing on their own experiences and ideas as well as on the work of other university- and school-based teachers and researchers.

Along with all members of the START community (cooperating teachers, university-based supervisors, project directors, and course instructors), student teachers write personal narrative essays about their lives and the experiences that have shaped their views of race, culture, and diversity. The intent in narrative essays is for all members of the community to explore for themselves but also to provide for other members a sense of who they are as teachers, as learners, and as human beings. Student teachers also write critical essays designed to promote thoughtful responses to program readings in which they pose their own questions about the topics they find central. The intent in these essays, in which student teachers are invited to address the generic question "What do you think you think about _____?" is for prospective teachers to use other people's research to uncover their own interpretive frameworks and to explore the implications of these connections in ways that are tentative and evolutionary. Both kinds of essays—those that are narrative and personal and those that link the student teacher's emerging understandings to empirical and conceptual research in education and related fields—are essential to a stance that enables prospective teachers to learn how to construct and confront the dilemmas of cultural diversity and to teach effectively both their own and others' children.

In the excerpts that follow, I draw on two essays written by student teachers, the first a narrative essay and the second a readings essay, to illustrate the ways student teachers use these formats in an inquiry-centered preservice program. In the first, Penny Sparks, an African American who spent the year student teaching in an urban public school in a poor area that was 100% African American, confronted the contradictions she realized were involved in trying to both escape from and embrace her community and her history.

Excerpt 1
(from Penny Sparks' narrative essay written for local publication for the Project START community)

I've known Gilda ever since I was eight years old. We attended the same elementary school, middle school, high school, and undergraduate university. We are products of the inner city. Although our community was not impoverished, opportunities for those who resided there were not plentiful.

Presently Gilda is a registered nurse, and I am a full-time graduate student at the University of Pennsylvania. . . . In the past we have looked back at our childhood years and frowned. We frowned upon where we have come from, because of where we are. We refused to return to our community, because of the communities we presently reside in. We looked down upon those who currently reside there, because of our present friends and acquaintances. Why? We feared the past, somehow convincing ourselves that to return equated to still being a part of. We convinced ourselves that we had escaped, so why turn back? We ceased communication because we believed that we could no longer relate to our past neighbors. Who were we? Who did we become?

We were African Americans afraid to acknowledge our community and history. We feared that acknowledgement would somehow send us two steps back. We were African Americans who shunned our African brothers and sisters, because they were not afforded the same opportunities and were not as lucky as we. We were African Americans with no sense of pride, culture, or love of our people. We often spoke about being African Americans but did not have a clue. We did not understand the plight of the African Americans or their struggle in this racist society. We were unaware of our history, thus knowing little about whence our people came. . . .

As the years progressed our view and perceptions have changed and continue to change as we become more enlightened about ourselves, our history, and our people. . . . As we began to see the world differently and critically, we began to understand why many of our brothers and sisters cannot escape the communities which keep them locked in a vicious cycle of oppression. We began to see why African Americans turn their backs on their communities in an attempt to assimilate into mainstream society.

Understanding these things has ultimately changed the way we view ourselves as African Americans, the way we view our people, and the way we view the world. I now believe that the lives of African Americans are not complete unless they use their capabilities to fight for their people . . .

In the second essay, Peggy Kaplan, a White, European-American student teacher who entered teaching after several years as a homemaker and mother, confronted the realization that the current arrangements of schools and society provided unearned privileges for members of the majority, including herself and her own children, but handicapped the children she was teaching in her student teaching classroom, children who were not part of that majority in either language or race.

Excerpt 2
(from Peggy Kaplan's critical readings essay)

*Hegemony* is a large and complex concept. It is also a lofty way to say prejudice—except this concept is covert, insidious, and oftentimes unconscious, which makes it much more difficult to battle. Many times it is even hard to recognize. However, it is a useful concept that has helped to clarify so much of what I am witnessing in my [student teaching] school and in my life.

McIntosh's article spoke about me when it said, "I think Whites are carefully taught not to recognize White privilege." I know I was. I was taught everyone was equal. It never occurred to me that I got what I did because I could fit into the system. . . . McIntosh must have shared my experiences because again she captured my sentiments when she wrote, "My schooling gave me no training in seeing myself as an oppressor, as an unfairly advantaged person, or as a participant in a damaged culture."[18] Because I succeeded through the system, am I more likely to perpetuate it, even if it is unwillingly or unknowingly?

Weiler says that reproduction theory "in general is concerned with the processes through which the existing social structures maintain and reproduce themselves."[19]. . . . I recognize I am a classic byproduct of this system. How, as a teacher, can I impart another set of values? Hunter [an urban public school with a large Hispanic population in a poor area] is a perfect example of hegemony, but, more importantly, so is Merion [a public school in an affluent White suburb where nearly all children go on to college]. I student teach at Hunter; I am the proud parent of a second grader at Merion. Neither school is trying to change the system, and therefore Merion will always succeed in reproducing the "future executives," and Hunter will always be struggling to have its children merely come to class daily. Merion will be able to win all the awards because standardized tests seem to be stacked in its favor while Hunter [won't] measure up.

Case in point: Hunter had been told to test all kindergartners and first graders in the fall on gross and small motor skills. However, a directive came down delaying it until spring. A new test was authorized, testing memorization, word, and letter skills. Over half the children in my [kindergarten] class speak Spanish at home and know only minimal English. The test will be given in English. . . . I see these young and eager children possibly being placed on the path of low expectation and failure.

I feel the unfairness is the consequence of hegemony. I am wrestling with its implications. But how do I fight against a system that gives my own children the life I want them to have? I moved from the city to give them the same advantages I had. My husband and I chose Lower Merion Township because it offered the lifestyle and schools we wanted. I will have a tough time bucking a system that works for myself and my children. Does that mean I am part of the problem and not the solution?

Each of these excerpts provides insights into the ways student teachers construct and confront the dilemmas of race, culture, and language in teaching by reconsidering and reconnecting their personal experiences and knowledge. Part of what is important in this sort of inquiry is that students struggle with the idea that racism includes not simply what McIntosh calls "individual acts of kindness or meanness"[20] but also, and in much larger measure, the privileges and disadvantages that both shape and are embedded in the institutions we live by, especially our educational institutions. For some students, the process was literally a re-seeing of their lives, not as morally neutral and average but as filled with the privileges conferred by race. The toughest part of this self-critical reflection was not accepting blame or guilt because they had been part of a system based on hegemony rather than meritocracy. Rather, the task was locating themselves as active agents within those institutions and reconsidering the ways they, as educators, could, from now on, understand and act on the successes and failures of individual students and groups of students, on the actions and apparent inactions of parents and community members, and on the educational categories and labels assigned by experts and other educators.

## Locating teaching in the culture of the school and community

Cazden and Mehan rightly argue that one of the most important things teacher education needs to do is provide opportunities for student teachers to learn "experientially about students and their families" and "how to gain information from the local community and transform it for pedagogical use."[21] A central aspect of this is for student teachers to understand that the teaching and learning they observe and participate in is located within the cultures of teaching in individual classrooms as well as the cultures of the schools and communities in which they work. This means understanding that any given instance of teaching occurs within a particular historical and social moment and is embedded within nested layers of context, including the social and academic structures of the classroom; the history and norms of teaching and learning at the school; and the attitudes, values, beliefs, and language uses of the community and its web of historical, political, and social relationships to the school.

One way to do this is to begin the student teaching experience by conducting group research projects to gather information about the schools and communities that they will come to know over the course of the year. In Project START, there is no pretense in the group inquiry that students will develop a full understanding of the culture of the school and community, but there is the intention that inquiry will help students begin to understand and raise questions by closely observing inside and outside school; interviewing teachers, students, parents, and other school personnel and community members; visiting community centers and action groups; and examining school documents as well as children's work and other artifacts of teaching and learning. What is important in an inquiry project of this kind is that prospective teachers try to understand what is going on in their schools from the meaning perspectives of the participants—teachers, parents, and children—and in relation to the history and values of the community.

Terri Campbell, Peggy Kaplan, Jennifer Lockwood, and Paige Menton, one African American and three White European-American student teachers, respectively, who were placed at Hunter Elementary, a public school in northeast Philadelphia, worked together to explore the culture of their school and its surrounding community. They began by gathering school data for pupils and staff from the student handbook and the Superintendent's Management Information Center (including statistics about programs, standardized achievement test scores, graduation, households, income, rental costs, race, language, occupation, and enrollments) and taking photos of the school, its facilities, classrooms, surrounding areas, and neighborhood. They also interviewed school personnel, families, and community members. They asked teachers, counselors, principal, and classroom aides questions such as "How would you describe the philosophy of Hunter? How would you describe the management structure of the school? How old is the school? Has it changed demographically? How are teachers evaluated? How much autonomy do teachers have? What kinds of relationships do they have with administrators? What is a typical day like? How long have you been associated with the school?" They asked parents and other community members questions such as "What do you think about Hunter? How did you decide to send your child to this school? What languages are used at the school and/or for talk about the school? How does language use vary? How long have you and/or your children and your family been associated with the school? In what ways do parents and community members have opportunities to be involved? What are the problems and priorities in the neighborhoods? What programs and groups are active in the community?" They asked children to draw pictures that represented Hunter School for them, and they asked them questions such as "What are your favorite things about Hunter? What is a typical day like for you? What languages do you hear at school, at home?" The group also consulted school documents such as site-management plans, grant applications, and histories as well as literature from community and cultural centers in the surrounding neighborhoods, newspaper articles, and promotional information. They attended teacher orientations, back-to-school nights, parent–teacher meetings and conferences, and faculty in-service programs, and they visited community centers and community action groups. All four of the student teachers also observed extensively in their own student teaching classrooms; consulted with and interviewed their cooperating teachers and the other teachers who were part of the school-site research group; and analyzed curriculum guides, textbooks, and other instructional materials.

Pooling their data, student teachers in each school-site group presented an overview of the culture of their school and community to others in the program, with special attention to the group who would *cross-visit* at their school four times during the school year, including a 2-week period when they would trade places with their cross-visit partners during the second semester. Individually, each student teacher also wrote about the culture of the school and community as the context within which he or she located all other inquiry projects. The excerpts below provide a sense of the ways in which the Hunter student teachers attempted to understand the school and the community during their first 2 months there.

### Excerpt 3
(from Terri Campbell's school culture description)

William H. Hunter Elementary School . . . is located in the predominantly [Latino] neighborhood of Kensington. [It] services a student body whose first language is Spanish and whose second language is English. Besides language, there are other barriers for the students to overcome. . . . The low income neighborhood surrounding Hunter is both crime- and drug infested. Not surprisingly, survival is the number one consideration for a large majority of the residents in the community. While a good education is very important to both students and parents, very often due to economic factors, the resources to ensure a good education are lacking in many of the homes.

### Excerpt 4
(from Peggy Kaplan's school culture description)

The neighborhood is trying to change itself, to become more organized in order to fight drugs, clean up the streets, and provide a better lifestyle. The effort is being spearheaded by the Norris Square Neighborhood Project with executive director Sister Carol Keck. Since I have been at the school, I have read three different newspaper articles about her work here. . . . The school administration as well as the majority of teachers are White and female. Some speak Spanish, [but] there is only one Hispanic teacher. Most live outside the community and return home without ever venturing out of the school. There is little commerce in the area, which limits interaction . . . (But) the school is also trying to serve the community better. It employs a local community representative whose job it is to go into the homes to find out why a child is truant.

Part of what is important in the excerpts above is that student teachers worked to understand what was going on in their school from the points of view of participants rather than simply making judgments about teachers' or parents' actions based on their own frames of reference. They also tried to locate schooling and curriculum issues within the history and politics of the community rather than treat them as ahistorical or value-free phenomena. Part of what this means is that as student teachers began to develop critiques, they realized the complexity of issues as the following excerpts suggest.

### Excerpt 5
(from Paige Menton's school culture description)

Because of the Chapter 1 and Schoolwide Project funding structures that maintain schools' fitting [their particular] profile, Hunter must demonstrate a steady improvement in students' test scores in language arts and math in order to qualify for federal funding, and, in the case of Schoolwide Project guidelines, in order to maintain a significant level of autonomy over its annual budget. . . . This pressure to maintain funding guidelines has a definite impact on curricular decisions, both schoolwide and by individual teachers in their classrooms. With this in mind, I find it interesting that Hunter has taken a position schoolwide favoring an approach which does not square smoothly with standardized testing models of language proficiency. While it is not a unified philosophical shift, the school principal voiced her support of whole language at the beginning of the year and appears concerned that teachers work to find what they perceive to be the most beneficial approaches for their children.

### Excerpt 6
(from Jennifer Lockwood's school culture description)

Almost all of the students speak Spanish. For many of them, Spanish is the only language spoken at home, and the parents have little or no knowledge of or use of English. Spanish is the primary language of the community; thus, it is the language which is reinforced outside of the school. Many of the children have lived in Puerto Rico at some point in their lives. Although almost all of the children are bilingual, the use of Spanish is discouraged in school. . . . In classes Spanish is not spoken during formal lessons, but some children use it in talking with each other. There are a few teachers who speak Spanish, but my observation has been that they only use Spanish to give directives. Although most of the teachers do not speak Spanish, all but two of the teaching assistants are Spanish speaking. They often interpret for teachers who need to communicate with parents or students who do not speak English. [But] the students are not permitted to speak or write in Spanish for the purpose of academic work. . . . The students do often speak to each other in Spanish when they are not in class.

The excerpts above touch on some of the tensions inherent when a school with a White European-American faculty serves a Latino population or when a principal and some teachers attempt to incorporate whole language perspectives while still having to answer at the central office level to achievement criteria based on skills-based standardized tests. What is most important about this kind of inquiry is that student teachers begin to understand that "the learner," "the teacher," "the school," and "the community" do not exist in teaching—rather, the condition within which teachers construct curriculum and make educational decisions is the local and messy context of "this learner," "this teacher," "this school," and "this community." A number of preservice structures support this kind of work—structures that focus on community work, using ethnographic methods in fieldwork classrooms and finding ways to collaborate with families. The examples that appear in the following sections make it clear how this kind of knowledge informs pedagogy and curriculum decisions.

## Analyzing children's learning opportunities

When student teachers conduct small-scale studies about their own schools and classrooms, they engage in active classroom teaching, curriculum construction, and analysis of classroom data, including children's written work, group discussions and other verbal interactions, group and individual child observations, and textbooks and other materials, in order to learn from teaching. This allows them to analyze the learning opportunities that are or are not available to children within various academic tasks and social participation structures, particularly those of scripted and unscripted programs of instruction. For example, student teachers teach one lesson from a set of elementary level basal reading materials, following as closely as possible the script in the teacher's manual. Based on data from this experience and on their reading of language and learning theory, critique, and practice, they then construct a modified lesson using similar materials and develop a focusing research question about children's opportunities for learning in the contrasting situations.

Student teachers formulate research questions in order to compare, for example: children's responses to original literature and to abridged or vocabulary-controlled stories, interaction patterns that result from open-ended questions and from single right-answer questions, quality of comprehension when children read complete connected text and when they read parceled-out smaller segments of texts punctuated frequently with interruptions in the form of teachers' questions, the number and range of vocabulary words children hear and use in scripted and unscripted discussion, the percentage of time spent actually reading connected texts and the range and variation of topics that occur in altered and unaltered lessons, and the questions and connections to prior experiences and knowledge that children themselves construct about texts with the questions and connections that scripted materials stipulate. In essence, through their own research, prospective teachers consider the impact on children's learning opportunities when control of understanding is shifted from text and teacher to children themselves and to the transactions of children, teachers, and texts. Data from scripted and from modified lessons are analyzed to explore the traditional realities as well as other possible realities of language learning opportunities and reading and writing instruction at the elementary school level.

To illustrate, I use an excerpt from the work of Sara McClain, a White, European-American student teacher who worked over the course of a year with a

sixth-grade class at Friends Select School, a Quaker school in center city Philadelphia with a population of about two-thirds White and one-third children of color.
She pointed out at the beginning of her report that, although the teacher's manual
suggested that only *teachers* could know the most effective use of the teacher's
guide, it also went on to say that teachers should not try to adapt the guide before
thoroughly understanding it through "close study and following all the suggested
procedures" (see Excerpt 7). McClain then described her first basal lesson in
which she followed the teacher's guide as closely as possible (see Excerpt 8).

**Excerpt 7**
(from Sara McClain's final report, based on her analysis of a set of basal
reading materials at the sixth-grade level)

According to publisher recommendations, I guess it is possible to try your
own ideas and teaching methods *after* all suggested procedures have been
followed and *if* time permits and *if* any student interest still exists—these,
I have seen, are unlikely.

**Excerpt 8**
(from Sara McClain's observation notes, written after teaching her first
by-the-script reading lesson)

Stage two [of the lesson] was silent reading. I asked the students to read the
story, and then we would discuss it. This was an agonizing twenty minutes, or
more, for me. The children all read at varying speeds; the faster readers
quickly turned page after page, while the slower readers took constant breaks
by glancing at the others, seeing where the others were in comparison to
where they were, counting how many pages remained, looking around the
room, laughing at hallway noise, and looking at their watches. The faster
readers set immediately to the task and seemed to become engrossed in the
story. The slower readers seemed somewhat self-conscious about reading
with the others. They weren't comfortable allowing themselves to forget their
classmates and become involved in the book. I never before had considered
what makes a slower reader, slower. Is it lack of interest in the material to be
read? Lack of proficiency in reading? The personality of the reader—easily
distracted, competitiveness with others, feeling pressure to read under time
constraints? . . . Susie finished first, then Janeen, followed by Jimmy, and then
Regina. (Actually I'm not really sure Regina ever did finish reading the story,
but the earlier finishers were becoming bored waiting for the others, and I'm
sure Regina sensed this.) Maybe the reason many basal programs require
reading aloud is to keep everyone at the same place at the same time . . .
     This experience prompted me to make my first conscious alteration for
the modified basal lesson—I [decided to] have my next group of students read
the story at their own pace at home the night before the lesson.

By doing research on contrasting lessons, student teachers often discover, as
McClain did, that management issues are, at least in part, artifacts of the structure
of lessons wherein everyone is supposed to proceed in unison, know the same
things, and interpret texts in the same ways. Further, they discover not only that
there are far fewer opportunities to learn to read connected and compelling literary discourse for children who are assigned to low and remedial reading groups
than there are for those in higher groups but also that there are few, if any,

possibilities for children to move into more advanced groups once they are labeled. On the other hand, student teachers also recognize the safety net of the teacher's manual and the power of workbook pages, exercises, and other unison social structures and academic tasks to avoid many behavioral problems in the first place. Close observations of students' and teachers' actions and interactions lead student teachers to construct the dilemmas inherent in moving away from the scripture of prepackaged programs and to see the interrelationships of language and interactional patterns, management strategies, grouping procedures, and reading content and materials.

As a result of teaching her first by-the-script lesson, McClain constructed these teacher research questions: Given the opportunity, what questions will the children themselves ask about the text? What areas will they find most interesting to explore further, question, debate, research? In essence, what will happen to discussion, to comprehension, and to student engagement when different kinds of questions are asked and when different group structures are developed?

**Excerpt 9**
(from analysis in Sara McClain's final report of the basal reading lessons inquiry project)

When I think back to these basal lessons, the difference in amount of student engagement is staggering. Moving from literal, one-correct-answer questions to open-ended questions generated and pursued by the students transformed a flat, boring lesson to one that was stimulating . . . I could not help but be painfully aware of the effect the first basal lesson was having on my students. The lines of authority were clearly demarcated. The teacher was the asker of questions and acknowledger of correct answers. The students were expected to be suppliers of these correct answers with little or no opportunities to ask questions of their own. As Goodman [suggests], "Since both the teaching and assessment of comprehension in the basals are confined almost entirely to the questions the teachers are instructed to use, the quality of the questions must be a major concern. . . ."[22] As evidenced by the tone of my [two] lessons, [I think] the basal approach to reading must be reconsidered. Basal reading systems that dominate reading instruction in many elementary classrooms are so comprehensive (including graded books for students to read, teachers' manuals telling teachers what and how to teach, workbooks and dittos for the students to complete, sets of tests to assess reading skills, etc.), very little room or time is left for the inclusion of other kinds of reading activities. I believe this approach to reading discourages students from developing and exercising the critical literacy and thinking skills needed to participate fully in a . . . democratic society.

Basal reading programs are controversial in the field of reading/language education: Although they have been soundly criticized by the scholarly community, they are regarded by some who control educational policy at local and larger levels as a complete technology for reading instruction, and they continue to dominate instruction. What is most important about inquiry projects such as the one I have described here, however, is that, through their own intentional and systematic inquiries, student teachers learn to critique dominant instructional materials and practices and begin to teach against the grain, not simply by eschewing convention or imitating the critiques of their professors or other scholars.

Rather, prospective teachers have the opportunity to treat reading groups and other social organizations for instruction as sites for research. They learn to look closely at how particular materials, instructional practices, and participation structures limit or support children's language learning opportunities and their chances of moving beyond the narrow constraints of reading groups, differentiated instruction, and homogeneous tracking.

## Understanding children's understanding

A fourth perspective that is central to learning to teach in a culturally and linguistically diverse society is *understanding children's understanding* or exploring what it means to know a child, to consider his or her background, behaviors, and interactions with others, and to try to do what Duckworth calls "give reason"[23] to the ways the child constructs meanings and interpretations, drawing on experiences and knowledge developed both inside and outside the classroom. A major site for this kind of inquiry during the preservice period is observation and interview of the individual child wherein the student teacher, in consultation with a more experienced school-based mentor, develops research questions about ways to support a particular aspect of one child's development in the classroom and then gathers multiple data sources in order to describe, or come to know, that child from various perspectives. The image of the teacher implicit in this kind of research is not one of a person who simply practices or applies other people's principles or accepts the knowledge of outside experts and what they may claim are the appropriate placements, groupings, labels, expectations, and limits for a particular child. Rather, the teacher is taken to be a builder of knowledge and theory to "interpret, understand and eventually transform the social life of schools."[24] Similarly, the child is not regarded as receiver or object of others' actions but as active knower and agent—always learning, always "on task,"[25] and always involved in the business of making sense of what is going on around him or her.

Through teacher research, student teachers work to understand individual children by analyzing classroom data. To do so, they draw on the theories of practice that they construct with other teachers in their local communities as well as the illuminating frameworks and categories for considering a child's many embedded contexts of family, community, and other sociocultural institutions developed by school- and university-based researchers, especially Carini's categories for *descriptive review*.[26] They also draw on various schemes for describing the uses of language and literacy in communities and schools. Through inquiries about individual children, prospective teachers recognize that their efforts to respond to cultural, linguistic, and social diversity in their classrooms are located not only in the nested contexts of families, communities, and institutions but also, and in large measure, in their own preconceptions, experiences, and assumptions about learning and teaching.

The following excerpts are drawn from the child observation inquiry project of Amanda Collins, a White, European-American student teacher, who chose to focus on Ho, a third-grade student at Lowell School, a public elementary school in northeast Philadelphia, where the population was about one-third Asian—including, children from Vietnam, Korea, Cambodia, Laos, and Thailand —one-third African American, and one-third White. Ho was born in Vietnam and had arrived in the United States from China 2 years earlier speaking no English. Collins' question emerged soon after she began observing: How can we, as teachers in this classroom, help to engage Ho more fully in classroom activities and help him become more motivated to learn in this setting?[27] The following excerpt from Collins' full description emphasizes her careful use of rich observational data and her attempts to come to know from the child's perspective:

### Excerpt 10
(from Amanda Collins' child observation inquiry project, drawing on journal entries and observations over the course of several months)

Ho loves to read, but he is not particularly fond of writing. When an unfamiliar format is introduced, he often looks at other children's work first to see what they are doing before starting his own. At times, he finds other things to do for as long as possible before getting to work. . . . When he is unfamiliar with a format, he seems to ask for more help with spelling. When he is comfortable with the format, as when he is making a journal entry, he is comfortable using invented spelling.

Ho's learning approaches vary from math to language arts. In math, he relies alternately on trial and error, observation of other students' work, and using a step-by-step approach (provided the steps are given to him one at a time). When he uses trial and error, he puts some thought into the process. It is not a haphazard approach. If his answer is not quite there, however, it usually takes some prodding to get him to try again. Often Ho will watch what the children around him are doing. While that can help him to reach the right answer, it does not help him to grasp the concept, as he often cannot tell me what he did or use the same operation with different numbers. When asked, he is reluctant to explain how he reached his answer, which makes it difficult to explore what he is thinking.

Ho is a good reader, but always insists on pictures. . . . He once wrote in his reading response journal that he didn't like a particular book because there was no color in the pictures. Questioning reveals that he does understand a story when it is read to him without pictures. He just seems to have a real need to know what [things] look like. . . . While most classroom reading is done in pairs (each child has a reading partner), Ho prefers to read alone. During one reading partner activity, Ho let his partner read the entire book. He told me this was because he prefers to read by himself. I asked if he would like to borrow the book and read it at home on his own. He did, and came back the following day excited about the story. When reading, Ho occasionally flips back a page or two and studies the pictures. I'm not sure why he does this, but wonder if he likes to read alone because it gives him the opportunity to take his time and squeeze every bit of meaning out of the book—pictures and text.

Collins attempted to understand Ho's understanding through the lenses of three patterns in his life at school that seemed to influence his learning, and then, as the descriptive review process calls for, she suggested a number of concrete recommendations for ways she and her cooperating teacher could alter the curriculum and classroom routines in order to support his learning. Although space limits do not permit detailed reporting of these patterns and recommendations, it is especially important to note her first one.

Excerpt 11
(from Amanda Collins' recommendations for action in her child observation inquiry final project)

Cazden and Mehan discuss the importance of looking at the relationship of an event to its context and in trying to understand a child's many embedded contexts—including family, community, and other sociocultural institutions —and looking at how those contexts might determine meaning for the child. I feel at a significant disadvantage in this respect, in that Ho is of a culture very different from my own and that culture must have a significant impact on how he makes sense of what happens in the classroom. I know very little of his culture. I don't know, for instance, how books are used at home, which according to Heath[28] might determine how Ho uses books in the classroom.

My first recommendation, then, is to learn more about his culture in order to better understand how Ho makes sense of his world in general and, more specifically, in the classroom.

As the semester progressed, Collins and her cooperating teacher developed a number of ways to learn more about Ho's family, his community, and his culture—including locating appropriate child- and adult-intended fiction and nonfiction about Vietnam and China, visiting with Ho's older sibling, taking to members of his family and community, and giving Ho opportunities to share information with the other children in the class. It is widely acknowledged that, as educators, we are most able to understand, make accurate predictions about, and provide strategic support for those students who are most like us in culture, race, and ethnicity. It takes much more effort and time to understand and support those who are not like us. For Collins and other student teachers, the process of constructing a knowing picture of the child conveyed an important image about the teacher's responsibility for knowing the children in her care and for educating herself about their language and cultural resources.

## *Constructing reconstructionist pedagogy*

When they are initiated into teaching in a community that promotes self-critical and systematic inquiries about teaching, student teachers also learn to *construct reconstructionist pedagogy*—that is, pedagogy intended to help children understand and then prepare to take action against the social and institutional inequities that are embedded in our society.[29] One of the potential sites for inquiry of this kind is the social studies, math, or literature study group. Like the basal reader inquiries described above, the study group inquiry also requires student teachers to engage in active teaching with children and to use classroom data in order to learn from and about learning and teaching. In planning for study groups, however, student teachers do not set out simply to modify scripted lessons or tinker with instructional practices but are, instead, invited to construct curriculum by locating and drawing on alternative texts and materials and to alter both the social participation and the academic task structures of conventional instruction. One group of students, who met to explore issues of race and racism in teaching by drawing on the data of their own teacher research over the course of their first semester of student teaching, referred to this kind of pedagogy as *proactive teaching*. The words of the group, composed of two

African American, one Puerto Rican, and three White, European-American women, provide some evidence that teacher research may be a vehicle through which students both raise questions about the status quo and take action to change it:

### Excerpt 12
(from "Teaching Ain't No Crystal Stair")[30]

In questioning our own practices, our experiences in school, and the state of American schooling, we have seen the alienation of the child of color and the low-income child regardless of race, from the whole system.

Now, what do we do about it?

As we looked at our writings and discussions [this semester] we found that we attempted to address our own understandings of race and class through specific lessons. [By closely] examining how we taught, we identified four common elements [in this kind of pedagogy]: self-examination; a view of the classroom as a place that is influenced by race and class; a view of the children . . . as knowers; and a desire to give children specific skills to help *them* challenge the status quo. We think of this effort as "proactive teaching" because it actively confronts the forces of racism and classism we see in our society and our schools.

These student teachers made it clear that they were working from the premise that skills for surviving in the system as well as skills for questioning the system need to be taught explicitly to children of all races, classes, and cultures beginning at an early age and in terms that make it clear how the injustices of society have an impact on their daily lives. Maldonado, a Puerto Rican woman with a predominantly Puerto Rican first-grade class at Crampp School in urban Philadelphia, wrote this about her teaching during the first semester:

### Excerpt 13
(from Maldonado Carmen's report on a social studies inquiry project in which she analyzed first-grade lessons about city life, poverty, and law)

Throughout the lesson, their ears and eyes were open to question and to begin debating real issues of life in poverty. Questioning society should never be something that is suddenly slapped onto you when you become 18 and can vote. Proper questioning and debating from an early age can help to increase a child's development of observation [skill]—a crucial point for survival in today's society, especially for children of color. . . . I have learned [from my teaching] not to fear discussing "real" issues with children—their insights, questions, answers, and suggestions need to be validated. In this way, and only in this way, will they learn and experience that their thoughts are important and that they must learn to question society.

Student teachers have constructed study groups and thematic explorations with children that centered on urban poverty and the law, the biographies of civil rights leaders, social and literary uses and consequences of standard and non-standard English, modern and historical novels with strong African-American or Latino or women characters, revisionist and critical perspectives on early explorations and exploitations of lands occupied by Native Americans, historical novels that deal with the impact of war, biographical and historical accounts of the

Holocaust, and fiction and nonfiction accounts of the growing-up experiences of children from different social and economic strata.

What follows are excerpts from the literature study inquiry project of Kecia Parham, an African-American teacher who worked with a group of fifth graders at Douglass School, a Philadelphia public school with a population that was 100% African American. Parham began her report of the group's work by remembering her own childhood reading experiences when she was encouraged by teachers to read stories with White, European-American characters and, as she later realized, White values and language (see Excerpt 14). Parham connected her own experiences to the responses she had observed in her student teaching class when the children read Laura Ingalls Wilder's *Little House on the Prairie* (see Excerpt 15).

**Excerpt 14**
(from Kecia Parham's reflections on her own childhood reading experiences)

Somehow I would always end up seeing the world as the White, middle class female [main character] saw it and viewing the other characters in the book as the main character would describe them. What shocks me more now is how adults and teachers encouraged my love for literature and reading by perpetuating the cycle of little [literary] exposure to my [own] cultural experiences and disguising it as gaining "power and knowledge" of the world through books . . .

[I realize now] I was being socialized linguistically and culturally without being aware of how this process was affecting my life. . . . It was true that I learned how to use the English language correctly through my love of books, but rarely were there any African Americans in these stories. . . . It is a concern that plagued me then and still does whenever I take the time to delve into a literary work [to be used with African-American children in school].

**Excerpt 15**
(from Kecia Parham's observation notes, written during the teaching of Wilder's novel, *Little House on the Prairie*)

The children were particularly interested in why the Indians in Laura's story were perceived as so bad and why Laura and her Pa were afraid of them or hated them so much. It was then that I realized how much attention the children pay to the use of descriptive words and language and what effect it has on how they view the characters in a book. Words such as "bad," "mean," "evil," or "shiftless" can weigh a lot on perceptions, particularly if they are being used to describe characters of races that these children relate to.

Parham's project centered on using several of the works of Mildred Taylor, an award winning African-American author of children's historical novels that chronicle the experiences of the Logans, an African-American family struggling courageously to survive the depression and the debilitating impact of racism and poverty.

Drawing on tape-recorded sessions of the group's discussions as well as the children's journal writing, Parham wanted to expose the children to powerfully written literature with positive African-American characters and help them explore the relationships among dialect, culture, and the perceptions of intelligence, status, and education that people (including the children themselves) tend to attach to these. She described the group's first session (see Excerpt 16) and then went on to recount more of the lesson (see Excerpt 17).

**Excerpt 16**
(from Kecia Parham's observation notes and audiorecorded transcriptions of group interaction during the teaching of Taylor's novel, *Roll of Thunder Hear My Cry*)

Several times during the reading we came across the word, *nigger*. [I] anticipated a response from the students. Nothing came from them with the use of that all too familiar word. I felt that this could be because many of the children have been exposed to this type of language from the streets and therefore did not need to question it. However, [when] I read several lines from the [dialogue] of the elderly Black man's character, I noticed the . . . most displeasure.

The first response of the students was laughter. Then one of the students said:

*One child:* That ain't funny. Why y'all laughin'? He talkin' all stupid. He can't even talk!!
*Another child:* I know, why he talkin' like that?
*Kecia:* Well, have you ever listened to the way that you talk sometimes? Do you think that you sound like Mr. Bee does when he talks in the book? Sometimes the way we talk now is the way people talked back in Cassie's day. There really was nothing wrong with the way he talked because he was speaking the way others around him spoke. Can you find other characters who spoke differently?
*Another child:* Yes, the White people do. They talk all proper, but in this book they were talking like the Black people do.
*Kecia:* What do you mean, "like the Black people do?"
*Another child:* Like talk's countrified, like "How y'all doin" (laughter) and stuff like that. White people don't really talk like that. It's really only Black people from down south that talk like that.
*Child:* But sometimes the White people down south talk like that too 'cause they never finished school, so they don't know no better.
*Kecia:* So what you're saying is that how long a person spends in school makes them use language better?
*Group:* Yes!
*Kecia:* Well, would you say that you talk like the White people in the book or the Black people in the book? We all go to school, right? Sometimes don't we still talk like Mr. Bee does, and does that mean that we don't know better?
*Child:* No, that just means that we talk like Black people talk.
*Kecia:* Do Black people always sound the same in different [situations]? Do White people always talk "proper"?

**Excerpt 17**
(from Kecia Parham's analysis of the above interaction in the final report of the literature study group inquiry project)

As the session continued, we grappled with the ways that language is represented in society, in the ways that African Americans use it and in the ways
that Whites construct language and use it. It seemed to be a general opinion
that African Americans do not know how really to use language as properly
as Whites and that the representation in literature is sometimes correct
when it [implies] that African Americans have less of a mastery of "proper
English."

The discussions Parham led were tricky. She missed some opportunities that a
more experienced teacher might have exploited and pursued some lines of discussion that were misleading or ineffective. But Parham herself was in the process of
learning to understand the interrelationships of race, culture, and language and
also in the process of learning to work with children. From the beginning, Parham
banked on the power of Taylor's characters, on the rich language she crafted, and
on the compelling story to help open up new ideas to the children. From the
beginning, she also believed in the children's ability to understand, to explore, and
to raise significant questions.

### Excerpt 18
(from Kecia Parham's analysis at the conclusion of the literature study group
in the final report of the inquiry project)

Taylor does a wonderful job of making the Logan family appear to be strong
and defensive of their own rights. The exchanges that the characters engage in
gave the children something to feel proud about since the Logans were able to
take up for themselves [in encounters with White characters] in a society
which at one point did not allow that type of rapport between races.

In the final session, many of the children concluded that, if they had a choice
between being Laura Ingalls (of *Little House on the Prairie*) or Cassie Logan (of
*Roll of Thunder*), they would choose Cassie "because she was strong" or
"because she was Black" and because there "weren't any Black people in Laura's
story anyway."

What is most significant about Parham's inquiry project is not that she got it all
right in her teaching but that she set out to alter the curriculum by offering a quite
complex and powerful text with rich vocabulary and language that featured
strong African-American characters and thus to construct culturally responsive
and challenging curriculum. She also set out to alter her children's perceptions of
themselves as African Americans by making issues of language, culture, dialect,
and power an examined part of the curriculum and of their lives.

Not all of the literature study inquiries that student teachers do are aimed so
directly at altering both the curriculum and the system. But all of them, like
Parham's, are based on a belief in the efficacy (rather than the efficiency) of
teachers, individually and collectively, to change their own teaching lives and the
course of the world of schooling. And every one of them is based on the premise
that children are active knowers, capable of dealing with rich and complicated
content, with the ability to think critically, to pose and solve real problems, to
construct interpretations of texts, and ultimately to participate in a democratic
society.[31] Hence, each literature study inquiry has the potential to function as
reconstructionist or transformative pedagogy by challenging the dominance of
tracking, abridged texts, and teacher control of knowledge transmission.

## Beyond color blindness and basket making

In describing research, Lawrence Stenhouse once wrote:

> [Research] is founded in curiosity and a desire to understand; but it is a stable, not a fleeting, curiosity, systematic in the sense of being sustained by a strategy. . . . Research nowadays is an everyday activity: an industry, a tool and a pastime. . . . It was not always so. People with questions and problems turned—as many still do—to answers from divine revelation, to the authority of a learned caste, to traditional lore, or the received opinion. And curiosity is as ever dangerous, because it leads to intellectual innovation which brings in its trail a press towards social change. To those who yearn for the support of faith, authority, and tradition, research presents a threat of heresy. Yet without the organized pursuit of curiosity we could not sustain our social life.[32]

Stenhouse's claims are reminiscent of Dewey's concerns earlier in the century about teachers' positions of *intellectual subserviency* in school organizations. He criticized teacher institutes and journals, on the one hand, for their eagerness to provide model lessons and clear-cut instructions in how to teach, and teachers, on the other hand, for their willingness to accept these without inquiry or criticism. Dewey believed that the "blind search" for "educational gospel" would be impossible if teachers were more intellectually vital and more "adequately moved by their own independent intelligence."[33]

What I have been suggesting in this article is that, if we are going to prepare teachers to work intelligently and responsibly in a society that is increasingly diverse in race, language, and culture, then we need more teachers who are moved by their own intelligence and actively involved in communities that engage in "the heresy" of systematic and critical inquiry. Teachers who are inquirers do not have to be color blind in order to be fair to all students, teach basket making in order to "do" multicultural education, or wait for the learned authorities of teacher education institutions or school administrations to tell them "*the* teaching strategies" that are most effective for "*the* culturally diverse learner." Rather, these teachers are involved in intellectually vital and independent pursuits to try to answer some of the toughest questions there are about how to work effectively in the local context with learners who are like them and not like them.

Student teachers who struggle to move beyond color blindness and basket making need to work in the company of experienced teachers and teacher educators who are also struggling to do so. Clearly, this approach to the issues of diversity in teaching and teacher education is fraught with obstacles and challenges. It is a process of working against the grain of much of current school practice and engaging in the risky business of constructing new roles for teachers as knowledge generators and curriculum creators as well as creating new relationships among teachers, supervisors, and administrators.[34] Despite efforts to establish closer connections between school and university, sometimes student teachers in these situations find themselves caught in the middle between what the university is encouraging them to think and do and what the school-based teachers they work with advocate. Sometimes new teachers who have been prepared in an inquiry and reform-centered program "fail" at certain aspects of their early teaching experiences because they do not fit smoothly into the system or because they view teaching as a process of questioning assumptions and challenging traditions rather than adopting the practices modeled by much more experienced educators.

Sometimes teacher educators are caught between helping their students learn the practices that will signify to many school administrators and supervisors that they are good beginning teachers (e.g., how to write and carry out lesson plans), on the one hand, and practices that aim to reinvent classroom knowledge and discourse so that they build on and are attentive to the resources of all children (e.g., how to construct curricula with materials from both the canon and alternative bodies of literature, history, and culture and how to make issues of diversity explicit parts of the curriculum), on the other.

Teacher educators can perhaps best handle the tension between the lesson plan stance and a transformative, inquiring stance on teaching by arming their student teachers with thorough knowledge of current practice as well as the ability to construct and act on a trenchant critique of that practice. Students cannot teach effectively against the grain if they do not have a thoughtful understanding of what "the grain" is and what its strengths as well as weaknesses are. Teacher education programs that aim to be transformative have a dual agenda, then, much like the dual agenda facing new teachers who are attempting to meet the needs of an increasingly diverse student population. For student teachers, the dilemma is how to teach children about the canon of literature, language, and history while also teaching them how to critique it as well as teaching them their own literature, language, and history. For teacher educators, the dilemma is how to teach student teachers about "best practice" while also teaching them alternative practice. Student teachers need to know not only how to display in traditional ways their competence as beginning teachers but also how to strategically justify and demonstrate a different kind of competence. How to resolve these dilemmas is a year-long theme for many of the student teachers I have worked with and, I would venture, a life-long theme for many of us as teachers and teacher educators.

Student teachers also need to learn about the power of collaboration in learning communities and networks where other teachers are struggling to understand and ultimately to improve the social relations of schools and classrooms. The days of the isolated, though exemplary, teacher who closes her classroom door and works miracles with her children are over. The odds against the efficacy of the lone teacher are overpowering, given the problems of urban poverty, family disintegration, and widespread social failure. The collaborative experiences student teachers have in learning communities with one another and with their experienced teacher mentors are among the most powerful influences during the critical preservice period. But an explicit part of the preservice curriculum also needs to be preparing student teachers to find and work in existing networks of reform-minded teachers in their own schools or across schools and school systems as they begin their careers as teachers. If such networks do not exist, student teachers need to know how to begin to build networks of their own and find colleagues with whom to collaborate.

As teacher educators struggling to promote a discourse of diversity among our students, we also need to open up this discourse among teacher-education faculty and staff and examine our own efforts to teach those who are like and not like us. In the period since I wrote the first draft of this article, I have been exploring more carefully and introspectively the assumptions about race, class, and culture that underlie my own work as a teacher educator and the assumptions that are implicit in the teacher education program that I direct. In this work, I have been grappling with the idea that student teachers and teacher educators are often unintentional but uncertain allies of children, teachers, and parents who are not like them in race or cultural background. I have come to think that the image of the center that is implicit in the pedagogy of preservice programs may be among the most potent informal influences on prospective teachers—the ways that teacher educators talk about "others," include or ignore multiple perspectives, express public uncertainty, and make efforts to alter their own teaching. I have come to see that embedded in our pedagogy—not simply what we say to student teachers about the kinds of teachers they should become but also what we show them about what the "norm" or the taken-for-granted point of view is—is a powerful subtext about teaching and about the boundaries of race and teaching in schools and larger educational systems.[35]

## Notes

1 See, for example, the well-known discussions of Molefi Asante, "The Afro-Centric Idea in Education," *Journal of Negro Education* 62, no. 2 (1991): 170–180; Lisa Delpit, "The Silenced Dialogue: Power and Pedagogy in Educating Other People's Children," *Harvard Educational Review* 58 (1988): 280–298; and Shirley Brice Heath, *Ways With Words: Language, Life and Work in Communities and Classrooms* (Cambridge: Cambridge University Press, 1983).

2 Marilyn Cochran-Smith and Susan L. Lytle, "Interrogating Cultural Diversity: Inquiry and Action," *Journal of Teacher Education* 43, no. 2 (1992): 104–115.

3 Thomas Popkewitz, "Cognitive Educational Sciences as Knowledge and Power," chap. 6 in *A Political Sociology of Educational Reform* (New York: Teachers College Press, 1991).

4 Courtney Cazden and Hugh Mehan, "Principles From Sociology and Anthropology: Context, Code, Classroom, and Culture," in *Knowledge Base for the Beginning Teacher*, ed. C. Reynolds (Oxford: Pergamon Press, 1989).

5 I have argued in some detail that student teachers need to regard teaching as a political activity and embark on the profession as activists as well as educators. See Marilyn Cochran-Smith, "Learning to Teach Against the Grain," *Harvard Educational Review* 61, no. 3 (1991): 279–310.

6 See the critique of the basket making and ivory carving focus of the Inupiat studies curriculum used in the Northwest Arctic region of Alaska in the 1980s in Paul Ongtooguk, "Their Silence About Us: The Absence of Alaska Natives in the Curriculum" (paper presented at the American Educational Research Association, Atlanta, April 1993) as well as criticisms of multicultural educational programs that emphasize single or several cultures by focusing on foods, folkways, and handiwork in Christine Sleeter and Carl Grant, "An Analysis of Multicultural Education in the United States," *Harvard Educational Review* 57, no. 4 (1987) 421–444.

7 There continue to be extensive discussions of the steps and procedures for lesson plans in recent textbooks on elementary teaching. See, for example, the lengthy discussion of the explicit steps student teachers should follow when planning in Dorothy Rubin, *Teaching Elementary Language Arts* (Englewood Cliffs, NJ: Prentice Hall, 1990), 32–37.

8 The thoughtful and thorough synthesis of research on teacher planning in Christopher Clark and Penelope Peterson, "Teachers' Thought Processes," in *Handbook of Research on Teaching*, ed. Merlin Wittrock (New York: Macmillan, 1986) provides specific empirical evidence for each of these conclusions about lesson plans.

9 I want to make it clear that I am *not* suggesting that student teachers should not plan for teaching or that they need not be thoroughly prepared in content, organizational and interactional strategies, and understandings of children as learners. I am also not suggesting that, as beginners, student teachers should be expected to plan for and understand teaching in the same ways as experienced teachers. But, as I point out in the next sections of this article, I *am* attempting to challenge the primacy of *the* lesson plan in preservice education—to challenge its step-by-step procedures, its transmission model of knowledge, and its implicit assumptions about the uniformity, rather than diversity, of children's and teachers' experiences, language and cultural resources, and ways of knowing.

10  The most well-known critiques of basal reading programs are Kenneth S. Goodman et al.'s *Report Card on Basal Readers* (New York: Richard C. Owen Publishers, 1988) and Patrick Shannon's *Merging Literacy: Reading Instruction in 20th Century America* (South Hadley, MA: Bergin and Garvey, 1988). These provide empirical evidence about patterns of usage of basal programs in American elementary education as well as historical and conceptual analyses of their origins and development.

11  John Dewey, "The Relation of Theory to Practice in Education," pt. 1 of *The Third NSSE Yearbook*, ed. C. A. McMurry (Chicago: University of Chicago Press, 1904), 157.

12  The preservice program that provides the data for this article is based on a conceptual framework for teacher research across the professional lifespan developed over a period of almost 10 years by myself and my colleague, Susan L. Lytle. See Marilyn Cochran-Smith & Susan L. Lytle, *Inside/Outside: Teacher Research and Knowledge* (New York: Teachers College Press, 1994) as well as Susan L. Lytle & Marilyn Cochran-Smith, "Inquiry, Knowledge, and Practice," in *Teacher Research and Education Reform. 94th Yearbook of the National Society for the Study of Education*, eds. S. Hollingsworth and H. Sockett (Chicago: University of Chicago Press). We have defined *teacher research* as systematic intentional inquiry by teachers about their own school and classroom work, drawing in part on the work of Lawrence Stenhouse and others who define *research*, in general, as systematic, self-critical inquiry and in part on an ongoing survey of the literature of teacher writing. The writing of Lawrence Stenhouse is compiled in *Research as a Basis for Teaching, Readings From the Work of Lawrence Stenhouse*, ed. Jean Rudduck and David Hopkins (London: Heinemann Educational Books, 1985). See also the writing of Stenhouse and his colleagues at the Center for Applied Research in Education at the University of East Anglia in John Nixon, ed., *A Teacher's Guide to Action Research* (London: Grant McIntyre, 1981); John Elliott, "Facilitating Action Research in Schools: Some Dilemmas," in *Field Methods in the Study of Education*, ed. R. Burgess (Lewes: Falmer Press, 1985); John Elliott and B. McDonald, "People in Classrooms," occasional paper no. 2, University of East Anglia, Center for Applied Research in Education, 1975.

Teacher research and a range of other reflective processes such as practitioner inquiry, action research, and critical inquiry are related to the work of those who have advocated educational action research (see, for example, Stephen Corey, *Action Research to Improve School Practices* [New York: Teachers College, Columbia University, 1953]); schools as centers for inquiry (see, for example, Robert Schaeffer, *The School as a Center of Inquiry* [New York: Harper and Row, 1967]; Miles Myers, "Institutionalizing Inquiry," *National Writing Project Quarterly*, 9, no. 3 [1985]); and teachers as active research partners with university-based researchers (see, for example, William Tikunoff, Betty Ward, and Gary Griffin, "Interactive Research and Development on Teaching Study," [final report, Far West Regional Laboratory for Educational Research and Development, San Francisco, Calif., 1979]).

Many action researchers draw on the work of Kemmis and McTaggart and others in Australia who envisioned collaborative curriculum planning as a way for teachers to participate in the larger agenda of human emancipation. See William Carr and Stephen Kemmis, *Becoming Critical: Education, Knowledge, and Action Research* (London: Falmer Press, 1986); Stephen Kemmis and Robert McTaggart, *The Action Research Planner* (Geelong, New Zealand: Deakin University Press, 1988). Many of the action research initiatives in Australia and the U.S. have aimed both to improve school and classroom practice and to contribute to knowledge about teaching and research itself. For more extensive discussions of the roots and emancipatory potential of action research, see D. Kyle and R. Hovda, "The Potential and Practice of Action Research, Parts I and II," *Peabody Journal of Education* 64, nos. 2–3 (1989): 80–95, 170–175; Sharon Oja and Lisa Smulyan, *Collaborative Action Research: A Developmental Approach* (London: Falmer Press, 1989); Susan Noffke, "Action Research: Towards the Next Generation," *Educational Action Research* 2 no. 1 (1994): 9–21; Susan Noffke and Robert Stevenson, ed., *Educational Action Research: Becoming Practically Critical* (New York: Teachers College Press, 1995); John Elliott, *Action Research for Educational Change* (Bristol, PA: Open University Press, 1991); Joe L. Kincheloe, *Teachers as Researchers: Qualitative Inquiry as a Path to Empowerment* (London:

Falmer Press, 1991); John McNiff, *Action Research: Principles and Practices* (London: Macmillan, 1986); Landon Beyer, *Knowing and Acting: Inquiry Ideology and Educational Studies* (London: Falmer Press, 1988).

Many recent iterations of teacher research are linked to national efforts to improve subject matter teaching, to reform the cultures of schools and school systems, and to revise school–university relationships. These tend to focus on teachers as problem posers who identify their own practice-based questions, systematically document their observations, and share their analyses with others in the educational community. See, for example, Dixie Goswami and Peter Stillman, *Reclaiming the Classroom: Teacher Research as an Agency for Change* (Upper Montclair, NJ: Boynton/Cook, 1987); Marion Mohr and Marian MacLean, *Working Together: A Guide for Teacher-Researchers* (Urbana, Ill.: National Council of Teachers of English, 1987); Glenda Bissex and Robert Bullock, *Seeing for Ourselves: Case Study Research by Teachers of Writing* (Portsmouth, NH: Heinemann, 1987); D. Daiker and M. Morenberg, ed. *The Writing Teacher as Researcher* (Portsmouth, NH: Boynton/Cook, Heinemann, 1990); N.H. Branscombe, Dixie Goswami, and Jeff Schwartz, *Students Teaching, Teachers Learning* (Portsmouth, NH: Boynton/Cook, Heinemann, 1992); Bay Area Writing Project, *Research in Writing: Working Papers of Teacher Researchers* (Berkeley: University of California, Bay Area Writing Project, 1990); Sandra Hollingsworth and Hugh Sockett, ed., *Teacher Research and Education Reform, Yearbook of the National Society for the Study of Education* (Chicago: University of Chicago Press, 1994); Faye Peitzman, ed., *The Power of Context: Studies by Teacher Researchers* (Los Angeles, Calif.: University of California, Center for Academic Interinstitutional Programs, 1990).

13  Teacher research, action research, and other forms of critical inquiry have been used in a number of preservice education programs in the U.S. Among the best documented efforts are, for example, Robert Tabachnik and Kenneth Zeichner, *Issues and Practices in Inquiry-Oriented Teacher Education* (London: Falmer Press, 1991); Jennifer Gore and Kenneth Zeichner, "Action Research and Reflective Teaching in Preservice Teacher Education," *Teaching and Teacher Education* 7 (1991): 119–136; Renee Clift, M. L. Veal, M. Johnson, and P. Holland, "Restructuring Teacher Education through Collaborative Action Research," *Journal of Teacher Education* 41 (1990): 52–62; Doreen Ross, "Action Research for Preservice Teachers: A Description of Why and How," *Peabody Journal of Education* 64 (1987): 131–150; David Hursh, "Reflective Practice and the Culture of Schools," in E. Wayne Ross, ed., *Reflective Practice and Social Studies Education* (Washington, D.C.: National Council for the Social Studies, 1994); Kenneth Teitelbaum and Deborah Britzman, "Reading and Doing Ethnography: Teacher Education and Reflective Practice," in Robert Tabachnik and Kenneth Zeichner, ed., *Issues and Practices in Inquiry-Oriented Teacher Education* (Bristol, PA: Falmer Press, 1991). At the same time that practitioner research has gained currency as a strategy for preservice teacher education, however, it also has been vigorously criticized. Critics have argued that we cannot advocate research by preservice teachers as a good thing in and of itself. Instead, we must interrogate what student teachers are doing research about, toward what social and political ends, and in relation to what larger frames of interpretation and analysis. These critics point out that various versions of research in preservice education are based on quite different concepts of knowledge, language, and the politics of schooling. See, for example, Peter Grimmett, "The Nature of Reflection in Schon's Conception in Perspective," in *Reflection in Teacher Education*, ed. Peter G. Grimmett and Gaelen Erickson (New York: Pacific Educational Press and Teachers College Press, 1988); Alan Tom, "Inquiring Into Inquiry-Oriented Teacher Education," *Journal of Teacher Education* 36 (1985): 5, 35–44; Kenneth Zeichner and Daniel Liston, "Teaching Student Teachers to Reflect," *Harvard Educational Review*, 57 (1987): 1–22; Marilyn Cochran-Smith, "The Power of Teacher Research in Teacher Education," in *Teacher Research and Education Reform. Yearbook of the National Society for the Study of Education* ed. S. Hollingsworth and H. Sockett (Chicago: University of Chicago Press, 1994).

14  A number of scholars have developed different, but related, concepts to challenge traditional divisions of theory, knowledge, and practice in teaching, schooling, and research. See, for example, Carole Edelsky, Barbara Altwerger, and Barbara Flores, *Whole Language: What's the Difference?* (Portsmouth, NH: Heinemann, 1991);

D. Sanders and Gail McCutcheon, "The Development of Practical Theories of Teaching," *Journal of Curriculum and Supervision* 2, no. 1 (1986): 50–67; Donald Schön, *The Reflective Practitioner* (San Francisco: Jossey-Bass, 1983); Lee Shulman, "Knowledge and Teaching: Foundations of the New Reform," *Harvard Educational Review* 51 (1983): 1–22.

15   Marilyn Cochran-Smith, "Learning to Teach Against the Grain," *Harvard Educational Review* 61, no. 3 (1991): 279–310.

16   All of the excerpts used in this article are drawn from the work of student teachers I worked with in Project START (Student Teachers as Researching Teachers) and either have been presented in public forums or local publications or are used here with student teachers' explicit permission. (Children's names that are included within these excerpts have been changed.) Project START is a fifth-year master's program in elementary education at the University of Pennsylvania. Developed 8 years ago in collaboration with Philadelphia area teachers, START centers around a year-long student teaching experience at the same school and classroom site where student teachers, cooperating teachers, and supervisors meet weekly as teacher–researcher groups. The program is based on the premise that teaching is both an intellectual and a political activity. It is assumed that prospective teachers learn to teach against the grain by working in the company of experienced classroom teachers and teacher educators who also see themselves as reformers and researchers and who regard learning to teach as a process that continues across the professional lifespan.

17   In an earlier article, I referred to a similar perspective as "making knowledge problematic." See Marilyn Cochran-Smith and Susan L. Lytle, "Interrogating Cultural Diversity: Inquiry and Action," *Journal of Teacher Education* 43, no. 2 (1992): 104–115. Although the examples I have constructed and interpreted in this article are different from the examples in the previous paper, the ideas have benefited greatly from conversations and writings with my colleague.

18   Peggy McIntosh, "White Privilege: Unpacking the Invisible Knapsack," *Peace and Freedom* (1989): 10–12.

19   Katherine Weiler, *Women Teaching for Change: Gender, Class and Power* (New York: Bergin Garvey, 1988).

20   McIntosh, "White Privilege," 12.

21   Courtney Cazden and Hugh Mehan, "Principles From Sociology and Anthropology: Context, Code, Classroom, and Culture," in *Knowledge Base for the Beginning Teacher*, ed. C. Reynolds (Oxford, England: Pergamon Press, 1989), 55.

22   Goodman et al., *Report Card on Basal Readers*, 78–79.

23   Eleanor Duckworth, *The Having of Wonderful Ideas* (New York: Teachers College Press, 1987), 134.

24   John Smyth, *A Rationale for Teachers' Critical Pedagogy: A Handbook* (Victoria, Australia: Deakin University Press, 1987), 12.

25   Frederick Erickson, 'Taught Cognitive Learning in Its Immediate Environments: A Neglected Topic in the Anthropology of Education," *Anthropology and Education Quarterly* 13 (1981): 149–180.

26   Patricia Carini, *Prospect's Documentary Processes* (Bennington, VT: The Prospect School Center, 1986).

27   The process of formulating a focusing question of this kind and then exploring that question through rich descriptions is drawn directly from Patricia Carini's discussion of "The Descriptive Review of a Child," in *Prospect's Documentary Processes* (Bennington, VT: The Prospect School Center, 1986).

28   Heath, *Ways With Words*.

29   A number of scholars have used similar terminology to describe this sort of critical pedagogy—including, Stanley Aronowitz and Henry Giroux, *Education Under Siege* (New York: New World Foundation, 1985); Henry Giroux, "Intellectual Label and Pedagogical Work: Rethinking the Role of Teachers as Intellectuals," *Phenomenology and Pedagogy* 3 (1985): 20–31; Ira Shor, *Critical Teaching in Everyday Life* (Boston: South End Press, 1980).

30   Angela Garcia, Debra Kauffman, Carmen Maldonado, Kecia Parham, Jessie Smith, and Katie Whitney, "Teaching Ain't No Crystal Stair" (paper presented at the Ethnography and Education Forum, Philadelphia, February 1992), 11.

31  This comment relies on Edelsky, Altwerger, and Flores' work, *Whole Language*, where they make a similar point about the political aspects of a whole language perspective on teaching and learning reading/language arts.
32  Lawrence Stenhouse, *An Introduction to Curriculum Research and Development* (New York: Holmes and Meier, 1975).
33  John Dewey, "The Relation of Theory to Practice," 12, 16.
34  Marilyn Cochran-Smith, "Learning to Teach Against the Grain." Also see Susan L. Lytle and Marilyn Cochran-Smith, "Understanding Teacher Research: The Questions That Persist" (paper presented at the Ethnography and Education Forum, Philadelphia, February 1994), 1–20, as well as Susan L. Lytle, "Risky Business," *The Quarterly of the National Writing Project and the Center for the Study of Writing and Literacy* 15 (1993) 1, 20–23.
35  See Marilyn Cochran-Smith, "Uncertain Allies: Understanding the Boundaries of Race and Teaching" (paper presented at the Annual Meeting of the American Educational Research Association, New Orleans, April 1994), 1–36 and "Blind Vision: Preservice Curriculum as Racial Text" (paper presented at the Annual Meeting of the American Educational Research Association, San Francisco, April 1995), 1–37.

# CHAPTER 10

# PREPARING TEACHERS FOR CULTURALLY DIVERSE SCHOOLS (2001)

Research and the overwhelming presence of whiteness

*Christine E. Sleeter*

It is widely recognized that the cultural gap between children in the schools and teachers is large and growing. In 1996, the enrollment in public elementary and secondary schools was 64% White, 17% Black, 14% Hispanic, 4% Asian/Pacific Islander, and 1% American Indian/Alaskan Native (National Center for Education Statistics, 1999). In contrast, the teaching force in 1994 was 87% non-Hispanic White, 7% Black, 4% Hispanic, 1% Asian/Pacific Islander, and 1% American Indian/Alaskan Native. Thirtynine percent of teachers had students with limited English proficiency in their classrooms, but only one quarter of those teachers had received training for working with them (U.S. Department of Education, 1997).

Education in many communities of color, as well as many poor White communities, is in a state of crisis. Students are learning far too little, becoming disengaged, and dropping out at high rates. Far too few students are going on to college. As a teacher educator, I am often asked what preservice education can do. I have plenty of ideas based on years of experience but decided to examine what the research is saying. When I reviewed research studies on teacher education for multicultural education 15 years ago (Sleeter, 1985), there was little to review. Today there is a sizable body. For this review, I focused on published data-based research studies that examine the preparation of teachers for schools that serve historically underserved, multicultural student populations. A longer discussion of how the research was framed can be found elsewhere (Sleeter, in press).

## The problem

Students of color tend to bring richer experiences and perspectives to multicultural teaching than do most White students, who dominate numerically. Several studies document this pattern, which has tremendous implications for teacher education.

A large proportion of White preservice students anticipate working with children of another cultural background. As a whole, however, they bring very little cross-cultural background, knowledge, and experience (Barry & Lechner, 1995; Gilbert, 1995; Larke, 1990; Law & Lane, 1987; McIntyre, 1997; Schultz, Neyhart, & Reck, 1996; R. Smith, Moallem, & Sherrill, 1997; Su, 1996, 1997; Valli, 1995). For example, Schultz et al. (1996) found that preservice student teachers are fairly naïve and have stereotypic beliefs about urban children, such as believing that urban children bring attitudes that interfere with education. Most White preservice students bring little awareness or understanding of discrimination, especially racism (Avery & Walker, 1993; King, 1991; Su, 1996, 1997). Su (1996, 1997) found that White preservice students interpret social change as meaning almost any kind of change except changing structural inequalities, and many regard programs to remedy racial discrimination as discriminatory against Whites. White preservice students tend to use colorblindness as a way of coping with fear and ignorance (McIntyre, 1997; Valli, 1995). These problems carry over into the classroom. Preservice students tend to have limited visions of multicultural teaching (Goodwin, 1994) as a technical issue and multicultural curriculum as mainly additions to the existing curriculum (Vavrus, 1994). Furthermore, many preservice as well as in-service teachers are ambivalent about their ability to teach African American children, and their feelings of efficacy seem to decline from the preservice to the in-service stage (Pang & Sablan, 1998).

Preservice students of color bring a richer multicultural knowledge base to teacher education than do White students. Students of color generally are more committed to multicultural teaching, social justice, and providing children of color with an academically challenging curriculum (Ladson-Billings, 1991; Rios & Montecinos, 1999; Su, 1996, 1997). Preservice students of color do not necessarily bring more knowledge about pedagogical practices than do White preservice students, however (Goodwin, 1997; Montecinos, 1994); both groups need well-designed preservice teacher education.

Predominantly White institutions have generally responded very slowly to the growing cultural gap. According to a survey of 19 Midwest Holmes Group teacher preparation programs, 94% of their faculty and students were Anglo (Fuller, 1992). Only 56% of these institutions required elementary education students to complete a multicultural education course; one institution did not even offer such a course. Preservice students generally were placed in field experiences "reminiscent of their childhood" (p. 192). A large proportion of teachers of color have been prepared by historically Black institutions. V. L. Clark (1987), for example, wrote that as of the mid 1980s, "even though the historically black institutions [HBIs] only represent 5% of the institutions of higher education, the HBIs have produced 66% of the black teachers in the United States" (p. 86). He argued that predominantly White institutions need to help.

Several case studies have examined predominantly White teacher education programs that do "business as usual" (Cannella & Reiff, 1994; Davis, 1995; Grant & Koskela, 1986; Parker & Hood, 1995; Weiner, 1990). On a superficial level, many White preservice students in these programs initially showed receptivity toward learning about diversity. The programs themselves provided disjointed multicultural content, dependent on the interests of individual professors. By the time they student taught, the preservice students were concerned mainly about surviving in the classroom. Those in primarily White schools had subordinated any interest in multicultural education to demands of their cooperating teachers. Those in urban schools were completely unprepared for the students and the setting and had great difficulty. Parker and Hood (1995) found that students of color in such programs are very critical of this superficial treatment of diversity. Although they brought life experiences they could draw on to construct multicultural pedagogy, their programs were not designed to extend what they already knew, nor to prepare their White peers to teach in schools like those with which the students of color were familiar.

The research reviewed in the remainder of this article provides no clear guidance about what to do in preservice education. This is a limitation of the research that has been done thus far rather than an indication that interventions are not needed. Continuing business as usual in preservice teacher education will only continue to widen the gap between teachers and children in schools. Certainly research can help to inform practice; as I point out in this review, the research that exists currently is piecemeal.

Preservice programs take two rather different lines of action to address the cultural gap between teachers and children in the school: (a) bring into the teaching profession more teachers who are from culturally diverse communities and (b) try to develop the attitudes and multicultural knowledge base of predominantly White cohorts of preservice students. Although these are not mutually exclusive, they differ in what they emphasize.

## Recruitment and selection of preservice students

Preservice teacher education programs use at least two strategies to alter the mix of who becomes teachers. One strategy is to recruit and prepare many more prospective teachers of color. The literature contains numerous descriptions of such programs (Becket, 1998; Brennan & Bliss, 1998; Dillard, 1994; Littleton, 1998; Love & Greer, 1995; Shade, Boe, Garner, & New, 1998; Torres-Karna & Krustchinsky, 1998; Yopp, Yopp, & Taylor, 1992) but little follow-up research of their impact on schools. For example, Shade et al. (1998) described EC3, an alternative teacher certification program for prospective teachers of color, created through collaboration between two higher education institutions. The program successfully certified three cohorts of a total of 49 teachers of color. Although the articles above are all program descriptions, not studies of program effectiveness, they do demonstrate that it is possible to recruit and prepare many more teachers of color than we do currently.

Another strategy to alter the mix of who becomes teachers is to recruit and select only those who bring experiences, knowledge, and dispositions that will enable them to teach well in culturally diverse urban schools. Martin Haberman (1996) has been the leading advocate and developer of this strategy. He argues that urban teachers succeed or fail based on what they bring to teaching more than on what they learn in a preservice program. His observations of star urban teachers identified seven main attributes they share (Haberman, 1995). Preservice students who bring these attributes generally are older (30 to 50 years of age), are of color, are from an urban area, have raised children and held other jobs, and have learned to live normally in a somewhat violent context (Haberman, 1996). Haberman argues that the best way to prepare successful urban teachers is to select candidates who bring those attributes, then prepare them pedagogically in urban schools. He has found that one can predict not only who will succeed in urban schools but also the degree to which they will succeed in the classroom using attributes of star urban teachers as predictive criteria (Haberman, 1993).

Haberman's research suggests that teacher education programs could potentially recruit and select many more preservice teachers who bring knowledge, experiences, commitments, and dispositions that will enable them to learn to teach culturally diverse student populations well. Although most research in multicultural teacher education examines how to prepare White preservice teachers, much more can be done to bring into the profession teachers who culturally match the children in the schools. Further research on the impact of alternative selection and recruitment processes is needed.

## Community-based cross-cultural immersion experiences

Community-based cross-cultural immersion programs are those in which teacher education students actually live in communities that are culturally different from their own while they are learning to teach. Several White educators have written autobiographically about how they learned to teach cross-culturally and emphasized the power of community-based learning (Sleeter, 1996; G. P. Smith, 1998; Weiner, 1993; Yeo, 1997). Yeo (1997), for example, described how he learned from students and community members in an inner-city school. His teacher preparation program was irrelevant to urban teaching; as a new teacher, he discovered that he needed to put that training aside and learn to listen to inner-city students and residents. Merryfield (2000) reported similar stories in her study of life histories of White teacher educators who lived for a time outside their own country. Conclusions based on these personal narratives have support in other forms of research.

Indiana University has several cross-cultural immersion projects that have been studied mainly through follow-up surveys of graduates. The projects include the American Indian Reservation Project in the Navajo Nation, the Hispanic Community Project in the lower Rio Grande Valley, the Urban Project in Indianapolis, and the Overseas Project. The semester prior to their immersion experience, students complete an intensive preparatory course. During the immersion experience, they have ongoing substantive community involvement, as well as student teaching. A survey of graduates of the American Indian Reservation Project reported that it made a positive impact on their attitudes, knowledge, and employability in Native as well as non-Native schools (Mahan, 1982). In a short qualitative study of that project, Melnick and Zeichner (1996) concurred, finding "much evidence of student teachers making efforts to connect their classrooms to community people, practices, and values, even when cooperating teachers did not support these practices" (p. 185). A follow-up survey of the Overseas Project reported similar positive findings (Mahan & Stachowski, 1990). In two additional follow-up surveys, a large number of preservice students reported that community people were highly significant sources of learning (Mahan & Stachowski, 1993–1994; Stachowski & Mahan, 1998).

Small-scale studies have examined other immersion programs (Aguilar & Pohan, 1998; Canning, 1995; Cooper, Beare, & Thorman, 1990; Marxen & Rudney, 1999; Noordhoff & Kleinfeld, 1993). All reported considerable learning, and authors emphasized the value of cross-cultural immersion projects and the power of learning from the community. For example, Cooper et al. (1990) compared 18 preservice students from Minnesota who had student taught in the Rio Grande Valley in Texas with 85 who had conventional student teaching placements in Minnesota. On all measures, such as reported comfort discussing racial or ethnic issues, expectations for students of diverse racial backgrounds, and willingness to visit students' families, those who had student taught in Texas scored higher. Noordhoff and Kleinfeld (1993) studied the impact of Teachers for Alaska on preservice students' teaching practice. They videotaped students teaching short lessons three times during the program and found that students shifted dramatically from teaching as telling to teaching as engaging students with subject matter, using culturally relevant knowledge.

When community-based immersion experiences are studied, researchers generally report a powerful impact, although much of the data are based on very small projects. When White educators describe their own learning, community-based experiences are also often extremely important and in some cases much more important than their formal teacher education programs. The researchers mentioned here attribute students' learning to the power of community-based, cross-cultural contexts in which they have to grapple with being in the minority, do not necessarily know how to act, and are temporarily unable to retreat to the comfort of a culturally familiar setting. Community-based immersion experiences require a good deal of work to organize and operate, however, and convincing others that such experiences should be a part of teacher education is difficult without a stronger research base. How long does an immersion project need to be? What kinds of settings work best? What impact does an immersion experience have on a teacher when he or she enters the profession? These are questions that need to be addressed through research.

## Multicultural education coursework

Many teacher preparation programs have added coursework in multicultural education, teaching the urban child, teaching English language learners, or some variation of these. A good deal of research examines student learning in these courses from various angles, focusing mainly on how or whether they change how predominantly White preservice students think. This review includes studies of stand-alone courses, as well as courses that include field experience.

### Stand-alone multicultural education courses

In the past few years, many faculty members have written about their own courses, reporting either action research or reflective analyses. For the most part, they examine teaching strategies that raise awareness about issues related to race and/or culture among predominantly White classes of students. Action research case studies use as data student papers, student reflective journals, and/or interviews with students. In many cases, the author is the instructor of the course. Teaching strategies that have been examined include using autobiography (C. Clark & Medina, 2000; Florio-Ruane, 1994; Xu, 2000), engaging students in a mail cultural exchange with others in very different cultural contexts (Fuller & Ahler, 1987), using a simulation of unequal opportunity (Frykholm, 1997), teaching about White privilege (Lawrence, 1997; Lawrence & Bunche, 1996), and engaging students in debate (Marshall, 1998). All of these teaching strategies seem to raise students' awareness about race, culture, and discrimination.

Many narratives reflect on the work that goes into making an impact on White preservice students in multicultural education courses (e.g., Larkin & Sleeter, 1995; Martin, 1995). There is some overlap between action research case studies and narrative research; the former emphasizes data collection more than the latter, whereas the latter may reflect on experience more than the former. For example, Ahlquist (1991) explored her predominantly White students' resistance to awareness raising about race. She contrasted her own sense of urgency about preparing teachers to grapple with race with her students' lack of background information about the issue. She argued for a need to teach in a way that allows students to reflect and digest in order to move forward. Thoughtful narratives that grow from and examine extensive experience help readers to see the basis on which experienced educators make recommendations or take action (e.g., Cochran-Smith, 2000). Narrative essays vary widely in degree of reflection and use of experience, however, and as a result can be criticized as substituting opinion and selective perception for data. The field needs more discussion of how to evaluate and interpret narrative research.

Most of the small-scale case studies and reflective narratives suggest strategies that make an impact on students, but a few critique coursework that is counterproductive. McDiarmid (1992), for example, studied a multicultural strand in Los Angeles Unified School District-based teacher certification training, which included 15 sessions on background information and pedagogical techniques for working with culturally diverse students. Through interviews with the students, he found that didactic presentations about various groups actually taught stereotypes and generalizations and did little to change the thinking among the preservice students.

Studies using experimental research designs are not as optimistic in their conclusions as are case studies and narratives; neither are they as textured. Eight used a pretest-posttest design to measure the effects of a multicultural education course on attitudes. The great majority of the participants in these studies were White women. These studies reported that after a course, students' attitudes are generally more positive than before (Baker, 1973, 1977; Bennett, 1979; Bennett, Niggle, & Stage, 1990; Hennington, 1981; Martin & Koppelman, 1991; Rios, McDaniel, & Stowell, 1998; Tran & Young, 1994). However, some studies found only small gains (Baker, 1973, 1977). Furthermore, the only study with a follow-up found that a month after the course, which lasted only 1 week, gains were lost (Hennington, 1981). Two more studies used a control group design to investigate the impact of coursework on students' ability to use culture and language to analyze a classroom case study (Guillaume, Zuniga-Hill, & Yee, 1995, 1998). In both, there was no difference in the quality of response between the two groups.

From this research, it is difficult to say how much impact multicultural education courses have on White students. Experimental studies examined mainly attitudes using Likert-type scales, which do not offer a very textured reading of what students learn. Case studies and narratives provided more depth and detail but may also have highlighted what the instructor saw as working because most of these were written by the course instructor, who may have a bias toward discussing successes of her or his work. Almost none of the studies above examined the impact of multicultural education coursework on how preservice students actually teach children in the classroom. Only Lawrence (1997) subsequently followed students into the classroom during their student teaching to find out how much carryover their learning had. She found the carryover varied widely, depending on the level of racial awareness students had developed earlier.

Intuitively, it makes sense to assume that preservice students who are taught something about culture and race will become better teachers in multicultural contexts than those who are not, but the research has not been designed to investigate this assumption. Those who wish to do research on multicultural education courses should attempt to follow students into the classroom after they finish teacher education to find out how much impact coursework has. Furthermore, unless one is critically examining one's own experience, researchers studying the impact of a particular course should take steps to gain some distance from the course itself, by studying another instructor's course for example.

## Multicultural education coursework with a field experience

A number of other studies examined how students experience a multicultural education course that includes a field experience in a school or community setting.

In most of these studies, the preservice student populations were primarily White, and a major focus of the experience was to raise awareness.

One approach was to teach students ethnographic research skills, then have them complete a research project in an urban community or school; in most cases, the community contexts were primarily African American (Fry & McKinney, 1997; Narode, Rennie-Hill, & Peterson, 1994; Olmedo, 1997; Ross & Smith, 1992; Sleeter, 1996). Authors emphasized that preparation for the community research and help processing the experience was very important. All of these studies described conceptual growth among the students and greater willingness among many to consider working in an urban school, although some authors noted students' reluctance to contextualize communities within broader relations of power (Ross & Smith, 1992; Sleeter, 1996).

Another approach was to have preservice students tutor children in cultural contexts that are not primarily White and middle-class (Aaronsohn, Carter, & Howell, 1995; Barton, 1999; Boyle-Baise & Sleeter, 2000; Bullock, 1997; Lazar, 1998; Moule, in press; Murtadha-Watts, 1998; Rodriguez, 1998). These case studies described insights that specific preservice students gained, including their growth in awareness of culture, knowledge of a context different from their own, and awareness of their own stereotypes. For example, Lazar studied two White preservice students who, over a semester and after tutoring children and talking personally with some of their primary caregivers, came to question their assumption that low-income African American parents do not care about their children's literacy development. At the same time, Murtadha-Watts (1998) emphasized how little awareness of larger issues the preservice students had, even after the experience. Many students found stereotypes disconfirmed by the experience, but some found confirmation of stereotypes. More broadly, they had little understanding of institutional racism within which to contextualize the program in which they tutored.

Pretest-posttest studies examining the effects of a course plus a field experience on predominantly White preservice students report mixed findings. Four studies reported a positive change (Bondy, Schmitz, & Johnson, 1993; Grottgau & Nickolai-Mays, 1989; Mason, 1997; Wiggins & Follo, 1999). For example, Bondy et al. (1993) studied a course in which students examined why poor and minority students perform less well in school than White, middle-class students. They also considered teaching strategies that might break that cycle, and students tutored in public housing neighborhoods. They found that participation in the course and the field experience together had a significant impact. Students who completed one or the other, or neither, however, did not show gains. Authors of these studies concluded that a course provides a support mechanism for students to interpret their tutoring experiences.

On the other hand, two studies found that field experience reinforced or produced more stereotypic attitudes (Haberman & Post, 1992; Reed, 1993). Haberman and Post found that most of the White preservice students they studied interpreted their inner-city field experience mainly through preconceptions they brought with them. Although students completed concurrent multicultural education coursework, its didactic pedagogical format did not sufficiently engage them in examining their perceptions. By the end of the experience, students felt more confident about themselves as teachers but characterized pupils with more negative descriptions than at the beginning.

Again, intuitively it would seem that teaching preservice students something about culturally diverse children and requiring them to work directly with children or their communities would help them to become better teachers. But does it? We do not really know because preservice students are not usually followed into teaching. The study that most closely examines this question is one that I did several years ago (Sleeter, 1989). I surveyed 456 teachers who had been certified in Wisconsin between 1981 and 1986 to find out how they used various dimensions of multicultural education in their teaching. The state requires infusion of multicultural course content plus a field experience. Overall, the teaching strategies teachers reported using most often were of the human relations variety. Teachers who had completed programs with more than four credits in multicultural education reported using multicultural teaching strategies in the classroom more often than those completing programs with less than four credits. However, the number of credits they had completed was less related to what they reported doing in the classroom than was the student population they were teaching. Teachers were more likely to incorporate multicultural content when their students were of color and/or from low-income backgrounds than when they were not.

It was unclear to me how much difference the multicultural education coursework and field experience, in themselves, had made. Even if preservice students learn and grow through the experience, are they growing enough to become strong teachers in culturally diverse schools? After studying what mostly White preservice students gained from one such course with a tutoring field experience, Murtadha-Watts (1998) wrote the following:

> The perspectives of the preservice teachers in this pilot program, most of whom will (regrettably) never get opportunities early in their teaching studies to question and challenge their own tightly held cultural assumptions, are commonplace. What will happen if the increasing numbers of teachers have no idea about what they are doing culturally, who they are working with, and what the students' circumstances are? Will we continue this cycle? Does the cycle of culturally incompetent teachers continue, or can teacher educators provide other opportunities for culturally responsive teaching?

## Interventions at a program level

Adding a course or a field experience does not necessarily address the rest of the program. What if programs are restructured or redesigned in some way?

In some traditionally structured programs, faculty members have infused multicultural course content and field experiences throughout. Two case studies found the impact of such programs limited, but for different reasons. Burstein and Cabello (1989) found that although students' thinking over 2 years shifted away from a deficiency orientation and they gained some strategies for motivating, teaching, and building on children's first languages, most students still struggled with deep cultural differences and belief systems about schooling. Artiles, Barreto, Peña, & McClafferty (1998) found that two graduates of such a program had actually experienced diverse and disconnected discourses while in the program: their own prior beliefs, conflicting theoretical perspectives with the program (such as critical theory vs. behaviorism), and beliefs of teachers they interacted with in the schools. As a result, they put much of what they had learned in the program aside and learned to teach on the job.

School-university collaborations constitute a form of program restructuring designed to connect theory with practice. Three articles reported experimental studies of such programs for preparing urban teachers. Two reported effects of

Teacher Corps training on subsequent classroom teaching behavior. Marsh (1975, 1979) compared 82 Teacher Corps graduates with a control group of other newly hired teachers. He found that the Teacher Corps graduates did not differ from graduates in the control group on most variables, including use of several instructional strategies, handling behavior, or acting as change agents. They were more likely than those in the control group to develop culturally relevant curricula, use community resources in teaching and initiate contact with parents, and show positive attitudes about reading development and causes of poverty. Pupils of Teacher Corps graduates gained more than pupils of control group teachers on a measurement of self-concept, but there were no differences between pupil groups in reading achievement or attendance. Marsh (1979) noted that whereas many Teacher Corps projects emphasize cultural awareness, there is less emphasis on specific instructional skills, which is why its graduates' teaching skills are no different from those of other new teachers. Stallings and Quinn (1991) examined the effects of the Houston Teaching Academy and found that its graduates used more effective teaching practices in inner-city classrooms than graduates of a traditional teacher preparation program. These three studies suggest that university-school collaboratives have the potential to teach skills that teachers will actually use in the classroom. The research did not examine whether they accomplished any of the broader rethinking of schooling that is part of multicultural education.

Cochran-Smith (1991) and Cochran-Smith and Lytle (1992) studied preservice students participating in school-based inquiry communities that were involved in reforming culturally diverse urban schools. There, teachers and preservice students frequently talked together about what it means to teach real students in their classes well and wrestled with significant pedagogical issues. They learned to ask more complex questions, examine themselves more deeply, and question how schools respond to student diversity. Preservice teachers experienced teaching against the grain (i.e., teaching in ways that the teacher believes benefit children more than predominant modes of teaching do) as a reality rather than a university professor's vision (Cochran-Smith, 1991).

Attempts to rework whole teacher education programs, whether by collaborating with schools, infusing multicultural course content, or both, might improve the preparation of teachers. There are too few data, however, to know how well teachers in such programs learn to teach in culturally diverse schools. Certainly the quality and nature of the experience in partner schools is as important to examine as is the nature of the teacher education program. Schools with strong culturally responsive teachers could partner well with a multicultural teacher education program; partnerships between schools and universities with predominantly White staffs doing business as usual would probably produce more business as usual.

## The overwhelming presence of whiteness

The great bulk of the research has examined how to help young White preservice students (mainly women) develop the awareness, insights, and skills for effective teaching in multicultural contexts. Reading the research, one gains a sense of the immense struggle that involves. For preservice students of color in predominantly White programs, the overwhelming presence of Whiteness can be silencing. Five studies examined how preservice students of color experience such contexts (Agee, 1998; Burant, 1999; Guyton, Saxton, & Wesche, 1996; Pailliotet, 1997;

Tellez, 1999). For example, Burant (1999) examined the process through which one Latina became silenced in a course organized around dialogue and collaborative constructivist work. Initially, she spoke up in class, but she "lost her voice" after White classmates expressed a lack of interest in multicultural and language issues. In predominantly White programs, not only are classmates mostly White, but so are professors and teachers in the field.

I would guess that most of the authors of the research reviewed here—both authors of color as well as White authors—are aware of the overwhelming presence of Whiteness in teacher education. Some scholars have examined this issue very insightfully with reference to their own work (Cochran-Smith, 1995, 2000).

Because of this overwhelming presence, many teacher educators have chosen to develop alternative teacher education programs for prospective teachers of color or for those who bring experiences and attributes that good urban teachers share. These alternative programs may develop a range of insights that do not emerge when focusing mainly on how to prepare traditional White students. For example, alternative programs value what students of color (who are often recruited from the ranks of paraprofessionals) bring, making their assets part of the selection process, and build on what they already know, often in highly field-based settings. What does a teacher education curriculum look like in such a program, and how well do such programs prepare strong teachers? Research on these questions could be immensely valuable.

Although working to shift who becomes teachers is essential, working with White prospective teachers is also essential. Working to improve White attitudes should not become a diversion from selecting and preparing the excellent, culturally responsive teachers that historically underserved schools need. Of the various strategies that are used in teacher education programs, extensive community-based immersion experiences, coupled with coursework, seem to have the most promise. However, a stronger research base is needed to strengthen this claim. The research suggests that community-based immersion experiences are more powerful than stand-alone multicultural education courses, yet it is likely that the latter are more prevalent because they are easier to institutionalize.

## A quest for research

I framed this review around a quest for research on the preparation of teachers who can teach well in schools serving communities that have been historically underserved. This way of framing the issue draws attention to what actually happens in classrooms when graduates of teacher preparation programs begin to teach. It is there that the fruit of our efforts has the most impact and there that we as teacher educators need to focus our energies.

A research base on good teaching in historically underserved classrooms does exist: for example, Ladson-Billings's (1994) study of effective teachers of African American children and Reyes, Scribner, and Scribner's (1999) collection of studies of high-performing Latino schools. Research on preparing such teachers, however, is very piecemeal, predominated by small-scale action research studies that—although useful locally for a program improvement—together produce a disjointed and somewhat repetitious knowledge base. After reviewing research on multicultural teacher education, Ladson-Billings (1999) commented that

> despite the changing demographics that make our public schools more culturally and linguistically diverse and the growing body of knowledge on

issues of diversity and difference, multicultural teacher education continues to suffer from a thin, poorly developed, fragmented literature that provides an inaccurate picture of the kind of preparation teachers receive to teach in culturally diverse classrooms. (p. 114)

Research in teacher education needs to follow graduates into the classroom, and our work needs to extend beyond preservice education, linking preservice education with community-based learning and with ongoing professional development and school reform.

# References

Aaronsohn, E., Carter, C., & Howell, M. (1995). Preparing monocultural teachers for a multicultural world. *Equity & Excellence in Education, 29*(1), 5–9.

Agee, J. (1998). Confronting issues of race and power in the culture of schools. In M. Dilworth (Ed.), *Being responsive to cultural differences* (pp. 21–38). Thousand Oaks, CA: Corwin Press.

Aguilar, T. E., & Pohan, C. A. (1998). A cultural immersion experience to enhance cross-cultural competence. *Sociotam, 8*(1), 29–49.

Ahlquist, R. (1991). Position and imposition: Power relations in a multicultural foundations class. *Journal of Negro Education, 60*(2), 158–169.

Artiles, A. J., Barreto, R. M., Peña, L., & McClafferty, K. (1998). Pathways to teacher learning in multicultural contexts. *Remedial and Special Education, 19*(2), 70–90.

Avery, P. G., & Walker, C. (1993). Prospective teachers' perceptions of ethnic and gender differences in academic achievement. *Journal of Teacher Education, 44*(1), 27–37.

Baker, G. (1973). Multicultural training for student teachers. *Journal of Teacher Education, 24,* 306–307.

Baker, G. (1977). Two preservice training approaches. *Journal of Teacher Education, 28*(3), 31–33.

Barry, N. H., & Lechner, J. V. (1995). Preservice teachers' attitudes about and awareness of multicultural teaching and learning. *Teaching and Teacher Education, 11,* 149–161.

Barton, A. C. (1999). Crafting a multicultural science teacher education: A case study. *Journal of Teacher Education, 50,* 303–314.

Becket, D. R. (1998). Increasing the number of Latino and Navajo teachers in hard-to-staff schools. *Journal of Teacher Education, 49*(1), 196–205.

Bennett, C., Niggle, T., & Stage, F. (1990). Preservice multicultural teacher education: Predictors of student readiness. *Teaching and Teacher Education, 6,* 243–254.

Bennett, C. T. (1979). The preparation of pre-service secondary social studies teachers in multiethnic education. *High School Journal, 62*(5), 232–237.

Bondy, E., Schmitz, S., & Johnson, M. (1993). The impact of coursework and fieldwork on student teachers' reported beliefs about teaching poor and minority students. *Action in Teacher Education, 15*(2), 55–62.

Boyle-Baise, L., & Sleeter, C. E. (2000). Community-based service learning for multicultural teacher education. *Educational Foundations, 14*(2), 33–50.

Brennan, S., & Bliss, T. (1998). Increasing minority representation in the teaching profession through alternative certification: A case study. *Teacher Educator, 34*(1), 1–11.

Bullock, L. D. (1997). Efficacy of a gender and ethnic equity in science education curriculum for preservice teachers. *Journal of Research in Science Teaching, 34,* 1019–1038.

Burant, T. J. (1999). Finding, using, and losing (?) voice: A preservice teacher's experiences in an urban educative practicum. *Journal of Teacher Education, 50,* 209–219.

Burstein, N. D., & Cabello, B. (1989). Preparing teachers to work with culturally diverse students: A teacher education model. *Journal of Teacher Education, 40*(5), 9–16.

Cannella, G. S., & Reiff, J. C. (1994). Teacher preparation for diversity. *Equity and Excellence in Education, 27*(3), 28–33.

Canning, C. (1995). Getting from the outside in: Teaching Mexican Americans when you are an "Anglo." *The High School Journal, 78*(4), 195–205.

Clark, C., & Medina, C. (2000). How reading and writing literacy narratives affect preservice teachers' understandings of literacy, pedagogy, and multiculturalism. *Journal of Teacher Education, 51*, 63–76.

Clark, V. L. (1987). Teacher education at historically Black institutions in the aftermath of the Holmes/Carnegie reports. *Planning and Change, 18*(2), 74–89.

Cochran-Smith, M. (1991). Learning to teach against the grain. *Harvard Educational Review, 61*, 279–310.

Cochran-Smith, M. (1995). Uncertain allies: Understanding the boundaries of race and teaching. *Harvard Educational Review, 65*, 541–570.

Cochran-Smith, M. (2000). Blind vision: Unlearning racism in teacher education. *Harvard Educational Review, 70*, 157–190.

Cochran-Smith, M., & Lytle, S. L. (1992). Interrogating cultural diversity: Inquiry and action. *Journal of Teacher Education, 43*(2), 104–115.

Cooper, A., Beare, P., & Thorman, J. (1990). Preparing teachers for diversity: A comparison of student teaching experiences in Minnesota and South Texas. *Action in Teacher Education, 12*(3), 1–4.

Davis, K. A. (1995). Multicultural classrooms and cultural communities of teachers. *Teaching and Teacher Education, 11*, 553–563.

Dillard, C. B. (1994). Beyond supply and demand: Critical pedagogy, ethnicity, and empowerment in recruiting teachers of color. *Journal of Teacher Education, 45*(1), 9–17.

Florio-Ruane, S. (1994). The future teachers' autobiography club. *English Education, 26*(11), 52–56.

Fry, P. G., & McKinney, L. J. A. (1997). A qualitative study of preservice teachers' early field experiences in an urban, culturally different school. *Urban Education, 32*(2), 184–201.

Frykholm, J. A. (1997). A stacked deck: Addressing issues of equity with preservice students. *Equity and Excellence in Education, 30*(2), 50–58.

Fuller, M. L. (1992). Teacher education programs and increasing minority school populations: An educational mismatch? In C. A. Grant (Ed.), *Research and multicultural education: From the margins to the mainstream* (pp. 184–200). London: Falmer.

Fuller, M. L., & Ahler, J. (1987). Multicultural education and the monocultural student: A case study. *Action in Teacher Education, 9*(3), 33–40.

Gilbert, S. L. (1995). Perspectives of rural prospective teachers toward teaching in urban schools. *Urban Education, 30*(3), 290–305.

Goodwin, A. L. (1994). Making the transition from self to other: What do preservice teachers really think about multicultural education? *Journal of Teacher Education, 45*(2), 119–131.

Goodwin, A. L. (1997). Multicultural stories. *Urban Education, 32*(1), 117–145.

Grant, C. A., & Koskela, R. A. (1986). Education that is multicultural and the relationship between campus learning and field experiences. *Journal of Educational Research, 79*(4), 197–204.

Grottgau, B. J., & Nickolai-Mays, S. (1989). An empirical analysis of a multicultural education paradigm for preservice teachers. *Educational Research Quarterly, 13*(4), 27–33.

Guillaume, A., Zuniga-Hill, C., & Yee, I. (1995). Prospective teachers' use of diversity issues in a case study analysis. *Journal of Research and Development in Education, 28*(2), 69–78.

Guillaume, A., Zuniga-Hill, C., & Yee, I. (1998). What difference does preparation make? In M. E. Dilworth (Ed.), *Being responsive to cultural differences* (pp. 143–159). Thousand Oaks, CA: Corwin Press.

Guyton, E., Saxton, R., & Wesche, M. (1996). Experiences of diverse students in teacher education. *Teaching and Teacher Education, 12*, 643–652.

Haberman, M. (1993). Predicting the success of urban teachers (the Milwaukee trials). *Action in Teacher Education, 15*(3), 1–6.

Haberman, M. (1995). *Star teachers of children in poverty*. West Lafayette, IN: Kappa Delta Pi.

Haberman, M. (1996). Selecting and preparing culturally competent teachers for urban schools. In J. Sikula, T. J. Buttery, & E. Guyton (Eds.), *Handbook of research on teacher education* (2nd ed., pp. 747–760). New York: Macmillan.

Haberman, M., & Post, L. (1992). Does direct experience change education students' perceptions of low-income minority students? *Midwest Educational Researcher, 5*(2), 29–31.

Hennington, M. (1981). Effect of intensive multicultural non-sexist instruction on secondary student teachers. *Educational Research Quarterly, 6*(1), 65–75.

King, J. E. (1991). Dysconscious racism: Ideology, identity, and the miseducation of teachers. *Journal of Negro Education, 60*(2), 133–146.

Ladson-Billings, G. (1991). Beyond multicultural illiteracy. *Journal of Negro Education, 60*(2), 147–157.

Ladson-Billings, G. (1994). The dreamkeepers. San Francisco: Jossey-Bass.

Ladson-Billings, G. (1999). Preparing teachers for diversity. In L. Darling-Hammond & G. Sykes (Eds.), *Teaching as the learning profession* (pp. 86–123). San Francisco: Jossey-Bass.

Larke, P.J. (1990). Cultural diversity awareness inventory: Assessing the sensitivity of pre-service teachers. *Action in Teacher Education, 12*(3), 23–30.

Larkin, J. M., & Sleeter, C. E. (Eds.). (1995). *Developing multicultural teacher education curricula*. Albany: State University of New York Press.

Law, S., & Lane, D. (1987). Multicultural acceptance by teacher education students: A survey of attitudes. *Journal of Instructional Psychology, 14*(1), 3–9.

Lawrence, S. M. (1997). Beyond race awareness: White racial identity and multicultural teaching. *Journal of Teacher Education, 48*(2), 108–117.

Lawrence, S. M., & Bunche, T. (1996). Feeling and dealing: Teaching White students about racial privilege. *Teaching and Teacher Education, 12*, 531–542.

Lazar, A. (1998). Helping preservice teachers inquire about caregivers: A critical experience for field-based courses. *Action in Teacher Education, 19*(4), 14–28.

Littleton, D. M. (1998). Preparing professionals as teachers for the urban classroom: A university/school collaborative model. *Action in Teacher Education, 19*(4), 149–158.

Love, F. E., & Greer, R. G. (1995). Recruiting minorities into teaching. *Contemporary Education, 67*(1), 30–32.

Mahan, J. (1982). Native Americans as teacher trainers: Anatomy and outcomes of a cultural immersion project. *Journal of Educational Equity and Leadership, 2*(2), 100–110.

Mahan, J. M., & Stachowski, L. (1990). New horizons: Student teaching abroad to enrich understanding of diversity. *Action in Teacher Education, 12*(3), 13–21.

Mahan, J. M., & Stachowski, L. (1993–1994). Diverse, previously uncited sources of professional learning reported by student teachers serving in culturally different communities. *National Forum of Teacher Education Journal, 3*(1), 21–28.

Marsh, D. D. (1975). An evaluation of sixth cycle Teacher Corps graduates. *Journal of Teacher Education, 26*(2), 139–140.

Marsh, D. D. (1979). The classroom effectiveness of Teacher Corps graduates: A national assessment. *Journal of Classroom Interaction, 15*(1), 25–33.

Marshall, P. L. (1998). Toward developmental multicultural education: Case study of the issues exchange activity. *Journal of Teacher Education, 49*(1), 57–65.

Martin, R., & Koppelman, K. (1991). The impact of a human relations/multicultural education course on the attitudes of prospective teachers. *Journal of Intergroup Relations, 18*(1), 16–27.

Martin, R. J. (Ed.). (1995). *Practicing what we teach: Confronting diversity in teacher education*. Albany: State University of New York Press.

Marxen, C. E., & Rudney, G. L. (1999). An urban field experience for rural preservice teachers. *Teacher Education Quarterly, 26*, 61–74.

Mason, T. (1997). Urban field experiences and prospective teachers' attitudes toward inner-city schools. *Teacher Education Quarterly, 24*(3), 29–40.

McDiarmid, G. W. (1992). What to do about differences? A study of multicultural education for teacher trainees in the Los Angeles Unified School District. *Journal of Teacher Education, 43*(2), 83–93.

McIntyre, A. (1997). *Making meaning of Whiteness*. Albany: State University of New York Press.

Melnick, S., & Zeichner, K. (1996). The role of community-based field experiences in preparing teachers for cultural diversity. In K. Zeichner, S. Melnick, & M. L. Gomez

(Eds.), *Currents of reform in preservice teacher education* (pp. 176–196). New York: Teachers College Press.

Merryfield, M. M. (2000). Why aren't teachers being prepared to teach for diversity, equity, and global interconnectedness? A study of lived experiences in the making of multicultural and global education. *Teaching and Teacher Education, 16,* 429–443.

Montecinos, C. (1994). Teachers of color and multiculturalism. *Equity and Excellence in Education, 27*(3), 34–42.

Moule, J. (in press). Safe and growing out of the box: Immersion for social change. In W. Ayres, T. Quinn, P. Bradfield-Kreider, R. Serrano, & J. Romo (Eds.), *Working in the margins: Becoming a transformative educator.* New York: Teachers College Press.

Murtadha-Watts, K. (1998). Teacher education in urban school-based, multiagency collaboratives. *Urban Education, 32*(5), 616–631.

Narode, R., Rennie-Hill, L., & Peterson, K. (1994). Urban community study by preservice teachers. *Urban Education, 29*(1), 5–21.

National Center for Education Statistics. (1999). http://nces.ed.gov/pubs99/condition99/SupTables/supp-table-46-1.html

Noordhoff, K., & Kleinfeld, J. (1993). Preparing teachers for multicultural classrooms. *Teaching and Teacher Education, 9,* 27–39.

Olmedo, I. M. (1997). Challenging old assumptions: Preparing teachers for inner city schools. *Teaching and Teacher Education, 13,* 245–258.

Pailliotet, A. W. (1997). I'm really quiet: A case study of an Asian language minority preservice teacher's experience. *Teaching and Teacher Education, 13,* 675–690.

Pang, V. O., & Sablan, V. A. (1998). Teacher efficacy. In M. E. Dilworth (Ed.), *Being responsive to cultural differences* (pp. 39–58). Thousand Oaks, CA: Corwin Press.

Parker, L., & Hood, S. (1995). Minority students vs. majority faculty and administrators in teacher education: Perspectives on the clash of cultures. *Urban Review, 27*(2), 159–174.

Reed, D. F. (1993). Multicultural education for preservice students. *Action in Teacher Education, 15*(3), 27–34.

Reyes, P., Scribner, J. D., & Scribner, A. P. (Eds.). (1999). *Lessons from high-performing Hispanic schools.* New York: Teachers College Press.

Rios, F., & Montecinos, C. (1999). Advocating social justice and cultural affirmation. *Equity & Excellence in Education, 32*(3), 66–76.

Rios, F. A., McDaniel, J. E., & Stowell, L. P. (1998). Pursuing the possibilities of passion: The affective domain of multicultural education. In M. E. Dilworth (Ed.), *Being responsive to cultural differences* (pp. 160–181). Thousand Oaks, CA: Corwin Press.

Rodriguez, A. J. (1998). Strategies for counterresistance: Toward sociotransformative constructivism and learning to teach science for diversity and understanding. *Journal of Research in Science Teaching, 35,* 589–622.

Ross, D. D., & Smith, W. (1992). Understanding preservice teachers' perspectives on diversity. *Journal of Teacher Education, 43*(2), 94–103.

Schultz, E. L., Neyhart, K., & Reck, U.M. (1996). Swimming against the tide: A study of prospective teachers' attitudes regarding cultural diversity and urban teaching. *Western Journal of Black Studies, 20*(1), 1–7.

Shade, B. J., Boe, B. L., Garner, O., & New, C. A. (1998). The road to certification: A different way. *Teaching and Change, 5*(3–4), 261–275.

Sleeter, C. E. (1985). A need for research on preservice teacher education for mainstreaming and multicultural education. *Journal of Educational Equity and Leadership, 5,* 205–215.

Sleeter, C. E. (1989). Doing multicultural education across the grade levels and subject areas: A case study of Wisconsin. *Teaching and Teacher Education, 5,* 189–203.

Sleeter, C. E. (1996). *Multicultural education as social activism.* Albany: State University of New York Press.

Sleeter, C. E. (in press). Epistemological diversity in research on preservice teacher preparation for historically underserved children. In W. G. Secada (Ed.), *Review of research in education* (Vol. 6). Washington, DC: AERA.

Smith, G. P. (1998). Who shall have the moral courage to heal racism in America? *Multicultural Education, 5*(3), 4–10.

Smith, R., Moallem, M., & Sherrill, D. (1997). How preservice teachers think about cultural diversity. *Educational Foundations, 11*(2), 41–62.

Stachowski, L. L., & Mahan, J. M. (1998). Cross-cultural field placements: Student teachers learning from schools and communities. *Theory Into Practice, 37*(2), 155–162.

Stallings, J. A., & Quinn, L. F. (1991). Learning how to teach in the inner city. *Educational Leadership, 49*(3), 25–27.

Su, Z. (1996). Why teach; Profiles and entry perspectives of minority students as becoming teachers. *Journal of Research and Development in Education, 29*(3), 117–133.

Su, Z. (1997). Teaching as a profession and as a career: Minority candidates' perspectives. *Teaching and Teacher Education, 13*, 325–340.

Tellez, K. (1999). Mexican-American preservice teachers and the intransigency of the elementary school curriculum. *Teaching and Teacher Education, 15*, 555–570.

Torres-Karna, H., & Krustchinsky, R. (1998). The early entry program. *Teacher Education and Practice, 14*(1), 10–19.

Tran, M. T., & Young, R. L. (1994). Multicultural education courses and the student teacher: Eliminating stereotypical attitudes in our ethnically diverse classroom. *Journal of Teacher Education, 45*(3), 183–189.

U.S. Department of Education. (1997). *America's teachers: Profile of a profession, 1993–94.* Washington, DC: National Center for Education Statistics.

Valli, L. (1995). The dilemma of race: Learning to be color blind and color conscious. *Journal of Teacher Education, 46*(2), 120–129.

Vavrus, M. (1994). A critical analysis of multicultural education infusion during student teaching. *Action in Teacher Education, 16*(3), 45–57.

Weiner, L. (1990). Preparing the brightest for urban schools. *Urban Education, 25*(3), 258–273.

Weiner, L. (1993). *Preparing teachers for urban schools.* New York: Teachers College Press.

Wiggins, R. A., & Follo, E. J. (1999). Development of knowledge, attitudes, and commitment to teach diverse student populations. *Journal of Teacher Education, 50*(2), 94–105.

Xu, H. (2000). Preservice teachers integrate understandings of diversity into literacy instruction: An adaptation of the ABC's model. *Journal of Teacher Education, 51*, 135–142.

Yeo, F. L. (1997). *Inner-city schools, multiculturalism, and teacher education.* New York: Garland.

Yopp, R. H., Yopp, H. K., & Taylor, H. P. (1992). Profiles and viewpoints of minority candidates in a teacher diversity project. *Teacher Education Quarterly, 19*(3), 29–48.

# CHAPTER 11

# REVEALING THE DEEP MEANING OF CULTURE IN SCHOOL LEARNING (1995)
## Framing a new paradigm for teacher preparation
*Etta R. Hollins*

Beginning teachers need to be helped to become simultaneously students and architects of their own professional development. They need assistance to develop frameworks for thinking contextually and reflectively about their development; they need to become students of schooling and those aspects of institutional life, school practice, and interpersonal relations that are likely to enable or inhibit their development as professionals (Bullough, Knowles, & Crow, 1992).

Each culture is not only an integrated whole but has its own rules for learning. These are reinforced by different patterns of over-all organization. An important part of understanding a different culture is learning how things are organized and how one goes about learning them in that culture. This is not possible if one persists in using the learning models handed down in one's own culture (Hall, 1977).

In the book *Emerging as a Teacher*, Bullough and his colleagues (1992) challenge the orientation to teacher education as training. They present an alternative vision of teacher development that encourages beginning teachers to negotiate a role and identity for themselves as participants within a professional community. This type of preservice teacher development is facilitated by reflecting on life histories related to schooling, analyzing teaching metaphors, writing classroom ethnographies, and engaging in action research. Twenty-five preservice teachers are organized into cohorts, led by one or two faculty members. Members of the cohorts study together, observe each other's field-based experiences, and provide feedback to each other. Faculty members lead seminars where preservice teachers examine ideas and problems.

Induction programs for beginning teachers include seminars and support groups, reasonable teaching assignments that allow time for planning and studying one's own practice, mentoring by proficient teachers, participation in decision-making affecting the school-community, meaningful feedback and evaluation, and support and encouragement. University faculty are part of the induction process for beginning teachers.

The concept of teacher development as described by Bullough and his colleagues (1992) is insightful and seems to have significant potential for improving teacher education, although on the surface it appears more promising for those who will teach students like themselves. For example, reflecting on one's own life history related to school learning may not provide a reliable basis for understanding productive practices in culturally diverse classroom settings. Demographic changes in the nation's population make it increasingly unlikely that teachers and their students will share common cultural and experiential backgrounds.

Culture is the medium for cognition and learning for *all* human beings, not just ethnic minority and low income children in the United States. It is not enough to add a course on multicultural education or attempt to integrate multicultural concepts across the curriculum in traditional preservice teacher education programs. The purpose of this paper is to present a six-part model for preservice teacher education that embraces the centrality of culture in human existence. In this model preservice teachers strive to construct an operational definition of culture that facilitates their understanding of teaching and learning and supports the design of productive classroom instruction.

The proposed model has important aspects in common with that developed by Bullough and his colleagues (1992), including university faculty who work collaboratively among themselves and with preservice teachers to facilitate their mutual development, systematic inquiry employing an ethnographic approach, cohorts of preservice teachers who work collaboratively to support each other's development, and professional development that extends beyond preservice education. The proposed model is a six-part process of reflection and inquiry that includes (a) objectifying culture, (b) personalizing culture, (c) inquiring about students' cultures and communities, (d) applying knowledge about culture to teaching, (e) formulating theory linking culture and school learning, and (f) transforming professional practice to better meet the needs of students from different cultural and experiential backgrounds. All aspects of the model are interrelated and interdependent. Each of the six parts that comprise the teacher education inquiry-oriented program is described next.

## Objectifying culture

It is important for classroom teachers to construct an operational definition of culture that makes explicit its centrality and systemic nature in the realities of human existence. This includes interpretative and explanatory functions that form culturally framed perceptions of the world. The definition of culture should include its function in human survival, societal arrangements, and in human development that is intellectual, psychological, social, and spiritual. The definition of culture should reveal the interconnectedness of its identifiable aspects and describe its dynamic quality in responding to fundamental changes in life conditions and circumstances.

Constructing a working definition of culture is not intended as a simple task to be completed easily. It is a dynamic process. Early definitions of culture may be transformed as preservice teachers examine culture in the United States, their own culture, and the culture of their students. New insights may be acquired in the process of rethinking classroom instruction and reframing curriculum for students from different cultural and experiential backgrounds.

## Personalizing culture

Personalizing culture refers to the act of developing a knowledge of one's own culture that allows for the type of deep introspection that reveals its centrality in one's own life. This includes acquiring an understanding of the longitudinal influence of early socialization, making explicit one's own personal and group identity, identifying personally held perceptions of the world that are culturally framed, and describing participation in culturally sanctioned practices and values.

Culture is such an integral part of human existence that it becomes the invisible script that directs our personal lives. This invisible script can encapsulate and blind us to the factors that make us simultaneously unique from and similar of those from other cultures. Cultural encapsulation can lead to a view of the world as an extension of self and of those who are culturally different as aberrant, quaint, or exotic. Teachers who hold this view are likely to base classroom practices on their own culture and encourage students to conform to their perceptions and values. These teachers may be more successful with students with whom they share a common cultural and experiential background than with those whose culture and experiences are different.

Personalizing culture is an important part of preservice teacher education because it has the potential to decrease cultural encapsulation by bringing subconscious aspects of culture to the conscious level for examination. Preservice teachers can become aware of those factors that distinguish their culture from that of their students while maintaining a positive regard for the commonality of functions served. This awareness can contribute to improving cross cultural communication and understanding and facilitate teaching and learning.

Examples of heuristics that can be employed to help preservice teachers personalize culture are: (1) The use of the history and origin of a particular family (sur)name and a study of the way of life of those to whom it is ascribed (Hollins, 1990) and (2) The use of Helms' (1990) stages of racial identity to examine the value of "race" in the American society. The careful examination of a particular line in one's own family heritage reveals the continuities and discontinuities of cultural transmission while illuminating the centrality of culture in shaping one's own life. Studying Helms' stages of racial identity encourages deep analysis and introspection into the influence, transmission, and maintenance of specific cultural values. Both of these heuristics support personalizing culture and constructing an increasingly complex operational definition.

## Learning about students' cultures

An approach to learning about students' cultures and experiential backgrounds in a way that informs classroom practices involves reflective-interpretive-inquiry (RIQ) which relies on ethnographic techniques for data gathering and analysis. This is a process of systematic inquiry and analysis that helps preservice teachers compile and examine information that supports understanding the relationship among culture, cognition, and school learning (Hollins, in press). RIQ involves seven categories of inquiry:

1  *teacher belief about students* reflects personal beliefs about students;
2  *teacher belief about instruction* reveals biases in beliefs about instruction that favor specific cultural perceptions, practices, and values;
3  *the social context of instruction* facilitates the examination of similarities and differences between social interaction in the classroom and in the students' home culture;
4  *students' experiential background* indicates significant experiences students have had within and outside of school;
5  *ethnic and cultural group* identifies practices and values characteristic of the students' cultures;
6  *the local community* examines the political and social structure within the students' local community; and

7   *societal context* reflects a particular culture in relationship to the larger societal context.

Preservice teachers may be expected to study one cultural group extensively, rather than dealing superficially with several that are different. Such extensive study of one cultural group supports the construction of a working definition of culture that promotes the formulation of a theory of the relationship among culture, cognition, and school learning. Working collaboratively with those studying other cultural groups broadens the experience.

## Applying knowledge about culture to teaching

Preservice teachers can use their emerging definition of culture and the data gathered using the RIQ approach to frame curriculum content and to design learning experiences for their students.

### Reframing the curriculum

Among the purposes served by the school curriculum are the transmission of culturally valued knowledge and the perpetuation of cultural values and practices. In the United States this means that public schools present a curriculum that serves the purpose of maintaining and perpetuating European American culture. At this point many preservice teachers will recognize that such a curriculum is inherently more meaningful to European American students than to those who identify themselves with other ethnic and cultural groups. This creates dissonance in school learning for some students. Some students will be able to tolerate this dissonance and do well; others will fail. Preservice teachers need to learn to reframe the curriculum to minimize dissonance.

One possibility for decreasing dissonance is to make the curriculum simultaneously particularistic and inclusive. That is, the curriculum can be designed to address the needs of particular cultures while addressing the need for national unity (Spears-Bunton, 1990). The particularistic aspect of the curriculum provides students from culturally diverse backgrounds (a) a sense of personal and group identity, (b) a historical perspective that supports a sense of intergenerational continuity and pride in the accomplishments of their ancestors, (c) a contemporary view of their ethnic or cultural group's position within the society and the world that presents a positive reality, (d) a vision of the future that encourages hopefulness based on personal commitment to self-improvement, self-determination, and cooperation and collaboration with others, and (e) the academic and intellectual preparation necessary for full and active participation within the society. Preservice teachers can use the insights they have acquired in the study of specific cultural groups to identify ways to reframe the curriculum to meet the particularistic needs of their students.

The inclusive aspect of the school curriculum promotes the understandings and knowledge that in turn support national unity, improving the quality of life for all human beings, and maintaining and improving the condition of the natural environment. Preservice teachers will be able to identify parts of the existing curriculum that are inclusive and those that need to be adjusted.

## Redesigning instruction

Classroom instruction is rarely discussed as a contributing factor in the disproportionately high rate of school failure found among some ethnic minority and low income students. The fact that there are exemplary schools and individual classroom teachers who foster uncharacteristically high academic outcomes for these youngsters seems to have little influence on attributions of blame proposed by many educators and researchers. Most explanations for school failure blame factors beyond the control of educators. Two positive exceptions are the theory of contextual interaction (Cortes, 1986) and the theory of cultural mismatch (Au, 1992; Au & Mason, 1981; Hollins, 1982). Preservice teachers need to become familiar with these theories as part of the process of constructing a working definition of culture and to facilitate their own formulation of a theory that will guide the planning of instruction for culturally diverse students.

The theory of contextual interaction (Cortes, 1986) posits academic achievement as a function of the dynamic interaction among the societal context, and the school context and within the school among educational input factors, instructional elements, and student qualities. The proponents of the contextual interaction model do not propose a particular intervention, but rather suggest that a combination of actions is more likely to have an effect. This could mean changing the entire schooling process along with specific aspects of the home-community relationship.

The theory of cultural mismatch, also referred to as the theory of cultural congruence (Au, 1980; Au & Mason, 1981; Hollins, 1982), posits that academic achievement is influenced by the relationship between school practices and the practices and values found in the students' home culture. The proponents of this theory contend that school practices are culturally derived and favor students from a particular cultural group. Successful interventions that improve the academic achievement of groups traditionally underserved in the nation's public schools focus on (a) legitimizing the knowledge the children bring to school (McCarty, Lynch, Wallace, & Benally, 1991; Moll, 1986, 1988); (b) making meaningful connections between school learning and cultural knowledge or knowledge acquired outside of school (McCarty et al., 1991; Moll, 1986); (c) creating a hybrid culture in school that is congruent with many of the practices and values children bring from the home and peer culture (Au & Mason, 1981); (d) creating a community of learners where collaboration rather than competition is the norm (Hollins, 1982; Moll, 1986, 1988); (e) balancing the rights of students and teachers (Au & Mason, 1981); and (f) providing curriculum content and pedagogical practices that support a consistent and coherent core of identity and intergenerational continuity with the past (McCarty et al., 1991; Spears-Bunton, 1990). Research studies supporting the theory of cultural mismatch include those related to Native Hawaiian students reported by Au (1992), Au and Mason (1981); Native American students reported by Philips (1983) and McCarty and colleagues (1991); Mexican American students reported by Moll (1986, 1988); and African American students reported by Moses, Kamii, Swap, and Howard (1989).

Preservice teachers need to formulate theory that will explain the relationship among culture, cognition, and school learning. The primary goal of such theorizing is to explain the conditions and practices that generate productive instruction in culturally diverse classroom settings. Preservice teachers can begin by examining research studies and making connections or by doing critiques of several existing theories. A summary of the theory of cultural mediation in instruction is presented here as an example of one that might be analyzed by preservice teachers. For a more detailed discussion of this theory, see Hollins (in press).

## The theory of cultural mediation in instruction

The premise of the theory of cultural mediation in instruction (Hollins, in press) is that school learning is facilitated or impeded by the proximal relationship between the school culture and the students' home culture. Similarities between the school culture and the home culture facilitate communication and learning. Differences between the school culture and home culture contribute to interference in communication and learning. This is particularly true in situations where teachers and their students are from different cultural and experiential backgrounds and do not share the same meanings even when using the same language. Based on the theory of cultural mediation, classroom instruction can be divided into three categories that include cultural meditation, cultural accommodation, and cultural immersion.

### Culturally mediated instruction

Cultural mediation in instruction is characterized by the use of culturally mediated cognition, culturally appropriate social situations for learning, and culturally valued knowledge in curriculum content. Culturally mediated cognition (Hollins, in press) refers to approaches to instruction that make use of the ways of knowing, understanding, representing, and expressing typically employed in a particular culture. For example, Hall (1989) describes different ways of knowing and understanding found among high-context and low-context cultures. High-context cultures are characterized by a holistic approach to information processing in which meaning is "extracted" from the environment and the situation. Low-context cultures use a linear, sequential approach to information processing in which meaning is "constructed." Culturally mediated cognition requires knowing and using these differences in classroom instruction.

Culturally appropriate social situations for learning refer to relationships among students and between teachers and students during classroom instruction that are consistent with cultural values and practices. For example, McCarty, et al. (1991) found that when instruction is consistent with "natural learning-teaching interactions outside the classroom" and articulate a "Navajo philosophy of knowledge," Navajo students traditionally described as nonanalytical and nonverbal engage in verbal interaction and inductive/analytical reasoning with an inquiry-based curriculum. Thus, social arrangements are important aspects of productive instruction.

Culturally valued knowledge in curriculum content refers to the inclusion of knowledge valued within the students' culture outside of school. Wigginton (1977) made use of culturally valued knowledge in the Foxfire Project, where the students documented the oral history of their own community for publication. Another example is Rison's (1990) application of cultural content such as that included in rap music and other cultural elements to raise the achievement levels of African American students in mathematics in several school districts in Texas. Cultural mediation can be divided into two subcategories, authentic cultural mediation and intermittent cultural mediation.

## Authentic cultural mediation

In authentic cultural mediation (Hollins, in press), schooling practices are an extension of the enculturation process found in the child's home and local community. The curriculum content is based on knowledge valued by the local community and reflects the history and culture of its people. The teachers and their students share a common cultural and experiential background, making it easy to employ culturally mediated cognition and culturally appropriate social situations for learning. Academic performance is enhanced in situations employing authentic cultural mediation. In public schools as they presently exist, authentic cultural mediation in instruction is available for some groups of European American students, but rarely for ethnic minority and low income students.

## Intermittent cultural mediation

In intermittent cultural mediation the teachers and their students share a common culture, but find themselves in a situation where the constraints of the schooling process prevent routine use of culturally appropriate social situations in learning and knowledge valued by their cultural group. Also, the history and culture of these teachers and their students are not well represented in the curriculum content. In intermittent cultural mediation, teachers have a full repertoire of cultural understandings and are able to support culturally mediated cognition as necessary to facilitate learning.

Some ethnic minority teachers are able to use intermittent cultural mediation with their students, while others have lost this ability due to the persistent acculturation process in public schools and the nation's colleges and universities. Teacher preparation programs offer little, if any, support for ethnic minority teachers to learn how to apply their cultural knowledge in teaching students who share their cultural background (Zeichner, 1992). If professionally prepared teachers who are mature learners are unable to bridge the gap between the school culture and the home culture for their students, it is unrealistic to expect the students who have little academic experience or preparation to do so.

## Cultural accommodation

Cultural accommodation appears to be the most accessible approach to supporting academic success in cases where the teacher and students do not share a common cultural or experiential background. In cultural accommodation selected aspects of the students' home culture are used to facilitate learning (Au, 1980; Philips, 1983).

Cultural accommodation most often employs culturally appropriate social situations for learning and culturally valued knowledge in curriculum content. For example, Au (1985) describes the use of a communicative practice from Native Hawaiian children's home culture called "talk story" to facilitate reading comprehension. Philips (1983) describes the academic benefits of employing participant structures that reflect social interaction patterns in Warm Springs Indian children's home culture in the classroom. Hollins (1982) describes aspects of African American culture employed by Marva Collins in the Chicago Westside Preparatory School. Similarly, preservice teachers can collaborate in identifying other cultural practices that can be used to facilitate school learning.

## Cultural immersion

The practice of cultural immersion involves repeated exposure of students to curriculum content, instructional approaches, and a context based on a culture other than their own (Hollins, in press). This does not involve the use of culturally mediated cognition, culturally appropriate social situations for learning, or culturally valued curriculum content. Within the United States those students who are not part of the European American culture from which schooling practices are drawn are often referred to as "culturally deprived" or "disadvantaged." Many of these students do not experience the same degree of success in school as European American children whose culture is practiced in the schools.

Teachers frequently attempt to re-socialize students from different cultural backgrounds to the culture of the school in order to increase the productivity of instruction. Many school districts have policies and programs designed to re-socialize or remediate students who are deemed to be "at-risk" for academic failure. Most of these programs are doomed to failure because they do not bridge the gap between what is taught in school and what the student already knows or has learned outside of school. For example, children enter school with cognitive schema in place. The most productive instruction links the content presented in school to the cognitive schema students have already developed (Nolan and Francis, 1992). Most elementary and secondary students are limited in their ability to act independently in linking new knowledge with what they already know. This function is best served by well-prepared professional educators.

The data gathered by preservice teachers can be used to challenge or test this or any other theory, to build upon and expand existing theories, or to formulate new theories. The process of formulating theory is intended to help preservice teachers develop a basis for instructional planning and decision-making and a mode of reflection and inquiry that will systematically improve professional practice.

## Transforming professional practice

Beginning teachers need a transition or induction period in which they are provided support from the more accomplished members of the professional community and are allowed adequate time for reflection and inquiry (Zimpher & Grossman, 1992). This induction period should allow beginning teachers to learn how to fully participate in all aspects of the professional community. The insights gained in the preservice program through study, inquiry, and reflection can provide important input for the more experienced teachers. This input may represent the beginning teacher's initial contribution to improving the larger community of professional practice.

Teacher development is a continuous process (Reynolds, 1992). Beginning teachers should be supported in designing a professional development plan that meets their particular needs. The types of experiences that enhance professional growth and enable teachers to contribute to improving the community of professional practice include studying one's own practice, studying expert practice, participating in teacher support groups and university sponsored courses and seminars, attending professional conferences, and being actively involved in research and scholarship.

## Summary

In summary, a model is outlined that frames a new paradigm for teacher preparation that facilitates the comprehension of the deep meaning of culture in school learning. Preservice teachers move in cohorts through a six-part process of inter-related program components employing strategies of introspection and reflective-interpretive-inquiry. During this process a complex operational definition of culture is constructed that ultimately reveals aspects of the relationship among culture, cognition, and school learning. The operational definition of culture and the data collected by preservice teachers are used to formulate a theory explaining the relationship between culture and school learning. This theory guides reframing the curriculum, redesigning classroom instruction, and creating a more responsive social context for school learning for students from different cultural and experiential backgrounds.

## References

Au, K. H. (1980). Participation structures in a reading lesson with Hawaiian children: Analysis of a culturally appropriate instructional event. *Anthropology and Education, 11*(2), 91–115.

Au, K. H. (1992). Constructing the theme of a story. *Language Arts, 69*, 106–111.

Au, K. H., & Kawakami, A. J. (1985). Research currents: Talk story and learning to read. *Language Arts, 62*(4), 406–411.

Au, K. H., & Mason, J. M. (1981). Social organizational factors in learning to read: The balance of rights hypothesis. *Reading Research Quarterly, 17*(1), 115–152.

Bullough, R. V., Knowles, J. Jr., & Crow, N. (1992). *Emerging as a teacher.* Baltimore, MD: Routledge Publishing Company.

Cortes, C. E. (1986). The education of language minority students: A contextual interaction model. In *Beyond language: Social and cultural factors in schooling language minority students* (pp. 3–34). Sacramento, CA: Bilingual Education Office, California State Department of Education.

Hall, E. T. (1977). *Beyond culture.* Garden City, NY: Doubleday Publishing Company.

Hall, E. T. (1989). Unstated features of the cultural context of learning. *The Educational Forum, 54*(1), 21–34.

Helms, J. E. (1990). *Black and White racial identity: Theory, research, and practice.* New York: Greenwood Press.

Hollins, E. R. (1982). The Marva Collins story revisited. *Journal of Teacher Education, 32*(1), 37–40.

Hollins, E. R. (1990). Debunking the myth of a monolithic white American culture; or, Moving toward cultural inclusion. *American Behavioral Scientist, 34*(2), 201–209.

Hollins, E. R. (in press). *Culture in school learning.* New York: Erlbaum Publishers.

McCarty, T. L., Lynch, R. H., Wallace, S., & Benally, A. (1991). Classroom inquiry and Navajo learning styles: A call for reassessment. *Anthropology and Education Quarterly, 22*, 42–59.

Moll, L. C. (1986). Writing as communication: Creating strategic learning environments for students. *Theory into Practice, 25*(2), 102–108.

Moll, L. C. (1988). Some key issues in teaching Latino students. *Language Arts, 65*(5), 465–472.

Moses, R. P., Kamii, M., Swap, S. M., & Howard, J. (1989). The Algebra Project: Organizing in the Spirit of Ella. *Harvard Educational Review, 59*(4), 423–443.

Nolan, J., & Francis, P. (1992). In C. D. Glickman (Ed.), *Supervision in transition* (pp. 44–60). Arlington, VA: Association for Supervision and Curriculum Development.

Philips, S. U. (1983). *The invisible culture: Communication in classroom and community on the Warm Springs Indian Reservation.* New York: Longman.

Reynolds, A. (1992). What is competent beginning teaching? A review of the literature. *Review of Educational Research, 62*(1), 1–35.

Rison, A. (1990). *How to teach Black children*. Austin, TX: Sunbelt Theatre Productions.
Spears-Bunton, L. A. (1990). Welcome to my house: African American and European American students' responses to Virginia Hamilton's House of Dies Drear. *Journal of Negro Education, 59*(4), 566–576.
Wigginton, E. (1977). The foxfire approach: It can work for you. *Media and Methods*, 49–52.
Zeichner, K. M. (1992). *Educating teachers for cultural diversity*. East Lansing, MI: National Center for Research on Teacher Learning, Michigan State University.
Zimpher, N. L., & Grossman, J. E. (1992). Collegial support by teacher mentors and peer consultants. In C. D. Glickman (Ed.), *Supervision in transition* (pp. 141–154). Arlington, VA: Association for Supervision and Curriculum Development.

# CHAPTER 12

# MAKING THE RHETORIC REAL (1996)
## UCLA's struggle for teacher education that is multicultural and social reconstructionist
### Jeannie Oakes

On a Thursday afternoon in April of 1992, the faculty of the Graduate School of Education and Information Studies at UCLA sat squabbling in its usual fashion over its agenda of bureaucratic minutiae at its regular faculty meeting. Because our building—historic Moore Hall at the center of the campus—was undergoing seismic renovation, faculty had relocated to the 17th floor of a high rise at the busy commercial intersection of Westwood and Wilshire Boulevards. A spacious corner office, formerly occupied by a mega-corporation CEO, now enhanced faculty meetings with its spectacular, sweeping view of the city. As we met that Thursday, someone noticed the first fire—a small bright spot to the south and east—and then another, and another, and another. We sat stunned as we watched our city's tenuous social contract go up in smoke just hours after the jury delivered its not guilty verdict in the Rodney King beating trial. Then we rushed to our cars and crawled slowly thorough the traffic toward our homes that were mostly far from the trouble.

I will not claim that we changed dramatically after that Thursday, but some things have not been quite the same. It has not been so comfortable since then for some of us to look past our city as we focus our educational research nationally and internationally. It has not been so easy to claim that our research and teaching interests rightfully claim a larger purview than schooling in our hometown. Some of us started feeling a bit foolish as we boarded planes for Washington, New York, Chicago, and elsewhere to struggle with issues of race, poverty, and inequality in schools. Some of us began to consider how we might bring our work closer to home.

In a very real sense, then, Center X (Where Research and Practice Intersect for Urban School Professionals) at UCLA actually began on that Thursday afternoon in April 1992. But, of course, we didn't know it then. And it wasn't until three years later in the Fall of 1995 that we welcomed our first cohort of teacher candidates who had signed on to our teacher education program expressly committed to social and educational justice for low-income children of color in urban Los Angeles.

Our discussions about what we might do in the months following the Rodney King verdict were premised on our understanding that, typically, the structures, cultures, and pedagogies practiced in schools (and rarely challenged or disrupted by university research and teaching) work to exacerbate the inequalities in the rest of our society. With seemingly neutral, sometimes even scientific, technology and language, schools compound the disadvantages of children who have less outside of school. Many with meager economic prospects, often racially diverse and bilingual and limited-English proficient students, are judged to be disabled, "not ready," lacking social capital, or, most pernicious, simply not as intelligent as their more advantaged peers. The upshot is that even though it's disappointing when children don't achieve, it's not really unexpected in urban schools. Everybody says that "all children can learn," but few really believe it. Too often, the one institution that low-income, racially diverse, bilingual and limited-English proficient, and immigrant families count on for access to a better life simply helps perpetuate the cycle of discrimination, poverty, and hopelessness.

This paper skips over the three years of reading, thinking, worrying, arguing, hestitating, persuading, waiting, and hoping that led to Center X—our effort to reshape UCLA's professional education programs in ways that could acknowledge, and perhaps even confront these conditions. Suffice it to say that we gobbled up Jim Banks, Jim Cummins, Antonia Darder, Carl Grant, Gloria Ladson-Billings, Marlin Cochran-Smith, Christie Sleeter, and Ken Zeichner to get a handle on linking teacher education, social justice, and multiculturalism. We wrestled with the ideas of Henry Giroux, bell hooks, and our own Peter McLaren about helping teachers become critical pedagogues. We sought counsel from Luis Moll, Roland Tharpe, and our own Ron Gallimore and Kris Gutierrez to better understand the implications of Vygotskyian sociocultural learning theory for diverse Los Angeles schools. We looked to Nel Noddings, our own Lynn Beck, and to the Macdonalds' work to help us struggle with helping teachers become caring advocates for students without reducing them to dependent clients. We kept in mind my tracking work as we thought about the power of structures to shape expectations and limit opportunities. And we considered the ideas of Sol Alinsky and his intellectual/activist descendants regarding the power of person-to-person organizing. We re-read John Dewey. Suffice it to say that we wrote lots of proposals and attended lots of meetings.

What I'd like to do here is to describe what we're actually trying to do in teacher education at UCLA to make our rhetoric about social justice and multiculturalism real.

## Center X: The power of many

Center X brings together under one mission and organizational umbrella a number of programs that were formerly quite separate, and it has dramatically changed the nature of those activities. Center X is UCLA's Teacher Education Program (formerly the Teacher Education Laboratory) that grants California CLAD/BCLAD (Cross-cultural Language and Academic Development/Bilingual Cross-cultural Language and Academic Development) elementary and secondary teaching credentials and M.Ed. degrees. It is also six of the state-sponsored California Subject Matter Projects, the UCLA Principals' Center, and other professional development projects for practicing educators. It is also the Graduate School of Education's Ed.D. program in Education Leadership.

We thought that by building on the synergy of these enterprises and developing long-term, positive, interdependent connections with schools and districts, Center X could integrate preservice teacher education, teachers' induction into the profession, and the continuing development of seasoned professionals. We also thought that we could blend our programs for professional educators with the training of our aspiring Ph.D.s. Finally, we thought that by bringing all of these people together, Center X might also itself be able to become what we want schools to be—caring, ethical, racially harmonious, and socially just.

Actually, we're a pretty motley crew. Some of us are faculty with programs of research and teaching to be attended to—both junior and senior ladder faculty, as well as visiting faculty and postdoctoral scholars. Some of us are what we call "clinical faculty" (although only the medical school is allowed to use this job title officially) with doctorates who teach courses in the M.Ed. program for our teacher candidates, provide non-degree, professional development activities for practicing educators, and administer our credentialling process. Some of us are practicing K-12 professionals who lead Center X programs and courses on campus or in schools and district offices. Some of us are graduate students hoping to use UCLA educations to launch careers as teacher educators, researchers, or educational leaders. Some of us are teacher candidates with ambitious goals for ourselves in urban schools and high hopes that the Center X teacher educators won't lead us into waters deeper than we can swim. We are Anglo, African American, Latino, and Asian. Some of us speak only English, but many of us also speak Spanish, Korean, Vietnamese, Tagalog, Armenian, and other languages. We are old, young, and in-between; male and female; gay and straight; and who knows what else.

## Some non-negotiables

We knew that many forces would conspire against our ambitious social and educational agenda. Not the least, we'd be pressed to be reasonable, to use our common sense, to be a bit less idealistic. We worried that unless we established a solid principled grounding for our new Center, we'd soon find ourselves on the slippery slopes of efficiency and expediency. So, when we were ready to go public with Center X, we began with a set of "non-negotiables"—things about which we would not compromise. These are our core values, and these would be the measuring stick by which we would measure our progress:

- **Embody a social justice agenda**—The racial, cultural, and linguistic diversity of our Los Angeles community is its strongest asset, and we will act on this by constructing extraordinarily high quality education for all children and particularly for low-income, children of color in Los Angeles' schools. We seek to turn policymakers' attention, educational resources, and teachers' talents toward those in our city who have the least outside of school.
- **Treat professional education "cradle-to-grave"**—Education is a seamless process that connects efforts to attract young people into teaching, with learning experiences for teacher candidates, with learning experiences for novice teachers, and with learning experiences for seasoned professionals. Further, it is a process that is focused on serving students—of all ages—and their families and communities.
- **Collaborate across institutions and communities**—Collaborative efforts provide the best means to address the entire ecology of settings and institutions that contribute to children's education. Center X is committed to develop and sustain long-term, positive, interdependent connections and equal status partnerships among K-12 schools and community colleges, UCLA, and the diverse communities of Los Angeles.
- **Focus simultaneously on professional education, school reform, and reinventing the university's role in K-12 schooling**—Center X must help new and experienced educators acquire the knowledge and skills necessary for social justice and educational quality in urban schools. At the

same time, the Center's work must press schools to develop cultures that encourage and support putting new knowledge and skills into practice. Moreover, UCLA itself will need to change as it crafts new roles and responsibilities for the university in these collaborative research/practice efforts. We all have much to learn.

- **Blend research and practice**—Center X will combine opportunities to acquire new knowledge and skills, with research aimed at creating new knowledge, and the practical application of that knowledge in schools. UCLA scholars must formulate and conduct their research and teaching in ways that reflect the realities of children, educators, schools, and communities. School professionals, in turn, must guide their practice by a process of critical inquiry, reflection, and social responsibility.
- **Bring together educators' and students' needs for depth of content knowledge, powerful pedagogies, and school cultures that enable serious and sustained engagement in teaching and learning**—We view these three domains of teaching and learning as inextricably connected. Our core work is to better understand this complex relationship and promote reform efforts that approach all three domains.
- **Remain self-renewing**—View change and problems as "normal" conditions that require a flexible, responsive, nonstatic, learning organization. Center X must resist efforts to shape its activities into a traditional control-oriented, bureaucratic organization. Rather it must remain a commitment-driven entity whose structures organize people around important problems, interests, and goals.

## A new culture of teacher education

Once we'd gone public with these principles, we decided that we'd better get a bit more concrete. We were going to educate our novice teachers in schools where most students are poor and non-white. We were going to send them into neighborhoods they may have only seen before on the nightly news. We knew that no matter how committed to our ideals they might be, we knew that being committed wouldn't be enough. We needed to develop and deliver a curriculum that would help them withstand their own and their families' anxieties—as well as their friends' puzzlement—about what they'd chosen to do. We needed to deliver on our promise to educate teachers who could transform urban schools and classrooms. To do this, we'd need to translate our "non-negotiable" principles into a pretty specific set of knowledge, skills, and experiences that would allow our novice teachers to see themselves as a grounded and prepared, as well as committed. Following Henry Giroux's notion of a "transformative intellectual" we wanted them to have "the courage to take risks, to look into the future, and to imagine a world that could be as opposed to simply what is" (Giroux, 1988, 215). But we also wanted them to have the capacity and confidence to act on what they could imagine.

How have we attempted to translate our principles into a teacher education program? We identified four interrelated roles that we thought students should learn to be transformative and efficacious urban teachers, and everything we do with our students—our curriculum—aims at their developing these roles. These are what we help Center X teachers become:

- Caring Advocates for All Students

- Reflective, Inquiry-Based Practitioners
- Community Builders
- Generative Change Agents

## *Caring advocates*

We knew we'd get no argument from our novice teachers when we shared James B. Macdonald and Susan Colberg Macdonald's view of the importance of educators having a fundamental commitment to a just and caring society: "Human life is experienced in the way we live our everyday lives, our relationships to ourselves and others, our sense of personal belonging in society and the cosmos. We believe this demands a human condition characterized by freedom, justice, equality, and love" (Macdonald & Macdonald, 1988, 480). But we also expected that our mostly-middle class novices would have had little experience with acting on such sentiments, particularly when they were confronted with the staggering increases in the numbers of Los Angeles children growing up in the physically, medically, and emotionally hazardous conditions that increasingly prevail in our inner city.

Frankly, we were worried that, like so many bright, idealistic, middle-class young people, they would approach this ethic of care with a missionary-like zeal for rescuing people who they saw as unable to rescue themselves. We had seen in our research too many well intentioned educators who, because they felt such sympathy, tried to make schools safe and comfortable places that didn't add to their disadvantaged students' burdens. As such, they expected very little of them.

Rather, we wanted to foster an ethic in which care would be expressed as high expectations, confidence in students' capacity, and support for persistence and high achievement. This meant, we believed, that our novice teachers must rethink such fundamental notions as "intelligence," "motivation," "a value for education," "parent support" and "sense of responsibility," that have acquired common-sense meanings that work against those who aren't white and middle class (or, at least, don't act like they are).

We also believed that caring advocacy meant that our teachers needed to learn to use the racial, cultural, and linguistic diversity of their students as a resource for constructing rich and meaningful learning opportunities. We also decided that that new teachers must have opportunities to approach learning, teaching, and curriculum from constructivist perspectives that reflect the diversity of our society in all its aspects: gender; race; cultural, linguistic and ethnic identification; multiple intelligences; socio-economic status; family structure, and others. We also decided that they needed to learn about socio-cultural approaches that could promote literacy and make content knowledge accessible to students from a range of ethnic and linguistic backgrounds, particularly those who have limited English proficiency. In addition, we thought they should connect with emerging research in the area of cultural congruence and culturally democratic pedagogy that suggests the importance of connecting students' school experiences to their home culture, in effect, making them congruent. Furthermore, this ethic of caring meant that all our teachers must learn bilingual and primary language instructional strategies and have a great deal of practice using them. It also meant that they needed to become familiar with the social supports that are available in Los Angeles communities, and they must learn how to help children and their families—not out of kindness alone, but because such supports enable learning and persistence.

## Teachers as reflective, inquiry-based practitioners

We decided that we needed to enable our novice teachers to be questioning and reflective about everything—even the wisdom we thought we were imparting. It would do little good, we decided, if they simply "learned" a new set of things that we thought were important in place of the old convention. In particular we wanted them to become ever mindful of how our culture and institutions seem to easily distort well-meant ideas and actions in ways that perpetuate discrimination and inequality. During their time at Center X, we decided, the teacher candidates must engage in a ongoing process of reflection and critical inquiry that connects theory, current research findings, scholarship, and practice. So, we decided to make inquiry our own primary pedagogical tool—and, importantly, to model teachers-as-inquirers with regular "inquiry sessions" of faculty and staff where no "business" could be conducted, only a serious consideration of the meaning of our enterprise, and a careful scrutiny of the beliefs, values, and assumptions that inform our decisions.

We also decided that reflective Center X teachers must remain actively engaged in the disciplines they teach, as well as learn about teaching. Writing teachers should write, history teachers should conduct original inquiries into historical topics, science teachers should do scientific investigations, and art teachers should perform. That way, they could learn how their disciplines create knowledge, have opportunities to reflect on the equitable dimensions of that knowledge, and more effectively understand the school and classroom contexts that permit teachers and learners to engage in creating discipline-based knowledge.

We charged the Directors and Teacher Leaders of the UCLA Subject Matter professional development projects with this task, and they have completely reconstructed our "methods" courses, and engage the novices in professional development in the content areas with the Los Angeles' basin's most talented teachers.

## Teachers as community builders

We knew that our teachers' knowledge, skills, and dispositions must not only extend beyond the classroom walls, but also beyond the schoolyard. Children grow up in an ecology of institutions and activities that educate—for good or for ill. **While schools may be the "official" and most formal of these educational agents, they are not necessarily the most powerful or influential.** Particularly in low-income, racially, culturally, and linguistically diverse neighborhoods, the influence of teachers and schools may pale in the face of countervailing informal educational agents, such as alienated peer groups and discouraged families. Consequently, we decided that Center X novice teachers must engage with the communities they serve, not so much to "educate" parents in the conventional meaning of the term, but rather to connect what children do in school to their experiences in the community. By engaging children and their families in finding and solving real problems that matter to them outside of school, we thought that they could help make schoolwork less abstract and detached (and thereby more likely to be learned) and that they could enhance the power and well-being of the larger educational ecology for children.

Furthermore, we wanted our teachers to know how to include parents and other community members in adult-centered inquiry into school practice and beliefs. We wanted them to learn that community members can inform discussion around curricular and extra-curricular issues and in this process develop more democratic relationships with the professional staff. Working with a range of community resources, such as public health, social welfare, and psychological support systems, we wanted our teachers to support programs that deal more comprehensively with the range of issues facing low-income, urban children, and schools. Toward this end, we knew that Center X teacher candidates must participate in community projects and connect with neighborhood organizations, head start programs, and engage parents in inquiry and discussion about their children's schooling. Some have mounted Social Justice Community Nights in their school communities.

## Teachers as generative change agents

Finally, we realized that even exceedingly well prepared teachers are not likely, through classroom practice alone, to counteract the impact of the deadening structures and cultures of most urban schools. Given this grim reality, we thought that we must prepare our Center X teachers to develop the commitment, capacity, and resilience to participate effectively in efforts to fundamentally reconceptualize, change, and renew urban schools. And we agreed with much of the current educational reform movement that suggests that fundamental change will require teachers who are willing and able to engage in continuous examination of every aspect of their structures and activities.[1]

Consequently, we decided that novice teachers in Center X must undertake an activist role in school reform that goes beyond the familiar search for "what works" to make conventional school practice "more effective" and "just" and even "visionary." Our program must engage perspective professionals in generative processes for implementing change that fundamentally challenges, reconceptualizes, and transforms now decaying urban schools into places of hope and opportunity for all students. Furthermore, our teachers must be prepared to view change and problems as "normal" conditions that require flexible, generative responses. They must have a life-long commitment to professional growth as part of their ongoing commitment to reaching the needs of all students. Toward these ends, we decided that Center X teacher candidates must have the opportunity to work collaboratively in teams to initiate change projects in their school and/or communities, and to see this work as a "normal" part of the job of teaching.

## A new structure of teacher education

Our first bold step toward a structure that had a prayer of helping novice teachers learn these four teaching roles was to announce that the standard UCLA 15-month teaching credential and master's program was insufficient, and that we were adding another year of scaffolded coursework and field experiences. (Remember, we're in California where teacher education doesn't begin until graduate school.) To our surprise, nearly everyone agreed! Where we thought we'd have battles, there were none. Even the California Teacher Credentialling Commission supported our application for "experimental" status to allow us to waive the state regulation that teacher education programs must permit students to become credentialled within one year.

We needed the extra year to accommodate three essential program components. The first is the M.Ed. core curriculum that integrates research-based methodologies with classroom practice by providing advanced study in such areas as multicultural foundations, instructional decision-making, and curriculum development. The second is the course sequence that guides students toward the development of instructional strategies and pedagogical skills needed to satisfy the state's credentialling requirements. The third component of the program prepares candidates to develop their knowledge and skills in methods and strategies of teaching students from diverse cultural and language backgrounds. This third component prepares teachers to provide (a) instruction for English language development and (b) specially designed academic subjects content instruction delivered in English. It also qualifies our teachers for the state's CLAD (Cross-cultural, Language, and Academic Development) Emphasis credential. The bilingual emphasis (BCLAD) that many of our students also complete provides students with methodology for primary language and content instruction delivered in Spanish and Korean. A two-year Center X program, we argued, would permit students to complete all three components and provide enough time for them to see themselves as Center X teachers.

During their first year, our students complete a program integrating theory and practice to fulfill the requirements for a basic credential. In addition to their coursework, during the fall of their first year, each team of novice teachers has a range of opportunities to observe schools and classrooms in a variety of urban settings that have racially, culturally, and linguistically diverse students. Throughout this period of observation and initial participation, students analyze effective strategies for achieving learning for all students, including constructivist instruction, socio-cultural approaches, cultural congruence, and educational technology. A key component of this phase is the students' active engagement in reflection on issues in the schools they are observing. In the Winter and Spring of the first year, students are assigned to an urban school site with a racially, culturally, and linguistically diverse student population for "student teaching." Throughout the student teaching period novice teachers will plan, implement, and assess daily lessons and units with the assistance of a mentor teacher. Key components of student teaching are the novice teachers' active engagement in reflection on issues in the schools in which they are teaching and their involvement in the larger school community.

During their second year, students take jobs in school districts to teach as teaching residents in school sites with low-income, and racially, culturally, and linguistically diverse student populations. During this time, they attend weekly seminars at UCLA, meet with fellow residents and Center X faculty at their school sites, and work in cooperative teams to initiate a Change Project in their local school and/or its community and complete a case study on the project. These teaching residencies continue the scaffolded university-field residency during the critical induction into teaching, as well as allowing the second-year "residents" additional time to complete their final CLAD/BCLAD-Emphasis credential requirements and Master's Degree in Education. At the end of this second year, students complete a portfolio assessment process that synthesizes their theoretical and practical experiences and defend it for their M.Ed. at the end of the second year.

## Cohorts

The Center X program is collegially-based so that the students move through the combined academic and field work program in a cohort. Each year, a total of 90 first-year students are admitted to the program and assigned to teams determined by either an elementary or secondary focus. Each team is composed of approximately 15 first-year students and 15 second-year students. These teams are coordinated by team leaders who are both ladder and clinical faculty members. Because the university curriculum and field component are comprehensively and sequentially designed, students must complete the entire program as full-time, UCLA students.

Some of our friends and probably lots of others predicted that we'd never get students to sign on to such an ambitious program. Our Office of Student Services was convinced that we wouldn't attract a large enough applicant pool to fill our enrollment targets. Frankly, we were a bit nervous ourselves, even though we thumbed our noses at the skeptics. In fact, we received as many applications as we had in years before with our high status, conventional, 15-month program, and we had more than four applicants for every available slot. The applicants had grades, scores, and letters that matched any in previous years. But they were also different in important ways. Many wrote passionately about their commitment to social and educational justice in Los Angeles; many had significant experiences working with diverse groups of low-income children in the past. We chose carefully, sifting through this embarrassment of riches, and wound up with a cohort that was about half students of color, and nearly a third bi- or tri-lingual. This first cohort is now working as teaching residents in Los Angeles urban schools. Our second cohort—every bit as talented and committed as the first—has begun its novice year.

## Partnerships

Because we are committed to integration of theory and practice, Center X has worked hard to develop a novice-mentor model of student teaching within university-school partnerships. These partnerships with local urban districts provide candidates with a rich and varied set of novice teaching experiences in racially, culturally, and linguistically diverse school sites, especially in classrooms with bilingual and limited-English proficient students. Each student begins his or her induction into the profession as a "novice teacher," rather than a student teacher, and each teacher in the field primarily responsible for working with a novice teacher assumes the role of "mentor teacher," rather than the traditional role of master or supervising teacher. The mentor teachers responsible for mentoring novice teachers work closely with other teachers at their schools, administrators, and clinical and ladder faculty members to redefine their roles in this new collaborative relationship. Through university-school partnerships, we work to operationalize the idea that "It takes a whole school to educate a teacher." Center X works with school site personnel to develop site-based approaches for mentoring novice teachers that will encourage them to become part of the larger school community. As part of these partnerships, Center X provides clinical and ladder faculty support for novice teachers in the field. Expert practitioners serve as UCLA lecturers in curriculum and methods courses. I teach my multicultural foundations course in a classroom at a partner middle school.

Of course these partnerships are difficult to initiate and sustain. While most local school systems are enamored by the idea of partnering with UCLA, the details of working together are not so glamorous. Much has been written about the problems of bridging the cultures of schools and universities. Our efforts are no different. Moreover, because we won't negotiate away our commitment to schools with low-income children of color, we may have lost as many partners as we've won. We have war stories of attacks by angry school administrators convinced that we were insulting them and abandoning our commitment to "all children" by not placing our students in their whiter and weather schools.

## Center X: A program of research

The need for teachers with the commitment, knowledge, and skills we claim to be fostering is well established, and Center X believes that its program design will enable students to develop them. However, we actually have little empirical evidence about the impact of efforts such as ours. Consequently, we have designed a strategy to document the implementation and test the efficacy of our work over the next five years.

The research component of our work examines the extent to which the Center X Program actually does prepare teachers to have the commitment, capacity, and resilience to provide depth of content knowledge, literacy, powerful pedagogies, and engaging school cultures for all students, especially those from racially, culturally, and linguistically diverse backgrounds. It investigates the extent to which our teachers actually assume the four interrelated core roles of transformative professionals described earlier: 1) a caring advocate for all students, 2) a reflective, inquiry-based practitioner, 3) a community builder, and 4) a generative change agent, to serve students from racially, culturally, and linguistically diverse communities. This research is being carried out by ladder faculty, clinical faculty, and graduate students, in collaboration with educators in our partner schools.

### Our questions

For the research side of our work, we're trying to answer the following hard questions:

1   How does our Center X program—oriented as it is toward issues of social justice, caring, and instructional equity—nurture and sustain novice teachers' commitment to become transformative professionals? Or does it?

2   How does our Center X approach to teacher education that more closely connects students' coursework and field experiences with racially, culturally, linguistically diverse students and communities help connect theory to their own practice? Or does it?

3   How does participation of novice teachers in collaborative and responsible learning communities both in the university and in the field that construct, use, and share knowledge build program graduates' commitment and capacity to work with communities to effect change in urban schools? Or does it?

4   How does the Center X supported residency in an urban school during the second year build teachers' efficacy and commitment to low-income racially, culturally, and linguistically diverse children and prepare teachers who will choose to teach in those children's schools? Or does it?

5   How does the Center X focus on the challenges and rewards of teaching low-income racially, culturally, and linguistically diverse students enhance new teachers' commitment, capacity, and resilience to teach in those children's schools? Or does it?

6   How does students' sustained engagement with the Center X program

ease their transition into teaching, including an ongoing commitment to change in professional development and renewal in the urban teaching profession? Or does it?

## Our design and methods

Our study began with a baseline year of data collection in 1994–95, before we instituted our two-year program, and it will extend over the next five years. In alignment with Center X's commitment to social justice and caring, the study is socially responsive research within the paradigm of critical inquiry (Sirotnik, 1991; Sirotnik & Oakes, 1990; Stringer, 1993). As critical inquiry, our data analysis and interpretation will be continuously subjected to reflection, discussion, and debate within the Center X community and serve as the basis for ongoing changes and renewal of the program. The study design is a longitudinal, multimethod research design based on qualitative and quantitative data. It attempts to understand the dynamics of the teacher education process in context and its impact on students.

We are following four two-year cohorts of teacher education credential and M.Ed. candidates, who have entered or will join the program respectively in 1995, 1996, 1997, and 1998. A series of interconnected data collection and analysis strategies will enable Center X to track novice teachers' development: Initial surveys of incoming students and follow-up surveys (both paper and pencil and interviews) of graduates, evaluation of key program elements through portfolios and portfolio defenses, and targeted case studies. The first two strategies involve the entire cohort of each entering class, and the last one focuses on a sub-sample of students from each entering cohort. The first two strategies aim to tell us what we've accomplished; the latter can help us understand how and why, and where we have rethinking to do.

## Surveys

We began our data collection with a survey adapted from the instrument developed by John Goodlad for his national Study of the Education of Educators, and we administer annual follow-up surveys. These surveys provide longitudinal data on novice teachers' socialization into teaching. To get greater depth of understanding of what our students mean by their responses to the survey questions, we supplement this paper and pencil survey with interviews about how students conceptualize teaching and social justice for children in central city schools.

## Portfolios and portfolio defenses

The impact of our program elements will be assessed through the students' M.Ed. portfolios, which include components that specially address CLAD/BCLAD credential and our M.Ed. requirements. The portfolio, based on student work, is a product that provides rich, in-depth data to determine the efficacy of the program. The portfolio is based on an integration of academic course work and field-based experiences and will focus on how each credential/M.Ed. candidate integrates his or her philosophy of teaching, theories of teaching, learning, language acquisition, culture, inquiry, community, change, and classroom practice. The portfolio will include three components: Theory to Practice, Practice to Theory, and Philosophical Perspective. In the Theory to Practice component, students will include a case study of a Change Project they implemented in their resident year in a racially, culturally, and linguistically diverse school or its community. The credential/M.Ed. candidate sits for a defense of his or her portfolio before a panel, consisting of academic, clinical, community, and student members. At the end of the defense, each candidate has the opportunity to assess the Teacher Education Program's strengths and weaknesses. A recorder will provide a record of each portfolio and defense, based on an established rubric.

## Targeted case studies

Targeted indepth initial and exit interviews and case studies of select students will provide rich, explanatory narratives of the context in which our students have learned to become teachers.

Importantly, our primary research goal is not to document and "prove" that we've figured out how to produce teachers who can make central city schools rich, rigorous, socially just, and caring learning communities where all children learn extraordinarily well. We know that we haven't figured it out, and that maybe we never will. Our research goal, rather, is to document the struggle of teacher educators and novice teachers who've decided that they can't **not** try.

## Asking for trouble

Using the powerful symbolism of the university and the extraordinary talent of the educators in the university and the schools, the staff at Center X have committed to the view—however idealistic—that schools and teaching for low-income, racially culturally, and linguistically diverse children can change. We've also asked for a whole lot of trouble, and in fact, we've gotten lots. As I read what I've written here, I realize that sentences and paragraphs strung together make our efforts sound far more tidy than they are. We're struggling to do something we really don't know how to do. We're asking questions we don't know how to answer. We frustrate many of our partnering educators who want more clarity and definition of our program than we can provide. We worry some of our colleagues who think we're too ideological. We anger some of our students when we won't give them a safety net of classroom management strategies and structured lesson-planning procedures that we think will create more problems that they will solve. We ask everyone to tolerate our ambiguity. We're not being realistic. We work too hard. We work our students too hard. We expect too much.

Frankly, we wouldn't have it any other way. We don't expect to stop the fires from coming again to Los Angeles. But next time, we'll know that we tried.

## Note

1   For a fuller explication of these ideas, see Paul Heckman, *The Courage to Change*, Newbery Park, CA: Corwin.

## References

Banks, James A. (1994). *An Introduction to Multicultural Education*. Boston, MA: Allyn and Bacon.
Beck, Lynn. (1994). *Reclaiming Educational Administration as a Caring Profession*. New York: Teachers College Press.

Cummins, Jim. (1989). *Empowering Minority Students.* Sacramento, CA: California Association for Bilingual Education.

Dewey, John. (1902). *The Child and the Curriculum.* Chicago, IL: University of Chicago Press.

Giroux, Henry A. (1988). *Schooling and the Struggle for Public Life: Critical Pedagogy in the Modern Age.* Minneapolis, MN: University of Minnesota Press.

Gutierrez, Kris D. (1992). "A Comparison of Instructional Contexts in Writing Process Classrooms with Latino Children." *Education and Urban Society* 42, no. 2: 244–62.

Gutierrez, Kris D. & Eugene E. Garcia. (1989). "Academic Literacy in Linguistic Minority Children: The Connections Between Language, Cognition and Culture." *Early Child Development and Care.* no. 51: 109–26.

Goodlad, John I. (1994). *Educational Renewal: Better Teachers, Better Schools.* San Francisco, CA: Jossey-Bass Publishers.

Hargreaves, Andy. (1994). *Changing Teachers, Changing Times.* New York: Teachers College Press.

Heckman, Paul E., Christine B. Confer, & Jean Peacock. (1995). "Democracy in a Multicultural School and Community." In Jeannie Oakes & Karen Quartz (Eds.), *Creating New Educational Communities. Ninety-fourth Yearbook of the National Society for Study of Education. Part I.* Chicago, IL: University of Chicago Press, pp. 187–201.

Moll, Luís. (1988). "Some Key Issues in Teaching Latino Students." *Language Arts* 65, no. 5:465–472.

Moll, Luís. Ed. (1990). *Vygotsky and Education: Instructional Implications and Applications of Sociohistorical Psychology.* New York: Cambridge University Press.

Noddings, Nel. (1984). *Caring.* Berkeley, Los Angeles, and London: University of California Press.

Noddings, Nel. (1992). *The Challenge to Care in Schools: An Alternative Approach to Education.* New York: Teachers College Press.

Oakes, Jeannie. (1985). *Keeping Track: How Schools Structure Inequality.* New Haven: Yale University Press.

Oakes, Jeannie. (1990b). *Multiplying Inequalities: The Effects of Race, Class, and Tracking on Opportunities to Learn Mathematics and Science.* Santa Monica, CA: RAND.

Sirotnik, Kenneth A. (1991). "Critical Inquiry: A Paradigm for Praxis." In Edmund C. Short, Ed., *Forms of Curriculum Inquiry.* Albany, NY: State University of New York Press, pp. 243–49.

Sirotnik, Kenneth A., & Jeannie Oakes. (1990). "Evaluation as Critical Inquiry: School Improvement as a Case in Point." *Evaluation and Social Justice* 45: 37–59.

Stringer, Ernest T. (1993). "Socially Responsive Educational Research: Linking Theory and Practice." In *Theory and Concepts in Qualitative Research: Perspectives from the Field,* Ed. David J. Flinders & Geoffrey E. Miles. New York and London: Teachers College Press, pp. 141–162.

Vygotsky, Lev S. (1962). *Thought and Language.* Cambridge, MA: MIT Press.

Vygotsky, Lev S. (1978). *Mind in Society.* Cambridge, MA: Harvard University Press.

# CHAPTER 13

# MULTICULTURE AND SPECIAL EDUCATION TEACHER EDUCATION ACCREDITATION (1979)

*William R. Carriker and William H. Berdine*

## Introduction

Concern for national accreditation standards in teacher education has evolved in the areas of special education and multicultural education over the past 10 to 15 years. The standards we do have, however, will probably not be very effective in bringing about changes unless they can be incorporated into a nationally recognized accreditation process. The National Council for Accreditation of Teacher Education (NCATE) has been using one set of standards for the preparation of elementary and secondary teachers as well as various administrative and support personnel, paraprofessionals, and college teachers, for over a quarter of a century. Authority for their accrediting activities has been authorized by the Council on Post-secondary Accreditation (COPA).

> The NCATE has been authorized by the Council on Post-secondary Accreditation (COPA) to adopt standards and procedures for accreditation and to determine the accreditation status of institutional programs for preparing teachers and other professional school personnel. The NCATE is also recognized by the U.S. Commissioner of Education. (NCATE, 1979, p. 1)

The revised NCATE standards are based on continuous review and involvement with representatives of accredited institutions and professional education organizations. Past history indicates that approximately 2 years are required to bring about revisions and/or additions, with an additional 18 months before the application of the new standard becomes mandatory.

The current (1979) revisions of the NCATE standards as they pertain to multicultural education are of particular interest to special educators. A significant proportion of the children receiving special education services are members of cultural and ethnic minorities. Special educators, therefore, must learn to deal with the cultural as well as the handicapping characteristics of the children in their programs. Familiarity with the NCATE standards on multicultural education may be of some assistance.

Special educators need to be familiar with at least two aspects of the NCATE accreditation process: (1) standards for multicultural education and how they were incorporated into the accreditation process and (2) the relationship of the multicultural standards to existing preservice special education teacher-training programs that are seeking accreditation.

## Multicultural education

The need to include multicultural education in teacher education programs seems to have been highlighted over the years by at least three major educational forces: the American Association of Colleges for Teacher Education (AACTE), the National Education Association (NEA), and committed professionals who are concerned about bilingual and multicultural education. The 1974 Bilingual Education Act, support for bilingual and multicultural educational research and development through the National Institute of Education (NIE), and the establishment of resource and training centers in multicultural-multilingual education by the Office of Bilingual Education have provided further and significant impetus.

The commitment of AACTE to multicultural education is clear in E. C. Pomeroy's statement in the foreword of Sutman, Sandstrom, and Shoemaker (1979).

> Multicultural education is one of the core missions of the Association. One of the AACTE's three basic commissions is responsible for promoting multiculturalism, especially within the hundreds of colleges and universities which are members of the Association. The Commission has publicly stated: "The preparation of educational personnel competent to serve effectively in a culturally pluralistic society and in an interdependent world is a professional task of utmost importance. AACTE national surveys reveal that American educational personnel preparation programs do not adequately meet this competency goal. (p. v)

This statement shows just one major organization's commitment to the concept. In concert with the other organizations, revisions in the NCATE standards were completed and adopted over a 2-year period, from 1975 through 1977, becoming effective January 1, 1979 (NCATE, 1979).

The new NCATE multicultural standard, particularly with regard to where the standard is placed in the total "set" of NCATE standards, has major impact for special education. The NCATE standards are divided into two levels—Part I: Basic Teacher Education Programs (Program for the Initial Preparation of Teachers Through the Fifth Year Level, including MAT Programs), and Part II Advanced Programs (Post-Baccalaureate Programs for the Advanced Preparation of Teachers and the Preparation of Other Professional School Personnel). Each part has a series of six standards developed around the following areas:

1 Governance
2 Curricula
3 Faculty
4 Students
5 Resources and facilities
6 Evaluation and program review

Within each standard are specific subsets of standards that add both depth and specificity to the general standards.

The standards for multicultural education have been placed in the undergraduate or basic teacher education programs as Standard 2, *Curricula for Basic Programs*; as a subset of 2.1, *Design of Curricula*; and in the graduate or advanced programs as standard G-2, *Curricula for Advanced Programs*; as a subset of G-2.1, *Design of Curricula*. The standard at the basic level reads:

2.1.1  The institution gives evidence of planning for multicultural education in its teacher education curricula including both the general and professional studies component.

As with all NCATE standards, a brief preamble describes the intent of the standard in question. The preamble for multicultural education describes it as a preparation for the social, political and economic realities that individuals experience in culturally diverse and complex human encounters. These realities have both national and international dimensions. This preparation provides a process by which an individual develops competencies to perceive, believe, evaluate, and behave in varied cultural settings. Thus, multicultural education is viewed as an intervention and an on-going assessment process to help institutions and individuals become more responsive to the human condition, to individual cultural integrity, and to cultural pluralism in society and the world.

While the standards are stated in broad and general terms, the requirements for meeting them become quite clear and stringent when a battery of questions are posed to the institutions by the accrediting on-site teams. Here are some examples of such questions:

2.1.1  Multicultural education
- In what ways is multicultural education reflected in the plan of study for all programs in regard to:
  (a)  General studies
  (b)  Professional education
  (c)  Preparation in clinical/laboratory experiences
  (d)  Practicum and field experiences
- What resources have been added to support multicultural education over the past 5 years?
- What efforts have been made to recruit new faculty in view of the multicultural concepts? What success has been attained?
- What efforts have been made to recruit students in view of multicultural concepts? What success? (NCATE, 1979, p. 21)

At the present time, additional questions are being generated by the Professional Standards Committee of the Teacher Education Division (TED) of CEC. Input from TED will add greater specificity to site-visit teams' inquiries regarding training competencies within the multicultural standards. In addition, the location of the multicultural standard within the "set" of standards requires that it be taken into account in each of the six major standards and their subcomponent standards.

## Special education

The process of establishing guidelines and standards came to the forefront in special education in the 1960s through the efforts of The Council for Exceptional Children. The initial guidelines focus on teacher education in special education. The statements are very general and appear as guidelines, not in the form of standards.

Concern for special education teacher education accreditation was evidenced by the Teacher Education Division of CEC in 1972–73, when a task force was established. This task force was instrumental in working with the various governing bodies of CEC in order to become a part of the mainstream of accreditation through NCATE. CEC is now completing its 4th year as a member of the NCATE Council. For the first 2 years, CEC was an associate member (no voting privileges); it is now a full constituent member with all privileges.

CEC's involvement with NCATE has lead NCATE to consider making major additions and revisions in the standards. These changes would reflect the need for special education teacher education to be a viable and recognized component in all teacher education. With the support of AACTE, NEA, and other organizations who are represented on the NCATE Council, special education teacher education concepts will eventually permeate all the NCATE standards.

Evidence of change is already reflected by the action of the Council to accredit special education teacher education as a separate program. Beginning in the Fall of 1979, it will no longer be subsumed, for example, under such headings as elementary, secondary, or K-12 teacher education programs. And special education curricular concept statements may be inserted in the preamble of Standards 2, *Curricula for Basic Programs*, and G-2, *Curricula for Advanced Program*, which would facilitate review of special education programs that are an integral component of regular teacher education programs.

Of particular significance to special education teacher education personnel are the possible training implications the multicultural standard may have for their programs. The impact of the multicultural standard will be greatest in, but not solely limited to, regions of the country where large groups of cultural minorities are living. As noted earlier and documented in Reynolds and Birch (1977), minorities tend to be overrepresented in special education programs. When provisions for accrediting special education training programs separately are included within the NCATE standards, these training institutions will need to include multicultural training at the preservice level. The training institutions are going to need to develop training competencies for preparing special educators to deal with multicultural and/or ethnic differences among learners. Baker (1973, 1977) demonstrated that positive attitudes about ethnic and cultural groups can be developed within preservice teacher-training programs through the use of workshops and specific courses of study. Laosa (1977) describes one area of needed research that is particularly relevant for special educators involved in multicultural settings or activities; that is, the influence of culture and its possible effect on cognitive styles that affect the ways individuals approach teaching. It seems reasonable to assume that teacher educators need to provide specific preservice training to take into account and develop instructional strategies to deal with the culturally different pupil as well as the culturally different teacher. In many instances, the teachers in special education classrooms will find themselves to be the cultural or ethnic minority. Teacher-training institutions need to prepare their students to adapt to various cultural and ethnic settings without compromising the effectiveness or efficiency of their instruction.

# References

Baker, G. C. Multicultural training for student teachers. *Journal of Teacher Education*, 1973, *24*, 306–307.

Baker, G. C. Multicultural education—Two preservice training approaches. *Journal of Teacher Education*, 1977, *28*, 31–33.

The Council for Exceptional Children. *Guidelines for personnel in the education of exceptional children*. Reston, Va.: Author, 1976.

Laosa, L. M. Multicultural education—How psychology can contribute. *Journal of Teacher Education*, 1977, *28*, 26–30.

National Council for Accreditation of Teacher Education. *Standards for accreditation of teacher education*. Washington, D.C.: Author, 1979.

Reynolds, M. C., & Birch, J. W. *Teaching exceptional children in all America's schools*. Reston, Va.: The Council for Exceptional Children, 1977.

Stutman, F. X., Sandstrom, E. L., & Shoemaker, F. *Educating personnel for bilingual settings: Present and future*. Washington, D.C.: AACTE and Temple University, MERIT, 1979.

# CHAPTER 14

# SPECIAL EDUCATION AND MULTICULTURAL EDUCATION (1984)

## A compatible marriage

*Oris Elizabeth Amos and Mary Frances Landers*

Children in schools represent not only many culturally diverse groups but also reflect differences in intellectual and physical capacities, including sensory and health impairments. These factors may limit opportunity to access learning unless modifications are made in the learning environments. Handicapped children and youth in schools include those with (a) specific learning disabilities, (b) mild, moderate, and severe mental retardation, (c) visual and hearing impairments, (d) emotional disturbance, and (e) multihandicaps. According to the 1980–1981 child count of the United States Department of Education, 8.65 percent of the school-age population was served under P.L. 94–142, the Education for All Handicapped Children Act of 1975. In addition to the approximately nine percent of children served in special education units, many children with disabilities are in the mainstream of general education.

The authors use the terms *disabilities* and *handicaps* in this paper but these terms are not synonymous. Brolin (1982) appropriately defines the two terms:

> A disability is a medical condition that may or may not be a handicap! An individual who loses an arm is disabled but not handicapped if he or she is able to resume normal duties and the disability isn't perceived as a handicap. Many people with disabilities lead normal, productive lives and are quite irritated by those who consider them handicapped despite their ability to carry on their business as usual and be happy and satisfied. Most definitions of handicap reflect a person who deviates below average in mental, physical, or social characteristics and who needs special education and rehabilitative services to assimilate into the requirements of community living and working. (p. 32)

In the past, most teachers did not have any orientation to teaching children with differences—whether those differences were cultural, intellectual, or physical. Prejudice and discrimination against learners with special education needs have been well documented in the literature (Hewett & Forness, 1977; MacMillan, 1982). In the past, individuals with disabilities have been categorized in groups, labeled with demeaning titles, and placed in segregated facilities and institutions. The treatment of the disabled has often been compared to the treatment of ethnic minority groups. Gliedman and Roth (1980) have called persons with disabilities "the unexpected minority." Comparing the isolation and discrimination experienced by the disabled with that of blacks and other minorities, Gliedman and

Roth state that "the able-bodied person sees that handicapped people rarely hold good jobs, become culture heroes, or are visible members of the community and concludes that this is 'proof' that they cannot hold their own in society" (p. 22). Wright (1960) also observes that minorities and disabled persons are restricted because of society's prejudicial attitudes. Comparing the disabled with minorities, Wright points out that employment opportunities for the disabled are limited especially at higher levels; social and recreational activities are also frequently restricted.

The area of special education has constantly experienced the negative aspects of limited school options for children and youth with different learning potential and special needs. In the past, classes for educable mentally retarded (EMR) and emotionally handicapped (EH) became overpopulated by children who were poor, bilingual, culturally different, or severely frustrated with the school (Dunn, 1968; Johnson, 1969; Jones, 1976; Mercer, 1977). In 1968, Dunn created a controversy in the fields of special education and psychology when he observed that 60–80 percent of the children taught by teachers of the retarded were "children from low status backgrounds—including Afro-Americans, American Indians, Mexicans, and Puerto Rican Americans; those from nonstandard English speaking, broken, disorganized, and inadequate homes; and children from other non-middle class environments" (p. 6).

Mercer (1972), having completed extensive research in the area of evaluation of minority children, stated:

> A large number of minority persons who can cope well with the requirements of their daily lives are being labeled mentally retarded. They acquire these labels not because they are unable to cope with the world, but because they have not had the opportunity to learn the cognitive skills necessary to pass Anglo oriented intelligence tests. They do not conform to the typical Anglo, middle-class pattern; thus they appear "retarded" to the white middle-class clinician or teacher. Yet their behavior outside of the test situation belies their test score. (p. 44)

Interestingly, 10 years after Mercer's comments in 1972, Ysseldyke, Algozzine, and Richey (1982) found professionals tend to estimate that a higher number of minority and low socioeconomic status children exhibit handicaps than children of higher socioeconomic status. They stated, "the number of minority and low socioeconomic status children thought to evidence academic difficulties and behavior problems was at least twice as high as the number of high-socioeconomic status children and girls; estimates for boys were medial" (p. 532).

Children and youth who can operate normally in their homes and neighborhoods have sometimes been identified as "six hour retarded" because they are retarded only during those hours when they are at school. It has been argued that standardized tests and teacher attitudes and expectations have caused a disproportionate number of minority and low socioeconomic individuals to be seen as handicapped. MacMillan (1982) summarizes the controversy related to testing minority children:

> Intelligence tests have been subjected to severe criticisms recently. They are implicated in the long-lasting debate over the relative importance of genetic and environmental determination of intelligence and challenged as unfair measures for use with mentally retarded ethnic minority individuals. In the

latter case the critics say the tests consist of items that do not reflect the cultural background of the child coming from a subculture that differs from the dominant culture and that the conditions under which a standardized test is administered depress the performance of the minority child (e.g., a standard test administration could be perceived as threatening by a minority child, resulting in poorer performance than if the administration procedure took cultural difference into account). (p. 9)

In the past, stereotypical attitudes toward persons with disabilities have been similar to attitudes toward minorities. Figure 14.1 indicates some of the similar attitudes held about the two groups.

| Culturally Different | Disabled |
|---|---|
| 1 Categorized—"all alike" within the group. Examples: "Black students score less than whites on tests." "The Indians reject modern ways." | 1 Categorized—"all alike" within the group. Examples: "The mentally retarded have poor memory." "The learning disabled are hyperactive." "The cerebral palsied score in the mentally retarded range." |
| 2 Labeled—disadvantaged, inner city, culturally deprived. | 2 Labeled—sometimes seen as mentally retarded or mentally ill. |
| 3 Segregated—Even after the laws prohibited segregation in housing and schools, segregation is still widespread. | 3 Segregated—in special classes, special schools, and institutions. |
| 4 Confronted with attitudinal barriers. Seen as misfits, aggressive, problems. | 4 Confronted with attitudinal and architectural barriers. Seen as slow, incapable of growth and progress, ill, handicapped.* |
| 5 Considered communication or language deficient. Seen as unable to speak English, low IQ. | 5 Seen as untestable, non-educable, deficient in academics, low IQ. |
| 6 Adjudged as genetically inferior. | 6 Adjudged as genetically inferior. |
| 7 Seen as lifelong children, happy, unmotivated, carefree, incapable of responsibility. | 7 Seen as lifelong children, with need to be patronized, protected, sheltered. |
| 8 Seen as financial drains on schools and agencies. | 8 Seen as financial drains with money being diverted from regular students. |
| 9 Seen as discipline problems—hard to manage and teach. | 9 Seen as too hard to manage or teach. |

*Figure 14.1* Stereotypical attitudes toward culturally different and disabled individuals

*Note:* Having a disability does not necessarily mean that person will be "handicapped." Many people with disabilities are able to adapt equipment, learning modalities, etc., and make their lives productive and "normal."

Parents and advocates for individuals with disabilities have sought and gained redress from some of the unfair and prejudicial practices which have curtailed equal opportunities to the disabled. An overrepresentation of ethnic minorities in special education helped to trigger the mandates for non-discriminatory testing, placement in the least restrictive environment, individual education programs, and due process procedures for parents, all included in the Education for All Handicapped Children Act, 1975. It is important to note that the legal arguments used in the *Brown v. Board of Education* case of 1954 against the "separate but equal" philosophy was the rationale for the right to education for the handicapped. Legal arguments against the segregation of black children in public schools were used to support lawsuits and decisions on behalf of handicapped individuals.

Since attitudes, expectations, and practices related to minorities and individuals with handicaps have been similar, education and training of personnel to serve both groups can also be similar. A marriage between special education and multicultural education should produce professionals who have knowledge, skills, and attitudes which increase educational opportunities for *all* learners in schools. Such a marriage should also enhance the efforts to serve more learners with differences in the mainstreams of our educational system. Kunzweiler (1982) discussed the need for "structures and processes to deal with emotional and spiritual growth to aid prospective teachers to reach higher levels of consciousness and awareness so as to affect their contact with all children." He states, "Because of this lack of formal structure and processes, if we come into college a bigot, the chances are we will leave the college as a bigot who has earned the academic credentials to teach" (p. 32).

We now have mandated responsibilities to develop formal structures and processes to help prospective teachers to develop skills to work with learners who are culturally different and/or handicapped. The content of the mandates are similar and compatible for both special education and multicultural education.

## The compatible components

Many professional organizations and learned societies, as well as certification and accreditation agencies, are supporting and mandating both special education and multicultural competencies for teachers. The National Council for Accreditation of Teacher Education (NCATE, 1977) described multicultural education as "an intervention and an ongoing assessment process to help institutions and individuals become more responsive to the human condition, individual cultural integrity and cultural pluralism in society" (p. 13). NCATE (1977, p. 13) further indicates that multicultural education could include but not be limited to experiences which:

1 promote analytical and evaluation abilities to confront issues such as participatory democracy, racism, and sexism and the parity of power;
2 develop skill for values clarification including the study of the manifest and latent transmission of values;
3 examine the dynamics of diverse cultures and the implications for developing professional education strategies.

The Council for Exceptional Children (1983), in proposed standards for preparation of personnel, included the NCATE standard relating to multicultural education. The proposed standard states: "It is important that all students in preparation have an opportunity to understand the issues relating to cultural differences and cultural pluralism in this society" (p. 3). New certification standards for teachers in the state of Ohio (Ohio Department of Education, 1975) require that the teacher education curriculum "include human relations related to both teaching in a pluralistic society and working effectively with students regardless of race, political affiliation, religion, age, sex, and socioeconomic status or exceptionality not requiring a fulltime special educational environment" (p. 4).

Under P.L. 94–142, the Education for All Handicapped Children Act of 1975, all children must receive a free public education in the least restrictive environment. To be educated in the least restrictive environment, many mildly handicapped children will be educated in the regular classroom. Among the mildly handicapped who are now in both regular and special classes, there is a disproportionate number of children from poor and culturally different families. Therefore, all educators, both special and general, must have training in working with children and youth who have learning difficulties and who may have language, economic, and/or cultural differences.

To support these mandates, teacher education institutions seeking accreditation or reaccreditation from NCATE must meet a standard relating to the preparation of education professionals for the education of exceptional students. The NCATE (1982) special education standard states, in part:

> All educators should have the knowledge and skills necessary to enable them to respond to the individual differences of learners. The presence of exceptional learners in regular classrooms requires that general and special educators perceive their professional roles as less distinct and more complementary. They must increasingly view themselves as differentiated members of an instructional team to provide an appropriate education for exceptional learners. . . .
>
> Professional education programs should prepare all school personnel to contribute to the education of exceptional learners. Such programs should prepare educators to be able to recognize and refer exceptional learners for diagnosis and to contribute to the design and implementation of curricular programs, instructional techniques, and classroom management strategies to accommodate their educational needs. (pp. 14–15)

Understanding and responding effectively to human conditions, diversity, and individual differences are compatible components of both special education and multicultural education.

Review of current literature on teacher effectiveness, multicultural education, mandates of NCATE, P.L. 94–142, and the State of Ohio Standards (Amos, Jones, Williams, & Brooks, 1982) points up broad areas in which education personnel should have competency. Suggested broad competency areas which overlap both special education and multicultural education are:

1   self awareness and knowledge of one's own values and potential helping skills
2   knowledge and skills in assessment of pupils, content, and methodology to meet individual as well as group needs and pupil evaluation
3   knowledge about the makeup of the multicultural/pluralistic society and schools and the implications for skills and attitudes for serving diverse populations—including learners with disabilities

4   knowledge, skills, and attitudes for conferencing and counseling with parents—including culturally different parents and parents with disabled learners

In a multicultural-special education teacher training program, knowledge, skills, and attitudes can follow the schema of:

INTRODUCTION AND AWARENESS—REINFORCEMENT OF KEY CONCEPTS—MASTERY OF KEY CONCEPTS

In the introduction phase of special education and multicultural education, students should have opportunities to:

1   evaluate their own beliefs and attitudes toward others
2   review concepts about different cultural/ethnic/religious, economic, and intellectually different groups and relate those concepts to learning and teaching
3   recognize the meaning of prejudice, stereotypes, segregation, and discrimination
4   recognize propaganda and controversial issues
5   recognize general characteristics of mildly, moderately, and severely handicapped children
6   recognize examples of the placement options available for handicapped children
7   recognize the general mandates of P.L. 94–142
8   participate in activities simulating handicapping conditions

In the reinforcement phase, students should have:

1   field experiences with members of culturally different groups and with learners receiving special education services
2   opportunities to evaluate books, media, and curricula and to observe the treatment of diverse groups including persons with disabilities
3   opportunities to observe special learners working in least restrictive environments—in regular classes, special classes in regular schools, learning centers, special schools, hospitals, and residential centers
4   opportunities to develop an instructional plan for a disabled student in an educational setting

In the mastery stage of special education-multicultural education, the student should be able to demonstrate skills in:

1   developing a unit, center of interest, or other project which relate to special education-multicultural education issues. (Such projects could be used in a student teaching or participation experience in a school or agency.)
2   guiding simulation of handicapping conditions in schools for children and teachers
3   developing reading lists or bibliographical materials which depict persons with disabilities as positive contributing members of society
4   participating with a team to write an individual education program (IEP)

5 participating in or observing a parent conference in a school or other agency

It should be pointed out that the mastery stage does not indicate the end of learning about diversity; this phase suggests that the individual has mastered skills which can be taught or used with others.

## Expected outcomes

Multicultural and special education training must begin in teacher education programs. Fuchigami (1980, p. 640), discussing "teacher education for culturally diverse exceptional students," summarizes his concerns by stating:

> A major barrier is a teacher education program that fails to provide information and skills about how to work with minority students and their parents. In essence, minority children must not be expected to carry the burden of teacher and administrator ignorance about minorities into the 1980s. Teacher trainers have an opportunity and a directive to make the necessary changes. The question remains: How will they respond?

Special education personnel—teachers, psychologists, speech and language clinicians—have the responsibility of serving very diverse populations and often have limited orientation to the special needs and differences among cultural groups. Recognizing the need for multicultural preparation of professionals in special education, Gonzales (1979) indicates:

> Until the last five (5) years, special education teachers have not been prepared to teach in a multicultural setting. The main emphasis has been on the evaluation of the culturally and linguistically different child. The question of diagnosis has, for the most part, been satisfactorily addressed, although most educational programs remain totally insensitive to the needs of the multicultural exceptional child. Now with the demands set forth by recent legislation and the courts to provide for individual needs, regardless of linguistic and cultural background, and in the least restrictive environment, universities have begun to retrain special educators to function more effectively in a multicultural setting. (p. 15)

How can multicultural and special education objectives and activities help teachers and other education personnel make classrooms more enriching for special and general education learners? Since many teachers have had little opportunity to have experiences with culturally different children or children with learning or physical disabilities, formal instruction and inservice training are important. Individuals *can* change behavior based on knowledge, skills, and experiences. Barnes (1977) states:

> Equipped with a knowledge of self and a body of information on minority cultures, needs, problems, and behavior patterns, teachers will be better able to analyze, synthesize, and integrate the positive elements of both bodies of knowledge into their teaching for the betterment of themselves and their students. Teachers will also be equipped to create a more conducive classroom environment for learning in which they do not (a) view minority students as

178 Oris Elizabeth Amos and Mary Frances Landers

dumb, trouble making radicals who are threats to their comfort and security; and (b) use the classrooms as prisons, indoctrinating cells, or filters through which to process minority students to make them come out after twelve years of schooling as ignorant, conformist, politicized passive citizens who cannot and dare not think for themselves. (p. 515)

Teachers have tremendous power in helping students to develop social skills. Teachers tend to be models and children learn much from how the teacher reacts to individuals in the classroom, as well as to adult peers. In discussing "teaching through modeling," Charles and Malian (1980) state:

The traits we wish to develop in fully functioning persons are heavily dependent on modeling. We best teach openness through being open, acceptance through accepting, courtesy through being courteous, responsibility through being responsible. Students are more likely to do as teachers do, rather than as teachers say. (p. 87)

Teidt and Teidt (1979) suggest the following to teachers:

You model appropriate language and behavior every day in the classroom. Referring to the groups of people by acceptable names as blacks, Caucasians, Irish Americans, and Native Americans, for example, demonstrates your respect for members of these ethnic groups no matter what your own origins are. The kinds of expectations that you have for the various students in your class should reflect realistic assessment of each child's abilities and should not be influenced by skin color or national origin. (pp. 12–13)

Garcia (1982) observes:

Teachers can make a difference in the lives of students. To make a difference in a pluralistic society, a teacher should understand how the ethnic factor impinges upon teaching and learning. Teachers should keep their focus first on transcending problems that are common in important ways to all cultures, nations, and students—ignorance, poverty, disease, hunger—and second on the cultural differences manifest in their students' learning styles and ways of behaving. A posture of cultural relativism, which views ethnic and cultural groups from their own vantage point, can assist the teacher with the awesome task of dealing with and teaching in a pluralistic society. (p. 16)

Teachers with training and skills in multicultural and special education should be better prepared to demonstrate acceptance and valuing of differences and should be prepared to develop programs which consider individual backgrounds, learning differences, and values. Children and youth with disabilities should be able to access various learning opportunities and placements which have been unavailable because of attitudinal and architectural barriers.

If children and youth are to live, learn, work, and play in a multicultural and pluralistic society, educational personnel must be trained to respect, value, and teach (help) learners who are culturally different or learners who have disabilities and handicaps.

We have the mandates from national and state laws and professional organizations to prepare educational personnel who have training in special education and multicultural education. The reasonable approach is a marriage between special education and multicultural education. The two areas are compatible and could produce fruitful and enriching changes in schools and communities.

# References

Abeson, A. (1976). Legal forces and pressures. In R. Jones (Ed.), *Mainstreaming and the minority child*. Reston, VA: Council for Exceptional Children.

Amos, O., Jones, M., Williams, M., & Brooks, D. (1982). *Teaching in a multicultural/ pluralistic society—A resource module*. Lexington, MA: Ginn.

Barnes, W. (1977). How to improve teacher behavior in multiethnic classrooms. *Educational Leadership, 34*, 515–518.

Brolin, D. (1982). *Vocational preparation of persons with handicaps* (2nd ed.). Columbus: Merrill.

Charles, C., & Malian, I. (1980). *The special student—Practical help for the classroom teacher*. St. Louis: C.V. Mosby Co.

Council for Exceptional Children. (1983). *Proposed CEC standards for preparation of special education personnel*. Reston, VA: Author.

Dunn, L. (1968). Special education for the mildly retarded—Is much of it justifiable? *Exceptional Children, 35*, 5–22.

Fuchigami, R. (1980). Teacher education for culturally diverse exceptional children. *Exceptional Children, 46*, 634–641.

Garcia, R. (1982). *Teaching in a pluralistic society—Concepts, models, strategies*. New York: Harper & Row.

Gliedman, J., & Roth, W. (1980). *The unexpected minority—Handicapped children in America*. New York: Harcourt Brace Jovanovich.

Gonzales, E. (1979, Summer). Preparation for teaching the multicultural exceptional child—Trends and concerns. *Teacher Education and Special Education, 2*, pp. 12–17.

Hewett, F., & Forness, S. (1977). *Education of exceptional learners*. Boston: Allyn & Bacon.

Johnson, J. (1969). Special education and the inner city: A challenge for the future or another means for cooling the mark out? *Journal of Special Education, 3*, 241–251.

Jones, R. (Ed.). (1976). *Mainstreaming and the minority child*. Reston, VA: Council for Exceptional Children.

Kunzweiler, C. (1982). Mainstreaming will fail unless there is a change in professional attitude and institutional structure. *Education*, 284–288.

MacMillan, D. (1982). *Mental retardation in school and society*. (2nd ed.). Boston: Little, Brown.

Mercer, J. (1972, September). I.Q.: The lethal label. *Psychology Today*, pp. 44–47; 95.

Mercer, J. (1977). *System of multicultural pluralistic assessment*, Riverside, CA: Institute for Pluralistic Assessment, Research & Training.

National Council for Accreditation of Teacher Education. (1977). *Standards for accreditation of teacher education*. Washington, DC: Author.

National Council for Accreditation of Teacher Education. (1982). *Standards for accreditation of teacher education*. Washington, DC: Author.

Ohio Department of Education. (1975). *Standards for colleges and universities preparing teachers*. Columbus: Author.

Teidt, P., & Teidt, I. (1979). *Multicultural teaching: A handbook of activities, information and resources*. Boston: Allyn & Bacon.

Wright, B. (1960). *Physical disability: A psychological approach*. New York: Harper & Row.

Ysseldyke, J., Algozzine, B., & Richey, L. (1982). Judgment under uncertainty: How many children are handicapped? *Exceptional Children, 48*, 531–534.

# CHAPTER 15

# EQUALITY IS EXCELLENCE (1986)
## Transforming teacher education and the learning process
*Ira Shor*

Teacher education programs are disturbingly alike and almost uniformly inadequate. . . . This nation cannot continue to afford the brief, casual, conforming preparation now experienced by those who will staff its classrooms. . . . We will only begin to get evidence of the potential power of pedagogy when we dare to risk and support markedly deviant classroom procedures. (Goodlad, 1983, pp. 249, 315, 317)

Only a few teachers used the difficult decade of the 1970s to teach themselves and their students with some new methods. . . . It is easy to claim that a radical restructuring of society or the system of education is needed for the kind of cultural bridging reported in this book [*Ways With Words*] to be large scale and continuous. (Heath, 1983, pp. 363, 369)

Far too many teachers give out directions, busy work, and fact-fact-fact lectures in ways that keep students intellectually passive, if not actually deepening their disregard for learning and schooling. (The Holmes Group, 1986, p. 29)

It is astonishing that so few critics challenge the system. . . . When one considers the energy, commitment, and quality of so many of the people working in the schools, one must place the blame [for school failure] elsewhere. The people are better than the structure. Therefore the structure must be at fault. (Sizer, 1984, pp. 29, 30)

## Reform in the name of authority since 1983

Wisdom says that where there is light there is heat, but experience shows the opposite is not always true. The current wave of school reform, "the great school debate" chronicled by many educators, has created the context for examining teacher education.[1] But the reform movement so far has generated more heat than light. Perhaps it is understandable that discussion of root causes and forward-looking solutions languishes in these conservative years. The Reagan administration commissioned *A Nation at Risk*, the report of the National Commission on Excellence in Education (1983), which accuses students and teachers of an alarming "mediocrity." According to the report, this "mediocrity" has helped Japan and Germany outpace our economy and has even threatened our national security. The recommended antidote fits the regressive tenor of the times – more traditional courses, more mechanical testing, a lust for "excellence," and a token glance at equality.

The influential Education Commission of the States (1983b) fired a second major salvo in its report, *Action for Excellence*. Highlighting "the teacher gap"— that is, the shortage of qualified teachers and the lower achievement of those entering the profession—this report echoed the White House alarm about the decline of schools. Many other studies and documents were released in that same year: *Academic Preparation for College* (The College Entrance Examination Board, 1983), *Making the Grade* (Twentieth Century Fund Task Force, 1983), *Educating Americans for the 21st Century* (The National Science Board, 1983), and *America's Competitive Challenge* (Task Force of the Business-Higher Education Forum, 1983). This great wave from above provoked statewide legislation and reviews of curriculum, and eventually swept the sad condition of teacher education into its nets.

## Fishy nets: Why the authorities launched their reforms

Unhappy with the costs and the outcomes of schooling, the highest policymakers turned their attention after 1983 to curricular reform, to restructuring their management of the teaching profession, and to teacher education. Business and the military complained about the quality of graduates entering the workforce and the service, especially in regard to literacy and to discipline in the workplace.[2] From another perspective, the new arms race and the high-tech boom in the economy during the early 1980s created an undersupply of computer workers and engineers (estimated at 40,000 a year by the Task Force of the Business-Higher Education Forum, 1983). In response to this labor shortage, the curriculum tipped towards technology and computer studies. Unfortunately, by 1986 sectors of the electronics industry were laying off workers in a period of economic recovery, sorry news for students who rushed to computer majors and for college planners who promoted business needs through curriculum.

Still another labor factor brought curriculum and teacher education into the spotlight. By 1984 the teacher surplus of the 1970s had become a teacher shortage. Although education programs had grown by 113 in number since 1973, by the 1980s they were producing 53 percent fewer teachers (see Feistritzer, 1984). Schools were experiencing disruptive spot shortages of teachers, especially in math, science, and foreign languages. Inner-city schools had unusually high turnover rates in their staffs each year. Substantial portions of the teacher corps were teaching out-of-license (for example, music majors instructing math courses) in nominally temporary arrangements that became a permanent and irrational way of life. The teacher supply problem is expected to grow worse in the coming decade. This has prompted "manpower" strategies to overhaul the professional pipeline training new teachers and to reorganize teaching in order to get more from current staff.

With few exceptions, the official reports explained away the real issues in the teacher shortage and in the decline of education. They chose instead "blaming-the-victim" formulas such as student-teacher "mediocrity," the need for "excellence" and higher "standards," the softness in a "cafeteria-style" high school curriculum, and the "breakdown of discipline" in school and the family.[3] In reality, the current crisis resulted from budget cuts that left class sizes too large, school buildings shabby, instructional materials in short supply, education programs unable to afford careful mentoring of student teachers, and aging academic departments deprived of new blood. Further, conservative educational policy in the 1970s imposed depressing programs of careerism and back-to-basics, making intellectual life in the classroom dull, vocational, and over-supervised.[4] These new curricula discouraged creativity and liberal education. They invited gifted teachers to leave the profession, while they dissuaded students from thinking of education as an exciting career. Also in the 1970s, the job market for liberal arts majors and for teachers collapsed at the same time that the number of business and computer majors expanded wildly. This vocational imbalance in college curriculum steered a generation of students away from education as a career; for those teachers already in service, fiscal austerity since the Nixon administration has led to wage losses and to decay in their schools. These depressing public-sector conditions are characteristic of the recent conservative era.

Two other factors contributed to the teaching crisis: higher wages in the private sector for some college graduates, and the appearance of a new baby boom. First, wages for technical-scientific graduates are better in the private sector than in education or in public-sector jobs. This difference draws labor to industry, attracting teachers out of low-paying education jobs into better-paying corporate ones. In an economy kept unbalanced by high military spending there is a domestic "brain drain" of math, science, and engineering teachers out of education into the booming military and electronics sectors of the job market.[5]

Second, the rising birthrate made its predictable impact on the elementary grades by 1984, creating a demand for new teachers after a decade of economic and social policy that undermined public education. This sudden demand for labor is as much a crisis in education as in any other labor-short part of the economy. The $130 billion-a-year school system will need about one million new teachers in the coming decade, according to the National Institute of Education (NIE, 1984a) report, *The Condition of Education*.

Evading criticism of economic policy and the arms race, the "excellence" reformers promised that renewal would come from high technology, greater emphasis on traditional subjects, more required testing, career ladders in the teaching profession, and something called "education for economic growth." Such proposals hid the causes of school decline, which included budget cuts, withdrawal of federal support for equality, redirection of funds from social services to the military, and the dramatic failure of the corporate job market to inspire graduates with employment equal to their educations.[6] Only a few years before the White House initiative in 1983, educators were debating the terrible predicament of "the overeducated American." Along with Freeman's (1976) book of that name, studies by Berg (1970), NIE (1983), Braverman (1974), and Levin and Rumberger (1983) pointed to a work force that was becoming more educated while the job market *deskilled* work through automation and *raised* the credentials needed to get routine jobs. The official reports were silent on the bizarre phenomenon of "overeducation" turning so quickly into "mediocrity." In reality, students are not overeducated, and are not mediocre. Such mystifications merely explain away the root causes of the current crisis. The stagnant economy of this conservative era cannot distribute equality or prosperity, the two legs of the American dream on which the corporate system stands. Myths of overeducation and mediocrity distract attention from the systemic causes of decline.

## The system of silence: Pushing liberal values to the margins

By ignoring uncomfortable political questions, the recent reform wave has prompted a remarkably unbalanced debate and legislative season. Official commissions, legislative groups, and the media have followed a narrow line of traditional frameworks and authoritarian remedies.[7] These "get tough" approaches caused visible dismay in out-of-favor liberal circles. Boyer (1983, p. 5; 1984) complained that proponents of the new regimens forgot that "education is to enrich the living individual" while Sizer declared that the current reform wave lacked the compassion for students that characterized earlier periods of change ("The bold quest," 1983, p. 66). Boyer, Sizer, and other skeptics like Goodlad (1983) and Howe (1985a, 1985b) doubted the claims of the "excellence" camp with regard to illiteracy, the SAT decline, and the need for heavy doses of back-to-basics.[8] The liberal dissenters noted the strident emphasis on more testing of teachers and students, more required courses, fewer electives, a reduced federal role in guaranteeing equity, and the call for standard English over bilingual teaching.

The liberal perspective deserved more attention than it received in a period dominated by conservatism. In addition to that in Boyer (1983), liberal departures can be found in Sizer's (1984) *Horace's Compromise* and Darling-Hammond's two studies, *Beyond the Commission Reports* (1984a) and *Equality and Excellence: The Educational Status of Black Americans* (1984b). Early liberal statements made by Kohl (1982) and Maeroff (1982) included a critique of the conservative politics behind the back-to-basics movement. These got far less attention than Adler's (1982) traditional *paideia* program. Also among the liberal departures, Heath (1983) offered a nontraditional ethnographic model of teaching and learning which unfortunately had no impact on state legislation or on district-wide curricular policies. In addition, Richardson, Fisk, and Okun (1983) did not blame working-class students for their learning deficits, but offered another pedagogical challenge. Richardson pointed to mechanical teaching styles, state under-funding of mass higher education, and the vocational bias of the community-college system as the principal obstacles to the development of "critical literacy" needed by working students.

Other meagerly discussed reports from this dissenting group were the NIE's (1984) *Involvement in Learning*, the New World Foundation's (Bastian et al., 1985) *Choosing Equality*, the Association of American Colleges' (AAC, 1985) *Integrity in the College Curriculum*, and Goodlad's (1983) monumental *A Place Called School*. These documents presented policy and pedagogical alternatives to the conservative tide of the 1980s. *Choosing Equality* boldly recommended egalitarian federal funding, public economic development to create jobs, and student/teacher/parent "empowerment" as the foundations for educational reform. It was one "grass-roots" correction to the "excellence" mystification launched by *A Nation at Risk* (National Commission, 1983) and *Action for Excellence* (Education Commission of the States, 1983b), and promoted by "excellence" networkers such as Finn and Ravitch (1984).[9]

Those taking an egalitarian perspective matched policy issues with presentations of alternative pedagogy. Heath's work in the Carolina Piedmont area of the East Coast demonstrated the power of student-centered teaching to break the traditional separation of school and community. The NIE (1984a, 1984b) and AAC (1985) reports took stands for an interactive, interdisciplinary curriculum. Goodlad (1983) supported experimental, participatory pedagogy in contrast to the traditional teacher-talk which dominated the thousand classrooms visited by his researchers. Sizer (1984), Boyer (1983), and Goodlad (1983) all acknowledged the failure of the regular school syllabus to address the needs and themes of adolescents. Darling-Hammond (1984b) discussed the unequal curriculum offered to black students. The NIE and AAC reports acknowledged the failure of traditional curricula to serve the educational needs of college students whose learning was hindered by the academy's departmental sectarianism, preference for lecture methods, and rewarding of professors for narrow research instead of teaching.[10] This dissenting body of literature did not support "get tough" programs to solve the school malaise.

## The heart in the dissenting body: An egalitarian synthesis

The liberal dissenters in this antiliberal period occupied marginal ground. Their defense of student-centered, egalitarian, and interactive values was a heroic holding action. Education as a change-agent, however, constituted one undeveloped value in this dissenting margin. *Choosing Equality* (Bastian et al., 1985) stands out for its advocacy of community empowerment and community-based school reform. This report called for including parents in school policy-making and for linking education to local leadership and existing community organizations. Even farther out in the margins, energetic networks of "participatory researchers" and adult or community educators developed a vision of the educator participating in social change.[11]

Besides greater attention to the idea of change-agency, the dissenting body of literature needs an egalitarian overview. Such a synthesis is too important to leave implicit or unrecognized. I suggest the following framework as one way to pose egalitarianism and change-agency in education: *Equality is excellence and inequality leads to alienation.* Excellence without equality produces only more inequality. Inequality leads to learning deficits and to resistance in the great mass of students. Alienation in schools is the number-one learning problem that depresses academic performance and elevates student resistance. Student resistance to intellectual life is socially produced by inequality and by authoritarian pedagogy in school, worsening the literacy problem and the crisis in teacher burnout.[12] Teacher burnout and student resistance are social problems of an unequal system and cannot be fully addressed by teacher-education reforms or by classroom remedies alone. Participatory and critical pedagogy, coupled with egalitarian policies in school and society, can holistically address the education crisis.

I am proposing that the education crisis is thus an expression of social inequality. Equality empowers people and raises aspirations in school and society. Power and hope are sources of motivation to learn and to do. Motivation produces student involvement, and involvement produces learning and literacy. Such participation also supports teacher morale, makes the hard work of teaching attractive and rewarding, and decreases burnout. Teacher and student morale will be increased from the heightened joy of learning; this morale will in turn inspire more people to choose teaching as a career—and to stay in teaching once there, thus easing the teacher shortage. Inspiring classroom experiences can also encourage teachers and students to take themselves more seriously as intellectuals who can critically grasp any issue, technical process, body of knowledge, moment in history, or political condition in society. Teachers and students oriented to debate and critical study will be better able to act as citizens democratically transforming society. Democratic participation in society may include action against the arms race and budget cuts, which could potentially shift spending priorities from guns to learning, and consequently improve the quality and appeal of intellectual life in schools.

My egalitarian perspective, outlined and synthesized above, simply recognizes that economics, community life and literacy, commercial mass culture, and political action outside the classroom grossly influence the fate of education. Apart from the billions of dollars spent on weapons, the most glaring social inequity is the greater amount of money invested in the education of richer students at all levels. Years after the landmark *Serrano v. Priest* (1971) decision against unequal school funding, children of poor and working-class families still have much less invested in their educations, according to Fiske (1981) and Sizer (1984, p. 36).[13] This inequality is only the tip of the iceberg because the daily lives, the language, and the job opportunities of poor and working-class students can also work against success in traditional classrooms.[14] This citing of the "arms race" and "inequality" to explain the school crisis did not appear in the official reports because it blames the business world and its educational subsystem, that is, the function of schools to socialize students for their places in the corporate economy. Rather, the reports chose to point haughty fingers at student-teacher "mediocrity," at "spongy" courses in high school, at open admissions to college, or at the alleged breakdown of discipline in the family. But the corporate education system itself gutted public education and invited students and teachers to go on a performance strike.

## Performance anxiety: Why teaching matters

While factors beyond the classroom greatly affect education, what goes on in school makes an important difference. This is true not only with respect to the quality of a student's life and learning, but also to the possible transformation of students, teachers, and the society that sets the curriculum. The strongest potential of teaching lies in studying the politics and student cultures that affect the classroom. It is politically naive or simply "technocratic" to see the classroom as a separate world where inequality, dominant ideology, and economic policy do not affect learning. It is equally damaging to think pessimistically that nothing good can be achieved in the classroom until the economic system and society are changed. Similarly, it is also a mistake to believe that education by itself can change society one classroom at a time.

Individual classrooms cannot change an unequal social system; only political movements can transform inequality. In working for transformation, egalitarian pedagogy can interfere with the disabling socialization of students. Schools are one large agency among several which socialize students; they can confirm or challenge socialization into inequality. Teachers can reinforce student alienation from critical thinking by confirming the *curricular* disempowerment of their intelligence, or teachers can employ critical pedagogy to counter the disabling character of students' prior educational experiences. As a dependent sector of society, schools can either play a role in reproducing alienated consciousness or they can challenge inequality through a curriculum critical of the dominant culture that offers such a disabling mass education.

When pedagogy and curricular policy reflect egalitarian goals, education can be empowered *to oppose dominant socialization with critical desocialization.* This involves developing critical consciousness in preference to commercial consciousness and transforming society rather than reproducing inequality. Efforts at critical desocialization could serve to illuminate the myths that support the elite hierarchy of society, to invite students to reflect on their own conditions, and to challenge them to consider how the limits they face might be overcome. Critical literacy programs and participatory courses can also raise awareness about the values expressed through language in daily life. They would further serve to distribute research skills and censored information useful for investigating power and policy in society.

Critical pedagogy recasts education as an opposition to the purpose of traditional curriculum, which is the reproduction of inequality (Apple, 1982; Bowles & Gintis, 1982; Carnoy & Levin, 1985; Giroux, 1983; Jencks et al., 1972; Willis, 1981; and others). Several roads can lead to critical classrooms that oppose the reproduction of subordinate consciousness in school. A number of educators have experimented, for example, with Freire's methods and approaches (Finlay & Faith, 1979; Fiore & Elsasser, 1982; Frankenstein, 1983; Shor & Freire, 1986; Shor, in press; Wallerstein, 1983). Heath (1983) tested an ethnographic model; Kohl (1982) offered a humanistic language program similar to Judy's (1980) proposals; and Pattison (1982) suggested a "bi-idiomatic" approach to teaching colloquial and formal discourse simultaneously. When we discuss teacher education programs or curriculum at any level of schooling, we can pose the questions of critical pedagogy and desocialization. Once we accept that education's role is to challenge inequality and dominant myths like student "mediocrity" or the alleged neutrality of "standards," rather than to socialize students into the status quo, we have set the foundation needed for inventing practical methods of desocialization.

Desocialization thus builds on the terrain already staked out by the liberal dissenters. Pattison (1982), for example, refused to define "correct usage" as a universal standard of excellence, referring to it simply as the idiom of the triumphant middle classes, useful for supporting authoritarian societies as easily as democratic ones (see esp. chaps. 5,6,7). Boyer (1983) asserted that equality constitutes an unfinished agenda for education. Darling-Hammond (1984b) reflected Boyer's view in her study of the education of black students whose progress toward equality during the 1960s has eroded since 1975. Further, Darling-Hammond (1984c) saw state-mandated testing and syllabi as depressing the performance of teachers.[15] Sizer (1984) acknowledged that social class has a great impact on educational choices but that class as a theme was not included in school curricula. Heath (1983) suggested reaching out into everyday life in an effort to build on the existing literacy of any school population. Her work was a refreshing break from routine assertions that students were "mediocre" or "illiterate." Goodlad (1983) offered the most systematic critique of traditional teaching, including the tendency for minority students to be placed in vocational tracks in school. Lastly, the AAC (1985) report strongly criticized the remoteness of college professors from teaching.

The liberal agenda and the aims of desocialization may yet make the more important contribution to education reform, if only because an authoritarian approach—memorization, mechanical testing, teacher-talk and student silence, abstract subjects remote from student interest, standardized syllabi, balkanized faculties, and Byzantine administrations—cannot solve the current school crisis. This is the regime which produced student alienation and teacher burnout in the first place. By proposing solutions that caused the problem, the commissions and legislatures offer water to a drowning school system. Conservative regimens will only intensify the dilemmas faced by teachers and students in school. The authorities are inviting a more severe crisis down the road;[16] at that point, in the vacuum of Reagan-era reforms, liberal humanists may find that their program is an idea whose time has come.

## Cleaner vacuums: The reform wave washes over teacher education

In the spinoff debate on reforming teacher education, liberal dissent once again has been overshadowed by conservative policy. Some of Goodlad's (1983) comments on teacher education, and Heath's (1983) teaching model, stand out from business-as-usual. Goodlad recommends experimental schools in each district, where future teachers would train to enter the profession. Teacher-apprentices would spend two years as interns in these experimental schools, learning their craft in settings that model student-centered pedagogy. This would introduce them to teaching through a participative approach rather than a traditional one. Heath's model of having both teachers and students engaged in ethnographic research is another alternate method for teacher training. Teachers would be ethnographers of their students' communities and cultures, while students would be trained as local ethnographers, studying scientifically the language and habits they had previously only experienced. Through such a pedagogy, students and teachers would teach and learn from one another. This mutual education also offers students a certain distance from reality and models the critical habit of mind, which can be defined as the habit of analyzing experience and questioning received knowledge. Heath's program collapses the wall between classroom and community, between research and teaching, and between research and living. It is an example of the experiential/conceptual approach to learning that Dewey (1900/1956, 1902/1956, 1938/1956) proposed.

In contrast, official reports after 1983 defined the teaching and learning crisis in ways that evaded the real needs of the classroom. One evasion focused on managing the profession—teacher testing, certification requirements, merit pay—while bypassing the three big-ticket items that most concern teachers: higher wages across the board, smaller class sizes, and lighter course loads. A second evasion concerned the learning process. The official view posed teaching and learning in terms of the "Great Books," a fixed authority based on standard reading lists. Accordingly, the teacher functioned as a delivery system in a one-way transfer of information and skills to students. This mechanical notion of education sought traditional material for its core curriculum: the American Heritage and Western Civilization.[17] Such rejections of the multicultural diversity that emerged from the 1960s are reflected by Hirsch (1985, pp. 8–15), who defines "cultural literacy" as a 130-page reading list of Eurocentric works.[18] Hirsch suggests that this list can be reduced, for curriculum purposes, to a more manageable size, but he maintains that without familiarity with these works— written predominantly by white, male, Western authors—a person could not be considered literate. Similarly, Adler's (1982, 1983) bookish *paideia* program posed another canonical thrust which endorsed the teaching of "classics" through a lecture-based pedagogy.

The notion of a core curriculum based on traditional values and classical texts appealed also to Finn, who, as assistant secretary of education in the Reagan administration, prepared a gray booklet called *What Works: Research About Teaching and Learning* (1986). This volume exhorts the family to do more at home for education. It insists that hard work and self-reliance, not social policy or school funding, are the heart of student success. Finn's traditional bent, as a key "excellence" spokesperson, was borne out by the many quotations from ancient and pre-1800 sources sprinkling the text, as well as by recommendations to teach a "shared" heritage to students that would instill national pride. This myth of a neutral, shared, national history reduces the critical and multicultural potentials of education.

The traditional models of Hirsch, Adler, and Finn informed legislative action. They denied the student-centered and experiential values of Goodlad (1983) and Heath (1983), and of Silberman (1971), who, during the upheavals of the 1960s, defined a community *paideia* (pp. 5, 49). Goodlad also referred to *paideia* as education in a whole community, not as a school-bound event alone. The house of authority, however, heard only Adler's *paideia*.

One lesson from this debate is that the learning process itself is a form of politics and ideology, not a neutral realm of activity. Another lesson is that the learning process we set for the schools is the model that socializes future teachers in how to teach. By reasserting an elite canon and a mechanical menu of testing and teacher-talk, the official commissions and legislative bodies after 1983 also reimposed a model of teaching. In-service teachers now feel great pressure to teach to the tests, while future teachers receive passive canonical instruction in high school, in collegiate liberal arts, and in their academic majors. A passive pedagogy that utilizes dismal texts and traditional reading lists is the curriculum modeled to students, including that fraction who will one day be teachers. This is why all of schooling is actually "teacher education," a *paideia* socializing teachers in how to teach and what to learn. To segregate "pedagogy" courses as *the* place to study teaching is one way to hide the authoritarian, mechanical ideology embedded in the standard curriculum.

## Cannons aimed at canons: The culture war over the learning process

For over a century, mechanical, factory models of teaching and learning have been at war with critical, interactive education.[19] The quality of the learning process was an issue for liberal dissenters after 1983, heirs as they are to the Deweyan side in the long culture war over curriculum. On the managerial side of this debate, a number of official reports from around the nation fail to give adequate attention to the learning process.[20] Instead of providing a systematic discussion of learning, these reports focus on managing the profession, on certification of teachers, on merit pay schemes and career ladders, on alternate routes to the profession, and on time spent in collegiate programs. The documents do acknowledge the importance of student teaching, and the California (1985) report, with Goodlad on the commission, does recommend deregulating teacher education in order to allow colleges to experiment. Their discussion, however, omits examination of the learning process and leaves intact the mechanical pedagogy that dominates teacher education as much as it dominates other classrooms.

While the reports differ in style and emphasis, they display a compatibility and a consensus. A policy agenda from this group could be synthesized as follows:

The teaching profession needs higher standards for training and licensure.

Teacher education programs should be more selective; in-service teachers need to meet more rigorous standards. Admissions and graduation standards in college programs should be raised.

Teachers need more in-service development. Veteran classroom teachers can train new teachers in school and future ones in campus programs.

Salaries need improvement, especially at entry-level, and career ladders should be instituted to give teachers incentives.

Teachers should be assigned fewer noninstructional duties, granted more autonomy in their classrooms, and included more in administrative and policy decisions.

More care and funds should be given to student teaching in college programs. Teacher preparation should include at least a one-year student-teaching internship.

The training of teachers should remain primarily on college campuses with some alternate, off-campus routes into the profession (a choice made by a number of states, most notably New Jersey and its alternate certification plan).

Education majors need more liberal arts courses in college.

For certification, new teachers should have to pass exams in subject matter, basic skills, and knowledge of pedagogy, in addition to completing successfully a one-year internship in student teaching.

Efforts should be made to attract the brightest students, especially high-achieving minority candidates, to teaching.

Research on teaching needs to be more widely disseminated in education courses and in public schools.

A five-year undergraduate teacher education program is needed. This would require liberal arts, a concentration in an academic major, education courses, and an internship in student teaching, all of which could not be completed within the current four-year degree programs.

A five-year undergraduate program was recommended by the National Commission for Excellence in Teacher Education (1983), by the California Commission on the Teaching Profession (1985), and by the NIE (1984b) statement. The heads of both teacher unions, Shanker of the American Federation of Teachers (AFT) and Futrell of the National Education Association (NEA), served on the National Commission, and strongly endorsed the recommendation for a five-year baccalaureate program. The five-year undergraduate education program is one way to paint yourself into a corner if you lose sight of the quality of a learning process. I will return to this point shortly to discuss "time" fallacies in mechanical approaches to learning.

Faults aside, this consensual agenda does suggest items beneficial to the teaching profession: higher pay, more classroom autonomy for teachers, carefully mentored internships, in-service development, and veteran schoolteachers serving as adjunct faculty in college programs (see Shanker, 1985).[21] The California Commission even recommended the teacher's nightly wish: reduced class size. The agenda, however, was undemocratically developed and imposed, with little or no input from teachers. The first high-profile reforms to be pushed through have suggested more testing and more required courses in the syllabus. Very little debate has focused on the learning process in teacher education or in the colleges and schools.

## The proof of the pudding is in the process: If more liberal arts is the answer, what is the question?

One repeated claim in the major reports is that education courses are soft on content while liberal arts courses are hard. Therefore, future teachers who need a better grasp of the canon should study more academic courses. Future secondary teachers already spend the largest part of their credits in liberal arts (natural sciences, social sciences, and literature courses) and only about 20 percent of their baccalaureate hours in education courses.[22] Still, the information mystique of the liberal arts reappears at a time when mechanical pedagogy fits the needs of authoritarian reform.

The humanities curriculum should be admired when it generates critical thought in students and inspires them to be interactive learners. Academic studies should not be bodies of knowledge consumed in gulps by information-hungry students. Liberal arts courses should develop conceptual habits of mind, critical methods of inquiry, and in-depth scrutiny that displays the relationship between intellect, politics, values, and society. Sending future teachers to liberal arts courses where they are lectured at and made passive recipients of information socializes them into an inadequate model of learning and teaching. The validity of every liberal arts course rests on how much critical thinking it generates, how much participation it mobilizes, and how it relates its body of knowledge to other disciplines and to the larger conditions of society. It should be noted that these are the pedagogical responsibilities of any course, not merely liberal arts.

## Soul repository: The spirit of qualitative learning

In proposing a qualitative process instead of mechanical learning, I want to suggest a pedagogy that is participatory, critical, values-oriented, multicultural, student-centered, experiential, research-minded, and interdisciplinary. Such a pedagogy focuses on the quality of an activity, not on the quantity of skills or facts memorized, or on the quantity of hours or credits spent on a task. Further, the quality approach addresses a major myth in the recent discussion of teacher education, that undergraduate preparation of teachers requires *five* years instead of *four*. Another myth is that teacher education should be done at the graduate level only. These are mechanical fallacies in the reports, which can nevertheless be credited for speaking of the need to make teacher education more clinical, more in touch with research, and more open to minorities (even though the new teacher tests are producing high minority failure rates).

Because the reforms propose a one- or two-year internship in student teaching prior to entering the profession, the four-year baccalaureate programs run out of time, not to mention money, in the limited budgets usually allocated to education schools. A seriously mentored internship requires more money and more faculty attention on campus and in the cooperating school than is likely to be invested. Clinical settings in real schools are the best places to learn a teacher's craft, but when the reports favor *more* subject-matter specialization and *more* liberal arts at the undergraduate level, they wind up adding a *fifth* year to squeeze in a teacher internship. This is the sad result of the quantitative approach to learning. If you measure knowledge by minutes, hours, courses, credits, semesters, and years, you are ruled by the clock, not by the intellect. Instead, the focus should be on the kind of learning and teaching modeled at every level of education. If a passive, authoritarian model of pedagogy dominates all levels of school and college classrooms, what good is it for future teachers to spend an extra year being socialized in the worst model of teaching? Four years of bad models will not be remedied by adding a fifth.

The Holmes Group (1986) understood this need for interactive pedagogy. But four years of good models—critical, participatory learning—will also make the Holmes call for graduate teacher-training far less urgent. The challenge here is the same one made to the information myth of the liberal arts. What kind of learning and teaching is modeled at every year and level of education? If the learning process is interactive and critical, then four years is enough to prepare future teachers. If the learning process models equality and critical thought on school and society, then teacher education will be a serious enterprise at the undergraduate level. If a curriculum at any degree level, for any number of years, is dominated by teacher talk, didactic lectures, canonical reading lists, commercial textbooks, and standardized testing, then five or six years of undergraduate work, or two years of graduate study, will not develop the teachers needed to inspire learning. Further, even the best teacher education will have limited results as long as low pay, large classes, heavy work loads, administrative oversupervision, standardized testing, and shabby conditions dominate the classroom.

It will be useful for teacher education reformers to confront the time fallacy. Concerns about more time in liberal arts, a five-year baccalaureate, or a two-year M.A.T. pale in comparison to the question of the learning process. The socializing power of any experience is greater in its quality than in its quantity, greater in the quality of social relations than in the quantity of statements or rules. A desocializing, egalitarian, and critical pedagogy is a quality process which can invite teachers and students to take their educations seriously. It is one not being modeled now. To help define a desocializing model for teacher education, I want to offer an agenda of themes for the learning process.

## Modeling new fashions: Egalitarian teacher education

### Dialogic teaching

The dialogic method discussed by Freire (1970, 1973) is one way to reduce student withdrawal and teacher-talk in the classroom. A dialogic class begins with problem posing and critical discussion. This interactive opening sends powerful signals to students that their participation is expected and needed to solve problems of mutual interest. It will not be easy to learn the arts of dialogue because education now offers so little critical discussion and so few constructive peer exchanges. Dialogue is the art of intervention and the art of restraint, so that the verbal facility of a trained intellectual (the teacher) does not silence the verbal styles of unscholarly students.

Practice in leading long dialogic inquiries in class will require making the curriculum itself dialogic. It also suggests study in group dynamics, the social relations of discourse, and the linguistic habits of students in their communities, in relation to their sex, class, race, region, age, and ethnic origin.

### Critical literacy

Literacy that provokes critical awareness and desocialization will involve more than minimal competency. It will require critical literacy across the curriculum and will ask that all academic subjects develop habits of reading, writing, thinking, speaking, and listening, in order to provoke conceptual inquiry into self, society, and the discipline itself. This means that future teachers in every subject specialization, from biology to architecture, will learn how to pose problems in an effort to develop thinking and language skills.

Critical literacy invites teachers and students to "problematize" all subjects of study—that is, to understand existing knowledge as an historical product deeply invested with the values of those who developed such knowledge. A critically literate person does not stay at the empirical level of memorizing data, or at the impressionistic level of opinion, or at the level of dominant myths in society, but goes beneath the surface to understand the origin, structure, and consequences of any body of knowledge, technical process, or object under study. This model of literacy establishes teaching and learning as forms of research and experimentation. It calls on us to test hypotheses, examine evidence and artifacts, and finally to question what we know. In addition, teaching/learning as research suggests that teachers constantly observe students' learning in order to make pedagogical decisions, while students are also researching their language, their society, and their own learning.

## Situated pedagogy

This goal asks teachers to situate learning in the students' cultures—their literacy, their themes, their present understandings, their aspirations, their daily lives. The goal is to integrate experiential materials with conceptual methods and academic subjects. Grounding economics, nursing, engineering, mathematics, or biology in student life and literacy will not only connect experience with critical thought, but will also demonstrate that intellectual work has a tangible purpose in our lives. Further, only a situated pedagogy can bring critical study to bear on the concrete conditions of life, which critical learning may help recreate.

## Ethnography and cross-cultural communication

A teacher's academic program needs components in ethnography and cultural anthropology. To situate critical literacy and dialogue inside the language, themes, and cognitive levels of the students, a teacher needs to study the population he or she is teaching. This study can be carried out using the ethnographic methods described by Heath (1983), the sociolinguistics demonstrated by Hoggart (1957) and Bisseret (1979), and the grounded-theory approach to research discussed by Glaser and Strauss (1967).

Further, experience in cross-cultural communications will be valuable for teachers who are likely to lead classrooms with diverse student populations. Bidialectalism and bilingualism in schools are academic themes that invite learning about the communication problems of teaching in a multicultural society. A final anthropological feature of teacher education is the need to study literatures outside the official canon, from labor culture, ethnic groups, and women's writings.

## Change-agency

To be egalitarian change-agents, teachers need to study community analysis and models of community change.[23] How do communities structure themselves? How do they change? How do outsiders identify and work with local leaders? How can classroom instruction model itself on key issues of community life?

Teachers will also need to study school organization, school-based curriculum design, the legislative environment for education, and professional politics. Inside the institution of a school or college, political methods for change can include staff-development seminars, community-school linkages, faculty committees and assemblies, internal publications, political lobbying, and union organization. Future teachers can benefit from studying histories of organizing change in the classroom, in schools or colleges, and in communities.

## Inequality in school and society

This academic interest can be studied through courses in sociology, economics, history, and psychology. How do inequalities in race, sex, and class influence school outcomes and expenditures? How did the current school system emerge in relation to the politics of each preceding age? What impact have egalitarian movements had on school and social policy? How have nontraditional, egalitarian programs affected student performance?[24]

## Performance skills

Teachers can benefit from voice and drama training to enhance their skills in problem posing and discussion leading. To be a creative problem poser in the classroom, drama and voice skills are helpful. The teacher needs to think of herself or himself as a creative artist whose craft is instruction. An exciting instructor is a communications artist who can engage students in provocative dialogue. Also, performing skills can habituate new teachers to the intimidating challenge of standing up each hour in front of a large group and taking charge of the session. Lastly, a dramatic teacher models the aesthetic joy of dialogue, the pleasure of thinking out loud with others.

This agenda of themes is meant to be suggestive rather than exhaustive. Each study item does not require a separate course; an ethnography class can demonstrate dialogic methods of teaching as well as provide background on literacy situated in student culture, which can be studied for the impact of social inequality on daily life and learning. The above program can be coordinated with student teaching. Further, there are other subjects worthy of study: child psychology and adolescent development, the history of pedagogical thought, international education, immigrant patterns of assimilation, a second language (preferably Spanish, for U.S. teachers), and survival during the teacher's first year in the classroom. The most valuable element is participatory learning, which mobilizes critical thought and democratic debate.

In conclusion, I would emphasize that learning is not the transfer of skills or information from a talking teacher to a passive student. Education is different from narrow training in business careers. These are negative recipes which will produce even more student alienation and teacher burnout.

A teacher must aspire to be much more than a talking textbook, more than a mere functionary who implements standardized tests and mandated syllabi. Teaching should offer an illumination of reality which helps all of us grasp the social limits that constrain us. Critical learning does not define students as empty vessels to be filled with packaged bits of facts and figures. Teachers must oppose the mechanical pedagogy and the unequal tracking that take some students to success and most others to low wages and underemployment, to despair and anti-intellectualism. Learning which is more than job training and more than socialization into subordinate lives involves the critical study of society. Such education is a charmingly utopian challenge to inequality and to authoritarian methods. It aims to foster a humorous, rigorous, and humanizing dialogue, with the April hope of lowering student resistance and teacher burnout, and the August desire of reknowing ourselves and history, within that vast arena of culture war called education.

## Notes

1  See Gross and Gross (1985), Passow (1984), Education Commission of the States (1983a, 1983b), Task Force on Education for Economic Growth (1983). For a summation that includes some critique, see Cross (1984, pp. 167–172).

2  See National Commission on Excellence in Teacher Education (1983, pp. 9–10), Task Force on Education for Economic Growth (1983, pp. 17–19), and Panel on Secondary School Education for the Changing Workplace (1984, pp. xi–xii, 17–19) for commentary on the business-military perception of literacy and work discipline in young graduates.

3  One exception to the routine assertions of the 1983 reform wave is *High Schools and the Changing Workplace* (National Academy Press, 1984), which did not wax grandiloquent on high-tech and computers, as did the other reports. Stanford economist Levin was on the panel producing this report, and its cool assessment of high-tech may reflect his research into the marginal impact computers would have on wages, opportunities, and employment in the future job market. Another exceptional source is the "Background Paper" by Peterson (1983), attached to the Twentieth Century Fund (1983) report, *Making the Grade*. Peterson's research found no educational crisis or collapse to justify the official claims of 1983. His lengthy study showed positive outcomes from federal equity programs in the 1960s, thus reversing the report's majority statement in favor of more emphasis on "excellence" and less on equality. A third exception is the California Commission on the Teaching Profession's (1985) report, *Who Will Teach Our Children?*, which recommended ending state regulation of teacher education programs, thus allowing each campus to experiment. Goodlad (1983) was on this commission, and this unusual recommendation reflected at least one concern in his study, *A Place Called School*.

4  See Shor (1986, chap. 2, on career education, and chap. 3 on the literacy crisis). For more background on the depressant political effects of vocationalism in the 1970s, see Karabel (1972) and Grubb and Lazerson (1975). An illuminating study of the economics of the 1970s and 1980s can be found in Bowles, Gordon, and Weiskopf (1983). Another spacious survey was done by Bowles and Gintis (1982) and the aggressive conservative politics of this age were studied by Piven and Cloward (1982).

5  For some analysis of the domestic brain drain, see Levin (1985). Levin's research points out that from 15–50 percent of all scientific personnel are employed directly or indirectly by the Defense Department.

6  For a discussion of the job market's impact on school performance, see National Coalition of Advocates for Children (1985). For another consideration of how economic decline after the 1960s affected student learning, see Levin (1981); for a discussion of businesses' tilting of curriculum in the 1980s, see Spring (1984).

7  For a sample of the restricted debate in the mass media, see the following cover stories on the education crisis: "The bold quest" (1983), "Can the schools be saved?" (1983, May 9), "Why teachers fail" (1982), and "What makes schools great" (1984).

8  Less discussed critiques of the post-1983 school reforms can be found in Leonard (1984), Hacker (1984), and Karp (1985).

9  Finn and Ravitch set up the National Network for Excellence in Education in 1984, and edited a compendium with Fancher. See Finn and Ravitch's (1984) "Conclusions and Recommendations: High Expectations and Disciplined Effort," for their traditional curricular position in the great debate. See Finn (1981, 1983) for his conservative view on educational policy. A liberal response to the elite impact of the "excellence" reforms is in Toch (1984).

10 The NIE (1984b) report deals more with learning process than does the AAC (1985) report. AAC focused on curricular policy for higher education, promoting inter-disciplinary and critical themes, in a desire to reorient a research professoriat back toward teaching.

11 Some networks supporting community-based, participatory, or change-agency educa-tion include the Institute for Responsive Education (Boston), the Public Education Information Network (St. Louis), The Association for Community-Based Education (Washington, DC), Basic Choices (Madison, WI), the Participatory Research Group (Toronto), the Center for Popular Economics (Amherst, MA), the Lindeman Center (Chicago), the Highlander Center (New Market, TN), and the Labor Institute (New York City). See, for example, Adams and Horton (1975), The Labor Institute (1982), and The Institute for Responsive Education (1984). For one experience in community-based, change-oriented education, see Minkler and Cox (1980).

12 In *The 1984 Metropolitan Life-Survey of the American Teacher* (Harris and Associates, 1984), teachers ranked lack of student interest as the most serious problem in the classroom, with budget cuts running a close second.

13 The study by Jencks et al. (1972) is the watershed document on this issue; see also Bowles and Gintis (1976, esp. pp. 4, 33, 133).

14 Heath's (1983) *Ways With Words* is an illuminating study of how community literacy and school literacy conflict. She examines how the idioms of black and white non-elite schoolchildren in the Carolina Piedmont clashed with elite usage favored by the schools. For another excellent study of the clash between language and culture in the schools, see Willis (1981).

15 See also Darling-Hammond's (1984c) critique of the testing craze in the 1983 reform wave.

16 Cuban (1984) wisely assessed the potential for failure in a mechanical reform program.

17 These were the curricular emphases in California's reform legislation Senate Bill 813 and in New York's Regents Action Plan with its Part 100 Regulations. Secretary of Education Bennett (1984) also took up these themes in his report.

18 Hirsch's (1985) quantitative canon is discussed in his essay. Cuban (1984) also offers a concise critique of the mechanical approach to learning. For some historical perspective on the politics of literacy, see Donald (1983). Donald offers an illuminating look at the literacy debate in 19th-century Britain, when state-sponsored literacy in official schools helped reduce dissent. For another fine discussion of literacy, see Ohmann (1985).

19 In a heated reform year Gibboney (1983, pp. 55–56) wrote a cheerful counter to the conservative agenda and a pointed reminder of the long debate over curriculum. He discussed Colonel Parker's reversal of educational decline in the Quincy, Massachusetts schools in the 1870s through "progressive" pedagogy. For a substantial history of the Progressive movement, see Cremin (1964).

20 See the Southern Regional Education Board (1985), Galambos (1985), Oregon State System of Higher Education (1984), California Commission on the Teaching Profession (1985) policy study, New York Education Department (1985), Feistzritzer (1984), and the most prominent of all, the National Commission for Excellence in Teacher Education (1985).

21 Shanker (1985) proposed hiring veteran teachers as mentors and adjunct faculty in teacher-education programs and confirmed his support of a national teacher-testing program and career ladders, including a category of "transient" teacher at the entry-level position.

22 How an education major spends her or his credits at the undergraduate level is dis-cussed in the National Commission for Excellence in Teacher Education (1985, p. 13).

23 For a well-defined program in community education, see Harris (1982).

24 For an informative survey of the unknown successes in non-traditional programs, see Jennings and Nathan (1977); see also Nathan (1983).

# References

Academy for Educational Development. (1985). *Teacher development in schools: A report to the Ford Foundation*. New York: Author.

Adams, F., & Horton, M. (1975). *Unearthing seeds of fire: The idea of highlander.* Winston-Salem, NC: Blair.

Adler, M. (1982). *The paideia proposal: An educational manifesto.* New York: Macmillan.

Adler, M. (1983). *Paideia problems and possibilities.* New York: Macmillan.

Apple, M. (1982). *Cultural and economic reproduction in education.* London: Routledge & Kegan Paul.

Association of American Colleges. (1985). *Integrity in the college curriculum.* Washington, DC: Author.

Bastian, A., Fruchter, N., Gittell, M., Greer, C., & Haskins, K. (1985). *Choosing equality: The case for democratic schooling.* New York: New World Foundation.

Bennett, W. (1984). *To reclaim a legacy: A report on the humanities in higher education.* Washington, DC: U.S. Government Printing Office.

Berg, I. (1970). *Education and jobs: The great training robbery.* New York: Praeger.

Bisseret, N. (1957). *Education, class language, and ideology.* London: Routledge & Kegan Paul.

The bold quest for quality. (1983, October 10). *Time,* pp. 58–66.

Bowels, S., & Gintis, H. (1976). *Schooling in capitalist America: Educational reform and the contradictions of economic life.* New York: Basic Books.

Bowles, S., & Gintis, H. (1982). The crisis of liberal democratic capitalism in the case of the United States. *Politics and Society, 2*(2), 51–93.

Bowles, S., Gordon, D., & Weiskopf, T. (1983). *Beyond the wasteland: A democratic alternative to economic decline.* New York: Anchor.

Boyer, E. L. (1983). *High school: A report on secondary education in America.* New York: Harper & Row.

Boyer, E. L. (1984). Reflections on the great debate of '83. *Phi Delta Kappan, 65,* 525–530.

Braverman, H. (1974). *Labor and monopoly capital.* New York: Monthly Review.

California Commission on the Teaching Profession. (1985). *Who will teach our children? A strategy for improving California's schools.* Sacramento: Author.

Can the Schools be Saved? (1983, May 9). *Newsweek* [Shaping Up], pp. 50–58.

Carnoy, M., & Levin, H. (1985). *Schooling and work in the democratic state.* Stanford: Stanford University Press.

The College Entrance Examination Board. (1983). *Academic preparation for college: What students need to know and be able to do.* New York: Author.

Commission for Excellence in Teacher Education. (1985). *A call for change in teacher education.* Washington, DC: Author.

Cremin, L. (1964). *The transformation of the school.* New York: Vintage. (Original work published in 1961).

Cross, K. P. (1984). The rising tide of school reform reports. *Phi Delta Kappan, 66,* 167–172.

Cuban, L. (1984). School reform by remote control: SB 813 in California. *Phi Delta Kappan, 66,* 213–215.

Darling-Hammond, L. (1984a). *Beyond the commission reports: The coming crisis in teaching.* Santa Monica: Rand Corporation.

Darling-Hammond, L. (1984b). *Equality and excellence: The educational status of black Americans.* New York: College Entrance Examination Board.

Darling-Hammond, L. (1984c, January 8). Mad-Hatter tests of good teaching. *New York Times,* II–2.

Dewey, J. (1956). *The school and society.* Chicago: University of Chicago Press. (Original work published in 1900)

Dewey, J. (1956). *The child and the curriculum.* Chicago: University of Chicago Press. (Original work published in 1902)

Dewey, J. (1956). *Experience and education.* New York: Collier. (Original work published in 1938)

Donald, J. (1983). How illiteracy became a problem (and literacy stopped being one). *Journal of Education, 165,* 33–52.

Education Commission of the States. (1983a, November). *A summary of major reports on education.* Denver: Author.

Education Commission of the States, Task Force on Education for Economic Growth. (1983b). *Action for excellence: A comprehensive plan to improve our nation's schools.* Denver: Author.

Feistritzer, C. E. (1984). *The making of a teacher: A report on teacher education and certification.* Washington, DC: National Center for Education Information.

Finlay, L. S., & Faith, V. (1979). Illiteracy and alienation in American colleges: Is Paulo Freire's pedagogy relevant? *Radical Teacher, 16,* 28–40.

Finn, C. E., Jr. (1981). Why public and private schools matter. *Harvard Educational Review, 52,* 510–514.

Finn, C. E., Jr. (1983, April). The drive for educational excellence: Moving toward a public consensus. *Change, 15,* pp. 15–22.

Finn, C. E., Jr. (1986). *What works: Research about teaching and learning.* Washington, DC: U.S. Department of Education.

Finn, C. E., Jr., & Ravitch, D. (1984). Conclusions and recommendations: High expectations and disciplined effort. In Finn, C. E., Jr., Ravitch, D., & Fancher, R. T. (Eds.). *Against mediocrity: The humanities in America's high schools.* (pp. 237–262). New York: Holmes & Meier.

Fiore, K., & Elsasser, N. (1982). Strangers no more: A liberatory literacy curriculum. *College English, 44*(2), 115–128.

Fiske, E. B. (1981, October 27). Court invalidates school financing in New York State. *New York Times,* p. II–3.

The Ford Foundation. (1985). *Teacher development in schools.* New York: Author.

Frankenstein, M. (1983). Critical mathematics education: An application of Paulo Freire's epistemology. *Journal of Education, 165,* 315–339.

Freeman, R. (1976). *The overeducated American.* New York: Academic Press.

Freire, P. (1970). *Pedagogy of the oppressed.* New York: Seabury.

Freire, P. (1973). *Education for critical consciousness.* New York: Seabury.

Galambos, Eva C. (1985). *Teacher preparation: The anatomy of a college degree.* Atlanta: Southern Regional Education Board.

Gibboney, R. A. (1983). Learning: A process approach from Francis Parker. *Phi Delta Kappan, 65,* 55–56.

Giroux, H. A. (1983). *Theory and resistance in education.* South Hadley, MA: Bergin & Garvey.

Glaser, B. G., & Strauss, A. L. (1967). *The discovery of grounded theory: Strategies for qualitative research.* Chicago: Aldine.

Goodlad, J. I. (1983). *A place called school: Prospects for the future.* New York: McGraw-Hill.

Gross, R. & Gross, B. (1985). *The great school debate: Which way for American education?* New York: Simon and Schuster.

Grubb, W. N., & Lazerson, M. (1975). Rally round the workplace: Continuities and fallacies in career education. *Harvard Educational Review, 45,* 451–474.

Hacker, A. (1984, April 12). The schools flunk out. *New York Review of Books,* pp. 35–40.

Harris, I. M. (1982). An undergraduate community education curriculum for community development. *Journal of the Community Development Society, 13,* 69–82.

Harris, L., & Associates. (1984). *The 1984 Metropolitan Life survey of the American teacher.* New York: Author.

Heath, S. B. (1983). *Ways with words.* New York: McGraw-Hill.

Hirsch, E. D. (1985). Cultural literacy and the schools. *American Educator, 9,* pp. 8–15.

Hoggart, R. (1957). *The uses of literacy.* London: Chatto & Windus.

The Holmes Group. (1986). *Tomorrow's teacher: A report of The Holmes Group.* East Lansing, MI: Author.

Howe, H. (1985a). Let's have another SAT score decline. *Phi Delta Kappan, 66,* 599–602.

Howe, H. (1985b). Education moves to center stage: An overview of recent studies. *Phi Delta Kappan, 67,* 167–172.

The Institute for Responsive Education. (1984). *Action for educational equity: A guide for parents and members of community groups* (Order No. 16C). Boston: Author.

Jencks, C., Smith, M., Acland, H., Bane, M. J., Cohen, D., Gintis, H., Heyns, B., & Michelson, S. (1972). *Inequality: A reassessment of the effect of family and schooling in America.* New York: Basic Books.

Jennings, W., & Nathan, J. (1977). Startling/disturbing research on school program effectiveness. *Phi Delta Kappa, 41,* 568–572.

Judy, S. (1980). *The ABCs of literacy.* New York: Oxford.

198    *Ira Shor*

Karabel, J. (1972). Community colleges and social stratification. *Harvard Educational Review, 42*, 521–562.

Karp, W. (1985, June). Why Johnny can't think: The politics of bad schooling. *Harper's*, pp. 69–73.

Kohl, H. (1982). *Basic skills*. New York: Bantam Books.

The Labor Institute (1982). *What's wrong with the U. S. economy? A popular guide for the rest of us*. Boston: Southend.

Leonard, G. (1984, April). The great school reform hoax. *Esquire*, pp. 47–56.

Levin, H. (1981). Back-to-basics and the economy. *Radical Teacher, 20*, 8–10.

Levin, H. (1985). Solving the shortage of mathematics and science teachers. *Education evaluation and policy analysis, 7*, 371–382.

Levin, H., & Rumberger, R. (1974). *The educational implications of high technology*. Institute for Research on Education Finance and Governance: Stanford University.

Maeroff, G. (1982). *Don't blame the kids: The trouble with America's schools*. New York: McGraw-Hill.

Minkler, M., & Cox, K. (1980). Creating critical consciousness in health. *International Journal of Health Services, 10*, 311–322.

Nathan, J. (1983). *Free to teach: Equity and excellence in schools*. New York: Pilgrim.

National Academy Press. (1984). *High schools and the changing workplace: The employers' view*. Washington, DC: Author.

National Coalition of Advocates for Children. (1985). *Barriers to excellence: Our children at risk*. Boston: Author.

The National Commission for Excellence in Teacher Education. (1985). *A call for change in teacher education*. Washington, DC: Author.

The National Commission on Excellence in Education. (1983). A *Nation at Risk: The Imperative for Educational Reform*. Washington, DC: U.S. Department of Education.

National Institute of Education. [Chaired by J. O'Toole]. (1983). *Work in America*. Washington, DC: Department of Health, Education and Welfare.

National Institute of Education. (1984a). *The condition of education*. Washington, DC: Author.

National Institute of Education. (1984b). *Involvement in learning*. Washington, DC: U.S. Department of Education.

The National Science Board Commission on Preschool Education in Mathematics, Science, and Technology. (1983). *Educating Americans for the 21st Century*. 2 vols. Washington, DC: National Science Foundation.

New York State Education Department. (1985). *Strengthening teaching in New York State*. Albany: Author.

Ohmann, R. (1985). Literacy, technology, and monopoly capital. *College English, 47*, 675–684.

Oregon State System of Higher Education. (1984). *Quality assurance: Teacher education in the Oregon State System of Higher Education*. Eugene: Author.

Panel on Secondary School Education for the Changing Workplace. *High school and the changing workplace: The employers' view*. (1984). Washington, DC: National Academy Press.

Passow, A. H. (1984). Tackling the reform reports of the 1980s. *Phi Delta Kappan, 65*, 674–683.

Pattison, R. (1982). *On literacy: The politics of the word from Homer to the age of rock*. New York: Oxford.

Peterson, P. E. (1983). (Background paper attached to *Making the grade*.) New York: Twentieth Century Fund.

Pincus, F. (1980). The false promise of community colleges: Class conflict and vocational education. *Harvard Educational Review, 50*, 332–361.

Piven, F., & Cloward, R. (1982). *The new class war: Reagan's attack on the welfare state*. New York: Pantheon.

Richardson, R. C., Fisk, E. C., & Okun, M. K. (1983). *Literacy in the open-access college*. San Francisco: Jossey Bass.

Serrano v. Priest. (1971). 5 Cal. 3d 584, 487 P. 2d 1241, 96 Cal. RPTR 601.

Shanker, A. (1985). *The making of a profession*. Washington, DC: American Federation of Teachers.

Shor, I. (1986). *Culture wars: School and society in the conservative restoration, 1969–1984.* New York: Routledge & Kegan Paul.

Shor, I. (in press). *Critical teaching and everyday life.* Chicago: University of Chicago Press. (Original work published in 1980)

Shor, I., & Freire, P. (1986). *A pedagogy for liberation.* South Hadley, MA: Bergin & Garvey.

Silberman, C. (1971). *Crisis in the classroom.* New York: Vintage.

Sizer, T. R. (1984). *Horace's compromise: The dilemma of the American high school.* Boston: Houghton Mifflin.

Southern Regional Education Board. (1985). *Improving teacher education.* Atlanta: Author.

Spring, J. (1984, April). From study hall to hiring hall. *The Progressive, 46,* 30–31.

Task Force of the Business-Higher Education Forum. (1983). *America's competitive challenge.* Washington, DC: Author.

The Twentieth Century Fund Task Force on Federal Elementary and Secondary Education Policy. (1983). *Making the grade.* New York: Twentieth Century Fund.

Toch, T. (1984). The dark side of the excellence movement. *Phi Delta Kappan, 65,* 173–176.

Wallerstein, N. (1983). *Language and culture in conflict: Problem-posing in the ESL classroom.* NJ: Addison-Wesley.

What makes great schools great. (1984, August 27). *U.S. News and World Report,* pp. 46–51.

Why teachers fail: How to make them better. (1984, September 24). *Newsweek,* pp. 64–70.

Willis, P. (1981). *Learning to labor: How working class kids get working class jobs.* New York: Columbia University Press.

# CHAPTER 16

# TEACHER EDUCATION AND THE POLITICS OF ENGAGEMENT (1986)

## The case for democratic schooling

### Henry A. Giroux and Peter McLaren

As far back as 1890, a teacher from New England named Horace Willard cogently argued that in contrast to members of other professions, teachers lived "lives of mechanical routine, and were subjected to a machine of supervision, organization, classification, grading, percentages, uniformity, promotions, tests, examination."[1] Nowhere, Willard decried, was there room in the school culture for "individuality, ideas, independence, originality, study, investigation."[2] Forty years later Henry W. Holmes, dean of Harvard University's new Graduate School of Education, echoed these sentiments in his criticism of the National Survey of the Education of Teachers in 1930. According to Holmes, the survey failed to support teachers as independent critical thinkers. Instead, it endorsed a view of the teacher as a "routine worker under the expert direction of principals, supervisors, and superintendents."[3] Holmes was convinced that if teachers' work continued to be defined in such a narrow fashion, schools of education would eventually respond by limiting themselves to forms of training that virtually undermined the development of teachers as critically-minded intellectuals.

At different times both of these noteworthy critics of American education recognized that any viable attempt at educational reform must address the issue of teacher education. Most important was their conviction that teachers should function professionally as intellectuals, and that teacher education should be inextricably linked to critically transforming the school setting and, by extension, the wider social setting.

In the early part of the century, a number of experimental teacher education programs managed to shift the terrain of struggle for democratic schooling from a largely rhetorical platform to the program site itself. One such program was organized around New College, an experimental teacher training venture affiliated with Columbia University, Teachers College between 1927 and 1953. Spokespersons from New College proclaimed "that a sound teacher education program must lie in a proper integration of rich scholarship, educational theory, and professional practice."[4] Furthermore, New College embarked on a training program based on the principle that "it is the peculiar privilege of the teacher to play a large part in the development of the social order of the next generation."[5] The College's first announcement claimed that if teachers were to escape from the usual "academic lock step ... [they] required contact with life in its various phases and understanding of it—an understanding of the intellectual, moral, social, and economic life of the people."[6]

The idea that teacher education programs should center their academic and moral objectives on the education of teachers as critical intellectuals, while simultaneously advancing democratic interests, has invariably influenced the debates revolving around the various "crises" in education over the last fifty years.[7] Moreover, it has been precisely because of the presence of such an idea that a rationale eventually could be constructed which linked schooling to the imperatives of democracy and classroom pedagogy to the dynamics of citizenship. This is not to suggest, however, that either public education or teacher training programs were overburdened by a concern for democracy and citizenship.[8] Nevertheless, the historical precedent for educating teachers as intellectuals and developing schools as democratic sites for social transformation might begin to define the way in which public education and the education of teachers *could* be appropriately perceived today. We wish, in other words, to build upon this precedent in order to argue for the education of teachers as transformative intellectuals. We use the term "intellectual" in the manner described by Frank Lentricchia:

> By "intellectual" I do not mean what traditional Marxism has generally meant—a bearer of the universal, the political conscience of us all. Nor do I mean "a radical intellectual" in the narrowest of understandings of Antonio Gramsci—an intellectual whose practice is overtly, daily aligned with and empirically involved in the working class. By intellectual I refer to the *specific intellectual* described by Foucault—one whose radical work of transformation, whose fight against repression is carried on at the specific institutional site where he finds himself and on the terms of his own expertise, on the terms inherent to his own functioning as an intellectual.[9]

By the term "transformative intellectual," we refer to one who exercises forms of intellectual and pedagogical practice which attempt to insert teaching and learning directly into the political sphere by arguing that schooling represents both a struggle for meaning and a struggle over power relations. We are also referring to one whose intellectual practices are necessarily grounded in forms of moral and ethical discourse exhibiting a preferential concern for the suffering and struggles of the disadvantaged and oppressed. Here we extend the traditional view of the intellectual as someone who is able to analyze various interests and contradictions within society to someone capable of articulating emancipatory possibilities and working towards their realization. Teachers who assume the role of transformative intellectuals treat students as critical agents, question how knowledge is produced and distributed, utilize dialogue, and make knowledge meaningful, critical, and ultimately emancipatory.[10]

We argue in this paper that within the current discourse on educational reform[11] there exists, with few exceptions,[12] an ominous silence regarding the role that both teacher education and public schooling should play in advancing democratic practices, critical citizenship, and the role of the teacher as intellectual. Given the legacy of democracy and social reform bequeathed to us by our educational forebears, such as John Dewey and George Counts, this silence not only suggests that some of the current reformers are suffering from political and historical amnesia; it also points to the ideological interests that underlie their proposals. Regrettably, such interests tell us less about the ills of schooling than they do about the nature of the real crisis facing this nation—a crisis which, in our view, not only augurs poorly for the future of American education, but underscores the need to reclaim a democratic tradition presently in retreat. Bluntly stated, much of the current literature on educational reform points to a crisis in American democracy itself.

The discourse of recent educational reform characteristically excludes certain proposals from consideration. For instance, missing from the various privileged discourses that have fashioned the recent reform movement, and absent among the practices of public school teachers whose participation in the current debate on education has been less than vigorous, are concerted attempts at democratizing schools and empowering students to become critical, active citizens. This reluctance on the part of teachers has had a particularly deleterious effect, since the absence of proposals for rethinking the purpose of schools of education around democratic concerns has further strengthened the ideological and political pressures that define teachers as technicians and structure teacher work in a demeaning and overburdening manner. Kenneth Zeichner underscores this concern when he writes:

> It is hoped that future debate in teacher education will be more concerned with the question of which educational, moral and political commitments ought to guide our work in the field rather than with the practice of merely dwelling on which procedures and organizational arrangements will most effectively help us realize tacit and often unexamined ends. Only after we have begun to resolve some of these necessarily prior questions related to ends should we concentrate on the resolution of more instrumental issues related to effectively accomplishing our goals.[13]

The current debate provides an opportunity to critically analyze the ideological and material conditions—both in and out of schools—that contribute to teacher passivity and powerlessness. We also believe that recognition of the failure to link the purposes of public schooling to the imperatives of economic and social reform provides a starting point both for examining the ideological shift in education that has taken place in the 1980s and for developing a new language of democracy, empowerment, and possibility in which teacher education programs and classroom practices can be defined. Our central concern is in developing a view of teacher education that defines teachers as transformative intellectuals and schooling as part of an ongoing struggle for democracy. In developing our argument, we will focus on four considerations. First, we will analyze the dominant new conservative positions that have generated current educational reforms in terms of the implications these viewpoints hold for the reorganization of teacher education programs. Second, we will develop a rationale for organizing teacher education programs around a critical view of teacher work and authority, one that we believe is consistent with the principles and practices of democracy. Third, we will present some programmatic suggestions for analyzing teacher education as a form of cultural politics. Finally, we will argue for a critical pedagogy that draws upon the many-sided conversations and voices that make up community life.

## Education reform and the retreat from democracy

Underlying the educational reforms proposed by the recent coalition of conservatives and liberals, conveniently labeled "the new conservatives," is a discourse that both edifies and mystifies their proposals. Capitalizing upon the waning confidence of the general public and a growing number of teachers in the effectiveness of public schools, the new conservatives argue for educational reform by faulting schools for a series of crises that include everything from a growing trade deficit to the breakdown of family morality.[14] As is the case with many public issues in the age of Ronald Reagan, the new conservatives have seized the initiative by framing their arguments in a terse rhetoric that resonates with a growing public concern about downward mobility in hard economic times, that appeals to a resurgence of chauvinistic patriotism, and that points toward a reformulation of educational goals along elitist lines. Such a discourse is dangerous not only because it misconstrues the responsibility schools have for wider economic and social problems—a position that has been convincingly refuted and need not be argued against here[15]—but also because it reflects an alarming ideological shift regarding the role schools should play in relation to society. The effect of this shift, launched by the new right's full-fledged attack on the educational and social reforms of the 1960s, has been to redefine the purpose of education so as to eliminate its citizenship function in favor of a narrowly defined labor market perspective. The essence and implications of this position have been well-documented by Barbara Finkelstein.

> Contemporary reformers seem to be recalling public education from its trad-itional utopian mission—to nurture a critical and committed citizenry that would stimulate the processes of political and cultural transformation and refine and extend the workings of political democracy. . . . Reformers seem to imagine public schools as economic rather than political instrumen-talities. They forge no new visions of political and social possibilities. Instead, they call public schools to industrial and cultural service exclusively. . . . Reformers have disjoined their calls for educational reform from calls for a redistribution of power and authority, and the cultivation of cultural forms celebrating pluralism and diversity. As if they have had enough of political democracy, Americans, for the first time in a one hundred and fifty-year history, seem ready to do ideological surgery on their public schools—cutting them away from the fate of social justice and political democracy completely and grafting them onto elite corporate, industrial, military, and cultural interests.[16]

It is important to recognize that the new conservative attack on the reforms of the last decade has resulted in a shift away from defining schools as agencies of equity and justice. There is little concern with how public education could better serve the interests of diverse groups of students by enabling them to understand and gain some control over the sociopolitical forces that influence their destinies. Rather, via this new discourse, and its preoccupation with accountability schemes, testing, accreditation, and credentializing, educational reform has become syn-onymous with turning schools into "company stores." It now defines school life primarily by measuring its utility against its contribution to economic growth and cultural uniformity. Similarly, at the heart of the present ideological shift is an attempt to reformulate the purpose of public education around a set of interests and social relations that define academic success almost exclusively in terms of the accumulation of capital and the logic of the marketplace. This represents a shift away from teacher control of the curriculum and toward a fundamentally techni-cist form of education that is more directly tied to economic modes of production. Moreover, the new conservatives provide a view of society in which authority derives from technical expertise and culture embodies an idealized tradition that glorifies hard work, industrial discipline, domesticated desire, and cheerful obedience. Edward Berman has deftly captured the political nature of this ideological shift.

> Architects of the current reform have, to their credit, dropped the rhetoric about the school as a vehicle for personal betterment. There is little pretense in today's reports or the resultant programs that individual improvement and social mobility are important concerns of a reconstituted school system. The former rhetoric about individual mobility has given way to exhortations to build educational structures that will allow individual students to make a greater contribution to the economic output of the corporate state. There are few rhetorical flourishes to obfuscate this overriding objective.[17]

The ideological shift that characterizes the current reform period is also evident in the ways in which teacher preparation and classroom pedagogy are currently being defined. The rash of reform proposals for reorganizing schools points to a definition of teacher work that seriously exacerbates conditions which are presently eroding the authority and intellectual integrity of teachers. In fact, the most compelling aspect of the influential reports, especially the widely publicized *A Nation at Risk, Action for Excellence,* and *A Nation Prepared: Teachers for the 21st Century,* is their studious refusal to address the ideological, social, and economic conditions underlying poor teacher and student performance.[18] For example, as Frankenstein and Louis Kampf point out, public school teachers constantly confront conditions "such as the overwhelming emphasis on quantification (both in scoring children and keeping records), the growing lack of control over curriculum (separating conception from execution) and over other aspects of their work, the isolation from their peers, the condescending treatment by administrators, and the massive lay-offs of veteran teachers."[19]

Instead of addressing these issues, many of the reforms taking place at the state level further consolidate administrative structures and prevent teachers from collectively and creatively shaping the conditions under which they work. For instance, at both the local and federal levels, the new educational discourse has influenced a number of policy recommendations, such as competency-based testing for teachers, a lockstep sequencing of materials, mastery learning techniques, systematized evaluation schemes, standardized curricula, and the implementation of mandated "basics."[20] The consequences are evident not only in the substantively narrow view of the purposes of education, but also in the definitions of teaching, learning, and literacy that are championed by the new management-oriented policymakers. In place of developing critical understanding, engaging student experience, and fostering active and critical citizenship, schools are redefined through a language that emphasizes standardization, competency, and narrowly-defined performance skills.

Within this paradigm, the development of curricula is increasingly left to administrative experts or simply adopted from publishers, with few, if any, contributions from teachers who are expected to implement the new programs. In its most ideologically offensive form, this type of prepackaged curriculum is rationalized as teacher-proof and is designed to be applied to any classroom context regardless of the historical, cultural, and socioeconomic differences that characterize various schools and students.[21] What is important to note is that the deskilling of teachers appears to go hand-in-hand with the increasing adoption of management-type pedagogies.

Viewing teachers as semiskilled, low-paid workers in the mass production of education, policymakers have sought to change education, to improve it, by "teacher-proofing" it. Over the past decade we have seen the proliferation of elaborate accountability schemes that go by acronyms like MBO (management by objectives), PBBS (performance-based budgeting systems), CBE (competency-based education), CBTE (competency-based teacher education), and MCT (minimum competency testing).[22]

The growing removal of curriculum development and analysis from the hands of teachers is related to the ways technocratic rationality is used to redefine teacher work. This type of rationality increasingly takes place within a social division of labor in which thinking is removed from implementation and the model of the teacher becomes that of the technician or white-collar clerk. Likewise, learning is reduced to the memorization of narrowly defined facts and isolated pieces of information that can easily be measured and evaluated. The significance of the overall effects of this type of rationalization and bureaucratic control on teacher work and morale has been forcefully articulated by Linda Darling-Hammond. She writes:

In a Rand study of teachers' views of the effect of educational policies on their classroom practices, we learned from teachers that in response to policies that prescribe teaching practices and outcomes, they spend less time on untested subjects, such as science and social studies; they use less writing in their classrooms in order to gear assignments to the format of standardized tests; they resort to lectures rather than classroom discussions in order to cover the prescribed behavioral objectives without getting "off the track"; they are precluded from using teaching materials that are not on prescribed textbook lists, even when they think these materials are essential to meet the needs of some of their students; and they feel constrained from following up on expressed student interests that lie outside of the bounds of mandated curricula. . . . And 45 percent of the teachers in this study told us that the single thing that would make them leave teaching was the increased prescriptiveness of teaching content and methods—in short, the continuing deprofessionalization of teaching.[23]

The ideological interests that inform the new conservative proposals are based on a view of morality and politics that is legitimated through an appeal to custom, national unity, and tradition. Within this discourse, democracy loses its dynamic character and is reduced to a set of inherited principles and institutional arrangements that teach students how to adapt rather than to question the basic precepts of society. What is left in the new reform proposals is a view of authority constructed around a mandate to follow and implement predetermined rules, to transmit an unquestioned cultural tradition, and to sanctify industrial discipline. Couple these problems with large classes, excessive paperwork, fragmented work periods, and low salaries, and it comes as no surprise that teachers are increasingly leaving the field.[24]

In effect, the ideological shift at work here points to a restricted definition of schooling, one that almost completely strips public education of a democratic vision where citizenship and the politics of possibility are given serious consideration. When we argue that the recent conservative or "blue-ribbon" reform recommendations lack a politics of possibility and citizenship, we mean that primacy is given to education as economic investment, that is, to pedagogical practices designed to create a school-business partnership and make the American economic system more competitive in world markets. A politics of possibility and citizenship, by contrast, refers to a conception of schooling in which classrooms are seen as active sites of public intervention and social struggle. Moreover, this view maintains that possibilities exist for teachers and students to redefine the nature of critical learning and practice outside of the imperatives of the corporate marketplace. The idea of a politics and project of possibility is grounded in Ernst Bloch's idea of "natural law" wherein "the standpoint of the victims of any society ought to always provide the starting point for the critique of that society."[25] Such a politics defines schools as sites around which struggles should be waged in the name of developing a more just, humane, and equitable social order both within and outside of schools.

We have spent some time analyzing the new conservative discourse and the ideological shift it represents because in our view the current reforms, with few exceptions, pose a grave threat to both public schooling and the nature of democracy itself. The definition of teaching and learning provided by this discourse ignores, as we have pointed out, the imperative of viewing schools as sites of social transformation where students are educated to become informed, active, and critical citizens. The gravity of this ideological shift is hardly ameliorated by the fact that even public schooling's more liberal spokespersons have failed to develop a critical discourse that challenges the hegemony of dominant ideologies. For example, the highly publicized reports by John Goodlad, Theodore Sizer, Ernest Boyer, and others neither acknowledge nor utilize the radical tradition of educational scholarship.[26] While the liberal position does take the concepts of equality of opportunity and citizenship seriously, we are, nevertheless, left with analyses of schooling that lack a sufficiently critical understanding of the ways in which power has been used to favor select groups of students over others. In addition, we are given only a cursory treatment of the political economy of schooling, with its scattered history of dishonorable linkages to corporate interests and ideology. Furthermore, we are provided with little understanding of how the hidden curriculum in schools works in a subtly discriminating way to discredit the dreams, experiences, and knowledges associated with students from specific class, racial, and gender groupings.[27]

In the absence of any competing critical agenda for reform, the new conservative discourse encourages teacher education institutions to define themselves primarily as training sites that provide students with the technical expertise required to find a place within the corporate hierarchy. Thomas Popkewitz and Allan Pitman have characterized the ideology underlying the current reform proposals, moreover, as betraying a fundamental elitism since it basically adopts a perspective of society that is undifferentiated by class, race, or gender. The logic endemic to these reports, the authors argue, demonstrates an attachment to possessive individualism and instrumental rationality. In other words: "Quantity is seen as quality. Procedural concerns are made objects of value and moral domains. The teacher is a facilitator . . . or a counselor. . . . Individualization is pacing through a common curriculum. . . . Flexibility in instruction is to begin 'where the student is ready to begin'. . . . There is no discussion of what is to be facilitated or the conceptions of curriculum to guide procedures."[28]

Furthermore, Popkewitz and Pitman see a distinctive shift from a concern with equity to a slavish regard for a restricted notion of excellence. That is, the concept of excellence that informs these new reports "ignores the social differentiations while providing political symbols to give credibility to education which only a few can appreciate."[29] What is rightly being stressed is that the concept of excellence fashioned in the reports is designed to benefit "those who have already access to positions of status and privilege through accidents of birth."[30]

Given the context in which teaching and learning are currently being defined, it becomes all the more necessary to insist on an alternative view of teacher education, one which, in refusing to passively serve the existing ideological and institutional arrangements of the public schools, is aimed at challenging and reforming them.

## Teacher education: Democracy and the imperative of social reform

We want to return to the idea that the fundamental concerns of democracy and critical citizenship should be central to any discussion of the purpose of teacher education. In doing so, we will organize our discussion around two arguments. The first represents an initial effort to develop a critical language with which to reconstruct the relationship between teacher education programs and the public schools, on the one hand, and public education and society on the other. The second, and more detailed, argument presents a view of authority and teacher work that attempts to define the political project we believe should underlie the purpose and nature of teacher education programs.

If teacher education programs are to provide the basis for democratic struggle and renewal in our schools, they will have to redefine their current relationship to such institutions. As it presently stands, schools of education rarely encourage their students to take seriously the imperatives of social critique and social change as part of a wider emancipatory vision. If and when education students begin to grapple with these concerns at the classroom level, it is invariably years after graduation. Our own experiences in teacher education institutions—both as students and as instructors—have confirmed for us what is generally agreed to be commonplace in most schools and colleges of education throughout the United States: that these institutions continue to define themselves essentially as service institutions which are generally mandated to provide the requisite technical expertise to carry out whatever pedagogical functions are deemed necessary by the various school communities in which students undertake their practicum experiences.[31] In order to escape this political posture, teacher education programs need to reorient their focus to the critical transformation of public schools rather than to the simple reproduction of existing institutions and ideologies.[32]

One starting point would be to recognize the importance of educating students in the languages of critique and possibility; that is, providing teachers with the critical terminology and conceptual apparatus that will allow them not only to critically analyze the democratic and political shortcomings of schools, but also to develop the knowledge and skills that will advance the possibilities for generating curricula, classroom social practices, and organizational arrangements based on and cultivating a deep respect for a democratic and ethically-based community. In effect, this means that the relationship of teacher education programs to public schooling would be self-consciously guided by political and moral considerations. Dewey expressed well the need for educators to make political and moral considerations a central aspect of their education and work when he distinguished between "education as a function of society" and "society as a function of education."[33] In simple terms, Dewey's distinction reminds us that education can function either to create passive, risk-free citizens or to create a politicized citizenry educated to fight for various forms of public life informed by a concern for justice, happiness, and equality. At issue here is whether schools of education are to serve and reproduce the existing society or to adopt the more critical role of challenging the social order so as to develop and advance its democratic imperatives. Also at issue is developing a rationale for defining teacher education programs in political terms that make explicit a particular view of the relationship between public schools and the social order, a view based on defending the imperatives of a democratic society.

## Public schools as democratic public spheres

Our second concern is directed to the broader question of how educators should view the purpose of public schooling. Our position echoes Dewey in that we believe public schools need to be defined as democratic public spheres. This means regarding schools as democratic sites dedicated to self- and social empowerment. Understood in these terms, schools can be public places where students learn the knowledge and skills necessary to live in a critical democracy. Contrary to the view that schools are extensions of the workplace or front-line institutions in the corporate battle for international markets, schools viewed as democratic public spheres center their activities around critical inquiry and meaningful dialogue. In this case, students are given the opportunity to learn the discourse of public association and civic responsibility. Such a discourse seeks to recapture the idea of a critical democracy that commands respect for individual freedom and social justice. Moreover, viewing schools as democratic public spheres provides a rationale for defending them, along with progressive forms of pedagogy and teacher work, as agencies of social reform. When defined in these terms, schools can be defended as institutions that provide the knowledge, skills, social relations, and vision necessary to educate a citizenry capable of building a critical democracy. That is, school practice can be rationalized in a political language that recovers and emphasizes the transformative role that schools can play in advancing the democratic possibilities inherent in the existing society.[34]

## Authority and intellectuals: Rethinking the nature and purpose of teacher work

Redefining the notion of authority in emancipatory terms is central to understanding and legitimating teacher work as a critical practice. The importance of such a task can be made clearer by highlighting the significance of authority as part of the fundamental discourse of schooling.

First, as a form of legitimation, authority is inescapably related to a particular vision of what schools should be as part of a wider community and society. Thus, questions about school and teacher authority help to make both visible and problematic the presuppositions of the officially sanctioned discourses and values that legitimate the institutional and social arrangements constituting everyday life in schools. For example, questions might be raised about the nature and source of the authority which legitimates a particular type of curriculum, the way school time is organized, the political consequences of tracking students, the social division of labor among teachers, and the patriarchal basis of authority. In this way, the concept of authority raises issues about the ethical and political basis of schooling. That is, it calls into serious question the role that school administrators and teachers play as intellectuals in both articulating and implementing their particular views or ideologies. In short, the category of authority reinserts the primacy of the political into the language of schooling by highlighting the social and ideological function that educators serve in elaborating, enforcing, and legit-imating schooling as a particular form of social life, that is, as a particular set of ideas and practices that occur within historically defined contexts.

Second, if the concept of authority is to provide a legitimating basis for rethink-ing the purpose and meaning of teacher education, it must be reconstituted around a view of community life in which morality in everyday existence is fun-damental to the meaning of democracy.[35] A form of *emancipatory* authority needs to be developed, one that can illuminate the connection and importance of two questions that teacher education programs should take as a central point of inquiry in structuring the form and content of their curricula. These are: What kind of society do educators want to live in? What kind of teaching and pedagogy can be developed and legitimated by a view of authority that takes democracy and critical citizenship seriously? Authority, in this view, rests on the assumption that public schooling should promote forms of morality and sociality in which stu-dents learn to encounter and engage social differences and diverse points of view. In addition, schools should prepare students for making choices regarding forms of life that have morally different consequences. This means that educators must replace pedagogical practices which emphasize disciplinary control and one-sided character formation with practices that are based on an emancipatory authority, ones which enable students to engage in critical analysis and to make choices regarding what interests and knowledge claims are most desirable and morally appropriate for living in a just and democratic state. Equally important is the need for students to engage in civic-minded action in order to remove the social and political constraints that restrict the victims of this society from leading decent and humane lives.

A reconstituted notion of emancipatory authority suggests, in this case, that teachers are bearers of critical knowledge, rules, and values through which they consciously articulate and problematize their relationship to each other, to stu-dents, to subject matter, and to the wider community. This view of authority exposes and challenges the dominant view of teachers as primarily technicians or public servants whose role is to implement rather than to conceptualize peda-gogical practice. Moreover, the category of emancipatory authority dignifies teacher work by viewing it as an intellectual practice with respect to both its formal characteristics and the nature of the content discussed. Teacher work becomes a form of intellectual labor opposed to the pedagogical divisions bet-ween conception and practice, and production and implementation, that are cur-rently celebrated in a number of educational reforms. The concept of teacher as intellectual carries with it the political and ethical imperative to judge, critique, and reject those approaches to authority that reinforce a technical and social division of labor that silences and disempowers both teachers and students. In other words, emancipatory authority is a concept which demands that teachers and others critically confront the ideological and practical conditions which enable or constrain them in their capacity as transformative intellectuals.

It is important to stress that the concept of emancipatory authority provides the theoretical basis for defining teachers not merely as intellectuals but, more specifically, as transformative intellectuals. The distinction is important because transformative intellectuals are not merely concerned with empowerment in the conventional sense, that is, with giving students the knowledge and skills they will need to gain access to some traditional measure of economic and social mobility in the capitalist marketplace. Rather, for transformative intellectuals, the issue of teaching and learning is linked to the more political goal of educating students to take risks and to struggle within ongoing relations of power in order to alter the oppressive conditions in which life is lived. To facilitate this goal, transformative intellectuals need to make clear the nature of the appeals to authority they are using to legitimate their pedagogical practices. In other words, educators need to specify the political and moral referents for the authority they assume in teaching particular forms of knowledge, in taking stands against forms of oppression, and in treating students as if they ought also to be concerned about social justice and political action.

In short, this reconstituted version of authority is important because it contains elements of a language of both criticism and possibility. As part of the language of critique, the notion of emancipatory authority provides a discourse through which educators can critically examine views of authority often used by conservatives and others to link the purpose of schooling to a reductionist view of patriotism and patriarchy. As part of the language of possibility, authority as an emancipatory practice provides the scaffolding with which one can connect the purpose of schooling to the imperatives of what Benjamin Barber calls a "strong democracy," a democracy characterized by citizens capable of seriously confronting public issues through ongoing forms of public debate and social action.[36]

In our view, the most important referent for this particular view of authority rests in a commitment to address the many instances of suffering that characterize the present society. This suggests a recognition and identification with "the perspective of those people and groups who are marginal and exploited."[37] In its practical dimension, such a commitment represents a break from the bonds of isolated liberal individuality and a desire to engage with others in political struggles that challenge the existing order of society as being institutionally repressive and unjust. It is important to note that transformative intellectuals can serve to act, as Welch points out, as bearers of dangerous memory.[38] This means that such intellectuals can link knowledge to power by bringing to light and teaching the subjugated histories, experiences, stories, and accounts of those who suffer and struggle within conditions that are rarely made public or analyzed through the official discourses of public schooling. Thus, we can point to the histories of women, blacks, working-class groups, and others whose histories challenge the moral legitimacy of the structures of society and therefore contain knowledge too "dangerous" to make visible. Of course, teachers of "dangerous memory" must do more than excavate historical reason and subjugated knowledge; they must also make clear that people are called to struggle, that political alternatives do in fact exist, and that such buried knowledge needs to be appropriated in the interest of creating more critically democratic societies.

## Rethinking the nature of teacher education

We would like to bring the foregoing discussion to bear on the more practical mission of reconstructing teacher education programs around a new vision of democratic schooling and teaching for critical citizenship. Consequently, we shall devote the remainder of our discussion to outlining, in more detailed and programmatic terms, what we feel are some essential components and categories for a teacher education curriculum and a critical pedagogy for the schools.

As we have argued, most teacher education programs have been, and continue to be, entirely removed from a vision and a set of practices dedicated to the fostering of critical democracy and social justice. A repeated criticism made by educators working within the radical tradition has been that, as it currently exists, teacher education rarely addresses either the moral implications of societal inequalities within our present form of industrial capitalism or the ways in which schools function to reproduce and legitimate these inequalities.[39]

Usually when classroom life is discussed in teacher education programs, it is presented fundamentally as a one-dimensional set of rules and regulative practices, rather than as a cultural terrain where a variety of interests and practices collide in a constant and often chaotic struggle for dominance. Thus, prospective teachers frequently receive the impression that classroom culture is essentially free from ambiguity and contradiction. According to this view, schools are supposedly devoid of all vestiges of contestation, struggle, and cultural politics.[40] Furthermore, classroom reality is rarely presented as if it were socially constructed, historically determined, and reproduced through institutionalized relationships of class, gender, race, and power. Unfortunately, this dominant conception of schooling vastly contradicts what the student teacher often experiences during his or her practicum or fieldsite work, especially if the student is placed in a school largely populated by economically disadvantaged and disenfranchised students. Yet, student teachers are nevertheless instructed to view schooling as a neutral terrain devoid of power and politics. It is against this transparent depiction of schooling that prospective teachers, more often than not, view their own ideologies and experiences through a dominant theoretical and cultural perspective that remains largely unquestioned. Most important, teachers in this situation have no grounds upon which to question the dominant cultural assumptions that shape and structure the ways in which they respond to and influence student behavior.

Consequently, many student teachers who find themselves teaching working-class or minority students lack a well-articulated framework for understanding the class, cultural, ideological, and gender dimensions that inform classroom life. As a result, cultural differences among students often are viewed uncritically as deficiencies rather than as strengths, and what passes for teaching is in actuality an assault on the specific histories, experiences, and knowledges that such students use both to define their own identities and to make sense of their larger world. We use the term "assault" not because such knowledge is openly attacked —but because it is devalued through a process that is at once subtle and debilitating. What happens is that within the dominant school culture, subordinate knowledge is generally ignored, marginalized, or treated in a disorganized fashion. Such knowledge is often treated as if it did not exist, or treated in ways that disconfirm it. Conversely, ideologies that do not aid subordinate groups in interpreting the reality they actually experience often pass for objective forms of knowledge. In this process prospective teachers lose an understanding of the relationship between culture and power as well as a sense of how to develop pedagogical possibilities for their students from the cultural differences that often characterize school and classroom life. In the section that follows, we will discuss the elements we feel should constitute a new model of teacher education, one that addresses the above issue more specifically.

## Teacher education as cultural politics

Our concern here is with reconstituting the grounds upon which teacher education programs are built. This means developing an alternative form of teacher education curriculum that supports what we call the construction of a cultural politics. In our view, such a programmatic approach to teacher education conceptualizes schooling as taking place within a political and cultural arena where forms of student experience and subjectivity are actively produced and mediated. In other words, we wish to stress the idea that schools do not merely teach academic subjects, but also, in part, produce student subjectivities or particular sets of experiences that are in themselves part of an ideological process. Conceptualizing schooling as the construction and transmission of subjectivities permits us to understand more clearly the idea that the curriculum is more than just an introduction of students to particular subject disciplines and teaching methodologies; it also serves as an introduction to a particular way of life.[41]

At this point, we must forego a detailed specification of teaching practices and instead attempt to briefly sketch out particular areas of study crucial to the development of a reconceptualized teacher education curriculum. We assign the term "cultural politics" to our curriculum agenda because we feel that this term permits us to capture the significance of the sociocultural dimension of the schooling process. Furthermore, the term allows us to highlight the political consequences of interaction between teachers and students who come from dominant and subordinate cultures. A teacher education curriculum as a form of cultural politics assumes that the social, cultural, political, and economic dimensions are the primary categories for understanding contemporary schooling.[42] Within this context, school life is conceptualized not as a unitary, monolithic, and ironclad system of rules and regulations, but as a cultural terrain characterized by varying degrees of accommodation, contestation, and resistance. Furthermore, school life is understood as a plurality of conflicting languages and struggles, a place where classroom and street-corner cultures collide and where teachers, students, and school administrators often differ as to how school experiences and practices are to be defined and understood.

The imperative of this curriculum is to create conditions for student self-empowerment and self-constitution as an active political and moral subject. We are using the term "empowerment" to refer to the process whereby students acquire the means to critically appropriate knowledge existing outside of their immediate experience in order to broaden their understanding of themselves, the world, and the possibilities for transforming the taken-for-granted assumptions about the way we live. Stanley Aronowitz has described one aspect of empowerment as "the process of appreciating and loving oneself."[43] In this sense, empowerment is gained from knowledge and social relations that dignify one's own history, language, and cultural traditions. But empowerment means more than self-confirmation. It also refers to the process by which students are able to interrogate and selectively appropriate those aspects of the dominant culture that will provide them with the basis for defining and transforming, rather than merely serving, the wider social order.

The project of "doing" a teacher education curriculum based on cultural politics consists of linking critical social theory to a set of stipulated practices through which student teachers are able to dismantle and critically examine preferred educational and cultural traditions, many of which have fallen prey to an instrumental rationality that either limits or ignores democratic ideals and principles.

One of our main concerns focuses on developing a language of critique and demystification that is capable of analyzing the latent interests and ideologies that work to socialize students in a manner compatible with the dominant culture. We are equally concerned, however, with creating alternative teaching practices capable of empowering students both inside and outside of schools. While it is impossible to provide a detailed outline of the courses of a curriculum for cultural politics, we want to comment on some important areas of analysis that should be central to such a program. These include the critical study of power, language, culture, and history.

## Power

A pivotal concern of a teacher education curriculum that subscribes to a cultural politics approach is to assist student teachers in understanding the relationship between power and knowledge. Within the dominant curriculum, knowledge is often removed from the issue of power and is generally treated in a technical manner; that is, it is seen in instrumental terms as something to be mastered. That such knowledge is always an ideological construction linked to particular interests and social relations generally receives little consideration in teacher education programs. An understanding of the knowledge/power relationship raises important issues regarding what kinds of knowledge educators can provide to empower students, not only to understand and engage the world around them, but also to exercise the kind of courage needed to change the social order where necessary. Of considerable concern, then, is the need for student teachers to recognize that power relations correspond to forms of school knowledge that both distort the truth and produce it. That is, knowledge should be examined not only for the ways in which it might misrepresent or mediate social reality, but also for the ways in which it actually reflects people's experiences and, as such, influences their lives. Understood in this way, knowledge not only reproduces reality by distorting or illuminating the social world; it also has the more concrete function of shaping the day-to-day lives of people through their felt, relatively unmediated world of commonsense assumptions. This suggests that a curriculum for democratic empowerment must not only examine the conditions of school knowledge in terms of how it is produced and what particular interests it might represent, but should also scrutinize the effects of such knowledge as it is lived day-to-day. In short, prospective teachers need to understand that knowledge does more than distort, it also produces particular forms of life. Finally, in Michel Foucault's terms, knowledge contains hopes, desires, and wants that resonate positively with the subjective experience of a particular audience and such knowledge needs to be analyzed for the utopian promises often implicit in its claims.[44]

## Language

In traditional and institutionally legitimated approaches to reading, writing, and second-language learning, language issues are primarily defined by technical and developmental concerns. While such concerns are indeed important, what is often ignored in mainstream language courses in teacher education programs is how language is actively implicated in power relations that generally support the dominant culture. An alternative starting point to the study of language recognizes the significance of Antonio Gramsci's notion that every language contains elements of a conception of the world. It is through language that we come to consciousness and negotiate a sense of identity, since language does not merely reflect reality, but plays an active role in constructing it. As language constructs meaning, it shapes our world, informs our identities, and provides the cultural codes for perceiving and classifying the world. This implies, of course, that within the available discourses of the school or the society, language plays a powerful role because it serves to "mark the boundaries of permissible discourse, discourage the clarification of social alternatives, and makes it difficult for the dispossessed to locate the source of their unease, let alone remedy it."[45] Through the study of language within the perspective of a cultural politics, prospective teachers can gain an understanding of how language functions to "position" people in the world, to shape the range of possible meanings surrounding an issue, and to actively construct reality rather than merely reflect it. As part of language studies, student teachers would become more knowledgeable about and sensitive to the omnipresence and power of language as constitutive of their own experiences and those of their potential students.[46] Student teachers would also benefit from an introductory understanding of European traditions of discourse theory and the textual strategies that characterize their methods of inquiry.[47] Furthermore, through an exposure to the semiotics of mass and popular cultures, students could at least learn the rudimentary methods of examining the various codes and meanings that are constitutive of both their own personal constructions of self and society and those of the students they work with during their practicum or on-site sessions.

## History

The study of history should play a more expansive role in teacher education programs.[48] A critical approach to history would attempt to provide student teachers with an understanding of how cultural traditions are formed; it would also be designed to bring to light the various ways that curricula and discipline-based texts have been constructed and read throughout different historical periods. Furthermore, such an approach would be self-consciously critical of the problems surrounding the teaching of history as a school subject, since what is conventionally taught overwhelmingly reflects the perspectives and values of white, middle-class males. Too often excluded are the histories of women, minority groups, and indigenous peoples. This exclusion is not politically innocent when we consider how existing social arrangements are partly constitutive of and dependent upon the subjugation and elimination of the histories and voices of those groups marginalized and disempowered by the dominant culture. In addition, the concept of history can also help illuminate what kinds of knowledge are deemed legitimate and promulgated through the school curriculum. Conventional emphasis on chronological history "which traditionally saw its object as somehow unalterably 'there,' given, waiting only to be discovered"[49] would be supplanted by a focus on how specific educational practices can be understood as historical constructions related to the economic, social, and political events of a particular time and place. It is primarily through this form of historical analysis that students can recover what we referred to previously as "subjugated knowledges."[50] Our use of this term directs us to those aspects of history in which criticism and struggle have played a significant role in defining the nature and meaning of educational theory and practice. For example, students will have the opportunity to examine critically the historical contexts and interests at work in defining what forms of school knowledge become privileged over others, how specific forms of school authority are sustained, and how particular patterns of learning become institutionalized.

Within the format of a curriculum as a form of cultural politics, it is also necessary that the study of history be theoretically connected to both language and reading. In this context, language can be subsequently studied as "the bearer of history" and history can be analyzed as a social construction open to critical examination. The important linkage between reading and history can be made by emphasizing that "reading occurs within history and that the point of integration is always the reader."[51] In analyzing this relationship, teachers can focus on the cultural meanings that students use to understand a text. Such a focus will better equip student teachers to understand how the process of reading occurs within a particular student's cultural history and in the context of his or her own concerns and beliefs. This will also assist student teachers to become more critically aware of how students from subordinate cultures bring their own sets of experiences, as well as their own dreams, desires, and voices to the reading act.

## Culture

The concept of culture, varied though it may be, is essential to any teacher education curriculum aspiring to be critical. We are using the term "culture" here to signify the particular ways in which a social group lives out and makes sense of its "given" circumstances and conditions of life.[52] In addition to defining culture as a set of practices and ideologies from which different groups draw to make sense of the world, we also want to refashion the ways in which cultural questions become the starting point for understanding the issue of who has power and how it is reproduced and manifested in the social relations that link schooling to the wider social order. The link between culture and power has been extensively analyzed in radical social theory over the past ten years. It is therefore possible to offer three insights from that literature that are particularly relevant for illuminating the political logic that underlies various cultural/power relations. First, the concept of culture has been intimately connected with the question of how *social relations are structured* within class, gender, and age formations that produce forms of oppression and dependency. Second, culture has been analyzed within the radical perspective not simply as a way of life, but as a *form of production* through which different groups in either their dominant or subordinate social relations define and realize their aspirations through asymmetrical relations of power. Third, culture has been viewed as a *field of struggle* in which the production, legitimation, and circulation of particular forms of knowledge and experience are central areas of conflict. What is important here is that each of these insights raises fundamental questions about the ways in which inequalities are maintained and challenged in the sphere of culture.

The study of cultures—or, more specifically, what has come to be known as "cultural studies"—should become the touchstone of a teacher education curriculum. We feel this to be the case because cultural studies can provide student teachers with the critical categories necessary for examining school and classroom relations as social and political practices inextricably related to the construction and maintenance of specific relations of power. Moreover, by recognizing that school life is often mediated through the clash of dominant and subordinate cultures, prospective teachers can gain some insight into the ways in which classroom experiences are necessarily intertwined with their students' home life and street-corner culture. This point is meant to be more than a rallying cry for relevance;

rather, it asserts the need for prospective teachers to understand the meaning systems that students employ in their encounters with forms of dominant school knowledge and social relations. It is important, therefore, that student teachers learn to analyze expressions of mass and popular culture, such as music videos, television, and film. In this way, a successful cultural studies approach would provide an important theoretical avenue for teachers to comprehend how ideologies become inscribed through representations of everyday life.

## Towards a critical pedagogy for the classroom

In the previous sections we have highlighted the importance of viewing schools as social and political sites involved in the struggle for democracy. In addition, we have reconsidered the relationship between authority and teacher work and have attempted to develop the theoretical rudiments of a program in which teacher education would be viewed as a form of cultural politics. In this final section, we shift the focus from questions of institutional purpose and teacher definition to the issues of critical pedagogy and student learning. In so doing, we point to some of the fundamental elements that we believe can be used to construct a critical pedagogy, one in which the issue of student interests or motivation is linked to the dynamics of self- and social empowerment. We wish to underscore here that the public schools shape and reinforce the attitudes that prospective teachers bring to their clinical experiences. By focusing on some of the theoretical elements that constitute a critical pedagogy, we attempt to clarify the link between our notion of a teacher education curriculum as a form of cultural politics and the actual dynamics of classroom pedagogy. With this in mind, we will now sketch out the rudiments of a critical discourse that defines classroom pedagogy within the parameters of a political project centering around the primacy of student experience, the concept of voice, and the importance of transforming schools and communities into democratic public spheres.

### The primacy of student experience

The type of critical pedagogy we are proposing is fundamentally concerned with student experience insofar as it takes the problems and needs of the students themselves as its starting point. On the one hand, a pedagogy of student experience encourages a critique of dominant forms of knowledge and cultural mediation that collectively shape student experiences; on the other hand, it attempts to provide students with the critical means to examine their own particular lived experiences and subordinate knowledge forms. This means assisting students in analyzing their own experiences so as to illuminate the processes by which they were produced, legitimated, or disconfirmed. R. W. Connell and his associates in Australia provide a cogent direction for this type of curricular approach in their formulation of the kinds of knowledge that should be taught to empower working-class students when they suggest:

> that working-class kids get access to formal knowledge via learning which begins with their own experience and the circumstances which shape it, but does not stop there. This approach neither accepts the existing organization of academic knowledge nor simply inverts it. It draws on existing school knowledge and on what working-class people already know, and organizes this selection of information around problems such as economic survival and

collective action, handling the disruption of households by unemployment, responding to the impact of new technology, managing problems of personal identity and association, understanding how schools work and why.[53]

Student experience is the stuff of culture, agency, and identity formation and must be given preeminence in an emancipatory curriculum. It is therefore imperative that critical educators learn how to understand, affirm, and analyze such experience. This means not only understanding the cultural and social forms through which students learn how to define themselves, but also learning how to engage student experience in a way that neither unqualifiedly endorses nor delegitimates such experience. This suggests that, first of all, knowledge has to be made meaningful to students before it can be made critical. School knowledge never speaks for itself; rather, it is constantly filtered through the ideological and cultural experiences that students bring to the classroom. To ignore the ideological dimensions of student experience is to deny the ground upon which students learn, speak, and imagine. Judith Williamson addresses this issue well.

> Walter Benjamin has said that the best ideas are no use if they do not make something useful of the person who holds them; on an even simpler level, I would add that the best ideas don't even exist if there isn't anyone to hold them. If we cannot get the "radical curriculum" across, or arouse the necessary interest in the "basic skills," there is no point to them. But in any case, which do we ultimately care more about: our ideas, or the child/student we are trying to teach them to?[54]

Students cannot learn "usefully" unless teachers develop an understanding of the various ways in which student perceptions and identities are constituted through different social domains. At stake is the need for student teachers to understand how experiences produced in the various domains and layers of everyday life give rise to the different voices students employ to give meaning to their worlds and, consequently, to their existence in the larger society. Of course, not all student experiences should be unqualifiedly affirmed or rendered legitimate since some of them undoubtedly will draw from an uncritical categorization and social construction of the world (as in racist and sexist stereotyping, for example). In this case, teachers must understand student experience as arising from multiple discourses and subjectivities, some of which must be interrogated more critically than others. It is crucial, therefore, that educators address the question of how aspects of the social world are experienced, mediated, and produced by students. Failure to do so will not only prevent teachers from tapping into the drives, emotions, and interests that give students their own unique voice, but will also make it equally difficult to provide the momentum for learning itself.

While the concept of student experience is being offered as central to a critical pedagogy, it should also be recognized as a central category of teacher education programs. This suggests that student practicums should be seen as sites where the question of how experience is produced, legitimated, and accomplished becomes an object of study for teachers and students alike. Unfortunately, most student practicums are viewed as either a rite of passage into the profession or merely a formal culminating experience in the teacher education program.

## Student voice and the public sphere

The concept of voice constitutes the focal point for a theory of teaching and learning that generates new forms of sociality as well as new and challenging ways of confronting and engaging everyday life. Voice, quite simply, refers to the various measures by which students and teachers actively participate in dialogue. It is related to the discursive means whereby teachers and students attempt to make themselves "heard" and to define themselves as active authors of their worlds. Displaying a voice means, to cite Mikhail Bakhtin, "retelling a story in one's own words."[55] More specifically, the term "voice" refers to the principles of dialogue as they are enunciated and enacted within particular social settings. The concept of voice represents the unique instances of self-expression through which students affirm their own class, cultural, racial, and gender identities. A student's voice is necessarily shaped by personal history and distinctive lived engagement with the surrounding culture. The category of voice, then, refers to the means at our disposal—the discourses available to us—to make ourselves understood and listened to, and to define ourselves as active participants in the world. However, as we have stressed previously, the dominant school culture generally represents and legitimates the voices of white males from the middle and upper classes to the exclusion of economically disadvantaged students, most especially females from minority backgrounds.[56] A critical pedagogy takes into account the various ways in which the voices that teachers use to communicate with students can either silence or legitimate them.

The concept of voice is crucial to the development of a critical classroom pedagogy because it provides an important basis for constructing and demonstrating the fundamental imperatives of a strong democracy. Such a pedagogy attempts to organize classroom relationships so that students can draw upon and confirm those dimensions of their own histories and experiences which are deeply rooted in the surrounding community. In addition, by creating active links with the community, teachers can open up their classrooms to its diverse resources and traditions. This presupposes that teachers familiarize themselves with the culture, economy, and historical traditions that belong to the surrounding community. In other words, teachers must assume a pedagogical responsibility for attempting to understand the relationships and forces that influence their students outside of the immediate context of the classroom. This responsibility requires teachers to develop their curricula and pedagogical practices around those community traditions, histories, and forms of knowledge that are often ignored within the dominant school culture. This can, of course, lead to a deeper understanding on the part of both teachers and students of how both "local" and "official" knowledges get produced, sustained, and legitimated.

Teachers need to develop pedagogical practices that link student experiences with those aspects of community life that inform and sustain such experiences. For example, student teachers could compile oral histories of the communities in which they teach, which could then be used as a school and curricula resource— particularly in reading programs. In addition, they could work in and analyze how different community social agencies function so as to produce, distribute, and legitimate particular forms of knowledge and social relations. This would broaden their notion of pedagogical practices and help them to understand the relevance of their own work for institutions other than schools. Similarly, prospective teachers could develop organic links with active community agencies such as business, religious organizations, and other public spheres in an attempt to develop a more meaningful connection between the school curriculum and the experiences that define and characterize the local community. The concept of voice can thus provide a basic organizing principle for the development of a relationship between knowledge and student experiences and, at the same time, create a forum for examining broader school and community issues. In other words, teachers must become aware of both the transformative strengths and structures of oppression of the community-at-large and develop this awareness into curriculum strategies designed to empower students toward creating a more liberating and humane society. In short, teachers should be attentive to what it means to construct forms of learning in their classrooms that enable students to affirm their voices within areas of community life, that is, within democratic public spheres needing constant criticism, safeguarding, and renewal.

Steve Tozer is worth quoting at length on this issue.

> The process of fitting students for community life, then, is an effort to prepare students both for the existing community and to bring them to understand and to appreciate the historical values and ideas which point to a more ideal community than the one that exists . . . the teacher's duty is to recognize the historical ideals which make community life worth living, ideals upon which the larger society is founded: ideals of human dignity and equality, freedom, and mutual concern of one person for another. . . . This is not to say that teachers should prepare students for some nonexistent utopia. Rather, teachers must develop an understanding of the community as it exists *and* an understanding of what kind of people will be required to make it better. They can try to develop for themselves an ideal of the community their students should strive for, and they should help their students with the knowledge, the values and the skills they will need if they are to be resilient enough to maintain high standards of belief and conduct in an imperfect society.[57]

It is an unfortunate truism that when communities are ignored by teachers, students often find themselves trapped in institutions that not only deny them a voice, but also deprive them of a relational or contextual understanding of how the knowledge they acquire in the classroom can be used to influence and transform the public sphere. Implicit in the concept of linking classroom experiences to the wider community is the idea that the school is best understood as a polity, as a locus of citizenship. Within this locus, students and teachers can engage in a process of deliberation and discussion aimed at advancing the public welfare in accordance with fundamental moral judgments and principles. To bring schools closer to the concept of polity, it is necessary to define them as public spaces which seek to recapture the idea of critical democracy and community. In effect, we want to define teachers as active community participants whose function is to establish public spaces where students can debate, appropriate, and learn the knowledge and skills necessary to live in a critical democracy.

By public space we mean, as Hannah Arendt did, a concrete set of learning conditions where people come together to speak, to engage in dialogue, to share their stories, and to struggle together within social relations that strengthen rather than weaken possibilities for active citizenship.[58] School and classroom practices should, in some manner, be organized around forms of learning which serve to prepare students for responsible roles as transformative intellectuals, as community members, and as critically active citizens outside of schools.[59]

220    *Henry A. Giroux and Peter McLaren*

## Conclusion

We began this essay by arguing that teacher education should be seriously rethought along the lines of the critical democratic tradition, a tradition which, regrettably, has been all but excluded from the current debates on American schooling. We have argued that this tradition provides the basis for rethinking the relationship of schooling to the social order and for restructuring the education of prospective teachers so as to prepare them for the role of transformative intellectual. Moreover, we have argued that teacher education programs must assume a central role in reforming public education and, in so doing, must assert the primacy of a democratic tradition in order to restructure school-community relations.

In our view, the search for a creative democracy undertaken at the beginning of the century by Dewey and others is presently in retreat, having been abandoned by liberals and radicals alike. This situation presents a dual challenge to critical educators: there is now an urgent need not only to resurrect the tradition of liberal democracy, but to develop a theoretical perspective that goes beyond it. In the current age of conservatism, public education must analyze its strengths and weaknesses against an ideal of critical democracy rather than the current corporate referent of the capitalist marketplace. Similarly, public education must fulfill the task of educating citizens to take risks, to struggle for institutional and social change, and to fight *for* democracy and *against* oppression both inside and outside of schools. Pedagogical empowerment necessarily goes hand-in-hand with social and political transformation.

Our position is indebted to Dewey but attempts to extend his democratic project. Dewey's struggle for democracy was primarily pedagogical and largely failed to develop an extended analysis of class relations and historically conditioned inequalities in society. Conversely, our position accentuates the idea that schools represent only one important site in the struggle for democracy. It is different from Dewey's view because it perceives the self- and social empowerment of students as involving not just the politics of classroom culture, but also political and social struggle outside of school sites. Such an approach acknowledges that critical pedagogy is but one intervention—albeit a crucial one—in the struggle to restructure the ideological and material conditions of everyday life. We are convinced that teacher education institutions and public schools can and should play an active and productive role in broadening the possibilities for the democratic promise of American schooling, politics, and society.

## Notes

1  Arthur G. Powell, "University Schools of Education in the Twentieth Century," *Peabody Journal of Education, 54* (1976), 4.
2  Powell, "University Schools," p. 4.
3  George Counts, quoted in Powell, "University Schools," p. 4.
4  As quoted in Lawrence A. Cremin, David A. Shannon, and Mary Evelyn Townsend, *A History of Teachers College, Columbia University* (New York: Columbia University Press, 1954), p. 222.
5  Cremin, Shannon, and Townsend, *A History*, p. 222.
6  As quoted by George Counts in Cremin, Shannon, and Townsend, *A History*, p. 222
7  For an interesting discussion of this issue, see Ira Katznelson and Margaret Weir, *Schooling for All: Class, Race, and the Decline of the Democratic Ideal* (New York: Basic Books, 1985).

8 See esp. the work of the revisionist historians of the 1960s. Among the representative works are Michael B. Katz, *The Irony of Early School Reform: Educational Innovation in Mid-Nineteenth Century Massachusetts* (Boston: Beacon Press, 1968); Colin Greer, *The Great School Legend* (New York: Basic Books, 1972); and Clarence J. Karier, Paul Violas, and Joel Spring, *Roots of Crisis: American Education in the Twentieth Century* (Chicago: Rand McNally, 1973).

9 Lentricchia, *Criticism and School Change* (Chicago: University of Chicago Press, 1983), pp. 6–7.

10 See Stanley Aronowitz and Henry A. Giroux, *Education under Siege: The Conservative, Liberal, & Radical Debate over Schooling* (South Hadley, MA: Bergin & Garvey, 1985).

11 We are using the term "discourse" to mean "a domain of language use subject to rules of formation and transformation," as quoted in Catherine Belsey, *Critical Practice* (London: Methuen, 1980, p. 160). Discourses may also be described as "the complexes of signs and practices which organize social existence and social reproduction. In their structured, material persistence, discourses are what give differential substance to membership of a social group or class or formation, which mediate at internal sense of belonging, and outward sense of otherness," as quoted in Richard Terdiman, *Discourse-Counter-Discourse* (New York: Cornell University Press, p. 54).

12 Aronowitz and Giroux, *Education under Siege*; and Ann Bastian, Colin Greer, Norm Fruchter, Marilyn Gittel, and Kenneth Haskins, *Choosing Equality: The Case for Democratic Schooling* (New York: New World Foundation, 1985).

13 Zeichner, "Alternative Paradigms of Teacher Education," *Journal of Teacher Education, 34* (1983), 8.

14 Some of the more representative writing on this issue can be found in Diane Ravitch, *The Troubled Crusade: American Education 1945–1980* (New York: Basic Books, 1983); John H. Bunzel, ed. *Challenge to American Schools: The Case for Standards and Values* (New York: Oxford University Press, 1985); Ravitch, *The Schools We Deserve: Reflections on the Educational Crises of Our Time* (New York: Basic Books, 1985); and Edward Wynne, "The Great Tradition in Education: Transmitting Moral Values," *Educational Leadership, 43* (1985), 7.

15 Some of the best analyses are Lawrence C. Stedman and Marshall S. Smith, "Recent Reform Proposals for American Education," *Contemporary Education Review, 53* (1983), 85–104; Walter Feinberg, "Fixing the Schools: The Ideological Turn," *Issues in Education, 3* (1985), 113–138; Edward I Berman, "The Improbability of Meaningful Educational Reform," *Issues in Education, 3* (1985), 99–112; Michael Apple, "National Reports and the Construction of Inequality," *British Journal of Sociology of Education*, in press; and Aronowitz and Giroux, *Education under Siege*.

16 Finkelstein, "Education and the Retreat from Democracy in the United States, 1979–198?," *Teachers College Record, 86* (1984), 280–281.

17 Berman, "Improbability," p. 103.

18 We are using the term "influential" to refer to those reports that have played a major role in shaping educational policy at both the national and local levels. These include The National Commission on Excellence in Education, *A Nation at Risk: The Imperative for Educational Reform* (Washington, DC: GPO, 1983); Task Force on Education for Economic Growth, Education Commission of the States, *Action for Excellence: A Comprehensive Plan to Improve Our Nation's Schools* (Denver: Education Commission of the States, 1983); The Twentieth Century Fund Task Force on Federal Elementary and Secondary Education Policy, *Making the Grade* (New York: The Twentieth Century Fund, 1983); Carnegie Corporation, *Education and Economic Progress: Toward a National Education Policy* (New York: Author, 1983); and Carnegie Forum on Education and the Economy, *A Nation Prepared: Teachers for the 21st Century* (Hyattsville, MD: Author, 1986).

Also considered are other recent reports on teacher education reform: The National Commission for Excellence in Teacher Education, *A Call for Change in Teacher Education* (Washington, DC: American Association of Colleges in Teacher Education, 1985); C. Emily Feistritzer, *The Making of a Teacher* (Washington, DC: National Center for Education Information, 1984); "Tomorrow's Teachers: A Report of the Holmes Group" (East Lansing, MI: Holmes Group, Inc., 1986); and Francis A. Maher and

Charles H. Rathbone, "Teacher Education and Feminist Theory: Some Implications for Practice," *American Journal of Education, 101* (1986), 214–235. For an analysis of many of these reports see Catherine Cornbleth, "Ritual and Rationality in Teacher Education Reform," *Educational Researcher, 15*, No. 4 (1986), 5–14.

19  Frankenstein and Kampf, "Preface," in Sara Freedman, Jane Jackson, and Katherine Boles, "The Other End of the Corridor: The Effect of Teaching on Teachers," *Radical Teacher, 23* (1983), 2–23. It is worth noting that the Carnegie Forum's *A Nation Prepared* ends up defeating its strongest suggestions for reform by linking teacher empowerment to quantifying notions of excellence.

20  Stedman and Smith, "Recent Reform Proposals," pp. 85–104.

21  We are not automatically opposed to all forms of curricular software and technologies, such as interactive video disks and computers, as long as teachers become aware of the limited range of applications and contexts in which these technologies may be put to use. Certainly, we agree that some prepackaged curricula are more salient than others as instruments of learning. Too often, however, the use of such curricula ignores the contexts of the immediate classroom situation, the larger social milieu, and the historical juncture of the surrounding community. Furthermore, classroom materials designed to simplify the task of teaching and to make it more cost-efficient often separate planning or conception from execution. Many of the recent examples of predesigned commercial curricula are largely focused on competencies measured by standardized tests, precluding the possibility that teachers and students will be able to act as critical thinkers. See Michael W. Apple and Kenneth Teitelbaum, "Are Teachers Losing Control of Their Skills and Curriculum?" *Journal of Curriculum Studies, 18* (1986), 177–184.

22  Darling-Hammond, "Valuing Teachers: The Making of a Profession," *Teachers College Record, 87* (1985), 209–218.

23  Darling-Hammond, "Valuing Teachers," p. 209.

24  For an excellent theoretical analysis of this issue, see Freedman, Jackson, and Boles, "The Other End of the Corridor." For a more traditional statistical treatment, see Darling-Hammond, *Beyond the Commission Reports: The Coming Crisis in Teaching*, R-3177-RC (Santa Monica, CA: Rand Corporation, July 1984); National Education Association, *Nationwide Teacher Opinion Poll, 1983* (Washington, DC: Author, 1983); and American Federation of Teachers, *School As a Workplace: The Realities of Stress*, Vol. I (Washington, DC: Author, 1983).

25  Dennis J. Schmidt, "Translator's Introduction: In the Spirit of Bloch," in Ernst Bloch, *Natural Law and Human Dignity*, trans. Dennis J. Schmidt (Boston: MIT Press, 1986), p. xviii.

26  Goodlad, *A Place Called School: Prospects for the Future* (New York: McGraw-Hill, 1983); Sizer, *Horace's Compromise: The Dilemma of the American High School* (Boston: Houghton Mifflin, 1984); and Boyer, *High School: A Report on Secondary Education in America* (New York: Harper & Row, 1983).

27  For an overview and critical analysis of this literature, see Henry A. Giroux, "Theories of Reproduction and Resistance in the New Sociology of Education: A Critical Analysis," *Harvard Educational Review, 53* (1983), 257–293.

28  Popkewitz and Pitman, "The Idea of Progress and the Legitimation of State Agendas: American Proposals for School Reform," *Curriculum and Teaching, 1* (1986), p. 21.

29  Popkewitz and Pitman, "The Idea of Progress," p. 20.

30  Popkewitz and Pitman, "The Idea of Progress," p. 22.

31  Zeichner, "Alternative Paradigms"; and Jesse Goodman, "Reflections on Teacher Education: A Case Study and Theoretical Analysis," *Interchange, 15* (1984), 7–26. The fact that many teacher education programs have defined themselves as synonymous with instructional preparation has often given them a debilitating practical slant, leading to a limited conception of teaching as exercises in classroom management and control. Isolated courses on classroom management have had a tragic effect on how teachers are able to critically interrogate the political implications of curricular decision-making and policy development. This predicament can be traced to a history of the academic politics that grew out of the separation of colleges of education from the liberal arts tradition and the arts and sciences faculty; see Donald Warren, "Learning from Experience: History and Teacher Education," *Educational Researcher, 14*, No. 10 (1985), 5–12.

32 For an excellent analysis of this issue, see National Coalition of Advocates for Students, *Barriers to Excellence: Our Children at Risk* (Boston: Author, 1985).

33 As quoted in Frank Lentricchia, *Criticism and Social Change* (Chicago: University of Chicago Press, 1985); see also Dewey, *Democracy and Education* (New York: Free Press, 1916) and *The Public and Its Problems* (New York: Holt, 1927).

34 Dewey, "Creative Democracy—The Task Before Us," in *Classic American Philosophers*, ed. Max Fisch (New York: Appleton-Century-Crofts, 1951), pp. 389–394; and Richard J. Bernstein, "Dewey and Democracy: The Task Ahead of Us," in *Post-Analytic Philosophy*, ed. John Rajchman and Cornell West (New York: Columbia University Press, 1985), pp. 48–62.

35 Henry A. Giroux, "Authority, Intellectuals and the Politics of Practical Learning," *Teachers College Record* (in press).

36 Barber, *Strong Democracy: Participating Politics for a New Age Theology of Liberation* (Berkeley: University of California Press, 1984).

37 Sharon Welch, *Communities of Resistance and Solidarity* (New York: Orbis Press, 1985), p. 31.

38 Welch, *Communities of Resistance*, p. 37.

39 Zeichner, "Alternative Paradigms"; Henry A. Giroux, *Ideology, Culture, and the Process of Schooling* (Philadelphia: Temple University Press, 1981); and John Sears, "Rethinking Teacher Education: Dare We Work Toward a New Social Order?" *Journal of Curriculum Theorizing*, 6 (1985), 24–79.

40 Of course, this is not true for all teacher education programs, but it does represent the dominant tradition characterizing them; see Zeichner, "Alternative Paradigms."

41 See John Ellis, "Ideology and Subjectivity," in *Culture, Media, Language*, ed. Stuart Hall, Dorothy Hobson, Andrew Lowe, and Paul Willis (Hawthorne, Australia: Hutchinson, 1980), pp. 186–194; see also Julian Henriques, Wendy Hollway, Cathy Urwin, Couze Venn, and Valerie Walkerdine, *Changing the Subject* (New York: Methuen, 1984).

42 Henry A. Giroux and Roger Simon, "Curriculum Study and Cultural Politics," *Journal of Education*, 166 (1984), 226–238.

43 Stanley Aronowitz, "Schooling, Popular Culture, and Post-Industrial Society: Peter McLaren Interviews Aronowitz," *Orbit*, 17 (1986), 18.

44 Foucault, "The Subject of Power," in *Beyond Structuralism and Hermeneutics*, ed. Hubert Dreyfus and Paul Rabinow (Chicago: University of Chicago Press, 1982), p. 221.

45 T. J. Jackson Lears, "The Concept of Cultural Hegemony: Problems and Possibilities," *American Historical Review*, 90 (1985), 569–570.

46 Gary Waller, "Writing, Reading, Language, History, Culture: The Structure and Principles of the English Curriculum at Carnegie-Mellon University." Unpublished manuscript, Carnegie-Mellon University, 1985, p. 12.

47 We are primarily referring to the French school of discourse theory, as exemplified in the writings of Foucault; see his *The Archaeology of Knowledge*, trans. A. M. Sheridan Smith (London: Tavistock; see also the following works by Foucault: *Language, Counter-Memory, Practice: Selected Essays and Interviews*, Donald F. Bouchard, trans. Donald F. Bouchard and Sherry Simon (Ithaca: Cornell University Press, 1979); and "Politics and the Study of Discourse," *Ideology and Consciousness*, 3 (1978), 7–26.

48 Waller, "Writing, Reading, Language," p. 12.

49 Waller, "Writing, Reading, Language," p. 14.

50 Foucault, "Two Lectures," in *Power/Knowledge*, ed. Colin Gordon (New York: Pantheon, 1980), pp. 78–108.

51 Waller, "Writing, Reading, Language," p. 14.

52 Henry A. Giroux, *Ideology, Culture, and the Process of Schooling* (Philadelphia: Temple University Press, 1981).

53 Robert W. Connell, Dean J. Ashenden, Sandra Kessler, and Gary W. Dowsett, *Making the Difference: Schools, Families, and Social Division* (Winchester, MA: Allen & Unwin, 1982), p. 199; see also Peter McLaren, *Schooling as a Ritual Performance: Towards a Political Economy of Educational Symbols and Gestures* (London: Routledge & Kegan Paul, 1986).

54   Williamson, "Is There Anyone Here From a Classroom?," *Screen, 26* (Jan./Feb. 1984), 24; see also Henry A. Giroux, "Radical Pedagogy and the Politics of Student Voice," *Interchange, 17* (1986), 48–69.
55   As quoted in Harold Rosen, "The Importance of Story," *Language Arts, 63* (1986), 234.
56   For a thorough analysis of this, see Arthur Brittan and Mary Maynard, *Sexism, Racism and Oppression* (New York: Blackwell, 1984).
57   Tozer, "Dominant Ideology and the Teacher's Authority," *Contemporary Education, 56* (1985), 152–153.
58   Arendt, *The Human Condition* (Chicago: University of Chicago Press, 1958).
59   Attempts to link classroom instruction to community contexts is nowhere more important than during teachers' clinical experiences. On these occasions, prospective teachers should be assisted in making connections with progressive community organizations, especially those affiliated with local governmental council meetings and to interview community leaders and workers in various community agencies linked to the school. This enhances the possibility that prospective teachers will make critically reflective links between classroom practices and the ethos and needs of the surrounding social and cultural milieu.

# CHAPTER 17

# THE USE OF EMANCIPATORY PEDAGOGY IN TEACHER EDUCATION (1986)

Beverly M. Gordon

## Introduction: The social Darwinian past vs. a democratic future

The recent report *A Nation at Risk: The Imperative for Educational Reform* attempts to grapple with the crisis in American education while overlooking some of the most critical and central issues. For although the report wrestles at great length with the ill-defined but politically explosive issue of school success or failure, this fundamental question cannot be examined at any significant depth without an understanding of the problematic nature of both the knowledge purveyed in the traditional school curriculum and the socio-economic and political role of schooling in our society. Henry A. Giroux focused on the implications of the failure of the educational community to come to terms with these issues, and advocates an overhaul of the American educational paradigm.[1]

Why do we educate our children? What are schools for? What is it that we expect to "happen" in schools to prepare children for the responsibilities and privileges of adult life? More specifically, what kind of knowledge is being purveyed in our schools in support of what kinds of future roles for which—and whose—children? And whose interest is this whole educational system really designed to serve? The current crisis in American education demands that the attention of teacher educators also be focused on these central issues, and that the methods and the knowledge content of teacher education programs be re-examined.

If we as educators are truly concerned with providing the American citizenry with the critical and reflective skills necessary for a full and meaningful participation in society, we must begin to question whether our educational system is truly designed to achieve this goal. It is this author's contention that the knowledge presently disseminated in teacher training programs is problematic and must be critiqued, because it is designed to legitimate and perpetuate the unjust hierarchial structuring of our society; and that the fundamental paradigm employed in today's teacher education programs must be overhauled, because it rests on an undemocratic and unscientific 19th-century psychological and administrative model which reflects 19th-century social Darwinist thought and social engineering theory.

## Teacher preparation and the issue of knowledge

Educational policy based on social Darwinist thought, social engineering philosophy, and administrative psychological approaches to education has been under attack by progressive elements in the educational community since this insidious phenomenon first began to take hold in this country.[2] The insidious paradigm underlying these policies prescribes, on Spencer's pretended "scientific" basis, an educational system designed to produce and maintain a social hierarchy which relegates ascribed categories of individuals to different caste roles in society. The educators Judd, Thorndike, and Snedden's models of societal stratification according to levels of natural cognitive abilities also rest on the sociological theories of Spencer's disciple William Sumner.

It is essential to remember, however, that Spencer's *Education: Intellectual, Moral and Physical* (1885)[3] arrived in this country in the late 1890's—after the collapse of Reconstruction, during a period of intensified racism, black urban migration and ghettoization, and the continuing pauperization of the black masses, and during a period of massive immigration of Eastern and Southern European peasants. Seen within this historical context, the acceptance of the Spencerian education paradigm and Sumner's sociology were—at best—attempts to rationalize the American urban socio-economic status quo. The differentiated curriculum approach outlined by Franklin Bobbitt and W.W. Charters, based on Thorndike's principles of "intelligence testing," can thus also be seen in context, as the "logical" way to put social Darwinist theory into educational practice. City planners as well as educators of that era recognized the potential role of the schools in societal development.[4]

In 1895, the *Report of the Committee of Fifteen on Elementary Education,*[5] in the section dealing with teacher education, described psychology, methodology, "school economy," and the history of education as the components of the science of teaching, and observation and practice as comprising the art of teaching. The *Report* then proceeded to debate the value of the history of education in teacher education programs, as well as the issue of professional versus academic studies, and the relationship between theory and practice. From today's perspective, however, the most striking aspect of the *Report of the Committee of Fifteen* is its overwhelming similarity to the discussions about today's educational situation. It is shocking to realize that neither the philosophy nor the methodology of teacher training has undergone any fundamental change in 89 years—i.e., that contemporary teacher training, and educators' theories and paradigms about the educational process and the preparation of the teachers, have not significantly changed or advanced since the 1890's. In the 1980's, teacher educators can no longer afford to resist examining alternative educational paradigms which go beyond the 19th-century "social efficiency"/educational psychology model of education as a system for reproducing the socio-economic status quo.

## Introducing emancipatory pedagogy teacher education programs

It is true that a variety of obstacles confronts us in the field of curriculum reform. For one thing, as Rosario and Lopes' study[6] of stability and change in a middle school indicates, the burdens of routine daily management and the demands of school discipline have relegated curriculum reform to low priority status for both administrators and teachers. It is also somewhat difficult to teach any innovative theory to young and unsophisticated students at the preservice level. Furthermore, at the inservice level, very few of today's public school teachers, however well trained and motivated, as yet have an adequate working knowledge of what emancipatory pedagogy might actually look like in an American classroom setting. It is also quite likely that emancipatory pedagogy would be completely unacceptable in certain milieux, and even where given fair consideration it would be perceived as a low priority item compared to other pressing curriculum concerns.

These potential obstacles, however, can be overcome; and the effort to implement such curriculum reform in teacher training programs would yield a number of significant benefits. First, the methods of emancipatory pedagogy will provide present and future teachers with the heuristic tools they need to analyze the crucial dynamics of the relationships between students and their teachers, including the problems of student/teacher conflict and student resistance.[7] Second the newest critical pedagogy would also provide student teachers with an opportunity to experience and experiment with a new critical perspective on education and a new intellectual awareness of their role as teachers which they would be able to convert into pedagogical materials and classroom activities and experiences. In essence, the critical perspective can become an alternative paradigmatic framework or "lens" through which teachers can re-examine and recreate the practice of teaching; and it can enable teachers to call upon their own newly-developed internal resources to develop workable solutions to some of the most basic and most profound problems of present-day education.

A third benefit to be obtained by introducing emancipatory pedagogy into existing teacher training programs is that it offers us a new epistemological perspective. As an alternative or competing paradigm which views conventional classroom knowledge itself as problematic, critical and emancipatory pedagogy also poses key questions about the classroom and its place in our society. This new paradigm requires us to become more aware of the socio-political-economic context of the classroom, and raises the question of whether our societal attitudes and values might not be shaped to a large extent *by the social and institutional structure* of our society—rather than the other way around.[8] This kind of gestalt not only enhances our social consciousness; it can also prove to be the first step in a paradigmatic overhaul or "revolution"[9] in social science theory.

There are several examples of critical and emancipatory pedagogy in the literature which could be used effectively in preservice teacher education programs. The richest sources can be found in the writings of a number of "master teachers," who made innovative changes in their classroom pedagogy and struggled to make schoolwork meaningful to their students and useful within the context of the students' lives. These writings provide student teachers with concrete examples of how to generate a curriculum based on the social realities that confront teachers and their students; and they also present clearly the analytical tools and skills necessary to understand and implement their ideas.

Most of these master teachers in emancipatory pedagogy worked with poor or working-class groups within their own societies. Sylvia Ashton-Warner's work with Maori children in New Zealand;[10] Chris Searle's work with poor, working-class, and "coloured" children in the East End of London;[11] Cynthia Brown's work with poor, working-class, and minority children in Berkeley, California;[12] Ira Shor's work with working-class adults at Staten Island College, CUNY,[13] and, of course, Paulo Freire's work with Brazilian peasants[14] are among many examples of a growing body of literature which integrates emancipatory theory and its quotidian classroom praxis.

It is critical to recognize that these master teachers are neither wild-eyed ideologues nor communists, and to note that they do not spend much time criticizing the schools for reinforcing class distinctions or perpetuating the societal status quo. Instead, working in the field, with students ranging from the primary grades to adult literacy classes to community colleges, their work and their thinking grows out of the hermeneutic demands of classroom praxis. They approach education creatively and, purposefully, and they respect education as a life-long and two-sided process—i.e., they view themselves as both teachers and learners.

One of the best known advocates of emancipatory pedagogy is Paulo Freire.[15] His writings describes the development of educational pedagogies designed to promote critical consciousness, to enable students to become critical thinkers and active societal participants, and to give people the emancipatory capability of redefining the nature of their own lives.

Freire's advocacy of education for critical consciousness and his model of emancipatory pedagogy for oppressed groups together heighten our awareness of the inherently and inescapably political nature of curriculum. His writings have also raised some fundamental questions which have enabled curriculum theorists to look anew at their role in the educative process. Freire stands fundamentally opposed to the positivistic rationality, which views the goal of schooling as merely facilitating the adaptation of students to the state's conception of reality.[16] To Freire, adaptation is a primary skill of the animal world—but it is not the proper goal of education.[17] Freire's thinking is sympathetic to reconceptualist criticisms of schooling, which regard positivism as a dehumanizing influence on society; but Freire's work also adds a global perspective which demonstrates that positivism is not an exclusively Euro-American rationality. American curriculum reconceptualists and public school teachers engaged in collaborative research efforts can benefit from Freire's insights. Freire's contention that adaptation is not the proper goal of education is also supported by this author's research,[18] which shows how students become alienated by the schools' attempts to "socialize" them and to push them into roles or categories they cannot accept, and how they develop various ways of resisting school pressures.

This author believes that Freire's theories help to illuminate the true nature and proper function of education in society, and that his methods of implementing emancipatory pedagogy in Brazil can offer our student teachers an important and unique perspective on the American school experience and its problems.

While Freire worked primarily with adults, the pedagogy employed by Brown, Warner, and Searle presents new ways in which teachers can work with children. Cynthia Brown used Freire's methodology with American primary school children. Sylvia Ashton-Warner talks about the organic vocabulary and learning that children bring with them into the classroom and shows how to tap into the "cultural capital" of the children and use it as a bridge to the more formalized knowledge that the schools wish the children to acquire.

Searle's use of the newspaper in his classroom of poor, working-class, and "coloured" students provides another example of how teachers can translate the critical perspective and analytic study into classroom activities meaningful to children, offering them an opportunity to learn and to use their reading and writing skills, as well as their analytical skills and aesthetic sensibility. Searle's pedagogy, geared toward societal participation, also provided his students with a sense of contributing to the "creation" of culture, an aspect which Freire also emphasizes; and it provided a transitional vehicle for demystifying the creation and dissemination of conventional classroom knowledge and the media by helping children to understand that what they read in school or see in the media is not necessarily true or "objective"—that it is not eternal truth engraved in stone, but merely someone else's necessarily subjective and selective perception of natural, scientific, political, social, economic, moral, or aesthetic phenomena. In essence, Searle does for his children what Freire did for the Brazilian peasants: he empowers the students with a sense of confidence in their own experiences and perceptions, with a sense that they can gain control over their own destiny, and with the rudimentary tools to start working towards a just society.

This kind of emancipatory education goes beyond using curriculum "relevance" for motivational purposes only, and actually helps students begin to deal with real-world issues that they face in their daily lives. In the emancipatory classroom, students begin to participate as an active citizenry and to overcome their feelings of despair and hopelessness, apathy and alienation.

Freire's and Searle's accounts of theory in action—of actual classroom praxis —provide concrete models of activities and experiences in which children can actively participate. Their accounts also show why these master teachers believe that reading is power, and that educating someone is an awesome responsibility and an unavoidably political act.

Another readable example of critical and emancipatory pedagogy, focusing on yet another clientele, is found in the work of Ira Shor. Not only is Shor's work illuminative and instructive for those already interested in incorporating emancipatory pedagogy, but it also deals with other themes and issues in present-day teacher education programs.

Working with adult students at the community college level, Shor used the critical issues in the lives of his students as the starting place for the educative process. By focusing discussions on the situations, circumstances, and contradictions in the daily lives of his students as they struggled to get an education, Shor developed and enhanced the students' critical awareness. His writing, in turn, enhances our understanding of how cultural and conceptual literacy can flow from social critique.

On another level, Shor's analysis demonstrates that in working-class colleges (which are, for the most part, the community colleges and technical institutes), the curriculum is designed to force students to commit intellectual suicide, in a false and unnecessary dilemma. The student is told, in effect, that s/he must choose between making a living—through skill development or vocationalism— and learning how to think critically (through liberal education). And then, "from these bottom (vocational) tracks of the school universe, worker-students get sent into the bottom levels of the job market".[19] The parallels between Shor's view of community college "vocationalism" and present-day teacher education programs are uncomfortably close! Vocationalism, Shor contends, leads to the stifling of the human potential and to the creation of a non-critical (non-political?) work force which effects, unfortunately, we also find among too many teachers and even teacher educators.

Using provocative, participatory, and open dialogue among educator and students instead of the traditional unidirectional lectures and "directed discussion" —this is the critical first step in the classroom implementation of an emancipatory paradigm (which Shor calls "liberatory" education). This method is emancipatory in two senses: because it makes learning a mutual and reciprocal process between educator and students, it liberates both from their traditional roles and because its object is the liberated creative intellect of free men. Far from being communist-inspired the methods and goals of emancipatory pedagogy bear a striking resemblance, respectively, to the Socratic method of provocatively questioning the conventional wisdom in order to reach more fundamental truths, and to the Western ideal of liberal education designed to create an enlightened and responsible, enfranchised citizenry. The differences between the modern American version of liberal education and emancipatory pedagogy are due partly to the erosion of the liberal tradition in our colleges; but more importantly, the differences occur in the emphasis in emancipatory pedagogy on using the indigenous cultural resources of the students instead of the "classical" curriculum materials of the dominant culture.

## Implications of critical and emancipatory education for teacher preparation

The implications of a critical and emancipatory curriculum and pedagogy in both the teacher training classes and elementary/secondary school classrooms are only now beginning to be addressed. In spite of today's overwhelming school discipline and management problems however, and in spite of the shrinking educational job market, the question, "Education for what?" remains the central question in both teacher education and in American schoolrooms. This basic question also forces us to focus on the many areas of contestation, conflict, and contradiction in our society and in the real lives of students. A fresh critical perspective in education could reawaken the thrust towards social reform, with the same enthusiasm Dewey had when he reconceptualized the role of schooling in the face of the scientific determinism and social efficiency movements of his time, in *The School and Social Progress*.[20]

Teacher education today is trapped in a "deceptive paradox",[21] or, in Kuhn's terms, a crisis.[22] While teachers are a part of the larger societal community and share "a very real need on the part of all socio-economic classes to learn about and transform the nature of their existence",[23] they are also part of the educational mechanism and its power structure. But it is precisely because teachers are of both worlds that they hold the key to transforming both worlds.

Our late-20th-century education system is in crisis and chaos in large part because it is based on teacher education paradigms which reflect 19th-century concepts of social efficiency and scientific determinism, and which employ 19th-century psychological models of authoritarian teaching and passive learning. If teacher education is to move forward, it must begin to re-examine the most fundamental questions concerning the goals and purposes of education, the nature of the learning process, and the role of teachers and schools in society. Then we must redesign teacher education methods and materials in accord with today's objectives and today's realities.

A critical and emancipatory perspective as one alternative model of teacher education merits serious consideration by teacher educators for three reasons. First, as practicing scientists, professional educators must continually look beyond and challenge the conventional wisdom; new paradigms must be debated in the educational scientific research community and must be allowed to stand or fall under the rigor of scientific scrutiny. Second, this particular alternative paradigm, which emphasizes critical thinking and awareness, provides student teachers with unique heuristic tools which will enable them to reflect critically on the values, meanings, and beliefs that they bring with them to their profession, and will help teachers to better understand their role in the teaching/learning process. Third, emancipatory pedagogy can help children become critical thinkers and constructive, creative, active citizen participants, capable of creatively redefining the nature of their future adult lives.

Emancipatory pedagogy does not afford teachers the comforts of naivete or selective amnesia or a pretense of non-involvement concerning the social and political dimensions inherent in the act of educating people. Instead, it implores them to think about and act on their ethical, moral, and social responsibilities and commitments, and to work towards increased opportunity for social justice and economic equity in society. Our present education system is floundering and foundering partly because it rests on a false premise of being politically "neutral." Only by re-examining the fundamental place of schooling in our society can teachers and teacher educators begin to participate constructively and effectively in the ongoing social debate about the state of education and directions for educational policy.

# Notes

1  Henry Giroux. "Public Philosophy and the Crisis in Education." *Harvard Educational Review*. Vol. 54, No. 2, May 1984: 186–194.
2  Carter G. Woodson. *The Education of the Negro Prior to 1861 (Orig. 1919)*. (New York: Arno Press, 1968). See also Benjamin Bowser "The Contribution of Blacks to Sociological Knowledge: A Problem of Theory and Role to 1950." *Phylon*. Vol. 42, 1981:180–193.
3  Herbert Spencer. *Education: Intellectual, Moral and Physical*. (New York: John B. Alden, Publisher, 1885).
4  Robert Park. "The Bases of Race Prejudice." *The Annals*. Vol. CXXXX, November, 1928:11–20; Robert Church. *Education in The United States*. (New York: Free Press, 1976); David Tyack. *The One Best System*. (Cambridge: Harvard University Press, 1976).
5  National Education Association. *Committee of Fifteen: Report on Elementary Education*. (New York: The American Book Company, 1895).
6  Jose Rosario and Lawrence Lopes. *Mechanisms of Continuity: A Study of Stability and Change in a Public School. Final Report: The Workings of Process and Order*. (Ypsilanti, MI: High/Scope Educational Research Foundation, 1983).
7  Beverly M. Gordon. *A Study of Conflict/Resolution in School-Community Relations. Final Report*. (Columbus: The Ohio State University & Teacher Corps Project. September, 1982(b)). See also Rosario & Lopes, *Mechanisms of Continuity*.
8  David T. Wellman. *Portraits Of White Racism*. (Cambridge: Cambridge University Press, 1977).
9  Thomas Kuhn. *The Structure of Scientific Revolutions*. (Chicago: University of Chicago Press, 1962).
10  Sylvia Ashton-Warner. *Teacher*. (New York: Basic Books, 1964).
11  Chris Searle. *Classrooms of Resistance*. (London: Writers & Readers Publishing Corp., 1975).
12  Cynthia Brown. *Literacy in Thirty Hours*. (Chicago: Alternative Schools Network, 1973).
13  Ira Shor. *Critical Teaching And Everyday Life*. (Boston: South End Press, 1980).
14  Paulo Freire. *Pedagogy of the Oppressed*. (New York: Seabury Press, 1970). Also see, Paulo Freire. *Education for Critical Consciousness*. (New York: Seabury Press, 1973).
15  Ibid.
16  Henry A. Giroux. *Ideology, Culture and the Process of Schooling*. (Philadelphia: Temple University Press, 1981): 21(p. 143) 23(p. 143).
17  Freire. *Education for Critical Consciousness*. p. 4.
18  Beverly M. Gordon. *The Educational History of Nine High School Dropouts*. Ph.D. diss., University of Wisconsin-Madison, 1979.
19  Shor. *Critical Teaching*. p. 24.

20  John Dewey. "The School and Social Progress" (1896). Excerpted in *John Dewey On Education: Selected Writings*, edited by Reginald Archambault. (New York: The Modern Library-Random House, 1964).
21  Giroux. *Ideology, Culture and the Process of Schooling.* p. 143.
22  Kuhn. *Scientific Revolutions.*
23  Giroux. *Ideology*, p. 143.

**PART 3**

# THE MODEL TEACHER

# CHAPTER 18

# TEACHERS OF CULTURALLY DISADVANTAGED AMERICAN YOUTH* (1963)

*Ronald J. Rousseve*

In this message, I want to talk with you about those youth who have come largely from slum backgrounds and who are called the disadvantaged, the culturally deprived, the underprivileged, the economically handicapped. Education is what the culturally disadvantaged need, true enough. But HOW, frankly, do you cope with the legions of youngsters in this country whose birthright is grinding poverty, ignorance, disease, unemployment, malnutrition, and the frustration that comes of all of these?

Their only goal appears to be to grow up; their only ambition, to get by. They don't dream of becoming engineers or nurses or firemen or secretaries or members of the Peace Corps. There is no urge to enter a race which they know they're doomed to finish last in.

Dr. James B. Conant, former president of Harvard, has said in his provocative study entitled *Slums and Suburbs* that "We are allowing social dynamite to accumulate in our cities. Leaving aside human tragedies, I submit that a continuation of this situation is a menace to the social and political health of our communities."

Another student of this strange American paradox—deprivation and despair in a land of plenty and opportunity—Attorney General Robert F. Kennedy, has had this to say: "A malignant cancer is spreading thru the American society. It is a cancer that weakens the moral and physical fiber of our nation, and it cannot be localized; its tenacles reach out in every direction. If a child is denied the opportunity to lead a wholesome, productive life, it is a loss to the nation, not just to his neighborhood."

Poverty, parents who don't seem to care, a childhood without much genuine love, encouragement to fail rather than succeed—these are some of the marks of the culturally disadvantaged.

The obvious thing, of course, is to blame parents. Yet, the parents are only an older generation of the disadvantaged. Obviously, they cannot pass on to their children ideals, values, and ambitions they themselves don't have.

This, then, is the problem facing the educator who works with culturally deprived youth: how to break the vicious circle so that disadvantaged children don't become disadvantaged parents producing another generation of disadvantaged children.

Please note that thus far we have been talking in general about the child from a low socio-economic level. If, however, the particular child we have in mind happens also to be a Negro or a Puerto Rican or a Mexican—in America he is segregated socially, economically, physically, and mentally all at once! The problem is poverty, to be sure—but poverty of every kind: cultural, intellectual, economic, and emotional.

Consequently, if he is to go to the root of the matter, the educator must look realistically at the social and economic conditions amid which the child exists. He must conceive of education as a total process, in which the conditions of society deeply affect the child's mind, the level of his achievement, and the range of his possibilities. It may be true that the curriculum, the classroom, the guidance office are all instruments for dealing with one part of the child's life. But they do not and cannot function in a social vacuum.

Nor is it permissible any longer to say that the social environment of the child is not the problem of the educator—that it belongs to city planners, social workers, economists, housing experts, or society. It belongs to everyone; but perhaps MOST of all, it belongs to the educator. For a real educator is a social and intellectual leader, and he begins to exercise his leadership when he recognizes the conditions of his society and brings to bear upon them the force of a humanitarian philosophy.

At this point, though, we may need to "back-track" a little, (so to speak) to demonstrate that these problems we're discussing are not far removed from us here in Texas. In order to show this, I want to tell you a little about the research study which a group of us at Prairie View A. and M. College conducted last year. The novel investigation of which I speak took the form of a descriptive study which was designed to provide information about the ideas or perceptions that Texas superintendents, principals, and counselors have concerning the cultural problems of Negro youth in the public high schools of the state. The study was also designed to point up implications arising from these perceptions which are relevant to the improving of programs of teacher education in the colleges and to increasing the awareness of in-service school personnel, generally, regarding the crucial importance of effective action in this area if Negro youth are to be in a position to take advantage of breakthroughs in the expanding arena of American opportunity.

With respect to background considerations, while it may be true, as Eli Ginzberg has put it, that "we expect education to furnish the individual with the necessary intellectual, social, moral, and technical clothing for a presentable appearance in the world community," it also appears to be true that the sub-culture to which the American caste system has assigned the Negro American child gives a peculiar twist to the normal gamut of cultural conflicts which accompany the experiences of the vast majority of youth who attend the public schools of this nation. That this is the case can be substantiated in available literature.

The social position of the Negro in the American scheme of things has made it difficult, if not impossible, for him to participate as actively in the cultural life of the nation as his white compatriots. The Negro American has the same language, the same religion, the same general social heritage as the dominant social group, but the Negro is a warped replica since his cultural participation has been limited and channelized quite differently from that of whites in the United States. By the attitudes of mingled fear, hostility, depreciation, discrimination, amused patronage, friendly domination, and rigid authoritarianism, the white caste generates opposite and complementary attitudes in the Negro caste. One of the results of this system of studied insult and contempt, of exploitation and deprivation, is a tormented, inefficient personality, straining under the load of suppressing its hostility to avoid punishment and further deprivation.

Thus, this study sought, in part, to determine whether or not in the cultural problems of Negro high school youth, as actually perceived and identified by Texas school officials who were contacted in the investigation, there is *in fact* tangible evidence which serves to validate these implications uncovered in the literature of the behavioral sciences.

Now with respect to the study itself—which, admittedly, was no "paragon of perfection"—a questionnaire-type instrument (that was largely unstructured) was developed and sent to superintendents, principals, and counselors in Texas who were in touch with Negro high school youth. Some 292 superintendents were contacted, while 620 instruments were forwarded to secondary principals and counselors. The Committee received a discouraging 26 per cent return and felt justified in using the data collected only for hypothesis purposes. While detailed information and a more penetrating description of the instrument that was devised for this investigation can be gleaned from the technical report of the study, suffice it to mention here that the respondents were asked to record their perceptions of the cultural problems of Negro youth in the areas of (1) personal behavior, (2) cultural appreciation, (3) cultural and occupational aspirations, (4) home and family life, (5) community organization, and (6) opportunities for cultural growth.

Some of the specific items which were treated in various ways by the respondents included: dress, speech, interpersonal relations, broken homes, inadequate discipline, parental neglect, lack of exposure to cultural media, inadequacy of opportunities for cultural growth because of segregation, no desire for personal betterment, low cultural and occupational aspirations, limited models for emulation, low educational goals, and lack of community organization—to identify but a few.

Especially worthy of note, perhaps, were the *behavioral descriptions* recorded by the respondents. They pointed up, generally, behavior characterized by nonconformity to patterns of expected conduct, submissiveness, academic passivity, ambivalent reactions toward their own reference groups, clowning, aggression, truancy, living-for-the-moment attitudes, unconscious "compensatory exhibitionism," and even tendencies to retreat from reality.

Frankly, from the standpoints of mental health, personal and social effiency, and seriousness of purpose, it was a most uninviting and sordid picture that was uncovered in this investigation. For, those of us who were afforded the opportunity to conduct the study, as a result of our painstaking analyses and "skull sessions," have envisioned all too vividly a perplexing set of circumstances. It is one that is characterized by *two cultural complexes*, somewhat removed one from the other, and *dramatically in conflict with each other!* That is to say, we have caught the image of (1) the marginal "Negro social world" on the one hand, (2) the dominant middle-class cultural mold on the other, and (3) caught between: the Negro youth—perhaps longing for the more positive aspects of the American promise, but invariably shackled to the disillusionment occasioned by a caste-like existence that is compounded of both a low socio-economic status and the ugly spectre of race in the United States.

I believe that most of us assembled here can extend the various aspects of this sordid picture into a most dismal maze of future low esteem, scholastic mediocrity, and shallow aspirations. But just in case there are some here present who want this spelled out more tangibly, please permit me to quote from the piece entitled "Negro Colleges—Preparing to Survive and Improve," which appeared in the December 15th, 1961 issue of *Time* magazine:

At Texas Southern University 90% of the freshmen have to take remedial math. or English or both. Half the freshman class of 1,000 drops out, and only about 1/4 lasts to graduation. About half the graduates of Negro colleges become schoolteachers. So goes the vicious circle: poor teachers turning out poor students, who in turn become poor teachers turning out poor students.

You recognize, I am sure, that the low academic performances of Negro students at the college level (which were just cited) are not, of course, a manifestation of innate deficiencies, but are, rather, the subtle results of cultural and social deprivation. In other words, the basic proposition here is that youth from culturally disadvantaged groups are significantly handicapped in their school work because of their cultural impoverishment.

At any rate, we must again raise the question of *how* to correct the social and economic conditions that stunt the promising intellectual potentials of many of the youth who come from culturally disadvantaged groups?

As you might have already surmised I stand with those who feel that the time is ripe for an imaginative and progressive movement to come forward and push farther back the frontiers of educational and social change. Happily, there are some forward-moving educators who are already at "the front lines"—educators like those in New York City who set up the unique "Higher Horizons" program as a result of the conviction that the education of a child in a depressed area constitutes a total problem, not just one relating to a lack of high I.Q. levels in the student body.

It is interesting to note that the main effort in New York City is aimed at enriching the disadvantaged child's total experience by using the whole city with its arts and culture as the educational environment, by extending the range of possibility for all the children beyond the limits of the local streets, by reaching out to the children and their parents with sympathetic guidance and improved instruction in every segment of the curriculum. The success of this "Higher Horizons" program (the details of which must be examined elsewhere), and the success of similar ventures spreading throughout this country are clear signs of the direction in which all of us must become prepared to move.

And specifically *what is required* to move ahead? Among other things, the experts in this area agree that the schools will need:

Enough guidance counselors so that each child can be given constant attention and encouragement to achieve in keeping with his capacities.

Imaginative community education efforts designed to win the vital assistance of parents and to capitalize upon the community's educational resources.

Social workers to bridge the gulf between home and school.

Enough qualified teachers so that certain classes can be limited to 10 to 15 students, if necessary.

Special remedial programs, especially in English.

Sufficient funds to keep the schools open nights and on week ends, particularly for those students who have no place else to study or do their homework.

It can't be done?! O yes it can! Because, you see, it's BEING done presently in several places throughout the country!

Now as we move into the "climactic" phase of these remarks, I should like to concentrate on just one dimension of the many-faceted challenge confronting us as teachers of culturally disadvantaged Negro American youth. Let me introduce this matter in the following manner:

A culturally disadvantaged youth gains no benefit from constant admonition unless the urging is accompanied by sensitive help in learning. All too often our perspective has been unbalanced, it seems to me, for, the youth who is unable to do well in math, or in English does not need goading or the threat of a bad grade. More than that, he needs GOOD TEACHING and a curriculum which does not aggravate his frustrations but helps him to overcome them.

Perhaps, though, the concerns I have in mind at this point in my presentation might best be driven home by sharing with you several items of interest which appear to be of pivotal significance here.

The *first* frame of reference I wish to set forth at this point in our discussion is a basic assumption that may be expressed as follows: Increasingly, the ultimate test of the quality of the educational experiences provided in our public schools is becoming the degree to which the graduates of these institutions can meet national standards of excellence as reflected in *standardized tests of proficiency.*

Secondly, with your indulgence, I should like to mention here one or two reactions which three of us from Prairie View A. and M. College experienced during our recent visits in New York with the staff personnel who are involved in the actual operation of the Higher Horizons Program (that was referred to earlier in these remarks). At the George Washington Senior High School in New York City, the following statement was made by a well-preserved and well-respected teacher of math. named Dr. Orleans: "All the talk about children from under-privileged backgrounds not being able to achieve admirably has been disproved. Our experience here has shown that once some of the barriers to effective learning are removed and the school gives them an opportunity to capitalize on their potentials, they do measure up!"

It is also worth noting here that when the principal of Manhattan's Junior High School 43 was asked by us what he would identify as the key element in the New York program (which, incidentally, had its beginnings at his school), without hesitation he said, "A dedicated, enthusiastic, and competent staff convinced of the value of the work they are doing."

Let me hasten to add, too, that if the three of us who journeyed to New York recently had any "reservations" about the excitement we perceived on the part of the staff personnel with whom we talked, believe me, such reservations were completely dispelled after we talked with three randomly selected 12th grade students who are in their final year of the program. These expressive and alert students (one a Puerto Rican; one a Negro American; and the other an Italian American) impressed us tremendously as they responded to our questions. And it will interest you to know that each of these young ladies placed high priority on the small classes they had participated in and on the individual guidance and interested personal attention they had received from their "truly dedicated" teachers.

A third frame of reference that should be called to the focus of attention at this point revolves around some of the observations that are treated in the (1959) monograph of the Association of Colleges and Secondary Schools called, "Improving the Academic Performances of Negro Students." One of the paragraphs in that well prepared publication reads in part as follows:

In many communities the average Negro teacher makes lower scores on standardized tests in English, mathematics, social science, and natural science than the average white teacher. Thus, the *lower average academic performance of Negro students is in part a reflection of the lower average performance of their teachers* . . .

Of interst here, too, is the following statement which appears in the concluding passage of this challenging report:

. . . What is being implied in this generalization is the central and important position of the TEACHER in the growth and learning of pupils . . . In the final analysis, *the academic performances of Negroes in elementary and secondary schools in the South can be changed by improving the performance of those who teach them.*

I should like to refer now, as we turn to a fourth and "culminating" observation or frame of reference for this phase of our discussion, to something which was highlighted at the annual meeting of the National Association of Personnel Workers held at A. and T. College in Greensboro, North Carolina recently. As a participant in a forum entitled "Desired Behavior Patterns for Full Participation in American Society," Dr. Patricia Harris (a brilliant young Negro woman on the staff of Howard University in Washington, D. C.) summarized her presentation by emphasizing the thought that what we're trying to do is "make our students increasingly middle-class in orientation."

What Pat Harris was saying—expressed in a different way—is that those of us who bear some responsibility for the growth and development of Negro American youth *must strive to minimize the points of difference performance-wise between Negroes and whites as a means of facilitating our more significant participation in American society.* Frankly, the point is very well taken and needs little (if any) elaboration.

Please permit me now (by way of ending this presentation) to state in very simple terms what I have tried to set before you this morning to stimulate your thinking and acting!

1   Despite the fact that Negro students in America today suffer from the effects of cultural deprivation, recent experimental efforts have demonstrated that these deficiences CAN be overcome when schools have set into motion systematic and highly structured programs designed to upgrade such youth academically and culturally.

2   Negro American youth MUST be upgraded academically and culturally if they are to begin to enjoy "equal opportunities" to a fuller degree. This proposition is based upon the observation that standardized tests are being used increasingly as a basis for assigning a variety of opportunities in American life. And, you see, in that regard, as long as racial disparities in test scores exist, the Negro will receive less than his proportionate share of all the opportunities dependent on test scores—and he will therefore remain a "marginal being" relative to the mainstream of American culture.

3   Because Negro teachers in many regions of our country (not unlike their Negro students) have *also* been affected negatively by the shameful inequities perpetuated by a society which has not yet adequately translated its ideals into practice, *there is a glaring NEED for RE-CONDITIONING*

*the TEACHERS of Negro American youth!* And we must look to this business of re-awakening and re-conditioning and sensitizing teachers *with dispatch*, lest all too many of us continue to be a part of the problem, rather than a part of the solution to it.

From my vantage point as a graduate level instructor at Prairie View A. and M. College, my continuing perception of the pitiable academic deficiencies of public school *teachers* employed in the schools of Texas leads me to say emphatically that many of us must act quickly to deepen and broaden ourselves in certain of the basic subject matter areas—English, reading, and mathematics, particularly, with respect to the usual format of most of the widely used standardized tests of scholastic proficiency. And make no mistake about it: the kind of psychological and academic and cultural re-conditioning of teachers about which I speak will require a considerable expenditure of time and energy above the confines of the so-called regular school day. The type of "depth in-service education" programs I am thinking about will require imaginative structuring and organization, and a liberal utilization of resource materials as well as competent consultants who know how to make learning an appealing and successful adventure for culturally impoverished youth from low socioeconomic backgrounds. Above all, the type of functional in-service education I have in mind will demand *creative leadership* from far-sighted school administrators who are inspired and secure and courageous enough themselves to create among their teachers the kinds of excitement, dedication, and professional exuberance which were manifested by those members of the Higher Horizons team with whom we talked in New York recently.

Although I would really welcome an expanded opportunity to explore the challenges in this area more fully, because I have already over-extended myself (as far as time limits are concerned), I must now quickly try to conclude this statement. In short, during this final phase of my discussion, I have tried to focus upon the singular role teachers must be prepared to discharge in upgrading American Negro youth academically and culturally. In this connection, there can be no substitute for *imaginative, functional in-service education programs* designed (1) to provide REMEDIAL and ENRICHMENT experiences aimed at improving the quality of instruction in basic subject matter areas, (2) to promote familiarity with useful but little used resource materials, and (3) to facilitate a positive modification of teacher *attitudes* and professional outlook so as to assure that our teachers will be inspired to attack the challenges confronting us with singular vigor and enthusiasm, a contagious "faith," and a genuine sense of personal fulfillment and social responsibility.

Fellow educators, you and I are in a position to help "lift up" the Negro youth in our respective communities who have not yet escaped the apathy, the loss of vision, the dread resignation before harsh circumstances that mark the "walking wounded" in a 300-year battle for freedom, equality of opportunity, and full citizenship. But to DO this we must become courageous men and women of principle who are secure enough professionally and personally to facilitate change. That is why I cry out to you: "Teachers of Culturally Disadvantaged American Youth, We Must Quickly Rally to Re-define our Purposes and Upgrade our Competencies."

# Note

* Keynote address delivered before the annual convention of the Central Texas District Teachers Association on March 16, 1962, Carver High School, Navasota, Texas.

## Selected references

Theodore Brameld, *Minority Problems in the Public Schools*. New York: Harper and Brothers, 1946.
James B. Conant, *Slums and Suburbs*. New York: McGraw-Hill, 1961.
Allison Davis, *Social-Class Influences Upon Learning*. Cambridge: Harvard University Press, 1948.
*Education and the Disadvantaged American* (Educational Policies Commission, 1962).
Eli Ginzberg, (ed.), *The Nation's Children*. New York: Columbia University Press, 1960.
Francis E. Merrill, *Culture and Society*. New Jersey: Prentice-Hall, 1962.
"Negro Colleges—Preparing to Survive and Improve," *Time* Magazine for December 15, 1961.
*Perceptions of the Cultural Problems of Negro Youth in the Public Schools of Texas.* (Educational Research Committee, Prairie View A. and M. College, March 1961.)
Waldo B. Phillips, "Counseling Negro Pupils: An Educational Dilemna" *The Journal of Negro Education*, 29:504–507, Fall, 1960.
J. St. Clair Price, *Improving the Academic Performance of Negro Students*. (Association of Colleges and Secondary Schools, 1959).
*"Project Uplift"—A Challenging New Program to Promote Higher Academic Achievement Through Enriched Cultural – Learning Experiences* (Educational Research Committee, March 1962).
Arnold M. Rose, *The Negro's Morale*. Minneapolis: University of Minnesota Press, 1949.
Ronald J. Rousseve, *Discord in Brown and White: Nine Essays on Intergroup Relations in the United States by a Negro American*. New York: Vantage Press, 1961.
P. C. Sexton. *Education and Income: Inequalities of Opportunity in Our Public Schools*. New York: Viking Press, 1961.
William O. Stanley, *et. al., Social Foundations of Education*. New York: Dryden Press, 1956.
Robert L. Sutherland, *Color, Class, and Personality*. (American Council on Education, 1942).
Harold Taylor, "The Whole Child: A Fresh Look." *Saturday Review* Dec. 16, 1961.
Paul A. Walter, *Race and Cultural Relations*. New York: McGraw-Hill, 1962.

# CHAPTER 19

# MULTICULTURAL EDUCATION (1978)
## NCATE standard rationale

*Richard L. James*

## Introduction

In recent years, the American educational community has witnessed a growing emphasis on the multicultural education concept. Many school districts have developed inservice programs on the subject for teachers and other school personnel. State departments of education have mandated multicultural requirements for candidates seeking certification and recertification. Additionally, colleges and universities have established various types of courses and programs multicultural in character. As a final step, the National Council for Accreditation of Teacher Education (NCATE)—the agency responsible for accrediting teacher education programs—incorporated multicultural education into its standards.

The preamble to NCATE's new standard, (2.1.1 Multicultural Education), which will be implemented on January 1, 1979, opens with this paragraph:

> Multicultural education is preparation for the social, political, and economic realities that individuals experience in culturally diverse and complex human encounters. These realities have both national and international dimensions. This preparation provides a process by which an individual develops competencies for perceiving, believing, evaluating, and behaving in differential cultural settings. Thus, multicultural education is viewed as an intervention and an on-going assessment process to help institutions and individuals become more responsive to the human condition, individual cultural integrity, and cultural pluralism in society.[1]

As the standard language indicates, the standard writers based their work on several assumptions:

1   Education, as it applies to formal learning experiences provided in schools, does not adequately prepare individuals to function effectively in a culturally diverse society.
2   Society in the United States is pluralistic in character, and this pluralism will become an increasingly important factor in the future development of the nation.
3   Educators and educational institutions play an important role in shaping social behavior and must assume a principal responsibility for leadership in the development of a multicultural society.

4   The monitoring and assessment of the educational enterprise is not complete unless educators and educational institutions are evaluated with
respect to providing educational experiences consistent with the concept
of multicultural education.

The assumptions that underlie the development of the multicultural standard
are not new. They reflect observations of many writers made about education
recently. For example, the U.S. Commissioner of Education in his 1974 report to
the Congress included the following statements:

> For generations Americans regarded their school system as the great melting
> pot and equalizer of society. In a social system characterized by cultural
> pluralism, the schools were expected to play a major role in imparting
> national culture and traditions. Since the 1960s, however, schools have also
> been called upon to make good on equality of opportunity in education for all.
>   This latter development, enhanced by massive support throughout the
> country for local autonomy, individualism, and self-determination, is mould-
> ing new trends in the education system. The demands of special interest
> groups are resulting in increased diversity in education services.[2]

The AACTE Bicentennial Commission on Education for the Profession of
Teaching address precisely the urgency of multicultural education. In its report the
commission states that:

> Teacher educators must maintain a profound commitment to human rights,
> particularly the rights of children. Unfortunately, teacher educators have not
> always been conscious exemplars of human rights. Few actively advocate the
> rights of minority groups or promote cultural pluralism. Today, leaders ask
> the education profession to develop in students those attitudes and beliefs
> which support cultural pluralism as a positive social force. Thus, the educa-
> tion of teacher educators must be substantive enough to develop a respect for
> the culture, life-styles, and contributions of nonmainstream cultures. Teacher
> educators also need a commitment to universal human values in order to
> promote harmonious coexistence.[3]

## Concept definition

It is not surprising that a great deal of anxiety exists concerning the new standard.
For many educators, multicultural education is a concept that lacks definition.
While the preamble to the standard may help to clarify multicultural education to
some degree, it does not adequately answer very basic questions such as: What
does the term multicultural education mean? How will one know when a teacher
education program is multicultural? What must an institution do to assure the
accrediting agency that the standard is met? Answers to these questions will
not come easily. However, it must be recognized that conscious application of
the multicultural education principles requires careful thought and planning
throughout the process of program design, development, and implementation.
This process must be based on an understanding and appreciation of multiculturalism as a positive force in American education.
   As the standard's preamble indicates, multicultural education is an on-going
process. It is not a subject to be easily packaged in separate courses and learning

experiences added to the teacher education program. Ideally, multicultural education should describe the total educational experience. Multicultural education presumes an acceptance of and a commitment to cultural pluralism. Without this acceptance and commitment, the development of a multicultural education program is difficult, if not impossible. Multicultural education is the process of making the educational experience more responsive to the cultural diversity that characterizes U.S. and world society.

Contrary to what many people seem to believe, multicultural education focuses on individual as well as group welfare. Teacher educators have always urged prospective teachers to consider the psychological characteristics that set one student apart from another. Teachers were told that the child learns better when instruction is fitted to unique individual needs and interests. In this respect, the role of addressing psychological differences in learning has received much work. On the other hand, little is known about the role of cultural factors. Cole Bembreck and Walker Hill call attention to this point in the introduction to their book, *Cultural Challenges to Education*, with these comments:

> Cultural Characteristics touch us (educators) at the level of feelings, emotion and prejudice. Instead of according them recognition and respect, as we do psychological differences, we tend to assign them "good" and "bad" designations, and we let our expectations of students be influenced by them. We tend to use cultural characteristics such as race, ethnic and national origins, language, and minority status for the purpose of sorting promising students from the unpromising. We apparently find it difficult to come at the matter of cultural diversity positively. We do not ask how cultural aptitudes might be used to support and enhance a child's classroom learning; instead, we tend to ignore or suppress these differences.[4]

Multicultural education presumes that cultural differences are as much of a child's background as psychological differences and that they influence learning. Therefore, multicultural education is the process of bringing together cultural and psychological differences to enhance each individual's learning environment.

Some educators believe that multicultural education is somehow synonymous with special programs for minorities and women. For persons who hold this view-point, such programs as Black Studies, Chicano Studies, and Native American Studies suffice for teaching and learning about cultural differences. The standard's preamble implies, however, that the aim of multicultural education is to produce multicultural individuals. The focus here is not on the creation and perpetuation of distinct cultural subunits. Multicultural education requries that American educational institutions acquaint all students with the broad range of cultural diversity that exists in the United States. It also requires the provision of learning experiences designed to teach students the analytical skills necessary to compete for the statuses of their choice. Ethnic Studies or Women's Studies may, indeed, be a part of multicultural education, but they do not represent the concept in its totality.

## Cross-cultural encounters

Multicultural education presumes an awareness of the teaching act as a cross-cultural encounter. Every student brings to the classroom a unique cultural identity. How classmates and, most importantly, the teacher perceive the student affects this identity significantly. A classroom with an instructional process insensitive to the existing cultural differences or with an essentially monocultural teaching-learning activity negatively affects students whose cultural background and experience differs from that being stressed. In a real sense, these students become outsiders. The most well-meaning teacher who plans and organizes instruction from a monocultural perspective is likely to encounter indifference, antagonism, or outright hostility. For the students whose cultural background is different, the educational experiences provided are viewed frequently as a "put down" or a denial of the legitimacy of their heritage. The effect of such experiences over a period of years can be devastating.

Benjamin Bloom, in his recent book, *Human Characteristics and School Learning*, states that students in school are taught at least two courses of study—the manifest curriculum and the latent curriculum.[5] Bloom's remarks about these two curricula seem to have special meaning for multicultural education.

The manifest curriculum is the one that the student is expected to learn.

> This curriculum includes the reading, mathematics, science, literature, social studies, and other school subjects that he or she is taught. This curriculum may be of great importance to the learner because of the competence he develops, the interests and attitudes he acquires, and the career opportunities which are made available to those who learn it well. . . . Some of it may be remembered and used repeatedly by the learners, while some of it may be forgotten quickly and discarded. The manifest curriculum is visible; it is documented in many ways; and most of the resources and personnel of the school are dedicated to the students' learning of this curriculum.[6]

The latent curriculum, writes Bloom, is uniquely taught to and differently learned by each student. He states:

> This is the curriculum which teaches the student who he is in relation to others. It may also teach each person his or her place in the world of people, of ideas, and of activities. While the student may learn this curriculum more slowly than the other, it is likely that he will not be able to forget it as easily as he can forget the details of history, the rules of grammar, or the specifics of any subject of study in the manifest curriculum.[7]

Multicultural education focuses on the latent curriculum, not at the expense of the manifest curriculum, but as a supplement to it. The multicultural standard rests on the assumption that teacher education programs can provide competencies and skills for enabling teachers to use qualities of the latent curriculum in the teaching-learning process.

Planning and teaching from a multicultural perspective requires the following:

1   Teachers should establish an environment in the classroom that enables each student to feel that his or her status is equal to that of every other student.
2   Each student should have a meaningful opportunity to participate in the formulation of the common goals to provide direction for the instructional activities.
3   Teachers should stimulate and promote the concept of cooperation and interdependence among students as they seek to accomplish the set goals.

4   Teachers should approve actively and encourage interaction among students maximizing opportunities for cross-cultural dialogue and communication.

Most teachers would probably insist that these conditions do exist in their classrooms. However, a look at the research regarding teacher-pupil interaction, classroom seating practices, or classroom discipline shows that serious deficiencies prevail, particularly with regard to students from racial and ethnic minorities.

## International dimensions

The standard preamble points out that multicultural education also has an international dimension. The cultural pluralism that characterizes society in the United States has its roots in the nations and peoples who came here from all over the world. In recent years, this nation has assumed a rapidly expanding role in world affairs—a role that requires more than a perfunctory knowledge of the cultures of other lands and other peoples. America has paid and continues to pay heavily for its lack of sensitivity to the culture and heritage of the people of Africa, Latin America, the Middle East, and Asia.

Current world events seem to indicate clearly that the era of U.S. and Western European dominance over international affairs is in a declining phase. As a result, more people will become more insistent on having a real voice in determining their destiny. A multicultural perspective is essential in the adjustment from a role of dominance to the required role of collaboration, cooperation, and negotiation. A prerequisite to acquiring the international multicultural perspective is attaining this perspective at home. In other words, a natural and significant relationship exists between multicultural education as it is practiced in a U.S. classroom and its application to international concerns. Education for an international multicultural perspective must include the study of cultures of non-Western people as an integral component. For example, such courses as the "History of Western Civilization" or "European Literature" will have their counterparts that deal with non-Western history and literature. Such courses and learning experiences must take their place in the regular curriculum and cease to be exotic experiences for those who have a special interest.

Clearly, it is imperative that those responsible for educating the nation's youth must provide learning experiences designed to eliminate the parochialism and national elitism characteristic of many Americans. Teachers and teacher educators can make a significant contribution toward this objective.

In *The World and the American Teacher*, written almost ten years ago, Harold Taylor describes the problem in words that still apply.

> If we ask the question bluntly, "To what extent are American teachers being prepared through their curriculum to understand and to teach about the nature of world society?" The answer is almost not at all. Not more than three to five percent of all teachers . . . have had in the course of their preparation to become teachers in the social sciences or any other area of the curriculum any formal study of cultures other than their own in the West, or have studied in a field which could properly be described as world affairs.[8]

Multicultural education can also be described as a process of making students become aware of and sensitive to the world as a community of cultures as well as gaining competencies and skills that will enable them to develop an international and domestic perspective in cross-cultural encounters. Such a perspective is necessary for Americans to fully appreciate their role and responsibilities in today's world.

## Institutional commitment

The new multicultural standard requires a serious review of teacher education programs in colleges and universities.

> Multicultural education is a great challenge to the teaching profession. It is not that the challenges themselves are new since championing the rights of children, striving to achieve a pedagogy responsive to all children's learning needs, and helping expand educational opportunities to include all social groups are inherent in the role of a teacher. What is new and significant is the commitment to preserve and enhance rather than melt away the uniqueness of cultural groups in the society. New also is the too seldom emphasized need for teachers to search for and emphasize the core values of American life which are the basis for unity amidst diversity.[9]

The foundation of an effective multicultural teacher program rests on institutional commitment. Without the support and commitment of the entire institution, there is little likelihood that the education unit can be successful in establishing a program consistent with the principles of multiculturalism. Ideally the institution's statement of its mission should explain it. The institution's commitment, which must be clear and unequivocal, must be reflected at the operational level. It should be evident in the selection, admission, and retention of students, in the recruitment and hiring of faculty, administrators, and staff; and in the institution's relationship to the community that it serves. A multicultural teacher education program depends on an institutional environment that is congruent with the goals of multiculturalism. As required by the new standard, the establishment of such an environment is a necessary step in the development of the systematic plan for multiculturalism in teacher education.

Once the proper environment for planning and implementing is established, the framework for task accomplishment can be determined. A first step in this process is arriving at agreement on stating the elements of a multicultural program at the institutional level. Within the standard's framework, each institution will have to develop its own definition of multicultural education; this should be the basis of the institution's plan. The development of the operational definition should, of course, involve persons who can bring a variety of perspectives to the task—persons who represent the diverse cultures found in the institution's constituency.

The revised standard clearly states that the institution's provisions for multicultural education are an integral part of its curriculum design. In formulating an operational definition and a plan that provides for multicultural education, institutions must remember that this process is part of the larger process of conceptualizing the teacher's role and establishing objectives based on that conceptualization. The 10 "essential understandings" compiled by Asa Hilliard[10] suggest elements of the conceptualization of the teacher's role from a multicultural perspective:

1  The teaching process is always a cross-cultural encounter.
2  The personality, values, and social background of the teacher are critical cultural inputs.
3  All teaching tools are culture bound.
4  The classroom is not a benign context but a potent matrix.
5  Teachers must know that students can be victims (of oppressive social and economic conditions).
6  Teachers must understand that all minds are equally complex.
7  Teachers must be helped to understand that the poor and racial or ethnic minorities can and actually have been able to learn at the same level as others when proper environmental support was provided.
8  Teachers must understand that learning is related to a sense of power over some of the forces which impinge upon our lives.
9  Teachers must understand how their own expectations are determining factors in building a climate of growth for students.
10  Teachers must understand intimately the culture of their students.

A conception of the teacher's role that incorporates elements like Hilliard's understandings provides a sound base for multicultural teacher education program development. They suggest concrete approaches that can be translated into content for courses and learning experiences and thus permit those planning a multicultural program to become more specific.

Banks writes that teacher education programs must be designed to prepare individuals to function successfully in multiethnic settings. These programs must help teachers acquire: (a) more democratic attitudes and values, (b) a clarified philosophical position related to pluralism, (c) a process conceptualization of ethnic studies, (d) the ability to view society from diverse ethnic perspectives, and (e) knowledge of the emerging stages of ethnicity, and their curricular and teaching implications.[11]

Banks describes five stages of ethnicity ranging from monoethnic to multiethnic. Multiethnic individuals participate in their ethnic culture, the mainstream ethnic culture, and within other ethnic cultures. A major goal of the school, Banks states, is to help individuals function at increasingly higher levels of ethnicity.[12]

The references to Hilliard, Banks, and others are just a sample from a growing amount of literature on multiculturalism in education. Teacher educators responsible for planning multicultural education programs in teacher education would profit from consulting this literature early in the planning process. A review of the literature will show that while there may be some ambiguity about the meaning of the term multicultural education, certain conclusions seem to be clear:

1  Learning experiences currently being provided by schools do not adequately meet the needs of all children and youth.
2  Cultural, racial, and ethnic factors do contribute to the inability of schools to meet the needs of all students.
3  Teachers play a central role in determining the nature of the instructional program and how it is implemented in the classroom. They also determine, to a substantial degree, the extent to which the instructional activities respond to the needs of all students.
4  Teacher education programs do not provide opportunities for prospective teachers to gain the skills and competencies needed for establishing

an environment where the success of all students is possible and is expected.

The purpose of the new multicultural standards is to stimulate teacher educators and teacher education institutions to assume a more active role in making educational institutions more responsive to the needs and aspirations of all Americans. The extent to which this is possible certainly depends on the dedication and commitment brought to the task. Educators cannot afford to avoid this responsibility. The American education community's future may depend on the choice made.

## Notes

1  *Standards for the Accreditation of Teacher Education* (Washington, D.C.: National Council for Accreditation of Teacher Education, 1977).
2  *Annual Report of the Commissioner of Education—Fiscal Year 1974* (Washington, D.C.: U.S. Department of Health, Education, and Welfare, 1975), p. 8.
3  Robert B. Howsam et al., *Educating a Profession* (Washington, D.C.: AACTE, 1976), pp. 108–109.
4  Cole S. Brembeck and Walter H. Hill, *Cultural Challenges to Education* (Lexington, Mass.: D.C. Heath, 1973), p. 3.
5  Benjamin S. Bloom, *Human Characteristics and School Learning* (New York: McGraw Hill, 1976), p. 142.
6  *Ibid.*
7  *Ibid.*
8  Harold Taylor, *The World and the American Teacher* (Washington, D.C.: AACTE, 1968), p. 26.
9  Howsam, *op. cit.*, p. 24.
10 Asa G. Hilliard, "Restructuring Teacher Education for Multicultural Imperatives," in *Multicultural Education Through Competency Based Teacher Education*, ed. William A. Hunter (Washington, D.C.: AACTE, 1974), pp. 44–47.
11 James A. Banks, "The Implications of Multicultural Education for Teacher Education," in *Pluralism and the American Teacher, Issues and Case Studies*, eds. Frank Klassen and Donna Gollnick (Washington, D.C.: AACTE, 1977), p. 26.
12 *Ibid.*

# CHAPTER 20

# MULTICULTURAL PREPARATION AND TEACHER EFFECTIVENESS IN DESEGREGATED SCHOOLS (1978)

*Geneva Gay*

The focus of much racial change in schools has been primarily on desegregation—the physical mixing of students of different races and ethnic groups . . .
We have not at the same time attended sufficiently to the definition and
realization of integration—high quality interracial education. The concentration on the technical problems of rearranging bodies overlooks the necessity
of reforms in human values, attitudes, and resources.[1]

Kathleen Smith's comments are a most astute description of the character of most
desegregation activities since the 1954 Supreme Court decision in *Brown v. Board
of Education*. Without a doubt, *desegregation* has been the single most pervasive
issue in American education for more than two decades now. It has prompted
both praise and criticism with respect to its potential for realizing the American
dream of equal educational opportunities for all students.

Desegregation in its most inclusive sense (e.g., integration) is a "people issue,"
and must be addressed by revamping human resources in the context of the
educational process, instead of it being merely a legal policy issue that can be
resolved through legislative and legalistic mandates. The fundamental question
is what happens or does not happen *after* the buses arrive that makes the difference between legal desegregation and operational integration. St. John suggests that less attention be given to achieving racial balance in schools and more
to improving conditions in biracial schools to achieve educational quality and
realize the promise of desegregation.[2] Smith supports this notion in her observations that:

> The mere physical movement of youngsters does little to provide or guarantee
> any changes in the quality of education; in the character of racism in American
> schools; in school achievement patterns; in the interpersonal relations exist-
> ing among black, brown, and white youngsters; or in the variety of patterns
> of ethnic plurality. No plan can settle for the mere physical mixing or
> desegregation of people. Provision must be made for an educational environ-
> ment encouraging academic and human growth for all students according to
> their particular talents and needs.[3]

One critical element of this "people issue" central to providing quality education and maximizing student growth in desegregated schools is teachers and
their readiness or preparedness for desegregation. To date teacher preparation for

desegregation has been largely neglected or terribly restrictive. Little attention has been given to the *systematic* preparation of teachers for the new socio-cultural classroom dynamics created by desegregation. Some sporadic, isolated, and fragmented crisis-oriented preparation efforts have occurred from time to time, but these have been lacking in careful conceptualization and planning, comprehensive implementation, and systematic follow-through. And, these efforts have been designed primarily for the purpose of orienting teachers to logistical and managerial matters related to relocating students, for gaining student conformity to school norms, and for avoiding racial conflict among different racial and ethnic groups of students.

Too often teachers have been thrown into desegregated situations with inadequate preparation in the differential values, attitudes, expectations, and behaviors they might find among multiethnic student populations, and the implications of these for restructuring the educational process. Yet, teachers are expected to facilitate the smooth psychological transition of students from segregation to desegregation. Little emphasis has been placed on understanding the content and implications of different ethnic cultures, value systems, and behavioral patterns for improving the educational process.

## Teacher apprehensions

Many teachers from middle class backgrounds who have been trained in middle class Anglo-American oriented colleges and universities approach desegregation with negative attitudes toward minority students, and some deep-seated apprehensions about teaching the culturally different. Buxton and associates have identified a list of apprehensions held by teachers toward culturally different students. Among the fourteen apprehensions expressed by white teachers toward black students are a lack of understanding of their interests, life styles, values, and language, lack of confidence in their own abilities to handle prejudices and other racial problems, and black students' vulgarity, disrespect for each other, defensiveness, and poor home training. Those things about white students that cause black teachers the most apprehension are their reluctance to interact with black students, their feelings of superiority, their isolation from the rest of the class, and tense atmospheres between the races. Black and white teachers are equally concerned about discipline, relating cross-racially to parents, being accused of prejudices, and the reading abilities of students.[4]

The available research on cross-racial student-teacher classroom interactions, although limited, indicate that anglo and minority (black and Mexican American) teachers act similarly in differentiating their verbal behaviors toward white and minority students. In terms of both quantative and qualitative measures, anglo students are treated significantly different from black and Mexican American students in desegregated classrooms. Teachers are less directive and more divergent in their interactions with white students, anglo students receive more opportunities to participate in *substantive* classroom interactions, and are praised or otherwise encouraged for their contributions more frequently than black and Mexican American students. Comparatively, teachers' interactions with minority students tend to be more authoritarian and convergent, black and Mexican American students receive fewer opportunities to engage in classroom activities, are critized more frequently, and tend to participate in *procedural* classroom matters more often than anglo students. These findings have led the U. S. Civil Rights Commission and Gay to conclude that if pupil-teacher interaction is the heart of the education process, and since anglo and minority students do not have equal access and opportunity to engage in this process, then minority students in desegregated schools are not receiving the same quality of education as anglo students.[5]

Although disturbing, it is not surprising that teachers exhibit such attitudes and behaviors toward culturally different students. Given the facts of the historical treatment and assessment of ethnic minorities in American society, that most teachers, like other Americans, live in ethnic enclaves in relative isolation from other ethnic groups, and that their professional preparation experiences are largely devoid of any instruction in ethnic diversity we should expect little more. How can we reasonably expect teachers untrained in cultural differences and the dynamics of interracial interactions to feel comfortable and confident in dealing with interracial situations, and be effective in providing quality educational experiences for students from different ethnic, racial, and cultural backgrounds. As Smith suggests, "one cannot take a faculty accustomed to segregated forms of instruction and expect it to be successful in desegregated settings without a great deal of retraining. We cannot expect people who grew up with, went to school in, got their early experience . . . in a segregated system to know how to teach in a desegregated milieu."[6]

## Preparing teachers for desegregation

Teacher preparation is critical to the effectiveness of desegregation. We cannot continue to assume that teachers who can teach at all can teach in desegregated settings. Nor can their preparation be left to chance. Such benign neglect is inexcusable, not to mention being terribly demoralizing to teachers. Rather, deliberately organized training programs must be designed to get teachers and other school personnel ready to *function differently and more effectively* in desegregated schools. Preparation that is planned deliberately to achieve specific objectives is essential, for we know from social science research on interracial relations that as age increases from young children to adults, people tend to space themselves at greater interpersonal distances, and that personal contact among races does not lead automatically to improved racial understanding.[7] In other words, just because teachers encounter different ethnic groups in desegregated schools, there is no reason to believe that their attitudes will change, that they will be sensitive and responsive to ethnic and cultural differences, or that they will teach differently than if they were in segregated schools. It seems more reasonable to expect the reverse to happen. Teachers do best what they know how to do *and* are comfortable with doing. Furthermore, how can we expect them to react responsibly to encounters they may not understand, and are likely to approach with some caution and skepticism.

Among the goals of programs designed to prepare teachers for desegregation should be recognizing the multiethnic nature of American history, life, and culture; accepting the probability of some cultural conflict in pluralistic settings; understanding racial attitudes and values of self and others; acquiring knowledge of the traditions and achievements of many different ethnic individuals and groups; and mastering principles and skill essential for interracial relations, crosscultural communication, and cultural-context teaching. These goals should provide the philosophy and substance for improving teacher effectiveness in desegregated schools.

## Self-awareness

If teachers are to improve their interracial behaviors, or even make a reasonable decision about whether their attitudes and behaviors need changing, first of all, they need to be *consciously aware* of what their racial attitudes and instructional behaviors are toward culturally different students. Often teachers do and say things that project negative racial attitudes, beliefs, and values, but are totally unconscious of what is taking place. The verbal language teachers use, the way they respond to or ignore ethnic students, and their nonverbal body language can convey to students that they are prejudiced, that they do not believe in the personal worth of all students whatever their racial identity or ethnicity, and that they do not value diversity. If teachers have negative attitudes toward ethnicity and feel uncomfortable in the presence of culturally and ethnically pluralistic populations, these attitudes will interfere with their effective functioning in desegregated classrooms. Thus, awareness of self and others' ethnic attitudes and values is a critical component of teacher preparation for desegregation, both as a means of helping teachers crystallize or clarify their own racial attitudes and values, and of providing them with experiential data and exemplary instructional techniques to use with students.

Such techniques as values analysis, introspection, process analysis, and systematic classroom observation schedules are useful devices for helping teachers become more sensitized to their personal racial attitudes, and for developing skills in discerning and interpreting their racial attitudes and values as exhibited in teaching behaviors. Teachers need to ask—and answer—of themselves such questions as: What are my beliefs and attitudes about racial and ethnic groups? How have my own life style, experiences, ethnic heritage, and cultural conditioning influenced the formation of my racial attitudes and beliefs? What do I know about different ethnic and racial groups? What are my expectations—academic, social, and relational—of different ethnic groups? What are some of my teaching behaviors and habits, both verbal and nonverbal, that are indicators of the beliefs and attitudes I hold toward different ethnic groups? How do my beliefs and what I think I know about ethnic groups compare with the scholarly data available on these groups? Are there some alternative ways for me to believe and behave toward ethnic groups that would be more congruent with the way ethnic groups really are?

Teachers also need to become more attuned to their teaching styles and instructional behaviors with different ethnic group students, and examine these critically to determine the racial attitudes, beliefs, and values embedded in them. Familiarity with systematic observation schedules used to record verbal and nonverbal classroom behaviors, and ethnographic observation techniques used to describe sociocultural activities and processes of groups in naturalistic settings, can serve to orient teachers toward becoming *participant-observers of their own instructional modes*. Teachers working in desegregated classrooms with ethnically diverse student populations should collect data on their teaching styles by asking themselves questions such as: Do I differentiate my teaching behaviors according to the ethnicity of my students? What kind of communication behaviors and habits do I use that are stereotypic, demeaning, and/or alienating to ethnically different students, and/or facilitative to cross-cultural and interracial interactions? Do I expect the academic performance of minority students to be lower than anglo students? Do I provide similar opportunities, in terms of frequency and quality, to ethnic minority students and majority students to participate in classroom activities, as expressed, for example, in the kinds of questions I ask and the praise and encouragement I give to students? Do I feel secure in discussing ethnic issues and racial problems with my students? Do I promote cultural diversity in my classroom and encourage my students to be proud of their ethnicity?

To answer these questions teachers need to begin to *consciously* record their attitudes, beliefs, and behaviors so that they can examine them reflectively, and better analyze the dynamics of their classrooms in order to determine the interface between attitudes, beliefs, and behaviors. These analytical exercises and processes will create a kind of psychological and cognitive dissonance that can provide a stimulus for mental growth and new learning. They also are requisites to behavior modification resulting from the exploration and discovery of new information about different ethnic groups.

The underlying premises of this recommended focus on self-awareness as an essential component of the preparation of teachers for desegregation are: (1) many teachers are not aware of their own racial beliefs, attitudes, values, and behaviors, and ethnic life styles; (2) teachers must learn to clarify their racial attitudes and cultural experiences before they can arrive at a state of readiness to understand, accept, and appreciate the cultural experiences and life styles of other ethnic groups; (3) teachers can, and need to, learn how to utilize the cultural experiences of different ethnic groups in preparing instructional designs for students in desegregated, pluralistic classrooms; and (4) similar issues and techniques teachers use to clarify their own racial beliefs and ethnic attitudes can be used to help students do likewise.

## Knowledge acquisition essential to promoting cultural differences

Knowledge about cultural and ethnic diversity is a prerequisite to teacher instructional effectiveness and responsiveness to cultural differences in desegregated classrooms. Respect and appreciation for cultural differences derive from understanding, and real understanding is based upon valid information about the cultural patterns, values, habits, and experiences of different ethnic groups. It is impossible for teachers to develop new instructional and relational styles that are responsive to different cultural traditions and ethnic learning patterns if they are not knowledgeable of cultural differences. While assuredly no panacea, some fundamental knowledge about different ethnic life styles and cultural experiences is imperative to teacher effectiveness in desegregated schools.

Among the cognitive knowledge teachers need to acquire in order to improve their understanding of cultural differences is: (1) the characteristics of different ethnic communication styles and the influences of cultural conditioning in shaping preferred communication modes; (2) the concept of ethnicity and its impact upon the identification process of ethnic minorities as well as "white ethnics"; (3) instructional materials, resources, and techniques for teaching ethnic life styles and cultural differences; (4) cognitive learning styles of different ethnic groups; and (5) the historical experiences and socialization or enculturation processes of different ethnic groups. These are important components to be included in preparing teachers for desegregation because of their significance in shaping student behavior in instructional settings, because insights derived from such understandings are useful in minimizing conflicts between ethnic values and school norms, and because teachers are better able to make more valid decisions about curriculum materials, learning alternatives, and instructional techniques most compatible with different ethnic backgrounds.

Teachers also need to understand the significance of Novak's statement that, "We are not atomic individuals. We appear for but one passing moment in a long line of our ancestors and our posterity. We carry forward a whole culture in every one of our gestures, acts, thoughts, and emotions,"[8] for interpreting the relational dynamics operating in desegregated classrooms. How students and teachers think and behave, what they value, and how they perceive the educational process are determined largely by the nature of their socialization, cultural conditioning, and the extent of their ethnic affiliation. The degree to which they have internalized the ethnic identification process has a profound effect on ethnic students' behaviors and perceptions. Ethnic identity is a persistent, emerging phenomenon. At any point in time members of ethnic groups are in different stages of questioning and clarifying their ethnic identities. This differential development can cause intra-group assertiveness, aggressiveness and conflict, what appears on the surface to be a lack of group solidarity, and great uncertainties in relationships with others.

Conflicting conceptions of self-identity may cause some black students to label each other "colored," "niggers," "honky-lovers," or "Toms." Hispanic students face the dilemma of whether to identify themselves as latinos, Spanish surnames, or Hispanics, and may accuse each other of being "gringos," "tito tacos," and unloyal to *La Raza*. Indians are torn between allegiance to their traditional cultures and the demands of urbanized living. White ethnics are just beginning a search to revitalize their "lost" ethnic identities. Depending on the stage of development ethnic students variously appear to be self-denigrating with strong negative self-concepts; self-centered and ethnocentric, avoiding contact with people outside their own ethnic group; oversolicitous or over-accommodating conformists to teacher and school expectations; and vacillating between complete denial of their ethnic identity, being totally consumed by their ethnicity, or proud of their ethnicity in nonethnocentric ways. Teachers in desegregated schools who are knowledgeable of and responsive to the ethnic identification process (1) plan classroom activities to help students understand what is happening to them and why; (2) provide guidance to students consonant with their stages of ethnic identification; and (3) design curriculum content congruent with particular stages of ethnic identification. For instance, if students have strong negative self-concepts, guidance techniques and curriculum content that highlight the cultural assets of their particular ethnic group may increase their self-esteem. Curriculum content that emphasizes value clarification and critical analysis of different ethnic group experiences is more appropriate for students who are secure in their own ethnic identity, whereas bicultural programs will help students in transition between their own ethnic cultures and the common culture of majority America better comprehend their social development.

Within the context of their cultural communities many ethnic groups ascribe to values that are at odds with school norms. For example students from Mexican American, Hawaiian, Korean, and Japanese American backgrounds are taught filial obligation, group affiliation, cooperation, and mutuality in their home communities. These orientations are likely to produce behaviors in school that are confusing to uninformed teachers, and that are in conflict with the institutional expectations of schools, which emphasize individuality, personal success, and competitiveness.

Different ethnic groups also have specific norms regulating relations among age groups, and determining conditions most conducive to learning. For instance, in traditional black and Hawaiian communities the peer group is a major socializing agency. After a certain age children are taught to avoid direct interactions or confrontations with adults in learning situations. Appeals are made to adult authority when the natural socializing process breaks down and some mechanism is needed to reestablish order. In schools teachers, representing authority, are the *primary* actors in the instructional or socializing process. Obviously, this causes students who do not share this cultural expectation some adjustment problems. Different relational norms of ethnic students and schools provide a challenge for teachers in desegregated classrooms to diversify their instructional styles and role behaviors so that they are not always at the center of teaching-learning activities. Student-directed, consensus-based, and group-focused activities are more congruent with peer-centered, cooperative cultural orientations toward learning than are teacher-directed, individualistic, and competitive activities.

If used wisely intercultural communication can be a most effective medium through which teachers in desegregated schools can express their respect and appreciation for cultural differences. After all, teaching is communicating, and without effective communication between students and teachers there can be no teaching and learning. Effective cross-cultural communication begins with knowledge of the fact that communication is a social process, and that communication patterns are largely culturally determined. Different ethnic groups have different vocabularies, attitudes toward language usage, nonverbal nuances, spatial relations, and communicative rules that can interfere with the smooth operation of classrooms. Communication is difficult in and of itself, and it becomes even more so when communicants do not share the same referential codes or experiential frames of reference. This is often the case in multiethnic desegregated classrooms. Words, gestures, and body movements are used by students and teachers that have different denotative and connotative meanings. These can easily polarize desegregated classrooms. Informed teachers are alerted to this possibility, are familiar with a variety of ethnic communication habits, and can facilitate their effective use in the classroom.

Knowledgeable teachers diversify curriculum content and courses to accommodate different cultural patterns. Opportunities are provided for students to use their vernaculars or "home languages" without being apologetic and threatened by retribution. Students from different ethnic groups are encouraged to share and learn from each other the "functional applied sociolinguistic communication styles" appropriate in their respective ethnic communities. Language arts and speech curricula incorporate contemporary ethnic vocabularies in lessons on vocabulary building, synonyms, language evolution, and selective communication. Students are encouraged to explore how interracial relations are affected by ethnic and racial stereotypes and prejudices projected through language and communication. This can be done by analyzing magazine advertisements, television commercials, and prime time situation comedy television programs with ethnic themes and/or characters for their subtle racial stereotyping. "Good Times," "Chico and the Man," "The Jeffersons," and "Sanford and Son" fall into the latter category and provide excellent case study materials for these analytical exercises. Examining words and phrases in the English language that are derivatives of "black" and "white" for their denotative and connotative meanings will sensitize students to how words and other communication habits can be powerful conveyors of both negative and positive racial attitudes and values.

Activities such as these are useful exercises in helping students and teachers learn to respect different "ethnic inclinations" in their interracial relations, and to develop skills of selective or situational word usage and communicative "style-shifting." The application of these skills in desegregated schools is indicative of the presence of accepting and valuing attitudes toward cultural differences on the part of students and teachers.

## Creating pluralistic classroom climates

The ecology or socio-psychological atmosphere that pervades desegregated class-rooms is a significant indicator of teachers' attitudes toward cultural differences. Valuing cultural differences is expressed through the environmental medium when ethnic and cultural diversity is an accurate description of the instructional techniques and materials, the general decorations, the themes and characters of bulletin board displays, and the audio and visual supplementary aids used in desegregated classrooms. A classroom in which teachers and students are open, comfortable, and eager to explore different ethnic issues, experiences, and heritages is suggestive of an environment where diversity is accepted as legitimate curriculum content, and as a viable source of personal growth and enrichment. The pictures of "heroes and heroines" and inspirational proverbs that appear in school hallways and on classroom walls, which are selected *consistently* from a wide variety of ethnic groups and sources, also are vibrant expressions of the acceptance of cultural differences. All of these environmental factors convey the message that teachers accept diversity as a real fact of life, and consider cultural pluralism as a fundamental ingredient of all aspects of the instructional process, both formal and informal.

Creating ethnically and culturally pluralistic classroom environments are easy to achieve and they are effective mechanisms through which teachers can help different ethnic students achieve a sense of ethnic affiliation and personal ownership in what goes on in the classroom. What better way for teachers to express their acceptance, appreciation, and endorsement of cultural pluralism, and for students to develop a sense of pride in their own and others' ethnicity than to cast the instructional process in an environmental context that radiates ethnic, racial, and cultural diversity.

## Cultural context teaching

Although knowledge of diversity, intercultural communication, and pluralistic classroom climates are essential means of responding positively to cultural differences they alone are not sufficient. Teachers need also to modify their instructional behaviors and curriculum content so that they too reflect and perpetrate ethnic and cultural diversity. This should be done such that instructional strategies complement and interact with teacher attitudes, the curriculum, the organizational structure, and the psycho-social climate of the classroom in order to have a total impact upon the education of students.

Teachers should strive to intersect or interface their instructional methodologies and curriculum content with the differential cognitive learning styles of various ethnic groups. This might be called ethnic-specific or cultural-context teaching. One way to do this is to modify school curricula to encompass multi-ethnic perspectives and culturally pluralistic content. For instance, reading skills such as listening, interpretation and translation, vocabulary building, comprehension, and word attack skills can be taught through the use of short stories, essays, autobiographies, novels, folktales, poetry, and song lyrics written by and about different ethnic group people. The list of candidates to be included in a study of "heroism" in America should include, among others, representation from black Americans, anglo Americans, Irish Americans, American Indian, Asian Americans, and Italian Americans. Examination of the concepts of ethnicity, identity, and "Americanness" is incomplete without the inclusion of different ethnic conceptualizations, such as "I Am Joaquin," "Black Is," "Ballard to America," "Half-Breed," and "Down These Mean Streets." Such approaches to teaching concepts and social issues validate ethnic diversity and cultural pluralism, have high motivational value and relevance potential, and expose students to a wide range of cultural options and perceptions of reality within the context of their daily classroom procedures.

Another way for teachers to demonstrate their commitment to cultural differences through ethnic-specific instruction if for them to develop repertoires for diversified multiethnic teaching examples. A great deal of teaching is done through examples, anecdotes, analogies, and vignettes. These are used to increase educational relevance by relating academic abstractions to daily experiential living. Teachers whose repertoires of instructional examples are comprised of anecdotal illustrations from many different ethnic experiences are very effective advocates of cultural pluralism. They are living exemplars of culturally pluralistic functioning.

Some necessary corollaries of multiethnic teaching examples are diversified teaching strategies, curriculum content, and learning activities to match cognitive patterns and learning styles of different ethnic groups. These techniques require thorough understanding of ethnic learning styles, the anthropological concept of cultural configurations, and the psychological concept of individual variation, the interaction between these, and the resulting educational implications. Teachers need to understand what it means to say an ethnic group has a particular learning style or pattern of cognitive processing; how, for example, field-sensitive learning styles compare with field-independent styles; which ethnic groups are more inclined toward what learning styles; and kinds of curriculum content and instructional, or relational, behaviors are most compatible with different cognitive patterns.

Teachers also should master a wide range of instructional modes, such as dyadic, democratic, directed, and inquiry teaching, and learn how to use a combination of these in any given teaching act to increase the probability of "reaching" more ethnic learning styles. Some instructional styles are more compatible with given ethnic patterns of cognitive processing than others. As a rule Asian and Indian children from traditional families are likely to respond more readily to teacher-directed instructional modes, Mexican American and Cuban students are more prone to be field-sensitive, learning in social, informal environments and hedonistic techniques are more congruent with the preferred inclinations of blacks, and anglo students are more at ease in independent, individualistic, competitive instructional settings. Therefore, differential instruction according to ethnic group *and* individual variation, or a concerted effort to match teaching styles with different ethnic learning styles, with due respect to individual differences, is imperative to respecting cultural differences and achieving quality education in desegregated schools.

# Remember . . .

Although still tentative and inconclusive data on ethnic learning styles, along with other cultural information, are helpful in assessing student behavior in pluralistic classrooms. These data provide a framework for teachers to observe inter-ethnic group interactions and to determine the "syncopation" between different ethnic life styles, value systems and cultures, and school norms and expectations. Teachers should remember "the socialization system of the child's home and community is influential in producing culturally unique preferred modes of relating to others, . . . incentive preferences, i.e., those environments, events which symbolize acceptance, recognition, and support, as well as preferred modes of thinking, perceiving, remembering, and problem-solving."[9] These characteristics should form the fundamental bases on which instructional program decisions are made and patterns of human interaction and the sociological dynamics of multiethnic, desegregated classrooms are assessed. However, care should be exercised not to limit or attribute interpretations of students' behaviors, values, and perceptions exclusively to ethnicity and cultural conditioning. Nor should teachers expect any *individual* student of a given ethnic group to conform, in entirety, to ethnic cultural characteristics and cognitive learning styles. Rather, teachers need to be mindful that learning styles are *patterns of cognitive processing generally exhibited by members of an ethnic group, and that cultural characteristics are descriptions of value configurations and propensities, or inclinations, of ethnic groups. They are not descriptions of individual behavior.* Unless teachers become "sensitized to the incredible complexity of inter-ethnic patterns in human interaction, the most dedicated educator cannot succeed in analyzing classroom problems clearly and objectively, nor is he able to devise instructional strategies based upon facts inherent in the situation,"[10] or truly appreciate and respond to the individuality of students within the context of the cultural diversity evident in desegregated schools.

While the specific examples discussed are merely illustrations and are not intended to be prescriptive, the ideas and concepts on teacher preparation for and performance in desegregated schools are. Teachers cannot be expected to work effectively with ethnically and culturally pluralistic student populations in desegregated schools, and demonstrate their acceptance of cultural differences if they are not adequately prepared. The necessary knowledge and skills are not acquired inherently or intuitively. They must be developed *consciously and deliberately.*

Teachers must become knowledgeable about the richness, the complexity, and the vitality of American cultural diversity; their own racial and ethnic attitudes and values, and how these affect their instructional and interactional behaviors; the cultural experiences, values, characteristics, and learning styles of different ethnic students that influence their orientations, perceptions, and behaviors; and develop concrete skills relative to curriculum design, instructional strategies, interaction abilities, and the sociological environment of desegregated classrooms for responding to cultural differences in positive, productive ways. Undoubtedly, these are difficult tasks, but not impossible ones. With carefully planned, continuous multicultural training and professional growth experiences teachers can indeed become the most significant variables in the desegregation process. Adequate knowledge about ethnic diversity and cultural differences, and the application of this knowledge in the instructional process, can be instrumental in the achievement of the real potential of desegregation—that is, quality integrated education wherein ethnically and culturally diverse groups of students receive instructional support in their academic and psycho-social development; where students and staffs from diverse ethnic and cultural backgrounds are engaged in mutual personal exchanges and the sharing of an educational experience; and where the "whole person" of different ethnic students, with full recognition of their "sociocultural being," is considered in the design and implementation of learning experiences, in order to maximize the intellectual, social, and emotional development of every individual student.

## Notes

1 Kathleen Smith, *Desegregation/Integration: Planning for School Change* (Washington, D. C.: National Education Association, 1974), p. 12.
2 Nancy H. St. John, *School Desegregation Outcomes for Children* (New York: John Wiley and Sons, 1975).
3 Smith, *Desegregation/Integration*, p. 56.
4 Thomas H. Buxton, Keith W. Richard, Charles M. Bingham, Charles E. Jackson, and Loutricia Talps, "Black and White Teachers and Desegregation," *Integrated Education*, 12 (January–April, 1974), pp. 19–22.
5 *Teachers and Students. Report V: Mexican American Study. Differences in Teacher Interaction with Mexican American and Anglo Students* (Washington, D.C.: U.S. Civil Rights Commission, March 1973); and Geneva Gay, *Differential Dyadic Interactions of Black and White Teachers with Black and White Pupils in Recently Desegregated Social Studies Classrooms: A Function of Teacher and Pupil Ethnicity* (Washington, D.C.: National Institute of Education, January 1974).
6 Smith, *Desegregation/Integration*, p. 62.
7 V. C. Dennis and E. P. Powell, "Nonverbal Communication Across Race Dyads," ERIC Documents, ED 069–429 (September 1972); and D. Sachdeva, "A Measurement of Changes in Interracial Student Attitudes in Desegrated Schools," *Journal of Educational Research*, 66 (May-June, 1973), pp. 418–422.
8 Michael Novak, "Variety is More Than a Slice of Life," *Momentum*, 6 (October 1975), p. 26.
9 Manuel Ramirez, III and Alfredo Castaneda, *Cultural Democracy, Bicognitive Development, and Education* (New York: Academic Press, 1974), p. 32.
10 E. C. Condon, "Cultural Conflict in Values, Assumptions, Opinions," ERIC Documents, ED 117–205 (1973), p. 10.

# CHAPTER 21

# TEACHERS FOR MULTICULTURAL SCHOOLS (1998)

## The power of selection

Martin Haberman and Linda Post

Multicultural education has much to offer our schools, particularly our urban schools, but simply adding a course or two will not bring about the changes that are needed. Likewise, adding multicultural education to the teacher education curriculum will not be sufficient. In this article, we argue that only teachers with a particular set of attributes and ideology can offer a multicultural curriculum. The stated goals of these curricula emphasize students' personal development. The achievement of such critically important but elusive objectives requires outstanding teachers.

We propose here 12 teacher attributes for offering a multicultural program, focusing on specific teacher qualities and ideology. We describe ways in which teachers explain how they learn, and present a profile of such teachers. Our argument proposes "what" (the content to be learned), "how" (the way it is learned), and "who" seems likely to learn it. The basic contention is that in order to perform the sophisticated expectations of multicultural teaching, selecting those predisposed to do it is a necessary precondition. Training, while vital, is only of value to teacher candidates whose ideology and predispositions reflect those of outstanding, practicing teachers. The article is prefaced by a brief analysis of the challenge presented by street values to multicultural initiatives.

## The urban setting

Urban schools are the battleground of a culture war. Traditional societal values are pitted against street values and are being beaten—badly. Not only are schools unable to contravene street values, they actually adopt and promulgate many of them. Elsewhere we have described 14 values that constitute unemployment training and by which urban schools systematically predispose graduates as well as dropouts to a life of unemployment and nonparticipation (Haberman, 1997).

Street values do not represent the diverse, minority culture groups that comprise urban communities any more than they represent the traditional American values promulgated in public schools. Being a member of a particular culture group is a source of strength and provides a platform for living a life of high self-esteem and self-realization. Living by street values portends a life of poverty, poor health, and antisocial behavior.

Before urban schools can become more multicultural, they must first become effective in resisting street values which, like other viruses, are carried into school each day by infected children. At present, students control the urban school's agenda by making educators spend most of their time and energy reacting to street values rather than proactively implementing the stated curriculum. Responding to street values is the school's primary business because maintaining a safe environment is a prerequisite for learning. But street values ultimately coalesce into an integrated behavior pattern that "works" for youngsters in urban schools.

For example, one street value is that personal relationships are determined by "who has the power to hurt you." This supports the tacit but ever-present threat of violence. One way students demonstrate this power value in school is by manifesting a "make me" attitude. This street value, which defines all interactions and relationships on the basis of power, forms the basis for the school game in which it becomes the job of the teachers to force students to learn and the role of the students to resist by functioning as observers rather than participants. Once the game is in progress, school authorities respond with more and more rules and attempts at greater coercion; students respond with noncompliance. This leads to even more complex rules which in turn engender more sophisticated forms of student resistance and detachment. The net effect is that urban students who have assimilated this street value do as little as possible, indeed nothing more than show up, and finesse the schools into legitimizing this "activity" with passing grades. The technical term for this exchange in which students are passed for merely showing up and not being disruptive is "the deal" and has been carefully documented (Payne, 1984).

Enter all those interested in restructuring or reform, including advocates for multicultural curriculum. Unfortunately, making school curriculum more multicultural will not necessarily decrease the power of street values. The communal and face-to-face values that characterize the minority cultures in our cities have been just as ineffective at overcoming the power of street values as the traditional associational values taught in public schools. (The Black Muslim community is a notable exception to this pattern and actually does contravene some street values.) Scenes of distraught family members and ministers sitting in courts, hospitals, and funeral parlors and wondering how they lost their children are just as well documented as those of educators expressing failure at turning their students on to learning or keeping them in school.

## Street values and multiculturalism

The goal of overcoming street values must be separated from the goal of making schools more multicultural. The former deals with issues such as whether or not schools should use metal detectors; the latter deals with teaching and learning about self-identity, enhancing community cultures, and functioning effectively in American society. Making the school curriculum more multicultural will not necessarily decrease violence, dropout rates, or gang activity. These are not valid criteria for initiating or judging the effects of multicultural curriculum. Greater multiculturalism in school programs has the potential for providing students with (a) powerful ideas for how to live successfully in the general American society, (b) useful skills for succeeding in the world of work, (c) understanding various culture groups, (d) gaining identity and strength from participating in one's own culture group, and (e) learning ways to contribute to greater equity and opportunity for all individuals and groups.

Some teachers offer such a curriculum by engaging, motivating, and interesting their students in ways that actively involve them and make them responsible for their learning. This leads to higher achievement in traditional school subjects.

More importantly, it also leads students to demonstrate high level skills for solving real life problems—even how to resist street values in some cases. We designate such teachers "stars" using the following criteria: they work in districts serving a majority of students in poverty; their classes surpass the average achievement level of their building; they are identified by other teachers, their principals, students' parents, outside observers, and themselves as superior or excellent. We estimate that even the most chaotic systems have as many as 8 percent of the teachers who meet these criteria (Haberman, 1995b).

Whether or not having a multicultural curriculum can overcome street values or merely provides a better education for youngsters who would resist street values anyway is a question in need of substantial future study. What we can be sure of is that multicultural curricula focus students on their current lives by studying real world problems rather than preparing them only for living later on in the best of all nonexistent worlds. In a society with the stated goals of equal opportunity and the enhancement of all culture groups, multicultural curriculum becomes a fundamental mission of public education.

Officially approved school-board positions adopting multiculturalism as a top priority are not typically found in small town or suburban school districts. "Can we all learn to live together?" is not a mission given schools in advantaged communities or in communities in which people expect societal institutions (i.e., government, the criminal justice system, health care, education) to function in their interest and actually meet their needs. Typically, multicultural mission statements are adopted in the 120 major urban districts that serve 7 million students in poverty and in which a majority of students are from diverse minority backgrounds. Consider the following statement of definition:

> Multicultural education is a process built on respect and appreciation of cultural diversity. Central to this process is gaining understanding of the cultures of the world and incorporating these insights into all areas of the curriculum and school life with a particular emphasis on those cultures represented in our school community. Growing from these insights is a respect for all cultures and commitment to creating equitable relationships between men and women, among people of different ethnic backgrounds, and for all categories of people. Viewed in this manner multicultural education builds respect, self-esteem, and appreciation of others and provides students with the tools for building a just and equitable society. (Milwaukee Public Schools, 1995)

The statement goes on to spell out an exhaustive list of goals for students that include an extensive understanding of American society derived from anthropological, historical, and economic concepts; sophisticated communication concepts and skills; the willingness and ability to self-reflect and change oneself; the causes and cures of a low self-concept; and in-depth knowledge of the causes of all forms of societal inequity as well as the proclivity and skills for making the world a better place.

## The knowledge base

Over the last 40 years we (Haberman and colleagues) have had the opportunity to develop, evaluate, and offer more teacher education programs preparing more teachers than anyone in the history of American teacher education. These programs have been notable failures if we use criteria such as the following: Did these models become institutionalized in universities after external funding was discontinued? Did the graduates remain as teachers in poverty schools longer than 3 years? Within each of these models, however, we have been able to identify program elements that do predict which candidates will be effective with children in poverty, who will remain as classroom teachers, what is the ideology of such teachers, and how are they selected and trained. In our current Metropolitan Multicultural Teacher Education Program (which is now replicated in several cities), we have a 7-year record of 97.5 percent retention of a teacher population that is 75 percent minority in the Milwaukee Public Schools.

In considering what we know about our teachers that predisposes them to offer multicultural programs as an integral part of their teaching, we have identified the nature of their knowledge base. Following are some of the essential elements of this knowledge base.

*Self-knowledge*—a thorough understanding of one's own cultural roots and group affiliations. An individual who says, "I'm not a member of any culture group, I'm just an American," is not sufficiently grounded to teach a multicultural curriculum. Teachers encourage students to search for more knowledge about their own and classmates' roots by sharing their own.

*Self-acceptance*—a high level of self-esteem derived from knowing one's roots. Nobodies do not make somebodies. It takes somebodies to make somebodies. Teachers foster self-confidence and pride of group identity by demonstrating a confident acceptance of their own.

*Relationship skills*—the ability to work with diverse children and adults who are different from oneself in ways that these others perceive as respectful and caring. The teacher shows "we can all live together" by treating all groups as equally fine.

*Community knowledge*—a knowledge of the cultural heritages of the children and their families. Teachers who make home visits and have continuing experiences in the community's churches, stores, businesses, and parks are able to offer a multicultural curriculum that derives from the specific life experiences of the children in their classes.

*Empathy*—a deep and abiding sensitivity and appreciation to the ways in which children and their families perceive, understand, and explain their world. The teacher truly understands what parents in particular culture groups may want for their children without lowering standards and expectations.

*Cultural human development*—an understanding of how the local community influences development. The teacher knows more than what is supposedly universal for all 7-year-olds or all 13-year-olds. What does it mean for a toddler, child, preadolescent, or adolescent who is of a particular language, racial, cultural, or economic group to "grow up" in this community?

*Cultural conflicts*—an understanding of the discrepancies between the values of the local community groups and the traditional American values espoused in schools. The teacher expects, prepares for, and deals with issues that arise from differences in religion, gender roles, and values.

*Relevant curriculum*—a knowledge of connections that can be made between general societal values and those of the culture groups in the community, and the skills needed to implement this knowledge. The teacher connects specific content goals to specific uses in the students' lives.

*Generating sustained effort*—a knowledge and set of implementation skills that will engage youngsters from this community to persist with schoolwork. The teacher's daily instruction is organized around and rewards effort rather than perceived ability.

*Coping with violence*—skills for preventing and de-escalating violence and the potential for violence. How do I work in and help students succeed in an environment where violence is a constant fact of life? The teacher demonstrates forms of conflict resolution based on criteria other than power.

*Self-analysis*—a capacity for reflection and change. How can I use my experiences to continue to learn, grow, and change? Teachers engage in systematic self-reflection. They develop and implement plans for professional development that impact on their classrooms.

*Functioning in chaos*—an ability to understand and the skills to cope with a disorganized environment. Urban school systems reflect the unstable, dysfunctional nature of their communities. Teachers who remain effective in such environments know and can implement behaviors that enable them to function effectively in spite of the irrationality of their school bureaucracies.

## How do teachers learn these things?

Teachers who can work with children in poverty in multicultural ways are neither born nor made; they develop as they integrate significant life experiences. A consideration of the elements of the knowledge base described above reveals that they are not forms of knowledge found in genes or gained in university courses. How then are these forms of knowledge developed and learned?

Star teachers of children in poverty offer some interesting perceptions and beliefs regarding how they got where they are in their development as teachers. Telling their stories, they state some things directly about their own development. In other cases they offer explanations after we ask them to explain things we have observed them doing in their teaching. The discussion that follows describes most, not all, of how they learned to teach. While the content of these learnings has changed, the procedures for learning them has remained fairly constant over the last 4 decades in which we have witnessed instruction and listened to teachers in urban schools across the nation.

Almost everything star teachers do that they regard as important is something they believe they learned on the job after they started teaching. When asked, "Where did you learn that?" about a practice or idea, they almost never attribute their learning to a university course, experience, or faculty. Teachers' preferred way of learning is to observe colleagues whom they regard as credible because they are successful with similar students in the same school system. Their focus is on craft knowledge. They are the ultimate pragmatists. Their test for knowledge is that they have seen it "work."

Having a credible teacher mentor actively coach them in their own classroom is the way star teachers prefer to practice and learn more effective procedures and make them their own. "Credible" mentors are teachers observed actually performing what they advise. Being part of an effective teacher team is also a powerful influence on teaching practice. Teaming is so influential that even when the team is functioning negatively it may continue to dominate their thinking and learning. Since teacher teams typically deal with the same students, teachers are especially sensitive to other teachers' practices that may be generating different student behaviors.

The perceived need to learn more subject matter is an unusual and minor influence on development of teachers. Practicing teachers rarely if ever attribute their students' lack of interest or achievement to their "inadequate" content knowledge. They strongly reject the contention that children in poverty are not learning more because their teachers do not know enough.

Developing more knowledge of teaching methods is regarded as an unimportant or easily met need. Teachers do not believe they need more workshops on teaching methods. They do seek more specific ways of making any method meet the particular needs of their students. They seek solutions to their perceived problems, not more subject matter content or teaching methodologies. Teachers regard workshops as useful if they come away with (a) specific strategies they can use to resolve their problems or (b) specific new materials or resources they can use in their classrooms. Again, such workshops must be offered by practicing teachers they regard as credible.

Networking with other teachers trying to resolve similar problems in the same school system seems to further teacher development and combat burnout. Some of the more influential activities frequently relate to methods of coping with system-imposed policies regarding new programs, testing, grade level requirements, recordkeeping, discipline, and school rules. The body of knowledge teachers learn in order to cope with such school mandates and other required conditions of employment constitutes a major portion of the knowledge they develop in the course of their careers. This essential knowledge for functioning in chaotic systems is shared by classroom teachers but is ignored in the professional literature. If it is noted it is deprecated as situation-specific information, or craft know-how, and not considered "professional knowledge."

Teacher practice is not seriously affected by theory or research. Rival explanations of human intelligence or summaries of phonics versus whole language research is not a determinant of how they plan or make instructional decisions. Activities that impact on teacher development in unimportant ways, if at all, include reading reports of research findings; listening to experts who are not regarded as credible because they are not teaching children in poverty; and reading analyses of "hot" topics at particular times, such as bilingual versus English-only instruction, or the pros and cons of tracking.

Substantial teacher development comes from using the lives of children as a rich source of study. Star teachers are constantly involved in learning more about their children, their families and communities, and what it means to grow up in particular settings. By using children's life experiences as a fundamental part of the classroom program, teachers continually learn more about children and community cultures. Teachers attribute almost all they know about child development to what they have learned about the lives of their students.

Much teacher development comes from the process of sharing their own interests, experiences, and talents with their students. The children, in effect, reward and shape their teachers by accepting and affirming what they share. The teachers, in turn, see the need for children to share their own backgrounds.

A great source of teacher development occurs by serendipity. Urban schools "try" almost everything. While projects are not systematically offered or evaluated, they abound. Inevitably this plethora of projects ("projectitis") has unintended consequences and unforeseen impact. Urban teachers and students who live with these erratic initiatives, reforms, programs, and models have daily encounters with unplanned events. In addition to developing general coping principles (e.g., "Just wait a year and it will go away"), teachers learn much from the specifics of each initiative. Working in chaotic systems—and urban school systems are examples of chaos theory in action—is a powerful learning opportunity.

Teachers in large urban settings become experts in discerning what to ignore, what to cope with, and what to learn from.

The most important source of teacher development is their ideology; that is, what they believe about the nature of teaching and learning, the nature of development, and the nature of the setting. They bring this ideology with them, but it is imbedded in a casing of prejudices, biases, preferences, beliefs, values, and perceptions. As they begin and move through their teaching experiences, some resist any new input. Such teachers have one year of experience 30 times. Others seek to reconcile their ideology with their experiences and have 30 years of growth —much of it on a painfully steep learning curve.

But teachers' experiences do not automatically lead to positive growth. We know that many teachers use their teaching experiences to solidify and rationalize their prejudices (Sleeter, 1992). Other teachers use their direct experiences to become increasingly supportive of children. Teaching is a process in which selective perception enhances what the teacher believes at the start. The ideology with which teachers begin their teaching has been shown to determine whether or not they will use their subsequent teaching experience to become more positive or more negative (Haberman & Post, 1992).

There are, of course, other ways in which teachers learn. Since Haberman started preparing teachers for children in poverty in the late 1950s, what teachers need to know has changed appreciably, but how teachers learn has not. Effective, growing teachers continue to use the same fundamental learning modes as practitioners of other human service crafts.

## Who should prepare for multicultural teaching?

In the programs we offer, we begin with college graduates (from all fields) who have had in-depth experiences with children and youth. They have initial summer experiences teaching children so that we can verify our selection interviews. In effect, how they actually interrelate with children in poverty is their final selection. They are hired as teachers by the Milwaukee Public Schools each September. The process by which they are prepared includes careful mentoring (one full-time mentor for each four teachers) and weekly classes. The mentors are star urban teachers as are the resource people who lead their weekly meetings. The role of university faculty, health and human service professionals, business consultants, parents, computer experts, and community resource people is to supplement the knowledge base of the practitioners who serve as mentors and resource people.

Not surprisingly, the "best and the brightest" teachers of children in poverty who complete this program are not young White females from small towns or suburbs with grades of A in student teaching and high grade point average (GPAs) who "always wanted to teach." The profile of the "best and the brightest" for culturally diverse children in urban poverty includes demographic as well as personal attributes such as the following:

- Did not decide to teach until after graduation from college.
- Tried (and succeeded) at several jobs or careers.
- Is between 30 and 50 years of age.
- Attended an urban high school.
- Has raised several children, is a parent, or has had close, in-depth, meaningful relations with children and youth.
- Currently lives in the city and plans to continue to do so.

- Is preparing for a teaching position in an urban school system.
- Doesn't believe "kids are kids" but comprehends and appreciates how cultural forces impact human development.
- Has had personal and continuing experiences with violence and of living "normally" in a violent community and city.
- Has majored in just about anything at the university.
- May or may not have an above-average grade point average.
- Expects to visit the homes of the children.
- Has some awareness of or personal experience with a range of health and human services available in the urban area.
- Expects that the school bureaucracy will be irrational and intrusive.
- Is likely not to be of Euro-American background but a person of color.
- Is likely to be sensitive to, aware of, and working on one's own racism, sexism, classism, or other prejudices.

These are some of the attributes that, taken together, provide a thumbnail sketch. Taken singly, each has no predictive validity. They characterize but do not explain teaching success. They are cited here merely to provide the real-world alternative to "the best and the brightest" stereotype that emphasizes high GPA college youth and continues to emanate from blue-ribbon committees, national panels, private foundations, the Office of Education, and other fantasy factories. High GPA has nothing to do with teaching children in poverty effectively or predicting who will remain in teaching. Indeed, we have much evidence that using high GPA to recruit and select will identify quitters and failures (Corwin, 1973).

In our current Milwaukee program (which has been replicated seven times in 7 years), we prepare individuals who share most if not all of the attributes cited above. They also share the experience of living in poverty for substantial periods themselves. Indeed, many of them are currently living in poverty and need not recollect former periods of their lives. In many ways these new teachers are "at risk" themselves because they live in communities characterized by violence. Since they are all carefully selected as having a commitment to the behaviors and ideology that matches those of star urban teachers, we know they will be successful. What we did not anticipate were the effects of their own low economic level on their lives and the stress this creates during their first year.

For example, we have had resident teachers die. They have also experienced the following: the death of a child; critical, life-threatening injuries to members of their immediate family; violence at home (either abuse from a spouse or child abuse); bankruptcy; forced moving, that is, the need to find a new residence for the family; inability to secure an affordable home or car insurance; serious illnesses requiring unforeseen surgery or rehabilitation; chemical or drug dependency; serious and continuing transportation problems; marital problems of all types and severity; child custody problems; law-suits related to a variety of out-of-school issues for which the teacher could not afford counsel; poor nutrition, exercise, and sleep habits; no preventive medicine for themselves or their families; mental and emotional problems, treated and untreated; and fear of deportation as illegal aliens.

We have been impressed, "floored" would be more accurate, by the ability of our resident teachers to both learn from and overcome their life experiences at the same time they were learning to teach in extremely demanding, urban poverty schools. The lesson we have learned is that carefully selected "best and brightest" (i.e., our definition) are individuals who are themselves frequently in poverty, close to poverty, or grew up in poverty. They are sensitive to what it means for a child to have to sneak to school early to avoid being beaten up by a gang, and why it is important for schools to have unlocked doors and serve breakfast. They not only show great understanding for the children but for the parents or caregivers.

At the same time such teachers follow through and insist upon parents and caregivers performing their responsibilities. While they appreciate and empathize with their students' stressful life conditions, they expect students to work at being successful in school. This profile has not precluded us from finding some teacher candidates from advantaged backgrounds. Our experience has been that one out of ten full-time, undergraduate students under 25 years of age, in full-time preservice teacher education programs, can pass our selection procedures.

One focus of our program is on preparing the interprofessional practitioner. This is no small feat. Anyone who has ever offered a teacher education program for children in poverty knows that it is typical for student teachers, beginning interns, and first-year resident teachers to be fearful: they fixate on the question, "Will I be able to control the children and manage what happens in my class?" To shift the focus off themselves and onto the total wellness of children frequently living in debilitating life conditions, once again, requires careful, appropriate selection of teacher candidates. The assumption that training alone can be sufficiently powerful to transform the immature and fearful into interprofessional practitioners is contrary to our experience. Teachers cannot themselves perform the range of health and human services their children need, but they can learn to identify conditions (such as abuse) and even more, expect and anticipate the needs of their children for services. Teachers can also be taught to help their children's families to make the connections they will need to get services they do not know they need, do not know are available, or do not know who to contact to access them. In poverty schools the client is not only the child but the child's family.

## Careful selection as a necessary condition

No school can be better than its teachers. And the surest and best way to improve the schooling for children and youth in poverty is to provide them with better teachers. The strategy for doing this is not mysterious. The premise is simple: Selection is more important than training. We have elsewhere described the attributes that predict success in urban poverty schools and the ones that may be identified in interviews (Haberman, 1995a).

Training is useful only for those with appropriate predispositions. The reason for this is that the functions performed by effective urban teachers are undergirded by a clear ideology derived from life experiences. Such teachers not only perform functions that quitters and burnouts do not, they also know why they do what they do. They have a coherent vision. It is a humane, respectful, caring, and nonviolent form of "gentle teaching" that we have described elsewhere (Haberman, 1994). Our point here is that star teachers' behaviors and the ideology that undergirds their behaviors cannot be unwrapped. They are of a piece.

Nor can this ideology be taught in traditional programs of teacher preparation. Writing a term paper on Piaget's concept of conservation or learning the seven steps in direct instruction will not provide neophytes with the ideology or skills of star teachers. This ideology and craft is open to development only in those predisposed to selectively perceive from their experiences in positive ways. What can be taught are effective teaching behaviors that are built on an already functioning belief system. Like the ideology, the teaching behaviors are not typically learned in coursework or in student teaching but on the job, with mentoring by a star teacher/coach, a support network, and some specific workshops and classes.

Reviews of college student learning and teaching provide overwhelming evidence that what students expect and value will determine what they will derive from their teacher education (Pintrich, 1990). Reviews of the relationship between development and learning indicate that what is learned is determined by the students' developmental stage. They must have attained an adult stage of development to benefit from teacher training (Sprinthall, Reiman, & Thies-Sprinthall, 1996). But knowing that college students' learning is controlled by their values and whether or not they have reached adulthood still has not changed the way they are selected into traditional programs of teacher education. GPA and written test scores still control the admission of late adolescents into traditional preparation programs (Haberman, 1996).

## Implications for the locus of programs

We have earlier discussed the ways in which teachers learn most effectively. Each of these ways is incorporated into an effective training program. Teachers-to-be should be actually engaged in responsible teaching; be able to observe star teachers in action; have a mentor who is a star teacher coaching them; be part of a team; participate in a network coping with a highly bureaucratized system; be students of their communities; and continually be faced with problems that cause them to reshape their ideology. In addition, the training is most effective when it is offered in the worst schools under the worst conditions of work.

Traditional teacher education and state certification agencies make the reverse assumption. They create professional development centers engaged in best practices and then certify graduates universally. The naive assumption is that graduates will be able to function in the worst school situations because they have observed good practices.

We make a more realistic assumption: Carefully selected and well prepared teachers who are educated to function in the worst situations will be able to function in poverty schools and other schools as well. They will not quit if they are "forced" to teach smaller classes, have fewer inclusion students, or receive adequate supplies and materials. Neither will they be shocked if every student has a seat and enough textbooks.

Since states assume license holders can teach all students in all situations, our philosophy of training in and for the worst situations is also the ethical position. In these "worst" training sites we have always found star teachers who can demonstrate that their ideology works (Haberman, 1995b). The fact that star teachers can actually function effectively in such "intolerable" situations has great impact on neophytes. Beginners are much more impressed by greatness operating in the real world than by observing best practices in a situation they will never again find. Our approach is to also work toward zero transfer, that is, learning to teach is most powerful when it is under the actual conditions in which one will serve. This means that ideal preparation would occur in the very school and community where one will remain as a teacher.

## Conclusion

We believe that getting better teachers is the best engine for driving school reform in poverty schools. The success of our program over the last 7 years tells us that implementing multicultural programs requires melding an extensive knowledge base with teacher ideology. The knowledge base can be identified in the work of star urban teachers, and neophytes with the ideology can be selected and then trained.

Emphasizing the work of star teachers means that the role of university education faculty with specific expertise must be reconceptualized from that of primary educator to resource person. We argue that the knowledge base is learned best in particular, specific school sites in the worst urban poverty schools and only those predisposed to learn what star teachers already know will accept and internalize the training. We make the issue of transfer of learning moot by preparing teachers to work in the very schools and communities where they will continue to teach after certification. After careful selection, training does have important value, provided such training emphasizes being mentored while on the job as a fully accountable teacher.

Our work has also identified neophytes who are "best and brightest" in ways not recognized by traditional teacher education programs. Successful candidates are over 30 years of age, frequently minorities, and have life experiences in urban areas. We have also shown that some European Americans may also demonstrate the predispositions of star teachers and are able to function effectively in poverty schools.

We hold several undergirding beliefs as guiding principals that need to be developed elsewhere to complement our argument. University faculty should be involved in but not in control of the preparation of teachers for children in poverty. Research and theory in the preparation of urban teachers must complement teacher ideology and the practices of star urban teachers. The university dedicated to accepting any candidate's belief system in a context of academic freedom is not the ideal place for selecting future teachers with an appropriate ideology. The process of mentoring on the job is extremely more powerful training than taking classes or going through traditional forms of laboratory experiences. Finally, and of greatest importance, is our contention that all teacher education programs for children in poverty must require candidates to demonstrate that the children they teach are actually learning important things (e.g., multicultural concepts) before granting certification.

# References

Corwin, R. (1973). *Reform and organizational survival: The Teacher Corps as an instrument of educational change*. New York: Wiley.

Haberman, M. (1994). Gentle teaching in a violent society. *Educational Horizons, 72*(3), 131–136.

Haberman, M. (1995a). Selecting star teachers for children and youth in urban poverty. *Phi Delta Kappan, 76,* 777–781.

Haberman, M. (1995b). *Star teachers of children in poverty*. West Lafayette, IN: Kappa Delta Pi.

Haberman, M. (1996). Selecting and preparing culturally competent teachers for urban schools. In J. Sikula (Ed.), *Handbook for research on teacher education* (2nd ed.; pp. 747–760). New York: Macmillan.

Haberman, M. (1997). Unemployment training: The ideology of nonwork learned in urban schools. *Phi Delta Kappan, 78*(7), 499–503.

Haberman, M., & Post, L. (1992). Does direct experience change students' perceptions of low income minority children? *Midwestern Educational Research, 5* (2), 29–31. (Special multicultural issue, University of Akron.)

Milwaukee Public Schools. (1995, January). *MPS Proposed Definition of Multicultural*

*Education*. Adopted by the Multicultural Curriculum Council of the Milwaukee Public Schools, Milwaukee, WI.

Payne, C.M. (1984). *Getting what we ask for: The ambiguity of success and failure in urban education*. Westport, CT: Greenwood Publishing.

Pintrich, P. (1990). Implications of psychological research on student learning and college teaching for teacher education. In W.R. Houston (Ed.), *Handbook for research on teacher education* (pp. 826–857). New York: Macmillan.

Sleeter, C.E. (1992). *Keepers of the American dream: A study of staff development and multicultural education*. London: The Falmer Press.

Sprinthall, N.A., Reiman, A.J., & Thies-Sprinthall, L. (1996). Teacher professional development. In J. Sikula (Ed.), *Handbook for research on teacher education* (2nd ed; pp. 666–703). New York: Macmillan.

# PART 4

# PROFESSIONAL DEVELOPMENT

# CHAPTER 22

# EXTENDING THE POSSIBILITIES OF MULTICULTURAL PROFESSIONAL DEVELOPMENT IN PUBLIC SCHOOLS (2001)

*Pepi Leistyna*

Hoping to accommodate the demographic shifts and mitigate the antagonistic social relations in their ever changing communities, educators and school systems are turning increasingly to the plethora of research, literature, and practices in multiculturalism to help ensure cross-cultural understanding (among students, faculty, and staff), academic success, and overall school/community harmony. Embodying this trend, the Changeton school district is making an effort to create a systemwide multicultural education program to combat the racism, cultural strife, and exclusionary practices that plague their schools and city.[1] A voluntary group, the Multicultural Central Steering Committee (CSC), has been established to shape and direct what the 17 members hope will be a foundation for working toward what they describe as "the affirmation of diversity through educational equity and social justice."

A three-year qualitative study produced research, on which this article is based, that documents and critiques the Changeton Multicultural CSC's work with curricula, professional development, staff diversification, and community outreach. The specific area of interest addressed here is the CSC's endeavors to better inform their schools' faculty and staff through multicultural professional development.

## Methodology

The study focused on the following research question: How did the Changeton Multicultural Central Steering Committee get created, and how did the members come to define multicultural education and go about putting this definition into operation (i.e., what were their goals, and what strategies did they use to meet these goals)? To answer the question, I used qualitative methods of participant observation and document collection.

The most important data collected consisted of recorded observations of all 54 CSC meetings—including 20 CSC subcommittee meetings and 5 inservice sessions. The observations included ideas presented, issues raised, points of debate, and decisions made. These data were central in describing the developments in the group's work. I collected data from secondary sources to provide more detail and to corroborate the recorded meetings. These sources consisted of official CSC minutes taken at each meeting by the committee's chairperson, official CSC progress reports that were publicly distributed, and clarification interviews. When information discussed during the CSC meetings was not clear, I briefly interviewed the person(s) afterward. For additional triangulation, I also used *member checks:*

I recognized that my own subjectivities would inevitably come into play in the collection, analysis, and interpretation of the data. To achieve a coherent depiction of the CSC's endeavors, during the descriptive stage of this research (capturing what the group discussed and accomplished), I had the committee's approval to select members to read my written descriptions to make sure that they were, in some respect, on target. This technique allowed the solicitation of alternative perspectives on what transpired.

## Efforts in Changeton

When I began this research, the city of Changeton had an estimated population of 74,449 whites, 12,028 blacks, 1,589 Asian/Pacific Islanders, 5,860 Latinos/as, 269 Native Americans, and 4,453 designated "others." In addition, the city had more women than men, more than 13,000 people were living in poverty, and the annual number of crimes committed in the city totaled 6,895, with 1,156 violent acts.

The city's educational system comprised 15 elementary schools, 4 middle schools, and 1 high school. Of a total student enrollment of 14,015, 13.6 percent were Latino/a, 29.7 percent were black, 3.0 percent were Asian American, and 53.2 percent were white. One in every 14 students in Changeton was limited-English proficient.

The school system was on probationary status with the state because of its inability to effectively desegregate its schools. In addition, Changeton had a high annual dropout rate—9.9 percent, or 296 students, many of them racially subordinated and low-income youths. The high school lost nearly a tenth of its population the year the research began (and the dropout rate for 9th graders was estimated at 12 to 14 percent). The retention rate (those held back) in the high school was 11.5 percent.[2]

The development of the Multicultural Central Steering Committee was a direct response to such statistics. It was also a critical reaction to public attitudes such as that expressed by a union representative who proclaimed, "The local gene pool in Changeton should be condemned."

The CSC is made up of individuals with diverse racial, ethnic, religious, and professional backgrounds, and it includes teachers, guidance counselors, administrators, and specialists in adult, bilingual, and special education. The committee, which is officially sanctioned by the superintendent of schools, has been given the responsibility to develop ideas that they believe will help their city's schools, based on their own individual experiences as well as the research and literature on cultural diversity.

Professional development should be a major component in any model of multicultural education.[3] It is admirable that the CSC was willing to make such an effort, with no pay and an almost nonexistent budget, to attempt to educate their school system's faculty and staff in the area of cultural diversity. The CSC understood the negative impact that educators can have on students' self-image and academic achievement, as well as on overall school social relations. As a result, the group diligently labored to conceptualize and implement workshops that would raise awareness about multiculturalism.

Throughout their 54 meetings the CSC's central focus was on changing the negative attitudes and biases of their faculty and staff. As revealed in their written mission statement and their individual lists of goals, they considered sensitivity training (which implied sensitizing teachers to other cultures) and the affirmation of diversity to be of the utmost importance:

. . . Teaching culturally different groups requires more sensitivity, it requires . . . placing equal value on all students. The committee should be involved in . . . providing retraining to all staff; i.e., sensitivity workshops . . .

Strategies to ensure that the faculty and staff would develop such sensitivity and affirmation preoccupied the committee and consumed their energies for the next three years.

Unfortunately, working from a theoretical model limited to issues of sensitivity and affirmation can create three fundamental problems. First, such a model can individualize discrimination and oppressive practices and thus take on a psychological perspective, abstracting one's identity from its ideological, sociohistorical, and institutional construction. Second, a sensitivity model often functions through the lens of *cultural relativism*—which values all cultures equally and uncritically. Cultural relativism not only limits the possibilities for critical dialogue, but it also allows discriminatory values, beliefs, and actions to go uncontested. Third, an exclusive focus on sensitivity and affirmation is likely to restrict awareness of the complexities of cultural politics.

The CSC's work illustrated these issues, and this article provides recommendations as to what additionally could be done to extend the possibilities of multicultural professional development. It is important to note that although this article contains extensive criticism, the goal of such research analysis is by no means to dismiss the crucial work being done by the CSC or to ridicule the individual contributions of its members. On the contrary, in deconstructing their work, the task at hand is to theoretically approach the complex social conditions that produce the disheartening statistics that gave rise to the committee in the first place. Such analysis is thus undertaken with the utmost optimism; however, hope for the future requires awareness of the grim realities that so many students in the United States face and the reconcilable limitations of mainstream efforts to democratize the nation's schools.

## The personality vacuum: Abstracting the social from the psychological

Psychology, with its notion of the isolated, developing individual, allows for the interpretation that all societal problems can be ultimately located at the door of the individual actor. This allows for an interpretation of society as an aggregate of individuals rather than a totality that is much greater than its individual parts.[4]

Centered on a *human relations* approach to professional development, which focuses on fostering positive interpersonal and intergroup interactions in schools by encouraging tolerance and unity,[5] the CSC concentrated on transforming individual psyches and thus directed its professional development energies toward "changing attitudes," "self-reflection," "asking yourself questions," "self-exploration," "addressing personal prejudice," and "self-examination, awareness, and sensitivity."

Most multiculturalists would agree that self-actualization and reducing prejudice are essential to social change, and that educators need to critically reflect on the assumptions that they carry about themselves, learning, different cultures, and so forth. However, the CSC was dealing with discrimination as if the abusive treatment of students and their poor academic performance were the end result of an educator's ignorance, personal affective character, or individual values and beliefs, rather than the product of historically and socially sanctioned practices and conditions. Epitomizing the tendency to individualize discrimination and extract the psychological from the social in the CSC's deliberations, a black male member stated, "Some don't know, some don't care, and some are truly racist."

Comments such as "We need to teach these kids to work and keep the system going," and "they [young black males] are bright and talented, but they turn outside rather than inside the system" risk communicating that the society is systemically structured to accommodate everyone, if educators can just get individual obstacles and the resulting student resistance out of the way of the existing educational process. In other words, if people are given the opportunity to learn in an environment that is welcoming, then everyone will stay in school and eventually succeed in the larger society. It would be inaccurate to tell students that if they study hard—assimilating mainstream values and beliefs—they will automatically succeed in the larger discriminatory society. So many of them already know that this simply isn't true.

The central problem and limitation with pathologizing individual behavior is that self-actualization and reduction of prejudice in and of themselves do not point out where the *self* or the discriminatory tendencies came from. It also risks implying that people are biologically predisposed to do the things that they do, driven by some innate fear and disdain of the unknown. The committee needs to explore in greater depth how schools, the media, and other institutions nationwide function to legitimate particular experiences and worldviews at the expense and distortion of others. Developing a sense of the social and political realities that shape people's lives shouldn't be limited to *"unlearning"* what people have come to know, because it is also imperative to identify how such values and beliefs were produced, distributed, and consumed. As one white female member of the CSC suggested in "The Multicultural Committee Draft of Goals" questionnaire, "We need experiential activities and opportunities to recognize and evaluate the ideological influences that shape our thinking about schooling, society, ourselves, and diverse others."

Critical educators need to understand that peering within oneself, disconnected from the rest of the world, one is unable to make the links to the larger sociopolitical reality that shapes the psychological. Only in critical dialogue with the world around them can educators begin to understand what is within. As Paulo Freire states, "I engage in dialogue because I recognize the social and not merely the individualistic character of the process of knowing."[6] In the spirit of a more critical form of multiculturalism. Henry Giroux adds that it is imperative

> to link approaches to human consciousness and action to forms of structural analysis that explore how they interpenetrate each other rather than appear as separate pedagogical concerns . . .[7]

A Latina at one of the inservice sessions emphasized the importance of engaging socially sanctioned values and beliefs:

> These are more than individual acts of meanness; it took a long time for it to become systemic . . . In reverse, it will take a long time to get back to individuals.

Expressing a similar viewpoint, near the end of the third year a black inservice facilitator informed the CSC that "educators need to examine the values and the institutions such as slavery that shape our society."

The committee needs to articulate the interconnecting linkages among macro-level political, economic, and social variables, the formation of identities (including their own), and subordinated groups' academic performance at the micro-level classroom.[8] In other words, to rupture the fallacy of education as the great equalizer, the group should explore the ways in which schools reflect the larger social order—

> how social, political, and economic conditions of society create either directly or indirectly some of the oppressive features of schooling . . . and the ways in which powerful institutions and groups influence the knowledge, social relations, and modes of evaluation that characterize the ideological texture of school life.[9]

In this way the CSC can continue its important goal of prejudice reduction and self-actualization while moving beyond its original premise that the institutions that structure society are okay, including their own school system, and it is simply the people who need changing.

## Embracing social theory

Theory, as defined by Barry McLaughlin, refers

> to a way of interpreting, criticizing, and unifying established generalizations. A theory is flexible and pliant, in that it allows its generalizations to be modified to fit data unforeseen in their formulation. And theory is heuristic, in the sense that theory itself provides a way of guiding the enterprise of finding new and more powerful generalizations.[10]

The important risk to be aware of with theorizing is that a fine line separates generalizing and stereotyping, which is precisely why people need to be critical of all of their assumptions, regardless of any empirical justifications. However, deterring people from analyzing and scrutinizing the world around and within them is a major shortcoming in any project of change.

A black female inservice facilitator encouraged the CSC and the representatives from the school-based committees to voice their individual opinions:

> We need to share and speak with "I" statements, from our own personal experience—"I believe," "I think"—so we can get out of the practice of generalizing.

Although it is extremely important for individuals to come to voice around their own life histories and to avoid any perpetuation of stereotypes, people nonetheless need a language with which they can examine and establish social patterns. Educators who embrace what the facilitators were calling for in the individualization of experience and history make it virtually impossible to analyze what it means to be exposed to a particular cultural reality or group history. As a result, it is difficult to understand how *I* is more often than not the product rather than the creator of meaning.

Without critical social theory, the group is likely to conclude that the central goal should be to look for mechanical strategies for responding to discriminatory incidents. For example, a white male principal, eager to confront harsh behavior from some members of his staff, stated, "I want to know strategies that teachers can use if they hear a racist remark in the teachers' lounge!" Before searching for an efficient technical response, which obviously is a vital step toward intervention, educators should first be apprenticed in theorizing oppressive behavior—all human behavior for that matter—so they can then act upon discriminatory tendencies from a more informed position.

To affirm and engage the complexity of diverse human histories and perceptions, a fundamental tenet of critical multicultural education in the area of professional development and/or teaching is the inclusion of facilitators' and inservice participants' voices in the learning process. This type of democratic participation calls into question everyone's identity, experiences, and the assumptions that guide one's actions. In listening to and engaging opinions and values that are made public, the idea is not that inservice facilitators or teachers should be disparaging or censorious. Rather, the interaction through dialogue is meant to leave people ill at ease to a point that everyone acknowledges and takes responsibility for their complicity in perpetuating forms of discrimination.

## Avoiding the pitfalls of cultural relativism

It is difficult to address multi*cultural*ism without first establishing a working definition of *culture*—how it is produced and what, in turn, it works to create and maintain. Overall, the committee was working toward solutions to enhance educational success by embracing cultural relativism—in which all differences are equally acceptable. The language of the CSC mission statement echoes this goal. It speaks of "appreciation of all cultures," being "inclusive," having a "common purpose," that "a celebration of diversities promotes unity," placing "equal value on all students," "acceptance," and promoting "staff respect for and sensitivity toward the diverse backgrounds of students and their families." The affirmation of diversity is extremely important if multicultural education of any kind is to gain the initial trust and participation of all groups in society. However, the celebration of difference can create an interactive process within which it is virtually impossible to engage all cultures for their strengths and shortcomings.

One young man, from a group of multiracial adults who had either dropped out, been pushed out, or been kicked out of Changeton schools, described his predicament in an interview:

> At one point, I just started sellin' guns for a livin'. Went to jail a couple times; moved to Providence; had a kid; got tired of sellin' drugs out there; came back over here; went to jail again.

Trapped in a language of affirmation, the liberal multicultural educator would be compelled to romanticize this worldview. There is no room for critique, cultural analysis, and ethical intervention. In fact, what usually happens in mainstream multicultural classrooms is that students never hear of this harsh reality in the context of formal learning, because teachers rarely investigate the existential realities of their students and the poverty, disenfranchisement, police brutality, and racism that shape these kids' lives and self-concept. As the social studies chair, a white woman, stated:

> They [teachers] think that these kids come from Nobel [the state capital]. . . . We go out to the bus stop to show people that these kids live here. . . .

A *human relations* approach openly avoids exploration of difficult cultural issues, arguing that it creates tensions and antagonisms rather than harmony.[11] However, multicultural education should be used as a way to prepare learners with exactly what they will need in order to excavate their history and cultural roots, and consequently the social nature of the self. It is only then that real substantive personal transformation and social agency can occur. In other words, it is only then that a society can begin to work against the culture of violence that it creates.

When professional development is based on inservice games, role plays, or ideas such as cultural fairs—all of which are generally devoid of any engagement with the core intergroup antagonisms of society—it can never achieve any kind of critical awareness among educators, or students for that matter. The CSC, brainstorming ideas for a faculty workshop, mentioned developing a convention that would use passports to move participants from one exhibit to another. The advocates of this creative and potentially informative idea should also propose visiting a ghetto where people actually live. As one youth interviewed during the research describes it: "The ghetto is everywhere; the hood ain't no joke and there's no way out." Tricia Rose observes that "the ghetto *exists* for millions of young blacks and other people of color—it is a profoundly significant location."[12] The facilitators of such a multicultural event should pose the question to educators, in order to encourage them to theorize culture, of what it is like to survive in a dilapidated housing project where drugs, violence, and hunger are everyday realities. They need to explore what it means to take care of sick parents, the feeling of having no schoolbooks, the inevitable ramifications of not trusting public education, what it's like to have your imprisoned brothers' mug shots posted around town, the experience of seeing battery acid poured over someone's face because of a gang deal gone bad, finding your mother's boyfriend dead in your house from an overdose of drugs, what it feels like to get stabbed or shot, or beaten by the police—all social realities described by the local youths interviewed.

To extend the virtues of multicultural professional development, inservice facilitators and workshop participants must move beyond internationalizing multiculturalism and reducing diversity to issues of immigration presented in limited discussions of life back in some other country that many children may have never even seen. (The families of many of the country's disenfranchised children have been in the United States for generations.) What is crucial here is the development of a deeper understanding of what defines culture in order to be able to move beyond an ahistorical sense of values, beliefs, group ethos, language, and practices, and to understand how these elements are produced within the context of abuses of power. In this way, educators can move beyond flag day, Japanese doll day, food festivals, and so on—events that reduce the complexities of culture to aesthetics and fun. Within the clashes of cultural capital—different languages, cognitive and learning styles, values and beliefs, literacies, knowledge, and so on—educators can also begin to address the kinds of academic failure that are endemic to Changeton. Multicultural professional development should thus be working to apprentice teachers into being ethnographers[13] so that they can begin to understand the communities that they are intended to serve and what their students are bringing to the arena of formal learning.

## Different from what?

Throughout their work, the CSC often referred to *difference* (e.g., "We are afraid of difference" and "We should see these kids not as culturally disadvantaged, but as different.") However, the committee needs to define what exactly the term implies and to recognize that difference exists only in relationship to a referent. The critical question is, What are the defining parameters of that referent—that is, of the person or group who is speaking?

The concept of *difference* in the United States is generally not examined in ways that name and call into question the dominant referent group—the invisible norm of the white, upper-middle-class, heterosexual, healthy, Christian male by which all others are evaluated and positioned. Educators are not simply individuals making random comparisons in the world. In reality, everyone is marked by group membership, whether or not that connection is understood or perceived as such. Whites, for example, are marked by membership in a category that has historically been used as the referent for negatively evaluating other racial groups.[14] It is precisely these social markings that shape identities and points of reference, that are far too often taken for granted, or seen as universal, or human.

The first three multicultural inservice sessions that the CSC developed and participated in did not take up the issue of *difference*, that is, beyond a relativistic approach, which is surprising given that the outside organizations that facilitated the sessions had the word *difference* in their names. At the first workshop, one of the facilitators, after categorically separating the group, asked if the participants felt labeled. One white male claimed, "It made everyone feel like a minority." Others referred to feeling "manipulated" or "segregated" and said they "didn't like to be white or nonwhite." Some were uncomfortable with the social class differentiation. The general consensus among the inservice participants was that "I felt good about some categories and bad about others."

This apolitical and ahistorical exercise would be more productive if it included a profound discussion of how these divisions among groups are legitimated in society, thus moving the experience into something more than just psychologically driven sensations. Otherwise, the end result will be much like that of a black male committee member's relativistic stance in response to the exercise: "We all mixed in the differences and belonged with each other at one point; we all have differences and commonalities." As Lawrence Grossberg warns:

> A theory that celebrates otherness fails to acknowledge the difference between experiences, real historical tendencies and cultural discourses and meanings, as well as the complex relations that exist between them.[15]

This first workshop included a number of opportunities to tease out some crucial points about the struggle over identity and difference. For example, one such opportunity occurred when a woman sat down in the middle of the floor, explaining to the larger group:

> I was born in the U.S. My family is from Cape Verde. They originated in Europe (Italy). Where am I? When I changed my descriptor, they changed my minority status.

A similar opportunity occurred at the central administration building, when the head of the bilingual education department explained to the CSC, "America wants you to come here and fit into categories that are already established, and millions of people are marked 'other.' " These types of situations—pedagogical moments —provide ample room to explore the history of socially and institutionally sanctioned racist and segregationist practices in the United States. Taking advantage of such pedagogical moments is crucial because, as Ana Maria Villegas states, "Teacher education must go beyond the acceptance of difference and help teachers analyze the sociopolitical system that gives rise to those differences."[16]

## Moving beyond the comfort zone

In developing inservice sessions for teachers throughout the school system, the committee talked about comfort and feeling free to speak and to share experiences. At one point in the workshop preparations, a Cape Verdean male informed the facilitator that he wanted to be able to talk about all groups and issues without emphasizing the negative: "Nothing negative, no violence; we are working on that." One of his white Jewish female colleagues agreed: "We shouldn't deal with all the negatives such as lynchings; rather, we need to accentuate the contributions of different groups." The chair of the social studies department, who would soon after resign from the committee, immediately rejected this position:

> I'm tired of dancing around with food and simple curriculum changes, and I don't like the idea of a fair; it trivializes multicultural education, as does Black History Month and Martin Luther King Jr. Month!

One of the inservice facilitators, who was helping the committee decide what to do in the first workshops, stated, "We can tailor the day to make everyone feel good." She told the CSC:

> There are some things that you don't want in the first session; some issues are difficult for the people that are in denial of living in a multicultural world.

This assurance of comfort was again reiterated when the same facilitator opened the inservice discussion with some words about "the need for safety and feeling comfortable" when dealing with diversity. As a result of this strategy, a variety of issues and tensions went unaddressed and thus uncontested.

After her opening statement about safety and comfort, the facilitator introduced an article on white privilege. After reading the essay out loud, some whites at the workshop voiced the opinion that they didn't think that their position was necessarily a privilege. There was general agreement among the group that "we don't want to shift the blame to white males in multicultural education." One woman argued:

> There is a backlash against the white male . . . What is the purpose of this inservice and the CSC? I think it's tolerance . . . Math, science, and language have no color . . . We need concrete strategies to go back with.

If given the opportunity, inservice participants who were challenged and felt under attack tried to move, perhaps unconsciously, away from the point of analysis—such as racism. They often accomplished this shift by calling for practical solutions and materials, as exemplified by the comment above. Unwilling to engage the ideological construction of whiteness, this speaker not only requested "concrete strategies" but also wanted to move out of the political and into what she believed to be neutral and objective ground—"Math, science, and language have no color."[17]

Along these same lines, confronted with issues of white supremacy, another white woman, expressing frustration with the inservice session, exclaimed:

> I don't feel that I'm getting anything here that I can use! I can't know every-
> thing about all groups, religions, or cultures. All students need certain things.
> Let's talk about that and their similarities.

A call for harmony and not engagement, this comment risks being translated as, "I am not comfortable with where this is going; let's talk about something else— abstract educational needs and materials, for example." If all kids have certain needs, and those needs are empathy, respect, encouragement, and to be treated with integrity, then that requires naming and engaging their experiences with racism, sexism, homophobia, classism, linguicism, and so forth. The participant's comment risks implying that students' needs have nothing to do with cultural politics. Perhaps using her position of privilege to avoid an analysis of the harsh realities that many people face, the speaker wanted to turn to a discussion of "similarities," which risks translating into, "Let's only talk about what you have in common with me so that I am not uncomfortable."

After the above statement, the facilitator took the floor, pointing out how the literature on privilege evoked "feelings of anger, confusion, and uncomfort-ableness." She added that this was "not simply a white/black thing" and that "gender, class, and sex were also important issues." What appeared to be a prime opportunity to discuss how the struggles over identity and difference cut across individual categories disappeared after this statement. It was as if the facilitator were using other categories to divert the group away from the tensions that were building around racial issues. Referring to the temporary discomfort, she argued that these feelings need to be dealt with, especially when working with students: "We want students to be comfortable. Then they will do better." However, in leaving the inservice participants' comments untouched, she didn't confront the assumptions and potential biases of the people directly in front of her. In this sense, the facilitator seemed to be "falling prey to a laissez-faire practice."[18] In other words, whatever the group wants, it gets, and in this case, it is to avoid the volatile issues. As Freire elaborates:

> In the end, the facilitator is renouncing his or her duty to teach—which is a
> dialogical duty. In truth, the teacher turned facilitator rejects the fantastic
> work of placing an object as a mediator between him or her and the students.
> That is, the facilitator fails to assume his or her role as a dialogical educator
> who can illustrate the object of study.[19]

If comfort was a strategy for keeping everyone open-minded at the workshop, members of the CSC, after years of working together, should have challenged their colleagues' assumptions and statements once they were back at the central office at a debriefing session. In support of the inservice experience and avoiding con-frontation altogether, a black committee member said:

> We recognized that we do have a problem and not to simply place blame
> ... There are things that you have to be aware of that came out in the
> exercises.

Chiming in on the theme of blame, a white principal informed the group that some people were upset because they felt that the Europeans were not mentioned at all. He also brought up the issue of white male-bashing:

> Many people don't support multiculturalism because they feel that it's against white males and females . . . Their concern is that we should not shift the blame from one group to another.

The willingness to embrace a world without culprits invoked a huge contradiction in the committee's logic: up until this point, the perception seemed to be that social institutions were functional, and once negative teacher attitudes were changed, schools would cater to all students. Suddenly it sounded like no one was to blame, that people are the products of what they have inherited from history and institutions. As a black male inservice facilitator said, "I'm not blaming anyone for that [discrimination] today . . . [people in present-day society] have inherited such conditions."

After the workshops, most committee members described the sessions as "nonthreatening," "comfortable," "inclusive," and "built on our sensitivity and camaraderie." It is more than likely that the participants were comfortable because of a tendency to avoid the real difficult issues and tensions among the group, as well as those in their schools, city, state, nation, and world.

The committee's future work should explore the ways in which people breathe life into existing institutions and socially sanctioned practices, which in turn breathe life into people. Insisting that no one is to blame risks shifting the power of human agency to historical determinism. In this uncritical sense, people become objects of history (passive recipients) and not subjects (shapers) capable of engaging and transforming both themselves and the world around them.[20]

## Color-blindness

Whiteness has played a significant role in shaping ethnic patterns, social identities, and institutions in the United States. However, whiteness has paradoxically been able to mask itself as a category—it is simultaneously everything and nothing.[21] The underlying evasive ideology that informs the social construction of whiteness is strategically infused in such a way that those who, for whatever reason, buy into its logic are unable, or simply unwilling, to see and thus name its oppressive nature.

By not recognizing whiteness as a racial identity, most whites see themselves as race-free and less ethnic than "others"; consequently they take for granted the privileges they secure by such an ideologically charged racial marker. Frances FitzGerald's data reveal that white, upper-middle-class professionals don't identify themselves as "ethnic, cultural, or powerful."[22] Ruth Frankenburg's research, which consisted of interviews with white women, showed that whiteness is "difficult for white people to name . . . those that are securely housed within its borders usually do not examine it."[23]

Limited to a multicultural discourse of sensitivity, affirmation, and comfort, and simultaneously an approach to multicultural education that focuses on the universal human experience and not a politics of identity and difference, members of the CSC embraced such ideas as "unity and common purpose," "working with teachers to help them view everyone as innately equal," "the concept of oneness," and "not pigeon-holing them [racially subordinated students] as black or brown." They made such statements as "I value all of my students in the same way;

[all groups go] under one umbrella," and "We are the same under the skin." The CSC also celebrated the fact that the high school was selling t-shirts with the slogan "Be Color Blind."

Although such efforts have the best intentions, not naming and working with the ideological markers of difference across race, class, gender, sexuality, and so forth can have detrimental results. Educators can't value "all" students if they deny any engagement with their diverse life experiences that are the very products of those socially constructed categories.[24] Educators shouldn't rely on what appears to be an objective and just way of dealing with all students—the idea that "I value all people as human beings"—if they truly hope to work toward significant social change. Because the process of racialization (ascribing behavioral characteristics to racial groupings) begins at an early age, by no means should experiences be denied or artificially homogenized in the name of equal treatment.

What is ironic is that in the very article that the inservice participants were required to read twice, the author Peggy McIntosh asserts:

> I think that whites are carefully taught not to recognize white privilege . . . My schooling gave me no training in seeing myself as an oppressor, as an unfairly advantaged person, or as a participant in a damaged culture.[25]

This social construction of "not seeing" was demonstrated in the laughter of the two white women at the first all-faculty workshop who commented to each other in response to the obvious implications of the video *The Eye of the Storm* (more popularly known as "Brown Eyes, Blue Eyes"): "It doesn't carry over; we don't see that . . . It's not racial; they like you or they don't." The CSC should explore how such educators disregard the realities of discrimination as expressed by these Changeton youths in an interview:

*Olavo:*  They treat you different, man. I had, like, three classes where I was the only nigger in the room. The teacher used to teach everybody in the class but me. I used to call her, "Can you explain this to me?" She used to ignore me.

*Roland:*  If you black, the attitude is, "You dumb."

Any depoliticized, ahistorical approach to multicultural education can provide window-dressing reforms; but simply acknowledging our differences, or avoiding them altogether in a color-blind approach, will not lead to an eradication of the abusive ideological and structural patterns of schools in the United States. If real substantive change is going to take place, then, as McIntosh states:

> to redesign social systems we need first to acknowledge their colossal unseen dimensions. The silences and denials surrounding privilege are the key political tool here. They keep the thinking about equality or equity incomplete, protecting unearned advantage and conferred dominance by making these subjects taboo.[26]

The long-term goal of any political project should be to achieve a world in which biological features such as color, gender, and sexual orientation have no negative social significance or unethical meaning. However, such an immediate transition is impossible because these categories play a major role in the production of social identities, interactions, and experience in the United States.

## Encouraging ongoing reflection and action

The CSC members seemed to share a de facto acceptance that an individual's subject position (the place that a person occupies within a set of social relationships) predisposes him or her to theoretical awareness. However, educators should be encouraged to understand that a person's race, ethnicity, gender, social class, and so on do not predispose critical consciousness—the ability to read the social and political realities that shape people's lives. As has been argued, critical forms of multicultural education should invite everyone to further explore the relationship between their own identities and individual experiences and society's larger historic, economic, and ideological constructs, and their inextricable connection to power. Part of this exploration for the Central Steering Committee should include an examination of social class, sexuality, and resistance.

### *The need to address social class*

The significance of social class emerged early on in the work of the CSC. The issue arose during the drafting of the mission statement, when members made comments such as these: "We treat poor kids poorly, what about them?" and "Sensitivity should not be limited to racial and ethnic differences alone, but should include gender, physical and mental challenges, and socioeconomic differences." It also came up in the preparation for the first inservice session: "We had a workshop that really made the participants feel class conscious . . . The people from Borton, in their Brooks Brothers suits, were embarrassed." When asked to separate themselves by social class at the first small workshop, many agreed that it made them feel uncomfortable. However, the CSC needs to develop a deeper theoretical understanding as to how socioeconomic status (beyond the mere quantity of money a person possesses) in part shapes the values, beliefs, worldviews, discourse styles, social relations, and actions of people.[27]

The first inservice facilitator included in his speech the history of exploitation of the poor in Changeton. However, the CSC considered his contributions to be "a bomb"—that is, a waste of time. The following comment expresses the general sentiment:

> Bur was atrocious—he was only going to speak for 10 minutes. He talked more about the blue-collar stuff and not about different populations—total irrelevance!

Capitalism and socioeconomic status should be considered significant issues when dealing with raising consciousness about multiculturalism. The committee needs to engage the interpenetrating relationship among power, economic resources, and social control, and thus how schools function as major socializing influences in preparing students for their place in a hierarchically divided labor force, one that includes a degree of poverty.[28] To better understand the social realities of their students and communities, the CSC—all citizens of Changeton, for that matter—should explore how historical materialism (i.e., the struggle of different classes over material and symbolic wealth) has shaped the city's past and historical present, as well as the ways in which class antagonisms have historically been used to incite racism and other forms of oppression.[29]

Throughout the three years, there was no mention of the fact that the affluent white minority in Changeton runs the schools (as it has historically controlled the city), and that many of the faculty and administrators don't actually live in the predominantly blue-collar community. In addition, the CSC should encourage a discussion of how its members' own social-class lenses have been shaping the ways in which they see their students (and vice versa), the kinds of expectations that they have for them, and the ways in which they have been approaching the entire debate over multiculturalism.

The Changeton youths interviewed during this research recognized the problem of social class and education:

*Stevie:*   You know what I notice, I noticed when I used to go to school, if the teachers knew you came from a nice, like, middle-class neighborhood, they'd treat you good. They give you special attention. But if they knew you came from the projects or somethin' . . .
*Carlos:*   If you come from a bad neighborhood they make sure you never make it.
*Stevie:*   They think that you are a troublemaker.
*Dion:*     Automatically, automatically!

The neglect of issues of class and capitalism (and the interconnecting relationships with race and gender) is disconcerting given that, as stated earlier, in the very year that the committee was formed, the city had 13,000 people living in poverty and nearly 7,000 crimes were committed.

### Addressing sexual orientation

Indifference toward sexual politics regularly surfaced in the CSC's work. An egregious example occurred during the registration process for a workshop being provided by the Center for Training and Health Education (not organized or related in any way to the committee's efforts). Part one of the conference was titled "Working and Living in Culturally Diverse Environments," and part two was called "Making Schools Safe for Gay, Lesbian, and Bisexual Youth." Not a single member of the CSC expressed the need to better inform themselves about the politics of sexuality. Instead, the committee strategically eliminated any mention of the gay/lesbian section of the workshop advertisement when they sought public funds to support their attendance at the first part of the conference. In addition, the group never actively, or even rhetorically, sought out an openly gay or lesbian person (or a disabled person, for that matter) for committee membership, as they had done with the various racial categories.

Multicultural educators need to attempt to develop an approach for honestly addressing sexuality, and they should explore the connections between sexual orientation and the cultural realities of everyday life. The real tangible tragedy would be to ignore the reality of people like one young man interviewed, a student who had dropped out of Changeton High School and turned to drugs and eventually suicide because of his public mistreatment for being gay.

### Developing a theory of resistance

*Resistance*, or the development of oppositional identities, is a legitimate (though not always conscious) response to domination, used to help individuals or groups deal with oppressive social conditions and injustice. Developing a theory of resistance could assist the CSC a great deal in understanding a number of the predicaments faced by educators in the everyday life of Changeton's classrooms, hallways, and streets. But, as argued throughout this article, the group was rarely encouraged to make linkages between student behavior and broader oppressive social practices and institutions. Perhaps the most striking example of the need to consider resistance theory came when a Latina committee member cited the fact that "in the behavior adjustment program, it's all boys and mostly minorities —especially black males." She asked an inservice facilitator:

> Is this an issue of poor parenting skills or what? It's not an issue of racism! I'm the principal, and I see that these kids can't control themselves. What are some ways to deal with this?

This comment not only risks blaming the victims for their predicament ("poor parenting skills or what"), but it does so with biological implications—"These kids can't control themselves." Instead, the committee needs to develop a theory to make sense of why these students, a majority of whom are poor and racially subordinated (and stigmatized for being in special education, bilingual education, and free lunch programs), are reacting as they do. This would help them understand, for example, the reaction of a young black female student, when driving by Changeton High School: " 'The big school,' you mean the prison . . . Changeton High—the big white lie!" Consider the feelings and reactions of two other youths interviewed about discrimination in the local schools:

*Carlos:*   I had teachers that were so prejudice against Puerto Ricans and blacks, and I am both.
*Roberto:*   I once threw a chair at a teacher who was racist against me, and I made the front page—we've all made the papers.
*Carlos:*   I jus' see it as, if teachers go out their way to make an ass out of you, . . . [Dion chimes in with Carlos, and together they say] you go out of your way to . . . make an ass outta dem.

Instead of trying to make sense of this kind of attitude and behavior, mainstream educators generally want to "deal with this"—implying a search for efficient ways to get this type of behavior (which is interpreted as deviance rather than resistance/opposition) to stop. On the contrary, as Bonny Norton Pierce argues:

> We need a theory of social identity that integrates the learner and the learning context, and how relations of power in the social world affect social interaction between learners and teachers and among peers.[30]

Resistance theory was also implicitly neglected in the following statement by a black male committee member who, in a concerned voice, argued that the inservice session "Name Game" (which dealt with family names and heritage) could be dangerous:

> What about those kids who don't have a heritage to fall back on, blacks for example? Some youngsters would feel embarrassed. "Mommy, where did we come from?"

Educators need to work against a cultural deprivation interpretation of the African American experience, which has been disseminated throughout the country since the enslavement of blacks. By not promoting the cultural importance of resistance to domination as a positive force, educators will be unable to celebrate the cultural realities of blacks in the United States. For example, African Americans, by reinventing the dominant communicative form of English into counter-discourses to fight white supremacy, were able to forge a culture of rebellion out of the oppressive nature of slavery and were thus able to work toward the political solidarity necessary for avoiding total domination. These new languages created the

> space for alternative cultural production and alternative epistemologies —different ways of thinking and knowing that were crucial to creating counter-hegemonic world views.[31]

Educators should be encouraged to recognize this incredible history of resistance, a history that would be extremely insightful and motivational to black students who have been told time and time again that they have done nothing. If, in fact, schools were doing a better job, then students wouldn't have to go home "and ask Mommy," because her participation and life story, as well as the long history of enslavement in this country, would already be a part of the school curriculum. These anecdotes and testimonies could then be linked to students' current experiences, predicaments, and active theorizing about the world around and within them.

## Hopes for the future

In their efforts to conceptualize and implement professional development for their colleagues, the Central Steering Committee worked tirelessly and altruistically to build a foundation that would enable multicultural education to become a fundamental part of the overall process of public schooling. One can hope that the contentious issues left on the table after three years of development will take center stage in the near future. The CSC should certainly continue its noble job of introducing multicultural education (avoiding the paralysis of an attitude that says, "We can't move until we've solved our ideological differences . . ."); however, they need to be openly honest, and insistent, about naming to the public (in hopes of larger debate) the very content and detail of those discrepancies.

From the research observations and pedagogical suggestions presented here, perhaps educators can open up new possibilities for developing the awareness necessary to extend the virtues of multicultural professional development in public schools and more effectively work to eradicate cultural tensions, low academic achievement, and high dropout rates. As a grander goal, educators and students can begin to influence and democratize the larger social realities that shape the very texture of school life.

## Notes

1   The name *Changeton* is a pseudonym, as are all of the other names of towns, cities, and people throughout this article.

2   The academic standings throughout Changeton's school system were also bleak: the percentage of high school seniors performing at grade-level goals in math was 25, and in science, 27. Of the 64 percent of the students who took the SATs that year, the average score was 801—as compared with the state average of 903. In addition,

13.5 percent of the students throughout the school system, overwhelmingly poor and racially subordinated boys and linguistic minorities, were in special education.

3 See James Banks. *An Introduction to Multicultural Education* (Boston: Allyn and Bacon, 1999); Christine Bennett, *Comprehensive Multicultural Education: Theory and Practice* (Boston: Allyn and Bacon, 1998); Geneva Gay, *Culturally Responsive Teaching: Theory, Research, and Practice* (New York: Teachers College Press, 2000); Sonia Nieto, *Affirming Diversity: The Sociopolitical Context of Multicultural Education* (New York: Longman, 2000); Vivian Pang, *Multicultural Education: A Caring-Centered Reflective Approach* (New York: McGraw Hill, 2000); and Christine Sleeter and Carl Grant, *Making Choices for Multicultural Education: Five Approaches to Race, Class, and Gender* (New York: John Wiley and Sons, 1999).

4 Edmund Sullivan, *Critical Psychology and Pedagogy: Interpretation of the Personal World* (New York: Bergin and Garvey, 1990), p. xii.

5 Christine Sleeter and Carl Grant, *Making Choices for Multicultural Education: Five Approaches to Race, Class, and Gender* (New York: John Wiley and Sons, 1999).

6 Paulo Freire and Donaldo Macedo, "A Dialogue: Culture, Language, and Race," in *Breaking Free: The Transformative Power of Critical Pedagogy*, ed. Pepi Leistyna, Arlie Woodrum, and Steven Sherblom (Cambridge, MA: Harvard Educational Review Publishing Group, 1996), p. 202.

7 Henry Giroux, *Theory and Resistance in Education: A Pedagogy for the Opposition* (South Hadley, MA: Bergin and Garvey, 1983), p. 61.

8 Lilia Bartolome, "Beyond the Methods Fetish: Toward a Humanizing Pedagogy." *Harvard Educational Review* 64 (Summer 1994): 173–194.

9 Henry Giroux, *Theory and Resistance in Education: A Pedagogy for the Opposition* (South Hadley. MA: Bergin and Garvey, 1983), p. 55.

10 Barry McLaughlin, *Theories of Second-Language Learning* (London: Arnold, 1987), p. 3.

11 Christine Sleeter and Carl Grant, *Making Choices for Multicultural Education: Five Approaches to Race, Class. and Gender* (New York: John Wiley and Sons, 1999).

12 Tricia Rose, *Black Noise: Rap Music and Black Culture in Contemporary America* (London: Wesleyan University Press, 1994), p. 12.

13 Shirley Brice Heath, *Ways with Words: Language, Life, and Work in Communities and Classrooms* (Cambridge, MA: Cambridge University Press, 1983).

14 See Theodore Allen, *The Invention of the White Race* (London: Verso, 1994); Mike Hill. *Whiteness: A Critical Reader* (New York: New York University Press, 1997); Alice Mcintyre, *Making Meaning of Whiteness: Exploring Racial Identity with White Teachers* (New York: SUNY Press, 1997); Martha Menchaca and Richard Valencia, "Anglo-Saxon Ideologies in the 1920s–1930s: Their Impact on the Segregation of Mexican Students in California," in *Antbropology & Education Quarterly* 21 (Spring 1990): 222–245; and Howard Winant, "Dictatorship, Democracy, and Difference: The Historical Construction of Racial Identity," in *The Bubbling Cauldron: Race, Ethnicity, and the Urban Crisis*, ed. M. P. Smith and J. R. Feagin (Minneapolis: University of Minnesota Press, 1995).

15 Lawrence Grossberg, "History, Politics and Postmodernism," in *Stuart Hall: Critical Dialogues in Cultural Studies*. ed. David Morley and Kuan-Hsing Chen (New York: Routledge, 1996). p. 169.

16 Ana Maria Villegas, "School Failure and Cultural Mismatch: Another View," in *The Urban Review* 20 (Fall 1988): 261.

17 Beyond a call for "*tolerance*," educators need to question the privilege that whites have in being in a position to decide who will and will not be tolerated.

18 Paulo Freire and Donaldo Macedo, "A Dialogue: Culture, Language, and Race," in *Breaking Free: The Transformative Power of Critical Pedagogy*. ed. Pepi Leistyna, Arlie Woodrum, and Steven Sherblom (Cambridge, MA: Harvard Educational Review Publishing Group, 1996), p. 202.

19 Ibid.

20 Paulo Freire, *Pedagogy of the Oppressed* (New York: Seabury Press, 1970).

21 Richard Dyer, "White," in *Screen* 29 (Spring 1988): 44–64.

22 Frances FitzGerald, *Cities on a Hill: A Journey Through Contemporary American Cultures* (New York: Simon and Schuster, 1986), p. 218.

23  Ruth Frankenburg, *The Social Construction of Whiteness: White Women, Race Matters* (Minneapolis: University of Minnesota Press, 1993), pp. 228–229.

24  Sonia Nieto, *Affirming Diversity: The Sociopolitical Context of Multicultural Education* (New York: Longman, 2000).

25  Peggy McIntosh, "White Privilege: Unpacking the Invisible Knapsack," in *Independent School* (Winter 1990): 31.

26  Ibid.: 36.

27  See Michael Apple, *Education and Power* (New York: Routledge, 1995); Stanley Aronowitz, *The Politics of Identity: Class, Culture, Social Movements* (New York: Routledge, 1992); Pierre Bourdieu and Jean-Claude Passeron, *Reproduction in Education, Society, and Culture* (London: Sage, 1977); Samuel Bowles and Herbert Gintis, *Schooling in Capitalist America: Educational Reform and the Contradictions of Economic Life* (New York: Basic Books, 1976); Noam Chomsky, Pepi Leistyna, and Steven Sherblom. "A Dialogue with Noam Chomsky," in Pepi Leistyna, *Presence of Mind Education and the Politics of Deception* (Boulder, CO: Westview Press, 1999); Amitava Kumar, *Class Issues* (New York: New York University Press, 1997); and C. Wright Mills, *White Collar: The American Middle Classes* (London: Oxford University Press, 1951).

28  See Jean Anyon. "Social Class and the Hidden Curriculum of Work," in *Journal of Education* 162 (Winter 1980); Michael Apple, *Ideology and Curriculum* (New York: Routledge, 1990); Peter McLaren, *Che Guevara, Paulo Freire, and the Pedagogy of Revolution* (Boulder, CO: Roman and Littlefield, 2000); and David Spener, "Transitional Bilingual Education and the Socialization of Immigrants," in *Breaking Free: The Transformative Power of Critical Pedagogy*, ed. Pepi Leistyna, Arlie Woodrum, and Steven Sherblom (Cambridge, MA: Harvard Educational Review Press, 1996).

29  See W. E. B. Du Bois, *Black Reconstruction in America, 1860–1880* (New York: Atheneum, 1935); and David Roediger, *Towards the Abolition of Whiteness* (New York: Verso, 1994).

30  Bonny Norton Pierce, "Social Identity, Investment, and Language Learning," in *TESOL Quarterly* 29 (Spring 1993): 7.

31  Bell Hooks. *Teaching to Transgress: Education as the Practice of Freedom* (New York: Routledge, 1994), p. 171.

# CHAPTER 23

# IMPROVING MULTICULTURAL TEACHER IN-SERVICE (1981)
## A CIPP planning model
John Gordon White

Educators, whether professors of education, teachers, or administrators, know that the measure of a program's success is often determined by its planning model. The choice of an evaluation strategy is critical in ascertaining whether the goals and objectives of an educational enterprise are adequately met. A formative/ process evaluation report can be significantly different from a summative/product report. Accordingly, the evaluation procedure selected, rather than the operation or outcome, can be the crucial part in evaluating the strength or weakness of an educational project. To evaluate teachers' sensitivity to ethnic differences, for example, a thorough evaluation model/plan must be adopted.

Multicultural teacher in-service programs have not always produced desired results. In fact, they might have produced the opposite, as Cross and Deslonde (1978) conclude: "In some instances, the inservicing itself seemed to cause a negative reaction to multicultural training" (p. 104). Part of the failure of such inservicing might be due not to the program but to the selection of an inadequate evaluation model in the beginning.

One evaluation model that warrants consideration in improving multicultural teacher in-service programs is Stufflebeam's Context, Input, Process, Product paradigm (CIPP). Using the CIPP model, a program planner can decide whether a multicultural teacher-training workshop should be retained, modified, or eliminated. The CIPP model provides a strong format to organize and evaluate a program. As Webster (1977) has observed:

> Probably the most comprehensive evaluation model was developed by Stufflebeam, et. al., (1971), and named the CIPP . . . Model. Evaluation was defined as the process of delineating, obtaining, and providing useful information for judging decision alternatives. The model identified four major types of evaluation: context evaluation to feed planning decisions, input evaluation to feed programming decisions, process evaluation to feed implementing decisions, and product evaluation to feed recycling decisions (p. 1).

Given this rationale of thoroughness of content, CIPP would appear to be a commendable option in structuring a multicultural teacher in-service program.

Although CIPP could be viewed as too comprehensive and time-consuming for all school districts to apply completely, such a model could help to formulate an educational program, even if program development is already in progress. Accordingly, an educator could use CIPP to structure and to initiate a multicultural teacher in-service program, or to evaluate a program development (Worthern and Sanders, 1973).

## The context phase

### Objective

The first phase in CIPP calls for analyzing the background, situation, or conditions of a proposed or existing in-service workshop, particularly noting programmatic needs and resources. Such operative context identification is illustrated by the 1969 California legislation conditionally requiring certain school districts to provide multicultural staff in-service sessions, which significantly, however, were without legislative funding (Blaylock, 1975).

As indicated by Jensen and Hopewell (1975), multicultural in-service programs must have at least two prerequisites: The superintendent must endorse and the board must fund voluntary staff participation.

### Method

Knowing the situational context in which teacher training is to take place becomes important after the goals are specified. To illustrate the implications for multicultural planning, Beebe (1978) notes that in Dade County, Florida, over a third of the students are native Spanish-speaking; monolingualism is a disadvantage. In this situation, to promote bilingualism would be a socially proper planning aim. Such aims, however, must be weighed programmatically because, despite legislative and judicial intervention, "the American academic community is not on the whole sympathetic to the concept of cultural pluralism or bilingual education" (Krug, 1977, p. 9). To ignore this negative climate would be a serious mistake in assessing situational variables in planning multicultural in-service sessions.

Krug's pessimistic pronouncement is echoed by Pacheco (1977), who admonishes us that, "schooling systems are inherently conservative" (p. 20), and that "Statistics continue to tell a tale of low achievement scores, high dropout rates" (p. 16). Nevertheless, Cross and Deslonde (1978) seem more optimistic about multicultural schooling as a situational variable (for context planning):

> If many educators have unicultural vision and/or are negative and seem unchanged after inservice in multicultural education, can the schools be turned around? The answer is yes (pp. 104–105).

To execute such a turnaround, Skjerwold (1975) outlines the following priorities:

> What we need to do is study our ethnic groups from a different perspective. This means focusing on their day-to-day lives rather than being concerned with the extent to which they are becoming Americanized, however that is defined (p. 64).

### Relation to decision making

Here, Stufflebeam advises addressing programmatic goals and objectives after the preceding context subphases have been ascertained and the discrepancies between actualities and intentions have been noted. In determining goals of multicultural inservicing, some examples are applicable to sharpen our decision making. For Baker (1978), "instruction [goals] have had a monocultural thrust" (p. 135), which echoes Bennett (1979) that such monoculturalism has "subjugated the validity of diverse . . . ethnic . . . groups" (p. 232). Geneva Gay (1978) proposes study goals of "the value systems, communication styles, relational patterns, and learning styles of different ethnic groups as component parts of distinctive socio-cultural systems" (p. 57). Paralleling this proposal, Ovando (1978) concentrates on curricular aims when he recommends an examination of ethnic roles (p. 120). Once such goals (ends) are determined and their objectives (means) are specified, the next step is to judge their effectiveness.

## The input phase
### Objective

"The purpose of input evaluation is to provide information for determining how to utilize resources to achieve project objectives" (Stufflebeam, 1973, p. 136). To accomplish this purpose, procedural barriers and implementational designs are considered, which should prompt the in-service educator to question the relevance of assessment techniques to the achievement of multicultural in-service goals and objectives.

The main procedural barrier to achieving project objectives, Valverde (1976) warns, could be labor antagonism between teachers and administrators during each workshop. Such potential labor antagonism as well as administrative or collegiate teacher assessment are procedural barriers requiring early scrutiny in planning for staff development.

### Method

This sequential subphase deals with an analysis of various techniques suggested by the preceding (object) input section. Once a method for problem solving is identified, the next step is to determine whether such a method should be used to assess certain instructional goals and objectives. The answer depends on two variables: a) whether a large or small solution is contemplated, such as participation by one or a hundred teachers, and b) whether a high or low information base is perceived as necessary support for the degree of desired change. For example, what is the consensus regarding teacher reaction to compulsory attendance of multicultural workshops?

The joint operation of these two variables requires different degrees of evaluation. Stufflebeam explains that "where small change is needed and where much information is available to support it, little formal evaluation is usually required" (p. 137). Contrariwise, where large change is needed and where little information is supplied, "then extensive efforts are required to provide the information" (p. 137), and much formal evaluation is required.

Bronaugh's (1977) specification of techniques affecting in-service staff behavior at the Racine Unified Schools Multicultural Training Center exemplify the methods of this subphase:

Three-day workshop trainees are exposed to readings, lectures, audiovisual materials, discussion of multicultural concepts as they pertain to various local ethnic groups. Lesson development with a multi-ethnic focus is required. Peer demonstration follows along with Center evaluation itself (p. 204).

Of course, educators can use several of these techniques for information about a solution to a context problem. Interviews and questionnaires, for instance, reveal staff attitudes about changes in workshop personnel.

### Relation to decision making

This subphase outlines the following considerations: a) the specification of procedures; b) budgets (for funding agencies); c) staff requirements; d) organizational schemes; e) schedules; f) equipment; g) materials. These elements denote available solutions if we adopt the CIPP classification (p. 137). To illustrate specifications of procedures, educators can refer to Beebe's (1978) Spanish immersion program on *la Isla Caribe* (p. 97). For English-speaking, monolingual pupils, this immersion consisted of 30 hours of intensive Spanish instruction which continued for five school days. Could such a program's immersion techniques be adapted to assist in multicultural staff development?

At this point, if the planner has selected the teacher-training goals and their specific behavioral objectives for achieving them, he would be ready for a trial run or pilot test of the workshop. After implementing workshop activities, a method must be identified to determine "feedback"; for this purpose an evaluation design will be proposed later.

## The process phase

### Objective

For Stufflebeam, a main purpose of process evaluation is to make programmatic decisions and to detect programmatic defects once a program is underway (p. 139). Although a lack of time is such a defect, a more subtle programmatic failure would be Banks' (1976) "ethnically encapsulated" teachers being trained in the same manner as others. Instructional adjustments must be provided for.

As stressed by Leiter and Cooper (1978), individual isolation and arbitrariness of workshop staff are other pitfalls to be avoided, not to mention the absence-of-principal-participation mistake spotlighted by Davison (1974). These errors may be unforeseen if accurate and complete programmatic records are not compiled.

### Method

Stufflebeam (1973) isolates at least four significant methods of evaluation in addressing the question of the means to detect programmatic dysfunction, such as workshop in-service mistakes. When feasible, he urges employment of a full-time evaluator; instruments for programmatic processing description; feedback meetings between the process evaluator and program personnel on a regular basis; "and frequent updating of the process evaluation design" (p. 138). (These instruments include various interviews, rating scales, and even suggestion boxes.)

## Relation to decision making

In this final subphase of process evaluation, multicultural in-service programs should be co-ordinated and revised. We are now ready for product evaluation.

## The product phase
### Objective

Product evaluation measures attainments both during and at the end of activities. Jones (1972), for instance, complains of the difficulty in assessing changes in teacher attitudes toward in-service programs during workshops, and Bronaugh (1977) concludes that a multicultural center's program afterwards met an "overwhelming positive response" (p. 204). The means best suited to obtain such measurements remain to be explored in the next product subphase.

### Method

To determine the most useful means for evaluating whether in-service aims have been achieved, workshop behavioral objectives should be formulated. Stufflebeam (1973) also examines the criteria behind such objectives (p. 138). These criteria are to be compared with absolute, or ideal criteria, as well as with relative criteria—what ought to be the rationale vs. what is the rationale in general practice.

### Relation to decision making

The final subphase of product evaluation is significant for deciding whether a program should be repeated, modified, refocused, or terminated (Stufflebeam, 1973, p. 138). The Spanish immersion program in Dade County, Florida, exemplifies the basis for such a decision: Despite changes in the staff development model, Beebe (1978) underscores the requests for similar programs. Accordingly, the decision-making role of product evaluation deals primarily with the recycling of programs.

It is obviously practical for the multicultural in-service planner to know whether his programmatic results are actually unpredictable consequences of outside influences, like new legislation or budget cuts. Recycling decisions depend on such knowledge as well as on the effectiveness of each part of the CIPP model applied to multicultural inservicing. Although the planner may select any means to make such an evaluation, Stufflebeam's (1973) evaluative design includes such components as the focusing of the evaluation; the collection, organization, analysis, and reporting of information; and the administration of the evaluation.

## Conclusion

Allowing for the sequential overlap of each applied stage of the CIPP evaluation model and its selected evaluation design, the multicultural in-service planner can organize and evaluate his workshops. The degree and stage of application of the CIPP approach should be a role geared for each situation, an approach which emphasizes that "Systems engineering provides an adaptation of systems thinking to the problem of developing effective in-service training systems in education"

300   *John Gordon White*

(Magliocca and Magliocca, 1978, p. 52). Comprehensive planning is, therefore, the key to in-service success.

# References

Baker, G. C. "The Role of the School in Transmitting the Culture of All Learners in a Free and Democratic Society." *Educational Leadership*, 36 (2): 134–138, November, 1978.
Banks, J. A. "The Implications of Multicultural Education for Teacher Education." Paper presented at the Leadership Training Institute in Teacher Education. American Association of Colleges for Teacher Education, Washington, D.C., April 1976.
Beebe, V. N. "Spanish Comes Alive on *la Isla Caribe*." *Phi Delta Kappan*, 60 (2): 95–98, October 1978.
Bennett, C. T. "The Preparation of Pre-service Secondary Social Studies Teachers in Multi-Ethnic Education." *High School Journal*, 54 (4): 232–237, October 1978.
Blaylock, E. V. "Article 3.3: California's Answer to Cultural Diversity in the Classroom." *Phi Delta Kappan*, 57(3): 203, November 1975.
Bronaugh, J. "The Multicultural Center: An Innovation In-Service Program." *Phi Delta Kappan*, 59 (3): 204–205, November 1977.
Cross, D. E. and J. Deslonde. "The Impact of Teacher In-Service Programs on Attitudes Toward Multicultural Education." *Educational Research Quarterly*, 2(4): 96–105, Winter 1978.
Davison, R. "The In-Service Response to Desegregated Schooling—Managing the Instructional Design Problem." *Urban Education*, 9(2): 149–150, July 1974.
Gay, G. "Viewing the Pluralistic Classroom as a Cultural Microcosm." *Education Research Quarterly*, 2(4): 45–59, Winter 1978.
Jensen, H. C. and A. C. Hopewell. "Inservice on Minority History, Culture, and Problems: One District's Progress Report." *California Journal of Teacher Education*, 2(5): 78–96, Summer 1975.
Jones, R. M., Jr. "The Effect of In-Service Training on the Performance and Attitudes of Inner-City Teachers." Unpublished doctoral dissertation. University of Southern California, 1972.
Krug, M. M. "Cultural Pluralism—Its Origins and Aftermath." *The Journal of Teacher Education*, 28(3), 5–9, June 1977.
Leiter, M. and M. Cooper. "How Teacher Unionists View In-Service Education." *Teachers College Record*, 80(1): 107–125, September 1978.
Magliocca, L. A. and J. A. Magliocca. "A Systems Approach to In-Service Education." *Viewpoints in Teaching and Learning*, 54(4): 41–54, October 1978.
Ovando, C. J. "Female and Male Latino College Aspirations: The Implications for Pluralistic Education." *Educational Research Quarterly*, 2(4): 106–122, Winter 1978.
Pacheco, A. "Cultural Pluralism: A Philosophical Analysis." *The Journal of Teacher Education*, 28 (3): 16–20, June 1977.
Skjerwold, C. K. "Ethnic Cultural Center Helps to Train Teachers." *Momentum*, 6(3): 55–58, October 1975.
Stufflebeam, D. L. "An Introduction to the PDK Book. Educational Evaluation and Decision Making." In B.R. Worthern and J.R. Sanders, eds. *Educational Evaluation: Theory and Practice*. Belmont, California: Wadsworth Publishing Co., 1973.
Valverde, L. A. "Leadership Compatible with Multicultural Community Schools." *Educational Leadership*, 33(5): 344–347, 1976.
Webster, W. J. "Sensible School District Evaluation." Paper presented at the AREA Evaluation Conference, San Francisco, September 1977, p. 1.
Worthern, B. R. and J. R. Sanders, eds. "Stufflebeam's Model: An Application." *Educational Evaluation: Theory and Practice*. Belmont, California: Wadsworth Publishing Co., 1973.

# CHAPTER 24

# A TRAINING PROGRAM IN ASIAN-AMERICAN CULTURE FOR ELEMENTARY SCHOOL TEACHERS* (1983)

*Esther Lee Yao*

## Nature of the project

The purpose of this project was to develop an awareness and understanding of the ethnic heritage of Asian-Americans in elementary school teachers. This project focused on a training program in ethnic studies for elementary school teachers in the southeastern counties of Texas. It was felt that most elementary school teachers needed to develop multicultural cognitive and affective teaching skills which would enable them to apply the newly gained competency in the classroom, in the local school districts, and in their interrelationships with all peoples. These trained teachers were "seed" teachers from whom a richer, goal-oriented, educated group would grow to form a nucleus of educators in and around Houston to strengthen teaching about our multiracial population.

A sequence of four graduate courses (12 credit hours over two semesters) was offered to twenty carefully screened elementary school teachers from seventeen school districts around Houston during the academic year of 1978. Most of these individuals applied these course offerings toward a master's degree (M.S.) with an emphasis in Multicultural Education at the University of Houston at Clear Lake City. The advisory council, required by the funding agency (DHEW) as part of the project, indicated that there was strong, committed interest and joint cooperation from the school districts in support of this proposed training program.

Due to the diverse content of ethnic studies, this one-year training program had its scope narrowed to specifically Asian-American ethnic heritages and their influences in the United States. The Asian culture merely served as a content area, while the methodology of teaching in ethnic heritage studies presented in this project was designed to reach all multiethnic audience.

A unique characteristic of this project was the involvement of public school administrators, elementary school teachers, parents with Asian-American ethnic backgrounds, and University faculty members with diverse expertise.

## Rationale behind this project

Despite the fact that the "melting pot" concept now is defunct from its earlier position (Banks, 1975) and that ethnic cultures are endemic in the American society, today many Americans still consciously or subconsciously believe that ethnic groups should and will eventually abandon their unique cultural components and assimilate those characteristics of Anglo-Americans, the dominant cultural group.

Social science specialists in ethnic relations have documented abundantly the fact that ethnicity and ethnic cultures are integral parts of our social system and that these aspect of American life are exceedingly resistant to change or eradication (Gordon, 1964). As Glazer and Moynihan (1970) have perceptively stated, ethnicity "is fixed deep in American life generally, the specific pattern of ethnic differentiation, however, in every generation is created by specific events" (p. 291).

Furthermore, ethnicity is a salient part of the American social order. A sophisticated understanding of our society cannot be grasped unless the separate ethnic communities (which exist regionally as well as socially) that constitute American society are seriously analyzed from the perspectives of the various social sciences and the humanities.

The following statements quoted from *Minorities: U.S.A.* succinctly point out the importance and the value of ethnic studies to both the majority and minority groups.

> Minority group problems are national problems. They affect all Americans, the majority as well as the minorities. Equal treatment for all is a key part of the American dream of a better future. It can make it possible for the members of minorities to and greatly to their country's life. (Finkelstein, Sandifer & Wright, 1971, p. ix).

Because ethnicity is a salient part of our social system, it is essential that students master the facts, concepts, generalizations, and theories needed to understand and interpret events which are related to intergroup and intragroup interaction and tensions. In recent years, educators have begun to realize the importance of ethnicity to American society and the need to help student develop more sophisticated understandings of the diverse ethnic groups that make up America and have a greater tolerance and acceptance of cultural differences. Responding largely to student demands and community pressure groups, educational institutions at all levels have made some attempts to put more information about ethnic groups into the social studies, language arts, and humanities curricula.

## Multicultural education at the University of Houston at Clear Lake City

In the State of Texas, the implications of multicultural education have been strongly recognized and emphasized by the Texas Education Agency (TEA) since 1971. According to a recent requirement from TEA, multicultural education will be a major task and educational issue. The understanding of the multicultural society and the children who come from various cultural backgrounds is particularly stressed by this organization.

In order to meet the multicultural requirements of TEA, University of Houston/Clear Lake City (UH/CLC) has developed a series of courses to be offered for graduate students who are working on their master's degrees as well as their educational certificates. Each course has its unique role as one of the required courses leading to teaching certification, endorsement, and/or master's degree in certain areas. For instance, **Educ. 5031: Acculturation through Education** is one of the suggested courses for all educational master's degrees, while **Educ. 5731: Children from Culturally Different Backgrounds** is required for the diagnostic teaching endorsement and supervision certificate.

Until 1977, only **Educ. 5031: Acculturation through Education** had been offered to graduate students on a regular basis. Meanwhile, a master's degree program with emphasis in multicultural education was in process. Now, the program has been developed and brochures of this program are available upon request.

The courses listed in the UH/CLC catalog for an M.S. in multicultural education provide a wide range of ethnic and cultural studies. The scope and content of these courses serve as a broad foundation for improving graduate students' value judgments and their competency in curriculum planning in teaching multicultural education. Nearly all graduate students enrolled in the program of Professional Education at the University are full-time public-school teachers who have great influence upon their classroom pupils while they are teaching and learning about multiethnic objectives. They represent the most important variable in the ethnic studies program, since their attitudes toward ethnic studies and ethnic cultures are crucial. Many teachers, especially Anglo-American teachers, may fear teaching ethnic content, particularly if their classes include ethnic minorities. Giving a teacher the opportunity to express his or her feelings and perceptions in graduate study, then comparing these developing sensitivities with the attitudes of other teachers and clarifying his or her racial feelings is necessary to the development of an understanding of various ethnic minorities.

Teaching about ethnic content is legitimate and acceptable in public schools today. Yet, integrating ethnic content into regular school curricula demands professional training. Sensitive and knowledgeable teachers may not be able to present ethnic material in terms of structure, sequencing, selection and emphasis, instructional tools, and methods used unless they are trained in methodology. The best approach to training teachers is not through inservice training, but in the university setting.

With qualified teachers and well planned ethnic curriculum content, school children can benefit greatly from ethnic studies as Banks (1975) indicates:

> Ethnic studies will teach them that there are other ways of living and being, and that to be racially and ethnically different does not mean that one is inferior or superior. More humanistic views of other cultures are imperative within our increasingly interdependent and ethnically polarized world. Humanistic views of other groups and cultures may help to create the kind of racial and ethnic harmony that our society must have to survive in the twenty-first century. (p. 460)

## Needs in studying Asian-Americans: Regional and national

The demands for new instructional materials and programs for ethnic minorities have not been widely met. In some regions and school districts in the United States, other ethnic minorities such as Chicanos and black Americans exceed the number of Anglo-Americans in the school population. In these districts, educators have been more sensitive to the need for programs which deal with these minorities. Yet, Asian-Americans, one of America's most diverse and interesting ethnic groups, are rarely systematically studied in the elementary and high school grades nationwide. One of the major reasons is the lack of knowledge by the public school teacher in understanding and becoming aware of the ethnic background of the Asian-American, and applying this knowledge to the school program.

In the history of Asian immigrants to the U.S., Japanese-Americans, Chinese-Americans, and Filipino-Americans have been the predominant subgroups since 1820. A series of Congressional actions such as the Gentlemen's Agreement between the U.S. and Japan in 1907–1908, the Chinese Exclusion Act of 1882, and the Tydings and McDuffie Act of 1934 limiting Filipino immigrants has restricted the Asian immigrants to the U.S. until 1968.

In 1965, Congress passed the Immigration Act that eliminated quotas based on national origins and instituted fair immigration policies. This act became effective in 1968. Since then, the number of Asian immigrants to the U.S. has increased substantially (U.S. Immigration and Naturalization Service, 1970–1979). In 1973, 23 percent of the total immigrants came from Europe, 31 percent from Asia, 45 percent from Canada and South America, and one percent from other regions. Compared to other groups, Asian immigrants are the only group that has had sharp increase since 1970. Unfortunately, there is no complete data available regarding the Vietnamese refugees after the fall of South Vienam of 1975. In the 1960s, the number of Oriental-Americans increased more than 55 percent while the entire U.S. population increased by 13.3 percent (U.S. Bureau of Census, 1970). On Census Day, 1970, the number of Japanese-Americans had increased 27 percent, the number of Chinese-Americans had increased 83 percent, and the number of Filipino-Americans had increased 95 percent over 1960 figures.

The majority of the Oriental American have remained a part of the nation's urban population. Today, 1.2 million—90 percent of the total—live in urban areas. In the greater Houston area, the population of Asian-American has also grown rapidly during the past decade. There were 2,731 Oriental Americans in 1960 and 11,949 in 1970 (Standard Metropolitan Census data, 1970). Since 1970, due to the Vietnam Conflict, there has been an increase of 46.6 percent of Oriental Americans in the Houston area (Texas Employment Manpower Commission, 1977).

Because of the statistical figures on the increasing population of Asian-Americans, their struggles in the U.S. cannot be overlooked. Amy Uyematsu indicates the following direction.

> Asian Americans can no longer afford to watch the black-and-white struggle from the sidelines. They have their own cause to fight, since they are also victims—with less visible scars of . . . white institutionalized racism. A yellow movement has been set into motion by the black power movement. Addressing itself to the unique problems of the Asian Americans, this "yellow power" movement is relevant to the black power movement in that both are part of the Third World strugglers to liberate all colored people. (Banks, 1975, p. 319).

Despite the fact that Japanese-Americans and Chinese-Americans have achieved high educational and economic mobility, such traditional measures of success are misleading and divert attention from the serious psychological and social problems that Asian-Americans still experience in American life because of their cultural characteristics. The economic mobility of Asian-Americans, and the factors which can explain it, could be researched in ethnic heritage studies. However, when Asian-Americans are studied, the focus should be on their values, identity, ethnic institutions, histories, and cultures, and not only on their economic success. Focusing on the economic and educational attainments of any ethnic group is much too narrow and will fail in help students fully understand

and appreciate the complex nature of any ethnic group's experience and culture. Chun-Hoon (1973), in commenting on aspects of the Asian-American life that should be included in the school curriculum, writes:

> There needs ... to be a recognition of Asian-American personalities in the teaching of the Asian-American experience so that there can be some discovery of the common human dimension shared by Asian and Americans alike. (p. 136)

In 1980 there were more than 3.26 million Asian-Americans in the United States (U.S. Bureau of Census, 1981) out of total national population of 204 million people. Oriental-Americans consist of many ethnic groups with many similarities and diversities. The attitudes, values, and ethnic institutions often differ within Japanese-American, Chinese-American, and Filipine-American communities. Nevertheless, Asian-Americans have had some similar experiences in the United States.

Because of their tremendous diversity, similarities and unique life experiences in the U.S., the study of Asian-Americans can greatly help elementary pupils increase the knowledge of their own ethnic heritage and develop respect for cultural differences. Thus, this training program was designed primarily to help equip classroom teachers with the information, strategies, and materials needed to help their students to become more ethnically aware and, consequently, more tolerant of cultural differences.

## Objective of the program

This training program has a twofold purpose as its goal. First, in terms of the cognitive domain, the selected elementary school teachers are expected to become knowledgeable of various diverse Oriental-American cultures, and become competent in curriculum planning of ethnic studies. The second purpose is in the affective domain. Through this training program, it is believed that the elementary school teachers' attitudes toward teaching ethnic studies and their attitudes toward Oriental-American ethnic groups will be positively improved. The overall goal is the implementation of the curriculum plan in the public school at the completion of this training program.

The specific educational objectives are stated as follows:

1   To help trainees clarify feelings about their own ethnicity and about the concept of cultural pluralism and related social issues
2   To provide information about ethnicity and the process through which ethnic groups adapt and change
3   To present the implications of multiculturalism for education in American society
4   To explore the characteristics of Oriental-Americans and their cultural backgrounds which affect their school-age children
5   To develop the skills in curriculum planning of ethnic studies, particularly of Oriental-American cultures
6   To gain innovative instructional methodology to be incorporated into the learner's background and scholastic work.

The more explicit objectives are:

1   To make known the fact that all contributing cultures in the U.S. make the interrelationships among them more crucial and multicultural understanding more imperative
2   To appreciate and accept the various cultures represented by school children through effective interpersonal communication with persons of diverse ethnic backgrounds—students, teachers, parents—especially those of Oriental-American backgrounds
3   To realize that multicultural education is the structuring of educational priorities, commitments, and processes in order to reflect the reality of cultural pluralism as a fact of life in the U.S.A.

## Contents of the program

There were twenty elementary school teachers participating in this training program. The selection of these teachers was competitive. Four major factors were considered during this screening process. First, the trainees for this program were to represent various school districts in different localities. Second, selected trainees were to have teaching experiences at several grade levels. Third, upon completion of this program the trainees were to be willing to share their experiences with their colleagues and administrators. Finally, the trainees were to possess unique cultural backgrounds and cultural experiences such as traveling, teaching overseas, etc. The final twenty trainees chosen consisted of two males and eighteen females and represented fourteen school districts. The ethnic composition of the group was four Hispanic-American, two Black, one Chinese, one Filipino, two German, four Irish, one Italian and five of British ancestry.

Regardless of their different school districts or their ethnic and cultural backgrounds, this group of trainees worked very closely in a cooperative and relaxed atmosphere. They were all highly motivated and interested in the materials presented by the instructors, Drs. Esther Lee Yao and Philip J. Lanasa. Classes often ran overtime. During the beginning of the semester, they even prepared and brought into class the kinds of food eaten by the ethnic group which was covered by the instructor on that night. However, such practice was "terminated" at the request of the instructor on the grounds of gaining too much weight!

During the two-semester training program, participants were required to take four graduate courses entitled Acculturation through Education, Education of the Culturally Different Learner, Curricular Needs of Culturally Different Students, and Children from Culturally Different Backgrounds. The outline of these four courses is presented as follows:

### Course one: Education 5031: Acculturation through Education (1st semester)

1   Historical studies of various ethnic groups in our American society
    (a)  Analysis and identification of the individual's ethnicity
    (b)  Early experiences of migration
    (c)  Problems encountered during assimilation and accommodation to the dominant society
    (d)  Process of acculturation
    (e)  The cultural contributions of diverse ethnic groups to American society.

2  Implication for teaching and for development of and emphasis on multicultural education
   (a) Educational opportunities in the U.S.
   (b) Socioeconomic status in America
   (c) Lifestyle in this land
   (d) Gaps among ethnic groups as a result of lacking mutual understanding
3  Creation of a teaching module (unit of study)
   (a) Philosophy development
   (b) Needs assessment of community and school
   (c) Behavioral objectives identified in cognitive, affective, and psycho-motor domain
   (d) Teacher-made and commercially available materials incorporated in module development

## Course two: Education 5032: Education of the Culturally Different Learner (1st semester)

1  Focus on Oriental cultural backgrounds
   (a) Historical ties among all oriental nations
   (b) Traditional cultures:
       family relations and structures
       child rearing techniques
       value systems
       religions
       languages and lifestyle
2  First generation immigrants and their descendants in the U.S.A.
   (a) Social adjustment
   (b) Financial conditions and establishments
   (c) Physical environments
   (d) Generation conflicts
3  Emotional conditions and needs of Oriental-American children
4  Different teaching strategies applied to Oriental-American children
   (a) Learning activities
   (b) Teaching materials
   (c) Teaching methods
   (d) Interpersonal relationships between teacher and students

## Course three: Education 5033: Curricular Needs Culturally Different Students (2nd semester)

1  Curriculum planning of ethnic heritage studies
   (a) The reality of cultural pluralism in classrooms
   (b) The consideration of learners' multicultural backgrounds
   (c) Unique learning process of culturally "exceptional" learners:
       • Aspects of learning: content learning, problem solving, and critical thinking
       • Motivation in learning
       • Learning conditions
       • Learning styles

- Learning abilities
(d) Steps in curriculum development of Oriental-American cultures:
    - Objectives of the curriculum
    - Content of the curriculum
    - Evaluation of the curriculum
2   Development of activities guide for use in public schools

## Course four: Education 5731: Children from Culturally Different Backgrounds (2nd semester)

1   Instructional methodology based on the developed curriculum
(a) Effective interpersonal communication among teacher, students, and parents, value clarifications and dynamics in the elementary classroom
    - Teacher's attitude toward parents and children
    - Involvement of all parents and children
    - Verbal and non-verbal expressions to parents and children
    - Daily self-evaluation in teacher's attitude
(b) Different teaching strategies applied to non-Oriental-American children
    - Learning activities
    - Teaching materials
    - Teaching methods
(c) Design and develop a teacher's handbook

The instructional methods used in this training program included lecture, group discussion, field trips, simulation games, class demonstration, panel discussion, resource persons, and presentation of slides and films. Students also had opportunities for large group involvement and also for small group interaction when several learning centers were set up by the students. During the first semester, six panel discussions presented by local resource persons were recorded on video tapes. The resource persons were invited by the students and represented the ethnic group during each discussion on Asian-Americans. The size of the panels ranged from three to six people. Their residential locality and educational and occupational backgrounds varied within each ethnic group. In other words, there were resource persons with doctoral degrees as well as those with only a grade school education. Each student was also required to develop one curriculum module which could be adapted by the trainee's classroom pupils. The designed modules consisted of a great variety of audio-visual teaching materials which reflected Asian-American cultural heritages. Based upon those modules, an activities book was developed the following spring semester.

The spring semester began with a series of celebrations of the Chinese Lunar New Year. First, the trainees participated in the one-day Chinese Cultural Festival sponsored by UH/CLC Chinese Student Organization. They were not only in charge of part of the program but also provided technical assistance to the art performance in the evening. This was well-received by the public and it created a cultural exchange at the regional level. Two local TV stations (ABC and CBS affiliates) provided regional coverage of this event. Two bilingual trainees from a local school district were responsible for a special program on the celebration of the Lunar New Year at the magnet center of an elementary school. The New Year's celebration was concluded with a potluck dinner at the home of the project director. All trainees were asked to prepare an oriental dish. A game of cross-cultural body language was played for entertainment following the dinner.

The trainees' major tasks for the spring semester were to instruct students using the developed materials and to prepare an activities handbook and a teachers' handbook. *A Handbook of Activities and Resources for Teaching about Asian-Americans in the Elementary School* was edited by Dr. Philip J. Lanasa, co-director of the project and photocopied by Ginn Custom Publishing Company. Copies of this handbook are available at the UH/CLC bookstore. *Teacher's Handbook for Teaching and Working with Oriental Students and Their Parents*, edited by Dr. Esther Lee Yao, has been included in ERIC (ED 187 095, 1979).

Asian-American EXPO 1979, an inservice workshop held on May 5, was the most stimulating event of this project. The contents of the workshop included twenty activity centers for cultural display, prepared and constructed by all train-ees, and three classroom sessions presented by the trainees on a rotating schedule. The cultural display centered on six regions: Japan, Korea, China, Southeast Asia, East India, and the Philippines. The display contained teaching modules, teacher made audio-visual materials, artifacts, and musical instruments. Three sessions of classroom presentations by trainees were made on a rotating basis. Topics of the classroom presentations were (1) the history/heritage of the six regions: differ-ences and similarities; (2) problems of Asian-American school children and their parents and how to work with them in the public school setting; and (3) curric-ulum design for Asian-American ethnic studies, including theory, methodology, and process.

## Evaluation of the training program

The success of this proposed training program for elementary school teachers was evaluated from two perspectives. Since the objectives of this program took both cognitive and affective domains into consideration, evaluation was made in these two areas.

The knowledge gained by the trainees in ethnic studies and curriculum plan-ning was determined by the difference of pre- and post-assessments. A Cognitive Test (CT) was constructed by Drs. Esther Lee Yao and Philip J. Lanasa based on the 12-credit-hour course content and given to the participants prior to course instruction. The CT was administered at the end of the first semester and upon completion of the 12-credit hour course in the spring semester as post-assessment. The same procedure was used for an Attitude Inventory (AI) which measured the changes in trainees' attitudes toward ethnic groups and teaching ethnic studies.

The t statistical analysis was applied to determine the gained knowledge and changing attitude of the trainees. The difference of CT between the pretest taken in September 1978 and the posttest taken in April 1979 was found significant at the .01 level with df=19 (t=11.30). The AI also demonstrated significant change (t=7.92) between September 1978 and April 1979.

The trainees' accomplishments are reflected not only by their scores on pre- and posttest, but also in the workshop on May 5 which was completely designed and executed by them. They were able to make use of the knowledge they had gained throughout the training project. They felt confident in sharing their know-ledge and experience with other school teachers during the inservice workshop. As compared with their colleagues not in the program, they found they were much more knowledgeable about Asian-American culture and heritage.

In addition to the achievement of the trainees, the performance of the instructors was also evaluated by the trainees. As required by the University, all instructors are rated by their students based upon their teaching efficiency and course evaluation. Both instructors were highly praised by the trainees in the program.

Such rewarding feelings and experiences did not end with the training project. Evidence that the interpersonal relationships, established and enjoyed during the project period, extended beyond the training project was shown when a potluck dinner was given by the entire group in honor of a trainee who was moving to California.

## Note

\*   This paper was presented at the Annual Meeting of the Southwest Educational Research Association, Dallas, Texas, January 28–31, 1981.

## References

Banks, J. A. Teaching strategies for ethnic studies. Boston Allyn and Bacon, 1975.

Chun-Hoon, L. K. Teaching the Asian-American experience. In J. A. Banks (Ed.), Teaching ethnic studies. Concept and strategies. Washington, DC: National Council for the Social Studies 43rd Yearbook, 1973.

Dunfee, M. Ethnic modification of the curriculum. Washington, DC: Association for Supervision and Curriculum Development, 1969.

Finkelstein, M., Sandifer, J. A. & Wright, E. S. Minorities, U.S.A. New York: Globe Book Company, 1971.

Glazer, N. & Moynihan, D. P. Beyond the melting pot: The Negroes, Puerto Ricans, Jews, Italians and Irish of New York City. Cambridge, MA: M.I.T. Press, 1970.

Gordon, M. M. Assimilation in American life: The role of race, religion, and national origins. New York: Oxford Book Company, 1964.

La Gumina, S. J. & Gavaioli, F. J. The ethnic dimension American society. Boston: Holbrook Press, Inc., 1974.

Lyman, S. M. Chinese Americans. New York: Random House, 1974.

Melendy, H. B. The Oriental American. Boston: Twayne Publishers, Inc., 1972.

Petersen, W. Japanese Americans. New York: Random House, 1971.

U.S. Bureau of the Census. Statistical abstract of the U.S.. Washington, DC: U.S. Government Printing Office, 1970.

U.S. Bureau of the Census. Statistical abstract of the U.S. Washington, DC: U.S. Government Printing Office, 1975.

U.S. Bureau of the Census. Statistical abstract of the U.S. Washington, DC: U.S. Government Printing Office, 1981.

U.S. Bureau of the Census. We, the Asian Americans. Washington, DC: U.S. Government Printing Office, 1973.

U.S. Immigration and Naturalization Service. Annual reports from 1970–1979. Washington, DC: U.S. Government Printing Office, 1979.

**PART 5**

# REFLECTIONS OF PRAXIS

# CHAPTER 25

# COMMUNITY INVOLVEMENT COMPONENTS IN CULTURALLY-ORIENTED TEACHER PREPARATION (1982)

*James M. Mahan*

NCATE papers (1977) emphasize the importance of practica and other field experiences in effective multicultural teacher preparation. Saville-Troike (1978) contends that cultural preparation of teachers should include trips into, and involvement with, various cultural and economic communities. Toelken (1976), focusing upon a specific cultural group, emphasizes how much can be learned if one looks thoughtfully at the Navajo world while actually living in a Navajo community.

For most preservice teachers, the student teaching assignment is the longest and most intense contact with teaching reality. However, this "reality" is often limited in scope to contact with pupils, teachers, principals, and a few parents who attend Parent Teacher Organization functions or who come to school for a conference over pupil achievement or deportment. There is a "community world" beyond the walls of the school shaped by economic, social, political, religious, cultural, and other forces too often unknown to the student teacher. One way to acquaint preservice teachers with the characteristics, values, needs, and achievements of the community which sponsors and supports the school is to supplement student teaching placements with required, non-school, community involvement assignments.

The objectives of this paper are to:

(a) identify some replicable community and community agency assignments currently functioning as integral parts of a student teaching semester.
(b) present longitudinal data reflecting participant acceptance in, reaction to, and evaluation of, community involvement assignments.
(c) illustrate the social and professional impact of community experiences upon student teachers as reflected in their subjective writings.
(d) encourage teacher educators to consider the inclusion of community assignments in all types of teacher preparation programs.

## Background

Indiana University, for nine consecutive years, has implemented an American Indian Reservation Project, a Hispanic Community Project, and an Urban Project. Each preservice participant completes a prerequisite course focusing upon the target cultural group before reporting for a sixteen to seventeen week assignment in the cultural community. In addition to fulfilling student teaching requirements by instructing Native American, Hispanic, or black students, the project participants must average at least fifteen hours per week in the performance of nonschool teaching work in the local community. They are to meet and work directly with people from various walks of life and become acquainted with "how a living is made" in that community.

Some of the assigned work is highly structured. For example, Hispanic and Urban Project participants are placed formally for forty hour work weeks in community social service agencies during the first five weeks of their student teaching semester. In week six, after classroom student teaching duties are assumed, the participants are still required to spend fifteen supplementary hours in a variety of less formal community (non-school) learning activities. The Reservation Project participants are not placed formally in social service agencies. There are fewer agencies on the Navajo and Hopi Reservations plus distances between agencies and living places preclude the agency assignments. However, a variety of formal and informal non-school activities totaling at least fifteen hours of non-teaching, community involvement per week are required on the Reservations.

## Feasible community involvement activities

A wide assortment of community activities in which preservice teachers can participate have emerged in Indianapolis, the lower Rio Grande Valley of Texas, in Arizona-Mexico border towns, and on the Navajo and Hopi Reservations. Similar opportunities exist in other locales, of course. List I presents some of the many viable and worthwhile activities engaged in over the years. This listing can

*List I*  Community Activities Included in a Student Teaching Semester

| *Hispanic and Urban Projects* | *Indian Reservation Project* |
|---|---|
| • Community agency internship—5 weeks | • Dormitory program assistant |
| • Aide in adult education—twice a week | • Student in adult education |
| • School board meeting attendance | • School board meeting attendance |
| • Town council meeting attendance | • Chapter House meeting attendance |
| • Attendance at cultural speeches/rallies | • Girl/Boy Scout assistant |
| • Festival preparation/attendance | • Bus route riding |
| • Interviews with community officials | • In-depth talk with adults |
| • Assisting migrant farm workers in the fields | • Visits to cultural centers |
| • In-depth talk with adults | • Attendance at ceremonials |
| • Visits to cultural centers | • Observation of jewelers/weavers |
| • Attendance at cultural ceremonies | • Dining at home of member of target cultural group |
| • Dining at home of member of cultural group | • Attendance at cultural fairs |
| • Volunteer church/civic work | • Assisting with sheepherding |
| • Attendance/communication at cultural fairs | • Babysitting for local families |
| • Tours of local industries | • Recreation program assistant |
| • Riding school bus routes | • Teaching/performing for community clubs/churches |

be expanded by teacher educators who are currently requiring community work/ learning experiences, and can be used as a starting point by those who desire to initiate community involvement components. List II indicates the functions of diverse social service agencies in which directors have been very willing to accept preservice teachers for a five week internship.

## Why require community involvement?

"What do you teach?" "I teach children, not a particular subject." This question and its answer are cliches in educational conversation. One must know a "subject" in order to teach it. Likewise, one must know "children" in order to teach "children." There is much to learn about children in any community—much that affects their attitude toward school, determines what they will value and what they will reject, how they will use their non-school time, what future goals they deem feasible to seek, how they will react to classroom discipline, etc. Not everything can be learned about children from books. Parents, employment or unemployment, the home, neighborhood peers, tradition, physical needs, cultural values are all among the forces that shape a child's perception of, and involvement with, classroom teaching. Cultural identity plays an important part in how people view and react to the world, how they view themselves, and how they learn. It is essential that teachers serving a different cultural group than their own become highly knowledgeable concerning the culture, conditions, and aspirations of the people they teach—for therein lies the key to understanding and communicating. Since the classroom is a contained, controlled environment where so many forces important to the learner are often hidden from, or unknown to, the teacher; the teacher needs to "go out there" and discover the non-school learnings of the child. Community folk and community events can be powerful teachers of teachers— can help the young teacher to understand where community children "are at" and why. Sullivan (1974) while discussing multicultural teacher preparation states that both schools and the cultural community must be used to extend the university classroom. Hilliard (1974) points out that language courses and a culture course are not sufficient for teacher candidates; interactions with the people to be taught are the grist for preservice teacher learning. Community involvement is required in the Indian Reservation, Hispanic Community, and Urban Projects so that the student teachers will directly experience some of the life and culture of

*List II* Types of Community Agency Activities Utilized

| | |
|---|---|
| Rural Legal Aid | Juvenile detention center training |
| Family planning | Employment/manpower projects |
| Child adoption | Meals-on-wheels programs |
| Urban League | Library outreach programs |
| City development projects | Door-to-door survey by newspaper |
| Food stamps | Salvation Army projects |
| Emergency housing | Headstart |
| Senior Citizen programs | Association for the Blind projects |
| Community health | Migrant clinic |
| Family guidance and counseling | Parental liaison out of central school office |
| Migrant council program | |
| Mayor's office civic projects | |

their students and parents, and, hopefully, modify curriculum and instructional procedures to fit community realities and aspirations.

## Participant evaluation of community involvement requirements

Do preservice teachers acknowledge that they benefit from community involve requirements and enjoy completing them? Cultural involvement/synthesis reports are submitted eight times per semester (biweekly) by Indian Reservation and Hispanic Community Project participants and five times per semester by Urban Project participants. As a part of each cultural report, the participants evaluate certain

*List III* Some Specific Reasons for Required Community Involvement for Student Teachers

---

- to develop knowledge of the housing patterns and conditions in the community
- to foster knowledge of employment/unemployment patterns in the community
- to acquaint the student teacher with social sub-groups—who interacts with whom
- to introduce the student teacher to family structure and family activities
- to develop knowledge of the major social needs in the community and current remedies for those needs
- to facilitate discovery of the decision-makers and power-brokers in the community
- to expose the student teacher to lay person attitudes towards schools and teachers (as opposed to the expectations of educators)
- to provide student teachers with opportunities to assess the responsiveness or unresponsiveness of economic, educational, political, and social institutions to the needs of the people of the community
- to provide student teachers with opportunities to assess the responsiveness or unresponsiveness of economic, educational, political, and social institutions to the needs of the people of the community
- to change the self-concept of the student teacher from "a visitor in town" to "an informed resident of the community"
- to acquaint the student teacher with cultural values and life styles important to the community
- to make it possible for the student teacher to have friends, contacts, and some "street savvy" *before* taking responsibility for a classroom
- to make the student teacher more aware of supplementary instructional resources—speakers, agencies, libraries, museums, social welfare projects, films, etc.
- to acquaint student teachers with youth play patterns, work activities, peer groups, communication styles, etc.
- to promote direct observation of cultural behavior thereby enhancing cultural understanding
- to provide student teachers with a reality base from which to make their classroom instruction more culturally relevant
- to expose teachers to the daily use and relative importance of dominant languages and second languages—and related language problems
- to make it possible for a teacher training institution to involve well qualified, non-certified personnel in the preparation of preservice teachers

---

aspects of the community involvement assignments. The survey items and tabular data that follow are based on the multiple responses each semester of all the project participants over a nine year period. The mean scores presented indicate that preservice teachers do accept community assignments, do benefit from them, are accepted into them by the local people, and do enjoy and value the experiences.

Tables 25.1 and 25.2 reveal positive evaluations by the student teachers of community involvement feasibility and of the outcomes of community involvement. The Reservation and Hispanic Project participants tend to be more positive about their community experiences than do the Urban Project participants. It should be noted that the Urban Project participants were not required to live in the urban community. Nightly they journeyed home to suburbia or wherever. Thus opportunities to informally socialize with urban Blacks were greatly reduced. The other two groups of participants lived at all times with Native American or Hispanic people, did not commute from anywhere, and regularly

*Survey I* Items Relating to the Feasibility of Community Involvement Components in Culturally-Oriented Teacher Preparation

---

(a) Is it truly possible to do meaningful community work at your placement site?
    seems impossible  1  2  3  4  5  6  7  very possible

(b) Does your community work put you in contact with adults from the target cultural group?
    promotes no contact  1  2  3  4  5  6  7  promotes extensive contact

(c) Do you feel accepted, wanted, and appreciated in your placement community?
    feel rejected  1  2  3  4  5  6  7  feel very accepted

(d) How valuable to you are these community involvement experiences?
    worthless  1  2  3  4  5  6  7  valuable

---

*Survey II* Items Relating to the Feasibility of Community Involvement Components in Culturally-Oriented Teacher Preparation

---

(a) How applicable are your community involvement assignments to the act of classroom teaching?
    not applicable  1  2  3  4  5  6  7  very applicable

(b) Will your community involvement better prepare you to promote cultural pluralism in the classroom?
    will not help  1  2  3  4  5  6  7  will help greatly

(c) How helpful are your community involvement assignments in promoting cultural understanding?
    no help  1  2  3  4  5  6  7  very helpful

(d) How valuable are your community involvement activities in facilitating friendship-making?
    of no value  1  2  3  4  5  6  7  of great value

(e) How much are you enjoying your community involvement assignments?
    not enjoying  1  2  3  4  5  6  7  enjoying thoroughly

---

*Table 25.1* Mean scores: Community involvement feasibility items

| Time span | Item | Project group | | | | | |
|---|---|---|---|---|---|---|---|
| | | Native American | | Hispanic | | Urban | |
| | | X | N | X | N | X | N |
| 9/72–5/75 | a feasible work | 5.4 | | 5.8 | | 5.8 | |
| | b adult contact | 4.9 | 78 | 6.1 | 41 | 5.6 | 21 |
| | c personal acceptance | 5.6 | | 5.8 | | 5.7 | |
| | d value | 6.2 | | 6.0 | | 5.8 | |
| 9/75–5/78 | a feasible work | 6.2 | | 6.2 | | 5.9 | |
| | b adult contact | 5.8 | 65 | 6.4 | 57 | 5.4 | 53 |
| | c personal acceptance | 5.8 | | 6.4 | | 5.6 | |
| | d value | 6.7 | | 6.3 | | 5.4 | |
| 9/78–5/81 | a feasible work | 6.0 | | 6.1 | | 5.8 | |
| | b adult contact | 5.7 | 150 | 6.3 | 54 | 5.8 | 39 |
| | c personal acceptance | 5.9 | | 6.1 | | 5.8 | |
| | d value | 6.5 | | 6.4 | | 5.7 | |

*Notes:*
8 responses × 293 participants = 2344 raw scores per each item for Reservation Project
8 × 152 participants = 1216 raw scores per each item for Hispanic Project
5 × 113 participants = 565 raw scores per each item for Urban Project

engaged in the local social and cultural events. It should also be noted that mean evaluative scores on most items for the Reservation and Hispanic groups tended to be lower for the 1972–75 period than they were for the 1975–78 and 1978–81 periods. It takes some time for the faculty of cultural field projects to identify productive social service agencies, meet key people in the various cultural settings, compile lists of activities in which participants can engage, choose cultural readings and films that facilitate community work, prepare guidelines for interaction at each site, etc. In other words, as the faculty became more knowledgeable about each community, its agencies, its events, its leaders, etc., it made more structured placements in more productive activities and provided more advice about "how to get started upon arrival."

In addition to responding to Likert-scale type evaluative items, project participants wrote adjectives describing each of several aspects of their cultural community experience. Three adjectives were associated with each aspect every time a cultural involvement and synthesis report was submitted. Project staff members classify and tally these adjectives as "positive" or "negative" upon receipt of the reports and keep summaries from year-to-year. Table 25.3 clearly indicates that the student teachers do enjoy life and the people in their cultural placement site. The only exceptions are the slightly negative views of the Urban participants toward the geographical/physical characteristics of the inner city.

A major goal of a cultural immersion teacher preparation program can be to

*Table 25.2* Mean scores: Community involvement outcome items

| Time span | Item | Project group | | | | | |
|---|---|---|---|---|---|---|---|
| | | Native American | | Hispanic | | Urban | |
| | | X | N | X | N | X | N |
| 9/72–5/75 | a classroom application | 5.5 | | 5.6 | | 5.3 | |
| | b promotion of pluralism | 5.9 | | 5.8 | | 5.6 | |
| | c foster understanding | 6.5 | 78 | 6.1 | 41 | 5.6 | 21 |
| | d friendship conducive | 6.5 | | 5.9 | | 6.1 | |
| | e enjoyment | 6.3 | | 6.2 | | 5.3 | |
| 9/75–5/78 | a classroom application | 6.2 | | 5.7 | | 4.6 | |
| | b promotion of pluralism | 6.2 | | 6.4 | | 5.7 | |
| | c foster understanding | 6.3 | 65 | 6.3 | 57 | 5.3 | 53 |
| | d friendship conducive | 6.3 | | 6.6 | | 5.5 | |
| | e enjoyment | 6.6 | | 6.6 | | 5.4 | |
| 9/78–5/81 | a classroom application | 6.0 | | 5.6 | | 5.1 | |
| | b promotion of pluralism | 6.4 | | 6.1 | | 5.6 | |
| | c foster understanding | 6.5 | 150 | 6.5 | 57 | 5.5 | 39 |
| | d friendship conducive | 6.2 | | 6.3 | | 5.9 | |
| | e enjoyment | 6.6 | | 6.6 | | 5.2 | |

*Table 25.3* Adjectival evaluation by student teachers of aspects of community involvement experiences

| Project aspect | Percent of evaluative adjectives classified "positive" | | |
|---|---|---|---|
| | Native American (24 × 293 = 7032 responses) | Hispanic (24 × 152 = 3648 responses) | Urban (15 × 113 = 1695 responses) |
| Community involvement | 88% | 89% | no data |
| Contact with adults | 87% | 90% | 81% |
| Living conditions | 75% | 82% | 85%* |
| Geographical area | 83% | 84% | 48% |
| Social life | 86% | 88% | no data |

* Many of these student teachers lived in suburbia and commuted to their agencies and schools.

forge a few close friendships between a preservice teacher and members of a cultural group that the teacher had not previously known, understood, or been in contact within the past. Reservation and Hispanic Project participants eight times per semester responded to this survey question. "Please name any person (who is a member of the target cultural group) who knows you as a person, who cares about you, whom you consider a good friend, etc. You are not obligated to name someone each time – name only those persons you truly consider close friends."

*Table 25.4* Close friendships made with members of target cultural group during full semester in placement site

| | Average number of friends reported per participant | | | | | |
|---|---|---|---|---|---|---|
| Project group | 75–76 | 76–77 | 77–78 | 78–79 | 79–80 | 80–81 |
| Native American | 4.0 | 4.0 | 7.2 | 7.0 | 5.3 | 6.1 |
| Latino | 6.6 | 5.5 | 10.0 | 7.8 | 8.3 | 9.3 |

Table 25.4 reveals that project participants do become friends with several people from the target cultural group. Although the mean scores fluctuate annually, more friendships have been made in each project in the most recent years. It should be noted that the student teachers involved had no close Native American or Hispanic friends before they left campus for their cultural placement sites. Four or more close Native American or Hispanic friends is rather impressive— probably more than a great many inservice teachers in the nation can claim.

## Community people evaluate involvement of preservice teachers in the community

Project participants periodically list close friends made. Do these community friends really hold positive views of the student teacher? Between September, 1972 and May, 1975 each Hispanic Project participant averaged listing 6.2 close friendships formed. Surveys were mailed to about 250 of the Hispanic people so listed. Over 60% of the survey recipients responded. Table 25.5 summarizes the very positive attitudes these Hispanic community people held toward the preservice teachers as individuals and toward their involvement in community work. The data suggest that teacher educators and preservice teachers can optimistically

*Table 25.5* Response of community members to involvement of preservice teachers in community activities

| Survey question | Percent of highly positive responses |
|---|---|
| Respondents identifying themselves as Mexican-American | 91% |
| Respondents identifying the student teacher as a friend | 82% |
| Respondents stating they would still recognize the student in three years and would eagerly extend an invitation to reminisce | 91% |
| Respondents stating that people who want to be teachers should learn about the community by working with adults through community agencies | 94% |
| Respondents stating the student teachers were of valuable service to the community via the agency | 92% |
| Respondents stating the student teachers were helpful to them personally | 88% |

expect to find acceptance and appreciation in the offices and homes of a placement community.

> "I believe that all universities ought to have similar programs so that teachers might be better prepared, not only to deal with students of their own background and age, but to go out into communities completely different than their own."

## Representative participants comments on the value of community involvement

Project participants have open-ended opportunities to evaluate their total cultural project experience at the end of the placement semester. The following quotations from participants support the contention that community people and community work assignments can be potent teachers of young educators.

- Through my talks and work with community people here, I have gained a much greater insight into the problems pupils face when they are caught between the Navajo and Anglo culture.
- Here in the community, I have seen how important a child's culture really is. Teachers need to learn how other cultural groups live and how they express themselves in and out of school.
- I used to be very selfish, but the Navajo people I work with have somehow changed that part of me.
- Working in this community has taught me that I am capable of things I never thought I could do. My view of others has changed as well. You must accept people, no matter how different, as they are. You cannot change people to suit your standards.
- After several Navajo people have shared their points of view with me, I have changed some of my ideas on government, man, marriage, family ties and teaching.
- By learning to work with community problems here, I think I am now better able to work with any problem a student from any cultural group might face.
- My experiences in this community have helped me to understand what it means to be a "minority."
- The best way to learn out here is to get out of your room and volunteer your help to everyone. There is so much to learn from everyone no matter from what walk of life.
- After four months I am beginning to envision "what is possible" for this community. I better understand what is in the community and how various aspects relate – church, school, business, home, entertainment.
- Through my work I have developed a sensitivity toward the people's cultural heritage and an awareness of the current issues and problems affecting their daily lives.
- My assignments have enabled me to learn about home life, religious beliefs, arts and crafts, and personal relationships.
- The contact with the community people and agency staff made every situation a new learning experience.
- Through community work I came into direct contact with pressing social

problems and conditions that I previously considered to be vague and distant.

- My community involvement has allowed me to see the strength common values can bring to a community (unity and direction) and also the limitations they can inflict (seclusion and conservatism). As I asked people "why", "how", "when", "how often" I realized that I had never asked myself those big questions. My answers would make me different in their eyes, too.

- Working in another culture has helped me to recognize the commonalities in humans, and to identify those commonalities which should be focused upon in the classroom.

- My community experiences have convinced me that all people are atypical. Stereotypes are harmful at worst, useless at best, and unacceptable.

## Conclusion

Evaluation of data collected over nine years indicates that structured, semester-long field experiences in cultural communities produce a significant, positive response from preservice teachers. Participants report a high degree of personal acceptance by community members. They also indicate very positive attitudes in regard to their own ability to work effectively in such settings. In addition, student teachers report making valuable friendships among members of the target cultural group. During the years when community members were surveyed regarding their contact with preservice teachers, eighty-two percent confirmed that real friendships had been made. Ninety-two percent verified that the student teachers were performing a valuable service through their community work.

Perhaps most encouraging is the data related to classroom outcomes of community involvement experiences. To a high degree, preservice teachers report that their community work has direct application to teaching and that it will help them to promote cultural pluralism and understanding in their classrooms. Open-ended comments from participants suggest that many of them have gained remarkable insights into themselves and others as a direct result of their community experience.

It must be pointed out, however, that the positive outcomes obtained are the result of carefully planned preservice training and site development. Such cultural immersion practica cannot be fully successful without the investment of considerable time and effort. The personnel of the preservice training component should have background knowledge of the cultures of the target communities as well as experience teaching and working in culturally diverse settings. Staff time must be dedicated to research of the current literature related to the target cultures and to the preparation of preservice course content. Time must also be invested in planning preservice seminars and workshops. Travel to community sites is essential in order to develop contacts in community agencies and to identify community members who may serve as resource persons. Adequate provisions must also be made for on-site supervision of students while they are engaged in community work.

Like other effective educational efforts, community-based multicultural teacher training requires hard work and careful planning. Longitudinal data suggest that the rewards of this endeavor can be seen in participants who are prepared to carry their new self-knowledge and cultural understanding into their own families, social groups, classrooms, and communities.

# References

Hilliard, A. G. "Restructuring Teacher Education for Multicultural Imperatives." In W. A. Unter (Ed.) *Multicultural Education Through Competency Based Teacher Education.* American Association of Colleges for Teacher Education, Washington, D.C., 1974.

National Council for Accreditation of Teacher Education (NCATE), *Standards for the Accreditation of Teacher Education.* Washington, D.C., May, 1977.

Saville-Troike, Muriel. *A Guide to Culture in the Classroom.* National Clearinghouse for Bilingual Education. Rosslyn, Virginia, 1978.

Sullivan, A. R. "Cultural Competence and Confidence: A Quest for Effective Teaching in a Pluralistic Society." In W. H. Hunter (Ed.), *Multicultural Education Through Competency Based Teacher Education.* American Association of Colleges for Teacher Education, Washington, D.C., 1974.

Toelkin, Barre. "Seeing With a Native Eye: How Many Sheep Will It Hold?" in Walter H. Capps (Ed.), *Seeing With a Native Eye: Essays on Native American Religion.* Harper and Row, New York, New York, 1976.

# CHAPTER 26

# POSITION AND IMPOSITION (1991)
## Power relations in a multicultural foundations class
### Roberta Ahlquist

> I could tell you
> if I wanted to.
> What makes me
> What I am.
> But I don't
> Really want to—
> And you don't
> Give a damn.
> (Langston Hughes, "Impasse," 1952)

## Understanding and knowing teachers' beliefs

My students, who are prospective high school teachers, reflect many of the common attitudes held by the larger general population; that is, they tend to be fairly apolitical, individualistic, and nonconfrontational, and most often they view situations and people from a personal point of view. My primary challenge as a White teacher educator is thus to intervene in such a way that my students do not reproduce in their teaching what they have experienced in their schooling. Two of my goals are that students develop the ability to be open and reflective about their learning histories, values, beliefs, and actions on those beliefs; and that they become conscious of the "hidden curriculum" of schooling (Chan & Rueda, 1979). Because I want my students to problematize (critically examine) the puzzling and contradictory aspects of their views of reality as well as their experiences, I strive to help them discover, experience, and construct powerful alternatives to their past experiences. I want them to become aware of the role that they may be asked to play in perpetuating oppressive structures and practices in the educational system and find ways to take an oppositional stance to an oppressive role. In effect, I try to teach my students to challenge the status quo in the hopes that they, as the teachers of the future, will choose to take a stand in the interests of social justice. Translating theory into practice, however, has proven difficult.

While I do not assume that all prospective teachers enter teacher education programs with racist and sexist values, I believe that a great majority of them do and that they tend either to be unconscious of this reality or want to deny it. As a teacher I have observed that a critical mass of students who are open to alternative points of view is necessary to challenge taken-for-granted views of teaching. Therefore, each semester I spend considerable time trying to understand and problematize the beliefs of prospective teachers: their views about race, gender, and social class as well as their beliefs about teaching and learning and the role they see themselves playing in that process. My experience has shown me that if teacher educators are to be successful in offering alternatives to the powerful forces of racism and sexism in today's society and challenging the far-too-prevalent behaviorist, authoritarian, and didactic practices of teachers, we must understand and speak to the preconceptions of beginning teachers. We must challenge student views as well as urge them to recast their views of reality into problems for critical assessment.

## Power and resistance—theirs and mine

Every class has its own unique dynamic based on the backgrounds, world views, and histories of its students. At the beginning of a recent semester I surveyed the students in my Multicultural Foundations of Education class to determine their levels of consciousness about multicultural education and about racism and other inequities. This particular class was composed of 31 students: 27 White women, 1 White man, 1 Black man (who dropped the class after the first week and subsequently dropped out of the program entirely), and 2 Mexican American women. The average student age was 29, yet many students were very young and held views that seemed politically naive. Ten women students were in their late thirties or early forties and had children in school. Nearly one-third of the class worked in addition to attending classes. The overwhelming majority of students defined themselves as middle-class. Several women students identified themselves as religious fundamentalists.

At the beginning of the semester most students indicated they were curious about multicultural education but did not have a good idea what it meant. A few students offered the typical definitions which revolved around foods, holidays, and customs, but the majority indicated little if any contact or experiences with people of color or poor people. One White working-class single parent revealed that her daughter's father was Black but that he had no contact with the family. A 45-year-old White woman student, who described herself as a disabled single parent, reported that she had been homeless several times and had ongoing experiences with people of color and poor people. Several students expressed the belief that poor people, people on welfare, and some minorities were poor because they were lazy. Others expressed anger because they felt the new immigrants were taking a disproportionate share of the diminishing number of available jobs. The level of political consciousness among most of the students was low regarding how American workers are divided around the issue of race. For many students, racism seemed to "make sense" based, as Hall (1980) explains, on the social construction of their consciousness and experiences.

Indeed, there was much to do to raise the critical consciousness of this class, and my goals for the course revolved around just that, particularly by making students reflect on what they knew—and how they came to know it—in a critical, reflective exchange. For the first three weeks of class I inventoried students' beliefs and values based upon the opinions they expressed during class discussions and in their writings about cultural and racial issues and their experiences with such issues. Examples of mechanistic thinking prevailed: "That's the way things are and always will be; poverty has been with us forever." Assimilation, many argued, was the only solution for the future of the world. Several students openly expressed condescending views of people they felt would not "make it" as adults.

When I spoke of the need to hear a multiplicity of viewpoints in order to clarify and articulate our own positions in relation to those of others, some students looked uncomfortable. They asserted that I was idealistic and utopian for advocating cultural diversity. Moreover, they claimed that racism and sexism no longer existed, that these injustices had ceased with the Civil Rights Movement and the Sixties. Racism and sexism were passé, they argued, and so was I for raising the issues. I had to keep reminding myself that time and conditions shape consciousness; these were not the students of the 1960s but rather those of the 1990s. Still, they had placed some of their thinking on the table for scrutiny. We were, I thought, setting the stage for dialogue.

The passivity and fear of failure I observed at the beginning of the semester was overwhelming. Never had I seen a group of students who were so cautious, so silent, so anxious, so tentative, so performance-oriented, and so unwilling to take risks. Never had so many students asked me so often how they were going to be graded. Many lacked a sense of agency about their education and questioned the uncertain direction of their lives in general. They mistrusted me as well as their own experiences. Although I had seen many prospective teachers exhibit this behavior, I had never seen it to the degree I experienced with this group. Nonetheless, their general demeanor was light, bubbly, and occasionally inane. They appeared excited about the prospects of becoming teachers, and many stated that they chose teaching as a profession because they liked children.

As the semester progressed I tried to provide my students with a view of teachers as agents of resistance. I challenged them to take active roles: to be critical, to question, to take risks, to assume responsibility for their learning, to critique their own education, and to evaluate themselves and each other. They were often bewildered by such requests—and resistant. They had little experience with such approaches to learning. They were particularly uncomfortable with the lack of traditional structure and direction in my class, and their discomfort was compounded by their fear of controversial issues. Some told me I was arbitrary and unfair in my evaluations of their work. When I asked these students what their expectations were for the course, at first they were timid: "This is your course, I don't know what to expect." Others offered the vague response: "Just tell [us] how to teach multiculturally." The following are typical early semester student reflections:

But, you're the teacher. I don't know what questions to ask.

Are we going to learn something today, or are we just going to talk about all the problems in society?

I've never had a class like this. Generally I just go to class, take out my notebook, take notes, occasionally tune out and think about what I have or haven't done for the next class, shut my notebook and go on to the next class. In this class I can't do that.

I've never before been asked what I think or what I believe is important in any other class.

It's frustrating because you don't give us the answers to the difficult questions you raise.

These statements are symptomatic of the historical perspectives grounded in these students' experiences of schooling. Their predominantly dualistic view of learning, lack of familiarity with abstraction, and limited experience with multiple ways of knowing had engendered in them a preference for and reliance upon the transmission of decontextualized factual information generated by so-called "experts." They were uncomfortable speaking out and wanted me to be a "talking head." They had little or no experience with higher levels of what Perry (1970) calls "contextualized discourse," or the analysis of concrete situations within which communication occurs. Consequently, they believed their primary role as students was to passively absorb content generated by teachers. They were unwilling to view knowledge (as I did) as either a constructed entity or a process in which students individually weigh their personal beliefs against a critical examination of alternative possibilities.

Thus, early in the class I was forced to ask myself: Why shouldn't these students resist other ways of knowing? Had they ever encountered such ideas before? How often had they encountered (and perhaps rejected) teachers who raised issues of racism and sexism and who encouraged the kinds of responses I sought from them? In response to their requests I gave in to their need for certainty. I prepared and distributed handouts that explicitly explained all class writing and project assignments and expectations. Appease and direct—this was certainly not very dialogic, despite my constant emphasis on the importance of participating in class discussions. I knew it was going to be a difficult semester.

Generally, I resisted their resistance. I began the course by attempting to define terms and locate the course in a social context. Although the class came to some agreement about the concept of racism, sexism, and social class as forces of inequality, many students were very reticent to talk about their experiences using these terms. The terms "racism" and "sexism" were as explosive to some as the term "communism" continues to be. All too often, they explained, the terms were used to make them feel guilty, ashamed, or angry, as if they were being held responsible for all the inequities in society. How, I pondered, could I get these students to understand that even well-intentioned people were capable of being racist, and that it was important for them to see that everyone—teachers, parents, students, and other community members—had a responsibility to take a position against racism as well as acknowledge how racism was embedded in their own behavior? I argued, as did Brandt (1986), that the trouble they were having accepting the terms indicated a lack of willingness on their part to acknowledge what the words meant or to claim any responsibility for such experiences. I urged students to develop working definitions of the terms, to render them in the form of concrete examples drawn from their own lives. We talked about "blaming the victim," internalizing oppression, and what these concepts meant in their own experience. In response, some students provided examples of what Sleeter and Grant (1988) refer to as the "illusion of progress"—small but mostly superficial examples of people of color and women in places of some power and responsibility that tend to obscure the reality that racism and sexism continue to be major forces in the lives of many people. I then distributed handouts that documented the political, economic, and social subordination of Blacks, Hispanics, and Native Americans. (Again, I knew this was not very dialogic, but I was hard-pressed to uncover a generative theme that *might* eventually bring them to this awareness or make them receptive to it.)

We then turned our attention to discussion of the impact of social class on race and gender. I raised questions about class domination and the way our economic system is structured. I encouraged students to discuss their own or their children's experiences in school, their families, and communities, and to consider these experiences within the framework of race, gender, and social-class issues. Although a few students shared stories of unequal treatment, the majority showed little "empathy or outrage" for the plight of those less fortunate than they (Berlak, 1988). Some students made vague references to people of color and poor people as "lazy," "undeserving," or "drug addicts." To challenge their defenses I provided the class with readings and several media presentations that addressed race, gender, and social-class issues. I often used self-disclosure, sharing with them my own experiences of growing up in a home where unconscious and conscious racism was a daily experience. I told them that I learned about equity and social justice not at home, not at church, but in the streets and at school. I shared many personal stories of my experiences with people of color and working-class people during my childhood, and I described incidents of discrimination I had experienced based on my class background and gender: how my teachers expected less of me because I was from the working class; how one geometry teacher had become frustrated with my board work and had shouted out in class, "Why are girls in this class, anyway? They weren't meant to do math!" I talked about what it meant to be a White female then and now, and I urged students to share their experiences and realities. I also encouraged students to keep a journal in which they were to record notes about class discussions and reflect upon the values, beliefs, and behaviors of their families; how race, gender, and class have influenced or shaped their view of the world and of education; the roles they wished to play as teachers; and their perspectives regarding the purposes of schooling. Some of their journal entries were shared in class, some I alone read, and some were reserved for the writer's privacy; but these writings provided substance for further dialogue and helped students clarify the points of view, attitudes, and questions we addressed in classroom discussions.

After several weeks of class discussion focussing on their personal experiences with discrimination and prejudice, most students agreed that racism and sexism were everywhere. They insisted, however, that they were neither responsible for nor engaged in racist or sexist practices. When we talked about personal fairness and equity, some students argued that they did not intentionally discriminate against anyone because of their race, ethnicity, or gender. The topic then turned to institutional racism in education, targeting particularly the practices of tracking, IQ testing, and unequal access to educational resources. To help facilitate the unveiling of racism and sexism in their own beliefs and in the beliefs of the majority of prospective teachers, I presented several videos such as "Racism 101" and "Killing us Softly: Images of Women in the Media." Most students were shocked by the blatant displays of racism and sexism depicted in these presentations.

Next we turned to the ways in which the media reinforces the racial/sexual status quo. To move students away from their tendency toward "tunnel vision," I had them engage in several exercises. They were asked to critique the White, middle-class, consumer-oriented media—especially television advertising and Saturday morning cartoons directed at impressionable young audiences—from the point of view of race, gender, and social-class issues. White students were asked to review television programs or discuss issues or conflicts from the perspective of a person of color; males were also asked to take a female perspective; middle-class students assumed a working-class view. It soon became apparent that this group of teachers had never considered the effect of point of view on their perception. For example, discussion of the idea that being White in American society results in one's seeing the world from a predominantly "White" perspective was an alarming revelation for several students. New awareness of the power of point of view provided students a basis for much reflection about their values and beliefs; however, many became angry and resistant when they found their attitudes about the reality they wanted to believe in were in conflict with the reality they experienced while "wearing the shoes" of another person.

Although role-playing helped break down several stereotypes, it also made some students hostile. When they felt they could not articulate their own position, they tended either to strike out in emotional outbursts or to blame and devalue themselves. I tried to address this hostility, a symptom of students' feelings of guilt and powerlessness, on an ongoing basis, but another trend emerged against which I was ultimately unsuccessful in fighting: I noticed that several students began to disengage from the process of self-examination and withdraw from class discussions. Growing awareness of their own biases proved more disturbing than these students wanted to admit. Comments such as the following, which one of the students in this class shared with me a semester later, reflect much: lack of power, fear of self-disclosure, guilt, passivity, fatalism, denial, and resistance. As one student confided:

> The course was an assault of horrors . . . every class some new injustice was presented . . . students were not sure what these had to do with them. [The teacher] went overboard in her concerns. Things aren't all that bad. And even if they were, one person couldn't do that much to change them. Some of them just didn't want to deal with this order of things because they were trying to do what they needed to do for their own life and they had no more energy. And besides they were nice people and not participating in these injustices.

I sincerely wanted to pierce the opaqueness (or, as Freire [1985] calls it, the "fog") that surrounded my students' thinking, but my advocacy may have gotten in the way of their problem posing. This was not my intention; my interest was to raise consciousness. I was depending upon "right" thought to lead to "right" action, but many of my students were unconvinced by my reasoning and disagreed about what was "right." Rather than see conflict as an opportunity to clarify their positions and to view learning as progression toward that clarification, my students had perceived the rigor of my arguments as an attempt to impose my point of view on them. As I asked myself: Did I provide hope for change, or was *I* responsible for their feelings of powerlessness? In my attempts to demystify the effects of the "system" on their thinking and to offer students a view of possibility, had I pushed them to the point of resistance?

## The myth of objectivity

Not surprisingly, the most heated classroom debate of the semester developed not over the issues of racism and sexism but over whether teachers should take a position on controversial issues. This debate represented one of several instances in which many of my students displayed their intolerance of diversity and their fear and anxiety about alternative points of view. It also represented a turning point in my ongoing process of self-critique.

The majority of the class took the position that it was wrong for teachers to state their viewpoints in class, even if doing so was in the interests of challenging racial, gender, or other forms of oppression. Deeply embedded in these students' world views was the notion that teachers must always present themselves as "objective" or "neutral," especially regarding controversial issues. My position was that if change was needed, teachers had a responsibility to take a position in support of change. Though I told students they did not have to agree with my view—in fact, I encouraged them to counter my position—I defended my right to state it. I quoted Freire's (1987) assertion, which I firmly believe, that "teachers should attempt to live part of their dreams within their educational space." My antiracist/antisexist position, I explained, was based not only on morality but on the grounds that demystifying racism and sexism also demystifies the inequalities of the economic system. For me to remain silent, feign neutrality, or claim no perspective on these issues, I told them, would have been dishonest. Thus, I argued strongly and at length in favor of reflective teaching from a critical, antiracist, and antisexist perspective.

I was dismayed by their response. On the one hand students were dependent upon teacher or "expert" authority, on the other hand they resisted it. The class was divided, but many of them fell back on the admonitions of teachers who told them not to take stands. Several of my most vocal students adamantly opposed partisan stands by teachers. For weeks one irate student came to class armed with arguments from other teachers, parents, and her own experience in favor of the position that teachers remain neutral. She argued that teachers should not play a role in taking a position on an issue, especially a controversial issue, because teachers by nature of their position had too much power. Moreover, she added, all sides of an issue need to be expressed, and students should be allowed to make up their own minds. Though I agreed with the latter part of her argument, I took issue with her position on teacher objectivity. I cited Maher (1987), who maintains that feminist and critical pedagogy challenge the concept of objectivity. I was insistent that teachers must counter or challenge a point of view if it is harmful, discriminatory, or privileges one person over another on the basis of race, gender, or social-class background.

This exchange lasted several class meetings. As the argument continued, tensions developed over the issue of teacher authority and power. The debate degenerated into a power struggle. I stood my ground because I felt it crucial for students to develop a clear point of view on this issue and be able to articulate and defend their view, but, unconsciously, I wanted the students to see and accept *my* view. Although I did not deliberately wish to violate, limit, or oppress their voices in the name of liberatory teaching, I could not bear the thought of students limiting or stifling discussion of visions of a better world. The manner in which I presented my views intimidated several students. They did not view my approach as an invitation to dialogue; instead, sides were taken and lines were drawn. The important issues of racism and sexism were diffused in the clash between teacher and student authority.

I was determined to get on with the rest of the course. For the first week after this exchange ended I attempted to ignore or downplay the effects the conflict had on the class. I soon realized that a chasm had been created between the students and me. I had invited a debate that no one had clearly won, yet my position remained the one most powerfully stated. Students viewed my interest in having them accept my view as an ultimatum: agree that racism and sexism must be eliminated, or else. I was guilty of the very dualism I was fighting against. The few students who tended to agree with me in class often withdrew from discussion, especially if they felt their classmates saw them as taking sides with the teacher. Some students who disagreed with me also withdrew. When I withdrew from a debate, support for my position was diminished; if I continued, I was perceived as exerting unfair authority and advantage. I was in a double bind situation; I felt simultaneously like the oppressor and the oppressed.

How could I get my students to reconsider their ways of viewing the world? How could I awaken students from their slumber, their limited consciousness, without being impositional? I asked myself the questions posed by Bridges and Hartman (1975): How can the teacher, as problem poser, reflect student reality back to the student in a nonthreatening, problematic way that will induce self-examination and critical questioning—without imposition? In effect, how can teachers use their power and authority to *abolish* power and authority? This is the major contradiction of teaching from a critical and dialogic perspective.

Many times I was tempted to return to a more fundamental approach, to methods of teaching that I had discarded years ago. I wondered if I should have relied more on factual data and articles to provide concrete evidence of both personal and institutional racism, sexism, and social-class bias? I asked myself whether I should change directions and merely respond to several students' repeated requests to "just tell [us] how to teach multiculturally" or "tell us how to teach a multicultural lesson; we can talk about these issues some other time."

## Reflections on resistance

... the whole process of education occurs within a social framework and is designed to perpetuate the aims of society. Thus, for example, the boys and girls who were born during the era of the Third Reich, when educated to the purposes of the Third Reich, became barbarians. The paradox of education is precisely this—that as one begins to become conscious one begins to examine the society in which he is being educated. The purpose of education, finally, is to create in a person the ability to look at the world for himself, to make his own decisions, to say to himself this is black or this white, to decide for himself whether there is a God in heaven or not. To ask questions of the universe, and then learn to live with those questions, is the way he achieves his own identity. But no society is really anxious to have that kind of person around. What societies really, ideally, want is a citizenry which will simply obey the rules of society. If a society succeeds in this, that society is about to perish. The obligation of anyone who thinks of himself as responsible is to examine society and try to change it and to fight it—at no matter what risk. This is the only hope society has. This is the only way societies change. (Baldwin, 1988, p. 4)

Teaching from an antiracist perspective often generates resistance (Banks, 1986; Rothenberg, 1985). Teaching from an inquiry-based and feminist perspective also creates resistance (Maher, 1987). Teaching from a critical, feminist, and antiracist perspective further compounds resistance (Sleeter & Grant, 1988; Berlak, 1988). I now understand that resistance is a complex and powerful dynamic in the classroom. It must be addressed, yet it can be viewed as a healthy response to controversial material, as critical questioning, and as a lack of willingness by students to conform blindly to the expectations of others. On the other hand, for teachers, there is a fine line between asserting one's world view and imposing it. In retrospect, I think I may have crossed that line. I may have presented my position too forcefully and too early in the discussion. The student who questioned the propriety of teachers taking a stand on controversial issues may not have been arguing merely for objectivity but rather for freedom from imposition. As other educators attempting to teach from a similar perspective have noted, when a position is imposed on students, resistance and alienation results and subsequent efforts to address conflict critically are often defeated (Hollins & King, 1989; Quintanar, 1989). My approach caused some students to resist my authority on not only the issue of teacher authority but on my other views as well. The students in my class resisted both the content as well as the methodology of my teaching, and my reaction to student resistance consequently led me to some pedagogical pitfalls.

Was my stand worth the alienation it created? As poet/critic Audrey Lorde (1987) says, the decision "still feels right to me." For too long, students and teachers alike have been socialized to believe that argument, conflict, debate, and disagreement are to be avoided, that they have no place in the classroom. If education cannot provide ways for students to critically examine and act on the world in the interests of change, then it merely serves to reproduce the status quo (Bowles & Gintis, 1976; Apple, 1982). To help students get beyond the common, unconscious process of mechanistic and dualistic thinking, teachers must provide more opportunities for discussion of controversy.

I also realize that the contradiction between authority and critical pedagogy that was problematized in this class was more striking for me as a female teacher. Power is automatically bestowed on the role of teacher, yet female teachers often have to prove themselves as authorities in ways that male teachers do not. I had never before considered, as Bridges and Hartman (1975) assert, that women teachers needed to establish their credibility before relinquishing their authority. I reflect now on Barbara Christian's (1987) caution: "One must distinguish the desire for power from the need to become empowered." Although I did not want to promote my views in opposition to student positions, the task for me (then and now) was to determine how to relinquish my power and authority as a teacher so that my students could become agents in their own learning. My gender was a factor in this dynamic; still, I believe the power imbalance between students and teachers must constantly be contested if we are to empower our students.

From my experiences with this class I discovered that too often I was asking students to provide information and answers on subjects they had scant likelihood of knowing. It was an exercise in futility to expect thoughtful discussions to evolve out of my questions, and I quickly became aware of my students' lack of sophistication about such issues. For example, Baldwin's words, though they were penned in 1963, still ring true to me; but when I asked this group of students to give consideration to the above quote, their resistance to his ideas made me feel as though the nation had taken two giant steps back. My own agenda and the urgency of the issues I sought to discuss led me away from the slower, more deliberative, and more haphazard process of focusing on students' lived experience and allowing generalizations to grow out of that process. Now I realize that deep understanding of an issue grows out of reflective examination of one's own experience, and true consciousness often comes very slowly. As Rothenberg (1985) and Brandt (1986) make clear, the ideologies of race, ethnicity, gender, and class (although the terms themselves are abstract and deserve skepticism) intersect and operate independently as well as interdependently in people's lives. Therefore, people must travel the road to understanding about racism, sexism, and other forms of oppression for themselves, otherwise they will only *think* they understand.

Perspectives such as these, my interpretations of some of the reasons for student resistance, and experience currently inform my teaching and the teaching of others working within the paradigm of critical pedagogy. The fear of addressing conflict, fear of taking a stand in the interests of justice, and the belief in pseudo-objectivity too often permeate the thinking of most prospective teachers. Teacher educators must acknowledge their student teachers' belief systems and experiences and work to assert antiracist and antisexist views in the least impositional way possible. The following are some lessons I have learned from my practice—examples of the limitations and possibilities which may inform others teaching from a critical perspective:

- We must become more cognizant of the problem of imposition and power relations and seek ways to constructively address both power and resistance. We have a responsibility to be explicit in our partisanship but not impositional.
- We must clarify the terms we use. For example, the very term "multicultural" is problematic; generally it does not mean "education for social justice," although it should.
- We must continually expose and critique hidden ideologies.
- To alleviate student anxieties about dialogical teaching, we must inform them, clearly and in advance, how our classes will be different or appear less structured (i.e., different grading policies, etc.) than traditional classes.
- We must be more patient with students who are unfamiliar with abstract ideas. We must also realize that sometimes we will not succeed, that new categories and approaches to teaching must often be reinvented with and for each class we teach.
- We must address student experience as a basis for critique and use this approach as a means to make students self-critically aware of their own and others' heritages and of the ways in which cultural background shapes individual character.
- We must work with students to provide clear direction, avenues, and possibilities for hope and change to counter student fatalism and feelings of powerlessness.
- We must provide students with early field experiences in diverse ethnic settings to help them overcome any misconceptions, fears, and anxieties they might have about working with diverse groups.
- We must avoid "blaming the victim" and internalizing oppression, and steer our students away from doing the same.
- We must foster an appreciation for the dialogical process as a powerful teaching tool to promote the value of social justice.
- We must find ways to support others who are attempting to teach from a critical perspective.
- We must support the revision or replacement of standardized teacher certification and evaluation methods, and seek ways to provide more accurate assessment of the talents of those who teach from a dialogical, antiracist view.
- We must urge the permeation of multicultural and antiracist content throughout all teacher education curricula, and resist its relegation to optional or elective course status.

Students are victims of the current educational system which has socialized them; teachers are also victims. Most teacher educators never received an education that was empowering, antiracist, problem-posing, or liberatory. If we teacher educators ourselves were taught no other way, how can we expect to provide alternatives to our students? To overcome the effects of my own mis-education, I have felt a growing need to examine critically and reflect on my own beliefs and on the constraints and formative influences that have shaped my practice. My own self-reflection is ongoing. I will continue to probe and unveil the contradictions between position and imposition, power and empowerment, and theory and practice in an effort to promote a more participatory, democratic, and socially responsible world view for prospective teachers.

## References

Apple, M. (1982). *Education and power*. New York: Routledge.

Baldwin, J. (1988). A talk to teachers. In R. Simonson (Ed.), *The Graywolf annual five: Multicultural literacy* (p. 4). St. Paul, MN: Graywolf.

Banks, J. (1986). Race, ethnicity and schooling in the United States: Past, present and future. In J. Banks (Ed.), *Multicultural education in western societies* (pp. 86–88). London: Holt.

Berlak, A. (1988). *Teaching for outrage and empathy in the liberal arts*. Paper delivered at the Annual Meeting of the American Education Research Association, New Orleans, Louisiana, April 1988.

Bowles, S., & Gintis, S. (1976). *Schooling in capitalist America*. New York: Basic Books.

Brandt, G. (1986). *The realization of anti-racist teaching*. Philadelphia: Falmer Press.

Bridges, A., & Hartman, H. (1975). Pedagogy by the oppressed. *Review of Radical Political Economics, 6*(4), 75–79.

Chan, K. S., & Rueda, R. (1979). Poverty and culture in education: Separate but equal. *Journal of the Council for Exceptional Children, 45*, 422–428.

Christian, B. (1987). The race for theory. *Cultural Critique, 6*, 51–63.

Ellsworth, E. (1989). Why doesn't this feel empowering? Working through the repressive myths of critical pedagogy. *Harvard Educational Review, 59*(3), 297–324.

Freire, P. (1985, February 5). Comments made at the Literacy Forum, Berkeley, California.

Hall, S. (1980). Teaching race. *Multicultural Education, 9*, 1.

Hollins, E., & King, J. (1989, March 13). Personal interview with the author.

Hughes, L. (1952). Impasse. In O. Williams (Ed.), *A little treasury of modern poetry*. New York: Scribner.

Lorde, A. (1984). *Sister outsider*. New York: Crossing Press.

Maher, F. (1987). Inquiry teaching and feminist pedagogy. *Social Education, 6*, 186–191.

Quintanar, R. (1989, February 2). Personal interview with the author.

Perry, W. (1970). *Intellectual and ethical development in the college years: A scheme*. New York: Holt, Rinehart & Winston.

Rothenberg, P. (1988). Integrating the study of race, gender and class: Some preliminary observations. *Feminist Teacher, 3*(3), 37–42.

Sleeter, C., & Grant, C. (1988). *Making choices for multicultural education: Five approaches to race, class and gender*. Columbus, OH: Merrill.

# CHAPTER 27

# DYSCONSCIOUS RACISM (1991)
## Ideology, identity, and the miseducation of teachers
*Joyce E. King*

They had for more than a century before been regarded as . . . so far inferior . . . that the negro might justly and lawfully be reduced to slavery for his benefit. . . . This opinion was at that time fixed and universal in the civilized portion of the white race. It was regarded as an axiom in morals as well as in politics, which no one thought of disputing . . . and men in every grade and position in society daily and habitually acted upon it . . . without doubting for a moment the correctness of this opinion. (*Dred Scott v. Sanford*, 1857)

Racism can mean culturally sanctioned beliefs which, regardless of the intentions involved, defend the advantages whites have because of the subordinated positions of racial minorities. (Wellman, 1977, p. xviii)

The goal of critical consciousness is an ethical and not a legal judgement [*sic*] about the social order. (Heaney, 1984, p. 116)

## Celebrating diversity

The new watchwords in education, "celebrating diversity," imply the democratic ethic that all students, regardless of their sociocultural backgrounds, should be educated equitably. What this ethic means in practice, particularly for teachers with little personal experience of diversity and limited understanding of inequity, is problematic. At the elite, private, Jesuit university where I teach, most of my students (most of whom come from relatively privileged, monocultural backgrounds) are anxious about being able to "deal" with all the diversity in the classroom. Not surprisingly, given recent neoconservative ideological interpretations of the problem of diversity, many of my students also believe that affirming cultural difference is tantamount to racial separatism, that diversity threatens national unity, or that social inequity originates with sociocultural deficits and not with unequal outcomes that are inherent in our socially stratified society. With respect to this society's changing demographics and the inevitable "browning" of America, many of my students foresee a diminution of their own identity, status, and security. Moreover, regardless of their conscious intentions, certain culturally sanctioned beliefs my students hold about inequity and why it persists, especially for African Americans, take White norms and privilege as givens.

The findings presented herein will show what these beliefs and responses have to do with what I call "dysconscious racism" to denote the limited and distorted understandings my students have about inequity and cultural diversity

—understandings that make it difficult for them to act in favor of truly equitable education. This article presents a qualitative analysis of dysconscious racism as reflected in the responses of my teacher education students to an open-ended question I posed at the beginning of one of my classes during the fall 1986 academic quarter to assess student knowledge and understanding of social inequity. Content analysis of their short essay responses will show how their thinking reflects internalized ideologies that both justify the racial status quo and devalue cultural diversity. Following the analysis of their responses and discussion of the findings I will describe the teaching approach I use to counteract the cognitively limited and distorted thinking that dysconscious racism represents. The concluding discussion will focus on the need to make social reconstructionist liberatory teaching an option for teacher education students like mine who often begin their professional preparation without having ever considered the need for fundamental social change (see also Ginsburg, 1988; and Ginsburg & Newman, 1985).

Critical, transformative teachers must develop a pedagogy of social action and advocacy that really celebrates *diversity*, not just random holidays, isolated cultural artifacts, or "festivals and food" (Ayers, 1988). If dysconscious racism keeps such a commitment beyond the imagination of students like mine, teacher educators need forms of pedagogy and counter-knowledge that challenge students' internalized ideologies and subjective identities (Giroux & McLaren, 1988). Prospective teachers need both an intellectual understanding of schooling and inequity as well as self-reflective, transformative emotional growth experiences. With these objectives in mind, I teach my graduate-level Social Foundations of Education course in the social reconstructionist tradition of critical, transformative, liberatory education for social change (see Gordon, 1985; Freire, 1971; Giroux & McLaren, 1986; Heaney, 1984; Shor, 1980; Searle, 1975; Sleeter & Grant, 1988). In contrast to a pedagogy for the oppressed, this course explores the dynamics of a liberatory pedagogy for the elite. It is designed to provide such teacher education students with a context in which to consider alternative conceptions of themselves and society. The course challenges students' taken-for-granted ideological positions and identities and their unquestioned acceptance of cultural belief systems which undergird racial inequity.

Thus, the course and the teaching methods I use transcend conventional social and multicultural Foundations of Education course approaches by directly addressing societal oppression and student knowledge and beliefs about inequity and diversity. By focusing on ways that schooling, including their own miseducation, contributes to unequal educational outcomes that reinforce societal inequity and oppression, students broaden their knowledge of how society works. I offer this analysis of dysconscious racism and reflections on the way I teach to further the theoretical and practical development of a liberatory praxis that will enable teacher education students to examine what they know and believe about society, about diverse others, and about their own actions.

## Discovering dysconscious racism

Dysconsciousness is an uncritical habit of mind (including perceptions, attitudes, assumptions, and beliefs) that justifies inequity and exploitation by accepting the existing order of things as given. If, as Heaney (1984) suggests, critical consciousness "involves an ethical judgement [*sic*]" about the social order, dysconsciousness accepts it uncritically. This lack of critical judgment against society reflects an absence of what Cox (1974) refers to as "social ethics"; it involves a subjective identification with an ideological viewpoint that admits no fundamentally alternative vision of society.[1]

Dysconscious racism is a form of racism that tacitly accepts dominant White norms and privileges. It is not the *absence* of consciousness (that is, not unconsciousness) but an *impaired* consciousness or distorted way of thinking about race as compared to, for example, critical consciousness. Uncritical ways of thinking about racial inequity accept certain culturally sanctioned assumptions, myths, and beliefs that justify the social and economic advantages White people have as a result of subordinating diverse others (Wellman, 1977). Any serious challenge to the status quo that calls this racial privilege into question inevitably challenges the self-identity of White people who have internalized these ideological justifications. The reactions of my students to information I have presented about societal inequity have led me to conceptualize dysconscious racism as one form that racism takes in this post-civil rights era of intellectual conservatism.

Most of my students begin my Social Foundations course with limited knowledge and understanding of societal inequity. Not only are they often unaware of their own ideological perspectives (or of the range of alternatives they have not consciously considered), most are also unaware of how their own subjective identities reflect an uncritical identification with the existing social order. Moreover, they have difficulty explaining "liberal" and "conservative" standpoints on contemporary social and educational issues, and are even less familiar with "radical" perspectives (King & Ladson-Billings, 1990). My students' explanations of persistent racial inequity consistently lack evidence of any critical ethical judgment regarding racial (and class/gender) stratification in the existing social order; yet, and not surprisingly, these same students generally maintain that they personally deplore racial prejudice and discrimination. However, Wellman (1977) notes that this kind of thinking is a hallmark of racism. "The concrete problem facing white people," states Wellman, "is how to come to grips with the demands made by blacks and whites while at the same time *avoiding* the possibility of institutional change and reorganization that might affect them" (p. 42). This suggests that the ability to imagine a society reorganized without racial privilege requires a fundamental shift in the way White people think about their status and self-identities and their conceptions of Black people.

For example, when I broach the subject of racial inequity with my students, they often complain that they are "tired of being made to feel guilty" because they are White. The following entries from the classroom journals of two undergraduate students in an education course are typical of this reaction[2]:

> With some class discussions, readings, and other media, there have been times that I feel guilty for being White which really infuriates me because no one should feel guilty for the color of their skin or ethnic background. Perhaps my feelings are actually a discomfort for the fact that others have been discriminated against all of their life [*sic*] because of their color and I have not.

> How can I be thankful that I am not a victim of discrimination? I should be ashamed. Then I become confused. Why shouldn't I be thankful that I have escaped such pain?

These students' reactions are understandable in light of Wellman's insights into the nature of racism. That White teacher education students often express such feelings of guilt and hostility suggests they accept certain unexamined assumptions, unasked questions, and unquestioned cultural myths regarding both the social order and their place in it. The discussion of the findings that follows will show how dysconscious racism, manifested in student explanations of societal inequity and linked to their conceptions of Black people, devalues the cultural diversity of the Black experience and, in effect, limits students' thinking about what teachers can do to promote equity.

## The findings

Since the fall academic quarter 1986 I have given the students teachers in my Social Foundations course statistical comparisons such as those compiled by the Children's Defense Fund (Edelman, 1987) regarding Black and White children's life chances (e.g., "Compared to White children, Black children are twice as likely to die in the first year of life"; see Harlan, 1985). I then ask each student to write a brief explanation of how these racial inequities came about by answering the question: "How did our society get to be this way?' An earlier publication (King & Ladson-Billings, 1990) comparing student responses to this question in the fall 1986 and spring 1987 quarters identifies three ways students explain this inequity. Content analysis of their responses reveals that students explain racial inequity as either the result of slavery (Category I), the denial or lack of equal opportunity for African Americans (Category II), or part of the framework of a society in which racism and discrimination are normative (Category III). In the present article I will again use these categories and the method of content analysis to compare student responses collected in the 1986 and 1988 fall quarters. The responses presented below are representative of 22 essay responses collected from students in 1986 and 35 responses collected in 1988.

Category I explanations begin and end with slavery. Their focus is either on describing African Americans as "victims of their original (slave) status," or they assert that Black/White inequality is the continuing result of inequity which began during slavery. In either case, historical determinism is a key feature; African Americans are perceived as exslaves, and the "disabilities of slavery" are believed to have been passed down intergenerationally. As two students wrote:

I feel it dates back to the time of slavery when the Blacks were not permitted to work or really have a life of their own. They were not given the luxury or opportunity to be educated and *each generation passed this disability on* [italics added]. (F6–21)[3]

I think that this harkens [*sic*] back to the origin of the American Black population as slaves. Whereas other immigrant groups started on a low rung of our economic (and social class) ladder and had space and opportunity to move up, Blacks did not. They were perceived as somehow less than people. This view may have been passed down and even on to Black youth . . . (F8–32)

It is worth nothing that the "fixed and universal beliefs" Europeans and White Americans held about Black inferiority/White superiority during the epoch of the Atlantic slave trade, beliefs that made the enslavement of Africans seem justified and lawful, are not the focus of this kind of explanation. The historical continuum of cause and effect evident in Category I explanations excludes any consideration of the cultural rationality behind such attitudes; that is, they do not explain *why* White people held these beliefs.

In Category II explanations the emphasis is on the denial of equal opportunity to Black people (e.g., less education, lack of jobs, low wages, poor health care). Although students espousing Category II arguments may explain discrimination as the result of prejudice or racist attitudes (e.g., "Whites believe Blacks are inferior"), they do not necessarily causally link it to the historical fact of slavery or to the former status of Black people as slaves. Rather, the persistently unequal status of African Americans is seen as an *effect* of poverty and systemic discrimination. Consider these two responses from 1986 and 1988:

> . . . Blacks have been treated as second class citizens. Caucasians tend to maintain the belief that Black people are inferior . . . *for this reason* [italics added] Blacks receive less education and education that is of inferior quality . . . less pay than most other persons doing the same job; (and) live in inferior substandard housing, etc. (F6–3)

> Because of segregation—overt and covert—Blacks in America have had less access historically to education and jobs, which has led to a poverty cycle for many. *The effects described are due to poverty* [italics added], lack of education and lack of opportunity. (F8–7)

In addition, some Category I and Category II explanations identify negative psychological or cultural characteristics of African Americans as effects of slavery, prejudice, racism, or discrimination. One such assertion is that Black people have no motivation or incentive to "move up" or climb the socioeconomic ladder. Consequently, this negative characteristic is presumed to perpetuate racial inequality: Like a vicious cycle, Whites then perceive Blacks as ignorant or as having "devalued cultural mores." The following are examples of Category II explanations; even though they allude to slavery, albeit in a secondary fashion, the existence of discrimination is the primary focus:

> Blacks were brought to the U.S. by Whites. They were/are thought to be of a "lower race" by large parts of the society . . . society has impressed these beliefs/ideas onto Blacks. (Therefore) Blacks probably have lower self-esteem and when you have lower self-esteem, it is harder to move up in the world. . . . Blacks group together and stay together. Very few move up . . . partly because society put them there. (F6–18)

> Past history is at the base of the racial problems evident in today's society. Blacks have been persecuted and oppressed for years . . . Discrimination is still a problem which results in lack of motivation, self-esteem and hence a lessened "desire" to escape the hardships with which they are faced. (F8–14)

In 1986 my students' responses were almost evenly divided between Category I and Category II explanations (10 and 11 responses, respectively, with one Category III response). In 1988 all 35 responses were divided between Category I (11) and Category II (24) responses, or 32% and 68%, respectively. Thus, the majority of students in both years explained racial inequality in limited ways— as a historically inevitable consequence of slavery or as a result of prejudice and discrimination—without recognizing the structural inequity built into the social order. Their explanations fail to link racial inequity to other forms of societal oppression and exploitation. In addition, these explanations, which give considerable attention to Black people's negative characteristics, fail to account for White people's beliefs and attitudes that have long justified societal oppression and inequity in the form of racial slavery or discrimination.

## Discussion

An obvious feature of Category I explanations is the devaluation of the African American cultural heritage, a heritage which certainly encompasses more than the debilitating experience of slavery. Moreover, the integrity and adaptive resilience of what Stuckey (1987) refers to as the "slave culture" is ignored and implicitly devalued. Indeed, Category I explanations reflect a conservative assimilationist ideology that blames contemporary racial inequity on the presumed cultural deficits of African Americans. Less obvious is the way the historical continuum of these explanations, beginning as they do with the effects of slavery on African Americans, fails to consider the specific cultural rationality that justified slavery as acceptable and lawful (Wynter, 1990). Also excluded from these explanations as possible contributing factors are the particular advantages White people gained from the institution of racial slavery.

Category II explanations devalue diversity by not recognizing how opportunity is tied to the assimilation of mainstream norms and values. These explanations also fail to call into question the basic structural inequity of the social order; instead, the cultural mythology of the American Dream, most specifically the myth of equal opportunity, is tacitly accepted (i.e., with the right opportunity, African Americans can climb out of poverty and "make it" like everyone else). Such liberal, assimilationist ideology ignores the widening gap between the haves and the have nots, the downward mobility of growing numbers of Whites (particularly women with children), and other social realities of contemporary capitalism. While not altogether inaccurate, these explanations are nevertheless *partial* precisely because they fail to make appropriate connections between race, gender, and class inequity.

How do Category I and Category II explanations exemplify dysconscious racism? Both types defend White privilege, which, according to Wellman (1977), is a "consistent theme in racist thinking" (p. 39). For example, Category I explanations rationalize racial inequity by attributing it to the effects of slavery on African Americans while ignoring the economic advantages it gave Whites. A second rationalization, presented in Category II explanations, engenders the mental picture many of my students apparently have of equal opportunity, not as equal access to jobs, health care, education, etc. but rather as a sort of "legal liberty" which leaves the structural basis of the racial status quo intact (King & Wilson, 1990). In effect, by failing to connect a more just opportunity system for Blacks with fewer white-skin advantages for Whites, these explanations, in actuality, defend the racial status quo.

According to Wellman, the existing social order cannot provide for unlimited (or equal) opportunity for Black people while maintaining racial privileges for Whites (p. 42). Thus, elimination of the societal hierarchy is inevitable if the social order is to be reorganized; but before this can occur, the existing structural inequity must be recognized as such and actively struggled against. This, however, is not what most of my students have in mind when they refer to "equal opportunity."

Category I and Category II explanations rationalize the existing social order in yet a third way by omitting any ethical judgment against the privileges White people have gained as a result of subordinating Black people (and others). These explanations thus reveal a dysconscious racism which, although it bears little resemblance to the violent bigotry and overt White supremacist ideologies of previous eras, still takes for granted a system of racial privilege and societal stratification that favors Whites. Like the Whites of Dred Scott's era, few of my students even think of disputing this system or see it as disputable.

Category III explanations, on the other hand, do not defend this system. They are more comprehensive, and thus more accurate, because they make the appropriate connections between racism and other forms of inequity. Category III explanations also locate the origins of racial inequity in the framework of a society in which racial victimization is *normative*. They identify and criticize both racist ideology and oppressive societal structures without placing the responsibility for changing the situation solely on African Americans (e.g., to develop self-esteem), and without overemphasizing the role of White prejudice (e.g., Whites' beliefs about Black inferiority). The historical factors cited in Category III explanations neither deny White privilege nor defend it. I have received only one Category III response from a student at the beginning of my courses, the following:

> [Racial inequity] is primarily the result of the economic system. . . . racism served the purposes of ruling groups; e.g., in the Reconstruction era . . . poor Whites were pitted against Blacks—a pool of cheap exploitable labor is desired by capitalists and this ties in with the identifiable differences of races. (F6–9)

Why is it that more students do not think this way? Given the majority of my students' explanations of racial inequity, I suggest that their thinking is impaired by dysconscious racism—even though they may deny they are racists. The important point here, however, is not to prove that students are racist; rather, it is that their uncritical and limited ways of thinking must be identified, understood, and brought to their conscious awareness.

Dysconscious racism must be made the subject of educational intervention. Conventional analyses—which conceptualize racism at the institutional, cultural, or individual level but do not address the cognitive distortions of dysconsciousness—cannot help students distinguish between racist justifications of the status quo (which limit their thought, self-identity, and responsibility to take action) and socially unacceptable individual prejudice or bigotry (which students often disavow). Teacher educators must therefore challenge both liberal and conservative ideological thinking on these matters if we want students to consider seriously the need for fundamental change in society and in education.

Ideology, identity, and indoctrination are central concepts I use in my Social Foundations of Education course to help students free themselves from miseducation and uncritically accepted views which limit their thought and action. A brief description of the course follows.

## The cultural politics of critiquing ideology and identity

One goal of my Social Foundations of Education course is to sharpen the ability of students to think critically about educational purposes and practice in relation to social justice and to their own identities as teachers. The course thus illuminates a range of ideological interests which become the focus of students' critical analysis, evaluation, and choice. For instance, a recurring theme in the course is that of the social purposes of schooling, or schooling as an instrument of educational philosophy, societal vision, values, and personal choice. This is a key concept about which many students report they have never thought seriously. Course readings, lectures, media resources, class discussions, and other experiential learning activities are organized to provide an alternative context of meaning within which students can critically analyze the social purposes of schooling. The range of ideological perspectives considered include alternative explanations of poverty and joblessness, competing viewpoints regarding the significance of cultural differences, and discussions of education as a remedy for societal inequity. Students consider the meaning of social justice and examine ways that education might be transformed to promote a more equitable social order. Moreover, they are expected to choose and declare the social changes they themselves want to bring about as teachers.

The course also introduces students to the critical perspective that education is not neutral; it can serve various political and cultural interests including social control, socialization, assimilation, domination, or liberation (Cagan, 1978; Freire, 1971; O'Neill, 1981). Both impartial, purportedly factual information as well as openly partisan views about existing social realities such as the deindustrialization of America, hunger and homelessness, tracking, the "hidden" curriculum (Anyon, 1981; Vallence, 1977), the socialization of teachers, and teacher expectations (Rist, 1970) allow students to examine connections between macrosocial (societal) and microsocial (classroom) issues. This information helps students consider different viewpoints about how schooling processes contribute to inequity. Alongside encountering liberal and conservative analyses of education and opportunity, students encounter the scholarship of radical educators such as Anyon (1981), Freire (1971), Kozol (1981), and Giroux and McLaren (1986), who have developed "historical identities" (Boggs et al., 1978) within social justice struggles and who take stronger ethical stances against inequity than do liberals or conservatives. These radical educators' perspectives also provide students with alternative role models; students discuss their thoughts and feelings about the convictions these authors express and reflect upon the soundness of radical arguments. Consequently, as students formulate their own philosophical positions about the purposes of education, they inevitably struggle with the ideas, values, and social interests at the heart of the different educational and social visions which they, as teachers of the future, must either affirm, reject, or resist.

Making a conscious process of the struggle over divergent educational principles and purposes constitutes the cultural politics of my Social Foundations course. In this regard my aim is to provide a context within which student teachers can recognize and evaluate their personal experiences of political and ethical indoctrination. In contrast to their own miseducation, and using their experience in my course as a point of comparison, I urge my students to consider the possibilities liberatory and transformative teaching offers. To facilitate this kind of conscious reflection, I discuss the teaching strategies I myself model in my efforts to help them think critically about the course content, their own world view, and the professional practice of teaching (Freire & Faundez, 1989). To demonstrate the questions critical, liberatory teachers must ask and to make what counts as "school knowledge" (Anyon, 1981) problematic, I use Freire's (1971) strategy of developing "problem-posing" counter-knowledge. For example, I pose biased instructional materials as a problem teachers address. Thus, when we examine the way textbooks represent labor history (Anyon, 1979) and my student teachers begin to realize all they do not know about the struggles of working people for justice, the problem of miseducation becomes more real to them. Indeed, as Freire, Woodson (1933), and others suggest, an alternative view of history often reveals hidden social interests in the curriculum and unmasks a political and cultural role of schooling of which my student teachers are often completely unaware.

Analysis of and reflection on their own knowledge and experience involves students in critiquing ideologies, examining the influences on their thinking and identities, and considering the kind of teachers they want to become. I also encourage my students to take a stance against mainstream views and practices that dominate in schools and other university courses. Through such intellectual and emotional growth opportunities, students in my course re-experience and re-evaluate the partial and socially constructed nature of their own knowledge and identities.

My approach is not free from contradictions, however. While I alone organize the course structure, select the topics, make certain issues problematic, and assign the grades, I am confident that my approach is more democratic than the unwitting ideological indoctrination my students have apparently internalized. For a final grade, students have the option of writing a final exam in which they can critique the course, or they may present (to the class) a term project organized around an analytical framework they themselves generate.

## Toward liberatory pedagogy in teacher education

Merely presenting factual information about societal inequity does not necessarily enable preservice teachers to examine the beliefs and assumptions that may influence the way they interpret these facts. Moreover, with few exceptions, available multicultural resource materials for teachers presume a value commitment and readiness for multicultural teaching and antiracist education which many students may lack initially (Bennett, 1990; Brandt, 1986; Sleeter & Grant, 1988). Teacher educators may find some support in new directions in adult education (Mezirow, 1984) and in theories of adult learning and critical literacy which draw upon Freire's work in particular (Freire & Macedo, 1987). This literature offers some useful theoretical insights for emancipatory education and liberatory pedagogy (Heaney, 1984). For example, the counter-knowledge strategies I use in my Social Foundations course are designed to facilitate the kind of "perspective transformation" Mezirow (1984) calls for in his work. It is also worth noting that a tradition of critical African American educational scholarship exists which can be incorporated into teacher preparation courses. Analyses of miseducation by Woodson (1933), DuBois (1935), and Ellis (1917) are early forerunners of critical, liberatory pedagogy. This tradition is also reflected in contemporary African American thought and scholarship on education and social action (see Childs, 1989; Gordon, 1990; Lee et al., 1990; Muwakkil, 1990; Perkins, 1986).

As Sleeter and Grant (1988, p. 194) point out, however, White students sometimes find such critical, liberatory approaches threatening to their self-concepts and identities. While they refer specifically to problems of White males in this regard, my experience is that most students from economically privileged, culturally homogeneous backgrounds are generally unaware of their intellectual biases and monocultural encapsulation. While my students may feel threatened by diversity, what they often express is guilt and hostility. Students who have lived for the most part in relatively privileged cultural isolation can only consider becoming liberatory, social-reconstructionist educators if they have both an adequate understanding of how society works and opportunities to think about the need for fundamental social change. The critical perspective of the social order offered in my course challenges students' world views as well as their self-identities by making problematic and directly addressing students' values, beliefs, and ideologies. Precisely because what my students know and believe is so limited, it is necessary to address both their knowledge (that is, their intellectual understanding of social inequity) and what they believe about diversity. As Angus and Jhally (1989, p. 12) conclude, "what people accept as natural and self-evident" is exactly what becomes "problematic and in need of explanation" from this critical standpoint. Thus, to seriously consider the value commitment involved in teaching for social change as an option, students need experiential opportunities to recognize and evaluate the ideological influences that shape their thinking about schooling, society, themselves, and diverse others.

The critique of ideology, identity, and miseducation described herein represents a form of cultural politics in teacher education that is needed to address the specific cultural rationality of social inequity in modern American society. Such a liberatory pedagogical approach does not neglect the dimension of power and privilege in society, nor does it ignore the role of ideology in shaping the context within which people think about daily life and the possibilities of social transformation. Pedagogy of this kind is especially needed now, given the current thrust toward normative schooling and curriculum content that emphasizes "our common Western heritage" (Bloom, 1987; Gagnon, 1988; Hirsch, 1987; Ravitch, 1990). Unfortunately, this neoconservative curriculum movement leaves little room for discussion of how being educated in this tradition may be a limiting factor in the effectiveness of teachers of poor and minority students (King & Wilson, 1990; Ladson-Billings, 1991). Indeed, it precludes any critical ethical judgment about societal inequity and supports the kind of miseducation that produces teachers who are dysconscious—uncritical and unprepared to question White norms, White superiority, and White privilege.

Myths and slogans about common heritage notwithstanding, prospective teachers need an alternative context in which to think critically about and reconstruct their social knowledge and self-identities. Simply put, they need opportunities to become conscious of oppression. However, as Heaney (1984) correctly observes: "Consciousness of oppression can not be the object of instruction, it must be discovered in experience" (p. 118). Classes such as my Social Foundations course make it possible for students to re-experience the way dysconscious racism and miseducation victimize them.

That dysconscious racism and miseducation of teachers are part of the problem is not well understood. This is evident in conventional foundations approaches and in the teacher education literature on multiculturalism and pluralism which examine social stratification, unequal educational outcomes, and the significance of culture in education but offer no critique of ideology and indoctrination (Gollnick & Chinn, 1990; Pai, 1990). Such approaches do not help prospective teachers gain the critical skills needed to examine the ways being educated in a racist society affects their own knowledge and their beliefs about themselves and culturally diverse others. The findings presented in this article suggest that such skills are vitally necessary. The real challenge of diversity is to develop a sound liberatory praxis of teacher education which offers relatively privileged students freedom to choose critical multicultural consciousness over dysconsciousness. Moving beyond dysconsciousness and miseducation toward liberatory pedagogy will require systematic research to determine how teachers are being prepared and how well those whose preparation includes critical liberatory pedagogy are able to maintain their perspectives and implement transformative goals in their own practice.

## Notes

1   It should be noted that dysconsciousness need not be limited to racism but can apply to justifications of other forms of exploitation such as sexism or even neocolonialism—issues that are beyond the scope of the present analysis.
2   I want to thank Professor Gloria Ladson-Billings, who also teachers at my institution, for providing these journal entries. See her discussion of student knowledge and attitudes in this issue of the *JNE*.
3   This and subsequent student comment codes used throughout this article identify individual respondents within each cohort. "F6–21," for example, refers to respondent 21 in the fall 1986 academic quarter.

## References

Angus, I., & Jhally, S. (Eds.). (1989). *Cultural politics in contemporary America.* New York: Routledge.
Anyon, J. (1979). Ideology and U.S. history textbooks. *Harvard Educational Review, 49,* 361–386.
Anyon, J. (1981). Social class and school knowledge. *Curriculum Inquiry, 11,* 3–42.
Ayers, W. (1988). Young children and the problem of the color line. *Democracy and Education, 3*(1), 20–26.
Banks, J. (1977). *Multiethnic education: Practices and promises.* Bloomington, IN: Phi Delta Kappa Educational Foundation.
Bennett, C. (1990). *Comprehensive multicultural education: Theory and practice.* Boston: Allyn & Bacon.
Bloom, A. (1987). *The closing of the American mind.* New York: Simon & Schuster.
Boggs, J. et al. (1979). *Conversations in Maine: Exploring our nation's future.* Boston: South End Press.
Brandt, G. (1986). *The realization of anti-racist teaching.* Philadelphia: The Falmer Press.
Cagan, E. (1978). Individualism, collectivism, and radical educational reform. *Harvard Educational Review, 48,* 227–266.
Childs, J. B. (1989). *Leadership, conflict and cooperation in Afro-American social thought.* Philadelphia: Temple University Press.
Cox, G. O. (1974). *Education for the Black race.* New York: African Heritage Studies Publishers.
DuBois, W. E. B. (1935). Does the Negro need separate schools? *Journal of Negro Education, 4,* 329–335.
Edelman, M. W. (1987). *Families in peril: An agenda for social change.* Cambridge, MA: Harvard University Press.
Ellis, G. W. (1917). Psychic factors in the new American race situation. *Journal of Race Development, 4,* 469–486.
Freire, P. (1971). *Pedagogy of the oppressed.* New York: Harper & Row.
Freire, P., & Faundez, A. (1989). *Learning to question: A pedagogy of liberation.* New York: Continuum.
Freire, P., & Macedo, D. (1987). *Literacy: Reading the word and the world.* South Hadley, MA: Bergin & Garvey.
Gagnon, P. (1988, November). Why study history? *Atlantic Monthly,* pp. 43–66.
Ginsburg, M. (1988). *Contradictions in teacher education and society: A critical analysis.* Philadelphia: The Falmer Press.
Ginsburg, M., & Newman, K. (1985). Social inequalities, schooling and teacher education. *Journal of Teacher Education, 36,* 49–54.
Giroux, J., & McLaren, P. (1986). Teacher education and the politics of engagement: The case for democratic schooling. *Harvard Educational Review, 56,* 213–238.

346    Joyce E. King

Gollnick, D., & Chinn, P. (1990). *Multicultural education in a pluralistic society.* Columbus, OH: Merrill.
Gordon, B. (1985). Critical and emancipatory pedagogy: An annotated bibliography of sources for teachers. *Social Education, 49*(5), 400–402.
Gordon, B. (1990). The necessity of African-American epistemology for educational theory and practice. *Journal of Education, 172,* in press.
Harlan, S. (1985, June 5). Compared to White children, Black children are . . . *USA Today,* p. 9-A.
Heaney, T. (1984). Action, freedom and liberatory education. In S. B. Merriam (Ed.), *Selected writings on philosophy and education* (pp. 113–122). Malabar, FL: Robert E. Krieger.
Hirsch, E. D. (1987). *Cultural literacy: What every American needs to know.* New York: Houghton Mifflin.
Howard, B. C. (1857). *Report of the decision of the Supreme Court of the United States and the opinions of the justices thereof in the case of Dred Scott versus John F. A. Sandford, December term, 1856.* New York: D. Appleton & Co.
Kozol, J. (1981). *On being a teacher.* New York: Continuum.
King, J., & Ladson-Billings, G. (1990). The teacher education challenge in elite university settings: Developing critical and multicultural perspectives for teaching in a democratic and multicultural society. *European Journal of Intercultural Studies, 1*(2), 15–30.
King, J., & Wilson, T. L. (1990). Being the soul-freeing substance: A legacy of hope in Afro humanity. *Journal of Education, 172*(2), in press.
Ladson-Billings, G. (1991). Beyond multicultural illiteracy. *Journal of Negro Education, 60*(2), 147–157.
Lee, C. et al. (1990). How shall we sing our sacred song in a strange land? The dilemma of double consciousness and complexities of an African-centered pedagogy. *Journal of Education, 172,*(2), in press.
Mezirow, J. (1984). A critical theory of adult learning and education. In S. B. Merriam (Ed.), *Selected writings on philosophy and adult education* (pp. 123–140). Malabar, FL: Robert E. Krieger.
Muwakkil, S. (1990). Fighting for cultural inclusion in the schools. *In These Times, 14*(37), 8–9.
O'Neill, W. F. (1981). *Educational ideologies: Contemporary expressions of educational philosophy.* Santa Monica, CA: Goodyear.
Pai, Y. (1990). *Cultural foundations of education.* Columbus, OH: Merrill.
Perkins, U. E. (1986). *Harvesting new generations: The positive development of Black youth.* Chicago: Third World Press.
Ravitch, D. (1990). Diversity and democracy. *The American Educator, 14,* 16–20.
Rist, R. (1970). Student social class and teacher expectations. *Harvard Educational Review, 40,* 411–451.
Searle, C. (Ed.). (1975). *Classrooms of resistance.* London: Writers and Readers Publishing Cooperative.
Shor, I. (1980). *Critical teaching in everyday life.* Boston: South End Press.
Sleeter, C., & Grant, C. (1988). *Making choices for multicultural education: Five approaches to race, class and gender.* Columbus, OH: Merrill.
Stuckey, S. (1987). *Slave culture: Nationalist theory and the foundations of Black America.* New York: Oxford University Press.
Vallance, E. (1977). Hiding the hidden curriculum: An interpretation of the language of justification in nineteenth-century educational reform. In A. Bellack & H. Kliebard (Eds.), *Curriculum and evaluation* (pp. 590–607). Berkeley, CA: McCutchan.
Wellman, D. (1977). *Portraits of White racism.* Cambridge, MA: Cambridge University Press.
Woodson, C. G. (1933). *The miseducation of the Negro.* Washington, DC: Associated Publishers.
Wynter, S. (1990, September 9). *America as a "world": A Black studies perspective and "cultural model" framework.* [Letter to the California State Board of Education.]

# CHAPTER 28

# TEACHING AND LEARNING THROUGH DESIRE, CRISIS, AND DIFFERENCE (2000)

## Perverted reflections on anti-oppressive education[1]

### Kevin K. Kumashiro

When I think about the concerns currently expressed by my student teachers, I hear the repetition of at least two sets of questions that my colleagues and I grappled with when I was a school teacher a few years ago. One, how do we motivate students to study, to think, to ask; in other words, how do we foster in students a *desire to learn*? Two, how do we teach uncomfortable and controversial material without upsetting students, parents, and community members; in other words, how do we *avoid crisis*? As reflected in numerous educational journals and books, video documentaries, and teacher certification courses, these questions play a central role in contemporary educational inquiry and practice. However, these questions do not necessarily go hand-in-hand with a form of education that actively and intentionally works against oppression (i.e., education that changes racism, sexism, heterosexism, etc.), what I call "anti-oppressive" education. In fact, my own teaching experiences suggest to me that these questions, with their commonsense or normalized notions of "desire" and "crisis," make possible only certain ways of thinking about and engaging in anti-oppressive education, and make impossible or unimaginable other, and perhaps more effective, approaches to teaching and learning against oppression.

In what follows, I reflect on my experiences teaching high school students and student teachers, and argue that teaching was made meaningful, and learning against oppression was made possible, only when we—consciously or unconsciously—made use of non-normalized or perverted forms of desire and crisis. My language, here, is intentional: reflections on the "perverted" involve not only a deviation from what is commonly considered good, right, or true in education, but also an incorporation of the "queer" into practices that often cling to the norm, as I will explain later on. Throughout the article, I include statements that some of my students have expressed orally and in writing to each other and to me as I attempt to represent some of the troubling conversations I hear in education.

## From desiring rationality to entering crisis

Three years ago, I taught a two-week workshop in a summer program for high school students of color. Of the seven afternoon workshops, my workshop was the only one that focused explicitly on oppression (in particular, on racist, sexist, and heterosexist stereotypes). All of my students had chosen to be in my workshop, which suggests to me that they desired to engage in anti-oppressive education. I, too, desired to engage in anti-oppressive education, and drawing on such

348 Kevin K. Kumashiro

theorists as Paulo Freire, Henry Giroux, and Peter McLaren, I envisioned my role as that of a "critical" educator, one who helps students to "critique and transform" oppressive social structures and ideologies. According to my syllabus, we were to do this rationally: the first week would be spent learning about the dynamics of oppression (as we examine a range of stereotypes and answer the question, "why are stereotypes harmful?"), and the second week would be spent acting on this knowledge as we engage in an activist project.

As the first week came to an end, my students' and my own reliance on rational learning and teaching brought us to a stuck place (I explain this in more depth in Kumashiro, 1999). For my students, learning about oppression exceeded the realm of the rational and abstract. Their participation could not remain at the level of intellectual and detached conversation and debates about "what are the stereotypes of this group" or "why are these stereotypes harmful to them?" Rather, they seemed to be confronting their own emotions and life experiences, and in the process, entering a form of "crisis." They became upset, saying they felt "bad" or "guilty" as they recounted times when they stereotyped others and were themselves stereotyped, and yet had not been aware that this was happening (because they had not considered such occurrences to be abnormal). I believe, that, as they learned about the dynamics of oppression, they were unlearning what they previously had learned was "normal," was not harmful, was just the way things are. And, as they unlearned what was "normal" and normative (i.e., the way things ought to be), they were learning about their own privileges and complicities with oppression, such as ways they were privileged by heterosexism, or ways they bought into and, thus, contributed to a racial hierarchy in which, say, Latinas were sexualized, Black men were dehumanized, and Asian Americans were considered unharmed by racism. Having learned about their own role in oppression, they now needed a way to feel better about themselves. Thus, we were "stuck," unable to move on with the more academic parts of the lesson because I had not incorporated into my lesson plan a way to address this emotional crisis.

Yet, as Shoshana Felman (1995) suggests, educators should expect students to enter crisis. In fact, she argues that "teaching in itself, teaching as such, takes place precisely only through crisis" (p. 55). How so? Consider the difference between education and repetition. "Education" is not about repeating what we already know, or affirming what we already believe, or reinforcing what we had previously learned. That is merely repetition. Education, I believe, is about learning something new, something different; education is about change. Perhaps this is all common sense, but what is significant, here, is the recognition that repetition (such as the affirmation of who we are and what we believe) is often a comforting process (because it tells us that we are smart or good). In contrast, education (especially the process of learning something that tells us that *the very ways in which we think and do things* is not only wrong but also harmful) can be a very discomforting process. Hence the notion that learning takes place "only through crisis." Educators should expect their students to enter crisis. And, since this crisis can lead in one of many directions—such as toward liberating change, or toward more entrenched resistance, etc.—educators need to provide a space in the curriculum for students to work through their crisis in a way that changes oppression. Elsewhere (Kumashiro, 1999) I describe this process of working through crisis in more detail.

My point, here, is that by realizing that anti-oppressive education necessarily involves crisis and getting stuck, educators can change the problematic ways in which their approaches to teaching and learning privilege rationality. For students, the desire to learn cannot be a desire to move forward rationally (meaning, to learn things that do not force the student to look within, to look back, to disrupt one's memories, to contradict one's worldview). Rather, the desire to learn must involve a desire to unlearn, a desire to return to what has already been learned, not to repeat or relearn it, but to unlearn it, to understand it in a different way, and to work through the resulting crisis.

Similarly, for teachers, the desire to teach cannot involve the facade of detachment. My students needed not an abstracted conversation about what they were going through, but a therapeutic activity in which they could work through their crisis. Leading such an activity required that I not be detached, impersonal, objective. Like my students, I needed to put myself into the lesson, to be *attached*, to listen to them, to share my own stories, and to address their needs. I needed to, and eventually did, rework my lesson plan and open a curricular space for my students to discuss their feelings and decide for themselves how they wanted to proceed with the lesson, which they did by writing and performing a skit for the other students in the program. They opened the skit by saying:

> Welcome! You are all gathered here for our group's play which is based on stereotypes, which was the focus of our workshop. Our play is called, "Just Think," which is something we all should do more often. Our play contains stereotypes, a lot of them, which may possibly offend some people but are not meant to. Please pay attention, enjoy, and think while viewing our play! Thank you!!

And they concluded by saying:

> We're feeling bad about what we did—that's why we're doing this [skit]. We're not trying to lecture you; we're trying to share what we learned.

By owning up to their prior complicity with stereotyping, and by critiquing the power of stereotypes to harm, the students, through the skit, were able to work through their crisis (and do something activist in the process). It is significant to note that, although my original lesson plan called for my students to do an "activist project," it did not leave open the space for them to work through emotional crisis while doing so.

Even well-intentioned pedagogies, then, can be problematic. Ironically, such pedagogies can further marginalize the very students they intend to liberate. Critiquing "critical" educators (like the ones who initially influenced my lesson planning), Elizabeth Ellsworth (1992) tells us that the reliance on rationality and assumption of detachment really privilege the "mythical norm" (White American, male, etc.), serving as "repressive myths that perpetuate relations of domination." In my own class, I believe that my initial privileging of rationality harmed my students because it could not account for the excesses of emotion. In particular, the life experiences of my students of color, especially with racism, brought a historical and personal connection to the lessons on oppression that those who fit the mythical norm do not typically have; they had difficulty separating their heart from their mind when "understanding" racism. Personal experiences as people not privileged on the basis of race exceeded the expectations of a pedagogy that relied on rationality and that repressed other ways of knowing and relating. I should note that even the ways my students were *privileged* required occasional departures from my lesson plan, such as when discussions of heterosexism and homophobia confronted a student with her own homophobia because they rubbed against and complicated memories of her favorite uncle, who happened to be gay. More than just acknowledging her privilege, this student wrestled with her privilege in a way that forced her to recognize parallels between heterosexual privilege and racial privilege, and the benefits both (unfairly) bestow on different dominant groups in society. Because my lesson plan could not address these emotional and unpredicted events, it missed my students, Othering them because they could not be engaged by a pedagogy that presumed to address the mythical norm.

Deborah Britzman (1998b) suggests that this should not be surprising: pedagogy's privileging of rationality (and repressing of other ways of knowing and relating, such as "touching") is its defense mechanism against what it cannot control or predict. And, like the ego's defense mechanisms, pedagogy's privileging of rationality harms itself, works against its own goals, and, as in my case, leads to stuck places that it cannot work through, and that, instead, it constantly tries to avoid or foreclose. Yet, as I argued earlier, when teaching and learning against oppression, crises cannot be avoided, should not be avoided, and must be worked through. This is not to say that rationality should be avoided. Rather, rationality must not be treated as the panacea, as the solution to our problems. While a rational pedagogy does make some teaching and learning possible, it make others impossible. The desire to teach, then, especially the desire to teach students outside the mythical norm, cannot revolve around solely the desire to reason; it must also involve a desire to attach and touch, a desire to enter stuck and uncontrollable places, and a desire for crisis.

## From desiring sameness to desiring crisis

I found myself in a different class entering a similarly stuck place last year when teaching a semester-long course on the relationship between school and society at a large Midwestern university. This introductory-level course consisted of over thirty undergraduate students, mostly White American, heterosexual women, most of whom were working towards certification in the teacher education program. We spent the first few weeks of the semester examining the paradoxical nature of schools that strive to give students equal educational opportunity but function to maintain various social hierarchies. As we discussed examples and theories of how and how often this happens, my students seemed to move, at least in their discussions, from feeling surprised, to critically reflecting on their own schooling experiences, to strategizing ways to address the problem. For this reason, I believe my students honestly desired to engage in anti-oppressive education. I, too, desired to engage in anti-oppressive education, wanting my students to think of schooling more critically, and to teach more critically.

Although I did not realize it at the time, both desires, while perhaps well-intentioned, revolved around affirming the self and remaining the same. For my students, the desire to learn involved learning only that which did not confront them with their own complicity with oppression. Some students felt that schools are not responsible for social change and, instead, should follow the course set by others in society:

> I don't think that schools are responsible to initiate change. I think that artists, writers, lobbyists, activists, performers, the new media, thinkers of all types, spiritual leaders and political leaders are all responsible to initiate the social change attitude. Education can then take it from there.

Some felt that teaching in ways that address oppression would detract from what schools were supposed to focus on, namely, academics:

> All the approaches deal so much with integrating racism, sexism, and hetero-sexism into the curriculum, but will this take away from the true intention of schools to teach children academics?

Besides detracting from academics, some felt that teachers should be morally neutral:

> There are only eight hours in a standard school day. If cultures, races, sexual orientations, etc., are going to be added to the curriculum, what is going to be taken out of the present system? The school day is already jam-packed with the basic classes. How can a curriculum incorporate all ideas and still leave room for math and science? Will not it seem like teachers are teaching their values on different ideas to their students?

Some felt that teachers are not part of the problem:

> I don't think that I have ever experienced a situation when students were directly oppressed by teachers in any way. The teachers were there to teach, not to impregnate their own beliefs or biases upon the students.

Many of my students acknowledged and condemned the ways schools per-petuate, say, racism, but asserted that, as a teacher, their job will be to teach academics, not disrupt racism. They separated the school's function from the individual teacher's role, remaining secure in their belief that they do not—and, as a future teacher, will not—contribute to these problems (Joy Lei, personal communication, March 19, 1999).

Some felt that teachers could blend anti-racist teaching with academics through a "multicultural" curriculum, but only one in which students learn about different cultures, not about their own privileges, i.e., about themselves. They did not believe their privileges made a difference in their education, and instead shifted the focus of our conversations to the people who were different from the norm at their school—they wanted to talk about *them*. As a several students kept repeating in class discussions and in their final projects, if people can learn about different groups, and develop empathy for them, then ignorance, and the prejudice based on it, will be effectively combated. For example, students who felt they were becoming more "open-minded about homosexuals" talked about realizing that there is "nothing wrong" with them, that they are just like the norm (or the normal folks), and that they hurt just like everyone else. Learn-ing, in this sense, was less an entry into difference, and more an affirmation of the self:

> I started the semester much more close-minded about the issue of homo-sexuality. After hearing many stories and reading the class materials, I finally have come to realize that there is nothing wrong with homosexuality. I think it helped that I got to know Kevin before he told us his sexuality, by that time it did not matter if he was gay[2] or not.

Not surprisingly, one student said:

This article made me sad. I had an uncle who was gay. I realize that he wasn't treated equal when he was in school. He was one of the greatest guys I ever knew. He died last year, so it really hurt me to know that other gay people are experiencing what he had to experience.

The expectation that information about the Other leads to empathy is often based on the assumption that learning about "them" helps students see that "they" are like "us" (Britzman, 1998a). In other words, learning about the Other helps students see the self in the Other, and thus, does not change how they see themselves.

Similarly, my desire to teach involved teaching in ways that affirmed my knowledge and projected myself onto others. As I imagine many teachers do, I had planned lessons thinking that I knew (1) what my students knew and felt, (2) how I wanted my students to end up thinking and acting, and (3) what I needed to do in the lesson to get them to that place. Furthermore, in choosing their reading and writing assignments and planning the lessons, I had wanted my students to become at least somewhat like me, to think of schools and oppression critically (the way I think), to teach subversively (the way I teach). I soon learned, however, that anti-oppressive education cannot revolve around affirmation and sameness.

As my students and I moved to the section of the course on how teachers and schools might address the ways they function to maintain social hierarchies, I had them read an essay I wrote (an earlier draft of Kumashiro, in press) that described four ways educators have talked about doing this (i.e., four approaches to anti-oppressive education), and I had planned an activity to generate discussion around these four approaches. In terms of the three areas described in the above paragraph, I had assumed that they (1) knew little about addressing oppression in schools but were committed to doing so, (2) could implement the four approaches if they learned them, and (3) therefore, should read about and discuss them in depth. However, when the class period began, we almost immediately got stuck at my use of the term "queer."[3] One student said:

> You use the term "queer" throughout the article and it struck me as derogatory and actually really upset me until you clarified why you used it on page 11. As a suggestion, maybe you should explain how you use the term "queer" for a feeling of "self-empowerment" at the beginning. It would make the reader feel more comfortable. The more I think about it, maybe you should not use the term at all. I don't really think it's appropriate for this type of paper. I know that I personally cringed every time I read it.

Another said:

> Really don't like the word queer. I understand better why you chose the word queer but it's still a bit much [when said] over and over again—it just has a negative feel to it.

I had hoped to discuss the ways that students from traditionally marginalized groups in society are Othered in schools, but in a conversation where even some of the normally quiet students were speaking, many kept expressing feelings of discomfort and even anger at my use of a term that often meant something derogatory. Although I neglected before assigning the paper to discuss the history of the term "queer," I did explain in the essay that "queer" has been claimed and appropriated by many queers to signify a conscious disassociation with normative sexuality and a sense of self-empowerment. Nonetheless, many were offended that I used a term that they had learned was politically correct to avoid. What they kept repeating in the discussion was the notion that "queer" meant something negative, and that I should instead use "homosexual" or "gay" since those terms will not upset the (presumably) predominantly straight readership of the journal in which I was hoping to publish the paper. (I had explained to them that this was a draft of an article I was trying to get published in an educational research journal.)

I believe there are two main reasons why we were stuck on "queer." One, it made explicit the constructedness and harmfulness of normalcy (i.e., how what is defined as "normal" is often normative in nature), and in doing so, confronted my students with the discomforting process of dis-identifying themselves with normalcy. The fluidity of sexuality signified by "queer" suggests that one's own sexual orientation is not fixed or given or natural, and thus, it forces one to denaturalize one's own identity. Two, it invoked a history of ignorance, bigotry, and hatred, and in doing so, confronted my students with their own role and complicity in that history (Lisa Loutzenheiser, personal communication, March 19, 1999). The preferred terms of "homosexual" and "gay" do not stir up such a history. In fact, the medically pathologizing history of "homosexual" and the assimilationist history of "gay" (Tierney & Dilley, 1998) perhaps make it easier to disclaim heterosexism/homophobia as a viable form of oppression. Indeed, several students asserted that they did not believe that heterosexism/homophobia was as much of a problem as racism, classism, and sexism, which were the other forms of oppression addressed in the essay:

> I saw the title about Anti-Oppressive Education, but the majority[4] of the examples used to explain the approaches dealt with homosexuality. I do not see homosexuality as the main problem. I would find it more helpful if more oppressive topics were discussed.

The hate-filled history of the term "queer" makes explicit the existence of heterosexism and homophobia, the severity of heterosexism/homophobia, and if the student had ever used the term in a harmful way (or failed to intervene in such a situation), the participation of the student in heterosexism/homophobia. So, although my students did desire to learn, their desire for normalcy and for affirmation of their belief that they do not oppress others was stronger, preventing many of them from confronting and tolerating these new yet discomforting forms of knowledge. In desiring to remain normal, they desired a repetition of the silence that normally surrounds heterosexism/homophobia, including their complicity with it, and thus, entered a crisis when they met "queer."

Our getting stuck on the term "queer" was also a crisis for me. I was completely surprised by their emotional reaction to my piece and unprepared for the resulting conversation. More importantly, I was upset not merely for being unprepared, but for being unprepared because I had fallen back on old habits. In the first place, yet again, I had planned a lesson that proceeded rationally: first, summarize the essay, second, extend the theories in the essay to other forms of oppression (since the essay focused on only four types of oppression). In other words, part of the problem was my failure to incorporate what I had learned from teaching the high schoolers two years earlier; I proceeded rationally, and left little space for uncertainty and for working through crisis. In the second place, I yet again presumed to know my students when I did not. I expected to know how they would respond to my essay. In particular, while I did anticipate a crisis, I was expecting a different kind of crisis, one based on learning about the many ways oppression played out in their schooling years, not one based on resisting the very theories being presented. Clearly, the students were not whom I thought I was addressing.

Elizabeth Ellsworth (1997) tells us this is not surprising. Educators can never fully know our students. Plus, our students are all different from one another, and they all have multiple identities. A mode of address that expects to know students and that expects students to be a unitary audience will always miss them. And that is what happened. My lesson plan missed many of my students.

There were, of course, a few students who expressed support for my use of the term "queer," and who thought of their experience reading the essay as a positive educational experience:

> Upon reading the essay, I felt very happy. For once, I was reading an essay that dealt directly with the topic of discrimination in schools (especially with homosexuality).

Some even felt the essay and its queerness was educationally useful:

> Personally, I had no problem with the use of the word "queer." I was not offended by the word. I was actually intrigued to read on and find out what the actual meaning of the word "queer" is.

Another said:

> This is a voice that I've never heard before. This brought a whole new dimension to my frame of thinking. I'm not sure what it is but information like this gets my mind going. It has been true for me that when I had to work through a crisis, I grew and gained from the experience like no other time in my life. This is what life's all about for me: learning.

One student told me that she did not initially understand why I was using "queer," but reasoned that the discomfort she felt was perhaps part of the learning process of reading my essay. She said that she wanted to learn, which for her meant learning something new, hearing a different voice, imagining the yet-unarticulated, doing the "unexpected." She preferred learning things that made her uncomfortable and complicated her "frame of thinking." In other words, her openness to my essay resulted from a desire to learn that involved not a desire for affirmation and repetition, but a desire for crisis and difference.

As the class discussion ensured, I encouraged my students to enter into discomforting places and to think of learning as taking place only through crisis. Modeling my own advice, I forced myself to enter an uncomfortable place, departing from my lesson plan and teaching the unpredicted. Such a move, I should note, is very difficult for me, as it is for many teachers who desire control over the direction of the lesson and over what students learn. Patti Lather (1998) tells us that educators often try to avoid crises and foreclose stuck places in order to maintain a sense of control over what students learn (and, for that matter, over how they behave). Yet, as my experiences show, we can never control what students learn. It is only when educators acknowledge the impossibilities, unknowabilities, and uncontrollabilities of teaching, and work within stuck places, that change is possible. Thus, teaching and learning against oppression cannot revolve around the desires for affirmation and sameness; students and teachers alike must be open to entering crisis and following the discomforting desire for difference.

Not until the end of the period did we discuss the four approaches. In retrospect, not expecting to address crisis not only led me to plan a lesson that could not be "achieved," but also, had I not departed from it, could have prevented me from working with my students where they were at. More and more, I am seeing that the goal of education needs to be change, i.e., getting students to a different place, out of repetition. This is not to say that they should get to "where I am." I cannot foretell where they (are to) go. And this is not to say that they should just go anywhere. Where they go could be as (or even more) harmful than before. The goal, then, needs to be a change informed by theories of anti-oppressive education, a change that works against multiple forms of oppression. Embracing difference, refusing complicity, troubling privilege, engaging in activism—I believe these are changes in the right direction. In my class, I can never fully know how I affected my students. But I can at least take comfort in knowing that the resulting discussion in our classroom gave us a space to begin to work through our own individual crises and get un-stuck.

In this article, I have tried to argue that education involves many desires and crises, and that traditional and even well-intentioned approaches to teaching and learning do not always allow for the (perverted) desires and crises that can help students and teachers to work against oppression. As educators and educational researchers continue to unmask the roles that our various desires can and do play in teaching and learning, we should also ask what differences are made possible when we confront various forms of crisis through anti-oppressive education, and what it might look like when we do this. Now, when I teach, I begin the semester by making explicit my expectations that we often desire repetition, that differences can be upsetting, and that, consequently, learning takes place "only through crisis." It is not the panacea, but such an approach has allowed me to engage students in conversations where they seem interested in learning about oppression, open to confronting their own privileges and complicities, and better prepared to address the emotions and discomfort that come in the process. I hope this article helps other educators address the complexities of anti-oppressive education.

# Notes

1   An earlier version of this article was presented at the Reclaiming Voice II Conference, held June 4 to 5, 1999, in Irvine, California. Thanks to Elizabeth Ellsworth, Lisa Loutzenheiser, Joy Lei, and especially my students for helping me think through the ideas in this article.

2   I should note that I came out to my class as "bisexual" and "queer," not "gay." Yet, most students (and people in general) referred to me as "gay." This reading practice (of placing me on one end of a sexual-orientation binary) reflects what I will soon argue is a desire by many people to think of sexual-orientation in ways that do not trouble their own sexual identities. To see me as (and to call me) "gay" is comforting because "gay" puts me on the "other" side of the binary. To see me as "bisexual" or "queer" is to acknowledge that sexual identity is not either-or but much more fluid, and that is not a concept that many were/are willing to embrace. They were resisting, in other words, the discomforting departure from binaries (e.g., straight-gay, self-other).

3   In the essay, as in this article, I use the term "queer" to mean "gay, lesbian, bisexual,

transgender, intersexed (neither male nor female) or in other ways 'queer' because of one's sexual identity or sexual orientation.* In addition to its inclusiveness, I choose to use the term "queer" for its pedagogical effect and political significance. As I will later argue, the term "queer" is discomforting to many people because it continues to invoke a history of bigotry and hatred, but for many queers, it has come to signify a rejection of normative sexualities and genders, a reclaiming of the terms of their identities, and a feeling of self-empowerment (Tierney and Dilley, 1998).

4   It is true that heterosexism is brought up in the essay more often than the other forms of oppression, but only slightly. I could not help but wonder if the reason students felt that heterosexism was given "too much emphasis" was because it was not given the kind of emphasis that it is normally given, by which I mean, only marginal attention. Perhaps my students could have tolerated a superficial discussion in which heterosexism was tokenized, but were unable and unwilling to mask their resistance to change when confronted with heterosexism head on.

## References

Britzman, D.P. (1998a). *Lost Subjects, Contested Objects: Toward a Psychoanalytic Inquiry of Learning.* Albany: State University of New York Press.

Britzman, D. P. (1998b). "On some psychical consequences of AIDS education." In W. F. Pinar (Ed.), *Queer Theory in Education.* Mahweh, NJ: Lawrence Erlbaum.

Ellsworth, E. (1992). "Why doesn't this feel empowering? Working through the repressive myths of critical pedagogy." In C. Luke & J. Gore (Eds.), *Feminisms and Critical Pedagogies.* New York: Routledge.

Ellsworth, E. (1997). *Teaching Positions: Difference, Pedagogy, and the Power of Address.* New York: Teachers College Press.

Felman, S. (1995). "Education and crisis, or the vicissitudes of teaching." In C. Caruth (Ed.), *Trauma: Explorations in Memory.* Baltimore, MD: The Johns Hopkins University Press.

Freire, P. (1995). *Pedagogy of the Oppressed.* (Translated by M. B. Ramos.) New York: Continuum.

Giroux, H. A., & McLaren, P. L. (1989). "Introduction: Schooling, cultural politics, and the struggle for democracy." In H. A. Giroux & P. McLaren (Eds.), *Critical Pedagogy, the State, and Cultural Struggle.* Albany: State University of New York Press.

Kumashiro, K. K. (1999). " 'Barbie,' 'big dicks,' and 'faggots': Paradox, performativity, and anti-oppressive pedagogy." *JCT: The Journal of Curriculum Theorizing*, 15(1), 27–42.

Kumashiro, K. K. (in press). "Toward a theory of anti-oppressive education." *Review of Educational Research*, 70(1).

Lather, P. (1998). "Critical pedagogy and its complicities: A praxis of stuck places." *Educational Theory*, 48(4), 487–497.

Tierney, W. G., & Dilley, P. (1998). "Constructing knowledge: Educational research and gay and lesbian studies." In W. F. Pinar (Ed.), *Queer Theory in Education.* Mahweh, NJ: Lawrence Erlbaum.

# APPENDIX 1: OTHER SUGGESTED READINGS

Ainsa, T. (1980). A broader approach to teacher training? *College Student Journal, 14*(3), 94–142.

Cochran-Smith, M. (1991). Learning to teach against the grain. *Harvard Educational Review, 61*(3), 279–310.

Darling-Hammond, L. (1983). Teacher education in the organizational context: A review of the literature. *Review of Educational Research, 53*(3), 285–328.

Darling-Hammond, L. (1996). What matters most: A competent teacher for every child. *Phi Delta Kappan, 78*(3), 193–200.

Davidman, L., & Davidman, P. (1988). Multicultural teacher education in the state of California: The challenge of definition and implementation. *Teacher Education Quarterly, 15*(2), 50–67.

Dilworth, M. E. (1988). A continuing critique of the Holmes Group. *Journal of Negro Education, 57*(2), 199–201.

Foster, M. (1990). The politics of race: Through the eyes of African American teachers. *Journal of Education, 172*(3), 123–141.

Futrell, M. H. (1988). Teachers in Reform. *Educational Administration, 24*(4), 374–380.

Gordon, B. (1986). The use of emancipatory pedagogy in teacher education. *The Journal of Educational Thought, 20*(2), 59–66.

Grant, C. A. (1994). Best practices in teacher preparation for urban schools: Lessons from the multicultural teacher education literature. *Action in Teacher Education, 16*(3), 1–18.

Justiz, M. J., & Darling, D. W. (1980). A multicultural perspective in teacher education. *Educational Horizons, 58*(4), 203–205.

Kleifgen, J. (1988). Learning from student teachers' cross-cultural communicative failures. *Anthropology and Education Quarterly, 19*, 218–234.

Latham, J. (1982). Exceptional children or exceptional teachers? An alternative policy for teacher education in a multi-racial society. *Journal of Future and Higher Education, 6*(2), 40–47.

Mahan, J., & Boyle, V. (1981). Multicultural teacher preparation: An attitudinal survey. *Educational Research Quarterly, 6*(3), 97–103.

Popkewitz, T. (1989). Teacher incentives as reforms: Teachers work and the changing control mechanisms in education. *Teachers College Record, 90*(4), 575–594.

Popkewitz, T. (1994). Professionalization in teaching and teacher education: Some notes on its history, ideology, and potential. *Teaching and Teacher Education, 10*(1), 1–14.

Sleeter, C. (1994). White racism. *Multicultural Education, 1*(4), 5–8, 39.

Smith, G. P. (1998). Who shall have the moral courage? *Multicultural Education, 5*(3), 4–10.

Solorzano, D., & Yosso, T. J. (2001). From racial stereotyping and deficit discourse toward a critical race theory in teacher education. *Multicultural Education, 9*(1), 2–8.

Tatum, B. D. (1994). Teaching white students about racism: The search for white allies and the restoration of hope. *Teachers College Record, 95*(4), 462–476.

Warren, R. L. (1968). Some determinates of the teacher's role in influencing educational aspirations: A cross-cultural perspective. *Sociology of Education, 41*(3), 291–304.
Zeichner, K. (1987). Teaching student teachers to reflect. *Harvard Educational Review, 57*(1), 23–48.

# APPENDIX 2: JOURNAL PUBLISHERS AND CONTACT INFORMATION

*Action in Teacher Education*
Association of Teacher Educators
1900 Association Drive, Suite ATE
Reston, VA 20191–1502
(703)620–2110; (703)620–9530
http://www.ate1.org

*American Association of Colleges for Teacher Education*
1307 New York Avenue, NW Suite 300
Washington, DC 20005–4701
(202)293–2450; (202)457–8096 (Fax)
www.aacte.org

*American Educational Research Association*
1230—17th Street NW
Washington, DC 20036
(202)223–9485, × 100; (202)775–1824
http://aera.net

*American Journal of Education*
University of Chicago Press
Permissions Department
1427 East 60th Street
Chicago, IL
(773)702–6096; (773)702–9756

*American Sociological Association*
1307 New York Avenue, NW Suite 700
Washington, DC 20005–4701
Jill Campbell
Publications Manager
(202)383–9005, × 303; (202)638–0882
www.asanet.org

*Anthropology and Education*
*Anthropology and Education Quarterly*
University of California Press
Journals and Digital Publishing Division
2000 Center Street, Suite 303
Berkeley, CA 94704

*Association for Supervision and Curriculum Development*
1703 N. Beauregard Street
Alexandria, VA 22311–1714
(703)578–9600; (703)575–5400 (Fax)
www.ascd.org

*Banks, Cherry A. McGee*
Professor, Education
University of Washington, Bothell
18115 Campus Way NE Room UW1 244
Bothell, WA 98011–8246

*Banks, James A.*
University of Washington
Box 353600, 110 Miller Hall
Seattle, WA 98195–3600
(206)543–3386; (206)542–4218 Fax
http://faculty.washington.edu/jbanks

*Comparitive Education Review*
University of Chicago Press
Permissions Department
1427 East 60th Street
Chicago, IL
(773)702–6096; (773)702–9756

*Curriculum and Teaching*
James Nicholas Publishers
PO Box 244
Albert Park, Australia, 3206

*Education*
Dr. George E. Uhlig
PO Box 8826
Spring Hill Station
Mobile, AL 36689

*Education and Urban Society*
Corwin Press, Inc.
2455 Teller Road
Thousand Oaks, CA 91320–2218
(805)499–9734; (805)499–0871 (Fax)
http://www.sagepub.com

*Educational Horizons*
National Association for Ethnic Studies, Inc. &
American Cultural Studies Department
Western Washington University
516 High Street—MS 9113
Bellingham, WA 98225–9113
(360)650–2349; (360)650–2690 (Fax)

*Educational Leadership*
Association for Supervision and Curriculum Development
PO Box 79760
Baltimore, MD 21279–0760
(703)578–9600; 1–800–933–2723; (703)575–5400 Fax
www.ascd.org

*Educational Research Quarterly*
113 Greenbriar Drive
West Monroe, LA 71291
(318)274–2355
hashway@alphagram.edu

*Educators for Urban Minorities*
Long Island University Press (No longer in operation)
Eugene E. Garcia, Ph.D.
Vice President Education Partnerships
Professor of Education
Arizona State University
Eugene.Garcia@asum.edu

*English Journal*
1111 W. Kenyon Road
Urbana, IL 61801–1096
(217)328–3870; (217)328–9645 (Fax)
http://www.ncte.org

*Exceptional Children*
Council for Exceptional Children
Permissions Department
1110 North Glebe Road Suite 300
Arlington, VA 22201–5704
(703)264–1637

*FOCUS*
Joint Center for Political Studies
1301 Pennsylvania Avenue, NW
Washington, DC 20004
(202)626–3500

*Ford Foundation*
320 East 43rd Street
New York, NY 10017

*Gibson, Margaret A.*
Professor of Education and Anthropology
Department of Education
University of California, Santa Cruz
1156 High Street
Santa Cruz, CA 95064
(831)459–4740; (831)459–4618 (Fax)

*Harvard Educational Review*
Harvard Graduate School of Education
8 Story Street, 1st Floor
Cambridge, MA 02138
(617)495–3432; (617)496–3584 (fax)
www.hepg.org
+
HarperCollins Publishers
10 East 53rd Street
New York, NY 10022
(212)207–7000

*Interchange*
Nel van der Werf
Assistant Rights and Permissions/Springer
Van Godewijckstraat 30
PO Box 17
3300 AA Dordrecht
The Netherlands
31 (0) 78 6576 298; 31 (0) 78 6576 323 (Fax)
Nel.vanderwerf@springer.com
www.springeronline.com

*Journal of Curriculum Studies*
Routledge (Taylor & Francis, Inc.)
4 Park Square, Milton Park
Abingdon, Oxon OX14 4RN United Kingdom
44–1235–828600; 44–1235–829000 (Fax)
http://www.routledge.co.uk

*Journal of Curriculum and Supervision*
Association for Supervision and Curriculum Development
1703 North Beauregard Street
Alexandria, VA 22311–1714
(703)578–9600/(800)933–2723; (703)575–3926 (Fax)
http://www.ascd.org

*Journal of Teacher Education*
American Association of Colleges for Teacher Education
1307 New York Avenue NW Suite 300
Washington, DC 20017–4701
(202)293–2450; (202)457–8095 (Fax)
www.aacte.org

*Journal of Research and Development in Education*
Julie P. Sartor, Editor
Office of the Associate Dean for Research,
Technology, & External Affairs
UGA College of Education
(706)542–4693; (706)542–8125 (Fax)
jsartor@uga.edu

*Journal of Negro Education*
Howard University Press
Marketing Department
2600 Sixth Street, NW
Washington, DC 20059
(202)806–8120; (202)806–8434 (Fax)

*Journal of Literacy Research* (formerly *Journal of Reading Behavior*)
Lawrence Erlbaum Associates, Inc.
10 Industrial Avenue
Mahwah, NJ 07430–2262
(201)258–2200; (201)236–0072 (Fax)

*Journal of Educational Thought*
University of Calgary
Faculty of Education – Publications Office
2500 University Drive N.W.
Education Tower, Room 1310
Calgary, Alberta, Canada T2N 1N4
(403)220–7499/5629; (403)284–4162 (Fax)
www.ucalgary.ca

*Journal of Teacher Education*
American Association of Colleges for Teacher Education
1307 New York Avenue NW 300
Washington, DC 20005–4701
(202)293–2450; (202)457–8095 (Fax)
www.aacte.org

*Language Arts*
The National Council of Teachers of English
1111 W. Kenyon Road
Urbana, IL 61801–1096
(217)278–3621
permissions@ncte.org

*Momentum*
National Catholic Educational Association
1077—30 Street, NW Suite 100
Washington, DC 2007
(202)337–6232; (202)333–6706 (Fax)
nceaadmin@ncea.org

*Multicultural Education*
Gaddo Gap Press
3145 Geary Boulevard PMB 275
San Francisco, CA 94118
(414)666–3012; (414)666–3552
http://www.caddogap.com

*National Catholic Educational Association*
1077—30 Street, NW Suite 100
Washington, DC 20007
(202)337–6232; (202)333–6706 (Fax)
nceaadmin@ncea.org

*National Council for the Social Studies*
8555 Sixteenth Street, Suite 500
Center for Multicultural Education
Silver Spring, MD 20910
(301)588–1800 × 122;
(301)588–2049 Fax

*National Educational Service*
1252 Loesch Road
PO Box 8 Department V2
Bloomington, IN 47402

*Negro Educational Review*
NER Editorial Offices
School of Education
1601 East Market Street
Greensboro, NC 27411
Alice M. Scales (scales@pitt.edu)
Shirley A. Biggs (biggs@pitt.edu)

*Peabody Journal of Education*
Lawrence Erlbaum Associates
10 Industrial Avenue
Mahwah, NJ 07430–2262

*Phi Delta Kappan*
Phi Delta Kappa International
408 N. Union Street
PO Box 789
(812)339–1156; 800–766–1156; (812)339–0018 fax

*Race, Class, and Gender*
Southern University at New Orleans (No Response)
Carl contact Jean Belkhir (jbelkhir@uno.edu)

*Radical Teacher*
Center for Critical Education
PO Box 382616
Cambridge, MA 02238
Saul Slapikoff, Permissions Editor
slap2@comcast.net

*Researching Today's Youth: The Community Circle of Caring Journal*
Dr. Carlos E. Cortes
Professor Emeritus
Department of History
University of California,
Riverside, CA 92521–0204
(951)827–1487
(951)827–5299 fax
carlos.cortes@ucr.edu

*Review of Educational Research*
American Educational Research Association
1230—17th Street NW
Washington, DC 20036–3078

*Sage Publications, Inc.*
*Corwin Press, Inc*
2455 Teller Road
Thousand Oaks, CA 91320
(805)410–7713; (805)376–9562 (Fax)
permissions@sagepub.com

*Southeastern Association of Educational Opportunity Program Personnel (SAEOPP)*
75 Piedmont Avenue NE
Suite 408
Atlanta, GA 30303–2518
(404)522–4642

*Teachers College Record*
Blackwell Publishing
PO Box 805
9600 Garsington Road
Oxford OX4 2ZG United Kingdom
44 (0) 1865 776868; 44 (0) 1865 714591 Fax
www.blackwellpublishing.com

*Teacher Education and Special Education*
Dr. Fred Spooner, Editor
Teacher Education and Special Education
SPCD/College of Education
University of North Carolina at Charlotte
Charlotte, NC 28223

(704)687–8851; (704)687–2916 Fax
fhspoone@email.uncc.edu

*The American Scholar*
1606 New Hampshire Avenue NW
Washington, DC 20009
(202)265–3808; (202)265–0083

*The Educational Forum*
Kappa Delta Pi
3707 Woodview Trace
Indianapolis, IN 46268–1158

*The High School Journal*
The University of North Carolina Press
PO Box 2288
Chapel Hill, NC 27515–2288
(919)966–3561; (919)966–3829
www.uncpress.unc.edu

*The Journal of Educational Research*
Heldref Publications
1319 Eighteenth Street, NW
Washington, DC 20036–1802
(202)296–6267; (202)296–5146 (Fax)
www.heldref.org

*The New Advocate*
Christopher-Gordon Publishers, Inc.
1502 Providence Hwy, Suite 12
Norwood, MA 02062–4643
(781)762–5577; (781)762–7261
http://www.christopher-gordon.com

*The Social Studies*
Heldref Publications
1319 Eighteenth Street, NW
Washington, DC 20038–1802
(202)296–6267; (202)296–5149 (Fax)
permissions@heldref.org

*The Teacher Educator*
Ball State University
Teachers College
TC 1008
Muncie, IN 47306
(765)285–5453; (765)285–5455

*The Urban Review*
Nel van der Werf
Assistant Rights and Permissions/Springer
Van Godewijckstraat 30
PO Box 17
3300 AA Dordrecht
The Netherlands
31 (0) 78 6576 298;  31 (0) 78 6576 323 (Fax)
Nel.vanderwerf@springer.com
www.springeronline.com

*Theory into Practice*
Lawrence Erlbaum Associates, Inc.
10 Industrial Avenue
Mahwah, NJ 07430–2262

*Viewpoints in Teaching and Learning*
Indiana University
School of Education
Education Building 109
Bloomington, IN 47405

*Young Children*
National Association for the Education of Young Children
1313 L Street, NW, Suite 500
Washington, DC 20036–1426
(202)232–8777; (202)328–1846 (Fax)
http://www.naeyc.org

# PERMISSION CREDITS

## Part 1: Teacher Dispositions

Wendy Leebov Gollub and Earline Sloan, "Teacher Expectations and Race and Socioeconomic Status." *Urban Education,* 13:1 (1978), 95–106. Copyright © 1978 by Sage Publications. Reprinted with permission.

Mary B. Giles and Thomas M. Sherman, "Measurement of Multicultural Attitudes of Teacher Trainees." *The Journal of Educational Research,* 75:4 (March/April 1982), 204–209. Copyright © 1982 by the Helen Dwight Reid Educational Foundation. Published by Heldref Publications. Reprinted with permission.

Valora Washington, "Implementing Multicultural Education: Elementary Teachers' Attitudes and Professional Practices." *Peabody Journal of Education,* 59:3 (April 1982), 190–200. Copyright © 1982 by Lawrence Erlbaum. Reprinted with permission.

Robert Rueda and Alfonso G. Prieto, "Cultural Pluralism: Implications for Teacher Education." *Teacher Education and Special Education,* 2:4 (1979), 4–10. Copyright © 1979 by the University of South Carolina at Charlotte. Reprinted with permission.

Mary Louise Gomez, "Prospective Teachers' Perspectives on Teaching Diverse Children: A Review with Implications for Teacher Education and Practice." *Journal of Negro Education,* 62:4 (1993), 459–474. Copyright © 1993 by Howard University. Reprinted with permission.

Gretchen McAllister and Jacqueline Jordan Irvine, "Cross Cultural Competency and Multicultural Teacher Education." *Review of Educational Research,* 70:1 (Spring 2000), 3–24. Copyright © 2000 by the American Association for Colleges of Teacher Education (AACTE). Reprinted with permission.

## Part 2: Teacher Preparation

James Mahan and Virginia Boyle, "Multicultural Teacher Preparation: An Attitudinal Survey." *Educational Research Quarterly,* 6:3 (Fall 1981), 97–103. Copyright © 1981 by the *Educational Research Quarterly.* Reprinted with permission.

Carl A. Grant and Ruth A. Koskela, "Education That Is Multicultural and the

## Part 3: The Model Teacher

## Part 4: Professional Development

## Part 5: Reflections of Praxis

# AUTHOR INDEX

# SUBJECT INDEX

critical pedagogy: classes 216–19;
curriculum 186; student experience
216–17; student voice and public sphere
218–19
cross cultural communication 192
cross cultural competency 63–82
cross cultural development: Developmental
Model of Intercultural Sensitivity
(Bennett) 64, 74–7; process models
64–77; Racial Identity Development
(Helms) 64, 66–71, 145;
recommendations 78–9; teacher
attitudes 64; teacher education 63–82;
Typology of Ethnicity (Banks) 64,
71–4
cross cultural encounters 245–7
cross cultural immersion 131–2
cultural accommodation 149
cultural differences: cognitive style 43–5;
cultural relativism 283–5; disability
compared 173; knowledge acquisition
255–8
cultural diversity: dilemmas 102–27;
schools 128–42
cultural immersion 131–2, 150
cultural mediation theory 148–50
cultural pluralism: classes 258; definition
40; teacher education 40–8
cultural politics: ideology and identity
341–3; teacher education 212–16
cultural relativism: pitfalls 282–8
culturally disadvantaged youth: African
Americans 236–41; teaching 235–42
**Culture**
Asian Americans 301–10; criteria 40;
cross cultural immersion 131–2; cultural
accommodation 149; cultural
immersion 150; deep meaning in
learning 143–53; knowledge applied to
culture 146–8; mediation 148–50;
objectifying 144; personalizing 144–5;
redesigning instruction 147–8; reflective-
interpretive-inquiry (RIQ) 145–6;
reframing curriculum 147; students
145–6; teacher education 215–16;
transforming professional practice 150
curriculum: bias 96; critical pedagogy 186;
hidden curriculum 95; reframing 147

democratic schooling 200–24
desegregation: teacher effectiveness
251–61; teacher preparation 253
desocialization 185–6
Developmental Model of Intercultural
Sensitivity (Bennett): process models 64,
74–7; studies 74–7

dialogic teaching 191
disability: *Brown* case (1954) 174;
cultural differences compared 173
dispositions: teachers *see* teacher
dispositions
diversity: celebrating diversity 335–6;
courses on diversity issues 54–5;
culture *see* cultural diversity; field
experiences 55–7; prospective
teachers 49–62; teacher education
53–4
Diversity Among Friends Scale 20,
22, 25
dysconscious racism: discovery 336–8;
study findings 338–40; teacher
education 335–46

education: anti-oppressive education
347–56; culturally associated variables
42; liberatory education 229, 343–5;
multicultural *see* multicultural education;
multiethnic 41; place of education 33;
special *see* special education; teachers *see*
teacher education; trainees *see* teacher
trainees
education that is multicultural: additional
instruction 93–4; affirmation 96;
assignments/projects 95–6; bias in
curriculum materials 96; campus
learning 93–5; classroom environment
95; classroom planning 94; comfort
level 96; comparison of studies 99;
contributions from various groups 95;
field experiences 95; hidden curriculum
95; multicultural education compared
91; non-negotiables 155–6; school-
community relations 94–5; student
activities 95–6; study discussion 97–9;
study methodology 91–3; study
observations 96–7; study results 93–7;
teacher education 90–101;
teaching strategies 94; UCLA
153–65
egalitarian synthesis 184–5
elementary schools: Asian Americans
301–10; *Report of the Committee of
Fifteen on Elementary Education* (1895)
226; teacher attitudes 29–39
**Emancipatory Pedagogy**
critical consciousness 228; critical
perspective 227, 230–1; epistemological
perspective 227; heuristic tools 227;
implications 230–1; liberatory
education 229; programs 226–30;
teacher education 225–32;
vocationalism 229

theory: cultural mediation theory  148–50;
   definition  281; resistance  290–2; social
   theory  281–2
tracking: teacher expectations  14–15
trainee teachers *see* teacher trainees
transformative intellectuals  201
Typology of Ethnicity (Banks): process
   models  64, 71–4; research studies  73–4;
   stages  71–2

UCLA: Center X  4, 153–65
University of Houston: multicultural
   education  302–3

White Racial identity Attitude Scale
   (WRIAS)  67–70
White Racial Identity Development model
   70
whiteness: overwhelming presence  136–7